American National Election Studies Data Sourcebook, 1952-1986

Warren E. Miller

Santa Traugott

Harvard University Press

Cambridge, Massachusetts, and

London, England

1989

LIBRARY OF CONGRESS CATALOGING-IN-PUBLICATION DATA

Miller, Warren E. (Warren Edward), 1924-
   American national election studies data sourcebook, 1952-1986/
   Warren E. Miller, Santa A. Traugott
      p.   cm.
   ISBN 0-674-02636-5 (alk. paper)
   1. Elections--United States--Statistics. 2. Politicians--United States--Statistics.
   3. Voting--United States--Statistics. 4. United States--Politics and government--1945-
   I. Traugott, Santa A.   II. Title
   JK1967.M54   1989
   324.973'092'021--dc20   89-7546
                                                            CIP

The American National Election Studies Data Sourcebook, 1952-1986, differs from the earlier NES Data Sourcebook both in the sponsorship of the work and in some features of possible substantive significance. The 1980 Sourcebook predated the National Science Foundation support of NES, and was produced entirely from resources supplied by the Center for Political Studies of the University of Michigan's Institute for Social Research. This volume was made possible by budgetary support authorized by the National Election Studies Board of Overseers to subvent preparation by the NES staff. Editorial decisions made by the editors were, of course, reviewed by others on the staff and Board. The organization and administration of the decisions were the sole responsibilities of Santa Traugott, who was ably aided by John Brehm, Fran Elliott, Patricia Luevano, Giovanna Morchio, and Laura San Facon.

New data include the addition of many items for which statistics had accumulated across at least two points in time. The major addition of new data is to be found in Chapter Seven, which includes the full array of data on the last five congressional elections, 1978-1986, data collected for the first time under the auspices of the National Election Studies.

The simple logical structure of the original presentation was reappraised at the urging, and with the assistance, of some of those who use the volume in their own research. As the table of contents indicates, the basic scheme of presenting nested series of bivariate relationships has been preserved in this new, completely redone, and updated version.

Also, this volume has been assembled from a cumulative data set that includes all eighteen biennial data files from 1952 to 1986. The cumulative data set may be obtained from the Inter-univeristy Consortium for Political and Social Research, located at the University of Michigan, by contacting Member Services, ICPSR, Institute for Social Research, P.O. Box 1248, Ann Arbor MI 48106-1248. The full data set includes detailed documentation on the coding conventions followed in generating data for the Sourcebook, as well as the original "raw" data from which derived summary measures were constructed. Finally, we have eliminated the graphic figures and all Normal Vote Analyses. These deletions may make selected searches a bit more difficult, but they do not reduce the data base in any way.

Any discrepancies discovered in comparing new data entries with those of the first edition should be the result of having done all of the calculations anew. Nevertheless, any and all discrepancies that may be discovered should be brought to the attention of Santa Traugott, Director of Studies, The National Election Studies, Center for Political Studies, University of Michigan, Ann Arbor MI 48106-1248

Contents

LIST OF TABLES

List of Tables

List of Tables

List of Tables

List of Tables

List of Tables

Introduction

Uses of the Book

This book is based on the premise that current events, including America's biennial and quadrennial national elections, are best understood in a historical context. The meaning which each national election should acquire from its antecedent conditions is often overlooked because so much in the world of electoral politics is focused on present and future candidates and so little on yesterday's incumbents and contenders. Our interest in overcoming the historical bias in contemporary political analysis and the interpretation of elections is not new. Our first major institutional contribution to the literature on mass electoral behavior in America, The American Voter, attempted to locate the historical past in a metatheoretical discussion of approaches to electoral analysis. The same volume, however, frequently noted the limitations inherent in evidence as sharply bounded in time as that produced by no more than the two Eisenhower elections on which the book was based. That volume and many other analyses emanating from our research during that period were limited in their historical sweep, and most often could not be pointedly informed by recent history because relevant aspects of that history had not been properly documented.

The American National Election Studies series has been extended by more than three decades beyond the Eisenhower era. The full set of eighteen biennial studies now makes it possible to present a longer and unbroken record of many of the attributes of national electoral behavior that are commonly examined in the course of exploring, interpreting, or attempting to understand any single national election. A part of the documentation of the complexity inherent in our national electoral politics, a quite diverse set of attributes with very substantial interyear comparability across the full set of biennial studies, is presented in this volume. When assembled in chronological sequence, the data on these attributes provide evidence of differing degrees of stability and change among a range of attributes useful to political analysis. Crucial elements of great stability, such as the voter's party loyalty, stand in sharp contrast to the more volatile elements, such as the voter's responses to different pairs of presidential candidates, as part of the documentation of the nature of our national electoral politics.

This volume has been assembled to enhance the understanding of individual elections and presidential periods and to provide a basis for broader generalizations about post-World War II American politics. It inevitably will serve other purposes as well. Some subsets of the data -- educational attainment, occupational status of women, attitudes relevant to the social status of black citizens -- are important for substantive concerns quite beyond the election of congressmen or presidents. For the regular user of data generated by academic survey research or public opinion polls, the displays will also serve more technical, methodological purposes implicit in time-series analysis. Teachers and students of public opinion, voting behavior, and attitude change should find an abundance of empirical material for classroom discussion as well as scholarly writing. The volume also provides a wide array of data which journalists, historians, and political decision makers can use as background material to enhance their interpretation of recent events.

The Reliability of Survey Data

Thanks to many efforts, such as those of the Professional Ethics Committee of the American Association for Public Opinion Research, it is now customary to see results of surveys and polls publicly reported with a caveat about "sampling error." The concept of sampling error and its manifestations are well known to the research community, but a visceral appreciation among poll clients and users of survey data is less common. Time-series data arrays, derived from data based on standardized and highly stable research methods and techniques of data collection, provide an invaluable tutorial in this domain. All of the data in this book are based on samples of the national electorate. All of the estimates of each attribute of the electorate are subject to sampling error, the variability that results when different samples are not equally faithful representations of the "true" values of the attribute in the total population being sampled. Data portraying a stable attribute of the national electorate, such as composition by race or sex, generally reflect that stability, as in the case of race (Table 1.11). However, in the case of male-female ratios (Table 1.9), for example, the data may suggest change where in fact the appearance of change is produced by growing response biases or shifts in field techniques. The presence of error in estimation can be readily seen when a single sample estimate of a value familiar to the reader, such as proportion of females in the electorate, is compared with validating Census figures or when successive sample estimates of male-female ratios are juxtaposed as in Table 1.9.

Other data less open to external validation, such as those describing the national electorate's "trust in government," are more difficult to interpret. The data may be read as portraying general trends, but a more critical eye will note perturbations around the trend line. The variability may be sampling error, as in the earlier instance of black-white ratios, or another kind of error, as in the estimation of sex ratios. It may be induced by short-lived variations in the real world; or, given the concept the data are intended to represent, the zigs and zags may be the result of measurement unreliability and the errors that result from poorly framed interviews or badly phrased questions.

Sampling error, other sorts of error, and real short-term fluctuations in attribute values all interfere with the depiction of steady state conditions or the capturing of true monotonic linear change over time. One of the best ways of comprehending the importance of these intrusions on survey or poll assessments of the public is to study time-series data for different variables where the evidence has been collected by standardized methods and techniques. As the reader examines each display, conclusions regarding stability and change should be drawn recognizing that the standard caveat on sampling error applies to all these data.

As a further aid to the reader's assessment of the reliability of survey estimates, a generalized table of sampling errors is presented in the introduction to Chapter 1. As that table suggests, the probable sampling error associated with any given estimated percentage (such as percent black or percent female) varies with the numerical size of the sample total on which the percentage is based. Larger samples are more reliable and the probable sampling error is smaller; smaller samples are less reliable and one must expect larger errors.

Sampling variability, and hence probable sampling error, is also a function of how even or how skewed the observed distribution of percentage is. Estimates that are close to 50 percent (a 50-50 division of the population, as in the male-female distribution) have larger sampling errors, while estimates of very large or of very small proportions (as in the skewed 10-90 division between blacks and whites) have smaller ranges of possible variation and, therefore, smaller probable sampling errors. Beyond this it is also true that each attribute sampled, such as sex, race, or age, has its own more or less unique sampling distribution; but the variation from one attribute to another is sufficiently limited to warrant reliance on average sampling errors such as those presented in the table. The table is, in fact, a presentation of averages computed on the basis of individual estimates of the sampling errors of a dozen or more of the "core" variables used in this volume. It has been constructed to take simultaneous account of differences in sample size and differences in skewedness of distributions.

It should be noted that the sampling errors presented are estimates of the largest errors likely to be encountered 95 percent of the time. That is, if 100 samples were drawn at any one time (instead of the single sample we have for each given year), and if proportions of a given variable were calculated for each of the 100 samples, 95 percent of the calculations would differ from the "true value" in the sampled population by no more than the specified sampling error. However, one sample in twenty (five out of the 100) could be expected to produce estimates that differed from the "true value" in the sampled population by more than the specified sampling error. The sampling errors in the table are, therefore, only the probable limits of error, and depict a magnitude of error that will probably not be exceeded more than 5 percent of the time. Any given estimate may be in error by more than the magnitude indicated, but the chances are 95 in 100 that this will not have occurred.

Assessing the Evidence

To preserve a basis for each reader's independent assessment of the data, we have included for each table the number of cases -- the number of respondents -- on which the sample estimates are based. Where the numerical size of the sample is not presented in a table, it can be found by going back to preceding tables from which the table in question has been derived. The introductions to the chapters, combined with the annotations in individual tables, specify most of the technical decisions which lie behind our effort to present data in a manner that facilitates direct substantive interpretation by the reader without demanding simultaneous attention to technical detail. Footnote references to changes in question wording, for example, should lead the interested reader to the original election study documentation, which presents the precise wording of each question asked in all eighteen national studies.

Among the many possible sources of confusion over apparently conflicting results from different surveys and polls, subtle differences in question wording are often named as villains. And rightly so. However, this volume will not be a significant aid to those interested in appraising the importance of question wording. In general, as each new variable is introduced, the relevant table includes the full text of the question used to elicit the data. We have annotated instances in which question wording has changed in the CPS series without, apparently, affecting the measure. But, where variations or changes in wording appear to have produced major changes in the data, destroying continuity of technique and interrupting the time series, we do not present the data. As a consequence, we judge all of the data presented in a given time series to be comparable.

At this point, it is worth noting that we did not attempt to second guess the decisions that had shaped the content of each of the CPS election studies by selecting only "interesting" attributes for display and analysis. Virtually every item in the volume has a history of use in two or more studies and was deemed of sufficient current interest to appear in a recent CPS study. More generally, we did not try to anticipate the interests and needs of those who will use this book by omitting what we thought to be the dull in favor of the exciting displays. We often enough find our own theoretical expectations darkened by "negative findings" to be aware that it is largely the reader's expectations that will determine whether a given data display is of real interest or not.

The Organization of the Volume

The structure of the volume reflects a handful of organizing principles that we, and many of our professional colleagues, use in thinking about mass electoral behavior, principles emphasizing stability and change, developmental ordering, and major referents for political evaluations.

For some purposes, we tend to order factors relevant to electoral behavior on a continuum ranging from the most stable to the most changeable. Thus major portions of the chapters proceed from considering such stable elements as sex, occupation, and religion to describing the enduring but less fixed attribute of party identification, then moving on to such topics as opinions on public policy and the relationships between voters' issue positions and their partisan choices.

In a closely related second theme, we often think in terms of a possible sequence in which the various elements acquire relevance for the voter's choice. In this setting, relatively fixed personal attributes, such as education or religion, provide the background, the social and economic context for one's politics. Party identification develops for many people at an early age, it often develops in accord with their location in the social structure, and it persists relatively unchanged through life as a predisposition coloring or governing subsequent views of political actors and events. The later perceptions and evaluations of candidates and parties are often anchored by the partisan predispositions, but they are also heavily influenced by the very real changes that occur as new problems create new issues and new candidates evoke different responses than did their predecessors. The voter's election-day choice develops last out of the interplay among all the preceding elements.

A third tradition has the political research scholar organizing his thinking around the three major concepts of parties, issues, and candidates. More recently, a fourth concept -- attitudes reflecting the individual's support for the political system -- has been recognized as separable from the other three and often important to an understanding of why some people participate in elections while others do not.

Chapter Content

All three organizing principles are reflected in the structure of each chapter and in the sequence of chapters. The book begins with the social composition of the eligible electorate. Data are presented for the ten social and economic attributes that are most relevant to ultimate decisions on partisan choice on election day and participation in the campaign or in voting.

The second chapter is on political partisanship. It begins with party identification and examines the party identification of persons in each of the social categories specified in the first chapter. The chapter then moves on, however, to the more volatile and changeable partisan attitudes evoked in evaluating political parties and presidential candidates. These evaluations, so heavily colored by the party identification of the citizens doing the evaluation, are then examined within the categories of party identification. The introduction of a third mode of defining partisanship, an effective rating of each of the two major parties, sets the pattern for the remainder of the book. The pattern is generally one of first providing the distribution of an attribute within the total population, the eligible electorate, for each year in the time series. In the initial presentation of the distribution, a summary is given as a single statistic. That summary statistic, a Percentage Difference Index (PDI), described below, is then used as the entry in tables displaying the summary within each of the personal data and party identification categories. This makes possible cross-year comparisons that take into account underlying changes in relevant social, economic, or party identification attributes.

The chapter on partisanship is followed by one about opinions on questions of public policy that have some enduring interest. Following the format described above, distributions of opinions on each issue are summarized with a PDI and the summaries are then presented for all of the categories of relatively stable social, economic, and political attributes introduced in the first two chapters. The analysis of the time-series data on attitudes toward public policies is thereby enhanced, as one is then able to sort out the categories of people whose patterns of attitudinal change differ from the average across the total electorate.

The fourth chapter is devoted to a variety of attitudes reflecting citizens' evaluations of different governmental institutions and classes of political figures, such as congressmen or public officials. These attitudes are not overtly partisan, as in the two preceding chapters; they are rather general descriptions of confidence, approval, or support. Some of the opinions, such as those reflecting trust or cynicism, have changed dramatically over time; others, such as the sense of civic obligation to vote, have been almost rocklike in their stability. The very fact that the various indicators of mass support for the political system have not all moved in tandem should forestall overgeneralization and unjustified extrapolation from a subset of the measures.

Chapter 5 is concerned with attitudinal involvement and actual participation in electoral politics. Current analyses of change in voter turnout suggest that the variations in turnout since World War II, including the continued slow decline through 1978, may be influenced by citizens' perceptions of the anticipated closeness of the race, their sense of the importance of the possible differences in outcome, and shifts in their perceptions of the responsiveness of the political system. In this chapter we treat those factors most directly related to the decision to vote or abstain, and we broaden the definition of electoral participation to include activities that are relevant to campaigns and electoral competition, but that go beyond the simple act of voting.

The sixth chapter, "The Vote," will be, for many, the heart of this volume. Here all the elements most relevant to the voters' ultimate partisan choice on election day are brought together. In the interest of simplicity, and in order to keep the reader close to the original data displays in earlier chapters, we have not attempted to present formally organized, multivariate analyses of vote choice. Given the many interrelationships among the data that are disclosed in the preceding five chapters, it is apparent that multivariate techniques to permit the simultaneous assessment of many factors related to the vote are needed if one wants to guard against specious interpretations based on the simple "zero-order" relationship between any one factor and the vote. An awareness of this possibility can be derived by paying close attention to the full set of two-variable relationships presented in the first five chapters. At the same time, it must be recognized that the precise configuration of factors that should be brought together for a truly multivariate analysis can be specified only by prior theory. The scholarly literature presents many such theories -- and often tests them with data from the studies contained in this volume -- but this book of time-series data was not organized for the purpose of testing alternate theories nor to demonstrate the superiority of any one theory. Its aims are more limited and will be served if readers' appetites are stirred to pursue such matters on their own.

The seventh and final chapter presents recently accumulated data on citizens' assessments of the Congress (the U.S. House of Representatives) and their Representative. This chapter relates measures of the warmth of feeling respondents have toward their Representative (the "feeling thermometer"), frequency of contact with Congressional candidates, rates of recall of Congressional candidates' names, and approval ratings of the Congress and their Representative.

The Use of Summarizing Statistics

To facilitate presentation, summary statistics have been used throughout the volume. In some places, the summary is simply one of the two percentage figures in a dichotomous (two-category) distribution. Thus, in the chapter on the vote, the entry is the Democratic proportion of the two-party vote; voting turnout is the proportion of a group which reports

having voted. In the presentation of affect ratings of the parties, the statistic is the mean of a distribution that ranges from 0 to 100 percent.

More often, the statistic is a Percentage Difference Index (PDI). The index is constructed by simple arithmetic, subtracting one percentage figure from another. Its meaning rests on an equally simple assumption about how people using these data will interpret differences in percentage distributions of attribute values. The answers to a question on how much interest people have in following a political campaign provide a ready example. The answers may be categorized as Very Much Interested, Somewhat Interested, or Not Much Interested. The PDI that summarizes this statement of interest is simply the proportion (percentage) of Not Much Interested responses subtracted from the proportion of Very Much Interested responses. The PDI therefore tells which of those two groups is larger, and by how many percentage points. The PDI assumes, however, that in comparing two or more distributions on popular interest in following campaigns, one will look for differences in both the Very Much Interested and the Not Much Interested categories and that one will attach equal weight to either set of differences -- for example, an increase of 10 percentage points in the proportion expressing high interest will be given the same meaning and the same weight in drawing conclusions about differences in interest as a 10-point decrease in the size of the low-interest category.

The PDI is in essence an average or a mean. It produces the same figure one would compute by trichotomizing a distribution of opinions, assigning a weight or score of +1 to all people falling at one end of the distribution, a score of -1 to all on the other end, and a score of 0 to everyone in the middle, summing all the scores, and dividing that sum by the total number of people in order to derive an average or a mean score. The PDI is not a good summary if one prefers to attach different weights to the two ends of the distribution. If readers consider expressions of high interest somehow less important, perhaps too socially acceptable, and are concerned only with the proportions expressing disinterest, they should compare only the latter proportions; the PDI may confuse and obscure what they think is important. Moreover, it does not indicate the size of the middle group. Some information contained in a full distribution is always lost in the computation of a single summarizing statistic. In this case, for example, plus, zero, and minus scores of 10, 60, and 30 produce a PDI of -20, just as do scores of 35, 10, and 55.

It should be noted that at times the percentages in tables do not total 100; also the PDI values sometimes differ from the figure which would be obtained by a hand calculation based on the table percentages. These discrepancies are the result of rounding rather than errors of computation.

Election Study Samples

Data for the CPS American National Election Studies are obtained from personal face-to-face interviews with national full probability samples of all citizens of voting age. The Survey Research Center's multistage area sample is used in all CPS studies. It is designed to represent dwelling units in the contiguous United States exclusive of those on military reservations. The 74 current sample points (66 before 1963) include the largest metropolitan areas, other Standard Metropolitan Statistical Areas (SMSAs), and counties or county groups representing the nonmetropolitan or rural sections of the country. First-stage stratification of SMSAs and counties is carried out independently within each of four major geographic regions, which are compounded of contiguous pairs of the eight regions of the Census Bureau and which are represented in the final sample in proportion to their respective populations. Thus, for any sample of 1000 dwellings based on 1970 Census information, we would expect to find about 240 dwellings from the Northeast, 280 from the North Central region, 310 from the South, and 170 from the West.

For all regions, the SMSAs and the counties are assigned to relatively homogeneous groups or strata. Twelve of these strata contain only one primary area each; they are the 2 Standard Consolidated Areas and the 10 largest SMSAs, outside the Consolidated Areas, which are included with certainty in each sample. The remaining strata (62 currently, 54 before 1963) may contain from 2 to 200 or more primary areas (SMSAs or county groups). From each stratum, one primary area is selected with probability proportionate to population. This process leads to approximately equal sample sizes. Unless research needs dictate otherwise, a self-weighted sample of dwelling units is drawn.

Instead of independent selections within each of these strata, controlled probability selection is introduced for a more efficient sample. Within each of the four geographic regions, the selection of primary areas is linked by a procedure that controls the distribution of sample areas by states and degree of urbanization beyond the controls effected through the formation of the strata. This controlled selection yields a more balanced sample and increases the precision of sample estimates.

As the multistage area sampling continues within the primary units, the area is divided and subdivided, in two to five stages, into successively smaller sampling units. By definition and procedure, each dwelling belongs uniquely to one sampling unit at each stage. Within the primary areas, cities, towns, and rural areas are the secondary selections. Blocks or clusters of addresses in cities and towns and chunks of rural areas are the third-stage units. In the fourth stage, there is a selection of small segments or clusters of dwellings, where interviews are conducted for a study. In the last stage of sampling, one or more respondents may be randomly selected from among household members by using a Kish selection table.

Probability selection is enforced at all stages of the sample selection. The interviewer has no freedom of choice either among dwelling units or among household members within designated dwelling units. The procedure yields a sample in which each individual member of the population has a known probability of selection, and, for the typical self-weighting cross-section design, the probabilities of selection at the level of the dwelling unit are equal.

The American National Election Studies, conducted originally by the Political Behavior Program of the Survey Research Center and later by the Center for Political Studies, have investigated citizen attitudes, beliefs, and behaviors in connection with all but one of the biennial presidential and off-year congressional elections since 1948. Until 1978, the samples were drawn in accordance with the multistage area probability sampling design and were intended to provide cross-section samples of citizens of voting age living in households within the contiguous United States.

Additional respondents were included and weighting procedures were instituted to produce a representative cross-section sample in those years when a reinterview panel design was also being carried out (1958, 1960, 1974, and 1976), or when additional respondents in some population subgroup (such as the black supplements in 1964, 1968, and 1970) were interviewed.

The data presented in this volume do not include any collected from the black supplements, nor from the sample of eighteen to twenty year olds taken in 1970 in anticipation of the lowering of the voting age by constitutional amendment. All of the data are weighted where weighting is called for.

The standard format for fieldwork surrounding presidential elections involves a pre-election interview conducted during the six or eight weeks before the election and a briefer post-election reinterview in November and December. For the off-year congressional elections, a single post-election interview has been conducted.

In 1978, research needs dictated a major change in the first state of the sampling design. The primary sampling units were recast to fit lines of congressional districts in the contiguous United States to facilitate analysis of the dynamics of congressional elections. The 432 eligible congressional districts were divided into 108 strata. Each stratum contained four districts of roughly comparable characteristics that, insofar as possible, were homogeneous with respect to geographic region, state, urbanization, and recent voting behavior. From each stratum, one district was chosen with a probability proportionate to its 1975 estimated population. The sample comprised a probability sample of both United States citizens and congressional districts but did not permit estimates of each district's constituency, since sampling and field costs prohibited within-district selections from being distributed across the district. As always, in all districts and at each stage of sampling, strict probability sampling procedures were used.

The Studies

The following studies provided data for this volume:

1952 American National Election Study: 1899 respondents.

1954 American National Election Study: 1139 respondents.

1956 American National Election Study: 1762 respondents (conducted in conjunction with the 1956 Fall Survey of Consumer Attitudes and Behavior).

1958 American National Election Study: 1450 respondents, weighted data.

1960 American National Election Study: 1181 respondents, weighted data.

1962 American National Election Study: 1297 respondents (conducted in conjunction with the 1962 Fall Survey of Consumer Attitudes and Behavior).

1964 American National Election Study: 1834 respondents, weighted data (1571 respondents in cross-section sample, 263 respondents in black supplement).

1966 American National Election Study: 1291 respondents (conducted in conjunction with the 1966 Fall Survey of Consumer Attitudes and Behavior).

1968 American National Election Study: 1673 respondents (1557 respondents in cross-section sample, 116 respondents in black supplement); combined sample and black sample are weighted; cross-section sample is self-weighting.

1970 American National Election Study: 1694 respondents (1580 respondents in cross-section sample, 114 respondents in black supplement); combined sample, black sample, and some questions in cross-section sample are weighted.

1972 American National Election Study: 2705 respondents.

1974 American National Election Study: 1575 respondents.

1976 American National Election Study: 2248 respondents.

1978 American National Election Study: 2304 respondents.

1980 American National Election Study: 1614 respondents.

1982 American National Election Study: 1575 respondents.

1984 American National Election Study: 2257 respondents.

1986 American National Election Study: 2176 respondents.

Given the need for brevity, this volume does not repeat much technical documentation available elsewhere. A detailed description of the sample of citizens selected for each study and detailed documentation of the data are preserved in the codebooks maintained by the Inter-university Consortium for Political and Social Research (ICPSR), which is a unit of the Center for Political Studies. Given the fact that original data have often been recoded to maximize comparability across the entire time series for the preparation of this volume, inquiries concerning coding rules applied to the time-series data should be addressed to National Election Studies Director, Center for Political Studies, Institute for Social Research, Box 1248, Ann Arbor, Michigan 48106-1248. The time-series data sets created for this volume and their documentation, as well as the original data and documentation for each of the eighteen studies, will be distributed by the ICPSR; inquiries should be directed to Ms. Janet Vavra, Assistant Director, Member Services, Inter-university Consortium for Political and Social Research, Institute for Social Research, Box 1248, Ann Arbor, Michigan 48106-1248.

How to Read The Tables

The reader should be familiar with three markings that appear in the tables throughout the Sourcebook. Two asterisks (**) denote a cell entry for which the data are unobtainable: a question may not have been asked during a given year, or a demographic group may not have been eligible for the sample (particularly the younger age cohorts). A single asterisk (*) following a cell entry indicates that the cell has between 20 and 50 cases. In such instances, the reader should be aware of the possible unreliability of the cell's estimate due to the small sub-sample size. A single hyphen (-) in a cell indicates that the cell has fewer than 20 cases. In these cases, the cell's estimate has been suppressed due to the very small sub-sample size.

Chapter 1. Social Characteristics of the Electorate

In an era when the presidential vote can oscillate from the Democratic landslide of 1964 to a massive Republican victory eight years later, it may seem that the relatively stable social attributes of voters can provide little insight into the nature of the national electoral choice. Nevertheless, it is a fact that the one-sided decisions of those years, as well as the photo finishes of the elections of the surrounding years 1960, 1968, and 1976, were constrained -- if not shaped -- by persistent differences in the partisanship of voters as they are separated into various social groups and sociological categories. The evidence for this conclusion is presented in Chapter 6 in our analysis of the vote.

Attributes such as age, education, and race also help to account for notable differences in the ways people think about politics. Social attributes, broadly defined to include the urbanism of one's place of residence as well as age, sex, and religion, may be overemphasized by campaign managers seeking "target groups" for their campaigns, or by political analysts who would unlock all the mysteries of electoral behavior with the keys of income, occupation, and social class. Nevertheless, life experiences, resources acquired through education, and immediate personal-social context all make important contributions to what one thinks about politics and how one behaves at election time. Few contemporary students of politics would accept the conclusion that a person thinks politically as he is socially. And yet studies of the ways in which citizens think about parties, issues, and candidates invariably examine social attributes. The indicators of past experience, present exposure to outside influences, and personal predisposition to respond to political events are provided by the personal socioeconomic attributes of citizens- - the so-called demographics of politics.

This chapter examines ten social characteristics of the electorate; age, education, urbanism, income, sex, race, union membership, region of residence, occupation, and religion. The first tables display the national distributions of the different values or categories for each attribute. The remainder present the distribution of each attribute _within_ each category of the other nine attributes. This simple device of examining attributes two at a time serves a number of analytic purposes. Thus Table 1.1 displays the changing age-cohort composition of the electorate, Table 1.3 reveals the changing educational attainment levels across the entire electorate, and Tables 1.21-1.22 present the distribution of educational attainment _within_ each of the age cohorts. Table 1.1 illustrates the fact that citizens who came of age before the 1932 election made up more than half of the electorate (53 percent) twenty years later in 1952, but constituted about one-twentieth of the electorate (5 percent) by 1986, the year in which the post-World War II cohorts (born after 1926) made up three-fourths (77 percent) of the potential voters. Table 1.21

and its summary in Table 1.22 show the intercohort differences in education, which suggest the not surprising conclusion that the change in the educational level of the total electorate presented in Table 1.3 is largely a result of the less well educated, older cohorts being replaced by better-educated, younger cohorts.

It is perhaps worth noting here that the treatment of age in this volume departs from the use of categories most familiar to users of survey and poll data. Rather than classify people by their age at the time of each survey, we have chosen to group them into somewhat broad age cohorts, defined by the year when they became eligible to vote.

This procedure facilitates tracking the same people across the full span of time during which any given age cohort or group is represented in successive biennial samples. In order to maximize the stability of age-related estimates, the age cohorts have been broadly defined to embrace political eras-- even though this means losing some information that would be retained if, say, four-year intervals were to define the groups. The oldest cohort (born before 1895) came of voting age before or during World War I; the cohort which followed (born 1895-1910) entered the electorate between the end of World War I and the Hoover-Roosevelt election of 1932; the third oldest cohort (born 1911-1926) reached their majority during the Roosevelt years and World War II; the next (born 1927-1942) came of age after the War through 1963; the next-to-youngest cohort (born 1943-1958) entered the electorate no earlier than the Johnson election of 1964; the youngest cohort reached majority in 1978, before the election of Reagan in 1980. The cohorts are thus bounded by landmark historic events, although for many the crucial period of political socialization may have preceded their coming of age or may have followed well after that signal birthday.

A systematic search through the tables in this chapter, guided by no more than common sense and straightforward logic, can provide a strong inferential base for specifying more or less precisely which subgroups in the population have produced the overall changes noted in the first section of the chapter.

For example, the data show that the change in sex roles in American society has sharply reduced the number of women who describe themselves as housewives. Table 1.17 indicates that the proportion of housewives in the total electorate (including men) has dropped from 35-36 percent in the early 1950s to less than 15 percent in the mid-1980s.

Table 1.88 confirms the assumption or inference that all change in the reported proportions of housewives is identified with women's reports of their own occupation. Table 1.32, presenting the proportion of housewives within each age cohort, indicates that the decline in the relative proportion of housewives has been quite uniform across all of the older cohorts, bringing them very much into line with all but the youngest cohorts. Table 1.46 suggests that the change has been largest within the middle education groups and smallest within the least educated, those with no more than a grade-school education. The same suggestion of greatest change within the modal social groups of the society is found when the income categories are inspected in Table 1.74. On the other hand, the change in the proportion of housewives within religious groupings is greatest among Jews, who are clearly the best educated (Table 1.153) and have the highest income of all religious groups (Table 1.157). At the other extreme, the change has just recently touched black households, in large part, we would infer from Table 1.104, because black women have been less often categorized as housewives throughout the studies until 1980. The remaining tables on region (Table 1.134) and urbanism of residence (Table 1.60) and on household union membership (Table 1.119) testify to the pervasiveness of the change in women's occupations.

It is clearly not only, or not even, the young, affluent, well-educated middle class in the nation's urban centers who provide the most dramatic evidence of change in the occupational status of American women. This rather cursory inspection of data is sufficient to counter a number of current theories about sex-role changes in the United States. The tables do not, however, provide a thorough exploration of the phenomenon. A reasonable next step would be to go beyond the two-by-two-by-two analysis of this volume and answer the next more complicated set of questions. For example, can we resolve the apparent anomaly of dramatic change among Jewish women by discovering that it has occurred only among the less wealthy and less well educated? To do this, one must simultaneously consider education, religion, and occupation (or income, religion, and occupation). Of course, even prior to asking whether the change in the proportion of housewives among Jews occurs at all education and income levels, we might well come closer to our goal of understanding the national decrease in the proportion of housewives by restricting the combined totals for men and women (which is what we have had to examine in every table except Table 1.88). In a like manner, the inferred differences between black and white women should be tested by first looking at only the occupations of women, and then comparing black and white women of similar age, education, income, and the like.

Analyses which focus on particular subgroups and test various possibilities with complex combinations of voter attributes are entirely possible with the data on which this volume is based. The data are available through the ICPSR (see page 6, above), and a computer-based data manipulation with available multivariate analysis techniques makes possible a host of complex analyses. Virtually no such analysis is presented in this or other chapters because of the problem of sheer size if even the more plausible of possible explanations

for documented temporal changes were logically and exhaustively explored. Instead, we hope that the organization of this chapter and the others will encourage readers to push well beyond our work and pursue their curiosities or theories by carrying out more thorough analyses of the various time-series data sets.

The illustrative exercise of tracking down the women who were once housewives but have now disappeared into the labor force was chosen in part because it draws attention to problems other than those pertaining to different levels of analytic complexity. For instance, when the income-occupation tables (1.73-1.74 and 1.143-1.144) are examined, the data appear quite "ragged," with interyear differences and between-occupation differences that vary a good bit. It is, consequently, more difficult to pick out trends across time in these tables than in many others. One major source of the problem lies with the definition of the income categories used in this volume. Because of the tremendous changes in personal income over the thirty-four years covered by the volume, an attempt was made to standardize income distribution by dividing the population into income percentiles (see the income categorization chart on p. 11). Unfortunately, this proved to be a troublesome task because, in many studies, income was recorded only in bracketed amounts (0-$4999, $5000-$7499, etc.), which did not fit perfectly a standardized percentile scheme. The percentile ranges that are used are, as a result, a kind of lowest common denominator of comparability. Table 1.7 indicates something of the magnitude of the problem. The PDI (proportion in the 68-100 percentile minus the proportion in the 0-33 percentile) should, by definition, be invariant year to year. It is not. Consequently, the reader must observe a general caveat where income data are concerned: all interpretations must carefully refer to Table 1.7 in an attempt to judge whether they are influenced by the unavoidable variations in the year-by-year definitions of the income categories.

A similar problem confounds time-series interpretations related to urbanism. Because of a series of changes in the definition of place of residence -- changes often imposed by Bureau of the Census procedures -- the operational definition of urbanism categories has varied over the period of the studies reported in this volume. The impact of these changes can be seen in Table 1.5, where it is apparent that only the most inexplicable ebb and flow of residential movement could have produced the interyear variations that are recorded. Any analysis of urbanism must take these definitional fluctuations into account.

Finally, attention should again be drawn to the problems of sample size and sampling error. The tables presenting the number of cases making up each category of each of the ten demographic attributes highlight the fragility of estimates based on analyses of the upper income category (containing as few as 54 individuals in 1970 and, at most, 146 persons in 1978), blacks (where the range is from 103 to 323), farmers (from 32 in 1980 to 131 in 1952), Jews (from 24 in 1982 to 68 in 1976), and the other religion category (with well under 100 until 1970). These numbers, laid against total sample sizes, remind us that politically significant groupings may constitute only minute fractions of the total electorate. When represented in proportion only to their numerical size, as in a national sample, their absolute numbers are small, and sample estimates based on them must be recognized as subject to great sampling variability. The table of sampling errors (p. 11) provides a guide to the assessment of data based on samples of different sizes.

With the possibility -- indeed, the known likelihood -- of sampling variability in mind, the users of this volume may be impressed, as we are, with the year-in-year-out stability of many estimates. At the same time, an awareness of the probability of sampling error should be used to guard against overinterpretation of the data; single data points that seem out of line with adjoining readings may be the result of sampling error -- but so may two consecutive readings that are consistent with the appearance of a substantively significant trend.

Income Categorization

Year	0-16 Percentile	17-33 Percentile	34-67 Percentile	68-95 Percentile	96-100 Percentile
1) 1952	$none-1,999	$2,000-2,999	$3,000-3,999	$4,000-9,999	$10,000 and over
2) 1954	$none-1,999	$2,000-2,999	$4,000-5,999	$4,000-9,999	$10,000 and over
3) 1956	$none-1,999	$2,000-3,999	$4,000-5,999	$6,000-9,999	$10,000 and over
4) 1958	$none-1,999	$2,000-3,999	$4,000-5,999	$6,000-14,999	$15,000 and over
5) 1960	$none-1,999	$2,000-3,999	$4,000-5,999	$6,000-14,999	$15,000 and over
6) 1962	$none-2,999	$3,000-3,999	$4,000-7,499	$7,500-14,999	$15,000 and over
7) 1964	$none-2,999	$3,000-4,999	$5,000-7,499	$7,500-14,999	$15,000 and over
8) 1966	$none-2,999	$3,000-3,999	$4,000-7,499	$7,500-14,999	$15,000 and over
9) 1968	$none-2,999	$3,000-5,999	$6,000-9,999	$10,000-19,999	$20,000 and over
10) 1970	$none-2,999	$4,000-4,999	$5,000-9,999	$10,000-24,999	$25,000 and over
11) 1972	$none-3,999	$4,000-5,999	$6,000-11,999	$12,000-24,999	$25,000 and over
12) 1974	$none-3,999	$4,000-6,999	$7,000-14,999	$15,000-34,999	$35,000 and over
13) 1976	$none-3,999	$4,000-7,999	$8,000-14,999	$15,000-34,999	$35,000 and over
14) 1978	$none-5,999	$6,000-10,999	$11,000-19,999	$20,000-34,999	$35,000 and over
15) 1980	$none-5,999	$7,000-11,999	$12,000-24,999	$25,000-49,999	$50,000 and over
16) 1982	$none-6,999	$7,000-12,999	$13,000-24,999	$25,000-49,999	$50,000 and over
17) 1984	$none-6,999	$7,000-12,999	$13,000-29,999	$30,000-59,999	$60,000 and over
18) 1986	$none-8,999	$9,000-14,999	$15,000-34,999	$35,000-74,999	$75,000 and over

Approximate Standard Errors of Percentages, Based on the 1986 Election Survey

Reported Percentages	Number of Respondents									
	2,250	2,000	1,500	1,000	750	500	400	300	200	100
50%	1.44	1.51	1.66	1.94	2.18	2.60	2.87	3.27	3.96	5.53
40% or 60%	1.41	1.48	1.62	1.90	2.14	2.54	2.81	3.20	3.87	5.42
30% or 70%	1.33	1.37	1.52	1.78	1.99	2.38	2.63	3.00	3.63	5.06
20% or 80%	1.15	1.20	1.33	1.54	1.74	2.08	2.29	2.62	3.17	4.42
10% or 90%	0.87	0.90	0.99	1.16	1.31	1.55	1.72	1.96	2.37	3.32

Table 1.1
Age Cohort of Respondent

	1952	1954	1956	1958	1960	1962	1964	1966	1968	1970	1972	1974	1976	1978	1980	1982	1984	1986
1959 or later	**	**	**	**	**	**	**	**	**	**	**	**	**	3%	7%	10%	16%	19%
1943 - 1958	**	**	**	**	**	**	2	7	10	17	28	34	36	39	37	37	37	38
1927 - 1942	9	7	18	21	22	28	33	31	32	31	27	23	24	25	23	21	21	20
1911 - 1926	39	48	41	39	38	34	34	32	31	27	25	24	24	21	22	24	19	18
1895 - 1910	31	33	26	26	27	25	22	22	21	21	16	16	15	10	11	8	8	5
Before 1895	22	13	15	15	14	13	10	8	6	5	4	3	2	1	1	1	0	0
Total	100%	100%	100%	100%	100%	100%	100%	100%	100%	100%	100%	100%	100%	100%	100%	100%	100%	100%
N	1773	1132	1742	1822	1950	1290	1566	1280	1552	1476	2688	2487	2850	2294	1612	1416	2232	2173
PDI#	44	39	24	20	19	10	-3	-8	-15	-21	-35	-38	-43	-56	-55	-59	-65	-73

PDI is proportion "born before 1911" minus proportion "born 1927 or later"

Table 1.2
Age Cohort of Respondent Sample Size

	1952	1954	1956	1958	1960	1962	1964	1966	1968	1970	1972	1974	1976	1978	1980	1982	1984	1986
1959 or later	**	**	**	**	**	**	**	**	**	**	**	**	**	74	114	140	346	416
1943 - 1958	**	**	**	**	**	**	26	91	152	248	744	838	1033	893	593	521	832	835
1927 - 1942	150	74	305	379	419	361	516	395	497	451	722	579	670	577	366	293	458	434
1911 - 1926	692	539	712	702	738	443	528	414	486	392	683	604	671	485	356	344	415	380
1895 - 1910	540	373	459	470	520	323	348	279	325	306	440	400	419	239	171	110	177	107
Before 1895	391	146	266	271	273	163	148	101	92	79	99	66	58	26	12	8	4	1
N	1773	1132	1742	1822	1950	1290	1566	1280	1552	1476	2688	2487	2850	2294	1612	1416	2232	2173

Table 1.3
Education of Respondent

	1952	1954	1956	1958	1960	1962	1964	1966	1968	1970	1972	1974	1976	1978	1980	1982	1984	1986
Grade School	41%	37%	31%	31%	30%	28%	25%	26%	23%	25%	20%	19%	17%	12%	12%	11%	11%	9%
High School	44	46	50	49	48	48	51	50	50	51	51	51	50	53	51	46	48	48
College	15	18	19	20	22	24	24	23	27	25	29	31	34	35	37	43	41	43
Total	100%	100%	100%	100%	100%	100%	100%	100%	100%	100%	100%	100%	100%	100%	100%	100%	100%	100%
N	1790	1135	1754	1802	1949	1291	1562	1285	1553	1500	2702	2503	2854	2292	1610	1413	2243	2152
PDI#	-27	-19	-12	-10	-8	-4	-1	-3	4	0	9	12	17	23	25	32	31	34

PDI is proportion "college" minus proportion "grade school"

Table 1.4
Education of Respondent Sample Size

	1952	1954	1956	1958	1960	1962	1964	1966	1968	1970	1972	1974	1976	1978	1980	1982	1984	1986
Grade School	740	416	542	550	584	359	388	337	359	368	539	469	476	274	194	159	242	194
High School	788	517	882	887	937	622	802	647	769	763	1374	1263	1423	1207	824	644	1073	1026
College	262	202	330	365	428	310	372	301	425	369	789	771	956	811	592	610	928	932
N	1790	1135	1754	1802	1949	1291	1562	1285	1553	1500	2702	2503	2854	2292	1610	1413	2243	2152

Table 1.5
Urbanism of Respondent's Residence

	1952	1954	1956	1958	1960	1962	1964	1966	1968	1970	1972	1974	1976	1978	1980	1982	1984	1986
Central cities	33%	34%	25%	25%	22%	25%	30%	29%	26%	27%	26%	28%	28%	27%	27%	28%	23%	25%
Suburbs	30	31	26	28	27	39	31	31	30	29	31	36	35	39	39	37	42	43
Non-urban areas	38	35	49	48	51	36	39	40	44	44	43	37	37	34	34	36	35	32
Total	100%	100%	100%	100%	100%	100%	100%	100%	100%	100%	100%	100%	100%	100%	100%	100%	100%	100%
N	1899	1139	1762	1822	1954	1297	1571	1291	1557	1507	2705	2523	2870	2304	1614	1418	2257	2176
PDI#	-5	-1	-24	-23	-28	-11	-9	-10	-18	-17	-17	-9	-9	-7	-6	-8	-12	-7

PDI is proportion "central cities" minus proportion "non-urban areas"

Table 1.6
Urbanism of Respondent's Residence Sample Size

	1952	1954	1956	1958	1960	1962	1964	1966	1968	1970	1972	1974	1976	1978	1980	1982	1984	1986
Central cities	620	390	438	448	433	328	469	378	406	405	698	698	801	624	442	392	525	552
Suburbs	560	348	466	506	532	500	490	403	471	441	840	902	1004	905	632	522	944	924
Non-urban areas	719	401	858	868	989	469	612	510	680	661	1167	923	1066	775	540	504	788	700
N	1899	1139	1762	1822	1954	1297	1571	1291	1557	1507	2705	2523	2870	2304	1614	1418	2257	2176

Table 1.7
Income of Respondent's Family Percentage Distributions

	1952	1954	1956	1958	1960	1962	1964	1966	1968	1970	1972	1974	1976	1978	1980	1982	1984	1986
Percentile 0-16	20%	21%	16%	16%	15%	22%	19%	20%	16%	15%	19%	16%	14%	17%	17%	17%	15%	17%
17-33	16	13	22	21	18	8	18	9	21	15	12	16	19	18	16	17	18	16
34-67	23	31	31	28	28	42	26	33	32	32	37	40	31	31	36	30	36	36
68-95	37	28	23	31	34	23	30	32	27	34	27	25	31	27	25	29	26	27
96-100	4	7	8	3	5	5	7	6	5	4	5	4	5	7	5	8	6	4
Total	100%	100%	100%	100%	100%	100%	100%	100%	100%	100%	100%	100%	100%	100%	100%	100%	100%	100%
N	1747	1096	1699	1743	1931	1229	1509	1246	1507	1450	2612	2363	2651	2000	1424	1253	1990	1985
PDI#	5	2	-8	-3	6	-1	-1	8	-5	8	1	-3	2	-1	-2	2	-1	-1

PDI is proportion "68-100 percentile" minus proportion "0-33 percentile"

Table 1.8
Income of Respondent's Family Sample Size

	1952	1954	1956	1958	1960	1962	1964	1966	1968	1970	1972	1974	1976	1978	1980	1982	1984	1986
Percentile 0-16	352	225	273	283	289	270	288	250	236	217	501	372	373	338	248	209	303	340
17-33	276	142	378	371	342	96	278	117	316	217	308	373	510	361	222	216	352	307
34-67	400	344	530	492	545	513	392	408	474	464	971	940	823	619	516	375	706	712
68-95	654	311	384	540	663	287	445	400	402	498	700	585	808	536	361	357	517	540
96-100	65	74	134	57	92	63	106	71	79	54	132	93	139	146	77	96	112	86
N	1747	1096	1699	1743	1931	1229	1509	1246	1507	1450	2612	2363	2651	2000	1424	1253	1990	1985

Table 1.9
Sex of Respondent

	1952	1954	1956	1958	1960	1962	1964	1966	1968	1970	1972	1974	1976	1978	1980	1982	1984	1986
Male	46%	47%	45%	47%	45%	45%	45%	44%	44%	43%	43%	42%	42%	44%	43%	45%	44%	44%
Female	54	53	55	53	55	55	55	56	56	57	57	58	58	56	57	55	56	56
Total	100%	100%	100%	100%	100%	100%	100%	100%	100%	100%	100%	100%	100%	100%	100%	100%	100%	100%
N	1799	1139	1762	1822	1954	1297	1571	1291	1557	1507	2705	2523	2870	2304	1614	1418	2257	2176

Table 1.10
Sex of Respondent Sample Size

	1952	1954	1956	1958	1960	1962	1964	1966	1968	1970	1972	1974	1976	1978	1980	1982	1984	1986
Male	821	532	787	851	881	583	703	572	684	647	1168	1053	1208	1017	695	634	989	952
Female	978	607	975	971	1073	714	868	719	873	860	1537	1470	1662	1287	919	784	1268	1224
N	1799	1139	1762	1822	1954	1297	1571	1291	1557	1507	2705	2523	2870	2304	1614	1418	2257	2176

Table 1.11
Race of Respondent

	1952	1954	1956	1958	1960	1962	1964	1966	1968	1970	1972	1974	1976	1978	1980	1982	1984	1986
White	90%	91%	92%	91%	91%	91%	90%	89%	90%	90%	90%	91%	90%	90%	88%	89%	89%	85%
Black	10	9	8	9	9	9	10	11	10	10	10	9	11	10	12	11	11	15
Total	100%	100%	100%	100%	100%	100%	100%	100%	100%	100%	100%	100%	100%	100%	100%	100%	100%	100%
N	1789	1125	1756	1805	1936	1286	1558	1274	1537	1485	2664	2473	2787	2250	1593	1402	2196	2127

Table 1.12
Race of Respondent Sample Size

	1952	1954	1956	1958	1960	1962	1964	1966	1968	1970	1972	1974	1976	1978	1980	1982	1984	1986
White	1618	1022	1610	1643	1764	1175	1399	1138	1388	1340	2397	2249	2494	2016	1406	1250	1946	1804
Black	171	103	146	162	172	111	159	136	149	145	267	224	293	234	187	152	250	323
N	1789	1125	1756	1805	1936	1286	1558	1274	1537	1485	2664	2473	2787	2250	1593	1402	2196	2127

Table 1.13
Union Membership in Respondent's Family

	1952	1954	1956	1958	1960	1962	1964	1966	1968	1970	1972	1974	1976	1978	1980	1982	1984	1986
Union household	27%	28%	27%	25%	27%	**	24%	28%	25%	24%	26%	26%	23%	26%	26%	21%	21%	20%
Non-union household	73	72	73	75	73	**	76	72	75	76	74	74	77	74	74	79	79	80
Total	100%	100%	100%	100%	100%	**	100%	100%	100%	100%	100%	100%	100%	100%	100%	100%	100%	100%
N	1781	1124	1757	1812	1922	**	1567	1282	1552	1488	2674	2466	2842	2290	1601	1407	2249	2165

Table 1.14
Union Membership in Respondent's Family Sample Size

	1952	1954	1956	1958	1960	1962	1964	1966	1968	1970	1972	1974	1976	1978	1980	1982	1984	1986
Union household	483	316	479	446	516	**	377	360	390	351	687	632	659	589	412	300	478	438
Non-union household	1298	808	1278	1366	1406	**	1190	922	1162	1137	1987	1834	2183	1701	1189	1107	1771	1727
N	1781	1124	1757	1812	1922	**	1567	1282	1552	1488	2674	2466	2842	2290	1601	1407	2249	2165

Table 1.15
Region of Respondent's Residence

	1952	1954	1956	1958	1960	1962	1964	1966	1968	1970	1972	1974	1976	1978	1980	1982	1984	1986
South	29%	31%	29%	30%	34%	35%	31%	30%	31%	35%	34%	36%	32%	35%	35%	36%	33%	36%
Non-South	71	69	71	70	66	65	69	70	69	65	67	64	68	65	65	64	67	64
Total	100%	100%	100%	100%	100%	100%	100%	100%	100%	100%	100%	100%	100%	100%	100%	100%	100%	100%
N	1899	1139	1762	1822	1954	1297	1571	1291	1557	1507	2705	2523	2870	2304	1614	1418	2257	2176

Table 1.16
Region of Respondent's Residence Sample Size

	1952	1954	1956	1958	1960	1962	1964	1966	1968	1970	1972	1974	1976	1978	1980	1982	1984	1986
South	555	351	513	548	657	452	480	384	481	521	906	907	931	811	571	510	750	779
Non-South	1344	788	1249	1274	1297	845	1091	907	1076	986	1799	1616	1939	1493	1043	908	1507	1397
N	1899	1139	1762	1822	1954	1297	1571	1291	1557	1507	2705	2523	2870	2304	1614	1418	2257	2176

Table 1.17
Occupation of Respondent

	1952	1954	1956	1958	1960	1962	1964	1966	1968	1970	1972	1974	1976	1978	1980	1982	1984	1986
Professional	15%	**	16%	18%	16%	**	19%	**	20%	21%	20%	22%	21%	25%	25%	25%	24%	26%
White collar	11	**	10	11	14	**	13	**	14	14	15	16	17	16	18	20	23	21
Blue collar	20	**	26	30	32	**	30	**	31	31	32	34	34	35	35	33	34	35
Unskilled	11	**	6	3	2	**	2	**	2	2	2	2	3	3	3	3	2	3
Farmers	7	**	7	5	6	**	5	**	4	4	3	3	3	2	2	3	4	3
Housewives	36	**	36	34	30	**	31	**	30	29	28	24	22	20	16	17	13	13
Total	100%	**	100%	100%	100%	**	100%	**	100%	100%	100%	100%	100%	100%	100%	100%	100%	100%
N	1774	**	1747	1803	1913	**	1544	**	1500	1472	2608	2422	2757	2224	1534	1364	2187	2093

Table 1.18
Occupation of Respondent Sample Size

	1952	1954	1956	1958	1960	1962	1964	1966	1968	1970	1972	1974	1976	1978	1980	1982	1984	1986
Professional	266	**	271	317	311	**	297	**	300	305	528	537	586	546	388	341	522	541
White collar	190	**	178	200	269	**	202	**	211	205	396	377	462	363	283	269	500	447
Blue collar	360	**	445	537	606	**	460	**	459	456	843	829	939	774	535	446	745	725
Unskilled	193	**	108	56	37	**	36	**	27	24	50	37	78	59	48	39	52	56
Farmers	131	**	113	89	109	**	74	**	60	63	72	74	83	44	32	44	80	57
Housewives	634	**	632	604	581	**	475	**	443	419	719	568	611	438	248	225	288	267
N	1774	**	1747	1803	1913	**	1544	**	1500	1472	2608	2422	2757	2224	1534	1364	2187	2093

Table 1.19
Religion of Respondent

	1952	1954	1956	1958	1960	1962	1964	1966	1968	1970	1972	1974	1976	1978	1980	1982	1984	1986
Protestant	72%	75%	73%	74%	74%	74%	70%	71%	72%	71%	69%	68%	65%	63%	64%	65%	62%	65%
Catholic	22	19	21	21	20	20	22	22	22	19	24	22	25	24	23	22	26	24
Jewish	3	3	3	3	3	3	3	3	3	3	2	2	2	3	3	2	2	2
Other and None	3	3	3	2	2	3	5	4	4	8	5	8	8	10	10	11	10	10
Total	100%	100%	100%	100%	100%	100%	100%	100%	100%	100%	100%	100%	100%	100%	100%	100%	100%	100%
N	1787	1138	1759	1818	1827	1295	1570	1280	1540	1502	2695	2500	2854	2283	1598	1409	2244	2154

Table 1.20
Religion of Respondent Sample Size

	1952	1954	1956	1958	1960	1962	1964	1966	1968	1970	1972	1974	1976	1978	1980	1982	1984	1986
Protestant	1281	857	1287	1338	1359	952	1105	911	1102	1059	1850	1704	1858	1439	1014	921	1387	1402
Catholic	387	217	372	386	368	261	349	280	337	289	640	541	707	548	370	314	582	511
Jewish	59	34	56	55	62	44	45	43	42	42	61	60	68	67	51	24	53	32
Other and None	60	30	44	39	38	38	71	46	59	112	144	195	222	229	163	150	222	209
N	1787	1138	1759	1818	1827	1295	1570	1280	1540	1502	2695	2500	2854	2283	1598	1409	2244	2154

Table 1.21
Education of Age Cohorts

	1952	1954	1956	1958	1960	1962	1964	1966	1968	1970	1972	1974	1976	1978	1980	1982	1984	1986	
1959 or later Cohort	**	**	**	**	**	**	**	**	**	**	**	**	**	1%	0%	2%	2%	1%	Grade School
	**	**	**	**	**	**	**	**	**	**	**	**	**	70	68	50	55	60	High School
	**	**	**	**	**	**	**	**	**	**	**	**	**	29	33	48	43	38	College
1943 - 1958 Cohort	**	**	**	**	**	**	8%*	24%	4%	3%	4%	2%	2%	2%	3%	3%	2%	3%	Grade School
	**	**	**	**	**	**	68*	53	47	62	55	56	53	51	49	41	43	42	High School
	**	**	**	**	**	**	24*	43	49	35	40	41	44	47	48	56	55	55	College
1927 - 1942 Cohort	23%	16%	12%	14%	10%	9%	9%	13%	9%	12%	9%	12%	10%	8%	7%	7%	10%	11%	Grade School
	57	62	69	67	69	57	61	60	59	58	54	52	52	56	53	51	52	45	High School
	20	22	19	19	22	34	30	27	32	30	36	36	38	36	40	42	38	44	College
1911 - 1926 Cohort	28%	26%	23%	22%	21%	21%	24%	21%	22%	27%	24%	25%	24%	20%	21%	23%	22%	21%	Grade School
	57	55	55	53	55	55	53	56	52	53	54	51	52	57	56	48	53	53	High School
	16	19	22	25	25	24	23	23	26	20	22	24	24	23	23	29	25	27	College
1895 - 1910 Cohort	48%	47%	41%	41%	45%	43%	40%	46%	47%	50%	48%	47%	46%	41%	39%	36%	45%	38%	Grade School
	36	37	41	40	33	39	41	39	36	34	38	37	38	40	39	39	36	35	High School
	16	16	18	19	22	18	19	16	17	16	14	16	16	19	22	20	20	27	College
Before 1895 Cohort	63%	62%	58%	59%	59%	60%	51%	64%	54%	53%	59%	43%	61%	56%*	–	–	–	–	Grade School
	27	24	32	29	27	28	32	21	34	29	30	43	26	28*	–	–	–	–	High School
	9	14	10	12	15	12	17	15	12	18	11	14	13	16*	–	–	–	–	College

Table 1.22
Education of Age Cohorts Summarized with a Percentage Difference Index#

	1952	1954	1956	1958	1960	1962	1964	1966	1968	1970	1972	1974	1976	1978	1980	1982	1984	1986
1959 or later Cohort	**	**	**	**	**	**	**	**	**	**	**	**	**	28	3	4	4	3
1943 - 1958 Cohort	**	**	**	**	**	**	16*	39	45	32	36	39	42	45	45	54	53	52
1927 - 1942 Cohort	-3	5	7	5	12	25	20	14	23	19	27	24	29	28	33	35	28	33
1911 - 1926 Cohort	-12	-7	-1	3	4	3	-1	2	4	-7	-2	-2	0	3	2	7	2	6
1895 - 1910 Cohort	-33	-31	-23	-22	-23	-24	-20	-30	-30	-40	-34	-32	-30	-40	-21	-10	-25	-11
Before 1895 Cohort	-54	-47	-48	-46	-44	-48	-34	-50	-42	-34	-48	-29	-48	-40*	–	–	–	–
Total PDI	-27	-19	-12	-10	-8	-4	-1	-3	4	0	9	12	17	23	25	32	31	34

PDI is proportion "college" minus proportion "grade school"

Table 1.23
Urbanism of Age Cohorts

	1952	1954	1956	1958	1960	1962	1964	1966	1968	1970	1972	1974	1976	1978	1980	1982	1984	1986	
1959 or later Cohort	**	**	**	**	**	**	**	**	**	**	**	**	**	27%	28%	29%	24%	27%	Central Cities
	**	**	**	**	**	**	**	**	**	**	**	**	**	39	38	37	41	39	Suburbs
	**	**	**	**	**	**	**	**	**	**	**	**	**	34	34	34	36	34	Non-urban areas
1943 or later Cohort	**	**	**	**	**	**	27%*	52%	32%	34%	27%	31%	27%	29%	29%	30%	23%	23%	Central Cities
	**	**	**	**	**	**	23*	23	23	27	33	39	38	39	40	37	43	44	Suburbs
	**	**	**	**	**	**	50*	25	45	39	40	30	35	32	32	33	33	33	Non-urban areas
1927 - 1942 Cohort	37%	45%	27%	26%	20%	28%	32%	29%	27%	25%	26%	28%	28%	24%	22%	26%	19%	25%	Central Cities
	31	31	25	24	28	44	37	34	35	38	35	38	41	44	47	36	45	47	Suburbs
	33	24	48	50	52	29	32	37	38	37	39	35	31	31	31	39	37	29	Non-urban areas
1911 - 1926 Cohort	32%	32%	25%	24%	23%	22%	26%	27%	23%	27%	25%	25%	28%	27%	29%	25%	25%	28%	Central Cities
	29	32	28	28	24	46	34	38	36	26	34	38	34	36	34	39	43	41	Suburbs
	39	36	47	48	53	32	40	36	41	46	41	37	39	37	37	36	32	31	Non-urban areas
1895 - 1910 Cohort	33%	38%	25%	26%	23%	27%	33%	29%	25%	23%	25%	24%	32%	26%	30%	32%	26%	27%	Central Cities
	29	28	25	29	28	31	26	25	21	22	21	28	21	36	33	30	31	34	Suburbs
	37	35	51	45	49	42	41	46	55	55	53	49	47	39	37	38	43	39	Non-urban areas
Before 1895 Cohort	32%	29%	21%	20%	19%	25%	29%	19%	32%	27%	22%	27%	16%	35%*	-	-	-	-	Central Cities
	31	34	25	31	34	22	16	19	15	25	13	14	29	39*	-	-	-	-	Suburbs
	37	38	54	49	47	54	55	62	53	48	65	59	54	27*	-	-	-	-	Non-urban areas

Table 1.24
Urbanism of Age Cohorts Summarized by a Percentage Difference Index#

	1952	1954	1956	1958	1960	1962	1964	1966	1968	1970	1972	1974	1976	1978	1980	1982	1984	1986
1959 or later Cohort	**	**	**	**	**	**	**	**	**	**	**	**	**	-7	-6	-6	-12	-8
1943 - 1958 Cohort	**	**	**	**	**	**	-23*	26	-14	-4	-12	1	-7	-4	-3	-3	-10	-9
1927 - 1942 Cohort	4	20	-21	-24	-32	-1	0	-8	-11	-12	-13	-7	-4	-7	-8	-13	-18	-4
1911 - 1926 Cohort	-7	-4	-22	-24	-29	-10	-13	-9	-17	-19	-17	-11	-11	-10	-9	-12	-7	-3
1895 - 1910 Cohort	-4	3	-26	-19	-26	-15	-8	-17	-30	-31	-28	-25	-16	-13	-7	-6	-17	-12
Before 1895 Cohort	-5	-9	-33	-29	-27	-30	-26	-44	-22	-22	-42	-32	-38	8*	-	-	-	-
Total PDI	-5	-1	-24	-23	-28	-11	-9	-10	-18	-17	-17	-9	-9	-7	-6	-8	-12	-7

PDI is proportion "central cities" minus proportion "non-urban areas"

Social Characteristics of Age Cohorts

Table 1.25
Family Income of Age Cohorts

	1952	1954	1956	1958	1960	1962	1964	1966	1968	1970	1972	1974	1976	1978	1980	1982	1984	1986	
1959 or later Cohort	**	**	**	**	**	**	**	**	**	**	**	**	**	26%	18%	31%	25%	22%	Percentile 0-16
	**	**	**	**	**	**	**	**	**	**	**	**	**	15	19	24	17	19	17-33
	**	**	**	**	**	**	**	**	**	**	**	**	**	28	32	20	35	36	34-67
	**	**	**	**	**	**	**	**	**	**	**	**	**	28	27	18	19	20	68-95
	**	**	**	**	**	**	**	**	**	**	**	**	**	3	5	7	5	3	96-100
1943 - 1958 Cohort	**	**	**	**	**	**	15%*	21%	14%	10%	15%	13%	10%	12%	13%	9%	9%	11%	Percentile 0-16
	**	**	**	**	**	**	42*	7	27	14	12	15	18	18	15	15	14	12	17-33
	**	**	**	**	**	**	19*	52	38	43	48	49	41	36	43	35	40	42	34-67
	**	**	**	**	**	**	23*	18	21	31	24	22	29	27	26	36	31	32	68-95
	**	**	**	**	**	**	0*	2	1	1	3	1	2	6	4	4	6	5	96-100
1927 - 1942 Cohort	15%	7%	9%	8%	5%	11%	8%	8%	6%	5%	7%	4%	6%	7%	5%	8%	10%	13%	Percentile 0-16
	20	19	25	29	17	7	15	7	16	10	8	12	9	14	10	11	10	12	17-33
	29	42	45	35	38	56	37	35	38	30	39	42	30	32	36	29	35	29	34-67
	35	30	18	28	37	23	34	43	35	49	39	36	45	35	38	37	36	39	68-95
	1	1	3	0	3	3	6	7	6	5	8	7	11	12	11	16	9	8	96-100
1911 - 1926 Cohort	11%	12%	8%	9%	5%	10%	10%	13%	7%	12%	15%	15%	13%	21%	23%	20%	18%	25%	Percentile 0-16
	14	12	20	14	13	7	20	8	17	9	10	13	20	18	17	21	27	21	17-33
	28	35	34	34	31	43	25	31	33	35	36	35	26	27	37	31	35	34	34-67
	46	34	30	39	46	33	36	40	36	39	32	30	34	26	20	20	18	17	68-95
	2	7	8	5	6	8	9	8	7	6	7	7	6	8	4	9	3	3	96-100
1895 - 1910 Cohort	17%	22%	13%	16%	18%	29%	30%	30%	33%	29%	42%	37%	35%	43%	49%	48%	34%	47%	Percentile 0-16
	14	13	23	24	20	10	20	16	30	26	22	30	38	29	27	26	42	26	17-33
	21	30	26	23	27	36	19	32	24	26	24	24	18	18	15	19	17	21	34-67
	42	28	25	34	29	20	22	19	9	16	10	8	7	9	7	7	7	6	68-95
	6	7	13	4	6	6	8	3	4	2	2	1	2	2	3	1	0	0	96-100
Before 1895 Cohort	42%	57%	52%	50%	54%	69%	67%	71%	60%	54%	72%	57%	62%*	72%*	-	-	-	-	Percentile 0-16
	20	15	24	25	24	8	18	10	28	24	14	13	29*	8*	-	-	-	-	17-33
	14	15	16	13	10	17	6	13	7	17	9	23	9*	16*	-	-	-	-	34-67
	19	7	5	7	9	4	7	6	2	5	5	8	0*	0*	-	-	-	-	68-95
	4	8	3	4	4	2	1	0	2	0	1	0	0*	4*	-	-	-	-	96-100

Table 1.26
Family Income of Age Cohorts Summarized with a Percentage Difference Index#

	1952	1954	1956	1958	1960	1962	1964	1966	1968	1970	1972	1974	1976	1978	1980	1982	1984	1986
1959 or later Cohort	**	**	**	**	**	**	**	**	**	**	**	**	**	-10	-6	-31	-18	-19
1943 - 1958 Cohort	**	**	**	**	**	**	-35*	-7	-19	8	0	-5	4	3	3	16	15	14
1927 - 1942 Cohort	1	6	-14	-9	18	7	16	35	19	39	32	28	40	26	34	34	25	21
1911 - 1926 Cohort	23	17	11	21	34	24	17	27	19	24	13	9	7	-6	-16	-13	-24	-27
1895 - 1910 Cohort	17	0	2	-3	-3	-12	-20	-24	-51	-36	-51	-57	-63	-61	-66	-66	-69	-67
Before 1895 Cohort	-40	-57	-68	-64	-65	-71	-77	-76	-84	-72	-80	-62	-91*	-76*	-	-	-	-
Total PDI	5	2	-8	-3	6	-1	-1	8	-5	8	1	-3	2	-1	-2	2	-1	-1

PDI is proportion "68-100 percentile" minus proportion "0-33 percentile"

Table 1.27
Percent Female within Age Cohorts

	1952	1954	1956	1958	1960	1962	1964	1966	1968	1970	1972	1974	1976	1978	1980	1982	1984	1986
1959 or later Cohort	**	**	**	**	**	**	**	**	**	**	**	**	**	**	60%	54%	61%	59%	57%
1943 - 1958 Cohort	**	**	**	**	**	**	**	46%*	53%	52%	60%	54%	61%	59%	54%	58%	52%	54%	54%
1927 - 1942 Cohort	55%	65%	61%	58%	58%	55%	58%	56%	59%	57%	55%	55%	54%	54%	54%	53%	54%	54%
1911 - 1926 Cohort	54%	50%	58%	55%	55%	55%	52%	56%	55%	55%	57%	55%	58%	55%	56%	56%	56%	60%
1895 - 1910 Cohort	54%	54%	50%	48%	50%	53%	57%	54%	53%	57%	61%	59%	61%	66%	64%	64%	63%	68%
Before 1895 Cohort	55%	55%	51%	52%	58%	59%	57%	55%	62%	61%	66%	61%	63%	77%*	-	-	-	-
Total Population	54%	53%	55%	53%	55%	55%	55%	56%	56%	57%	57%	58%	58%	56%	57%	55%	56%	56%

Table 1.28
Percent Black within Age Cohorts

	1952	1954	1956	1958	1960	1962	1964	1966	1968	1970	1972	1974	1976	1978	1980	1982	1984	1986
1959 or later Cohort	**	**	**	**	**	**	**	**	**	**	**	**	**	11%	12%	10%	16%	17%
1943 - 1958 Cohort	**	**	**	**	**	**	4%*	16%	6%	11%	11%	11%	12%	11%	13%	12%	11%	14%
1927 - 1942 Cohort	11%	6%	12%	13%	13%	8%	13%	10%	12%	10%	11%	9%	9%	11%	11%	11%	10%	17%
1911 - 1926 Cohort	11%	11%	8%	8%	8%	10%	10%	12%	9%	11%	8%	6%	11%	10%	11%	11%	12%	16%
1895 - 1910 Cohort	10%	9%	9%	10%	9%	8%	8%	9%	10%	8%	8%	9%	11%	6%	11%	9%	6%	6%
Before 1895 Cohort	7%	7%	5%	4%	6%	7%	8%	7%	8%	6%	8%	6%	10%	8%*	-	-	-	-
Total Population	10%	9%	8%	9%	9%	9%	10%	11%	10%	10%	10%	9%	11%	10%	12%	11%	11%	15%

Table 1.29
Percent Union Households within Age Cohorts

	1952	1954	1956	1958	1960	1962	1964	1966	1968	1970	1972	1974	1976	1978	1980	1982	1984	1986
1959 or later Cohort	**	**	**	**	**	**	**	**	**	**	**	**	**	26%	22%	12%	20%	14%
1943 - 1958 Cohort	**	**	**	**	**	**	39%*	30%	25%	29%	28%	29%	27%	26%	27%	26%	23%	24%
1927 - 1942 Cohort	34%	36%	35%	32%	37%	**	27%	31%	28%	26%	29%	30%	25%	30%	32%	29%	26%	23%
1911 - 1926 Cohort	34%	33%	32%	27%	28%	**	27%	34%	31%	30%	30%	27%	26%	29%	25%	18%	20%	18%
1895 - 1910 Cohort	26%	26%	25%	23%	25%	**	23%	22%	18%	13%	13%	14%	11%	9%	13%	5%	9%	8%
Before 1895 Cohort	15%	11%	11%	11%	13%	**	8%	11%	4%	6%	7%	3%	2%	12%*	-	-	-	-
Total Population	27%	28%	27%	25%	27%	**	24%	28%	25%	24%	26%	26%	23%	26%	26%	21%	21%	20%

Table 1.30
Region within Age Cohorts: Percent South

	1952	1954	1956	1958	1960	1962	1964	1966	1968	1970	1972	1974	1976	1978	1980	1982	1984	1986
1959 or later Cohort	**	**	**	**	**	**	**	**	**	**	**	**	**	42%	40%	36%	37%	42%
1943 - 1958 Cohort	**	**	**	**	**	**	39%*	28%	29%	38%	35%	32%	30%	32%	35%	35%	33%	33%
1927 - 1942 Cohort	31%	28%	32%	27%	29%	34%	27%	24%	29%	32%	32%	36%	29%	35%	32%	35%	33%	37%
1911 - 1926 Cohort	30%	31%	29%	32%	34%	38%	32%	27%	29%	36%	31%	34%	33%	38%	39%	38%	32%	35%
1895 - 1910 Cohort	25%	30%	29%	32%	38%	32%	31%	39%	37%	34%	37%	43%	44%	41%	33%	40%	36%	34%
Before 1895 Cohort	27%	34%	27%	27%	33%	34%	37%	39%	38%	38%	30%	46%	28%	27%*	-	-	-	-
Total Population	29%	31%	29%	30%	34%	35%	31%	30%	31%	35%	34%	36%	32%	35%	35%	36%	33%	36%

Table 1.31
Occupation of Age Cohorts

Cohort	1952	1954	1956	1958	1960	1962	1964	1966	1968	1970	1972	1974	1976	1978	1980	1982	1984	1986	Occupation
1959 or later Cohort	**	**	**	**	**	**	**	**	**	**	**	**	**	9%	6%	18%	16%	14%	Professional
	**	**	**	**	**	**	**	**	**	**	**	**	**	32	26	29	28	25	White collar
	**	**	**	**	**	**	**	**	**	**	**	**	**	40	45	38	39	40	Blue collar
	**	**	**	**	**	**	**	**	**	**	**	**	**	5	10	3	3	6	Unskilled
	**	**	**	**	**	**	**	**	**	**	**	**	**	0	2	2	4	3	Farmers
	**	**	**	**	**	**	**	**	**	**	**	**	**	14	10	10	10	13	Housewives
1943 - 1958 Cohort	**	**	**	**	**	**	8%*	**	19%	19%	19%	20%	21%	25%	28%	27%	29%	31%	Professional
	**	**	**	**	**	**	20*	**	19	20	21	21	22	20	20	20	24	21	White collar
	**	**	**	**	**	**	32*	**	35	27	32	35	33	34	33	33	31	34	Blue collar
	**	**	**	**	**	**	4*	**	1	2	3	2	4	3	3	3	3	2	Unskilled
	**	**	**	**	**	**	4*	**	2	3	1	0	1	1	1	2	2	2	Farmers
	**	**	**	**	**	**	32*	**	25	29	24	23	20	17	15	15	11	11	Housewives
1927 - 1942 Cohort	7%	**	11%	11%	17%	**	17%	**	23%	25%	25%	27%	28%	27%	32%	27%	25%	33%	Professional
	21	**	11	11	13	**	15	**	14	14	16	14	15	15	19	21	21	19	White collar
	24	**	24	30	30	**	31	**	27	28	31	31	33	35	35	32	36	30	Blue collar
	10	**	6	3	2	**	2	**	1	1	2	2	2	2	1	3	2	3	Unskilled
	4	**	2	2	3	**	2	**	2	2	2	2	2	2	1	2	4	1	Farmers
	35	**	47	43	36	**	34	**	33	30	25	25	20	19	12	15	12	15	Housewives
1911 - 1926 Cohort	12%	**	16%	20%	17%	**	22%	**	21%	20%	21%	25%	21%	24%	22%	24%	20%	21%	Professional
	12	**	12	13	16	**	12	**	15	14	15	15	15	12	16	17	22	20	White collar
	24	**	26	29	33	**	32	**	32	37	36	39	36	38	37	33	35	40	Blue collar
	10	**	6	2	2	**	3	**	3	1	1	1	3	3	2	2	2	2	Unskilled
	5	**	5	3	4	**	4	**	3	4	2	3	3	3	3	6	4	4	Farmers
	37	**	35	32	28	**	28	**	26	24	25	17	22	21	20	18	18	14	Housewives
1895 - 1910 Cohort	20%	**	21%	21%	19%	**	29%	**	15%	19%	15%	16%	13%	24%	23%	23%	22%	21%	Professional
	10	**	9	10	15	**	12	**	13	12	8	10	11	12	13	14	17	28	White collar
	18	**	29	34	32	**	38	**	34	33	32	34	37	30	31	31	31	28	Blue collar
	12	**	5	4	1	**	1	**	2	3	2	2	2	1	4	1	3	1	Unskilled
	9	**	8	6	8	**	8	**	8	5	7	9	8	5	5	6	7	7	Farmers
	31	**	28	25	25	**	13	**	29	28	37	30	30	29	25	26	21	15	Housewives
Before 1895 Cohort	16%	**	9%	15%	8%	**	19%	**	14%	11%	15%	19%	7%	19%*	-	-	-	-	Professional
	7	**	5	8	11	**	7	**	7	11	7	14	11	12*	-	-	-	-	White collar
	16	**	21	24	30	**	23	**	25	23	24	17	32	46*	-	-	-	-	Blue collar
	11	**	9	3	3	**	1	**	2	1	2	0	3	0*	-	-	-	-	Unskilled
	10	**	14	13	11	**	15	**	6	15	12	14	15	4*	-	-	-	-	Farmers
	41	**	41	37	37	**	35	**	44	38	41	36	33	19*	-	-	-	-	Housewives

Table 1.32
Incidence of Occupations within Age Cohorts

Percent Professional

	1952	1954	1956	1958	1960	1962	1964	1966	1968	1970	1972	1974	1976	1978	1980	1982	1984	1986	
	**	**	**	**	**	**	**	**	**	**	**	**	**	9%	6%	18%	16%	14%	1959 or later
	**	**	**	**	**	**	8%*	**	19%	19%	19%	20%	21%	25%	28%	27%	29%	31%	1943 - 1958
	7%	**	11%	11%	17%	**	17%	**	23%	25%	25%	27%	28%	27%	32%	27%	25%	33%	1927 - 1942
	12%	**	16%	20%	17%	**	22%	**	21%	20%	21%	25%	21%	24%	22%	24%	20%	21%	1911 - 1926
	20%	**	21%	21%	19%	**	19%	**	15%	19%	15%	16%	13%	24%	23%	23%	22%	21%	1895 - 1910
	16%	**	9%	15%	8%	**	19%	**	16%	11%	15%	19%	7%	19%*	-	-	-	-	Before 1895

Percent White collar

	1952	1954	1956	1958	1960	1962	1964	1966	1968	1970	1972	1974	1976	1978	1980	1982	1984	1986	
	**	**	**	**	**	**	**	**	**	**	**	**	**	32%	26%	29%	28%	25%	1959 or later
	**	**	**	**	**	**	20%*	**	19%	20%	21%	21%	22%	20%	20%	20%	24%	21%	1943 - 1958
	21%	**	11%	11%	13%	**	15%	**	14%	14%	16%	14%	15%	15%	19%	21%	21%	19%	1927 - 1942
	12%	**	12%	13%	16%	**	12%	**	15%	14%	15%	15%	15%	12%	16%	17%	22%	20%	1911 - 1926
	10%	**	9%	10%	15%	**	14%	**	13%	12%	8%	10%	11%	12%	13%	14%	17%	28%	1895 - 1910
	7%	**	5%	8%	11%	**	7%	**	7%	11%	7%	14%	11%	12%*	-	-	-	-	Before 1895

Percent Blue collar

	1952	1954	1956	1958	1960	1962	1964	1966	1968	1970	1972	1974	1976	1978	1980	1982	1984	1986	
	**	**	**	**	**	**	**	**	**	**	**	**	**	40%	45%	38%	39%	40%	1959 or later
	**	**	**	**	**	**	32%*	**	35%	27%	32%	35%	33%	34%	33%	33%	31%	34%	1943 - 1958
	24%	**	24%	30%	30%	**	31%	**	27%	28%	31%	31%	33%	35%	35%	32%	36%	30%	1927 - 1942
	24%	**	26%	29%	33%	**	32%	**	32%	37%	36%	39%	36%	38%	37%	33%	35%	40%	1911 - 1926
	18%	**	29%	34%	32%	**	29%	**	34%	33%	32%	34%	37%	30%	31%	31%	31%	28%	1895 - 1910
	16%	**	21%	24%	30%	**	23%	**	25%	23%	24%	17%	32%	46%*	-	-	-	-	Before 1895

Percent Unskilled

	1952	1954	1956	1958	1960	1962	1964	1966	1968	1970	1972	1974	1976	1978	1980	1982	1984	1986	
	**	**	**	**	**	**	**	**	**	**	**	**	**	5%	10%	3%	3%	6%	1959 or later
	**	**	**	**	**	**	4%*	**	1%	2%	3%	2%	4%	3%	3%	3%	3%	2%	1943 - 1958
	10%	**	6%	3%	2%	**	2%	**	1%	1%	2%	2%	2%	2%	1%	3%	2%	3%	1927 - 1942
	10%	**	6%	2%	2%	**	3%	**	3%	1%	1%	1%	3%	3%	2%	2%	2%	2%	1911 - 1926
	12%	**	5%	4%	1%	**	3%	**	2%	3%	2%	2%	2%	1%	4%	1%	3%	1%	1895 - 1910
	11%	**	9%	3%	3%	**	1%	**	2%	1%	2%	0%	3%	0%*	-	-	-	-	Before 1895

Percent Farmers

	1952	1954	1956	1958	1960	1962	1964	1966	1968	1970	1972	1974	1976	1978	1980	1982	1984	1986	
	**	**	**	**	**	**	**	**	**	**	**	**	**	0%	2%	2%	4%	3%	1959 or later
	**	**	**	**	**	**	4%*	**	2%	3%	1%	0%	1%	1%	1%	2%	2%	2%	1943 - 1958
	4%	**	2%	2%	3%	**	2%	**	2%	2%	2%	2%	2%	2%	1%	2%	4%	1%	1927 - 1942
	5%	**	5%	3%	4%	**	4%	**	3%	4%	2%	3%	3%	3%	3%	6%	4%	4%	1911 - 1926
	9%	**	8%	6%	8%	**	6%	**	8%	5%	7%	9%	8%	5%	5%	6%	7%	7%	1895 - 1910
	10%	**	14%	13%	11%	**	15%	**	6%	15%	12%	14%	15%	4%*	-	-	-	-	Before 1895

Percent Housewives

	1952	1954	1956	1958	1960	1962	1964	1966	1968	1970	1972	1974	1976	1978	1980	1982	1984	1986	
	**	**	**	**	**	**	**	**	**	**	**	**	**	14%	10%	10%	10%	13%	1959 or later
	**	**	**	**	**	**	32%*	**	25%	29%	24%	23%	20%	17%	15%	15%	11%	11%	1943 - 1958
	35%	**	47%	43%	36%	**	34%	**	33%	30%	25%	25%	20%	19%	12%	15%	12%	15%	1927 - 1942
	37%	**	35%	32%	28%	**	28%	**	26%	24%	25%	17%	22%	21%	20%	18%	18%	14%	1911 - 1926
	31%	**	28%	25%	25%	**	29%	**	29%	28%	37%	30%	30%	29%	25%	26%	21%	15%	1895 - 1910
	41%	**	41%	37%	37%	**	35%	**	44%	38%	41%	36%	33%	19%*	-	-	-	-	Before 1895

Social Characteristics of Age Cohorts

Table 1.33
Religion of Age Cohorts

	1952	1954	1956	1958	1960	1962	1964	1966	1968	1970	1972	1974	1976	1978	1980	1982	1984	1986	
1959 or later Cohort	**	**	**	**	**	**	**	**	**	**	**	**	**	67%	52%	53%	58%	59%	Protestant
	**	**	**	**	**	**	**	**	**	**	**	**	**	18	28	31	29	26	Catholic
	**	**	**	**	**	**	**	**	**	**	**	**	**	O	1	1	O	O	Jewish
	**	**	**	**	**	**	**	**	**	**	**	**	**	15	19	15	13	15	Other
1943 - 1958 Cohort	**	**	**	**	**	**	77%*	73%	61%	65%	63%	63%	59%	59%	58%	62%	55%	62%	Protestant
	**	**	**	**	**	**	19*	21	29	20	27	23	27	25	24	21	29	24	Catholic
	**	**	**	**	**	**	0*	2	3	2	2	2	3	3	3	2	3	2	Jewish
	**	**	**	**	**	**	4*	3	7	13	8	12	12	14	15	15	13	13	Other
1927 - 1942 Cohort	70%	65%	70%	76%	72%	71%	65%	67%	68%	66%	67%	69%	63%	65%	64%	66%	69%	68%	Protestant
	23	24	26	21	23	22	27	25	25	22	25	23	26	26	26	23	22	22	Catholic
	3	3	1	2	2	3	3	5	3	4	2	2	3	2	3	2	1	3	Jewish
	5	8	3	1	3	4	5	4	4	9	6	6	8	8	7	8	8	7	Other
1911 - 1926 Cohort	69%	75%	70%	71%	71%	72%	70%	70%	72%	73%	68%	68%	69%	66%	72%	71%	65%	74%	Protestant
	25	21	24	24	23	23	22	23	22	19	26	24	24	24	20	22	25	22	Catholic
	2	2	3	3	3	3	3	4	3	3	3	3	2	5	3	2	4	2	Jewish
	4	2	3	2	2	2	5	3	4	5	3	5	5	6	5	6	6	2	Other
1895 - 1910 Cohort	72%	76%	77%	74%	77%	76%	73%	76%	77%	76%	77%	76%	73%	66%	71%	78%	77%	66%	Protestant
	22	18	16	18	17	18	20	18	17	15	17	17	21	19	18	16	17	29	Catholic
	5	4	5	4	6	4	3	3	3	3	2	2	2	6	7	2	2	2	Jewish
	2	2	2	4	1	3	4	3	3	6	3	5	4	9	5	4	5	3	Other
Before 1895 Cohort	78%	82%	79%	76%	82%	79%	82%	79%	86%	80%	90%	88%	85%	77%*	-	-	-	-	Protestant
	16	10	16	20	14	14	14	12	12	14	7	6	11	23*	-	-	-	-	Catholic
	4	3	2	2	1	4	2	1	1	3	2	6	2	0*	-	-	-	-	Jewish
	3	4	3	2	2	3	2	8	1	4	1	O	3	0*	-	-	-	-	Other

Table 1.34
Incidence of Religions within Age Cohort Groups

	1952	1954	1956	1958	1960	1962	1964	1966	1968	1970	1972	1974	1976	1978	1980	1982	1984	1986	
Percent Protestant	**	**	**	**	**	**	**	**	**	**	**	**	**	67%	52%	53%	58%	59%	1959 or later
	**	**	**	**	**	**	77%*	73%	61%	65%	63%	63%	59%	59%	58%	62%	55%	62%	1943 - 1958
	70%	65%	70%	76%	72%	71%	65%	67%	68%	66%	67%	69%	63%	65%	64%	66%	69%	68%	1927 - 1942
	69%	75%	70%	71%	71%	72%	70%	70%	72%	73%	68%	68%	69%	66%	72%	71%	65%	74%	1911 - 1926
	72%	76%	77%	74%	77%	76%	73%	76%	77%	76%	77%	76%	73%	66%	71%	78%	77%	66%	1895 - 1910
	78%	82%	79%	76%	82%	79%	82%	79%	86%	80%	90%	88%	85%	77%*	-	-	-	-	Before 1895
Percent Catholic	**	**	**	**	**	**	**	**	**	**	**	**	**	18%	28%	31%	29%	26%	1959 or later
	**	**	**	**	**	**	19%*	21%	29%	20%	27%	23%	27%	25%	24%	21%	29%	24%	1943 - 1958
	23%	24%	26%	21%	23%	22%	27%	25%	25%	22%	25%	23%	26%	26%	26%	23%	22%	22%	1927 - 1942
	25%	21%	24%	24%	23%	23%	22%	23%	22%	19%	26%	24%	24%	24%	20%	22%	25%	22%	1911 - 1926
	22%	18%	16%	18%	17%	18%	20%	18%	17%	15%	17%	17%	21%	19%	18%	16%	17%	29%	1895 - 1910
	16%	10%	16%	20%	14%	14%	14%	12%	12%	14%	7%	6%	11%	23%*	-	-	-	-	Before 1895
Percent Jewish	**	**	**	**	**	**	**	**	**	**	**	**	**	0%	1%	1%	0%	0%	1959 or later
	**	**	**	**	**	**	0%*	2%	3%	2%	2%	2%	3%	3%	3%	2%	3%	2%	1943 - 1958
	3%	3%	1%	2%	2%	3%	3%	5%	3%	4%	2%	2%	3%	2%	3%	2%	1%	3%	1927 - 1942
	2%	2%	3%	3%	3%	3%	3%	4%	3%	3%	3%	3%	2%	5%	3%	2%	4%	2%	1911 - 1926
	5%	4%	5%	4%	6%	4%	3%	3%	3%	3%	2%	2%	2%	6%	7%	2%	2%	2%	1895 - 1910
	4%	3%	2%	2%	1%	4%	2%	1%	1%	3%	2%	6%	2%	0%*	-	-	-	-	Before 1895
Percent Other and None	**	**	**	**	**	**	**	**	**	**	**	**	**	15%	19%	15%	13%	15%	1959 or later
	**	**	**	**	**	**	4%*	3%	7%	13%	8%	12%	12%	14%	15%	15%	13%	13%	1943 - 1958
	5%	8%	3%	1%	3%	4%	5%	4%	4%	9%	6%	6%	8%	8%	7%	8%	8%	7%	1927 - 1942
	4%	2%	3%	2%	2%	2%	5%	3%	4%	5%	3%	5%	5%	6%	5%	6%	6%	2%	1911 - 1926
	2%	2%	2%	4%	1%	3%	4%	3%	3%	6%	3%	5%	4%	9%	5%	4%	5%	3%	1895 - 1910
	3%	4%	3%	2%	2%	3%	2%	8%	1%	4%	1%	0%	3%	0%*	-	-	-	-	Before 1895

Table 1.35
Age Cohorts of Education Groups

	1952	1954	1956	1958	1960	1962	1964	1966	1968	1970	1972	1974	1976	1978	1980	1982	1984	1986	
Grade School	**	**	**	**	**	**	**	**	**	**	**	**	**	0%	0%	2%	3%	3%	1959 or later
	**	**	**	**	**	**	1%	1%	2%	2%	6%	4%	5%	6	9	9	7	12	1943 - 1958
	5%	3%	7%	10%	7%	9%	12	15	12	15	13	15	13	18	13	13	19	25	1927 - 1942
	26	33	30	28	26	26	32	26	30	30	31	33	34	36	39	49	38	40	1911 - 1926
	36	42	35	35	40	38	35	38	43	43	39	41	40	35	34	25	32	21	1895 - 1910
	34	22	28	28	27	27	19	20	14	11	11	6	8	5	5	3	1	0	Before 1895
High School	**	**	**	**	**	**	**	**	**	**	**	**	**	4%	9%	11%	18%	24%	1959 or later
	**	**	**	**	**	**	2%	8%	9%	20%	30%	38%	39%	38	35	33	33	34	1943 - 1958
	11%	9%	24%	28%	31%	33%	39	37	39	35	29	24	25	27	23	23	22	19	1927 - 1942
	50	58	45	42	43	39	35	36	33	28	27	25	24	23	24	26	21	19	1911 - 1926
	25	27	21	21	18	20	18	17	15	14	12	12	11	8	8	7	6	4	1895 - 1910
	14	7	10	9	8	7	6	3	4	3	2	2	1	1	0	1	0	0	Before 1895
College	**	**	**	**	**	**	**	**	**	**	**	**	**	3%	6%	11%	16%	17%	1959 or later
	**	**	**	**	**	**	2%	13%	18%	24%	38%	45%	48%	52	49	48	50	49	1943 - 1958
	12%	8%	18%	20%	21%	40%	41	36	37	38	33	27	27	26	25	20	19	20	1927 - 1942
	42	52	49	47	43	35	32	32	30	21	19	19	17	14	14	17	11	11	1911 - 1926
	32	30	26	24	27	19	18	14	13	14	8	8	7	6	6	5	4	3	1895 - 1910
	14	11	8	9	9	7	7	5	3	4	1	1	1	1	0	0	0	0	Before 1895

Table 1.36
Age Cohorts of Education Groups Summarized with a Percentage Difference Index#

	1952	1954	1956	1958	1960	1962	1964	1966	1968	1970	1972	1974	1976	1978	1980	1982	1984	1986
Grade School	65	61	56	53	60	56	42	41	42	37	32	27	29	16	16	4	4	-19
High School	28	25	7	1	-5	-6	-18	-24	-29	-38	-44	-48	-51	-60	-59	-60	-68	-74
College	35	33	16	13	15	-14	-18	-30	-39	-44	-62	-63	-67	-74	-73	-74	-81	-83
Total PDI	44	39	24	20	19	10	-3	-8	-15	-21	-35	-38	-43	-56	-55	-59	-65	-73

PDI is proportion "born before 1911" minus proportion "born 1927 or later"

Table 1.37
Urbanism of Education Groups

	1952	1954	1956	1958	1960	1962	1964	1966	1968	1970	1972	1974	1976	1978	1980	1982	1984	1986	
Grade School	30%	30%	23%	22%	21%	26%	30%	26%	25%	21%	22%	22%	27%	25%	32%	21%	23%	22%	Central cities
	25	25	22	23	24	27	18	20	20	20	18	19	20	24	23	23	31	33	Suburbs
	46	45	55	55	55	47	53	55	54	59	60	59	53	52	45	56	46	45	Non-urban areas
High School	35%	37%	27%	26%	24%	24%	28%	29%	26%	27%	25%	28%	28%	27%	25%	28%	22%	25%	Central cities
	33	31	26	28	26	44	35	34	33	32	31	39	35	38	40	31	39	39	Suburbs
	33	32	48	46	50	32	37	37	41	41	44	33	37	36	35	41	39	36	Non-urban areas
College	37%	37%	22%	24%	19%	27%	35%	33%	27%	33%	29%	31%	27%	28%	29%	29%	25%	26%	Central cities
	33	41	36	35	35	42	37	39	34	33	40	41	43	47	43	46	48	49	Non-urban areas
	30	23	42	41	46	31	29	29	39	34	31	28	30	25	28	25	28	25	Non-urban areas

Table 1.38
Urbanism of Education Groups Summarized with a Percentage Difference Index#

	1952	1954	1956	1958	1960	1962	1964	1966	1968	1970	1972	1974	1976	1978	1980	1982	1984	1986
Grade School	-16	-15	-32	-33	-35	-21	-23	-29	-29	-38	-38	-37	-27	-27	-13	-35	-23	-23
High School	2	5	-21	-20	-26	-8	-9	-7	-15	-14	-18	-6	-8	-9	-9	-13	-17	-11
College	7	14	-19	-17	-26	-5	6	4	-12	-1	-2	4	-3	3	1	5	-3	1
Total PDI	-5	-1	-24	-23	-28	-11	-9	-10	-18	-17	-17	-9	-9	-7	-6	-8	-12	-7

PDI is proportion "central cities" minus proportion "non-urban areas"

Table 1.39
Family Income of Education Groups

	1952	1954	1956	1958	1960	1962	1964	1966	1968	1970	1972	1974	1976	1978	1980	1982	1984	1986	
Grade School	36%	39%	34%	36%	31%	48%	43%	43%	41%	36%	44%	40%	37%	49%	50%	44%	44%	56%	Percentile 0-16
	21	17	30	31	32	12	26	16	30	21	18	26	35	24	20	28	34	20	17-33
	22	27	24	20	21	32	18	26	20	31	28	26	17	23	23	19	17	21	34-67
	21	15	10	13	15	8	13	14	8	12	10	7	10	4	6	9	6	0	68-95
	1	2	2	1	1	0	1	0	2	1	1	2	1	1	1	0	0	0	96-100
High School	11%	12%	10%	10%	8%	14%	14%	13%	10%	9%	15%	13%	12%	15%	18%	19%	17%	19%	Percentile 0-16
	14	12	21	21	14	7	18	9	22	15	12	15	19	21	18	21	21	20	17-33
	26	36	37	34	36	51	32	36	38	37	44	47	36	34	40	33	40	38	34-67
	45	35	26	34	39	25	31	38	27	37	26	23	29	26	22	23	20	21	68-95
	4	5	6	2	3	4	6	5	4	2	3	3	3	4	3	4	2	2	96-100
College	4%	5%	3%	3%	8%	9%	6%	10%	5%	6%	9%	6%	6%	8%	8%	9%	7%	7%	Percentile 0-16
	7	6	12	10	6	6	11	4	12	9	8	12	12	12	11	12	10	9	17-33
	16	29	29	26	21	35	23	32	29	24	32	37	29	30	36	29	34	36	34-67
	61	39	35	52	51	38	45	41	43	52	39	39	42	35	36	38	38	39	68-95
	11	21	22	10	14	13	16	13	11	10	12	7	11	15	10	13	11	8	96-100

Table 1.40
Family Income of Education Groups Summarized with a Percentage Difference Index#

	1952	1954	1956	1958	1960	1962	1964	1966	1968	1970	1972	1974	1976	1978	1980	1982	1984	1986
Grade School	-35	-39	-53	-53	-47	-52	-55	-44	-61	-43	-50	-57	-61	-68	-63	-63	-72	-73
High School	24	17	1	5	20	9	5	22	-2	14	2	-3	1	-7	-11	-11	-16	-17
College	60	50	43	50	52	37	44	39	37	48	34	29	35	30	28	30	32	31
Total PDI	5	2	-8	-3	6	-1	-1	8	-5	8	1	-3	2	-1	-2	2	-1	-1

PDI is proportion "68-100 percentile" minus proportion "0-33 percentile"

Table 1.41
Percent Female within Education

	1952	1954	1956	1958	1960	1962	1964	1966	1968	1970	1972	1974	1976	1978	1980	1982	1984	1986
Grade School	51%	51%	53%	50%	48%	52%	51%	54%	53%	51%	55%	54%	56%	57%	51%	48%	53%	55%
High School	60%	57%	60%	58%	58%	60%	61%	61%	63%	63%	63%	63%	63%	60%	63%	60%	61%	60%
College	48%	49%	46%	46%	58%	48%	48%	45%	48%	51%	47%	53%	52%	49%	51%	52%	52%	53%
Total Population	54%	53%	55%	53%	55%	55%	55%	56%	56%	57%	57%	58%	58%	56%	57%	55%	56%	56%

Table 1.42
Percent Black within Education

	1952	1954	1956	1958	1960	1962	1964	1966	1968	1970	1972	1974	1976	1978	1980	1982	1984	1986
Grade School	15%	14%	14%	15%	13%	17%	16%	16%	17%	14%	14%	14%	18%	17%	20%	22%	15%	25%
High School	6%	7%	7%	6%	7%	7%	9%	11%	9%	11%	10%	9%	10%	11%	13%	11%	13%	17%
College	4%	3%	3%	7%	6%	4%	6%	4%	5%	3%	7%	6%	7%	7%	7%	8%	8%	11%
Total population	10%	9%	8%	9%	9%	9%	10%	11%	10%	10%	10%	9%	11%	10%	12%	11%	11%	15%

Table 1.43
Percent Union Households within Education

	1952	1954	1956	1958	1960	1962	1964	1966	1968	1970	1972	1974	1976	1978	1980	1982	1984	1986
Grade School	26%	27%	29%	25%	28%	**	24%	30%	25%	23%	22%	18%	17%	20%	25%	13%	15%	11%
High School	33%	35%	31%	31%	32%	**	29%	33%	30%	30%	32%	33%	28%	31%	29%	26%	23%	24%
College	14%	14%	14%	9%	13%	**	13%	15%	17%	12%	18%	18%	20%	19%	21%	19%	21%	19%
Total population	27%	28%	27%	25%	27%	**	24%	28%	25%	24%	26%	26%	23%	26%	26%	21%	21%	20%

Table 1.44
Percent South within Education

	1952	1954	1956	1958	1960	1962	1964	1966	1968	1970	1972	1974	1976	1978	1980	1982	1984	1986
Grade School	35%	41%	33%	35%	41%	40%	38%	39%	42%	40%	40%	47%	43%	49%	49%	48%	48%	56%
High School	22%	25%	26%	28%	29%	30%	28%	26%	27%	35%	33%	34%	32%	34%	33%	37%	36%	38%
College	27%	25%	30%	30%	34%	39%	28%	28%	29%	28%	30%	31%	27%	32%	34%	32%	26%	30%
Total population	29%	31%	29%	30%	34%	35%	31%	30%	31%	35%	34%	36%	32%	35%	35%	36%	33%	36%

Social Characteristics of Education Groups

Table 1.45
Occupation of Education Groups

	1952	1954	1956	1958	1960	1962	1964	1966	1968	1970	1972	1974	1976	1978	1980	1982	1984	1986	
Grade School	7%	**	5%	6%	4%	**	7%	**	6%	6%	6%	9%	4%	5%	6%	7%	4%	2%	Professional
	3	**	3	3	5	**	6	**	6	3	4	1	4	4	7	5	9	7	White collar
	24	**	32	39	43	**	42	**	44	49	45	49	48	55	49	45	52	60	Blue collar
	18	**	12	6	4	**	6	**	5	3	4	4	4	5	7	9	4	3	Unskilled
	12	**	12	11	12	**	11	**	10	11	8	10	11	8	7	13	11	10	Farmers
	35	**	36	34	31	**	28	**	29	29	35	28	29	25	24	22	21	19	Housewives
High School	13%	**	11%	13%	12%	**	15%	**	11%	13%	11%	13%	11%	13%	12%	10%	9%	10%	Professional
	15	**	14	14	18	**	15	**	17	18	18	19	19	18	20	20	26	22	White collar
	22	**	27	32	34	**	32	**	34	33	37	39	40	42	44	44	43	46	Blue collar
	7	**	5	2	1	**	2	**	1	2	2	1	3	3	3	3	3	4	Unskilled
	4	**	5	3	4	**	3	**	3	3	2	2	2	2	2	3	4	3	Farmers
	39	**	39	36	31	**	34	**	35	32	30	26	24	22	19	21	15	16	Housewives
College	45%	**	46%	45%	43%	**	43%	**	49%	54%	47%	46%	46%	50%	51%	46%	46%	49%	Professional
	18	**	12	16	18	**	17	**	16	16	18	20	20	18	20	24	24	24	White collar
	7	**	11	12	10	**	12	**	13	8	15	16	17	17	17	17	19	17	Blue collar
	1	**	1	0	0	**	0	**	0	0	1	1	2	1	2	1	1	1	Unskilled
	2	**	2	1	0	**	3	**	2	2	1	1	0	1	1	1	1	2	Farmers
	27	**	29	26	29	**	26	**	20	19	18	16	15	15	10	10	9	8	Housewives

Table 1.46
Incidence of Occupations within Education Groups

	1952	1954	1956	1958	1960	1962	1964	1966	1968	1970	1972	1974	1976	1978	1980	1982	1984	1986	
Percent Professional	7%	**	5%	6%	4%	**	7%	**	6%	6%	6%	9%	4%	5%	6%	7%	4%	2%	Grade School
	13%	**	11%	13%	12%	**	15%	**	11%	13%	11%	13%	11%	13%	12%	10%	9%	10%	High School
	45%	**	46%	45%	43%	**	43%	**	49%	54%	47%	46%	46%	50%	51%	46%	46%	49%	College
Percent White collar	3%	**	3%	3%	5%	**	6%	**	6%	3%	4%	1%	4%	4%	7%	5%	9%	7%	Grade School
	15%	**	14%	14%	18%	**	15%	**	17%	18%	18%	19%	19%	18%	20%	20%	26%	22%	High School
	18%	**	12%	16%	18%	**	17%	**	16%	16%	18%	20%	20%	18%	20%	24%	24%	24%	College
Percent Blue collar	24%	**	32%	39%	43%	**	42%	**	44%	49%	45%	49%	48%	55%	49%	45%	52%	60%	Grade School
	22%	**	27%	32%	34%	**	32%	**	34%	33%	37%	39%	40%	42%	44%	44%	43%	46%	High School
	7%	**	11%	12%	10%	**	12%	**	13%	8%	15%	16%	17%	17%	17%	17%	19%	17%	College
Percent Unskilled	18%	**	12%	6%	4%	**	6%	**	5%	3%	4%	4%	4%	5%	7%	9%	4%	3%	Grade School
	7%	**	5%	2%	1%	**	2%	**	1%	2%	2%	1%	3%	3%	3%	3%	3%	4%	High School
	1%	**	1%	0%	0%	**	0%	**	0%	0%	1%	1%	2%	1%	2%	1%	1%	1%	College
Percent Farmers	12%	**	12%	11%	12%	**	11%	**	10%	11%	8%	10%	11%	8%	7%	13%	11%	10%	Grade School
	4%	**	5%	3%	4%	**	3%	**	3%	3%	2%	2%	2%	2%	2%	3%	4%	3%	High School
	2%	**	2%	1%	0%	**	3%	**	2%	2%	1%	1%	0%	1%	1%	1%	1%	2%	College
Percent Housewives	35%	**	36%	34%	31%	**	28%	**	29%	29%	35%	28%	29%	25%	24%	22%	21%	19%	Grade School
	39%	**	39%	36%	31%	**	34%	**	35%	32%	30%	26%	24%	22%	19%	21%	15%	16%	High School
	27%	**	29%	26%	29%	**	26%	**	20%	19%	18%	16%	15%	15%	10%	10%	9%	8%	College

Table 1.47
Religion of Education Groups

	1952	1954	1956	1958	1960	1962	1964	1966	1968	1970	1972	1974	1976	1978	1980	1982	1984	1986	
Grade School	72%	76%	73%	71%	76%	74%	75%	74%	79%	75%	74%	71%	71%	66%	72%	69%	65%	71%	Protestant
	20	20	22	24	17	19	20	20	17	18	21	22	24	25	20	21	29	24	Catholic
	3	2	2	2	3	3	1	1	1	1	1	2	0	2	4	0	1	1	Jewish
	5	2	4	3	4	3	4	5	3	6	4	6	6	8	4	10	5	5	Other
High School	70%	75%	73%	73%	71%	75%	69%	71%	70%	72%	68%	71%	66%	66%	65%	69%	66%	67%	Protestant
	26	21	22	23	25	22	24	24	25	21	26	23	27	23	25	23	24	23	Catholic
	3	3	3	3	3	2	3	3	2	2	1	2	1	1	2	1	1	1	Jewish
	2	2	2	2	1	2	4	2	3	5	5	4	6	9	9	7	9	9	Other
College	77%	76%	74%	80%	80%	71%	69%	69%	67%	63%	66%	61%	62%	58%	59%	60%	56%	61%	Protestant
	15	14	18	14	14	18	21	19	21	18	22	20	22	25	22	22	27	25	Catholic
	4	5	6	4	4	7	5	7	6	5	5	4	5	6	5	4	4	3	Jewish
	5	5	3	2	2	5	6	5	6	14	8	15	11	12	14	15	13	11	Other

Table 1.48
Incidence of Religions within Education Groups

	1952	1954	1956	1958	1960	1962	1964	1966	1968	1970	1972	1974	1976	1978	1980	1982	1984	1986	
Percent Protestant	72%	76%	73%	71%	76%	74%	75%	74%	79%	75%	74%	71%	71%	66%	72%	69%	65%	71%	Grade School
	70%	75%	73%	73%	71%	75%	69%	71%	70%	72%	68%	71%	66%	66%	65%	69%	66%	67%	High School
	77%	76%	74%	80%	80%	71%	69%	69%	67%	63%	66%	61%	62%	58%	59%	60%	56%	61%	College
Percent Catholic	20%	20%	22%	24%	17%	19%	20%	20%	17%	18%	21%	22%	24%	25%	20%	21%	29%	24%	Grade School
	26%	21%	22%	23%	25%	22%	24%	24%	25%	21%	26%	23%	27%	23%	25%	23%	24%	23%	High School
	15%	14%	18%	14%	14%	18%	21%	19%	21%	18%	22%	20%	22%	25%	22%	22%	27%	25%	College
Percent Jewish	3%	2%	2%	2%	3%	3%	1%	1%	1%	1%	1%	2%	0%	2%	4%	0%	1%	1%	Grade School
	3%	3%	3%	3%	3%	2%	3%	3%	2%	2%	1%	2%	1%	1%	2%	1%	1%	1%	High School
	4%	5%	6%	4%	4%	7%	5%	7%	6%	5%	5%	4%	5%	6%	5%	4%	4%	3%	College
Percent Other and None	5%	2%	4%	3%	4%	3%	4%	5%	3%	6%	4%	6%	6%	8%	4%	10%	5%	5%	Grade School
	2%	2%	2%	2%	1%	2%	4%	2%	3%	5%	5%	4%	6%	9%	9%	7%	9%	9%	High School
	5%	5%	3%	2%	2%	5%	6%	5%	6%	14%	8%	15%	11%	12%	14%	15%	13%	11%	College

Table 1.49
Age Cohorts of Urbanism Groups

	1952	1954	1956	1958	1960	1962	1964	1966	1968	1970	1972	1974	1976	1978	1980	1982	1984	1986	
Central Cities	**	**	**	**	**	**	**	**	**	**	**	**	**	3%	7%	10%	16%	20%	1959 or later
	**	**	**	**	**	**	2%	13%	12%	21%	30%	38%	36%	42	38	40	38	36	1943 - 1958
	9%	9%	19%	22%	20%	31%	35	31	33	29	27	23	23	23	19	19	17	20	1927 - 1942
	38	45	42	38	40	30	30	30	28	27	24	22	23	21	23	22	20	19	1911 - 1926
	31	36	26	28	28	27	25	22	20	18	16	14	17	10	12	9	9	5	1895 - 1910
	21	11	13	12	12	12	9	5	7	5	3	3	1	2	1	0	0	0	Before 1895
Suburbs	**	**	**	**	**	**	**	**	**	**	**	**	**	3%	7%	10%	15%	17%	1959 or later
	**	**	**	**	**	**	1%	5%	8%	16%	29%	37%	39%	39	38	37	38	40	1943 - 1958
	9%	7%	16%	18%	22%	32%	39	34	38	40	30	24	28	28	27	20	22	22	1927 - 1942
	38	49	44	39	33	41	37	39	38	24	28	26	23	19	19	26	19	17	1911 - 1926
	30	30	25	27	28	20	18	17	15	16	11	12	9	10	9	6	6	4	1895 - 1910
	23	14	15	16	18	7	5	5	3	5	2	1	2	1	0	1	0	0	Before 1895
Non-urban areas	**	**	**	**	**	**	**	**	**	**	**	**	**	3%	7%	10%	16%	20%	1959 or later
	**	**	**	**	**	**	2%	5%	10%	15%	26%	28%	34%	37	35	34	36	39	1943 - 1958
	7%	5%	17%	22%	22%	22%	27	29	28	26	24	22	20	23	21	22	22	18	1927 - 1942
	41	49	39	39	39	30	34	29	29	28	24	25	25	23	25	25	17	17	1911 - 1926
	30	33	27	24	26	29	24	25	26	26	20	21	19	12	12	8	10	6	1895 - 1910
	22	14	17	15	13	19	13	12	7	6	6	4	3	1	1	1	0	0	Before 1895

Table 1.50
Age Cohorts of Urbanism Groups Summarized with a Percentage Difference Index#

	1952	1954	1956	1958	1960	1962	1964	1966	1968	1970	1972	1974	1976	1978	1980	1982	1984	1986
Central cities	43	38	20	18	21	8	-3	-16	-18	-27	-37	-45	-41	-56	-52	-60	-62	-70
Suburbs	45	37	23	26	23	-4	-17	-17	-28	-35	-47	-48	-56	-59	-62	-60	-69	-75
Non-urban Areas	45	42	27	18	16	26	8	4	-4	-9	-24	-24	-32	-51	-50	-57	-63	-71
Total PDI	44	39	24	20	19	10	-3	-8	-15	-21	-35	-38	-43	-56	-55	-59	-65	-73

PDI is proportion "born before 1911" minus proportion "born 1927 or later"

Table 1.51
Education of Urbanism Groups

	1952	1954	1956	1958	1960	1962	1964	1966	1968	1970	1972	1974	1976	1978	1980	1982	1984	1986	
Central cities	37%	32%	29%	28%	28%	29%	25%	23%	23%	19%	17%	15%	16%	11%	14%	8%	11%	8%	Grade School
	46	49	54	53	52	46	48	51	49	51	50	50	51	53	47	46	45	48	High School
	17	19	17	20	19	25	28	26	28	30	33	35	33	37	39	46	44	45	College
Suburbs	35%	30%	25%	25%	26%	19%	14%	16%	16%	17%	11%	10%	10%	7%	7%	7%	8%	7%	Grade School
	49	47	49	49	46	55	58	55	54	56	51	55	50	50	53	39	45	43	High School
	16	24	26	26	28	26	28	29	31	28	37	35	41	43	41	54	47	50	College
Non-urban areas	50%	47%	35%	35%	33%	37%	34%	36%	29%	33%	28%	30%	24%	18%	16%	18%	14%	13%	Grade School
	38	42	49	48	48	43	49	47	47	48	51	46	49	56	53	53	53	54	High School
	12	12	16	17	20	21	18	17	24	19	21	23	27	26	31	30	33	34	College

Table 1.52
Education of Urbanism Groups Summarized with a Percentage Difference Index#

	1952	1954	1956	1958	1960	1962	1964	1966	1968	1970	1972	1974	1976	1978	1980	1982	1984	1986
Central cities	-21	-13	-12	-8	-9	-3	3	3	6	11	16	20	17	26	24	37	34	37
Suburbs	-18	-6	0	1	2	7	14	12	15	11	26	25	31	35	34	47	39	43
Non-urban Areas	-39	-35	-19	-18	-13	-16	-16	-19	-4	-14	-7	-7	3	8	15	12	18	21
Total PDI	-27	-19	-12	-10	-8	-4	-1	-3	4	0	9	12	17	23	25	32	31	34

PDI is proportion "college" minus proportion "grade school"

Social Characteristics of Urbanism Groups

Table 1.53
Family Income of Urbanism Groups

	1952	1954	1956	1958	1960	1962	1964	1966	1968	1970	1972	1974	1976	1978	1980	1982	1984	1986	
Central Cities	14%	16%	11%	12%	10%	20%	18%	21%	16%	14%	22%	13%	14%	23%	24%	18%	17%	20%	Percentile 0-16
	16	13	23	20	17	9	17	9	24	14	13	19	21	21	17	20	22	18	17-33
	24	34	30	33	32	44	26	34	33	33	37	41	31	29	35	35	37	40	34-67
	44	31	27	33	38	22	31	34	25	37	24	23	28	21	18	24	19	17	68-95
	3	6	8	3	4	5	8	2	3	3	4	5	6	7	5	4	5	4	96-100
Suburbs	19%	16%	12%	14%	13%	13%	9%	10%	7%	10%	10%	11%	10%	10%	11%	12%	11%	12%	Percentile 0-16
	16	13	18	17	18	5	11	6	16	12	8	11	14	15	13	14	15	12	17-33
	20	30	34	27	25	43	28	32	31	30	36	40	30	32	36	27	34	31	34-67
	39	32	26	37	38	34	42	42	36	44	39	35	41	34	33	34	33	38	68-95
	6	9	10	5	6	6	10	10	10	4	7	3	6	10	6	14	8	6	96-100
Non-urban areas	27%	29%	21%	20%	18%	33%	28%	27%	22%	19%	24%	22%	18%	20%	20%	21%	20%	21%	Percentile 0-16
	16	14	24	25	18	11	25	13	23	18	14	18	23	20	18	19	19	18	17-33
	25	30	30	27	29	39	24	33	31	33	38	39	33	32	37	30	37	38	34-67
	30	23	18	26	31	13	19	23	21	27	20	16	23	24	22	26	22	20	68-95
	2	6	7	3	5	4	4	5	4	4	4	4	4	4	4	4	3	2	96-100

Table 1.54
Family Income of Urbanism Groups Summarized with a Percentage Difference Index#

	1952	1954	1956	1958	1960	1962	1964	1966	1968	1970	1972	1974	1976	1978	1980	1982	1984	1986
Central cities	17	8	2	5	15	-1	4	6	-12	13	-7	-4	-1	-16	-18	-9	-14	-17
Suburbs	11	13	6	11	13	23	31	36	23	26	28	16	22	19	16	21	16	20
Non-urban Areas	-10	-14	-20	-16	-1	-27	-31	-11	-20	-7	-14	-20	-14	-12	-11	-10	-13	-17
Total PDI	5	2	-8	-3	6	-1	-1	8	-5	8	1	-3	2	-1	-2	2	-1	-1

PDI is proportion "68-100 percentile" minus proportion "0-33 percentile"

Table 1.55
Percent Female within Urbanism

	1952	1954	1956	1958	1960	1962	1964	1966	1968	1970	1972	1974	1976	1978	1980	1982	1984	1986
Central Cities	57%	57%	57%	50%	55%	54%	55%	52%	59%	57%	58%	59%	62%	57%	58%	57%	57%	58%
Suburbs	56%	55%	55%	53%	56%	57%	53%	56%	52%	60%	55%	60%	56%	55%	57%	54%	57%	56%
Non-urban areas	51%	49%	55%	55%	54%	54%	57%	58%	57%	55%	58%	56%	57%	56%	56%	55%	55%	55%
Total Population	54%	53%	55%	53%	55%	55%	55%	56%	56%	57%	57%	58%	58%	56%	57%	55%	56%	56%

Table 1.56
Percent Black within Urbanism

	1952	1954	1956	1958	1960	1962	1964	1966	1968	1970	1972	1974	1976	1978	1980	1982	1984	1986
Central Cities	15%	16%	14%	18%	18%	17%	20%	27%	21%	24%	21%	17%	21%	26%	30%	24%	26%	30%
Suburbs	8%	7%	8%	7%	7%	5%	4%	4%	6%	3%	4%	5%	7%	3%	4%	5%	4%	9%
Non-urban areas	6%	4%	6%	6%	6%	7%	8%	5%	6%	6%	8%	7%	6%	7%	6%	7%	10%	12%
Total Population	10%	9%	8%	9%	9%	9%	10%	11%	10%	10%	10%	9%	11%	10%	12%	11%	11%	15%

Table 1.57
Percent Union Households within Urbanism

	1952	1954	1956	1958	1960	1962	1964	1966	1968	1970	1972	1974	1976	1978	1980	1982	1984	1986
Central Cities	38%	36%	38%	36%	37%	**	31%	35%	27%	28%	29%	29%	26%	28%	27%	23%	22%	20%
Suburbs	27%	25%	31%	27%	29%	**	27%	32%	31%	30%	30%	27%	26%	27%	30%	23%	24%	24%
Non-urban areas	18%	23%	20%	18%	21%	**	16%	21%	20%	17%	20%	21%	19%	22%	20%	18%	18%	15%
Total Population	27%	28%	27%	25%	27%	**	24%	28%	25%	24%	26%	26%	23%	26%	26%	21%	21%	20%

Table 1.58
Percent South within Urbanism

	1952	1954	1956	1958	1960	1962	1964	1966	1968	1970	1972	1974	1976	1978	1980	1982	1984	1986
Central cities	19%	19%	15%	12%	16%	29%	25%	26%	28%	29%	31%	29%	28%	33%	30%	34%	34%	36%
Suburbs	27%	28%	20%	23%	24%	27%	23%	19%	19%	23%	20%	30%	25%	24%	29%	28%	27%	27%
Non-urban areas	41%	45%	41%	44%	47%	48%	41%	41%	41%	46%	45%	47%	43%	50%	47%	46%	41%	48%
Total Population	29%	31%	29%	30%	34%	35%	31%	30%	31%	35%	34%	36%	32%	35%	35%	36%	33%	36%

Table 1.59
Occupation of Urbanism Groups

	1952	1954	1956	1958	1960	1962	1964	1966	1968	1970	1972	1974	1976	1978	1980	1982	1984	1986	
Central Cities	16%	**	15%	20%	16%	**	21%	**	21%	22%	21%	25%	22%	26%	25%	25%	25%	26%	Professional
	15	**	13	12	20	**	15	**	17	19	18	22	23	18	20	25	27	24	White Collar
	24	**	29	40	36	**	35	**	34	33	34	30	32	38	37	33	35	36	Blue Collar
	12	**	6	3	2	**	3	**	3	2	3	2	2	3	3	3	2	3	Unskilled
	1	**	1	0	0	**	0	**	0	1	0	0	1	1	1	0	1	1	Farmers
	34	**	36	25	27	**	28	**	26	24	24	22	20	14	14	14	10	10	Housewives
Suburbs	16%	**	19%	21%	21%	**	23%	**	24%	22%	24%	25%	25%	28%	27%	32%	28%	29%	Professional
	13	**	13	13	16	**	14	**	17	16	18	18	18	18	22	20	23	22	White Collar
	24	**	31	32	33	**	30	**	28	26	28	32	31	29	32	26	30	31	Blue Collar
	11	**	6	2	2	**	1	**	1	1	1	1	3	2	3	3	2	3	Unskilled
	3	**	1	1	0	**	1	**	0	1	0	1	1	1	0	2	3	1	Farmers
	34	**	31	32	27	**	31	**	30	35	28	23	21	22	17	18	14	14	Housewives
Non-urban areas	14%	**	14%	14%	14%	**	15%	**	16%	19%	17%	18%	17%	20%	23%	19%	18%	21%	Professional
	6	**	8	10	10	**	11	**	10	10	11	8	10	13	14	15	20	18	White Collar
	15	**	21	23	29	**	26	**	31	33	34	39	38	40	37	39	38	39	Blue Collar
	10	**	7	4	2	**	3	**	2	2	2	2	3	3	4	3	3	3	Unskilled
	17	**	13	10	11	**	11	**	9	9	6	8	7	4	5	7	7	6	Farmers
	39	**	39	39	34	**	33	**	32	27	29	25	25	21	17	17	14	13	Housewives

Table 1.60
Incidence of Occupations within Urbanism Groups

	1952	1954	1956	1958	1960	1962	1964	1966	1968	1970	1972	1974	1976	1978	1980	1982	1984	1986	
Percent Professional	16%	**	15%	20%	16%	**	21%	**	21%	22%	21%	25%	22%	26%	25%	25%	25%	26%	Central cities
	16%	**	19%	21%	21%	**	23%	**	24%	22%	24%	25%	25%	28%	27%	32%	28%	29%	Suburbs
	14%	**	14%	14%	14%	**	15%	**	16%	19%	17%	18%	17%	20%	23%	19%	18%	21%	Non-urban areas
Percent White Collar	15%	**	13%	12%	20%	**	15%	**	17%	19%	18%	22%	23%	18%	20%	25%	27%	24%	Central cities
	13%	**	13%	13%	16%	**	14%	**	17%	16%	18%	18%	18%	18%	22%	20%	23%	22%	Suburbs
	6%	**	8%	10%	10%	**	11%	**	10%	10%	11%	8%	10%	13%	14%	15%	20%	18%	Non-urban areas
Percent Blue Collar	24%	**	29%	40%	36%	**	35%	**	34%	33%	34%	30%	32%	38%	37%	33%	35%	36%	Central cities
	24%	**	31%	32%	33%	**	30%	**	28%	26%	28%	32%	31%	29%	32%	26%	30%	31%	Suburbs
	15%	**	21%	23%	29%	**	26%	**	31%	33%	34%	39%	38%	40%	37%	39%	38%	39%	Non-urban areas
Percent Unskilled	12%	**	6%	3%	2%	**	3%	**	3%	2%	3%	2%	2%	3%	3%	3%	2%	3%	Central cities
	11%	**	6%	2%	2%	**	1%	**	1%	1%	1%	1%	3%	2%	3%	3%	2%	3%	Suburbs
	10%	**	7%	4%	2%	**	3%	**	2%	2%	2%	2%	3%	3%	4%	3%	3%	3%	Non-urban areas
Percent Farmers	1%	**	1%	0%	0%	**	0%	**	0%	1%	0%	0%	1%	1%	1%	0%	1%	1%	Central cities
	3%	**	1%	1%	0%	**	1%	**	0%	1%	0%	1%	1%	1%	0%	2%	3%	1%	Suburbs
	17%	**	13%	10%	11%	**	11%	**	9%	9%	6%	8%	7%	4%	5%	7%	7%	6%	Non-urban areas
Percent Housewives	34%	**	36%	25%	27%	**	28%	**	26%	24%	24%	22%	20%	14%	14%	14%	10%	10%	Central cities
	34%	**	31%	32%	27%	**	31%	**	30%	35%	28%	23%	21%	22%	17%	18%	14%	14%	Suburbs
	39%	**	39%	39%	34%	**	33%	**	32%	27%	29%	25%	25%	21%	17%	17%	14%	13%	Non-urban areas

Table 1.61
Religion of Urbanism Groups

	1952	1954	1956	1958	1960	1962	1964	1966	1968	1970	1972	1974	1976	1978	1980	1982	1984	1986	
Central Cities	58%	61%	52%	54%	55%	65%	61%	60%	60%	61%	62%	54%	57%	60%	59%	60%	52%	58%	Protestant
	31	27	34	34	30	25	27	31	28	24	28	27	29	24	23	23	31	26	Catholic
	8	8	10	9	12	7	6	5	6	5	4	6	5	5	7	3	5	2	Jewish
	3	4	4	4	3	3	6	4	6	10	7	14	9	11	11	14	13	14	Other and None
Suburbs	70%	77%	71%	70%	68%	67%	60%	63%	62%	56%	59%	66%	59%	56%	56%	57%	56%	61%	Protestant
	25	21	25	25	27	26	31	29	32	29	31	25	31	30	30	30	31	28	Catholic
	2	1	2	3	2	4	4	4	3	4	3	2	3	3	3	3	3	2	Jewish
	4	1	2	2	3	3	5	4	3	11	7	7	8	10	11	11	10	9	Other and None
Non-urban areas	85%	88%	85%	86%	86%	86%	85%	86%	85%	86%	80%	81%	78%	73%	76%	79%	75%	77%	Protestant
	11	10	13	12	12	11	12	10	11	10	16	15	16	17	15	13	17	16	Catholic
	1	0	0	0	0	0	0	1	1	1	1	0	0	1	0	0	0	0	Jewish
	3	2	2	2	1	3	3	3	3	4	3	4	6	9	9	8	8	7	Other and None

Table 1.62
Incidence of Religions within Urbanism Groups

	1952	1954	1956	1958	1960	1962	1964	1966	1968	1970	1972	1974	1976	1978	1980	1982	1984	1986	
Percent Protestant	58%	61%	52%	54%	55%	65%	61%	60%	60%	61%	62%	54%	57%	60%	59%	60%	52%	58%	Central Cities
	70%	77%	71%	70%	68%	67%	60%	63%	62%	56%	59%	66%	59%	56%	56%	57%	56%	61%	Suburbs
	85%	88%	85%	86%	86%	86%	85%	86%	85%	86%	80%	81%	78%	73%	76%	79%	75%	77%	Non-urban areas
Percent Catholic	31%	27%	34%	34%	30%	25%	27%	31%	28%	24%	28%	27%	29%	24%	23%	23%	31%	26%	Central Cities
	25%	21%	25%	25%	27%	26%	31%	29%	32%	29%	31%	25%	31%	30%	30%	30%	31%	28%	Suburbs
	11%	10%	13%	12%	12%	11%	12%	10%	11%	10%	16%	15%	16%	17%	15%	13%	17%	16%	Non-urban areas
Percent Jewish	8%	8%	10%	9%	12%	7%	6%	5%	6%	5%	4%	6%	5%	5%	7%	3%	5%	2%	Central Cities
	2%	1%	2%	3%	2%	4%	4%	4%	3%	4%	3%	2%	3%	3%	3%	3%	3%	2%	Suburbs
	1%	0%	0%	0%	0%	0%	0%	1%	1%	1%	1%	0%	0%	1%	0%	0%	0%	0%	Non-urban areas
Percent Other and None	3%	4%	4%	4%	3%	3%	6%	4%	6%	10%	7%	14%	9%	11%	11%	14%	13%	14%	Central Cities
	4%	1%	2%	2%	3%	3%	5%	4%	3%	11%	7%	7%	8%	10%	11%	11%	10%	9%	Suburbs
	3%	2%	2%	2%	1%	3%	3%	3%	3%	4%	3%	4%	6%	9%	9%	8%	8%	7%	Non-urban areas

Table 1.63
Age Cohorts of Income Groups

	1952	1954	1956	1958	1960	1962	1964	1966	1968	1970	1972	1974	1976	1978	1980	1982	1984	1986	
Income Percentile 0-16	**	**	**	**	**	**	**	**	**	**	**	**	**	5%	7%	18%	26%	25%	1959 or later
	**	**	**	**	**	**	1%	7%	9%	12%	22%	28%	26%	29	28	22	23	24	1943 - 1958
	6%	2%	10%	11%	7%	15%	15	13	12	10	10	6	11	10	7	10	14	15	1927 - 1942
	22	28	20	21	11	15	17	20	14	20	20	23	22	26	28	29	20	24	1911 - 1926
	26	35	21	26	32	32	34	33	43	39	35	35	34	25	29	21	16	12	1895 - 1910
	46	35	48	43	50	38	33	26	23	19	13	8	7	5	2	1	1	0	Before 1895
Income Percentile 17-33	**	**	**	**	**	**	**	**	**	**	**	**	**	3%	8%	13%	15%	24%	1959 or later
	**	**	**	**	**	**	4%	5%	13%	16%	27%	33%	34%	42	36	34	30	30	1943 - 1958
	11%	9%	20%	28%	21%	26%	27	22	24	22	18	18	11	19	15	13	12	16	1927 - 1942
	34	43	36	26	29	31	36	28	26	16	22	20	25	21	23	28	26	23	1911 - 1926
	27	34	27	29	31	31	24	37	29	37	29	28	27	16	18	11	17	7	1895 - 1910
	28	14	16	16	20	13	9	8	8	9	4	2	3	1	1	1	0	0	Before 1895
Income Percentile 34-67	**	**	**	**	**	**	**	**	**	**	**	**	**	3%	5%	6%	15%	20%	1959 or later
	**	**	**	**	**	**	1%	11%	12%	23%	36%	42%	49%	47	46	44	44	46	1943 - 1958
	11%	9%	26%	26%	28%	39%	48	34	39	28	28	26	23	26	23	20	21	16	1927 - 1942
	48	54	45	47	41	35	33	31	33	29	25	22	20	18	22	24	17	16	1911 - 1926
	28	32	22	21	26	21	16	22	15	17	10	9	8	6	4	5	3	3	1895 - 1910
	14	6	8	7	5	5	2	3	1	3	1	1	1	1	0	0	0	0	Before 1895
Income Percentile 68-95	**	**	**	**	**	**	**	**	**	**	**	**	**	3%	7%	6%	12%	14%	1959 or later
	**	**	**	**	**	**	1%	4%	8%	16%	24%	30%	36%	42	39	49	46	46	1943 - 1958
	8%	7%	14%	19%	23%	28%	39	42	42	44	39	36	35	33	35	27	29	28	1927 - 1942
	48	58	55	50	51	48	41	40	43	30	30	29	27	20	17	16	12	10	1911 - 1926
	33	33	28	28	22	21	16	13	7	10	6	5	3	3	2	2	1	1895 - 1910
	11	3	3	3	4	2	2	1	1	1	1	1	0	0	0	0	0	Before 1895
Income Percentile 95-100	**	**	**	**	**	**	**	**	**	**	**	**	**	1%	5%	8%	13%	12%	1959 or later
	**	**	**	**	**	**	0%	3%	1%	6%	16%	12%	16%	33	30	22	45	42	1943 - 1958
	2%	1%	6%	0%	12%	16%	28	38	38	43	42	41	48	40	46	43	34	35	1927 - 1942
	22	49	44	54	44	51	46	47	43	39	34	44	29	22	14	26	9	12	1911 - 1926
	52	34	44	28	33	29	25	13	15	13	8	3	6	3	5	1	0	0	1895 - 1910
	25	15	6	18	12	5	2	0	3	0	1	0	0	1	0	0	0	0	Before 1895

Table 1.64
Age Cohorts of Income Groups Summarized with a Percentage Difference Index#

	1952	1954	1956	1958	1960	1962	1964	1966	1968	1970	1972	1974	1976	1978	1980	1982	1984	1986
Income Percentile 0-16	66	68	59	58	75	55	51	38	44	36	16	9	5	-14	-10	-28	-46	-52
Income Percentile 17-33	44	39	24	17	30	17	1	17	0	8	-12	-21	-15	-47	-41	-50	-40	-62
Income Percentile 34-67	31	29	4	1	2	-13	-31	-21	-35	-31	-53	-58	-63	-69	-70	-66	-77	-79
Income Percentile 68-95	36	29	18	12	3	-5	-22	-32	-43	-49	-57	-60	-67	-74	-78	-80	-85	-88
Income Percentile 95-100	75	48	44	46	33	18	-1	-28	-22	-35	-49	-50	-59	-71	-75	-72	-91	-88
Total PDI	44	39	24	20	19	10	-3	-8	-15	-21	-35	-38	-43	-56	-55	-59	-65	-73

PDI is proportion "born before 1911" minus proportion "born 1927 or later"

Table 1.65
Education of Income Groups

	1952	1954	1956	1958	1960	1962	1964	1966	1968	1970	1972	1974	1976	1978	1980	1982	1984	1986	
Income Percentile 0-16	73%	70%	66%	67%	63%	60%	56%	57%	59%	60%	45%	46%	41%	34%	32%	27%	28%	28%	Grade School
	24	26	32	30	25	31	37	31	32	31	41	43	44	48	51	50	52	53	High School
	3	4	3	3	12	10	7	12	9	9	14	12	14	18	17	23	20	18	College
Income Percentile 17-33	53%	49%	42%	43%	54%	43%	35%	44%	32%	34%	29%	30%	28%	16%	14%	17%	19%	11%	Grade School
	40	43	49	48	39	40	51	45	52	51	51	47	51	61	60	53	58	62	High School
	7	9	10	9	7	18	14	10	16	14	20	23	21	24	26	30	24	27	College
Income Percentile 34-67	39%	32%	24%	21%	22%	21%	17%	21%	14%	24%	15%	12%	9%	9%	7%	6%	5%	5%	Grade School
	50	52	59	60	62	58	62	56	60	57	60	60	60	57	55	50	54	50	High School
	11	16	18	18	16	21	21	23	26	19	26	29	32	35	38	44	41	45	College
Income Percentile 68-95	22%	19%	14%	13%	13%	9%	11%	12%	7%	9%	7%	5%	5%	2%	3%	3%	2%	1%	Grade School
	54	56	57	53	54	52	54	58	49	54	50	47	49	51	44	37	36	36	High School
	24	24	30	34	33	40	36	30	44	38	43	48	46	47	54	60	62	63	College
Income Percentile 95-100	12%	11%	7%	7%	7%	2%	5%	1%	8%	7%	4%	8%	3%	1%	1%	0%	0%	0%	Grade School
	45	34	41	29	28	36	41	45	33	28	28	35	26	25	26	26	21	22	High School
	43	55	53	64	65	63	54	54	60	65	68	58	70	73	73	74	80	78	College

Table 1.66
Education of Income Groups Summarized with a Percentage Difference Index#

	1952	1954	1956	1958	1960	1962	1964	1966	1968	1970	1972	1974	1976	1978	1980	1982	1984	1986
Income Percentile 0-16	-70	-66	-63	-64	-52	-50	-49	-45	-50	-50	-31	-34	-27	-17	-16	-4	-8	-10
Income Percentile 17-33	-46	-40	-32	-34	-47	-25	-21	-34	-17	-20	-9	-7	-7	8	12	13	5	15
Income Percentile 34-67	-29	-16	-6	-3	-6	0	4	2	11	-5	11	17	23	26	30	37	36	39
Income Percentile 68-95	2	5	16	22	20	31	25	18	38	29	36	43	41	45	51	57	59	62
Income Percentile 95-100	31	45	46	57	59	61	50	52	52	57	64	50	67	72	71	74	80	78
Total PDI	-27	-19	-12	-10	-8	-4	-1	-3	4	0	9	12	17	23	25	32	31	34

PDI is proportion "college" minus proportion "grade school"

Table 1.67
Urbanism of Income Groups

	1952	1954	1956	1958	1960	1962	1964	1966	1968	1970	1972	1974	1976	1978	1980	1982	1984	1986	
Income Percentile 0-16	22%	27%	17%	17%	15%	23%	27%	31%	26%	25%	29%	23%	28%	37%	38%	28%	25%	29%	Central Cities
	28	24	20	24	24	22	15	16	13	19	16	25	25	23	25	27	30	31	Suburbs
	50	49	63	59	62	55	58	53	61	56	55	52	48	40	37	45	44	40	Non-urban areas
Income Percentile 17-33	33%	34%	26%	23%	21%	28%	28%	28%	29%	24%	29%	33%	30%	31%	30%	31%	28%	29%	Central Cities
	29	30	21	22	28	22	19	19	23	24	21	24	26	32	33	31	35	33	Suburbs
	37	37	53	55	52	50	53	53	47	52	50	43	44	37	37	38	36	38	Non-urban areas
Income Percentile 34-67	34%	38%	24%	28%	25%	27%	30%	31%	28%	28%	26%	29%	27%	26%	27%	31%	24%	28%	Central Cities
	25	29	29	27	24	39	34	30	30	28	30	36	34	41	40	34	40	38	Suburbs
	41	33	47	45	51	34	36	40	42	45	44	36	39	34	34	36	36	35	Non-urban areas
Income Percentile 68-95	39%	38%	30%	26%	25%	24%	31%	31%	24%	29%	23%	26%	25%	21%	19%	23%	17%	15%	Central Cities
	31	34	30	33	30	55	45	41	42	37	45	50	47	50	52	45	54	61	Suburbs
	31	28	40	40	45	20	25	29	34	34	32	24	28	29	28	32	29	24	Non-urban areas
Income Percentile 95-100	28%	31%	26%	23%	16%	27%	35%	11%	14%	24%	22%	33%	30%	25%	27%	14%	21%	24%	Central Cities
	51	41	33	39	36	48	43	52	56	33	42	29	40	55	47	67	60	62	Suburbs
	22	28	41	39	48	25	22	37	30	43	36	38	30	20	26	20	19	14	Non-urban areas

Table 1.68
Urbanism of Income Groups Summarized with a Percentage Difference Index#

	1952	1954	1956	1958	1960	1962	1964	1966	1968	1970	1972	1974	1976	1978	1980	1982	1984	1986
Income Percentile 0-16	-28	-22	-46	-41	-47	-32	-30	-22	-35	-31	-26	-29	-20	-3	0	-17	-19	-12
Income Percentile 17-33	-4	-3	-27	-33	-31	-22	-25	-25	-18	-28	-22	-10	-14	-6	-8	-8	-8	-9
Income Percentile 34-67	-7	5	-23	-17	-26	-7	-7	-9	-14	-17	-19	-7	-12	-8	-7	-5	-12	-7
Income Percentile 68-95	8	10	-9	-14	-21	4	6	3	-10	-5	-9	2	-2	-8	-9	-9	-12	-9
Income Percentile 95-100	6	3	-15	-16	-32	2	13	-25	-17	-19	-14	-4	0	5	1	-6	3	10
Total PDI	-5	-1	-24	-23	-28	-11	-9	-10	-18	-17	-17	-9	-9	-7	-6	-8	-12	-7

PDI is proportion "central cities" minus proportion "non-urban areas"

Table 1.69
Percent Female within Income

	1952	1954	1956	1958	1960	1962	1964	1966	1968	1970	1972	1974	1976	1978	1980	1982	1984	1986
Income Percentile 0-16	65%	58%	63%	60%	68%	63%	66%	62%	71%	68%	68%	70%	71%	71%	68%	70%	70%	70%
Income Percentile 17-33	54%	54%	62%	58%	57%	60%	57%	61%	58%	66%	59%	58%	61%	56%	64%	58%	57%	62%
Income Percentile 34-67	56%	52%	51%	50%	55%	54%	57%	55%	55%	56%	54%	57%	57%	52%	53%	51%	55%	52%
Income Percentile 68-95	49%	51%	51%	48%	49%	46%	46%	51%	49%	50%	51%	53%	49%	48%	50%	50%	49%	48%
Income Percentile 95-100	39%	50%	46%	56%	51%	52%	53%	52%	43%	46%	48%	40%	48%	48%	47%	42%	40%	52%
Total Population	54%	53%	55%	53%	55%	55%	55%	56%	56%	57%	57%	58%	58%	56%	57%	55%	56%	56%

Table 1.70
Percent Black within Income

	1952	1954	1956	1958	1960	1962	1964	1966	1968	1970	1972	1974	1976	1978	1980	1982	1984	1986
Income Percentile 0-16	24%	21%	23%	24%	24%	18%	21%	20%	19%	22%	20%	17%	29%	21%	22%	25%	27%	29%
Income Percentile 17-33	13%	13%	12%	14%	11%	19%	12%	14%	11%	17%	15%	15%	12%	14%	16%	13%	13%	21%
Income Percentile 34-67	9%	7%	5%	6%	5%	6%	8%	10%	8%	8%	8%	7%	8%	7%	8%	9%	9%	12%
Income Percentile 68-95	3%	4%	2%	2%	5%	3%	5%	7%	5%	4%	5%	5%	5%	4%	7%	7%	6%	6%
Income Percentile 95-100	0%	1%	0%	0%	0%	5%	4%	1%	3%	2%	2%	0%	1%	2%	0%	1%	3%	8%
Total Population	10%	9%	8%	9%	9%	9%	10%	11%	10%	10%	10%	9%	11%	10%	12%	11%	11%	15%

Table 1.71
Percent Union Households within Income

	1952	1954	1956	1958	1960	1962	1964	1966	1968	1970	1972	1974	1976	1978	1980	1982	1984	1986
Income Percentile 0-16	7%	8%	8%	8%	7%	**	11%	11%	9%	7%	7%	8%	5%	9%	7%	5%	5%	7%
Income Percentile 17-33	19%	22%	24%	22%	22%	**	21%	22%	20%	15%	19%	12%	17%	21%	15%	12%	15%	10%
Income Percentile 34-67	38%	41%	41%	37%	37%	**	32%	35%	36%	28%	33%	33%	27%	30%	33%	26%	26%	24%
Income Percentile 68-95	37%	37%	33%	28%	32%	**	32%	37%	31%	31%	35%	34%	34%	37%	36%	35%	32%	32%
Income Percentile 95-100	12%	10%	10%	2%	5%	**	15%	17%	9%	15%	11%	13%	13%	23%	22%	20%	21%	20%
Total Population	27%	28%	27%	25%	27%	**	24%	28%	25%	24%	26%	26%	23%	26%	26%	21%	21%	20%

Table 1.72
Percent South within Income

	1952	1954	1956	1958	1960	1962	1964	1966	1968	1970	1972	1974	1976	1978	1980	1982	1984	1986
Income Percentile 0-16	51%	49%	47%	42%	54%	43%	41%	42%	41%	47%	46%	52%	51%	47%	42%	45%	47%	54%
Income Percentile 17-33	30%	39%	32%	33%	35%	40%	38%	39%	34%	37%	39%	38%	36%	35%	38%	43%	36%	40%
Income Percentile 34-67	24%	23%	26%	26%	30%	30%	30%	29%	28%	36%	34%	35%	34%	32%	32%	34%	33%	34%
Income Percentile 68-95	20%	23%	21%	26%	28%	33%	20%	19%	25%	27%	24%	30%	23%	30%	29%	32%	25%	27%
Income Percentile 95-100	11%	14%	22%	19%	32%	29%	33%	31%	27%	22%	22%	22%	18%	38%	34%	31%	24%	38%
Total Population	29%	31%	29%	30%	34%	35%	31%	30%	31%	35%	34%	36%	32%	35%	35%	36%	33%	36%

Social Characteristics of Income Groups

Table 1.73
Occupation of Income Groups

	1952	1954	1956	1958	1960	1962	1964	1966	1968	1970	1972	1974	1976	1978	1980	1982	1984	1986	
Income Percentile 0-16	8%	**	5%	4%	3%	**	6%	**	6%	7%	9%	8%	8%	11%	10%	8%	7%	9%	Professional
	4	**	3	6	7	**	7	**	8	8	12	11	9	12	15	17	17	13	White Collar
	10	**	22	32	33	**	40	**	38	37	37	43	44	47	46	42	50	50	Blue Collar
	25	**	12	7	3	**	3	**	4	2	2	3	4	5	7	5	3	6	Unskilled
	13	**	19	14	16	**	13	**	8	10	6	5	9	4	4	6	7	6	Farmers
	40	**	39	38	38	**	31	**	37	35	34	29	26	22	19	23	15	18	Housewives
Income Percentile 17-33	10%	**	5%	10%	5%	**	15%	**	11%	8%	11%	13%	10%	16%	15%	16%	13%	14%	Professional
	8	**	10	8	15	**	14	**	14	14	13	14	16	17	22	19	22	25	White Collar
	19	**	29	34	40	**	30	**	39	42	42	49	45	44	40	42	43	43	Blue Collar
	19	**	8	6	3	**	5	**	3	3	3	2	4	3	5	3	2	3	Unskilled
	10	**	7	6	6	**	7	**	6	8	4	3	2	3	3	4	4	3	Farmers
	34	**	41	36	31	**	30	**	27	26	27	19	23	17	15	16	16	11	Housewives
Income Percentile 34-67	10%	**	14%	13%	10%	**	15%	**	17%	15%	18%	22%	18%	21%	23%	26%	24%	25%	Professional
	11	**	9	13	16	**	15	**	17	16	16	17	19	18	21	21	25	23	White Collar
	26	**	31	37	39	**	30	**	34	34	36	36	36	38	37	34	33	36	Blue Collar
	8	**	6	2	1	**	2	**	2	2	2	2	3	3	3	3	3	2	Unskilled
	6	**	3	3	3	**	2	**	3	4	1	2	2	1	2	2	3	2	Farmers
	41	**	37	33	31	**	36	**	28	29	26	23	22	20	13	14	12	12	Housewives
Income Percentile 68-95	21%	**	24%	30%	27%	**	27%	**	33%	33%	31%	32%	33%	36%	38%	35%	39%	42%	Professional
	16	**	18	16	18	**	16	**	16	16	18	18	20	18	17	23	24	22	White Collar
	25	**	25	24	25	**	29	**	23	26	25	25	28	27	27	26	27	24	Blue Collar
	3	**	4	1	2	**	2	**	1	1	2	1	1	2	1	2	1	2	Unskilled
	4	**	2	2	3	**	1	**	1	1	1	2	1	1	1	1	1	1	Farmers
	31	**	28	28	26	**	24	**	26	24	24	22	18	16	15	13	8	11	Housewives
Income Percentile 95-100	45%	**	49%	54%	61%	**	43%	**	51%	59%	50%	46%	51%	46%	53%	47%	55%	51%	Professional
	12	**	10	7	3	**	8	**	12	11	10	15	14	16	19	15	17	20	White Collar
	6	**	6	0	3	**	9	**	4	4	10	3	3	14	8	12	11	12	Blue Collar
	2	**	1	0	0	**	0	**	0	0	0	0	2	1	1	1	2	2	Unskilled
	9	**	3	0	1	**	5	**	4	0	3	12	7	1	1	4	4	0	Farmers
	26	**	31	39	31	**	36	**	30	26	26	23	24	21	16	20	12	14	Housewives

Table 1.74
Incidence of Occupations within Income Groups

	1952	1954	1956	1958	1960	1962	1964	1966	1968	1970	1972	1974	1976	1978	1980	1982	1984	1986	
Percent Professional	8%	**	5%	4%	3%	**	6%	**	6%	7%	9%	8%	8%	11%	10%	8%	7%	9%	Percentile 0-16
	10%	**	5%	10%	5%	**	15%	**	11%	8%	11%	13%	10%	16%	15%	16%	13%	14%	Percentile 17-33
	10%	**	14%	13%	10%	**	15%	**	17%	15%	18%	22%	18%	21%	23%	26%	24%	25%	Percentile 34-67
	21%	**	24%	30%	27%	**	27%	**	33%	33%	31%	32%	33%	36%	38%	35%	39%	42%	Percentile 68-95
	45%	**	49%	54%	61%	**	43%	**	51%	59%	50%	46%	51%	46%	53%	47%	55%	51%	Percentile 95-100
Percent White Collar	4%	**	3%	6%	7%	**	7%	**	8%	8%	12%	11%	9%	12%	15%	17%	17%	13%	Percentile 0-16
	8%	**	10%	8%	15%	**	14%	**	14%	14%	13%	14%	16%	17%	22%	19%	22%	25%	Percentile 17-33
	11%	**	9%	13%	16%	**	15%	**	17%	16%	16%	17%	19%	18%	21%	21%	25%	23%	Percentile 34-67
	16%	**	18%	16%	18%	**	16%	**	16%	16%	18%	18%	20%	18%	17%	23%	24%	22%	Percentile 68-95
	12%	**	10%	7%	3%	**	8%	**	12%	11%	10%	15%	14%	16%	19%	15%	17%	20%	Percentile 95-100
Percent Blue Collar	10%	**	22%	32%	33%	**	40%	**	38%	37%	37%	43%	44%	47%	46%	42%	50%	50%	Percentile 0-16
	19%	**	29%	34%	40%	**	30%	**	39%	42%	42%	49%	45%	44%	40%	42%	43%	43%	Percentile 17-33
	26%	**	31%	37%	39%	**	30%	**	34%	34%	36%	36%	36%	38%	37%	34%	33%	36%	Percentile 34-67
	25%	**	25%	24%	25%	**	29%	**	23%	26%	25%	25%	28%	27%	27%	26%	27%	24%	Percentile 68-95
	6%	**	6%	0%	3%	**	9%	**	4%	4%	10%	3%	3%	14%	8%	12%	11%	12%	Percentile 95-100
Percent Unskilled	25%	**	12%	7%	3%	**	3%	**	4%	2%	2%	3%	4%	5%	7%	5%	3%	6%	Percentile 0-16
	19%	**	8%	6%	3%	**	5%	**	3%	3%	3%	2%	4%	3%	5%	3%	2%	3%	Percentile 17-33
	8%	**	6%	2%	1%	**	2%	**	2%	2%	2%	2%	3%	3%	3%	3%	3%	2%	Percentile 34-67
	3%	**	4%	1%	2%	**	2%	**	1%	1%	2%	1%	1%	2%	1%	2%	1%	2%	Percentile 68-95
	2%	**	1%	0%	0%	**	0%	**	0%	0%	0%	0%	2%	1%	1%	1%	2%	2%	Percentile 95-100
Percent Farmers	13%	**	19%	14%	16%	**	13%	**	8%	10%	6%	5%	9%	4%	4%	6%	7%	6%	Percentile 0-16
	10%	**	7%	6%	6%	**	7%	**	6%	8%	4%	3%	2%	3%	3%	4%	4%	3%	Percentile 17-33
	6%	**	3%	3%	3%	**	2%	**	3%	4%	1%	2%	2%	1%	2%	2%	3%	2%	Percentile 34-67
	4%	**	2%	2%	3%	**	1%	**	1%	1%	1%	2%	1%	1%	1%	1%	1%	1%	Percentile 68-95
	9%	**	3%	0%	1%	**	5%	**	4%	0%	3%	12%	7%	1%	1%	4%	4%	0%	Percentile 95-100
Percent Housewives	40%	**	39%	38%	38%	**	31%	**	37%	35%	34%	29%	26%	22%	19%	23%	15%	18%	Percentile 0-16
	34%	**	41%	36%	31%	**	30%	**	27%	26%	27%	19%	23%	17%	15%	16%	16%	11%	Percentile 17-33
	41%	**	37%	33%	31%	**	36%	**	28%	29%	26%	23%	22%	20%	13%	14%	12%	12%	Percentile 34-67
	31%	**	28%	28%	26%	**	24%	**	26%	24%	24%	22%	18%	16%	15%	13%	8%	11%	Percentile 68-95
	26%	**	31%	39%	31%	**	36%	**	30%	26%	26%	23%	24%	21%	16%	20%	12%	14%	Percentile 95-100

Table 1.75
Religion of Income Groups

	1952	1954	1956	1958	1960	1962	1964	1966	1968	1970	1972	1974	1976	1978	1980	1982	1984	1986	
Income Percentile 0-16	87%	84%	86%	80%	91%	84%	79%	79%	83%	80%	74%	76%	74%	71%	68%	73%	67%	70%	Protestant
	7	11	11	17	8	12	15	14	14	12	19	18	16	19	20	19	22	18	Catholic
	2	3	1	0	0	2	0	1	0	1	2	1	2	1	4	0	1	1	Jewish
	3	2	2	3	2	3	6	7	3	7	5	5	7	9	9	9	10	11	Other and None
Income Percentile 17-33	70%	76%	73%	80%	76%	77%	78%	77%	73%	77%	77%	67%	69%	66%	66%	65%	67%	76%	Protestant
	24	19	21	16	20	19	16	19	19	16	17	19	23	21	22	20	23	16	Catholic
	2	1	2	1	1	2	1	2	3	1	2	2	1	2	1	2	1	1	Jewish
	5	4	4	3	4	2	5	3	5	7	5	13	8	11	11	13	9	8	Other and None
Income Percentile 34-67	71%	74%	72%	69%	71%	71%	69%	72%	71%	69%	68%	68%	65%	62%	62%	66%	61%	65%	Protestant
	24	22	24	27	21	23	25	22	25	19	25	23	24	26	26	24	28	23	Catholic
	3	2	3	2	6	3	3	3	2	2	2	3	2	2	3	1	2	1	Jewish
	3	2	2	2	3	3	3	3	3	9	5	7	9	11	10	10	9	10	Other and None
Income Percentile 68-95	65%	71%	66%	69%	70%	72%	65%	64%	67%	65%	64%	65%	59%	59%	62%	62%	57%	58%	Protestant
	28	23	26	25	25	21	28	28	24	24	28	24	31	29	25	27	29	32	Catholic
	4	3	5	5	3	5	3	6	5	4	2	2	3	3	4	2	3	2	Jewish
	3	4	3	2	2	2	4	3	4	8	5	8	7	8	9	9	11	8	Other and None
Income Percentile 95-100	66%	72%	74%	79%	74%	65%	57%	69%	56%	70%	59%	58%	63%	51%	53%	63%	54%	53%	Protestant
	20	19	16	11	16	19	29	27	30	15	25	19	20	26	23	19	23	21	Catholic
	11	8	9	11	11	13	8	3	6	9	9	13	8	13	8	7	11	9	Jewish
	3	1	2	0	0	3	7	1	8	6	7	10	9	10	16	12	13	17	Other and None

Table 1.76
Incidence of Religions within Income Groups

	1952	1954	1956	1958	1960	1962	1964	1966	1968	1970	1972	1974	1976	1978	1980	1982	1984	1986	
Percent Protestant	87%	84%	86%	80%	91%	84%	79%	79%	83%	80%	74%	76%	74%	71%	68%	73%	67%	70%	Percentile 0-16
	70%	76%	73%	80%	76%	77%	78%	77%	73%	77%	77%	67%	69%	66%	66%	65%	67%	76%	Percentile 17-33
	71%	74%	72%	69%	71%	71%	69%	72%	71%	69%	68%	68%	65%	62%	62%	66%	61%	65%	Percentile 34-67
	65%	71%	66%	69%	70%	72%	65%	64%	67%	65%	64%	65%	59%	59%	62%	62%	57%	58%	Percentile 68-95
	66%	72%	74%	79%	74%	65%	57%	69%	56%	70%	59%	58%	63%	51%	53%	63%	54%	53%	Percentile 95-100
Percent Catholic	7%	11%	11%	17%	8%	12%	15%	14%	14%	12%	19%	18%	16%	19%	20%	19%	22%	18%	Percentile 0-16
	24%	19%	21%	16%	20%	19%	16%	19%	19%	16%	17%	19%	23%	21%	22%	20%	23%	16%	Percentile 17-33
	24%	22%	24%	27%	21%	23%	25%	22%	25%	19%	25%	23%	24%	26%	26%	24%	28%	23%	Percentile 34-67
	28%	23%	26%	25%	25%	21%	28%	28%	24%	24%	28%	24%	31%	29%	25%	27%	29%	32%	Percentile 68-95
	20%	19%	16%	11%	16%	19%	29%	27%	30%	15%	25%	19%	20%	26%	23%	19%	23%	21%	Percentile 95-10
Percent Jewish	2%	3%	1%	0%	0%	2%	0%	1%	0%	1%	2%	1%	2%	1%	4%	0%	1%	1%	Percentile 0-16
	2%	1%	2%	1%	1%	2%	1%	2%	3%	1%	2%	2%	1%	2%	1%	2%	1%	1%	Percentile 17-33
	3%	2%	3%	2%	6%	3%	3%	3%	2%	2%	2%	3%	2%	2%	3%	1%	2%	1%	Percentile 34-67
	4%	3%	5%	5%	3%	5%	3%	6%	5%	4%	2%	2%	3%	3%	4%	2%	3%	2%	Percentile 68-95
	11%	8%	9%	11%	11%	13%	8%	3%	6%	9%	9%	13%	8%	13%	8%	7%	11%	9%	Percentile 95-100
Percent Other	3%	2%	2%	3%	2%	3%	6%	7%	3%	7%	5%	5%	7%	9%	9%	9%	10%	11%	Percentile 0-16
	5%	4%	4%	3%	4%	2%	5%	3%	5%	7%	5%	13%	8%	11%	11%	13%	9%	8%	Percentile 17-33
	3%	2%	2%	2%	3%	3%	3%	3%	3%	9%	5%	7%	9%	11%	10%	10%	9%	10%	Percentile 34-67
	3%	4%	3%	2%	2%	2%	4%	3%	4%	8%	5%	8%	7%	8%	9%	9%	11%	8%	Percentile 68-95
	3%	1%	2%	0%	0%	3%	7%	1%	8%	6%	7%	10%	9%	10%	16%	12%	13%	17%	Percentile 95-100

Social Characteristics of Income Groups

Table 1.77
Age Cohorts of Sex Groups

	1952	1954	1956	1958	1960	1962	1964	1966	1968	1970	1972	1974	1976	1978	1980	1982	1984	1986	
Males	**	**	**	**	**	**	**	**	**	**	**	**	**	3%	8%	9%	15%	19%	1959 or later
	**	**	**	**	**	**	2%	8%	11%	16%	29%	31%	36%	41	36	39	39	41	1943 - 1958
	8%	5%	15%	19%	20%	28%	31	30	30	31	28	25	26	26	24	22	21	21	1927 - 1942
	40	51	39	37	37	35	36	32	32	28	25	26	24	22	22	24	19	16	1911 - 1926
	31	32	29	29	30	26	22	23	23	21	15	16	14	8	9	6	7	4	1895 - 1910
	22	13	17	15	13	12	9	8	5	5	3	3	2	1	1	1	0	0	Before 1895
Females	**	**	**	**	**	**	**	**	**	**	**	**	**	3%	7%	11%	16%	19%	1959 or later
	**	**	**	**	**	**	1%	7%	9%	18%	27%	36%	37%	38	38	35	36	37	1943 - 1958
	9%	8%	19%	23%	23%	28%	35	31	34	31	26	22	22	24	22	20	20	19	1927 - 1942
	39	45	43	40	38	34	32	33	31	26	26	23	24	21	22	25	19	19	1911 - 1926
	30	34	24	23	24	24	23	21	20	21	18	16	16	12	12	9	9	6	1895 - 1910
	22	13	14	15	15	14	10	8	7	6	4	3	2	2	0	1	0	0	Before 1895

Table 1.78
Age Cohorts of Sex Groups Summarized with a Percentage Difference Index#

	1952	1954	1956	1958	1960	1962	1964	1966	1968	1970	1972	1974	1976	1978	1980	1982	1984	1986
Males	44	40	31	25	23	10	-3	-7	-13	-21	-40	-38	-46	-61	-57	-63	-68	-77
Females	44	39	19	15	16	10	-3	-9	-17	-22	-31	-39	-41	-52	-54	-56	-63	-69
Total PDI	44	39	24	20	19	10	-3	-8	-15	-21	-35	-38	-43	-56	-55	-59	-65	-73

PDI is proportion "born before 1911" minus proportion "born 1927 or later"

Table 1.79
Education of Sex Groups

	1952	1954	1956	1958	1960	1962	1964	1966	1968	1970	1972	1974	1976	1978	1980	1982	1984	1986	
Males	45%	39%	32%	33%	34%	30%	27%	27%	25%	28%	21%	21%	18%	12%	14%	13%	12%	9%	Grade School
	39	42	45	44	45	43	45	44	42	44	43	45	44	48	44	41	43	44	High School
	17	20	23	23	21	28	28	29	33	28	36	35	39	41	42	46	46	47	College
Females	39%	35%	30%	29%	26%	26%	23%	26%	22%	22%	19%	17%	16%	12%	11%	10%	10%	9%	Grade School
	49	49	55	54	51	53	57	56	55	56	57	54	54	57	57	49	52	50	High School
	13	16	16	18	23	21	21	19	23	22	24	28	30	31	33	41	38	41	College

Table 1.80
Education of Sex Groups Summarized with a Percentage Difference Index#

	1952	1954	1956	1958	1960	1962	1964	1966	1968	1970	1972	1974	1976	1978	1980	1982	1984	1986
Males	-28	-19	-10	-9	-14	-2	0	2	8	0	15	14	21	29	29	33	34	37
Females	-26	-19	-14	-11	-3	-5	-2	-7	2	0	5	11	14	19	22	31	28	32
Total PDI	-27	-19	-12	-10	-8	-4	-1	-3	4	0	9	12	17	23	25	32	31	34

PDI is proportion "college" minus proportion "grade school"

Table 1.81
Urbanism of Sex Groups

	1952	1954	1956	1958	1960	1962	1964	1966	1968	1970	1972	1974	1976	1978	1980	1982	1984	1986	
Males	31%	32%	24%	26%	22%	26%	30%	32%	24%	27%	25%	27%	26%	26%	27%	27%	23%	25%	Central Cities
	28	30	27	28	27	37	33	31	33	27	33	35	37	40	39	38	42	42	Suburbs
	41	39	49	46	51	37	38	37	43	46	42	38	38	33	34	36	36	33	Non-urban areas
Females	34%	36%	26%	23%	22%	25%	30%	27%	28%	27%	26%	28%	30%	28%	28%	29%	24%	26%	Central Cities
	30	31	26	28	28	40	30	31	28	31	30	37	34	39	39	36	42	43	Suburbs
	35	32	48	49	50	35	40	41	44	42	44	35	37	34	33	35	34	31	Non-urban areas

Table 1.82
Urbanism of Sex Groups Summarized with a Percentage Difference Index#

	1952	1954	1956	1958	1960	1962	1964	1966	1968	1970	1972	1974	1976	1978	1980	1982	1984	1986
Males	-9	-7	-25	-19	-29	-11	-8	-5	-19	-19	-17	-11	-12	-7	-8	-10	-13	-9
Females	-1	4	-23	-26	-28	-11	-10	-14	-17	-15	-17	-7	-7	-6	-5	-7	-11	-5
Total PDI	-5	-1	-24	-23	-28	-11	-9	-10	-18	-17	-17	-9	-9	-7	-6	-8	-12	-7

PDI is proportion "central cities" minus proportion "non-urban areas"

Table 1.83
Family Income of Sex Groups

	1952	1954	1956	1958	1960	1962	1964	1966	1968	1970	1972	1974	1976	1978	1980	1982	1984	1986	
Males	15%	19%	13%	14%	11%	18%	14%	17%	10%	11%	14%	11%	9%	11%	13%	11%	10%	12%	Percentile 0-16
	16	13	19	19	17	7	18	8	20	12	11	16	17	17	13	16	17	13	17-33
	22	32	34	30	28	42	25	33	32	33	39	40	31	33	39	32	36	39	34-67
	42	29	25	34	39	28	35	36	31	40	30	27	36	31	29	31	30	32	68-95
	5	7	10	3	5	5	7	6	7	5	6	6	6	8	7	10	8	5	96-100
Females	24%	22%	19%	18%	19%	25%	23%	23%	20%	18%	23%	19%	18%	22%	21%	21%	19%	22%	Percentile 0-16
	16	13	25	23	18	9	19	10	22	17	13	16	21	19	18	19	18	17	17-33
	24	31	29	27	28	41	27	33	31	32	36	39	31	30	34	28	35	34	34-67
	34	28	21	28	30	20	25	29	24	30	24	23	26	23	23	26	23	24	68-95
	3	6	7	4	4	5	7	5	4	3	4	3	4	6	5	6	4	4	96-100

Table 1.84
Family Income of Sex Groups Summarized with a Percentage Difference Index#

	1952	1954	1956	1958	1960	1962	1964	1966	1968	1970	1972	1974	1976	1978	1980	1982	1984	1986
Males	16	6	3	4	17	9	11	16	7	22	11	6	16	11	10	14	10	12
Females	-4	-2	-16	-10	-2	-9	-10	2	-14	-2	-7	-10	-8	-11	-12	-8	-10	-11
Total PDI	5	2	-8	-3	6	-1	-1	8	-5	8	1	-3	2	-1	-2	2	-1	-1

PDI is proportion "68-100 percentile" minus proportion "0-33 percentile"

Table 1.85
Percent Black within Sex Groups

	1952	1954	1956	1958	1960	1962	1964	1966	1968	1970	1972	1974	1976	1978	1980	1982	1984	1986
Males	9%	9%	7%	9%	9%	8%	8%	11%	8%	8%	9%	7%	8%	8%	11%	9%	9%	15%
Females	10%	9%	9%	9%	9%	10%	12%	11%	11%	11%	11%	11%	12%	12%	12%	12%	13%	16%
Total Population	10%	9%	8%	9%	9%	9%	10%	11%	10%	10%	10%	9%	11%	10%	12%	11%	11%	15%

Table 1.86
Percent Union Households within Sex Groups

	1952	1954	1956	1958	1960	1962	1964	1966	1968	1970	1972	1974	1976	1978	1980	1982	1984	1986
Males	33%	30%	29%	25%	30%	**	28%	34%	29%	27%	29%	26%	27%	30%	32%	23%	25%	25%
Females	23%	27%	26%	24%	24%	**	21%	24%	22%	21%	24%	25%	21%	23%	21%	20%	19%	17%
Total Population	27%	28%	27%	25%	27%	**	24%	28%	25%	24%	26%	26%	23%	26%	26%	21%	21%	20%

Table 1.87
Percent South within Sex Groups

	1952	1954	1956	1958	1960	1962	1964	1966	1968	1970	1972	1974	1976	1978	1980	1982	1984	1986
Males	27%	31%	29%	29%	30%	35%	29%	29%	30%	35%	33%	34%	31%	36%	35%	36%	33%	35%
Females	30%	31%	29%	31%	36%	35%	32%	31%	31%	35%	34%	37%	33%	35%	36%	36%	33%	37%
Total Population	29%	31%	29%	30%	34%	35%	31%	30%	31%	35%	34%	36%	32%	35%	35%	36%	33%	36%

Table 1.88
Occupation of Sex Groups

	1952	1954	1956	1958	1960	1962	1964	1966	1968	1970	1972	1974	1976	1978	1980	1982	1984	1986	
Males	24%	**	26%	29%	24%	**	30%	**	32%	32%	31%	32%	29%	32%	33%	33%	28%	30%	Professional
	10	**	9	10	11	**	12	**	11	9	11	10	10	11	10	12	15	13	White Collar
	37	**	42	45	50	**	44	**	46	46	48	48	49	49	47	43	46	47	Blue Collar
	14	**	11	7	4	**	5	**	4	4	4	4	6	5	6	6	4	5	Unskilled
	15	**	12	9	11	**	9	**	8	9	6	7	6	4	4	6	7	5	Farmers
	0	**	1	0	0	**	0	**	0	0	0	0	0	0	0	0	0	0	Housewives
Females	7%	**	7%	8%	10%	**	11%	**	11%	13%	12%	15%	16%	19%	20%	19%	21%	23%	Professional
	12	**	11	12	17	**	14	**	17	17	19	20	22	21	25	26	29	28	White Collar
	7	**	12	16	16	**	18	**	19	20	20	24	24	24	26	24	25	25	Blue Collar
	8	**	2	0	0	**	0	**	0	0	0	0	1	1	1	0	1	1	Unskilled
	1	**	2	1	1	**	1	**	1	1	1	0	1	1	0	1	1	1	Farmers
	65	**	65	63	56	**	56	**	52	49	48	40	38	35	28	30	24	22	Housewives

Original data set for 1956 is in error. All housewives are female.

Table 1.89
Incidence of Occupations within Sex Groups

	1952	1954	1956	1958	1960	1962	1964	1966	1968	1970	1972	1974	1976	1978	1980	1982	1984	1986	
Percent Professional	24%	24%	26%	29%	24%	**	30%	**	32%	32%	31%	32%	29%	32%	33%	33%	28%	30%	Male
	7%	9%	7%	8%	10%	**	11%	**	11%	13%	12%	15%	16%	19%	20%	19%	21%	23%	Female
Percent White collar	10%	10%	9%	10%	11%	**	12%	**	11%	9%	11%	10%	10%	11%	10%	12%	15%	13%	Male
	12%	11%	11%	12%	17%	**	14%	**	17%	17%	19%	20%	22%	21%	25%	26%	29%	28%	Female
Percent Blue collar	37%	33%	42%	45%	50%	**	44%	**	46%	46%	48%	48%	49%	49%	47%	43%	46%	47%	Male
	7%	7%	12%	16%	16%	**	18%	**	19%	20%	20%	24%	24%	24%	26%	24%	25%	25%	Female
Percent Unskilled	14%	17%	11%	7%	4%	**	5%	**	4%	4%	4%	4%	6%	5%	6%	6%	4%	5%	Male
	8%	9%	2%	0%	0%	**	0%	**	0%	0%	0%	0%	1%	1%	1%	0%	1%	1%	Female
Percent Farmers	15%	15%	12%	9%	11%	**	9%	**	8%	9%	6%	7%	6%	4%	4%	6%	7%	5%	Male
	1%	1%	2%	1%	1%	**	1%	**	1%	1%	1%	0%	1%	1%	0%	1%	1%	1%	Female
Percent Housewives	0%	2%	1%	0%	0%	**	0%	**	0%	0%	0%	0%	0%	0%	0%	0%	0%	0%	Male
	65%	64%	65%	63%	56%	**	56%	**	52%	49%	48%	40%	38%	35%	28%	30%	24%	22%	Female

Table 1.90
Religion of Sex Groups

	1952	1954	1956	1958	1960	1962	1964	1966	1968	1970	1972	1974	1976	1978	1980	1982	1984	1986	
Males	70%	76%	74%	72%	73%	71%	67%	68%	71%	70%	67%	66%	61%	58%	60%	63%	59%	60%	Protestant
	23	19	20	22	21	21	24	23	21	19	23	21	27	24	23	22	25	25	Catholic
	3	3	3	3	4	4	2	4	2	3	2	3	3	3	4	1	3	2	Jewish
	4	3	4	4	3	5	7	5	6	8	8	11	10	15	14	14	13	13	Other and None
Females	73%	75%	73%	75%	76%	76%	73%	74%	72%	71%	70%	70%	68%	67%	66%	67%	64%	69%	Protestant
	21	20	22	21	20	19	21	21	23	20	24	23	24	24	24	23	27	23	Catholic
	4	3	4	3	3	3	3	3	3	3	2	2	2	3	3	2	2	1	Jewish
	3	3	2	1	1	2	3	2	2	7	4	5	6	6	7	8	7	7	Other and None

Table 1.91
Incidence of Religions within Sex Groups

	1952	1954	1956	1958	1960	1962	1964	1966	1968	1970	1972	1974	1976	1978	1980	1982	1984	1986	
Percent Protestant	70%	76%	74%	72%	73%	71%	67%	68%	71%	70%	67%	66%	61%	58%	60%	63%	59%	60%	Male
	73%	75%	73%	75%	76%	76%	73%	74%	72%	71%	70%	70%	68%	67%	66%	67%	64%	69%	Female
Percent Catholic	23%	19%	20%	22%	21%	21%	24%	23%	21%	19%	23%	21%	27%	24%	23%	22%	25%	25%	Male
	21%	20%	22%	21%	20%	19%	21%	21%	23%	20%	24%	23%	24%	24%	24%	23%	27%	23%	Female
Percent Jewish	3%	3%	3%	3%	4%	4%	2%	4%	2%	3%	2%	3%	3%	3%	4%	1%	3%	2%	Male
	4%	3%	4%	3%	3%	3%	3%	3%	3%	3%	2%	2%	2%	3%	3%	2%	2%	1%	Female
Percent Other and None	4%	3%	4%	4%	3%	5%	7%	5%	6%	8%	8%	11%	10%	15%	14%	14%	13%	13%	Male
	3%	3%	2%	1%	1%	2%	3%	2%	2%	7%	4%	5%	6%	6%	7%	8%	7%	7%	Female

Table 1.92
Age Cohorts of Racial Groups

	1952	1954	1956	1958	1960	1962	1964	1966	1968	1970	1972	1974	1976	1978	1980	1982	1984	1986	
Whites	**	**	**	**	**	**	**	**	**	**	**	**	**	3%	7%	10%	15%	19%	1959 or later
	**	**	**	**	**	**	2%	7%	10%	16%	27%	33%	36%	38	36	37	37	39	1943 - 1958
	8%	7%	17%	20%	20%	28%	32	31	31	31	26	23	24	25	23	21	20	20	1927 - 1942
	39	47	41	39	39	34	34	32	32	26	26	25	24	22	22	24	19	18	1911 - 1926
	31	33	26	26	27	25	23	23	21	21	17	16	15	11	11	8	9	6	1895 - 1910
	23	13	16	16	15	13	10	8	6	6	4	3	2	1	1	1	0	0	Before 1895
Blacks	**	**	**	**	**	**	**	**	**	**	**	**	**	3%	7%	9%	22%	21%	1959 or later
	**	**	**	**	**	**	1%	11%	6%	19%	31%	41%	40%	41	40	40	36	36	1943 - 1958
	10%	4%	24%	30%	30%	26%	41	29	38	30	30	24	20	27	22	20	18	22	1927 - 1942
	44	54	39	35	33	38	33	36	30	30	22	17	24	21	21	24	19	18	1911 - 1926
	31	32	28	29	28	25	18	19	21	17	14	16	15	6	10	7	5	2	1895 - 1910
	15	10	9	6	9	11	8	5	5	4	3	2	2	1	1	0	0	0	Before 1895

Table 1.93
Age Cohorts of Racial Groups Summarized with a Percentage Difference Index#

	1952	1954	1956	1958	1960	1962	1964	1966	1968	1970	1972	1974	1976	1978	1980	1982	1984	1986
Whites	45	40	25	22	21	10	-1	-7	-14	-20	-33	-37	-42	-54	-54	-59	-64	-71
Blacks	37	38	13	6	7	9	-16	-16	-19	-28	-44	-47	-42	-64	-58	-63	-71	-78
Total PDI	44	39	24	20	19	10	-3	-8	-15	-21	-35	-38	-43	-56	-55	-59	-65	-73

PDI is proportion "born before 1911" minus proportion "born 1927 or later"

Table 1.94
Education of Racial Groups

	1952	1954	1956	1958	1960	1962	1964	1966	1968	1970	1972	1974	1976	1978	1980	1982	1984	1986	
Whites	39%	34%	29%	28%	28%	25%	23%	25%	21%	23%	19%	17%	15%	11%	11%	10%	10%	8%	Grade School
	46	46	51	51	49	49	52	50	50	51	51	51	50	52	51	46	47	47	High School
	16	19	20	21	23	25	25	25	29	26	30	32	35	37	39	45	43	45	College
Blacks	67%	57%	53%	49%	46%	54%	39%	38%	40%	36%	27%	28%	29%	20%	21%	22%	14%	15%	Grade School
	27	37	40	35	40	36	47	53	46	57	52	52	48	57	57	48	55	55	High School
	7	6	7	15	14	10	14	10	15	7	21	20	24	23	23	30	31	30	College

Table 1.95
Education of Racial Groups Summarized with a Percentage Difference Index#

	1952	1954	1956	1958	1960	1962	1964	1966	1968	1970	1972	1974	1976	1978	1980	1982	1984	1986
Whites	-23	-15	-9	-8	-5	0	2	1	8	3	11	15	20	26	28	35	33	37
Blacks	-60	-52	-46	-34	-32	-44	-25	-28	-25	-29	-6	-8	-5	3	2	7	17	15
Total PDI	-27	-19	-12	-10	-8	-4	-1	-3	4	0	9	12	17	23	25	32	31	34

PDI is proportion "college" minus proportion "grade school"

Table 1.96
Urbanism of Racial Groups

	1952	1954	1956	1958	1960	1962	1964	1966	1968	1970	1972	1974	1976	1978	1980	1982	1984	1986	
Whites	31%	31%	23%	22%	20%	23%	26%	24%	22%	23%	22%	25%	24%	22%	22%	23%	20%	21%	Central cities
	30	32	27	29	28	40	34	34	32	32	33	37	36	43	42	39	46	46	Suburbs
	39	37	50	50	53	37	40	42	46	46	45	38	39	35	36	37	35	33	Non-urban areas
Blacks	51%	61%	42%	48%	44%	49%	59%	73%	56%	64%	54%	51%	55%	67%	69%	61%	53%	50%	Central cities
	25	23	24	23	23	23	11	10	18	10	13	21	25	11	14	18	16	24	Suburbs
	25	16	34	29	33	28	30	17	26	26	33	28	21	23	17	22	31	26	Non-urban areas

Table 1.97
Urbanism of Racial Groups Summarized with a Percentage Difference Index#

	1952	1954	1956	1958	1960	1962	1964	1966	1968	1970	1972	1974	1976	1978	1980	1982	1984	1986
Whites	-8	-6	-27	-28	-33	-14	-14	-19	-24	-23	-22	-13	-15	-13	-14	-14	-15	-12
Blacks	26	46	8	19	11	21	28	56	30	38	21	23	34	44	52	39	22	24
Total PDI	-5	-1	-24	-23	-28	-11	-9	-10	-18	-17	-17	-9	-9	-7	-6	-8	-12	-7

PDI is proportion "central cities" minus proportion "non-urban areas"

Table 1.98
Family Income of Racial Groups

	1952	1954	1956	1958	1960	1962	1964	1966	1968	1970	1972	1974	1976	1978	1980	1982	1984	1986	
Whites	17%	18%	14%	14%	13%	20%	17%	18%	14%	13%	17%	15%	11%	15%	15%	14%	13%	14%	Percentile 0-16
	15	12	21	20	17	7	18	9	20	14	11	15	19	17	15	17	17	14	17-33
	23	33	32	29	29	43	27	33	32	33	38	41	32	32	38	31	37	37	34-67
	41	30	24	34	36	25	31	34	28	37	28	26	32	29	26	30	28	30	68-95
	4	7	9	4	5	5	8	6	6	4	6	4	6	8	6	9	6	5	96-100
Blacks	49%	48%	44%	42%	40%	44%	39%	37%	32%	34%	38%	29%	40%	37%	35%	38%	36%	34%	Percentile 0-16
	21	17	32	32	22	17	22	12	25	25	17	26	22	26	22	20	21	22	17-33
	21	23	19	19	17	30	22	30	26	27	29	31	24	23	27	24	27	30	34-67
	9	12	5	7	21	7	14	20	15	14	14	14	14	12	15	18	15	11	68-95
	0	1	0	0	0	3	3	1	1	1	1	0	1	2	0	1	1	3	96-100

Table 1.99
Family Income of Racial Groups Summarized with a Percentage Difference Index#

	1952	1954	1956	1958	1960	1962	1964	1966	1968	1970	1972	1974	1976	1978	1980	1982	1984	1986
Whites	13	7	-2	3	12	4	4	13	0	14	5	1	8	5	3	7	4	6
Blacks	-60	-51	-71	-67	-42	-50	-44	-29	-41	-44	-40	-41	-47	-50	-42	-39	-41	-43
Total PDI	5	2	-8	-3	6	-1	-1	8	-5	8	1	-3	2	-1	-2	2	-1	-1

PDI is proportion "68-100 percentile" minus proportion "0-33 percentile"

Table 1.100
Percent Female within Racial Groups

	1952	1954	1956	1958	1960	1962	1964	1966	1968	1970	1972	1974	1976	1978	1980	1982	1984	1986
Whites	54%	53%	55%	53%	55%	55%	54%	56%	55%	57%	56%	57%	57%	55%	57%	55%	55%	56%
Blacks	56%	52%	62%	53%	55%	60%	66%	56%	62%	64%	62%	68%	67%	66%	60%	63%	66%	59%
Total Population	54%	53%	55%	53%	55%	55%	55%	56%	56%	57%	57%	58%	58%	56%	57%	55%	56%	56%

Table 1.101
Percent Union Households within Racial Groups

	1952	1954	1956	1958	1960	1962	1964	1966	1968	1970	1972	1974	1976	1978	1980	1982	1984	1986
Whites	27%	28%	27%	25%	27%	**	24%	27%	25%	24%	26%	25%	23%	26%	26%	21%	22%	21%
Blacks	25%	28%	26%	21%	25%	**	23%	31%	25%	21%	25%	29%	23%	26%	25%	23%	20%	19%
Total Population	27%	28%	27%	25%	27%	**	24%	28%	25%	24%	26%	26%	23%	26%	26%	21%	21%	20%

Table 1.102
Percent South within Racial Groups

	1952	1954	1956	1958	1960	1962	1964	1966	1968	1970	1972	1974	1976	1978	1980	1982	1984	1986
Whites	24%	29%	27%	29%	32%	33%	27%	29%	29%	32%	31%	34%	29%	33%	33%	34%	29%	32%
Blacks	67%	54%	57%	47%	55%	53%	61%	43%	52%	57%	59%	57%	56%	57%	51%	55%	60%	57%
Total Population	29%	31%	29%	30%	34%	35%	31%	30%	31%	35%	34%	36%	32%	35%	35%	36%	33%	36%

Social Characteristics of Racial Groups

Table 1.103
Occupation of Racial Groups

	1952	1954	1956	1958	1960	1962	1964	1966	1968	1970	1972	1974	1976	1978	1980	1982	1984	1986	
Whites	16%	**	16%	19%	17%	**	21%	**	21%	22%	21%	24%	23%	26%	27%	26%	25%	28%	Professional
	12	**	11	12	15	**	14	**	15	15	15	16	17	17	20	20	23	23	White collar
	21	**	25	28	29	**	28	**	29	28	31	32	32	33	33	31	32	32	Blue collar
	7	**	5	3	2	**	2	**	2	1	2	1	3	2	3	2	2	3	Unskilled
	7	**	6	5	6	**	4	**	4	4	3	3	3	2	2	3	4	3	Farmers
	38	**	37	35	32	**	32	**	30	30	29	24	23	21	16	17	14	13	Housewives
Blacks	7%	**	7%	7%	12%	**	8%	**	11%	9%	11%	10%	8%	12%	13%	15%	13%	15%	Professional
	4	**	3	8	6	**	7	**	11	11	15	18	15	13	12	17	20	16	White collar
	16	**	36	53	52	**	47	**	43	54	50	51	54	54	51	47	54	51	Blue collar
	46	**	21	7	4	**	7	**	5	4	5	4	6	6	8	8	5	3	Unskilled
	9	**	12	7	8	**	9	**	8	7	3	1	4	3	0	2	3	4	Farmers
	19	**	22	18	19	**	23	**	23	17	17	16	13	12	16	12	6	12	Housewives

Table 1.104
Incidence of Occupations within Racial Groups

	1952	1954	1956	1958	1960	1962	1964	1966	1968	1970	1972	1974	1976	1978	1980	1982	1984	1986	
Percent Professional	16%	**	16%	19%	17%	**	21%	**	21%	22%	21%	24%	23%	26%	27%	26%	25%	28%	White
	7%	**	7%	7%	12%	**	8%	**	11%	9%	11%	10%	8%	12%	13%	15%	13%	15%	Black
Percent White collar	12%	**	11%	12%	15%	**	14%	**	15%	15%	15%	16%	17%	17%	20%	20%	23%	23%	White
	4%	**	3%	8%	6%	**	7%	**	11%	11%	15%	18%	15%	13%	12%	17%	20%	16%	Black
Percent Blue collar	21%	**	25%	28%	29%	**	28%	**	29%	28%	31%	32%	32%	33%	33%	31%	32%	32%	White
	16%	**	36%	53%	52%	**	47%	**	43%	54%	50%	51%	54%	54%	51%	47%	54%	51%	Black
Percent Unskilled	7%	**	5%	3%	2%	**	2%	**	2%	1%	2%	1%	3%	2%	3%	2%	2%	3%	White
	46%	**	21%	7%	4%	**	7%	**	5%	4%	5%	4%	6%	6%	8%	8%	5%	3%	Black
Percent Farmers	7%	**	6%	5%	6%	**	4%	**	4%	4%	3%	3%	3%	2%	2%	3%	4%	3%	White
	9%	**	12%	7%	8%	**	9%	**	8%	7%	3%	1%	4%	3%	0%	2%	3%	4%	Black
Percent Housewives	38%	**	37%	35%	32%	**	32%	**	30%	30%	29%	24%	23%	21%	16%	17%	14%	13%	White
	19%	**	22%	18%	19%	**	23%	**	23%	17%	17%	16%	13%	12%	16%	12%	6%	12%	Black

Table 1.105
Religion of Racial Groups

	1952	1954	1956	1958	1960	1962	1964	1966	1968	1970	1972	1974	1976	1978	1980	1982	1984	1986	
Whites	70%	74%	72%	72%	73%	72%	69%	70%	70%	69%	67%	67%	64%	61%	61%	64%	59%	62%	Protestant
	23	20	22	22	21	21	24	23	23	20	25	23	26	26	25	24	28	27	Catholic
	4	3	4	3	4	4	3	4	3	3	3	3	3	3	4	2	3	2	Jewish
	3	3	3	2	2	3	5	4	4	7	5	8	7	10	10	11	10	9	Other and None
Blacks	91%	93%	93%	93%	96%	90%	93%	89%	93%	89%	88%	88%	82%	86%	82%	82%	82%	83%	Protestant
	4	5	6	5	3	7	4	10	5	4	8	7	9	6	9	10	10	7	Catholic
	O	O	O	O	O	O	O	O	O	O	O	O	O	O	1	O	O	O	Jewish
	6	2	1	2	1	3	3	2	2	7	5	5	9	9	9	9	8	10	Other and None

Table 1.106
Incidence of Religions within Racial Groups

	1952	1954	1956	1958	1960	1962	1964	1966	1968	1970	1972	1974	1976	1978	1980	1982	1984	1986	
Percent Protestant	70%	74%	72%	72%	73%	72%	69%	70%	70%	69%	67%	67%	64%	61%	61%	64%	59%	62%	White
	91%	93%	93%	93%	96%	90%	93%	89%	93%	89%	88%	88%	82%	86%	82%	82%	82%	83%	Black
Percent Catholic	23%	20%	22%	22%	21%	21%	24%	23%	23%	20%	25%	23%	26%	26%	25%	24%	28%	27%	White
	4%	5%	6%	5%	3%	7%	4%	10%	5%	4%	8%	7%	9%	6%	9%	10%	10%	7%	Black
Percent Jewish	4%	3%	4%	3%	4%	4%	3%	4%	3%	3%	3%	3%	3%	3%	4%	2%	3%	2%	White
	0%	0%	0%	0%	0%	0%	0%	0%	0%	0%	0%	0%	0%	0%	1%	0%	0%	0%	Black
Percent Other and None	3%	3%	3%	2%	2%	3%	5%	4%	4%	7%	5%	8%	7%	10%	10%	11%	10%	9%	White
	6%	2%	1%	2%	1%	3%	3%	2%	2%	7%	5%	5%	9%	9%	9%	9%	8%	10%	Black

Table 1.107
Age Cohorts of Union Membership Groups

	1952	1954	1956	1958	1960	1962	1964	1966	1968	1970	1972	1974	1976	1978	1980	1982	1984	1986	
Union Household	**	**	**	**	**	**	**	**	**	**	**	**	**	3%	6%	6%	15%	14%	1959 or later
	**	**	**	**	**	**	3%	8%	10%	21%	30%	39%	42%	40	39	44	40	47	1943 - 1958
	10%	8%	22%	27%	30%	**	37	34	36	34	31	27	25	29	28	28	25	23	1927 - 1942
	48	57	47	42	39	**	37	39	39	33	30	25	26	24	22	20	17	15	1911 - 1926
	30	30	24	24	25	**	21	17	15	11	8	9	7	3	5	2	3	2	1895 - 1910
	12	5	6	7	7	**	3	3	1	1	1	0	0	1	0	0	0	0	Before 1895
Non-union Household	**	**	**	**	**	**	**	**	**	**	**	**	**	3%	7%	11%	16%	21%	1959 or later
	**	**	**	**	**	**	1%	7%	10%	16%	27%	32%	35%	39	36	35	37	36	1943 - 1958
	8%	6%	16%	19%	19%	**	32	30	31	30	26	22	23	24	21	19	19	19	1927 - 1942
	36	44	38	37	38	**	33	30	29	24	24	24	23	20	22	26	19	18	1911 - 1926
	31	34	27	26	28	**	23	24	23	24	19	19	17	13	13	10	9	6	1895 - 1910
	26	16	19	18	16	**	11	10	8	7	5	3	2	1	1	1	0	0	Before 1895

Table 1.108
Age Cohorts of Union Membership Groups Summarized with a Percentage Difference Index#

	1952	1954	1956	1958	1960	1962	1964	1966	1968	1970	1972	1974	1976	1978	1980	1982	1984	1986
Union Household	31	27	8	4	2	**	-16	-21	-29	-42	-51	-57	-60	-68	-67	-76	-76	-81
Non-union Household	49	44	30	25	25	**	1	-3	-10	-15	-29	-32	-39	-51	-51	-54	-62	-70
Total PDI	44	39	24	20	19	10	-3	-8	-15	-21	-35	-38	-43	-56	-55	-59	-65	-73

PDI is proportion "born before 1911" minus proportion "born 1927 or later"

Table 1.109
Education of Union Membership Groups

	1952	1954	1956	1958	1960	1962	1964	1966	1968	1970	1972	1974	1976	1978	1980	1982	1984	1986	
Union Household	39%	35%	33%	31%	32%	**	25%	28%	23%	24%	17%	13%	12%	9%	12%	7%	7%	5%	Grade School
	54	56	58	61	58	**	62	59	59	64	63	65	59	64	58	54	52	55	High School
	8	9	10	8	11	**	13	13	19	13	20	22	29	27	30	39	41	40	College
Non-union Household	42%	37%	30%	30%	30%	**	25%	25%	23%	25%	21%	21%	18%	13%	12%	12%	12%	10%	Grade School
	40	42	48	45	44	**	48	47	46	47	47	45	47	49	49	43	47	46	High School
	18	21	22	25	26	**	27	28	30	28	33	34	35	38	39	45	42	44	College

Table 1.110
Education of Union Membership Groups Summarized with a Percentage Difference Index#

	1952	1954	1956	1958	1960	1962	1964	1966	1968	1970	1972	1974	1976	1978	1980	1982	1984	1986
Union Household	-32	-26	-23	-23	-21	**	-12	-15	-4	-11	3	9	17	18	19	32	34	35
Non-union Household	-25	-16	-8	-6	-3	**	3	2	7	4	12	14	17	26	27	32	30	34
Total PDI	-27	-19	-12	-10	-8	-4	-1	-3	4	0	9	12	17	23	25	32	31	34

PDI is proportion "college" minus proportion "grade school"

Table 1.111
Urbanism of Union Membership Groups

	1952	1954	1956	1958	1960	1962	1964	1966	1968	1970	1972	1974	1976	1978	1980	1982	1984	1986	
Union Household	46%	44%	34%	36%	31%	**	38%	36%	29%	32%	29%	32%	31%	30%	29%	30%	24%	25%	Central Cities
	30	28	31	30	29	**	36	35	37	37	37	39	40	42	45	40	48	51	Suburbs
	25	28	35	34	40	**	26	29	35	31	34	29	30	28	26	30	29	24	Non-urban areas
Non-union Household	28%	31%	21%	21%	19%	**	27%	27%	25%	25%	25%	27%	27%	26%	27%	27%	23%	25%	Central Cities
	29	32	25	27	27	**	30	30	28	27	29	35	34	38	37	36	40	40	Suburbs
	43	38	54	52	54	**	43	44	47	48	46	38	39	35	36	37	37	34	Non-urban areas

Table 1.112
Urbanism of Union Membership Groups Summarized with a Percentage Difference Index#

	1952	1954	1956	1958	1960	1962	1964	1966	1968	1970	1972	1974	1976	1978	1980	1982	1984	1986
Union Household	21	16	-1	2	-10	**	12	7	-6	1	-5	3	1	1	4	0	-5	1
Non-union Household	-15	-7	-32	-31	-35	**	-16	-17	-21	-22	-21	-12	-12	-9	-9	-10	-13	-9
Total PDI	-5	-1	-24	-23	-28	-11	-9	-10	-18	-17	-17	-9	-9	-7	-6	-8	-12	-7

PDI is proportion "central cities" minus proportion "non-urban areas"

Table 1.113
Family Income of Union Membership Groups

	1952	1954	1956	1958	1960	1962	1964	1966	1968	1970	1972	1974	1976	1978	1980	1982	1984	1986	
Union Household	5%	6%	5%	5%	4%	**	9%	7%	6%	4%	5%	5%	3%	6%	5%	4%	3%	6%	Percentile 0-16
	11	10	19	19	15	**	15	7	16	9	9	8	14	15	9	9	12	8	17-33
	32	45	46	42	39	**	34	40	44	39	47	52	36	36	46	35	42	41	34-67
	50	37	27	34	41	**	38	42	32	46	37	34	44	38	35	45	37	42	68-95
	2	2	3	0	1	**	4	3	2	2	2	2	3	6	5	7	5	4	96-100
Non-union Household	26%	26%	21%	20%	19%	**	22%	25%	19%	18%	24%	19%	17%	21%	22%	20%	19%	20%	Percentile 0-16
	18	14	23	22	19	**	19	10	23	16	13	18	21	19	18	20	19	18	17-33
	20	26	25	24	24	**	24	30	27	30	33	36	30	29	32	29	34	35	34-67
	33	25	21	30	32	**	27	29	25	31	24	22	27	23	22	24	23	23	68-95
	5	9	10	4	6	**	8	7	6	4	6	5	6	8	6	8	6	4	96-100

Table 1.114
Family Income of Union Membership Groups Summarized with a Percentage Difference Index#

	1952	1954	1956	1958	1960	1962	1964	1966	1968	1970	1972	1974	1976	1978	1980	1982	1984	1986
Union Household	36	24	6	11	23	**	18	30	12	35	25	24	31	24	26	39	27	32
Non-union Household	-6	-6	-13	-8	0	**	-7	0	-11	1	-7	-11	-6	-9	-12	-8	-9	-10
Total PDI	5	2	-8	-3	6	-1	-1	8	-5	8	1	-3	2	-1	-2	2	-1	-1

PDI is proportion "68-100 percentile" minus proportion "0-33 percentile"

Social Characteristics of Union Membership Groups

Table 1.115
Percent Female within Union Membership Groups

	1952	1954	1956	1958	1960	1962	1964	1966	1968	1970	1972	1974	1976	1978	1980	1982	1984	1986
Union Household	45%	50%	52%	52%	49%	**	47%	47%	50%	51%	52%	57%	51%	49%	47%	52%	49%	47%
Non-union Household	58%	55%	56%	54%	57%	**	58%	59%	58%	59%	58%	58%	60%	58%	60%	56%	58%	59%
Total Population	54%	53%	55%	53%	55%	55%	55%	56%	56%	57%	57%	58%	58%	56%	57%	55%	56%	56%

Table 1.116
Percent Black within Union Membership Groups

	1952	1954	1956	1958	1960	1962	1964	1966	1968	1970	1972	1974	1976	1978	1980	1982	1984	1986
Union Household	9%	9%	8%	8%	8%	**	10%	12%	10%	9%	10%	10%	10%	11%	11%	12%	11%	14%
Non-union Household	10%	9%	9%	9%	9%	**	10%	10%	10%	10%	10%	9%	11%	10%	12%	11%	12%	15%
Total Population	10%	9%	8%	9%	9%	9%	10%	11%	10%	10%	10%	9%	11%	10%	12%	11%	11%	15%

Table 1.117
Percent South within Union Membership Groups

	1952	1954	1956	1958	1960	1962	1964	1966	1968	1970	1972	1974	1976	1978	1980	1982	1984	1986
Union Household	16%	17%	17%	18%	22%	**	15%	17%	21%	22%	22%	22%	18%	20%	19%	21%	22%	22%
Non-union Household	33%	36%	34%	34%	38%	**	35%	34%	34%	39%	38%	41%	37%	40%	41%	40%	36%	39%
Total Population	29%	31%	29%	30%	34%	35%	31%	30%	31%	35%	34%	36%	32%	35%	35%	36%	33%	36%

Table 1.118
Occupation of Union Memberships Groups

		1952	1954	1956	1958	1960	1962	1964	1966	1968	1970	1972	1974	1976	1978	1980	1982	1984	1986	
Union Household		6%	**	6%	5%	6%	**	10%	**	10%	12%	10%	15%	15%	18%	21%	20%	19%	23%	Professional
		10	**	10	8	12	**	11	**	13	13	15	18	16	16	15	14	24	18	White Collar
		42	**	39	51	53	**	51	**	49	46	47	42	46	46	48	46	42	47	Blue Collar
		14	**	9	4	3	**	3	**	4	2	3	4	4	5	4	4	4	4	Unskilled
		0	**	1	0	0	**	0	**	1	0	0	1	0	0	0	0	1	0	Farmers
		29	**	34	31	27	**	25	**	24	27	24	21	20	15	13	17	11	8	Housewives
Non-union Household		19%	**	19%	22%	20%	**	22%	**	23%	24%	24%	25%	23%	27%	27%	26%	25%	27%	Professional
		11	**	10	12	15	**	14	**	15	14	15	15	17	17	20	21	23	22	White Collar
		12	**	20	23	24	**	23	**	24	26	27	31	31	31	31	29	32	32	Blue Collar
		10	**	5	3	2	**	2	**	1	1	2	1	3	2	3	3	2	2	Unskilled
		10	**	9	6	8	**	6	**	5	6	4	4	4	3	3	4	5	3	Farmers
		38	**	37	34	31	**	33	**	31	29	29	25	23	21	17	17	14	14	Housewives

Table 1.119
Incidence of Occupations within Union Membership Groups

	1952	1954	1956	1958	1960	1962	1964	1966	1968	1970	1972	1974	1976	1978	1980	1982	1984	1986	
Percent Professional	6%	6%	6%	5%	6%	**	10%	**	10%	12%	10%	15%	15%	18%	21%	20%	19%	23%	Union household
	19%	20%	19%	22%	20%	**	22%	**	23%	24%	24%	25%	23%	27%	27%	26%	25%	27%	Non-union household
Percent White collar	10%	7%	10%	8%	12%	**	11%	**	13%	13%	15%	18%	16%	16%	15%	14%	24%	18%	Union household
	11%	11%	10%	12%	15%	**	14%	**	15%	14%	15%	15%	17%	17%	20%	21%	23%	22%	Non-union household
Percent Blue collar	42%	40%	39%	51%	53%	**	51%	**	49%	46%	47%	42%	46%	46%	48%	46%	42%	47%	Union household
	12%	11%	20%	23%	24%	**	23%	**	24%	26%	27%	31%	31%	31%	31%	29%	32%	32%	Non-union household
Percent Unskilled	14%	12%	9%	4%	3%	**	3%	**	4%	2%	3%	4%	4%	5%	4%	4%	4%	4%	Union household
	10%	13%	5%	3%	2%	**	2%	**	1%	1%	2%	1%	3%	2%	3%	3%	2%	2%	Non-union household
Percent Farmers	0%	1%	1%	0%	0%	**	0%	**	1%	0%	0%	1%	0%	0%	0%	0%	1%	0%	Union household
	10%	10%	9%	6%	8%	**	6%	**	5%	6%	4%	4%	4%	3%	3%	4%	5%	3%	Non-union household
Percent Housewives	29%	35%	34%	31%	27%	**	25%	**	24%	27%	24%	21%	20%	15%	13%	17%	11%	8%	Union household
	38%	35%	37%	34%	31%	**	33%	**	31%	29%	29%	25%	23%	21%	17%	17%	14%	14%	Non-union household

Table 1.120
Religion of Union Membership Groups

	1952	1954	1956	1958	1960	1962	1964	1966	1968	1970	1972	1974	1976	1978	1980	1982	1984	1986	
Union Household	62%	69%	63%	63%	66%	**	63%	65%	65%	62%	60%	61%	58%	59%	57%	61%	56%	62%	Protestant
	33	25%	31	31	29	**	30	29	28	28	33	30	32	30	29	28	32	29	Catholic
	3	2	3	4	4	**	2	3	3	3	2	3	1	2	3	1	2	2	Jew
	3	4	3	2	2	**	5	3	4	7	6	7	9	9	11	11	10	7	Other and None
Non-union Household	75%	78%	77%	77%	78%	**	73%	73%	74%	73%	72%	71%	67%	65%	66%	67%	64%	66%	Protestant
	18	17	18	18	17	**	20	19	20	17	21	19	23	22	21	21	24	22	Catholic
	4	3	3	3	3	**	3	4	3	3	3	2	3	3	3	2	3	1	Jew
	4	2	2	2	2	**	5	4	4	7	5	8	8	10	10	11	10	10	Other and None

Table 1.121
Incidence of Religions within Union Membership Groups

	1952	1954	1956	1958	1960	1962	1964	1966	1968	1970	1972	1974	1976	1978	1980	1982	1984	1986	
Percent Protestant	62%	69%	63%	63%	66%	**	63%	65%	65%	62%	60%	61%	58%	59%	57%	61%	56%	62%	Union household
	75%	78%	77%	77%	78%	**	73%	73%	74%	73%	72%	71%	67%	65%	66%	67%	64%	66%	Non-union household
Percent Catholic	33%	25%	31%	31%	29%	**	30%	29%	28%	28%	33%	30%	32%	30%	29%	28%	32%	29%	Union household
	18%	17%	18%	18%	17%	**	20%	19%	20%	17%	21%	19%	23%	22%	21%	21%	24%	22%	Non-union household
Percent Jewish	3%	2%	3%	4%	4%	**	2%	3%	3%	3%	2%	3%	1%	2%	3%	1%	2%	2%	Union household
	4%	3%	3%	3%	3%	**	3%	4%	3%	3%	3%	2%	3%	3%	3%	2%	3%	1%	Non-union household
Percent Other	3%	4%	3%	2%	2%	**	5%	3%	4%	7%	6%	7%	9%	9%	11%	11%	10%	7%	Union household
	4%	2%	2%	2%	2%	**	5%	4%	4%	7%	5%	8%	8%	10%	10%	11%	10%	10%	Non-union household

Table 1.122
Age Cohorts of Region Groups

	1952	1954	1956	1958	1960	1962	1964	1966	1968	1970	1972	1974	1976	1978	1980	1982	1984	1986	
South	**	**	**	**	**	**	**	**	**	**	**	**	**	4%	8%	10%	17%	23%	1959 or later
	**	**	**	**	**	**	2%	7%	9%	19%	29%	31%	34%	35	36	36	37	35	1943 - 1958
	9%	6%	19%	19%	19%	27%	29	25	30	28	26	23	21	25	21	20	20	20	1927 - 1942
	42	48	40	40	38	37	36	30	29	27	24	23	24	23	25	25	18	17	1911 - 1926
	28	32	26	28	30	23	23	29	25	20	18	20	20	12	10	9	8	5	1895 - 1910
	21	14	14	14	14	13	11	10	7	6	3	3	2	1	1	0	0	0	Before 1895
Non-south	**	**	**	**	**	**	**	**	**	**	**	**	**	3%	7%	10%	15%	17%	1959 or later
	**	**	**	**	**	**	2%	7%	10%	16%	27%	36%	37%	41	37	37	38	40	1943 - 1958
	8%	7%	17%	22%	23%	28%	35	33	33	32	27	23	25	25	24	21	21	20	1927 - 1942
	38	47	41	38	38	33	33	33	32	26	26	25	24	20	21	24	19	18	1911 - 1926
	32	34	27	25	25	26	22	19	19	21	15	14	12	10	11	7	8	5	1895 - 1910
	22	12	16	16	14	13	9	7	5	5	4	2	2	1	1	1	0	0	Before 1895

Table 1.123
Age Cohorts of Region Groups Summarized with a Percentage Difference Index#

	1952	1954	1956	1958	1960	1962	1964	1966	1968	1970	1972	1974	1976	1978	1980	1982	1984	1986
South	40	40	21	23	25	9	3	8	-7	-21	-33	-31	-34	-51	-54	-57	-65	-73
Non-south	46	39	25	19	16	10	-6	-15	-19	-22	-35	-42	-48	-58	-56	-60	-65	-72
Total PDI	44	39	24	20	19	10	-3	-8	-15	-21	-35	-38	-43	-56	-55	-59	-65	-73

PDI is proportion "born before 1911" minus proportion "born 1927 or later"

Table 1.124
Education of Region Groups

	1952	1954	1956	1958	1960	1962	1964	1966	1968	1970	1972	1974	1976	1978	1980	1982	1984	1986	
South	52%	49%	36%	35%	37%	32%	31%	35%	31%	29%	24%	25%	22%	17%	17%	15%	16%	14%	Grade School
	34	37	45	45	41	41	47	44	44	52	50	49	50	51	48	47	52	50	High School
	14	14	19	20	22	27	22	22	25	20	26	27	28	32	35	38	33	36	College
Non-south	37%	31%	29%	29%	27%	25%	22%	23%	20%	22%	18%	15%	14%	9%	10%	9%	8%	6%	Grade School
	48	50	52	51	52	52	53	53	52	50	51	52	50	54	53	45	46	46	High School
	15	19	19	20	22	23	25	24	28	27	31	33	36	37	38	46	46	48	College

Table 1.125
Education of Region Groups Summarized with a Percentage Difference Index#

	1952	1954	1956	1958	1960	1962	1964	1966	1968	1970	1972	1974	1976	1978	1980	1982	1984	1986
South	-38	-35	-16	-15	-15	-5	-9	-13	-6	-9	2	2	6	16	19	23	17	22
Non-south	-22	-12	-10	-8	-5	-3	2	1	9	5	13	18	22	28	28	37	37	41
Total PDI	-27	-19	-12	-10	-8	-4	-1	-3	4	0	9	12	17	23	25	32	31	34

PDI is proportion "college" minus proportion "grade school"

Table 1.126
Urbanism of Region Groups

	1952	1954	1956	1958	1960	1962	1964	1966	1968	1970	1972	1974	1976	1978	1980	1982	1984	1986	
South	21%	21%	13%	10%	10%	21%	25%	26%	23%	23%	24%	23%	24%	26%	23%	26%	24%	25%	Central cities
	27	28	18	21	19	29	23	20	19	19	18	30	26	27	32	28	34	32	Suburbs
	52	52	69	69	71	50	52	54	58	58	58	48	49	48	44	46	43	43	Non-urban areas
Non-south	38%	40%	30%	31%	28%	28%	32%	31%	27%	29%	27%	31%	30%	28%	30%	29%	23%	25%	Central cities
	31	32	30	31	31	43	35	36	35	35	38	39	39	46	43	42	46	49	Suburbs
	32	28	40	38	41	29	33	33	37	36	36	30	31	26	28	30	31	26	Non-urban areas

Table 1.127
Urbanism of Region Groups Summarized with a Percentage Difference Index#

	1952	1954	1956	1958	1960	1962	1964	1966	1968	1970	1972	1974	1976	1978	1980	1982	1984	1986
South	-32	-31	-57	-60	-60	-29	-28	-29	-35	-35	-34	-25	-25	-22	-21	-20	-19	-18
Non-south	6	13	-10	-7	-13	-1	-1	-2	-10	-7	-9	0	-2	2	2	-1	-8	-1
Total PDI	-5	-1	-24	-23	-28	-11	-9	-10	-18	-17	-17	-9	-9	-7	-6	-8	-12	-17

PDI is proportion "central cities" minus proportion "non-urban areas"

Table 1.128
Family Income of Region Groups

	1952	1954	1956	1958	1960	1962	1964	1966	1968	1970	1972	1974	1976	1978	1980	1982	1984	1986	
South	37%	34%	26%	23%	24%	27%	25%	29%	21%	21%	26%	23%	22%	23%	21%	21%	21%	25%	Percentile 0-16
	17	17	25	23	19	9	23	12	23	16	14	16	21	18	17	20	19	17	17-33
	19	24	28	25	25	37	25	32	29	34	38	39	32	29	34	28	35	33	34-67
	26	22	16	27	28	23	19	21	22	27	19	20	21	23	22	25	20	20	68-95
	1	3	6	2	5	4	8	6	5	2	3	2	3	8	5	7	4	5	96-100
Non-south	14%	15%	12%	13%	10%	19%	16%	16%	13%	12%	16%	12%	10%	14%	15%	14%	12%	13%	Percentile 0-16
	16	11	21	20	17	7	17	8	20	14	11	15	18	18	15	16	17	15	17-33
	24	34	33	30	30	44	26	33	33	31	37	41	31	32	37	31	36	38	34-67
	42	31	25	33	38	24	34	37	29	38	31	27	35	29	27	31	29	31	68-95
	5	8	9	4	5	6	7	6	6	4	6	5	6	7	5	8	6	4	96-100

Table 1.129
Family Income of Region Groups Summarized with a Percentage Difference Index

	1952	1954	1956	1958	1960	1962	1964	1966	1968	1970	1972	1974	1976	1978	1980	1982	1984	1986
South	-26	-26	-28	-18	-10	-9	-21	-15	-18	-8	-18	-16	-20	-10	-12	-9	-17	-17
Non-south	17	13	0	3	15	3	8	18	1	17	10	5	13	4	3	9	7	8
Total PDI	5	2	-8	-3	6	-1	-1	8	-5	8	1	-3	2	-1	-2	2	-1	-1

PDI is proportion "68-100 percentile" minus proportion "0-33 percentile"

Table 1.130
Percent Female within Region Groups

	1952	1954	1956	1958	1960	1962	1964	1966	1968	1970	1972	1974	1976	1978	1980	1982	1984	1986
South	57%	53%	55%	56%	59%	55%	57%	57%	57%	57%	57%	61%	59%	55%	57%	55%	56%	58%
Non-south	53%	53%	55%	52%	53%	55%	54%	55%	56%	57%	57%	57%	57%	56%	57%	56%	56%	56%
Total Population	54%	53%	55%	53%	55%	55%	55%	56%	56%	57%	57%	58%	58%	56%	57%	55%	56%	56%

Table 1.131
Percent Black within Region Groups

	1952	1954	1956	1958	1960	1962	1964	1966	1968	1970	1972	1974	1976	1978	1980	1982	1984	1986
South	23%	16%	16%	14%	15%	13%	20%	15%	16%	16%	18%	14%	18%	17%	17%	16%	21%	24%
Non-south	4%	6%	5%	7%	6%	6%	6%	9%	7%	6%	6%	6%	7%	7%	9%	8%	7%	10%
Total Population	10%	9%	8%	9%	9%	9%	10%	11%	10%	10%	10%	9%	11%	10%	12%	11%	11%	15%

Table 1.132
Percent Union Households within Region Groups

	1952	1954	1956	1958	1960	1962	1964	1966	1968	1970	1972	1974	1976	1978	1980	1982	1984	1986
South	16%	15%	15%	15%	17%	**	12%	16%	17%	15%	17%	16%	13%	15%	14%	13%	14%	13%
Non-south	32%	34%	32%	29%	32%	**	29%	33%	29%	28%	30%	31%	28%	32%	32%	26%	25%	25%
Total Population	27%	28%	27%	25%	27%	**	24%	28%	25%	24%	26%	26%	23%	26%	26%	21%	21%	20%

Social Characteristics of Regional Groups

Table 1.133
Occupation of Region Groups

	1952	1954	1956	1958	1960	1962	1964	1966	1968	1970	1972	1974	1976	1978	1980	1982	1984	1986	
South	12%	**	15%	18%	18%	**	17%	**	21%	17%	18%	20%	17%	24%	26%	23%	20%	21%	Professional
	9	**	9	14	15	**	14	**	11	13	14	14	15	15	20	19	20	19	White collar
	16	**	22	23	26	**	25	**	32	34	36	35	39	36	31	33	39	39	Blue collar
	16	**	8	4	1	**	4	**	2	2	2	1	3	3	4	3	2	4	Unskilled
	11	**	11	7	9	**	9	**	6	6	3	3	4	3	2	3	6	3	Farmers
	36	**	36	34	31	**	31	**	28	29	28	27	23	19	17	18	12	15	Housewives
Non-south	16%	**	16%	18%	16%	**	20%	**	20%	23%	22%	24%	23%	25%	25%	26%	26%	29%	Professional
	11	**	11	10	14	**	13	**	15	15	16	17	18	17	18	20	24	23	White collar
	22	**	27	33	35	**	32	**	30	30	31	34	32	34	37	32	32	32	Blue collar
	9	**	6	3	2	**	2	**	2	2	2	2	3	3	3	3	2	2	Unskilled
	6	**	5	4	4	**	3	**	3	3	3	3	3	2	2	3	3	3	Farmers
	36	**	36	33	30	**	31	**	30	28	27	22	22	20	16	16	14	12	Housewives

Table 1.134
Incidence of Occupations within Region Groups

	1952	1954	1956	1958	1960	1962	1964	1966	1968	1970	1972	1974	1976	1978	1980	1982	1984	1986	
Percent Professional	12%	**	15%	18%	18%	**	17%	**	21%	17%	18%	20%	17%	24%	26%	23%	20%	21%	South
	16%	**	16%	18%	16%	**	20%	**	20%	23%	22%	24%	23%	25%	25%	26%	26%	29%	Non-South
Percent White collar	9%	**	9%	14%	15%	**	14%	**	11%	13%	14%	14%	15%	15%	20%	19%	20%	19%	South
	11%	**	11%	10%	14%	**	13%	**	15%	15%	16%	17%	18%	17%	18%	20%	24%	23%	Non-South
Percent Blue collar	16%	**	22%	23%	26%	**	25%	**	32%	34%	36%	35%	39%	36%	31%	33%	39%	39%	South
	22%	**	27%	33%	35%	**	32%	**	30%	30%	31%	34%	32%	34%	37%	32%	32%	32%	Non-South
Percent Unskilled	16%	**	8%	4%	1%	**	4%	**	2%	2%	2%	1%	3%	3%	4%	3%	2%	4%	South
	9%	**	6%	3%	2%	**	2%	**	2%	2%	2%	2%	3%	3%	3%	3%	2%	2%	Non-South
Percent Farmers	11%	**	11%	7%	9%	**	9%	**	6%	6%	3%	3%	4%	3%	2%	3%	6%	3%	South
	6%	**	5%	4%	4%	**	3%	**	3%	3%	3%	3%	3%	2%	2%	3%	3%	3%	Non-South
Percent Housewives	36%	**	36%	34%	31%	**	31%	**	28%	29%	28%	27%	23%	19%	17%	18%	12%	15%	South
	36%	**	36%	33%	30%	**	31%	**	30%	28%	27%	22%	22%	20%	16%	16%	14%	12%	Non-South

Table 1.135
Religion of Region Groups

	1952	1954	1956	1958	1960	1962	1964	1966	1968	1970	1972	1974	1976	1978	1980	1982	1984	1986	
South	90%	94%	94%	92%	91%	90%	89%	91%	90%	87%	83%	84%	79%	75%	75%	78%	75%	80%	Protestant
	5	4	4	5	5	8	9	7	7	7	13	10	14	14	17	12	16	12	Catholic
	1	1	1	2	2	0	0	0	1	1	0	0	0	2	1	1	1	1	Jewish
	5	1	1	1	3	2	2	2	2	5	4	5	7	9	6	9	8	6	Other and None
Non-south	64%	67%	65%	66%	66%	65%	62%	63%	63%	62%	61%	59%	59%	57%	57%	58%	55%	57%	Protestant
	28	26	28	28	28	27	28	28	29	26	29	28	30	29	27	28	31	30	Catholic
	4	4	4	4	4	5	4	5	4	4	3	4	3	3	4	2	3	2	Jewish
	3	3	3	3	2	4	6	4	5	9	6	9	8	11	12	12	11	12	Other and None

Table 1.136
Incidence of Religions within Region Groups

	1952	1954	1956	1958	1960	1962	1964	1966	1968	1970	1972	1974	1976	1978	1980	1982	1984	1986	
Percent Protestant	90%	94%	94%	92%	91%	90%	89%	91%	90%	87%	83%	84%	79%	75%	75%	78%	75%	80%	South
	64%	67%	65%	66%	66%	65%	62%	63%	63%	62%	61%	59%	59%	57%	57%	58%	55%	57%	Non-South
Percent Catholic	5%	4%	4%	5%	5%	8%	9%	7%	7%	7%	13%	10%	14%	14%	17%	12%	16%	12%	South
	28%	26%	28%	28%	28%	27%	28%	28%	29%	26%	29%	28%	30%	29%	27%	28%	31%	30%	Non-South
Percent Jewish	1%	1%	1%	2%	2%	0%	0%	0%	1%	1%	0%	0%	0%	2%	1%	1%	1%	1%	South
	4%	4%	4%	4%	4%	5%	4%	5%	4%	4%	3%	4%	3%	3%	4%	2%	3%	2%	Non-South
Percent Other and None	5%	1%	1%	1%	3%	2%	2%	2%	2%	5%	4%	5%	7%	9%	6%	9%	8%	6%	South
	3%	3%	3%	3%	2%	4%	6%	4%	5%	9%	6%	9%	8%	11%	12%	12%	11%	12%	Non-South

Table 1.137
Age Cohorts of Occupation Groups

	1952	1954	1956	1958	1960	1962	1964	1966	1968	1970	1972	1974	1976	1978	1980	1982	1984	1986	
Professional	**	**	**	**	**	**	**	**	**	**	**	**	**	1%	1%	6%	9%	9%	1959 or later
	**	**	**	**	**	**	1%	**	8%	14%	24%	28%	35%	39	40	39	46	47	1943 - 1958
	4%	**	12%	13%	22%	**	29	**	39	38	34	29	32	28	30	23	22	26	1927 - 1942
	32	**	43	45	40	**	39	**	33	26	27	28	24	21	19	24	16	14	1911 - 1926
	41	**	35	31	32	**	22	**	15	19	12	12	9	10	10	7	8	4	1895 - 1910
	23	**	9	12	7	**	9	**	5	3	3	2	1	1	0	0	0	0	Before 1895
White collar	**	**	**	**	**	**	**	**	**	**	**	**	**	5%	8%	13%	18%	21%	1959 or later
	**	**	**	**	**	**	3%	**	11%	22%	35%	43%	45%	47	39	38	39	37	1943 - 1958
	16%	**	18%	20%	20%	**	37	**	32	29	29	21	22	24	25	22	20	18	1927 - 1942
	44	**	50	46	42	**	32	**	35	26	25	23	22	16	20	21	18	17	1911 - 1926
	27	**	24	24	28	**	23	**	19	18	9	11	10	8	7	6	6	7	1895 - 1910
	13	**	8	11	11	**	5	**	3	4	2	2	1	1	1	0	0	0	Before 1895
Blue collar	**	**	**	**	**	**	**	**	**	**	**	**	**	3%	7%	10%	16%	21%	1959 or later
	**	**	**	**	**	**	2%	**	10%	14%	26%	32%	34%	37	35	36	35	37	1943 - 1958
	10%	**	16%	21%	20%	**	34	**	29	28	26	22	23	26	24	21	22	18	1927 - 1942
	46	**	42	38	40	**	36	**	34	32	29	28	25	24	24	25	20	21	1911 - 1926
	28	**	30	29	27	**	21	**	23	22	16	16	16	9	10	8	7	4	1895 - 1910
	17	**	13	12	13	**	7	**	5	4	3	1	2	2	0	0	0	0	Before 1895
Unskilled	**	**	**	**	**	**	**	**	**	**	**	**	**	5%	19%*	10%*	19%	38%	1959 or later
	**	**	**	**	**	**	3%*	**	4%*	21%*	40%*	32%*	47%	49	38*	44*	42	25	1943 - 1958
	8%	**	15%	21%	16%*	**	25*	**	22*	21*	22*	30*	14	15	10*	23*	15	20	1927 - 1942
	37	**	40	30	46*	**	36*	**	44*	21*	18*	22*	29	25	17*	21*	14	16	1911 - 1926
	33	**	22	32	19*	**	31*	**	22*	33*	16*	16*	8	5	13*	3*	10	2	1895 - 1910
	22	**	22	16	19*	**	6*	**	7*	4*	4*	0*	2	0	4*	0*	0	0	Before 1895
Farmers	**	**	**	**	**	**	**	**	**	**	**	**	**	0%*	6%*	5%*	16%	23%	1959 or later
	**	**	**	**	**	**	1%	**	5%	12%	6%	4%	14%	16*	25*	23*	25	30	1943 - 1958
	4%	**	5%	7%	13%	**	12	**	20	17	16	14	15	25*	6*	14*	23	11	1927 - 1942
	28	**	29	24	25	**	30	**	27	25	19	23	21	32*	31*	43*	19	25	1911 - 1926
	38	**	32	30	36	**	28	**	39	27	44	47	40	25*	25*	14*	15	12	1895 - 1910
	31	**	34	39	27	**	28	**	9	20	16	12	10	2*	6*	2*	3	0	Before 1895
Housewives	**	**	**	**	**	**	**	**	**	**	**	**	**	2%	4%	5%	11%	19%	1959 or later
	**	**	**	**	**	**	2%	**	7%	16%	23%	32%	31%	34	33	33	32	32	1943 - 1958
	8%	**	22%	27%	25%	**	36	**	36	33	25	25	22	25	18	19	19	23	1927 - 1942
	40	**	40	38	36	**	30	**	28	23	24	18	24	23	28	28	25	19	1911 - 1926
	27	**	21	20	22	**	21	**	20	21	23	21	21	15	17	13	13	6	1895 - 1910
	25	**	18	16	17	**	17	**	9	7	6	4	3	1	1	2	0	0	Before 1895

Table 1.138
Age Cohorts of Occupation Groups Summarized with a Percentage Difference Index#

	1952	1954	1956	1958	1960	1962	1964	1966	1968	1970	1972	1974	1976	1978	1980	1982	1984	1986
Professional	61	**	33	30	17	**	1	**	-27	-30	-43	-44	-56	-57	-61	-61	-69	-78
White collar	25	**	14	15	19	**	-11	**	-22	-29	-54	-51	-56	-67	-64	-67	-70	-70
Blue collar	36	**	26	20	21	**	-7	**	-11	-16	-33	-37	-39	-55	-56	-59	-66	-72
Unskilled	48	**	30	27	22*	**	8*	**	4*	-4*	-42*	-46*	-52	-65	-50*	-74*	-67	-80
Farmers	65	**	62	63	50	**	43	**	22	18	39	42	21	-14*	-6*	-25*	-46	-51
Housewives	44	**	16	9	14	**	-6	**	-15	-21	-20	-32	-29	-44	-37	-42	-49	-68
Total PDI	44	**	24	20	19	**	-3	**	-15	-21	-35	-38	-43	-56	-55	-59	-65	-73

PDI is proportion "born before 1911" minus proportion "born 1927 or later"

Table 1.139
Education of Occupation Groups

	1952	1954	1956	1958	1960	1962	1964	1966	1968	1970	1972	1974	1976	1978	1980	1982	1984	1986	
Professional	20%	**	10%	11%	8%	**	9%	**	7%	7%	6%	8%	3%	2%	3%	3%	2%	1%	Grade School
	38	**	36	37	34	**	39	**	28	31	29	30	27	28	24	19	19	18	High School
	43	**	54	52	58	**	53	**	65	62	66	63	70	70	73	78	80	82	College
White Collar	13%	**	8%	9%	12%	**	11%	**	10%	5%	5%	1%	4%	3%	5%	3%	4%	3%	Grade School
	62	**	71	63	60	**	59	**	60	67	62	61	58	60	57	46	54	50	High School
	25	**	22	28	29	**	30	**	31	28	34	38	38	37	39	51	42	47	College
Blue Collar	48%	**	40%	40%	42%	**	35%	**	33%	39%	28%	27%	24%	19%	17%	16%	17%	16%	Grade School
	47	**	53	52	52	**	55	**	56	55	59	59	60	64	66	62	61	64	High School
	5	**	8	8	7	**	9	**	11	6	13	14	16	17	17	22	23	21	College
Unskilled	70%	**	59%	63%	68%*	**	64%*	**	67%*	48%*	38%*	43%*	26%	20%	27%*	36%*	20%	9%	Grade School
	29	**	39	36	32*	**	33*	**	33*	48*	50*	38*	56	68	54*	46*	61	79	High School
	1	**	2	2	0*	**	3*	**	0*	4*	12*	19*	19	12	19*	18*	20	13	College
Farmers	70%	**	58%	68%	64%	**	59%	**	57%	60%	58%	62%	62%	46%*	41%*	46%*	33%	32%	Grade School
	25	**	36	30	35	**	27	**	33	30	33	31	35	43*	38*	41*	55	46	High School
	5	**	5	2	1	**	14	**	10	10	8	7	3	11*	22*	14*	13	23	College
Housewives	41%	**	31%	32%	31%	**	23%	**	23%	25%	26%	23%	22%	15%	18%	15%	17%	13%	Grade School
	49	**	54	53	48	**	57	**	59	59	56	57	56	59	61	59	55	60	High School
	11	**	15	16	21	**	20	**	18	16	18	21	22	26	21	26	28	27	College

Table 1.140
Education of Occupation Groups Summarized with a Percentage Difference Index#

	1952	1954	1956	1958	1960	1962	1964	1966	1968	1970	1972	1974	1976	1978	1980	1982	1984	1986
Professional	23	**	45	41	50	**	44	**	58	55	60	55	67	67	70	74	78	81
White collar	12	**	14	19	17	**	19	**	21	22	29	36	34	34	34	49	38	44
Blue collar	-43	**	-32	-32	-35	**	-26	**	-21	-33	-15	-13	-8	-2	0	6	6	5
Unskilled	-69	**	-57	-61	-68*	**	-61*	**	-67*	-44*	-26*	-24	-7	-8	-8*	-18*	0	4
Farmers	-65	**	-53	-66	-63	**	-45	**	-47	-51	-50	-55	-59	-34*	-19*	-32*	-20	-9
Housewives	-30	**	-17	-16	-10	**	-3	**	-5	-9	-8	-2	1	11	4	11	10	14
Total PDI	-27	**	-12	-10	-8	**	-1	**	4	0	9	12	17	23	25	32	31	34

PDI is proportion "college" minus proportion "grade school"

Table 1.141
Urbanism of Occupation Groups

	1952	1954	1956	1958	1960	1962	1964	1966	1968	1970	1972	1974	1976	1978	1980	1982	1984	1986	
Professional	35%	**	24%	28%	21%	**	32%	**	27%	29%	26%	30%	29%	28%	27%	27%	24%	25%	Central Cities
	31	**	32	33	35	**	37	**	37	31	38	40	41	46	42	46	50	49	Suburbs
	35	**	44	39	44	**	31	**	36	40	37	29	30	27	31	27	26	26	Non-urban areas
White collar	45%	**	31%	27%	32%	**	33%	**	31%	36%	31%	38%	39%	29%	29%	35%	27%	28%	Central Cities
	35	**	33	32	31	**	35	**	37	33	38	43	38	44	46	38	42	44	Suburbs
	20	**	36	42	37	**	32	**	32	32	31	20	23	27	25	28	31	28	Non-urban areas
Blue collar	38%	**	29%	33%	25%	**	35%	**	29%	29%	27%	24%	26%	29%	28%	27%	24%	26%	Central Cities
	34	**	32	29	28	**	32	**	28	24	28	34	32	33	36	29	37	39	Suburbs
	28	**	39	38	47	**	34	**	44	47	46	42	42	38	36	43	39	36	Non-urban areas
Unskilled	36%	**	24%	23%	24%*	**	33%*	**	37%*	25%*	34%*	30%*	21%	32%	29%*	31%*	23%	25%	Central Cities
	29	**	24	20	30*	**	17*	**	19*	17*	14*	30*	36	32	31*	36*	39	41	Suburbs
	35	**	52	57	46*	**	50*	**	44*	58*	52*	41*	43	36	40*	33*	39	34	Non-urban areas
Farmers	2%	**	2%	2%	0%	**	0%	**	0%	3%	0%	3%	4%	9%*	9%*	2%*	4%	12%	Central Cities
	12	**	4	5	2	**	8	**	3	10	4	7	9	16*	6*	18*	29	14	Suburbs
	86	**	95	93	98	**	92	**	97	87	96	91	87	75*	84*	80*	68	74	Non-urban areas
Housewives	31%	**	25%	18%	20%	**	27%	**	22%	22%	22%	25%	25%	19%	24%	23%	18%	20%	Central Cities
	28	**	23	26	24	**	31	**	31	36	32	36	34	45	42	40	44	47	Suburbs
	41	**	52	56	56	**	42	**	47	42	46	39	42	36	34	38	38	33	Non-urban areas

Table 1.142
Urbanism of Occupation Groups Summarized with a Percentage Difference Index#

	1952	1954	1956	1958	1960	1962	1964	1966	1968	1970	1972	1974	1976	1978	1980	1982	1984	1986
Professional	0	**	-19	-11	-23	**	1	**	-9	-11	-11	1	-1	1	-4	0	-2	-2
White collar	25	**	-5	-16	-6	**	1	**	-1	4	-1	18	16	3	4	7	-4	1
Blue collar	10	**	-11	-4	-21	**	1	**	-15	-18	-19	-18	-15	-9	-7	-16	-16	-10
Unskilled	1	**	-28	-34	-22*	**	-17*	**	-7*	-33*	-18*	-11	-22	-3	-10*	-2*	-15	-9
Farmers	-84	**	-93	-91	-98	**	-92	**	-97	-84	-96	-88	-83	-66*	-75*	-77*	-64	-61
Housewives	-10	**	-27	-38	-37	**	-15	**	-25	-20	-24	-14	-17	-16	-10	-15	-19	-13
Total PDI	-5	**	-24	-23	-28	**	-9	**	-18	-17	-17	-9	-9	-7	-6	-8	-12	-7

PDI is proportion "central cities" minus proportion "non-urban areas"

Social Characteristics of Occupational Groups

Table 1.143
Family Income of Occupation Groups

	1952	1954	1956	1958	1960	1962	1964	1966	1968	1970	1972	1974	1976	1978	1980	1982	1984	1986	
Professional	10%	**	5%	4%	-2%	**	6%	**	4%	5%	8%	6%	5%	8%	6%	5%	4%	5%	Perc. 0-16
	11	**	7	12	6	**	14	**	11	5	6	10	9	12	9	11	9	9	17-33
	15	**	27	21	18	**	21	**	27	23	33	40	26	27	34	31	35	34	34-67
	53	**	36	53	57	**	43	**	44	55	41	36	47	39	39	39	40	44	68-95
	11	**	25	10	17	**	16	**	14	11	12	9	13	14	11	14	12	9	96-100
White collar	6%	**	5%	9%	7%	**	10%	**	8%	9%	15%	11%	7%	12%	13%	14%	11%	10%	Perc. 0-16
	12	**	21	15	18	**	20	**	20	14	10	14	18	18	18	16	17	18	17-33
	22	**	28	31	31	**	30	**	37	36	40	43	34	34	41	32	39	39	34-67
	55	**	39	43	43	**	36	**	31	38	32	29	36	29	23	33	28	28	68-95
	4	**	8	2	1	**	4	**	4	3	3	4	4	7	5	6	4	4	96-100
Blue collar	10%	**	14%	17%	16%	**	25%	**	18%	17%	21%	19%	17%	21%	22%	21%	22%	23%	Perc. 0-16
	15	**	25	24	22	**	18	**	26	20	15	22	25	22	18	22	22	19	17-33
	29	**	38	35	35	**	26	**	35	35	42	42	33	33	39	32	35	38	34-67
	45	**	22	25	27	**	29	**	20	28	21	17	25	20	20	23	20	19	68-95
	1	**	2	0	1	**	2	**	1	0	2	0	1	3	1	3	2	2	96-100
Unskilled	47%	**	29%	35%	24%*	**	25%*	**	30%*	22%*	22%*	32%*	19%	28%	33%*	27%*	20%*	34%	Perc. 0-16
	27	**	29	37	30*	**	36*	**	30*	26*	20*	18*	28	20	22*	18*	16*	17	17-33
	17	**	27	15	16*	**	19*	**	33*	39*	37*	41*	36	28	36*	30*	47*	30	34-67
	10	**	13	13	30*	**	19*	**	7*	13*	20*	9*	13	20	7*	21*	13*	15	68-95
	1	**	1	0	0*	**	0*	**	0*	0*	0*	0*	3	4	2*	3*	4*	4	96-100
Farmers	37%	**	49%	48%	44%	**	50%	**	31%	36%	43%	28%	44%	34%*	30%*	32%*	31%	37%*	Perc. 0-16
	21	**	24	27	20	**	28	**	35	27	19	16	15	29*	22*	22*	22	20*	17-33
	18	**	17	15	17	**	8	**	22	27	19	23	19	17*	30*	22*	31	31*	34-67
	20	**	7	11	18	**	7	**	7	10	13	17	9	14*	15*	14*	9	12*	68-95
	5	**	4	0	1	**	7	**	6	0	6	16	13	6*	4*	11*	6	0*	96-100
Housewives	23%	**	18%	19%	19%	**	19%	**	19%	19%	23%	19%	17%	19%	21%	23%	19%	23%	Perc. 0-16
	15	**	25	23	18	**	18	**	20	14	12	13	20	17	16	17	23	14	17-33
	27	**	32	29	29	**	31	**	31	34	36	40	32	33	32	27	36	34	34-67
	33	**	18	26	30	**	24	**	25	30	24	24	25	23	26	24	17	23	68-95
	3	**	7	4	5	**	8	**	6	4	5	4	6	9	6	10	6	5	96-100

Perc. is the abbreviation for Percentile; this appears to the right of the 1986 column.

Table 1.144
Family Income of Occupation Groups Summarized with a Percentage Difference Index#

	1952	1954	1956	1958	1960	1962	1964	1966	1968	1970	1972	1974	1976	1978	1980	1982	1984	1986
Professional	43	**	49	47	66	**	39	**	42	56	39	30	46	34	34	37	39	38
White collar	42	**	21	22	19	**	11	**	7	18	11	8	15	6	-3	9	3	4
Blue collar	22	**	-15	-16	-10	**	-12	**	-24	-9	-14	-23	-17	-20	-19	-17	-22	-23
Unskilled	-63	**	-44	-59	-24*	**	-42*	**	-52*	-35*	-22*	-41*	-31	-24	-47*	-21*	-18*	-32
Farmers	-33	**	-63	-63	-45	**	-64	**	-53	-53	-43	-10	-36	-43*	-33*	-30*	-39	-45*
Housewives	-2	**	-18	-12	-2	**	-5	**	-8	0	-6	-5	-6	-4	-5	-6	-20	-9
Total PDI	5	**	-8	-3	6	**	-1	**	-5	8	1	-3	2	-1	-2	2	-1	-1

PDI is proportion "68-100 percentile" minus proportion "0-33 percentile"

Table 1.145
Percent Female within Occupation Groups

	1952	1954	1956	1958	1960	1962	1964	1966	1968	1970	1972	1974	1976	1978	1980	1982	1984	1986
Professional	27%	**	26%	23%	33%	**	30%	**	32%	35%	34%	40%	43%	43%	45%	41%	48%	50%
White Collar	58%	**	62%	59%	65%	**	59%	**	68%	72%	70%	74%	76%	71%	78%	73%	71%	73%
Blue Collar	18%	**	27%	29%	28%	**	34%	**	36%	37%	36%	41%	40%	38%	42%	40%	41%	42%
Unskilled	42%	**	20%	0%	5%*	**	0%*	**	4%*	4%*	8%*	0%*	10%	14%	17%*	5%*	21%	20%
Farmers	6%	**	20%	11%	10%	**	15%	**	13%	14%	11%	8%	20%	18%*	9%*	16%*	19%	19%
Housewives	100%	**	99%	100%	100%	**	100%	**	100%	100%	100%	100%	100%	100%	100%	99%	100%	100%
Total Population	54%	**	55%	53%	55%	**	55%	**	56%	57%	57%	58%	58%	56%	57%	55%	56%	56%

Original data set for 1956 is in error. All housewives are female.

Table 1.146
Percent Black within Occupation Groups

	1952	1954	1956	1958	1960	1962	1964	1966	1968	1970	1972	1974	1976	1978	1980	1982	1984	1986
Professional	5%	**	4%	4%	6%	**	4%	**	5%	4%	5%	4%	4%	5%	6%	6%	6%	8%
White Collar	3%	**	3%	7%	4%	**	5%	**	7%	7%	10%	10%	9%	8%	7%	9%	9%	11%
Blue Collar	8%	**	12%	16%	15%	**	16%	**	13%	17%	15%	14%	16%	16%	17%	16%	17%	22%
Unskilled	41%	**	28%	20%	19%*	**	31%*	**	26%*	22%*	27%*	24%*	20%	21%	27%*	32%*	22%*	18%
Farmers	12%	**	15%	12%	12%	**	19%	**	19%	17%	10%	3%	15%	17%*	0%*	7%*	10%	22%
Housewives	5%	**	5%	5%	6%	**	8%	**	7%	6%	6%	6%	6%	6%	11%	8%	5%	13%
Total Population	10%	**	8%	9%	9%	**	10%	**	10%	10%	10%	9%	11%	10%	12%	11%	11%	15%

Table 1.147
Percent Union Households within Occupation Groups

	1952	1954	1956	1958	1960	1962	1964	1966	1968	1970	1972	1974	1976	1978	1980	1982	1984	1986
Professional	10%	**	11%	8%	9%	**	13%	**	13%	13%	13%	18%	16%	19%	21%	17%	17%	18%
White Collar	25%	**	26%	19%	22%	**	21%	**	23%	22%	27%	29%	22%	25%	21%	15%	23%	17%
Blue Collar	56%	**	42%	42%	45%	**	41%	**	41%	36%	38%	32%	31%	35%	36%	30%	27%	28%
Unskilled	34%	**	42%	32%	38%*	**	28%*	**	52%*	35%*	42%*	61%*	34%	45%	29%*	31%*	35%	29%
Farmers	2%	**	4%	1%	1%	**	0%	**	3%	0%	4%	8%	1%	5%*	3%*	0%*	4%	2%
Housewives	22%	**	26%	23%	24%	**	20%	**	21%	23%	23%	22%	21%	20%	22%	22%	17%	14%
Total Population	27%	**	27%	25%	27%	**	24%	**	25%	24%	26%	26%	23%	26%	26%	21%	21%	20%

Table 1.148
Percent South within Occupation Groups

	1952	1954	1956	1958	1960	1962	1964	1966	1968	1970	1972	1974	1976	1978	1980	1982	1984	1986
Professional	23%	**	27%	30%	37%	**	28%	**	32%	29%	29%	32%	27%	34%	35%	33%	28%	29%
White Collar	24%	**	25%	37%	36%	**	32%	**	25%	32%	31%	32%	29%	32%	38%	35%	29%	31%
Blue Collar	23%	**	25%	23%	28%	**	26%	**	33%	37%	37%	37%	37%	36%	31%	37%	38%	40%
Unskilled	42%	**	36%	41%	24%*	**	53%*	**	30%*	38%*	2%*	32%*	34%	34%	42%*	39%*	33%	55%
Farmers	41%	**	49%	45%	53%	**	57%	**	48%	48%	33%	41%	40%	48%*	34%*	36%*	55%	33%
Housewives	29%	**	29%	31%	35%	**	31%	**	29%	35%	34%	41%	33%	34%	38%	40%	31%	40%
Total Population	29%	**	29%	30%	34%	**	31%	**	31%	35%	34%	36%	32%	35%	35%	36%	33%	36%

Social Characteristics of Occupational Groups

Table 1.149
Religion of Occupation Groups

	1952	1954	1956	1958	1960	1962	1964	1966	1968	1970	1972	1974	1976	1978	1980	1982	1984	1986	
Professional	70%	**	73%	75%	79%	**	68%	**	66%	67%	68%	64%	62%	59%	60%	60%	58%	60%	Protestant
	22	**	19	16	12	**	22	**	24	18	19	21	24	22	22	22	24	24	Catholic
	5	**	6	7	6	**	4	**	5	5	5	5	7	6	6	4	5	3	Jewish
	4	**	2	2	3	**	6	**	5	10	8	10	8	12	12	14	13	13	Other and None
White Collar	64%	**	74%	78%	69%	**	71%	**	66%	65%	64%	65%	62%	59%	65%	63%	60%	66%	Protestant
	28	**	20	20	23	**	23	**	26	20	27	26	26	29	24	27	30	24	Catholic
	5	**	3	2	8	**	4	**	5	5	3	4	4	4	3	1	2	2	Jewish
	3	**	2	1	0	**	3	**	2	10	6	6	9	8	9	9	8	8	Other and None
Blue Collar	63%	**	72%	68%*	71%	**	67%	**	74%	74%	69%	69%	66%	65%	65%	67%	63%	66%	Protestant
	30	**	24	28*	26	**	25	**	19	18	25	23	26	23	24	22	25	23	Catholic
	2	**	1	1*	1	**	1	**	1	1	1	1	0	1	2	0	0	1	Jewish
	4	**	3	4*	3	**	7	**	5	7	5	8	8	11	10	12	11	10	Other and None
Unskilled	78%	**	73%	80%	68%*	**	78%*	**	93%*	75%*	70%*	81%*	65%	59%	60%*	77%*	67%	64%	Protestant
	16	**	19	14	29*	**	22*	**	7*	13*	20*	11*	19	22	23*	10*	29	21	Catholic
	2	**	0	0	0*	**	0*	**	0*	4*	0*	0*	1	0	2*	0*	0	0	Jewish
	4	**	8	5	3*	**	0*	**	0*	8*	10*	8*	15	19	15*	13*	4	14	Other and None
Farmers	89%	**	91%	85%	93%	**	92%	**	93%	86%	90%	82%	77%	73%*	81%*	84%*	70%	70%	Protestant
	8	**	7	10	5	**	5	**	5	11	9	16	18	16*	6*	12*	20	19	Catholic
	0	**	0	0	0	**	0	**	0	0	0	0	0	2*	0*	0*	0	0	Jewish
	3	**	2	5	2	**	3	**	2	3	1	1	5	9*	13*	5*	10	11	Other and None
Housewives	74%	**	70%	74%	75%	**	71%	**	72%	70%	71%	74%	70%	67%	66%	68%	65%	72%	Protestant
	20	**	24	22	20	**	23	**	24	23	24	21	25	26	25	24	27	23	Catholic
	4	**	4	4	4	**	4	**	2	2	2	2	1	2	3	3	4	2	Jewish
	3	**	2	1	2	**	2	**	2	5	3	3	5	5	7	5	5	3	Other and None

Table 1.150
Incidence of Religions within Occupation Groups

	1952	1954	1956	1958	1960	1962	1964	1966	1968	1970	1972	1974	1976	1978	1980	1982	1984	1986	
Percent Protestant	70%	**	73%	75%	79%	**	68%	**	66%	67%	68%	64%	62%	59%	60%	60%	58%	60%	Professional
	64%	**	74%	78%	69%	**	71%	**	66%	65%	64%	65%	62%	59%	65%	63%	60%	66%	White Collar
	63%	**	72%	68%	71%	**	67%	**	74%	74%	69%	69%	66%	65%	65%	67%	63%	66%	Blue Collar
	78%	**	73%	80%	68%*	**	78%*	**	93%*	75%*	70%*	81%*	65%	59%	60%*	77%*	67%	64%	Unskilled
	89%	**	91%	85%	93%	**	92%	**	93%	86%	90%	82%	77%	73%*	81%*	84%*	70%	70%	Farmers
	74%	**	70%	74%	75%	**	71%	**	72%	70%	71%	74%	70%	67%	66%	68%	65%	72%	Housewives
Percent Catholic	22%	**	19%	16%	12%	**	22%	**	24%	18%	19%	21%	24%	22%	22%	22%	24%	24%	Professional
	28%	**	20%	20%	23%	**	23%	**	26%	20%	27%	26%	26%	29%	24%	27%	30%	24%	White Collar
	30%	**	24%	28%	26%	**	25%	**	19%	18%	25%	23%	26%	23%	24%	22%	25%	23%	Blue Collar
	16%	**	19%	14%	29%*	**	22%*	**	7%*	13%*	20%*	11%*	19%	22%	23%*	10%*	29%	21%	Unskilled
	8%	**	7%	10%	5%	**	5%	**	5%	11%	9%	16%	18%	16%*	6%*	12%*	20%	19%	Farmers
	20%	**	24%	22%	20%	**	23%	**	24%	23%	24%	21%	25%	26%	25%	24%	27%	23%	Housewives
Percent Jewish	5%	**	6%	7%	6%	**	4%	**	5%	5%	5%	5%	7%	6%	6%	4%	5%	3%	Professional
	5%	**	3%	2%	8%	**	4%	**	5%	5%	3%	4%	4%	4%	3%	1%	2%	2%	White Collar
	2%	**	1%	1%	1%	**	1%	**	1%	1%	1%	1%	0%	1%	2%	0%	0%	1%	Blue Collar
	2%	**	0%	0%	0%*	**	0%*	**	0%*	4%*	0%*	0%*	1%	0%	2%*	0%*	0%	0%	Unskilled
	0%	**	0%	0%	0%	**	0%	**	0%	0%	0%	0%	0%	2%*	0%*	0%*	0%	0%	Farmers
	4%	**	4%	4%	4%	**	4%	**	2%	2%	2%	2%	1%	2%	3%	3%	4%	2%	Housewives
Percent Other and None	4%	**	2%	2%	3%	**	6%	**	5%	10%	8%	10%	8%	12%	12%	14%	13%	13%	Professional
	3%	**	2%	1%	0%	**	3%	**	2%	10%	6%	6%	9%	8%	9%	9%	8%	8%	White Collar
	4%	**	3%	4%	3%	**	7%	**	5%	7%	5%	8%	8%	11%	10%	12%	11%	10%	Blue Collar
	4%	**	8%	5%	3%*	**	0%*	**	0%*	8%*	10%*	8%*	15%	19%	15%*	13%*	4%	14%	Unskilled
	3%	**	2%	5%	2%	**	3%	**	2%	3%	1%	1%	5%	9%*	13%*	5%*	10%	11%	Farmers
	3%	**	2%	1%	2%	**	2%	**	2%	5%	3%	3%	5%	5%	7%	5%	5%	3%	Housewives

Social Characteristics of Occupational Groups

Table 1.151
Age Cohorts of Religion Groups

	1952	1954	1956	1958	1960	1962	1964	1966	1968	1970	1972	1974	1976	1978	1980	1982	1984	1986	
Protestants	**	**	**	**	**	**	**	**	**	**	**	**	**	3%	6%	8%	15%	17%	1959 or later
	**	**	**	**	**	**	2%	7%	9%	16%	25%	31%	33%	37	34	35	33	37	1943 - 1958
	8%	6%	17%	22%	21%	27%	30	29	30	29	26	24	23	26	23	21	23	21	1927 - 1942
	38	47	39	37	36	34	34	32	32	28	25	24	25	22	25	26	20	20	1911 - 1926
	30	33	28	26	28	26	23	23	23	22	18	18	17	11	12	9	10	5	1895 - 1910
	24	14	17	15	15	14	11	9	7	6	5	3	3	1	1	1	0	0	Before 1895
Catholics	**	**	**	**	**	**	**	**	**	**	**	**	**	2%	9%	14%	17%	21%	1959 or later
	**	**	**	**	**	**	1%	7%	13%	18%	31%	36%	39%	40	38	34	42	38	1943 - 1958
	9%	8%	22%	21%	25%	31%	40	36	36	35	28	24	25	27	25	22	18	19	1927 - 1942
	44	53	47	43	44	39	33	35	31	27	27	27	23	21	20	25	18	16	1911 - 1926
	31	32	20	22	23	22	20	18	16	17	12	12	13	8	8	6	5	6	1895 - 1910
	16	7	11	14	10	9	6	4	3	4	1	1	1	1	1	0	0	0	Before 1895
Jews	**	**	**	**	**	**	**	**	**	**	**	**	**	0%	2%*	4%*	2%*	3%*'	1959 or later
	**	**	**	**	**	**	0%*	5%*	12%*	14%*	27%	23%	39%	33	30*	38*	47*	38*	1943 - 1958
	7%	6%*	7%	15%	15%	25%*	31*	42*	34*	38*	23	21	26	14	22*	29*	12*	34*	1927 - 1942
	28	36*	43	40	37	34*	40*	35*	32*	24*	30	33	23	33	22*	21*	33*	19*	1911 - 1926
	41	42*	41	36	44	27*	22*	16*	20*	19*	17	16	11	20	24*	8*	6*	6*	1895 - 1910
	24	15*	9	9	5	14*	7*	2*	2*	5*	3	7	2	0	0*	0*	0*	0*	Before 1895
Other and No Religion	**	**	**	**	**	**	**	**	**	**	**	**	**	5%	13%	14%	20%	30%	1959 or later
	**	**	**	**	**	**	1%	7%*	17%	28%	43%	55%	54%	53	54	53	49	50	1943 - 1958
	12%	20%*	19%*	5%*	32%*	35%*	39	33*	34	34	31	20	24	20	17	16	16	14	1927 - 1942
	51	33*	42*	31*	42*	27*	34	24*	29	18	16	15	15	13	10	13	11	4	1911 - 1926
	19	27*	19*	49*	11*	24*	21	20*	19	17	9	11	7	9	5	3	4	1	1895 - 1910
	19	20*	21*	15*	16*	14*	4	17*	2	3	1	0	1	0	1	1	0	0	Before 1895

Table 1.152
Age Cohorts of Religion Groups Summarized with a Percentage Difference Index#

	1952	1954	1956	1958	1960	1962	1964	1966	1968	1970	1972	1974	1976	1978	1980	1982	1984	1986
Protestants	46	42	28	19	22	12	2	-4	-9	-16	-28	-33	-37	-53	-50	-54	-60	-70
Catholics	38	30	10	15	8	0	-16	-21	-30	-32	-47	-47	-50	-60	-63	-64	-71	-72
Jews	59	52*	43	31	34	16*	-2*	-28*	-24*	-29*	-30	-21	-52	-27	-30*	-63*	-55*	-69*
Other and No Religion	25	27*	21*	59*	-5*	3*	-15	-2*	-31	-42	-64	-63	-70	-69	-77	-79	-81	-93
Total PDI	44	39	24	20	19	10	-3	-8	-15	-21	-35	-38	-43	-56	-55	-59	-65	-73

PDI is proportion "born before 1911" minus proportion "born 1927 or later"

Table 1.153
Education of Religion Groups

	1952	1954	1956	1958	1960	1962	1964	1966	1968	1970	1972	1974	1976	1978	1980	1982	1984	1986	
Protestants	42%	37%	31%	29%	31%	28%	27%	27%	26%	26%	22%	20%	18%	13%	14%	12%	11%	10%	Grade School
	43	45	50	49	46	49	50	50	49	52	50	53	50	55	53	48	51	49	High School
	16	18	19	22	24	23	23	23	26	22	28	28	32	32	34	40	38	41	College
Catholics	38%	38%	32%	35%	26%	27%	22%	24%	18%	23%	18%	19%	16%	12%	11%	11%	12%	9%	Grade School
	52	49	52	53	59	52	56	56	56	54	56	53	55	51	54	48	45	46	High School
	10	13	16	13	16	21	22	20	26	23	27	28	29	36	35	42	43	45	College
Jews	43%	27%*	18%	22%	29%	27%*	11%*	7%*	10%*	10%*	12%	12%	0%	6%	14%*	0%*	6%	3%*	Grade School
	40	39*	50	49	44	25*	49*	42*	31*	43*	30	42	27	24	26*	13*	23	19*	High School
	17	33*	32	29	27	48*	40*	51*	60*	48*	59	47	73	70	60*	88*	71	78*	College
Other and No Religion	57%	33%*	46%*	47%*	55%*	32%*	22%	35%*	17%	20%	13%	13%	12%	9%	5%	11%	5%	4%	Grade School
	23	37*	34*	34*	26*	32*	46	30*	41	35	44	28	40	48	45	30	41	46	High School
	20	30*	21*	18*	18*	37*	32	35*	42	46	43	59	49	43	50	59	54	50	College

Table 1.154
Education of Religion Groups Summarized with a Percentage Difference Index#

	1952	1954	1956	1958	1960	1962	1964	1966	1968	1970	1972	1974	1976	1978	1980	1982	1984	1986
Protestants	-26	-19	-12	-7	-7	-5	-4	-5	0	-4	6	8	14	20	20	28	26	31
Catholics	-28	-24	-15	-22	-10	-5	0	-4	8	-1	9	10	13	24	25	31	31	36
Jews	-26	6*	14	7	-2	20*	29*	44*	50*	38*	48	35	73	64	46*	88*	65	75*
Other and No Religion	-37	-3*	-25*	-29*	-37*	5*	10	0*	26	26	30	45	37	33	45	48	49	45
Total PDI	-27	-19	-12	-10	-8	-4	-1	-3	4	0	9	12	17	23	25	32	31	34

PDI is proportion "college" minus proportion "grade school"

Table 1.155
Urbanism of Religion Groups

	1952	1954	1956	1958	1960	1962	1964	1966	1968	1970	1972	1974	1976	1978	1980	1982	1984	1986	
Protestants	27%	28%	18%	18%	16%	22%	26%	25%	22%	23%	23%	22%	24%	26%	26%	26%	20%	22%	Cent. cities
	29	31	26	27	25	35	27	28	26	23	27	35	32	35	34	32	38	40	Suburbs
	45	41	57	56	59	42	47	48	52	53	50	43	44	39	40	43	42	38	Non-U. areas
Catholics	47%	48%	40%	39%	33%	31%	36%	41%	34%	34%	30%	34%	33%	27%	28%	29%	27%	27%	Cent. cities
	33	34	31	33	36	49	44	41	43	44	40	41	43	49	51	50	50	51	Suburbs
	19	19	30	28	31	20	20	18	23	22	30	25	24	24	22	21	23	22	Non-U. areas
Jews	78%	94%*	79%	69%	77%	50%*	58%*	47%*	52%*	48%*	43%	67%	59%	45%	61%	42%*	47%	38%*	Cent. cities
	15	6*	18	26	16	50*	38*	37*	36*	41*	36	32	38	42	35	54*	49	59*	Suburbs
	7	0*	4	6	7	0*	4*	16*	12*	12*	21	2	4	13	4	4*	4	3*	Non-U. areas
Other and No Religion	28%	57%	39%	41%	32%	29%	42%	33%	39%	36%	33%	48%	34%	30%	28%	36%	31%	35%	Cent. cities
	33	13	23	23	37	34	34	33	24	42	43	32	38	41	43	37	41	40	Suburbs
	38	30	39	36	32	37	24	35	37	22	24	20	29	29	29	27	28	24	Non-U. areas

Table 1.156
Urbanism of Religion Groups Summarized with a Percentage Difference Index#

	1952	1954	1956	1958	1960	1962	1964	1966	1968	1970	1972	1974	1976	1978	1980	1982	1984	1986
Protestants	-18	-13	-39	-38	-43	-20	-21	-23	-30	-30	-27	-21	-20	-13	-14	-17	-23	-16
Catholics	28	29	10	11	2	11	16	23	11	12	1	9	8	4	6	8	5	6
Jews	71	94	75	64	71	50	53	30	41	36	21	65	55	31	57	38	43	34
Other and No Religion	-10	27	0	5	0	-8	18	-2	2	13	8	29	5	1	-1	9	2	11
Total PDI	-5	-1	-24	-23	-28	-11	-9	-10	-18	-17	-17	-9	-9	-7	-6	-8	-12	-7

PDI is proportion "central cities" minus proportion "non-urban areas"

Table 1.157
Family Income of Religion Groups

	1952	1954	1956	1958	1960	1962	1964	1966	1968	1970	1972	1974	1976	1978	1980	1982	1984	1986	Percentile
Protestants	25%	23%	19%	18%	18%	25%	21%	22%	18%	17%	21%	18%	16%	19%	19%	19%	17%	18%	0-16
	16	13	22	23	18	8	20	10	22	16	13	16	20	19	16	17	19	18	17-33
	23	31	31	27	27	40	25	33	31	32	37	40	31	31	36	30	35	36	34-67
	34	27	20	29	33	23	27	29	25	31	25	24	28	25	25	27	24	24	68-95
	3	6	8	4	5	5	6	6	4	4	4	3	5	6	4	7	5	4	96-100
Catholics	7%	12%	9%	13%	6%	14%	13%	12%	10%	9%	16%	13%	9%	13%	15%	14%	13%	13%	0-16
	17	13	23	15	17	8	13	8	18	12	8	14	18	16	15	15	16	11	17-33
	25	36	36	35	30	49	28	33	36	32	39	42	31	33	40	31	38	35	34-67
	48	33	28	35	44	25	37	40	29	43	32	27	39	32	26	34	29	37	68-95
	3	7	6	2	4	5	9	7	7	3	5	4	4	8	5	6	5	4	96-100
Jews	13%	23%*	4%	0%*	2%	10%*	3%*	5%*	2%*	7%*	14%	4%	14%	7%	20%	0%	7%	7%	0-16
	7	7*	11	10*	3	5*	8*	5*	22*	7*	9	11	10	11	7	23	9	7	17-33
	19	23*	25	22*	50	33*	33*	29*	17*	27*	26	44	26	18	30	18	27	32	34-67
	48	27*	38	55*	31	33*	33*	56*	46*	46*	30	21	32	30	30	27	31	29	68-95
	13	20*	23	12*	15	19*	22*	5*	12*	12*	21	21	18	34	13	32	27	26	96-100
Other and No Religion	20%	14%*	12%*	21%*	11%*	20%*	25%	39%*	12%	14%	18%	9%	12%	16%	15%	15%	15%	20%	0-16
	22	18*	38*	26*	29*	6*	19	7*	27	13	12	26	19	20	17	23	15	12	17-33
	22	18*	19*	26*	34*	49*	19	25*	24	37	38	34	35	34	35	29	34	38	34-67
	32	46*	26*	26*	26*	20*	25	27*	27	34	26	26	28	23	24	25	29	23	68-95
	3	4*	5*	0*	0*	6*	10	2*	10	3	7	5	6	7	9	9	7	7	96-100

Table 1.158
Family Income of Religion Groups Summarized with a Percentage Difference Index#

	1952	1954	1956	1958	1960	1962	1964	1966	1968	1970	1972	1974	1976	1978	1980	1982	1984	1986
Protestants	-3	-3	-13	-9	2	-6	-9	2	-10	2	-4	-6	-3	-7	-6	-1	-7	-9
Catholics	28	15	3	9	25	9	20	27	8	25	13	4	16	11	2	12	6	17
Jews	41	17*	45	57*	40	38*	44*	51*	34*	44*	28	28	25	47	17*	36*	42*	42*
Other and No Religion	-7	18*	-19*	-21*	-13*	0*	-9	-16*	-2	10	3	-4	4	-5	0	-3	5	-1
Total PDI	5	2	-8	-3	6	-1	-1	8	-5	8	1	-3	2	-1	-2	2	-1	-1

PDI is proportion "68-100 percentile" minus proportion "0-33 percentile"

Table 1.159
Percent Female within Religion Groups

	1952	1954	1956	1958	1960	1962	1964	1966	1968	1970	1972	1974	1976	1978	1980	1982	1984	1986
Protestants	55%	53%	55%	54%	56%	57%	58%	58%	56%	58%	58%	60%	61%	59%	60%	57%	58%	60%
Catholics	51%	54%	58%	52%	54%	53%	52%	53%	59%	58%	58%	60%	55%	56%	58%	57%	57%	55%
Jews	66%	56%*	61%	58%	50%	50%*	62%*	54%*	64%*	50%*	54%	52%	56%	52%	49%	63%*	53%	31%*
Other and No Religion	43%	53%*	36%*	23%*	32%*	32%*	31%	35%*	32%	52%	38%	41%	44%	35%	41%	41%	41%	42%
Total Population	54%	53%	55%	53%	55%	55%	55%	56%	56%	57%	57%	58%	58%	56%	57%	55%	56%	56%

Table 1.160
Percent Black within Religion Groups

	1952	1954	1956	1958	1960	1962	1964	1966	1968	1970	1972	1974	1976	1978	1980	1982	1984	1986
Protestants	12%	11%	11%	11%	11%	11%	13%	13%	13%	12%	13%	12%	13%	14%	15%	14%	15%	19%
Catholics	2%	2%	2%	2%	1%	3%	2%	5%	3%	2%	3%	3%	4%	3%	4%	5%	4%	4%
Jews	0%	0%*	0%	0%	0%	0%*	0%*	0%*	0%*	0%*	0%	0%	0%	0%	2%	0%*	0%	0%*
Other and No Religion	17%	7%*	5%*	8%*	6%*	8%*	6%	4%*	5%	9%	9%	5%	13%	9%	11%	9%	10%	17%
Total Population	10%	9%	8%	9%	9%	9%	10%	11%	10%	10%	10%	9%	11%	10%	12%	11%	11%	15%

Table 1.161
Percent Union Households within Religion Groups

	1952	1954	1956	1958	1960	1962	1964	1966	1968	1970	1972	1974	1976	1978	1980	1982	1984	1986
Protestants	23%	26%	23%	21%	24%	**	21%	26%	23%	21%	23%	23%	21%	24%	23%	20%	19%	19%
Catholics	41%	37%	40%	36%	39%	**	32%	37%	32%	34%	35%	36%	30%	32%	32%	27%	26%	25%
Jews	22%	21%*	29%	31%	29%	**	20%*	23%*	26%*	21%*	16%	27%	14%	21%	26%	8%*	17%	25%*
Other and No Religion	22%	37%*	34%*	21%*	24%*	**	25%	24%*	29%	24%	27%	21%	26%	23%	27%	22%	22%	15%
Total Population	27%	28%	27%	25%	27%	**	24%	28%	25%	24%	26%	26%	23%	26%	26%	21%	21%	20%

Table 1.162
Percent South within Religion Groups

	1952	1954	1956	1958	1960	1962	1964	1966	1968	1970	1972	1974	1976	1978	1980	1982	1984	1986
Protestants	36%	53%	37%	38%	41%	43%	39%	38%	39%	42%	41%	44%	39%	42%	42%	43%	40%	44%
Catholics	6%	54%	5%	7%	8%	15%	12%	9%	9%	13%	18%	17%	19%	21%	26%	19%	21%	19%
Jews	7%	6%*	11%	15%	15%	5%*	4%*	0%*	10%*	17%*	7%	7%	2%	28%	16%	25%*	17%	25%*
Other and No Religion	38%	17%*	16%*	18%*	42%*	18%*	13%	17%*	19%	23%	23%	25%	28%	31%	22%	31%	25%	23%
Total Population	29%	31%	29%	30%	34%	35%	31%	30%	31%	35%	34%	36%	32%	35%	35%	36%	33%	36%

Table 1.163
Occupation of Religion Groups

	1952	1954	1956	1958	1960	1962	1964	1966	1968	1970	1972	1974	1976	1978	1980	1982	1984	1986	
Protestants	14%	**	16%	18%	18%	**	19%	**	18%	20%	20%	20%	20%	23%	24%	23%	23%	24%	Professional
	10	**	10	12	13	**	13	**	13	13	14	15	16	15	19	19	22	22	White collar
	18	**	25	27	30	**	29	**	32	33	32	34	34	36	35	33	35	35	Blue collar
	12	**	6	3	2	**	3	**	2	2	2	2	3	3	3	3	3	3	Unskilled
	9	**	8	6	7	**	6	**	5	5	4	4	4	2	3	4	4	3	Farmers
	37	**	35	34	31	**	31	**	30	28	28	25	24	21	17	17	14	14	Housewives
Catholics	15%	**	14%	13%	10%	**	19%	**	22%	19%	17%	21%	20%	23%	24%	25%	22%	27%	Professional
	14	**	10	10	16	**	13	**	17	14	18	18	17	20	19	24	26	22	White collar
	28	**	28	38	41	**	33	**	27	29	35	36	36	33	36	31	33	34	Blue collar
	8	**	5	2	3	**	2	**	1	1	2	1	2	2	3	1	3	2	Unskilled
	3	**	2	2	1	**	1	**	1	3	1	2	2	1	1	2	3	2	Farmers
	32	**	41	35	30	**	32	**	33	34	28	22	22	21	17	17	14	13	Housewives
Jews	20%	**	31%	42%	27%	**	28%*	**	37%*	39%*	44%	48%	60%	54%	49%*	61%*	53%	47%*	Professional
	17	**	11	6	31	**	16*	**	24*	27*	18	27	29	25	15*	13*	24	28*	White collar
	14	**	9	13	11	**	12*	**	15*	10*	16	7	2	8	19*	0*	4	13*	Blue collar
	7	**	0	0	0	**	0*	**	0*	2*	0	0	2	0	2*	0*	0	0*	Unskilled
	0	**	0	0	0	**	0*	**	0*	0*	0	0	0	2	0*	0*	0	0*	Farmers
	42	**	49	40	31	**	44*	**	24*	22*	23	18	8	12	15*	26*	20	13*	Housewives
Other and No Religion	17%	**	11%*	13%*	26%*	**	28%	**	28%*	28%	32%	33%	22%	31%	31%	33%	31%	34%	Professional
	10	**	9*	5*	3*	**	7	**	10*	19	17	14	20	13	16	17	19	17	White collar
	25	**	30*	50*	37*	**	46	**	44*	29	31	39	37	39	36	37	39	37	Blue collar
	13	**	21*	8*	3*	**	0	**	0*	2	4	2	6	5	5	4	1	4	Unskilled
	7	**	5*	11*	5*	**	3	**	2*	2	1	1	2	2	3	1	4	3	Farmers
	28	**	25*	13*	26*	**	16	**	16*	21	16	12	14	10	11	9	6	5	Housewives

Social Characteristics of Religious Groups

Table 1.164
Incidence of Occupations within Religion Groups

	1952	1954	1956	1958	1960	1962	1964	1966	1968	1970	1972	1974	1976	1978	1980	1982	1984	1986	
Percent Professional	14%	**	16%	18%	18%	**	19%	**	18%	20%	20%	20%	20%	23%	24%	23%	23%	24%	Protestant
	15%	**	14%	13%	10%	**	19%	**	22%	19%	17%	21%	20%	23%	24%	25%	22%	27%	Catholic
	20%	**	31%	42%	27%	**	28%*	**	37%*	39%*	44%	48%	60%	54%	49%*	61%*	53%	47%*	Jewish
	17%	**	11%*	13%*	26%*	**	28%	**	28%	28%	32%	33%	22%	31%	31%	33%	31%	34%	Oth. and None
Percent White collar	10%	**	10%	12%	13%	**	13%	**	13%	13%	14%	15%	16%	15%	19%	19%	22%	22%	Protestant
	14%	**	10%	10%	16%	**	13%	**	17%	14%	18%	18%	17%	20%	19%	24%	26%	22%	Catholic
	17%	**	11%	6%	31%	**	16%*	**	24%*	27%*	18%	27%	29%	25%	15%*	13%*	24%	28%*	Jewish
	10%	**	9%*	5%*	3%*	**	7%	**	10%*	19%	17%	14%	20%	13%	16%	17%	19%	17%	Oth. and None
Percent Blue collar	18%	**	25%	27%	30%	**	29%	**	32%	33%	32%	34%	34%	36%	35%	33%	35%	35%	Protestant
	28%	**	28%	38%	41%	**	33%	**	27%	29%	35%	36%	36%	33%	36%	31%	33%	34%	Catholic
	14%	**	9%	13%	11%	**	12%*	**	15%*	10%*	16%	7%	2%	8%	19%*	0%*	4%	13%*	Jewish
	25%	**	30%*	50%*	37%*	**	46%	**	44%*	29%	31%	39%	37%	39%	36%	37%	39%	37%	Oth. and None
Percent Unskilled	12%	**	6%	3%	2%	**	3%	**	2%	2%	2%	2%	3%	3%	3%	3%	3%	3%	Protestant
	8%	**	5%	2%	3%	**	2%	**	1%	1%	2%	1%	2%	2%	3%	1%	3%	2%	Catholic
	7%	**	0%	0%	0%	**	0%*	**	0%*	2%*	0%	0%	2%	0%	2%*	0%*	0%	0%*	Jewish
	13%	**	21%*	8%*	3%*	**	0%	**	0%*	2%	4%	2%	6%	5%	5%	4%	1%	4%	Oth. and None
Percent Farmers	9%	**	8%	6%	7%	**	6%	**	5%	5%	4%	4%	4%	2%	3%	4%	4%	3%	Protestant
	3%	**	2%	2%	1%	**	1%	**	1%	3%	1%	2%	2%	1%	1%	2%	3%	2%	Catholic
	0%	**	0%	0%	0%	**	0%*	**	0%*	0%*	0%	0%	0%	2%	0%*	0%*	0%	0%*	Jewish
	7%	**	5%*	11%*	5%*	**	3%	**	2%*	2%	1%	1%	2%	2%	3%	1%	4%	3%	Oth. and None
Percent Housewives	37%	**	35%	34%	31%	**	31%	**	30%	28%	28%	25%	24%	21%	17%	17%	14%	14%	Protestant
	32%	**	41%	35%	30%	**	32%	**	33%	34%	28%	22%	22%	21%	17%	17%	14%	13%	Catholic
	42%	**	49%	40%	31%	**	44%*	**	24%*	22%*	23%	18%	8%	12%	15%*	26%*	20%	13%*	Jewish
	28%	**	25%*	13%*	26%*	**	16%	**	16%*	21%	16%	12%	14%	10%	11%	9%	6%	5%	Oth. and None

Oth. and None is the abbreviation for Other and None; this appears to the right of the 1986 column.

Chapter 2. Party Identification, Ideology and Evaluations of Political Actors

Party identification refers to the psychological feeling of attachment to a political party. Therefore it is to be distinguished from such behavior as party registration for primary elections or voting for candidates of a particular party. Although self-identification as a Republican or Democrat is separable from the act of voting, it nevertheless has a substantial impact on political attitudes, participation, and vote choice, as later chapters will demonstrate.

Partisan identifications form relatively early in the development of political attitudes, either through the transmission of attitudes and values from parent to child or through experiencing major political events (e.g., the depression) at an early age. Because this early socialization is often reinforced by subsequent voting behavior and because parties are more enduring political objects than specific candidates or issues, partisan identification generally acts as a predisposition which influences how citizens respond to particular leaders or policy proposals. Unique candidates or important issues may influence partisan attitudes, especially among younger citizens, but, once established, partisan orientations appear quite enduring. Partisan loyalty can remain strong even after the original reason for distinguishing between parties begins to fade. It is the relative stability of the impact that party identification has on subsequent evaluations of candidates and policies which makes it an important attitude to monitor over time.

Despite a marked decrease in the proportion of avowed party identifiers after the mid-1960s (Table 2.1), the concept of partisanship remained applicable to more than eight out of every ten voting-age citizens toward the end of the seventies. Assessing the political relevance of the growth in the number of Independents (those who do not initially categorize themselves as partisans) is somewhat complicated because it is clear that Independents who feel closer to one of the parties than to the other often think and behave very much as partisans. If such "leaners" are included with self-declared partisans, the proportion of Independents shrinks substantially and the decline in partisan attachment appears much less consequential. We have not adopted a single a priori choice between these alternatives in presenting the data. Rather, we present first the data for the full array of possible party identification categories and then alternative summary statistics so readers can ascertain the answer to this puzzle for themselves.

The first tables in this chapter display the demographic correlates of party identification. Table 2.2, for example, presents party identification by age cohorts. Monitoring the relationship between age and party identification on a continuing basis provides evidence relevant to theories of generational differences in partisan orientation. With this in

mind, it is interesting to note that the greatest increase in Independents occurred among the younger cohort as they entered the electorate and that there is only limited evidence that older cohorts have actively rejected partisan labels.

Another noteworthy trend is visible in Table 2.12, which displays party identification among blacks. Prior to the passage of the Voting Rights Act in the mid-1960s, a significant proportion of blacks were excluded from national politics and therefore gave responses which classified them as apolitical on the party identification measure. After the mid-1960s, the proportion of apoliticals among blacks declined while the proportion identifying themselves as Democrats increased as a result of the party's visible efforts to mobilize blacks into the electorate.

Tables 2.24-2.27 show the relationship between party identification and political ideology represented as (a) self-placement on a liberal-conservative scale (Tables 2.24-2.25) and (b) "thermometer" ratings of liberals and conservatives (Tables 2.26-2.27). The liberal-conservative scale in Table 2.22 is a 7-point measure which we have collapsed into five categories. Survey respondents were presented with the seven options and asked to indicate how they would classify themselves. A substantial proportion, 27-33 percent, were unable or unwilling to place themselves on the scale and are not included in subsequent tables. The seven categories were collapsed into five as follows: (1) Extremely Liberal or Liberal; (2) Slightly Liberal; (3) Moderate, Middle of the Road; (4) Slightly Conservative; (5) Conservative or Extremely Conservative. The liberal-conservative index in Table 2.23, on the other hand, is derived from affective, thermometer ratings of liberals and conservatives. This measure was described to our respondents as analogous to a temperature thermometer. Ratings between zero and 49 degrees represent cold or unfavorable feelings, while ratings of 51 to 100 degrees indicate warm or favorable feelings; 50 degrees is a neutral rating. To calculate the liberal-conservative index, the thermometer rating of liberals is subtracted from the conservative thermometer score. Next 97 is added and the result is divided by 2 so that 0 is the most liberal score, 97 the most conservative score, and 49 is the midpoint representing balanced evaluations. (The constant 97 is used, rather than 100, because of coding conventions which prohibit the use of 98 or 99 as numerical values.) The first category of the index reflects the combination of a high rating of liberals and a low rating of conservatives, scores of 0 to 25; the next most liberal category contains scores of 26 to 48; a score of 49 is neutral; the moderately conservative category ranges from 50 to 75; and the fifth category, from 76 to 97, indicates a low rating of liberals and a high rating of conservatives.

Having completed a detailed description of party identification and ideology for various demographic and political groups, we present a brief series of tables (2.32-2.39) which use four summary measures as parsimonious descriptions of the trends in partisanship. The first two measures assess Democratic-Republican ratios; they differ only in their treatment of the Independent leaners. The second pair assesses degrees of partisanship and independence; they differ in their treatment of weak identifiers and leaning Independents.

Party preference, the first summary measure, indicates the relative proportions of Democratic and Republican preferrers and is calculated as (percent strong + weak + leaning Independent Democrats) - (percent strong + weak + leaning Independent Republicans).

Party identification balance, the second measure, is calculated as (percent strong + weak Democrats) - (percent strong + weak Republicans).

Partisan-Independent balance, the third measure, represents the preponderance of strong partisans relative to pure Independents and is computed as (percent strong Democrats + strong Republicans) - (percent Independent-Independents + Apoliticals).

Strength of party identification, the fourth measure, is calculated by scoring strong Democrats and Republicans as +2, weak Democrats and Republicans as +1, Independent leaners as 0, and Independent-Independents and Apoliticals as -1.

The remainder of the chapter goes beyond party identification to explore attitudes toward the candidates who have represented the major parties in the presidential elections, toward the political parties, and toward a series of political leaders who have been associated with the two parties over a period of time. Tables 2.40-2.65 are based on responses to open-ended questions which ask the survey respondents what they like and dislike about each of the presidential candidates and each of the two political parties. From responses to these questions, we have developed indices, described in the tables themselves, which measure positive and negative feelings about the parties and candidates as well as how salient they are to the public. The next series of tables (2.66-2.95) shows thermometer ratings of political figures who have been prominent in American politics over the years. The statistic used in all these tables is the mean thermometer rating. The purpose of the extensive set of tables 2.40-2.95 is to explore partisanship in a broader sense than may be captured by party identification alone. Political parties are an important institution of American government, and the data presented in this part of this chapter provide evidence based on the responses which this institution and its representatives have drawn from citizens over the years. The final section of the chapter (Tables 2.96-2.114) lay out, by party, our respondents' feelings about the major political actor in our system, the President. Tables 2.96-2.98 are an overall evaluation of how the President is doing his job, and tables 2.99-2.114 show affects toward and trait assessment of Ronald Reagan, by party.

Table 2.1
Party Identification

QUESTION: Generally speaking, do you usually think of yourself as a Republican, a Democrat, an
Independent, or what? (IF REPUBLICAN OR DEMOCRAT) Would you call yourself a strong (R/D) or a
not very strong (R/D)? (IF INDEPENDENT OR OTHER) Do you think of yourself as closer to the
Republican or Democratic Party?

	1952	1954	1956	1958	1960	1962	1964	1966	1968	1970	1972	1974	1976	1978	1980	1982	1984	1986
Strong Democrat	22%	22%	21%	27%	20%	23%	27%	18%	20%	20%	15%	18%	15%	15%	18%	20%	17%	18%
Weak Democrat	25	26	23	22	25	23	25	28	25	24	26	21	25	24	23	24	20	22
Independent Democrat	10	9	6	7	6	7	9	9	10	10	11	13	12	14	11	11	11	10
Independent Independent	6	7	9	7	10	8	8	12	11	13	13	15	15	14	13	11	11	12
Independent Republican	7	6	8	5	7	6	6	7	9	8	11	9	10	10	10	8	12	11
Weak Republican	14	14	14	17	14	16	14	15	15	15	13	14	14	13	14	14	15	15
Strong Republican	14	13	15	11	16	12	11	10	10	9	10	8	9	8	9	10	12	11
Apolitical	3	4	4	4	3	4	1	1	1	1	1	3	1	3	2	2	2	2
Total	100%	100%	100%	100%	100%	100%	100%	100%	100%	100%	100%	100%	100%	100%	100%	100%	100%	100%
N	1784	1130	1757	1808	1911	1287	1550	1278	1553	1501	2694	2505	2850	2283	1612	1411	2236	2166

Table 2.2
Party Identification of Age Cohort Groups

	1952	1954	1956	1958	1960	1962	1964	1966	1968	1970	1972	1974	1976	1978	1980	1982	1984	1986	
1959 or later cohort	**	**	**	**	**	**	**	**	**	**	**	**	**	7%	11%	8%	9%	13%	Strong Dem
	**	**	**	**	**	**	**	**	**	**	**	**	**	16	21	26	21	20	Weak Dem
	**	**	**	**	**	**	**	**	**	**	**	**	**	16	18	13	16	9	Indep Dem
	**	**	**	**	**	**	**	**	**	**	**	**	**	27	18	15	13	16	Indep Dem
	**	**	**	**	**	**	**	**	**	**	**	**	**	7	9	8	15	12	Indep Rep
	**	**	**	**	**	**	**	**	**	**	**	**	**	8	15	17	15	15	Weak Rep
	**	**	**	**	**	**	**	**	**	**	**	**	**	7	3	7	9	10	Strong Rep
	**	**	**	**	**	**	**	**	**	**	**	**	**	11	5	5	4	5	Apolitical
1943 - 1958 Cohort	**	**	**	**	**	**	20%*	11%	8%	13%	8%	14%	10%	9%	12%	16%	12%	14%	Strong Dem
	**	**	**	**	**	**	32*	30	24	24	25	22	25	25	25	25	21	22	Weak Dem
	**	**	**	**	**	**	12*	11	22	15	18	18	16	19	13	14	12	14	Indep Dem
	**	**	**	**	**	**	8*	16	17	19	18	20	19	17	17	14	13	13	Indep Dem
	**	**	**	**	**	**	8*	13	15	11	14	8	12	10	11	10	13	12	Indep Rep
	**	**	**	**	**	**	12*	11	7	12	9	10	13	12	13	13	16	15	Weak Rep
	**	**	**	**	**	**	4*	8	4	6	6	4	5	5	6	7	12	8	Strong Rep
	**	**	**	**	**	**	4*	0	3	1	1	4	1	3	3	2	2	2	Apolitical
1927 - 1942 Cohort	22%	14%	17%	26%	18%	18%	24%	14%	20%	17%	13%	16%	13%	13%	16%	21%	20%	20%	Strong Dem
	30	27	24	24	27	27	26	31	26	24	26	21	24	28	22	24	23	22	Weak Dem
	9	12	11	9	8	11	13	12	11	14	11	12	12	14	11	12	11	10	Indep Dem
	6	10	10	9	12	9	9	13	10	13	15	14	16	11	10	10	7	10	Indep Rep
	9	11	13	6	6	10	7	9	11	11	12	12	10	11	13	8	13	10	Indep Rep
	11	11	13	14	10	16	13	14	15	15	14	17	16	15	16	15	14	13	Weak Rep
	8	8	7	7	15	6	8	6	6	7	8	7	8	7	11	10	11	14	Strong Rep
	4	7	5	5	4	3	1	1	2	0	1	2	1	2	1	2	2	1	Apolitical
1911 - 1926 Cohort	20%	23%	20%	26%	19%	23%	27%	18%	19%	24%	19%	17%	19%	21%	26%	29%	26%	28%	Strong Dem
	31	28	26	26	27	27	26	28	26	25	27	22	27	24	23	21	18	25	Weak Dem
	10	9	7	7	9	6	9	9	10	8	9	13	8	11	9	9	8	8	Indep Dem
	5	7	9	7	10	10	9	11	11	12	9	12	10	11	8	7	10	7	Indep Dem
	9	6	8	6	7	5	6	5	8	5	8	7	9	9	10	8	11	7	Indep Rep
	15	13	14	16	14	14	14	17	17	16	16	16	14	13	14	14	13	14	Weak Rep
	7	10	12	8	13	10	9	10	9	9	12	10	11	10	7	11	15	11	Strong Rep
	3	4	3	4	2	4	0	2	1	1	1	3	1	2	1	1	1	1	Apolitical
1895 - 1910 Cohort	22%	22%	21%	28%	23%	29%	32%	23%	27%	21%	22%	25%	23%	29%	27%	25%	27%	27%	Strong Dem
	23	25	21	19	22	19	23	23	24	23	25	18	23	18	22	26	12	18	Weak Dem
	11	7	4	7	4	5	6	6	5	8	6	9	9	8	8	3	6	3	Indep Dem
	6	8	9	7	9	4	7	13	10	11	10	9	9	9	9	7	10	7	Indep Dem
	5	7	7	4	9	5	3	7	6	6	7	8	6	5	5	2	7	10	Indep Rep
	14	14	15	18	15	16	13	16	14	16	13	16	14	13	11	18	16	16	Weak Rep
	16	16	19	13	16	18	15	13	15	14	16	14	15	16	18	16	21	17	Strong Rep
	2	2	4	3	3	5	1	0	1	1	2	2	2	3	1	3	1	2	Apolitical
Before 1895 Cohort	25%	23%	26%	24%	23%	25%	27%	25%	23%	27%	13%	32%	19%	36%*	–	–	–	–	Strong Dem
	17	19	16	17	21	15	19	27	26	19	23	21	16	24*	–	–	–	–	Weak Dem
	7	7	3	5	3	5	3	3	4	3	5	0	3	0*	–	–	–	–	Indep Dem
	7	7	6	5	9	4	10	3	9	3	9	3	3	8*	–	–	–	–	Indep Dem
	6	1	6	4	2	3	6	4	2	3	5	5	6	0*	–	–	–	–	Indep Rep
	13	19	14	19	17	21	17	15	15	23	23	12	37	8*	–	–	–	–	Weak Rep
	22	19	24	24	25	22	24	14	22	17	24	21	13	24*	–	–	–	–	Strong Rep
	4	6	4	3	2	4	1	3	4	0	4	0	3	0*	–	–	–	–	Apolitical

Party Identification

Table 2.3
Age Cohort Groups Having Party Identification, Sample size&

	1952	1954	1956	1958	1960	1962	1964	1966	1968	1970	1972	1974	1976	1978	1980	1982	1984	1986
1959 or later Cohort	**	**	**	**	**	**	**	**	**	**	**	**	**	73	114	138	343	416
1943 - 1958 Cohort	**	**	**	**	**	**	25	88	152	248	740	831	1029	885	591	518	824	832
1927 - 1942 Cohort	149	73	305	377	413	361	513	389	495	449	721	576	664	571	366	293	456	432
1911 - 1926 Cohort	689	535	710	696	720	438	515	413	486	391	681	600	664	484	356	343	410	376
1895 - 1910 Cohort	536	370	456	468	511	319	346	276	323	304	439	396	416	235	171	110	175	106
Before 1895 Cohort	387	145	266	267	267	162	146	101	92	78	97	66	58	25	12	7	4	1

&Party ID includes 7 political categories and apoliticals (see Table 2.1)

Table 2.4
Party Identification of Education Groups

	1952	1954	1956	1958	1960	1962	1964	1966	1968	1970	1972	1974	1976	1978	1980	1982	1984	1986	
Grade School	25%	27%	22%	28%	26%	32%	38%	26%	31%	27%	24%	25%	24%	32%	31%	37%	31%	40%	Strong Democrat
	26	25	20	22	24	21	27	26	31	26	26	23	30	27	23	22	16	20	Weak Democrat
	8	6	4	6	3	6	6	7	5	6	6	8	8	7	8	11	7	7	Ind Democrat
	7	8	7	8	9	5	8	13	9	15	12	11	12	9	12	10	19	10	Ind Independent
	5	3	6	4	7	3	3	3	3	6	5	6	3	6	5	2	5	3	Ind Republican
	12	13	15	14	11	13	10	14	11	12	13	11	14	7	9	12	11	10	Weak Republican
	11	10	16	12	15	12	7	8	8	7	11	11	7	6	8	6	8	7	Strong Repub
	6	8	10	7	5	9	1	3	3	1	3	6	3	6	5	1	3	3	Apolitical
High School	21%	22%	21%	27%	21%	21%	25%	16%	19%	20%	14%	19%	16%	14%	18%	22%	17%	17%	Strong Democrat
	27	27	26	24	27	26	26	31	28	25	27	21	26	27	25	25	21	23	Weak Democrat
	11	10	7	7	9	8	11	10	10	11	12	14	12	14	10	10	11	10	Ind Democrat
	6	7	11	8	10	10	8	14	12	14	15	16	17	17	16	12	12	15	Ind Independent
	7	7	9	6	6	7	6	7	8	7	11	9	9	7	10	6	13	9	Ind Republican
	14	14	13	17	13	16	14	15	15	15	12	13	14	12	12	14	14	14	Weak Republican
	13	13	12	8	12	10	10	7	8	8	9	5	7	6	7	8	10	9	Strong Repub
	1	1	2	3	2	3	1	1	2	1	1	3	1	3	3	3	2	3	Apolitical
College	16%	13%	17%	23%	12%	18%	19%	13%	12%	13%	10%	10%	9%	11%	13%	14%	13%	15%	Strong Democrat
	18	22	20	20	21	21	21	23	17	20	23	21	21	19	21	23	20	22	Weak Democrat
	13	11	9	8	6	7	10	10	14	14	14	16	14	18	15	12	11	11	Ind Democrat
	3	7	6	5	10	8	8	9	10	8	11	14	13	11	8	10	8	9	Ind Independent
	13	11	10	6	7	8	9	11	16	11	14	10	14	14	12	11	14	15	Ind Republican
	17	17	18	20	18	20	16	17	18	19	16	17	16	16	18	16	17	16	Weak Republican
	21	18	20	17	25	17	18	16	13	14	13	11	13	11	11	12	16	13	Strong Repub
	0	1	0	1	1	0	0	0	0	1	1	1	0	1	1	1	1	1	Apolitical

Table 2.5
Education Groups Having Party Identification, Sample size&

	1952	1954	1956	1958	1960	1962	1964	1966	1968	1970	1972	1974	1976	1978	1980	1982	1984	1986
Grade School	734	412	539	549	577	356	378	332	357	365	534	462	468	270	194	157	237	194
High School	784	513	881	880	909	616	797	642	768	760	1371	1253	1416	1198	822	643	1064	1023
College	261	201	329	362	420	309	367	299	424	369	786	771	952	807	592	606	924	926

&Party ID includes 7 political categories and apoliticals (see Table 2.1)

Table 2.6
Party Identification of Urbanism Groups

	1952	1954	1956	1958	1960	1962	1964	1966	1968	1970	1972	1974	1976	1978	1980	1982	1984	1986	
Central cities	25%	20%	24%	35%	26%	27%	32%	23%	25%	23%	20%	25%	21%	21%	28%	24%	23%	24%	Strong Democrat
	23	24	26	23	22	25	24	29	23	26	27	22	28	27	25	25	24	26	Weak Democrat
	12	10	7	8	9	8	11	11	14	12	13	15	11	16	12	12	13	12	Ind Democrat
	7	9	9	5	10	7	9	14	11	12	9	13	11	13	10	10	10	9	Ind Independent
	7	8	7	5	7	7	3	5	10	6	9	6	9	7	8	8	11	9	Ind Republican
	12	12	11	12	8	11	11	10	9	12	11	9	10	9	8	10	9	11	Weak Republican
	12	13	13	10	14	12	9	7	7	9	9	6	9	6	7	9	9	9	Strong Repub
	2	4	2	3	4	3	1	1	2	1	2	4	1	2	2	1	2	1	Apolitical
Suburbs	20%	24%	20%	23%	16%	22%	21%	13%	17%	16%	11%	13%	11%	12%	13%	16%	15%	14%	Strong Democrat
	25	27	18	20	24	23	23	22	25	25	24	20	23	24	24	24	17	22	Weak Democrat
	8	7	5	8	5	9	11	12	8	12	13	15	15	15	12	13	11	10	Ind Democrat
	6	6	9	10	9	10	8	13	10	14	15	18	18	13	15	9	10	12	Ind Independent
	8	7	9	6	6	7	8	11	10	7	12	8	10	11	11	10	14	12	Ind Republican
	15	13	18	19	19	16	14	18	18	16	13	16	14	15	16	16	17	15	Weak Republican
	16	14	19	14	20	11	14	11	11	10	11	8	9	9	9	10	13	12	Strong Repub
	3	4	3	2	2	3	0	1	1	1	1	2	1	2	2	3	2	2	Apolitical
Non-urban Areas	21%	22%	19%	25%	20%	22%	28%	18%	19%	21%	14%	17%	14%	14%	16%	21%	15%	18%	Strong Democrat
	27	26	24	24	27	23	27	31	27	22	26	21	24	23	21	24	21	20	Weak Democrat
	9	9	6	6	6	5	7	6	9	9	9	10	9	13	11	8	9	10	Ind Democrat
	5	7	9	7	10	6	7	11	11	13	14	13	15	16	13	14	13	13	Ind Independent
	7	4	9	5	7	5	6	6	7	9	10	11	10	10	11	5	11	11	Ind Republican
	14	17	14	17	13	20	15	17	15	17	14	15	18	14	17	16	15	17	Weak Republican
	13	12	14	11	14	13	10	10	10	9	11	9	9	8	10	10	14	9	Strong Repub
	4	4	5	5	2	6	1	2	2	1	2	3	1	3	3	2	2	2	Apolitical

Table 2.7
Urbanism Groups Having Party Identification, Sample size&

	1952	1954	1956	1958	1960	1962	1964	1966	1968	1970	1972	1974	1976	1978	1980	1982	1984	1986	Sample Size
Central cities	586	386	438	440	424	326	460	373	406	402	696	688	794	614	441	387	521	548	
Suburbs	523	346	465	503	523	498	485	398	469	439	837	901	998	899	631	521	937	922	
Non-urban Areas	675	398	854	865	964	463	605	507	678	660	1161	916	1059	770	540	503	778	696	

&Party ID includes 7 political categories and apoliticals (see Table 2.1)

Table 2.8
Party Identification of Income Groups

	1952	1954	1956	1958	1960	1962	1964	1966	1968	1970	1972	1974	1976	1978	1980	1982	1984	1986	
Income Percentile 0-16	27%	27%	23%	27%	22%	22%	34%	19%	28%	28%	20%	21%	23%	21%	30%	28%	25%	25%	Strong Democrat
	23	25	21	19	25	23	25	29	31	23	28	20	27	27	19	27	18	24	Weak Democrat
	7	7	4	3	0	6	6	7	5	8	10	14	10	11	12	11	13	11	Ind Democrat
	4	7	7	9	7	4	9	13	9	15	10	11	13	14	11	14	15	13	Ind Independent
	5	3	4	3	2	3	4	5	5	4	8	7	6	6	8	5	13	7	Ind Republican
	10	10	11	13	15	20	10	17	10	14	12	9	12	9	9	9	8	11	Weak Republican
	14	13	17	17	20	14	9	7	11	6	10	10	8	8	8	4	6	6	Strong Repub
	11	10	13	10	9	9	3	2	3	3	3	8	1	4	4	2	3	3	Apolitical
Income Percentile 17-33	25%	24%	25%	29%	22%	20%	31%	27%	23%	23%	17%	25%	20%	19%	17%	24%	22%	22%	Strong Democrat
	25	22	25	23	28	26	29	25	24	25	27	22	29	27	32	27	22	23	Weak Democrat
	9	9	5	9	5	4	7	9	8	8	9	12	11	13	14	12	12	9	Ind Democrat
	8	11	9	9	11	4	9	17	13	14	16	15	12	14	11	8	12	12	Ind Independent
	7	5	6	5	6	8	4	6	8	7	10	5	7	6	7	6	7	7	Ind Republican
	14	11	16	15	13	14	11	7	12	16	10	9	13	13	14	13	13	15	Weak Republican
	11	14	12	7	13	18	10	9	9	6	11	8	8	5	5	9	11	10	Strong Repub
	3	6	4	3	2	5	0	1	3	0	1	4	1	3	1	2	2	2	Apolitical
Income Percentile 34-67	22%	22%	21%	28%	22%	25%	28%	16%	19%	19%	14%	17%	14%	13%	16%	24%	16%	18%	Strong Democrat
	29	27	24	26	26	24	28	31	25	26	28	25	26	26	23	23	20	23	Weak Democrat
	9	8	7	7	7	8	10	8	11	11	11	13	15	16	11	11	12	11	Ind Democrat
	5	7	10	5	11	10	8	10	11	13	15	16	15	14	16	11	10	12	Ind Independent
	8	7	11	6	7	7	4	6	10	9	10	9	10	9	12	8	13	12	Ind Republican
	14	16	15	15	12	15	12	16	14	12	12	13	13	12	13	14	15	16	Weak Republican
	12	10	10	9	15	8	9	11	10	11	8	5	7	8	7	9	12	9	Strong Repub
	2	2	2	4	1	2	1	1	1	0	2	2	1	2	2	1	2	2	Apolitical
Income Percentile 68-95	19%	20%	19%	25%	19%	23%	21%	18%	15%	18%	13%	14%	11%	11%	14%	16%	13%	12%	Strong Democrat
	27	28	22	22	24	22	22	26	25	22	23	19	23	23	24	22	20	21	Weak Democrat
	12	10	9	9	10	8	12	12	13	12	13	13	12	17	11	12	10	11	Ind Democrat
	5	7	10	7	11	8	6	12	11	11	10	15	18	13	10	11	8	11	Ind Independent
	8	6	8	6	8	9	8	8	10	9	13	11	12	13	12	11	16	15	Ind Republican
	15	15	13	19	14	16	18	14	18	18	15	19	16	16	18	18	18	15	Weak Republican
	14	12	18	11	14	13	12	10	8	9	13	8	9	6	11	10	14	14	Strong Repub
	0	2	1	2	1	1	1	1	1	0	1	1	1	0	1	1	1	0	1	Apolitical
Income Percentile 95-100	9%	7%	12%	21%	11%	13%	21%	11%	13%	11%	7%	10%	7%	14%	3%	6%	7%	13%	Strong Democrat
	6	14	21	9	12	21	14	21	19	17	19	3	12	18	18	21	14	15	Weak Democrat
	13	11	4	2	1	5	9	10	9	9	9	16	4	14	12	8	7	8	Ind Democrat
	13	6	5	5	8	11	8	11	6	9	13	5	9	7	13	4	9	7	Ind Independent
	11	12	14	9	17	2	11	13	15	7	11	14	20	18	17	14	18	17	Ind Republican
	22	22	18	21	23	18	17	20	24	20	24	22	22	15	16	20	23	17	Weak Republican
	27	29	27	33	29	31	20	14	13	26	17	30	25	14	21	25	22	21	Strong Repub
	0	0	0	0	0	0	1	0	1	0	0	0	0	1	1	1	0	1	Apolitical

Party Identification

Table 2.9
Income Groups Having Party Identification, Sample size&

	1952	1954	1956	1958	1960	1962	1964	1966	1968	1970	1972	1974	1976	1978	1980	1982	1984	1986	
Income Percentile 0-16	350	224	272	281	287	267	280	247	236	214	498	368	369	332	247	208	301	338	Sample Size
Income Percentile 17-33	274	141	376	371	333	93	274	116	315	217	308	367	506	358	222	215	350	307	
Income Percentile 34-67	398	340	528	488	538	512	390	406	473	464	966	940	819	616	515	375	703	711	
Income Percentile 68-95	652	310	384	538	650	286	442	395	400	496	698	581	804	534	361	356	514	537	
Income Percentile 95-100	64	73	134	57	84	62	105	71	79	54	132	93	139	146	77	95	111	86	

&Party ID includes 7 political categories and apoliticals (see Table 2.1)

Table 2.10
Party Identification of Sex Groups

	1952	1954	1956	1958	1960	1962	1964	1966	1968	1970	1972	1974	1976	1978	1980	1982	1984	1986	
Males	24%	25%	22%	29%	21%	25%	28%	20%	20%	20%	15%	15%	14%	14%	20%	19%	16%	18%	Strong Democrat
	23	25	23	19	22	24	22	26	23	23	22	20	22	24	18	19	17	18	Weak Democrat
	11	10	9	9	10	8	11	9	11	12	12	16	14	15	12	12	13	11	Ind Democrat
	7	8	10	7	10	9	8	12	10	13	15	16	17	16	15	13	12	12	Ind Independent
	7	6	9	5	8	6	6	9	10	9	13	10	12	12	12	10	14	14	Ind Republican
	13	13	13	15	15	15	11	13	16	13	13	13	13	12	14	16	15	14	Weak Republican
	13	12	13	13	13	11	11	11	9	10	10	10	7	6	8	10	13	11	Strong Repub
	2	2	2	3	1	2	1	1	1	1	1	1	1	2	2	2	1	2	Apolitical
Females	21%	20%	19%	24%	20%	22%	26%	17%	20%	20%	14%	19%	15%	16%	16%	21%	18%	18%	Strong Democrat
	27	26	23	26	27	23	27	29	27	25	29	22	27	25	27	28	23	25	Weak Democrat
	8	8	5	5	3	6	8	9	9	9	11	11	11	14	11	10	10	10	Ind Democrat
	5	7	8	7	10	7	8	12	11	13	12	14	13	12	11	10	11	11	Ind Independent
	7	6	8	5	6	6	5	6	8	7	9	7	8	8	9	7	11	8	Ind Republican
	15	15	15	18	13	18	15	17	13	17	13	15	15	13	14	13	15	15	Weak Republican
	14	14	17	10	18	13	11	9	10	8	11	7	10	9	9	9	12	11	Strong Repub
	4	5	5	5	4	6	1	2	2	1	2	4	1	3	2	2	2	2	Apolitical

Table 2.11
Sex Groups Having Party Identification, Sample size&

	1952	1954	1956	1958	1960	1962	1964	1966	1968	1970	1972	1974	1976	1978	1980	1982	1984	1986	
Males	813	531	782	847	865	577	693	566	681	644	1164	1052	1202	1011	694	631	980	945	Sample Size
Females	971	599	975	961	1046	710	857	712	872	857	1530	1453	1648	1272	918	780	1256	1221	

&Party ID includes 7 political categories and apoliticals (see Table 2.1)

Table 2.12
Party Identification of Racial Groups

	1952	1954	1956	1958	1960	1962	1964	1966	1968	1970	1972	1974	1976	1978	1980	1982	1984	1986	
Whites	21%	22%	20%	26%	20%	22%	24%	17%	16%	17%	12%	15%	13%	12%	14%	16%	15%	14%	Strong Democrat
	26	25	23	23	25	23	25	27	25	23	25	20	23	24	23	24	18	21	Weak Democrat
	10	9	6	7	6	8	9	9	10	11	12	13	11	14	12	11	11	10	Independent Dem
	6	8	9	8	9	8	8	12	11	13	13	15	15	14	14	11	11	12	Independent Ind
	7	6	9	5	7	7	6	8	10	9	11	9	11	10	11	9	13	13	Independent Rep
	14	15	14	17	14	17	15	16	16	16	14	15	16	14	16	16	17	17	Weak Republican
	14	13	16	12	17	13	12	11	11	10	11	9	10	9	9	11	14	12	Strong Rep
	2	3	3	3	1	3	1	1	1	1	1	3	1	2	2	2	2	2	Apolitical
Blacks	31%	24%	27%	32%	25%	35%	52%	30%	56%	43%	37%	40%	35%	37%	45%	53%	32%	42%	Strong Democrat
	22	29	23	19	19	25	22	31	29	34	31	26	36	30	27	26	31	30	Weak Democrat
	10	6	6	7	7	4	8	11	7	8	8	15	15	15	9	12	14	12	Independent Dem
	4	5	7	4	16	6	6	14	3	10	12	13	8	9	7	5	11	8	Independent Ind
	4	6	1	4	4	2	1	2	1	0	3	0	1	2	3	1	6	2	Independent Rep
	8	5	12	11	9	7	5	7	1	4	4	0	3	3	2	2	1	3	Weak Republican
	5	11	7	7	7	6	2	2	1	0	4	3	2	3	3	0	2	2	Strong Rep
	17	15	18	16	14	15	5	3	3	1	2	4	1	2	4	1	2	2	Apolitical

Table 2.13
Racial Groups Having Party Identification, Sample size

	1952	1954	1956	1958	1960	1962	1964	1966	1968	1970	1972	1974	1976	1978	1980	1982	1984	1986	
Whites	1608	1015	1606	1630	1722	1167	1383	1129	1384	1334	2387	2235	2480	2002	1404	1247	1931	1795	Sample Size
Blacks	169	101	145	161	171	109	156	132	149	145	266	224	289	227	187	148	247	322	

&Party ID includes 7 political categories and apoliticals (see Table 2.1)

Table 2.14
Party Identification of Union Membership Groups

	1952	1954	1956	1958	1960	1962	1964	1966	1968	1970	1972	1974	1976	1978	1980	1982	1984	1986	
Union Household	25%	27%	26%	36%	28%	**	38%	24%	23%	23%	19%	22%	20%	18%	23%	24%	22%	26%	Strong Democrat
	29	30	25	25	28	**	26	32	28	31	27	22	27	31	23	25	23	20	Weak Democrat
	12	10	8	8	9	**	13	10	11	11	13	15	15	15	12	14	13	12	Independent Dem
	5	6	9	6	11	**	6	11	10	14	16	18	16	13	17	12	10	11	Independent Ind
	6	4	9	6	8	**	4	4	8	6	10	8	9	7	10	5	12	10	Independent Rep
	12	11	12	11	8	**	9	15	13	11	9	8	9	9	9	11	11	12	Weak Republican
	10	9	9	5	7	**	4	3	6	4	6	5	3	4	5	7	7	8	Strong Rep
	1	3	2	3	2	**	0	1	1	0	1	2	1	3	2	1	2	1	Apolitical
Non-union Household	21%	20%	19%	23%	18%	**	23%	16%	19%	19%	13%	16%	13%	14%	16%	19%	16%	16%	Strong Democrat
	24	24	22	22	24	**	25	26	25	22	25	21	24	22	23	24	19	23	Weak Democrat
	9	8	6	7	6	**	8	9	9	10	11	13	11	14	11	10	10	10	Independent Dem
	6	8	9	8	9	**	8	13	11	12	12	13	14	14	12	11	11	12	Independent Ind
	7	7	8	5	7	**	6	8	9	9	11	9	10	10	11	9	13	11	Independent Rep
	14	15	15	18	16	**	15	15	15	17	15	16	16	14	16	15	16	15	Weak Republican
	15	15	17	13	19	**	13	12	11	11	12	9	11	9	10	10	14	11	Strong Rep
	4	4	5	4	3	**	1	1	2	1	2	3	1	3	2	2	2	2	Apolitical

Table 2.15
Union Membership Groups Having Party Identification, Sample size&

	1952	1954	1956	1958	1960	1962	1964	1966	1968	1970	1972	1974	1976	1978	1980	1982	1984	1986	
Union Household	482	316	477	443	507	**	373	357	388	349	686	631	657	586	411	298	474	436	Sample Size
Non-union Household	1289	800	1275	1357	1394	**	1174	912	1160	1133	1977	1817	2167	1687	1188	1102	1756	1720	

&Party ID includes 7 political categories and apoliticals (see Table 2.1)

Table 2.16
Party Identification of Region Groups

	1952	1954	1956	1958	1960	1962	1964	1966	1968	1970	1972	1974	1976	1978	1980	1982	1984	1986	
South	32%	32%	29%	33%	24%	27%	36%	21%	27%	24%	17%	20%	19%	18%	23%	27%	21%	22%	Strong Democrat
	33	29	32	29	34	26	30	32	29	26	32	27	31	28	25	25	23	25	Weak Democrat
	7	6	4	5	4	5	5	9	9	9	8	10	10	13	10	9	9	10	Independent Dem
	2	7	5	6	11	7	7	11	11	15	13	16	14	12	11	9	14	12	Independent Ind
	5	3	6	4	3	6	5	7	10	9	9	6	8	8	8	10	11	9	Independent Rep
	8	8	9	11	8	13	8	11	8	10	10	11	11	11	13	11	11	12	Weak Republican
	6	9	8	6	12	8	8	7	4	6	9	7	7	7	8	7	9	8	Strong Rep
	8	7	8	7	5	9	2	2	2	0	2	4	1	3	3	2	2	2	Apolitical
Non-south	18%	17%	18%	24%	19%	21%	23%	17%	17%	18%	13%	16%	13%	13%	15%	16%	15%	16%	Strong Democrat
	22	24	19	20	20	22	22	26	24	23	23	18	22	22	22	23	19	21	Weak Democrat
	11	10	7	8	8	9	11	9	10	11	12	15	13	15	12	12	12	11	Independent Dem
	7	7	10	8	10	8	8	13	10	12	13	14	15	14	14	12	10	11	Independent Ind
	8	7	9	6	9	6	7	8	7	11	10	11	10	12	7	13	12	Weak Republican
	16	17	17	19	17	18	16	17	17	18	15	16	16	14	15	16	17	16	Weak Republican
	17	15	18	14	18	15	13	11	12	11	11	9	10	8	9	11	14	12	Strong Rep
	1	2	2	3	1	1	0	1	1	1	1	2	1	2	2	2	2	2	Apolitical

Table 2.17
Region Groups Having Party Identification, Sample size&

	1952	1954	1956	1958	1960	1962	1964	1966	1968	1970	1972	1974	1976	1978	1980	1982	1984	1986	
South	504	343	511	545	645	447	475	377	479	518	901	900	923	803	570	509	740	776	Sample Size
Non-south	1280	787	1246	1263	1266	840	1075	901	1074	983	1793	1605	1928	1480	1042	902	1496	1390	

&Party ID includes 7 political categories and apoliticals (see Table 2.1)

Table 2.18
Party Identification of Occupation Groups

	1952	1954	1956	1958	1960	1962	1964	1966	1968	1970	1972	1974	1976	1978	1980	1982	1984	1986	
Professional	17%	**	16%	26%	16%	**	20%	**	14%	14%	10%	13%	11%	11%	13%	17%	14%	16%	Strong Democrat
	22	**	21	17	19	**	20	**	20	16	23	26	21	22	21	18	21	20	Weak Democrat
	13	**	8	7	9	**	10	**	9	15	13	15	12	17	13	11	11	12	Independent Dem
	7	**	8	9	11	**	8	**	12	10	11	12	14	11	11	11	8	9	Independent Ind
	8	**	12	6	8	**	9	**	15	11	12	8	15	15	13	12	10	14	Independent Rep
	14	**	17	19	15	**	16	**	18	20	17	17	16	15	19	15	20	15	Weak Republican
	20	**	18	15	20	**	18	**	11	15	14	8	12	9	11	15	16	14	Strong Rep
	0	**	1	1	2	**	0	**	1	0	1	0	0	1	0	1	0	1	Apolitical
White collar	20%	**	20%	21%	16%	**	25%	**	18%	18%	14%	17%	13%	13%	16%	15%	16%	4%	Strong Democrat
	25	**	23	29	28	**	26	**	21	24	27	21	23	24	23	19	23		Weak Democrat
	10	**	7	12	6	**	10	**	12	10	13	14	16	18	10	12	9	9	Independent Dem
	8	**	13	5	8	**	6	**	11	15	12	17	13	13	12	13	9	12	Independent Ind
	8	**	6	4	7	**	7	**	11	8	12	10	10	10	12	11	18	10	Independent Rep
	15	**	15	16	13	**	17	**	17	15	14	11	14	12	16	14	15	17	Weak Republican
	14	**	15	14	22	**	12	**	10	10	9	9	11	9	9	10	13	12	Strong Rep
	1	**	1	2	0	**	0	**	0	1	1	1	0	2	1	1	2	3	Apolitical
Blue collar	28%	**	24%	33%	27%	**	33%	**	23%	24%	18%	23%	19%	18%	22%	25%	22%	24%	Strong Democrat
	25	**	23	20	25	**	25	**	29	27	27	17	28	29	24	26	20	23	Weak Democrat
	13	**	9	9	9	**	12	**	11	8	11	14	11	13	10	11	12	10	Independent Dem
	6	**	10	7	12	**	9	**	10	14	15	14	16	16	15	12	13	13	Independent Ind
	5	**	9	5	6	**	4	**	7	7	11	10	8	6	8	5	12	10	Independent Rep
	12	**	12	15	11	**	9	**	11	12	9	11	12	9	10	13	10	11	Weak Republican
	10	**	12	8	9	**	7	**	8	7	8	7	5	5	7	6	9	7	Strong Rep
	1	**	3	4	1	**	0	**	1	1	1	5	1	3	3	3	2	2	Apolitical
Unskilled	30%	**	28%	36%	14%*	**	67%*	**	41%*	38%*	18%*	8%*	17%	17%	17%*	18%*	18%	16%	Strong Democrat
	22	**	27	29	24*	**	14*	**	19*	38*	20*	35*	19	26	17*	32*	20	27	Weak Democrat
	8	**	6	5	14*	**	3*	**	19*	13*	20*	8*	15	14	23*	16*	16	20	Independent Dem
	6	**	5	4	8*	**	6*	**	4*	0*	16*	14*	18	28	17*	11*	8	9	Independent Ind
	4	**	4	0	11*	**	3*	**	0*	8*	10*	11*	13	9	10*	5*	10	5	Independent Rep
	10	**	13	11	8*	**	3*	**	7*	0*	8*	5*	13	3	4*	16*	10	14	Weak Republican
	6	**	8	11	19*	**	3*	**	7*	4*	6*	16*	5	2	6*	3*	14	7	Strong Rep
	14	**	9	5	3*	**	3*	**	4*	0*	2*	3*	0	2	6*	0*	6	2	Apolitical
Farmers	25%	**	25%	31%	22%	**	30%	**	32%	27%	19%	15%	19%	16%*	16%*	32%*	6%	21%	Strong Democrat
	26	**	25	18	14	**	29	**	20	32	25	18	24	35*	28*	11*	17	19	Weak Democrat
	5	**	4	1	3	**	3	**	2	8	4	7	4	5*	3*	5*	9	9	Independent Dem
	5	**	4	6	13	**	6	**	12	7	11	4	13	9*	9*	9*	23	12	Independent Ind
	8	**	7	6	6	**	3	**	5	7	4	8	4	12*	13*	0*	11	9	Independent Rep
	15	**	10	16	17	**	18	**	20	10	14	26	22	16*	22*	27*	15	18	Weak Republican
	14	**	20	15	22	**	10	**	8	10	21	23	11	7*	3*	11*	19	9	Strong Rep
	1	**	6	8	4	**	3	**	2	0	1	0	2	0*	6*	5*	0	4	Apolitical
Housewives	18%	**	19%	22%	18%	**	24%	**	18%	19%	14%	17%	13%	14%	17%	21%	15%	14%	Strong Democrat
	27	**	22	25	29	**	27	**	29	24	27	22	26	22	25	31	21	22	Weak Democrat
	8	**	4	5	3	**	8	**	8	10	9	8	8	12	9	9	8	9	Independent Dem
	5	**	9	8	8	**	8	**	9	13	13	16	14	10	13	7	11	12	Independent Ind
	9	**	8	6	6	**	6	**	7	7	9	6	9	8	9	6	9	10	Independent Rep
	15	**	16	19	16	**	15	**	16	19	15	18	17	18	14	15	21	20	Weak Republican
	15	**	17	11	16	**	11	**	11	8	12	8	12	12	10	9	13	12	Strong Rep
	3	**	5	5	5	**	2	**	3	1	2	5	2	5	3	3	2	3	Apolitical

Party Identification

Table 2.19
Occupation Groups Having Party Identification, Sample size&

	1952	1954	1956	1958	1960	1962	1964	1966	1968	1970	1972	1974	1976	1978	1980	1982	1984	1986	
Professional	262	**	270	314	307	**	293	**	299	305	527	537	584	545	387	340	517	538	Sample Size
White collar	190	**	178	200	269	**	200	**	211	205	394	377	462	361	283	268	498	446	
Blue collar	359	**	443	532	598	**	452	**	456	453	840	825	932	768	534	444	737	721	
Unskilled	192	**	106	56	37	**	36	**	27	24	50	37	78	58	48	38	51	56	
Farmers	130	**	113	88	109	**	73	**	60	62	72	74	83	43	32	44	79	57	
Housewives	629	**	632	600	576	**	470	**	443	417	715	554	603	434	248	224	286	267	

&Party ID includes 7 political categories and apoliticals (see Table 2.1)

Table 2.20
Party Identification of Religion Groups

	1952	1954	1956	1958	1960	1962	1964	1966	1968	1970	1972	1974	1976	1978	1980	1982	1984	1986	
Protestants	20%	22%	19%	25%	18%	19%	26%	16%	19%	19%	13%	16%	14%	15%	18%	20%	16%	18%	Strong Dem
	24	25	22	22	23	23	25	26	24	23	24	21	23	21	22	21	19	22	Weak Dem
	8	7	5	5	5	6	7	8	9	9	9	11	10	12	10	10	9	9	Indep Dem
	5	7	8	7	9	8	7	12	9	11	13	13	15	13	12	11	9	11	Indep Ind
	7	6	9	6	8	7	6	8	9	9	11	10	9	11	11	8	13	11	Indep Rep
	16	15	15	19	15	18	16	17	17	17	16	16	18	15	15	17	18	16	Weak Rep
	16	15	18	13	19	14	13	12	12	11	13	10	11	10	10	12	14	12	Strong Rep
	4	3	4	4	3	5	1	1	2	1	1	3	1	3	2	1	2	2	Apolitical
Catholics	29%	24%	25%	31%	28%	34%	31%	25%	23%	22%	19%	24%	17%	17%	18%	22%	19%	20%	Strong Dem
	27	27	26	24	33	24	27	30	29	30	31	24	32	32	24	33	23	24	Weak Dem
	12	13	9	11	11	9	11	10	13	12	13	15	14	16	13	11	10	11	Indep Dem
	7	7	11	9	9	7	9	14	10	13	12	15	11	12	14	11	13	11	Indep Ind
	7	6	7	4	3	5	5	4	8	6	10	7	9	7	11	7	12	11	Indep Rep
	10	12	13	10	10	11	8	12	10	12	8	10	9	10	13	9	11	13	Weak Rep
	8	8	8	7	6	8	8	5	6	5	6	6	6	4	6	6	10	9	Strong Rep
	O	4	3	3	1	2	O	1	1	O	1	O	1	2	1	2	1	2	Apolitical
Jews	28%	21%*	25%	43%	21%	40%*	27%*	19%*	33%*	24%*	26%	28%	24%	21%	28%*	21%*	29%	26%*	Strong Dem
	40	32*	34	24	28	35*	27*	47*	19*	31*	25	33	31	30	46*	33*	31	13*	Weak Dem
	16	18*	16	13	19	16*	22*	16*	24*	24*	25	12	7	27	14*	4*	14	16*	Indep Dem
	9	6*	5	4	14	2*	13*	7*	17*	14*	10	12	13	9	2*	17*	8	i3*	Indep Ind
	7	6*	5	6	14	O*	2*	2*	2*	2*	3	5	17	6	8*	4*	10	10*	Indep Rep
	O	9*	9	9	5	5*	7*	7*	5*	2*	8	3	4	5	2*	13*	4	13*	Weak Rep
	O	6*	5	2	O	2*	2*	2*	O*	2*	2	7	3	2	O*	8*	6	10*	Strong Rep
	2	3*	O	O	O	O*	O*	O*	O*	O*	2	O	O	2	O*	O*	O	O*	Apolitical
Other and No Religion	13%	20%*	25%*	26%*	16%*	22%*	17%	20%*	12%	18%	12%	11%	7%	9%	10%	17%	11%	14%	Strong Dem
	23	17*	11*	21*	24*	24*	17	26*	31	15	20	15	20	23	20	20	17	21	Weak Dem
	22	13*	11*	13*	3*	19*	20	11*	9	19	23	26	22	23	17	20	23	15	Indep Dem
	10	13*	14*	8*	18*	14*	16	20*	24	25	19	28	23	21	22	12	16	16	Indep Ind
	5	3*	9*	O*	3*	3*	12	7*	9	6	11	3	13	9	8	10	12	11	Indep Rep
	10	10*	14*	18*	16*	11*	12	11*	14	12	8	11	8	8	14	11	9	13	Weak Rep
	8	10*	2*	11*	21*	5*	4	7*	3	3	4	2	3	4	6	4	9	5	Strong Rep
	8	13*	14*	3*	O*	3*	1	O*	O	2	3	5	4	3	4	6	4	6	Apolitical

Table 2.21
Religion Groups Having Party Identification, Sample size&

	1952	1954	1956	1958	1960	1962	1964	1966	1968	1970	1972	1974	1976	1978	1980	1982	1984	1986	
Protestants	1272	850	1282	1329	1337	945	1092	902	1098	1054	1843	1690	1844	1428	1013	916	1377	1397	Sample Size
Catholics	387	215	372	385	359	260	344	278	337	289	638	537	706	546	370	313	578	510	
Jews	58	34	56	54	58	43	45	43	42	42	61	60	68	67	50	24	52	31	
Other and No Religion	60	30	44	38	38	37	69	46	59	111	143	195	218	226	163	149	218	207	

&Party ID includes 7 political categories and apoliticals (see Table 2.1)

Table 2.22
Liberal - Conservative Self Placement

QUESTION: We hear a lot of talk these days about
liberals and conservatives. I'm going to show you
a seven-point scale& on which the political views
that people might hold are arranged from
extremely liberal to extremely conservative.
Where would you place yourself on this scale, or
haven't you thought much about this?

	1972	1974	1976	1978	1980	1982	1984	1986
Liberal 1	9%	13%	8%	10%	8%	7%	9%	7%
2	10	8	8	10	9	8	9	11
Neutral 3	27	26	25	27	20	22	23	28
4	15	12	12	14	14	13	14	15
Conservative 5	12	14	13	14	15	14	15	15
Don't know	28	27	33	27	36	36	30	25
Total	100%	100%	100%	100%	100%	100%	100%	100%
N	2155	2478	2839	2284	1565	1400	2229	2170
PDI#	-8	-5	-10	-8	-12	-13	-11	-12

\# PDI is proportion "pro liberal" (codes 1,2) minus proportion "pro conservative" (codes 4,5)

& Original 7-point scale is collapsed to a 5-point scale: two categories between most liberal (code 1 above)
  and neutral (3 above) were combined into a single category (2 above); similarly, two categories between most
  conservative (5 above) and neutral were combined into a single category (4 above).

Table 2.23
Liberal to Conservative Index

DESCRIPTION: The Liberal - Conservative thermometer index is
constructed from the Liberals and Conservatives thermometers.
The Liberals thermometer score is subtracted from the Conservatives
thermometer score.   Ninety-seven is added and the result is
divided by two and added to .5, so that zero becomes the most
liberal score and ninety-seven becomes the most conservative score,
and forty-nine is the midpoint representing equal evaluation.   The
result is then collapsed as follows: 0-25=1, 26-48=2, 49=3, 50-75=4, 76-97=5.

	1964	1966	1968	1970	1972	1974	1976	1978	1980	1982	1984	1986
Liberal 1	6%	4%	4%	5%	3%	3%	2%	**	3%	4%	3%	4%
2	19	18	20	17	18	21	16	**	17	14	24	22
Neutral 3	42	42	38	24	23	26	29	**	21	34	29	24
4	27	30	33	32	33	31	30	**	36	26	28	30
Conservative 5	6	7	6	9	7	7	6	**	9	7	5	7
Don't know&	**	**	**	13	16	12	17	**	15	15	10	13
Total	100%	100%	100%	100%	100%	100%	100%	**	100%	100%	100%	100%
N	1524	1262	1492	1482	2137	2403	2351	**	1398	1405	1923	2167
PDI#	-8	-14	-15	-20	-19	-14	-17	**	-26	-15	-6	-11

\# PDI is proportion "pro liberal" (codes 1,2) minus proportion "pro conservative" (codes 4,5).

& Don't know includes respondents without evaluation of either Liberals or Conservatives.
  In 1964, 1966, and 1968, Dont Know was coded as a score of 50 and as a result are included
  in Neutral rather than in a separate category.

Table 2.24
Party Identification of Liberal - Conservative Self Placement Groups&

	1972	1974	1976	1978	1980	1982	1984	1986	
Liberal Self Placement 1	34%	29%	29%	23%	36%	44%	39%	42%	Strong Democrat
	24	23	32	24	24	23	21	20	Weak Democrat
	23	20	19	28	25	18	17	18	Independent Democrat
	8	17	8	14	9	6	8	9	Independent Independent
	4	4	6	4	3	2	7	3	Independent Republican
	4	4	4	4	3	5	2	4	Weak Republican
	3	2	2	2	1	1	7	4	Strong Republican
	0	0	0	1	0	1	1	1	Apolitical
Liberal Self Placement 2	15%	25%	18%	18%	19%	29%	19%	22%	Strong Democrat
	25	29	31	30	30	27	28	31	Weak Democrat
	22	17	21	25	20	20	24	18	Independent Democrat
	12	9	11	10	9	9	6	4	Independent Independent
	12	6	9	9	7	9	6	10	Independent Republican
	11	9	8	6	11	5	12	10	Weak Republican
	4	5	2	1	4	2	6	4	Strong Republican
	0	2	0	1	0	0	0	1	Apolitical
Neutral Self Placement 3	13%	14%	13%	15%	17%	20%	16%	17%	Strong Democrat
	29	22	25	26	27	27	24	24	Weak Democrat
	11	17	13	17	14	15	13	12	Independent Democrat
	12	15	19	15	13	9	13	13	Independent Independent
	11	8	11	9	10	10	11	11	Independent Republican
	14	16	15	12	14	14	16	15	Weak Republican
	10	6	5	5	4	3	6	7	Strong Republican
	1	2	0	1	2	2	2	2	Apolitical
Conservative Self Placement 4	6%	12%	8%	7%	7%	9%	7%	7%	Strong Democrat
	21	17	18	21	19	19	17	19	Weak Democrat
	8	6	9	10	10	9	5	8	Independent Democrat
	12	13	8	11	12	10	8	12	Independent Independent
	18	12	16	17	15	14	22	15	Independent Republican
	22	25	24	24	26	22	26	27	Weak Republican
	13	16	17	9	12	18	16	13	Strong Republican
	0	0	0	1	1	0	0	0	Apolitical
Conservative Self Placement 5	7%	11%	8%	10%	10%	11%	11%	11%	Strong Democrat
	21	12	15	13	14	12	5	12	Weak Democrat
	6	9	5	5	7	6	5	5	Independent Democrat
	7	15	9	10	7	9	6	7	Independent Independent
	13	13	18	15	17	11	17	17	Independent Republican
	19	19	20	21	17	19	18	17	Weak Republican
	28	22	26	26	27	32	38	31	Strong Republican
	0	1	0	1	1	1	0	1	Apolitical

& For liberal-conservative self-placement description, see table 2.22

Party Identification

Table 2.25
Party Identification of Liberal - Conservative Self Placement Groups, Sample size&

	1972	1974	1976	1978	1980	1982	1984	1986	
Liberal Self Placement 1	188	315	231	217	118	100	197	153	Sample Size
Liberal Self Placement 2	212	198	229	224	136	104	200	232	
Neutral Self Placement 3	577	654	717	609	307	313	517	601	
Conservative Self Placement 4	321	302	353	309	211	177	312	328	
Conservative Self Placement 5	245	339	372	309	232	201	324	313	

& For liberal-conservative self-placement description, see table 2.22

Table 2.26
Party Identification of Liberal - Conservative Index Groups&

	1964	1966	1968	1970	1972	1974	1976	1978	1980	1982	1984	1986	
Liberal Index 1	51%	33%*	46%	49%	38%	42%	35%	**	56%*	57%	50%	42%	Strong Democrat
	19	17%*	24	29	30	25	30	**	28*	22	16	32	Weak Democrat
	13	21*	22	14	18	21	15	**	14*	16	26	18	Independent Democrat
	6	19*	5	4	7	8	10	**	3*	2	7	6	Independent Independent
	4	2*	0	0	3	0	0	**	0*	4	0	0	Independent Republican
	5	6*	2	3	4	5	4	**	0*	0	2	1	Weak Republican
	2	2*	2	1	0	0	6	**	0*	0	0	0	Strong Republican
	1	0*	0	0	0	0	0	**	0*	0	0	1	Apolitical
Liberal Index 2	37%	23%	31%	31%	22%	26%	19%	**	26%	31%	23%	25%	Strong Democrat
	25	32	24	30	25	24	32	**	30	30	29	25	Weak Democrat
	15	13	13	14	21	20	23	**	17	17	15	17	Independent Democrat
	6	12	10	11	12	13	14	**	10	6	7	8	Independent Independent
	3	5	3	4	8	3	6	**	6	7	9	9	Independent Republican
	9	9	14	6	8	9	5	**	7	7	11	10	Weak Republican
	5	5	4	4	5	4	2	**	2	2	5	5	Strong Republican
	0	0	1	0	0	1	0	**	1	1	0	1	Apolitical
Neutral Index 3	28%	17%	18%	17%	14%	16%	14%	**	15%	18%	14%	17%	Strong Democrat
	27	33	29	26	26	23	27	**	27	26	18	23	Weak Democrat
	8	8	10	14	11	12	12	**	14	14	12	12	Independent Democrat
	10	14	11	14	16	20	19	**	18	15	16	17	Independent Independent
	4	5	7	10	12	7	9	**	8	8	14	10	Independent Republican
	13	17	15	15	12	12	14	**	10	14	15	14	Weak Republican
	7	5	8	4	8	4	5	**	5	4	9	4	Strong Republican
	1	2	2	1	1	5	1	**	2	2	2	4	Apolitical
Conservative Index 4	16%	16%	16%	15%	8%	10%	11%	**	10%	12%	9%	12%	Strong Democrat
	23	23	24	19	24	18	18	**	19	19	17	21	Weak Democrat
	7	8	7	9	8	12	9	**	10	7	8	7	Independent Democrat
	6	10	11	13	10	14	12	**	11	9	8	10	Independent Independent
	9	10	13	8	13	14	14	**	15	12	17	15	Independent Republican
	18	19	16	22	19	19	20	**	22	23	21	19	Weak Republican
	19	13	13	13	16	12	17	**	11	18	21	15	Strong Republican
	1	1	1	0	1	1	0	**	2	1	1	1	Apolitical
Conservative Index 5	7%	7%	5%	11%	7%	7%	3%	**	7%	4%	7%	4%	Strong Democrat
	19	13	14	15	19	8	16	**	6	11	4	7	Weak Democrat
	3	2	6	2	7	7	5	**	6	7	1	3	Independent Democrat
	4	11	7	10	9	12	7	**	7	7	2	5	Independent Independent
	12	15	27	19	14	19	24	**	24	14	18	21	Independent Republican
	19	11	17	14	22	21	17	**	21	20	20	22	Weak Republican
	36	40	25	28	22	27	29	**	31	38	49	39	Strong Republican
	0	0	0	0	1	0	0	**	0	0	0	0	Apolitical

& For liberal-conservative index description, see table 2.23

Table 2.27
Party Identification of Liberal - Conservative Index Groups, Sample size&

	1964	1966	1968	1970	1972	1974	1976	1978	1980	1982	1984	1986	
Liberal Index 1	85	48	59	70	71	77	57	**	36	51	62	88	Sample Size
Liberal Index 2	291	227	295	248	378	492	387	**	230	203	462	478	
Neutral Index 3	634	522	564	354	491	631	684	**	297	470	554	512	
Conservative Index 4	406	371	484	477	704	736	695	**	508	358	546	648	
Conservative Index 5	93	82	88	136	142	173	128	**	121	104	101	156	

& For liberal-conservative index description, see table 2.23

Table 2.28
Liberal - Conservative Self Placement by Social Groups, Summarized by a Percentage Difference Index#

	1972	1974	1976	1978	1980	1982	1984	1986
1959 or later Cohort	**	**	**	7	-6	-14	-2	-3
1943 - 1958 Cohort	9	15	3	2	-8	-7	-8	-10
1927 - 1942 Cohort	-13	-19	-17	-15	-17	-17	-22	-17
1911 - 1926 Cohort	-17	-15	-20	-18	-15	-15	-10	-20
1895 - 1910 Cohort	-16	-12	-12	-11	-16	-15	-15	-15
Before 1895 Cohort	-8	-14	-14	-17*	-	-	-	-
Grade School	-6	-5	-7	-3	-7	-3	-3	2
High School	-12	-6	-9	-10	-13	-16	-11	-13
College	-2	-3	-11	-6	-13	-11	-13	-14
Central cities	6	7	-4	5	-1	-7	1	-4
Suburbs	-11	-8	-8	-11	-16	-16	-12	-15
Non-urban Areas	-13	-12	-15	-14	-16	-13	-17	-15
Income Percentile 0-16	0	3	0	-1	-4	-3	-2	-4
Income Percentile 17-33	-1	8	-2	-1	-9	-9	-6	-10
Income Percentile 34-67	-9	-3	-9	-10	-10	-7	-9	-13
Income Percentile 68-95	-13	-13	-13	-9	-21	-21	-18	-14
Income Percentile 95-100	-17	-48	-38	-27	-27	-35	-28	-26
Males	-9	-10	-10	-11	-16	-20	-14	-17
Females	-7	-2	-9	-6	-9	-7	-8	-8
Whites	-12	-8	-13	-11	-15	-14	-12	-15
Blacks	23	20	22	15	5	-1	4	6
Union Household	-5	-1	1	-4	-9	-10	-6	-11
Non-union Household	-9	-7	-13	-9	-13	-13	-12	-13
South	-11	-11	-12	-11	-15	-14	-12	-11
Non-south	-6	-2	-8	-6	-10	-11	-10	-12
Professional	-11	-5	-19	-8	-15	-16	-9	-11
White collar	-4	-6	-7	-2	-12	-10	-13	-15
Blue collar	-4	-4	-3	-7	-11	-14	-8	-13
Unskilled	3*	14*	-8	0	-11*	-5*	-8*	-7
Farmers	-21	-11	-15	-28*	-13*	-16*	-26	-12
Housewives	-17	-11	-18	-17	-13	-12	-15	-12
Protestants	-11	-10	-15	-15	-17	-17	-18	-18
Catholics	-7	-7	-8	-4	-7	-14	-6	-9
Jews	37*	30	46	21	24	33*	15	0*
Other and No Religion	14	31	10	19	-2	10	15	15
Total Population	-8	-5	-10	-8	-12	-13	-11	-12

PDI is proportion "pro liberal" minus proportion "pro conservative" per table 2.22

Party Identification

Table 2.29
Liberal - Conservative Self Placement by Political Groups, Summarized by a Percentage Difference Index#

	1972	1974	1976	1978	1980	1982	1984	1986
Strong Democrats	20	16	12	11	12	13	15	15
Weak Democrats	-3	7	4	3	-1	-2	6	1
Independent Democrats	22	15	13	22	12	8	21	11
Independent Independents	-5	-5	-4	-3	-10	-12	-7	-15
Independent Republicans	-25	-27	-32	-32	-36	-32	-35	-32
Weak Republicans	-29	-31	-32	-41	-34	-34	-34	-36
Strong Republicans	-41	-53	-59	-58	-62	-69	-54	-54
Liberal Index 1	66	74	59	**	80*	76	68	73
Liberal Index 2	49	54	41	**	38	39	21	25
Neutral Index 3	2	-1	-3	**	-3	-7	-7	-9
Conservative Index 4	-41	-42	-40	**	-33	-46	-42	-38
Conservative Index 5	-76	-79	-84	**	-84	-83	-84	-84
Total Population	-8	-5	-10	-8	-12	-13	-11	-12

PDI is proportion "pro liberal" minus proportion "pro conservative" per table 2.22

Table 2.30
Liberal - Conservative Index by Social Groups, Summarized by a Percentage Difference Index#

	1964	1966	1968	1970	1972	1974	1976	1978	1980	1982	1984	1986
1959 or later Cohort	**	**	**	**	**	**	**	**	-23	-14	-4	0
1943 - 1958 Cohort	-12*	0	-5	-11	-4	1	-2	**	-20	-11	-4	-10
1927 - 1942 Cohort	-2	-16	-12	-19	-20	-20	-23	**	-33	-19	-12	-17
1911 - 1926 Cohort	-9	-12	-17	-26	-31	-25	-28	**	-31	-18	-6	-17
1895 - 1910 Cohort	-14	-17	-19	-21	-26	-20	-20	**	-30	-15	-9	-21
Before 1895 Cohort	-11	-24	-20	-22	-17	-30	-29*	**	-	-	-	-
Grade School	3	-14	-7	-10	-14	-13	-6	**	-16	-3	1	-4
High School	-11	-14	-18	-24	-23	-19	-20	**	-27	-21	-5	-10
College	-13	-16	-15	-21	-15	-6	-16	**	-27	-12	-10	-15
								**				
Central cities	3	-3	-8	-5	0	1	-8	**	-9	-4	8	-5
Suburbs	-14	-14	-12	-29	-22	-18	-15	**	-31	-17	-11	-12
Non-urban Areas	-12	-23	-20	-24	-26	-22	-24	**	-34	-21	-10	-15
Income Percentile 0-16	-2	-15	-13	-4	-7	5	-3	**	-14	-6	6	-1
Income Percentile 17-33	0	-11	-13	-10	-13	3	-8	**	-29	-5	8	-9
Income Percentile 34-67	-4	-10	-12	-21	-23	-16	-13	**	-21	-13	-5	-13
Income Percentile 68-95	-16	-18	-20	-28	-22	-24	-27	**	-34	-25	-12	-15
Income Percentile 95-100	-20	-11	-9	-30	-28	-54	-38	**	-53	-35	-45	-19
Males	-9	-13	-14	-23	-20	-19	-18	**	-30	-19	-9	-16
Females	-8	-15	-15	-18	-18	-11	-15	**	-22	-12	-5	-7
Whites	-12	-16	-18	-27	-25	-19	-21	**	-31	-18	-9	-16
Blacks	23	2	13	36	34	30	30	**	9	12	13	14
Union Household	3	-6	-8	-14	-19	-13	-7	**	-22	-9	2	-5
Non-union Household	-12	-18	-17	-22	-19	-15	-19	**	-27	-17	-9	-13
South	-13	-22	-17	-19	-22	-16	-18	**	-29	-20	-7	-14
Non-south	-6	-11	-13	-21	-17	-14	-16	**	-25	-12	-6	-10
Professional	-18	**	-16	-25	-22	-9	-19	**	-31	-19	-9	-12
White collar	-8	**	-11	-18	-14	-13	-15	**	-31	-18	-4	-16
Blue collar	-1	**	-12	-14	-13	-15	-11	**	-28	-11	-1	-8
Unskilled	0*	**	0*	9*	-6*	5*	-14	**	-23*	-8*	14*	-5
Farmers	-15	**	-40	-8	-33	-35	-34	**	-25*	-19*	-30	-14
Housewives	-9	**	8	-29	-30	-22	-26	**	-17	-17	-16	-16
Protestants	-12	-20	-18	-25	-22	-20	-23	**	-32	-23	-11	-15
Catholics	-5	-6	-15	-23	-20	-19	-15	**	-19	-12	-3	-10
Jews	38*	21*	29*	34*	37*	33	24	**	23*	29*	24*	-23*
Other and No Religion	8	2*	11	16	13	31	18	**	-18	15	10	11
Total Population	-8	-14	-15	-20	-19	-14	-17	**	-26	-15	-6	-11

PDI is proportion "pro liberal" minus proportion "pro conservative" per table 2.23.

Table 2.31
Liberal - Conservative Index by Political Groups, Summarized by a Percentage Difference Index#

	1964	1966	1968	1970	1972	1974	1976	1978	1980	1982	1984	1986
Strong Democrats	20	2	13	8	14	18	4	**	9	16	26	19
Weak Democrats	-6	-5	-11	-5	-15	-2	0	**	-8	-2	14	0
Independent Democrats	16	9	7	-1	12	5	10	**	-7	6	20	19
Independent Independents	-6	-8	-17	-24	-13	-15	-10	**	-23	-17	-5	-12
Independent Republicans	-43	-41	-59	-47	-35	-59	-43	**	-61	-36	-28	-37
Weak Republicans	-31	-29	-22	-47	-45	-39	-41	**	-60	-45	-28	-35
Strong Republicans	-55	-58	-49	-66	-55	-61	-64	**	-72	-74	-55	-59
Liberal Self Placement 1	**	**	**	**	68	64	57	**	73	61	49	61
Liberal Self Placement 2	**	**	**	**	44	52	36	**	22	55	40	47
Neutral Self Placement 3	**	**	**	**	-28	-20	-18	**	-28	-12	4	-8
Conservative Self Placement 4	**	**	**	**	-65	-68	-54	**	-66	-54	-40	-46
Conservative Self Placement 5	**	**	**	**	-80	-78	-71	**	-71	-77	-64	-68
Total Population	-8	-14	-15	-20	-19	-14	-17	**	-26	-15	-6	-11

PDI is proportion "pro liberal" minus proportion "pro conservative" per table 2.23

Table 2.32
Party Preference by Social Groups, Summarized by a Percentage Difference Index#

	1952	1954	1956	1958	1960	1962	1964	1966	1968	1970	1972	1974	1976	1978	1980	1982	1984	1986
1959 or later Cohort	**	**	**	**	**	**	**	**	**	**	**	**	**	18	24	15	7	5
1943 - 1958 Cohort	**	**	**	**	**	**	40*	21	27	24	21	33	22	26	21	25	4	14
1927 - 1942 Cohort	32	23	18	32	23	23	36	29	25	22	16	13	14	22	8	25	15	16
1911 - 1926 Cohort	30	31	19	29	20	27	33	23	21	27	19	20	21	25	28	26	13	28
1895 - 1910 Cohort	21	18	5	20	10	14	31	15	21	15	17	15	20	21	22	17	1	5
Before 1895 Cohort	9	9	2	-2	3	-1	1	22	14	6	-10	15	-18	28*	-	-	-	-
Grade School	31	32	11	26	19	30	50	33	46	36	27	29	38	46	41	51	29	46
High School	23	25	19	28	25	22	33	27	26	25	21	26	23	30	23	29	13	18
College	-4	0	-1	7	-12	2	8	2	-4	2	5	9	1	7	8	11	-2	4
Central cities	30	21	26	38	28	29	44	41	35	33	32	40	33	41	43	35	32	33
Suburbs	13	25	-2	12	-1	20	18	7	11	20	12	15	16	16	12	18	0	7
Non-urban Areas	24	24	13	22	19	11	31	22	23	16	14	13	11	18	10	20	3	11
Income Percentile 0-16	28	33	15	17	9	13	41	26	39	36	27	28	35	35	36	48	30	36
Income Percentile 17-33	27	26	21	34	24	11	42	39	25	28	22	37	33	34	37	36	25	22
Income Percentile 34-67	28	24	17	31	21	26	41	22	21	25	23	28	24	27	18	28	8	15
Income Percentile 68-95	20	25	13	20	18	15	17	24	17	16	8	9	9	15	7	11	-5	0
Income Percentile 95-100	-31	-32	-22	-32	-44	-11	-4	-4	-11	-17	-18	-37	-45	-1	-21	-23	-33	-20
Males	25	29	20	24	17	25	31	22	18	22	13	18	18	22	15	16	4	9
Females	20	18	7	22	14	14	31	24	26	22	21	24	19	25	23	30	12	19
Whites	20	21	10	21	14	17	26	18	15	15	12	15	10	18	12	16	1	3
Blacks	46	37	37	37	30	48	74	61	89	81	65	77	80	74	73	87	68	79
Union Household	38	42	29	47	42	**	60	43	35	44	34	39	40	43	35	40	27	29
Non-union Household	17	15	6	15	6	**	22	15	18	15	12	16	12	17	14	19	4	11
South	53	47	41	45	38	30	51	36	41	33	29	33	34	34	30	33	23	27
Non-south	11	13	1	13	4	13	22	17	14	16	12	15	11	18	14	18	1	8
Professional	10	**	-2	10	0	**	6	**	0	0	2	21	2	10	4	5	0	5
White collar	18	**	14	29	8	**	25	**	13	19	19	23	17	23	14	14	-2	6
Blue collar	39	**	24	35	35	**	49	**	37	34	28	27	34	40	32	39	23	28
Unskilled	39	**	37	48	14*	**	75*	**	63*	75*	34*	19*	20	43	36*	42*	20	36
Farmers	20	**	17	14	-7	**	32	**	20	42	10	-18	10	21*	9*	9*	-14	14
Housewives	16	**	4	17	12	**	27	**	23	19	15	15	9	10	18	31	1	3
Protestants	13	18	5	15	3	8	24	14	15	14	7	13	9	12	14	15	0	10
Catholics	43	38	32	46	53	43	48	44	42	40	40	41	39	45	26	43	19	23
Jews	76	50¹	55	63	48	84*	65*	70*	69*	72*	62	58	39	66	78*	33*	54	23*
Other and No Religion	35	27*	23*	32*	3*	46*	28	33*	25	32	32	36	26	34	20	31	21	20
Total Population	23	23	13	23	15	19	31	23	22	22	18	21	19	24	20	23	8	15

Party Preference is proportion "Strong Democrat", "Weak Democrat", and "Independent Democrat" minus proportion "Strong Republican", "Weak Republican", and "Independent Republican" (see categories in table 2.1).

Party Identification

Table 2.33
Party Preference by Political Groups, Summarized by a Percentage Difference Index#

	1964	1966	1968	1970	1972	1974	1976	1978	1980	1982	1984	1986
Liberal Self Placement 1	**	**	**	**	70	62	67	65	80	77	60	69
Liberal Self Placement 2	**	**	**	**	34	52	51	57	47	61	47	47
Neutral Self Placement 3	**	**	**	**	18	23	21	31	29	35	19	20
Conservative Self Placement 4	**	**	**	**	-19	-18	-23	-13	-17	-17	-34	-21
Conservative Self Placement 5	**	**	**	**	-27	-22	-36	-35	-31	-33	-51	-37
Liberal Index 1	72	60*	88	87	79	82	69	**	97*	90	90	91
Liberal Index 2	61	49	47	61	47	56	60	**	60	62	42	42
Neutral Index 3	40	31	27	29	18	27	23	**	33	32	6	24
Conservative Index 4	1	4	6	0	-9	-4	-14	**	-9	-15	-25	-9
Conservative Index 5	38	-43	-45	-32	-25	-45	-47	**	-57	-51	-74	-68
Total Population	31	23	22	22	18	21	19	24	20	23	8	15

Party Preference is proportion "Strong Democrat", "Weak Democrat", and "Independent Democrat" minus
  proportion "Strong Republican", "Weak Republican", and "Independent Republican" (see categories in table 2.1).

Table 2.34
Party Identification Balance by Social Groups, Summarized by a Percentage Difference Index#

	1952	1954	1956	1958	1960	1962	1964	1966	1968	1970	1972	1974	1976	1978	1980	1982	1984	1986
1959 or later Cohort	**	**	**	**	**	**	**	**	**	**	**	**	**	8	14	10	6	8
1943 - 1958 Cohort	**	**	**	**	**	**	36*	22	20	19	18	23	17	17	19	21	6	13
1927 - 1942 Cohort	33	22	20	30	21	22	30	25	25	19	18	14	12	20	10	21	18	16
1911 - 1926 Cohort	29	28	20	29	19	26	30	18	19	24	18	13	22	23	28	25	16	27
1895 - 1910 Cohort	15	17	8	17	15	14	28	16	22	14	17	14	17	18	20	16	2	12
Before 1895 Cohort	8	4	4	-2	2	-3	.4	23	12	7	-10	20	-16	28*	-	-	-	-
Grade School	28	28	12	24	24	27	48	30	44	35	26	27	33	45	38	42	27	42
High School	20	22	22	27	22	21	28	25	24	21	20	21	21	23	24	25	14	17
College	-4	1	-1	6	-10	3	6	3	-2	-1	5	3	1	3	4	9	1	7
Central cities	24	19	26	36	26	28	36	35	32	27	28	31	31	33	39	31	30	30
Suburbs	13	24	2	10	0	18	16	6	13	15	11	8	10	13	11	15	3	9
Non-urban Areas	22	19	15	20	20	10	29	23	21	17	15	14	11	15	10	18	6	12
Income Percentile 0-16	26	29	15	16	11	11	39	24	39	31	25	22	30	30	31	42	30	31
Income Percentile 17-33	25	22	22	29	25	14	39	36	25	27	23	31	29	27	30	29	20	19
Income Percentile 34-67	27	24	21	30	21	25	35	20	20	22	22	23	19	19	19	25	9	16
Income Percentile 68-95	16	21	11	17	15	16	13	21	14	13	8	7	9	12	8	10	1	4
Income Percentile 95-100	-33	-30	-12	-25	-29	-15	-2	-1	-5	-19	-15	-39	-29	3	-16	-18	-23	-11
Males	21	25	20	21	15	23	26	21	17	19	14	12	16	19	15	13	6	12
Females	19	16	10	22	17	14	28	21	24	19	19	20	17	19	21	26	13	17
Whites	18	19	13	20	14	16	23	17	14	13	12	11	10	14	12	14	3	6
Blacks	40	37	32	34	28	46	67	52	83	73	60	63	66	61	67	76	60	69
Union Household	32	37	30	44	41	**	50	38	32	38	31	32	34	36	32	31	26	27
Non-union Household	16	14	9	13	7	**	20	14	18	13	12	11	11	13	13	17	6	12
South	50	44	44	44	37	31	51	35	42	34	30	29	32	29	27	34	24	26
Non-south	8	10	3	11	5	11	17	15	12	12	11	9	9	13	14	13	3	9
Professional	5	**	3	10	0	**	5	**	5	-5	2	14	5	9	4	5	-1	7
White collar	16	**	13	21	9	**	22	**	12	17	18	19	11	14	16	13	7	7
Blue collar	32	**	24	31	32	**	42	**	32	33	28	22	30	33	30	32	24	28
Unskilled	35	**	35	43	11*	**	75*	**	45*	71*	24*	22*	18	38	23*	32*	14	22
Farmers	22	**	20	18	-4	**	32	**	23	40	10	-16	10	28*	19*	5*	-11	14
Housewives	16	**	8	18	15	**	25	**	21	15	15	13	10	6	18	28	2	4
Protestants	12	17	9	15	7	9	22	14	15	14	9	11	8	11	15	13	4	12
Catholics	38	31	30	39	45	39	42	38	37	35	36	33	34	36	24	39	21	23
Jews	67	38*	45	56	43	67*	44*	56*	48*	50*	41	52	48	45	72*	33*	50	16*
Other and No Religion	18	17*	21*	19*	3*	30*	19	28*	26	19	20	13	17	20	11	22	11	16
Total Population	20	20	15	21	16	18	27	21	21	19	17	17	17	19	18	20	10	15

Party Identification Balance is proportion "Strong" and "Weak Democrat" minus proportion "Strong" and "Weak Republican"
  (see categories in table 2.1).

Table 2.35
Party Identification Balance by Political Groups, Summarized by a Percentage Difference Index#

	1964	1966	1968	1970	1972	1974	1976	1978	1980	1982	1984	1986
Liberal Self Placement 1	**	**	**	**	51	46	54	41	57	61	50	54
Liberal Self Placement 2	**	**	**	**	25	41	39	42	35	49	29	39
Neutral Self Placement 3	**	**	**	**	19	14	19	23	26	29	18	19
Conservative Self Placement 4	**	**	**	**	-9	-12	-16	-6	-12	-12	-17	-14
Conservative Self Placement 5	**	**	**	**	-20	-18	-23	-25	-21	-28	-40	-26
Liberal Index 1	62	42*	66	73	63	61	54	**	83*	78	65	73
Liberal Index 2	49	41	37	51	34	39	43	**	48	53	37	34
Neutral Index 3	36	28	24	24	20	22	21	**	27	26	8	22
Conservative Index 4	3	7	11	-1	-3	-3	-9	**	-4	-10	-16	-1
Conservative Index 5	-29	-31	-24	-15	-18	-34	-27	**	-39	-43	-57	-49
Total Population	27	21	21	19	17	17	17	19	18	20	10	15

Party Identification Balance is proportion "Strong" and "Weak Democrat" minus proportion "Strong" and "Weak Republican" (see categories in table 2.1).

Table 2.36
Partisan - Independent Balance by Social Groups, Summarized by a Percentage Difference Index#

	1952	1954	1956	1958	1960	1962	1964	1966	1968	1970	1972	1974	1976	1978	1980	1982	1984	1986
1959 or later Cohort	**	**	**	**	**	**	**	**	**	**	**	**	**	-25	-11	-5	0	2
1943 - 1958 Cohort	**	**	**	**	**	**	12*	3	-9	-1	-5	-6	-6	-6	-2	7	8	6
1927 - 1942 Cohort	20	6	10	18	17	12	22	7	14	11	5	7	4	7	15	19	23	23
1911 - 1926 Cohort	19	22	20	23	20	19	27	15	17	20	21	13	20	19	24	33	31	32
1895 - 1910 Cohort	30	29	26	31	27	37	38	23	32	23	27	28	27	32	35	31	38	36
Before 1895 Cohort	37	29	40	40	37	39	45	26	37	35	30	44	26	52*	-	-	-	-
Grade School	23	21	22	26	27	30	36	17	28	18	19	19	16	23	22	32	17	35
High School	28	27	21	24	21	18	26	9	14	13	7	5	5	1	5	15	13	8
College	33	23	31	34	27	28	29	21	15	19	11	6	9	10	16	15	20	19
Central cities	28	20	25	36	27	30	31	16	20	19	18	15	18	12	22	22	21	23
Suburbs	27	28	27	25	24	21	28	11	16	12	7	2	1	6	5	14	17	12
Non-urban Areas	25	24	20	23	22	23	29	16	17	15	9	10	8	3	10	15	14	12
Income Percentile 0-16	26	22	20	25	26	23	31	11	28	16	16	11	16	11	23	16	13	15
Income Percentile 17-33	26	21	25	24	22	29	31	17	16	14	12	14	16	7	9	23	19	18
Income Percentile 34-67	27	23	19	28	25	21	28	16	17	16	5	4	5	4	5	20	17	13
Income Percentile 68-95	28	24	26	27	21	28	26	15	12	15	15	6	2	3	13	13	18	14
Income Percentile 95-100	23	30	34	49	31	32	32	14	18	28	11	34	23	20	9	26	20	26
Males	28	27	24	32	23	25	30	17	18	16	9	7	5	2	10	15	16	15
Females	25	21	23	22	25	22	28	12	18	15	12	9	11	10	12	18	17	15
Whites	28	25	24	28	26	24	28	14	14	14	9	7	6	4	8	13	17	11
Blacks	15	15	9	19	2	20	44	14	51	32	27	26	27	29	37	47	22	35
Union Household	29	28	23	32	22	**	36	15	18	13	8	7	6	6	10	18	18	21
Non-union Household	26	23	23	25	25	**	27	14	18	16	12	8	9	7	12	17	17	13
South	27	27	23	25	21	18	34	15	18	14	11	6	12	10	17	23	14	16
Non-south	26	22	23	28	25	27	27	14	18	16	10	9	7	5	8	13	18	14
Professional	30	21	**	31	24	**	30	**	13	18	13	9	9	8	13	21	21	20
White collar	25	22	**	28	30	**	31	**	16	12	9	8	10	8	12	11	17	11
Blue collar	32	27	**	29	23	**	30	**	19	16	10	11	7	4	11	16	16	15
Unskilled	16	22	**	38	22*	**	61*	**	41*	42*	6*	8*	5	10	0*	11*	18	13
Farmers	33	31	**	32	28	**	32	**	27	31	28	34	16	14*	3*	30*	3	14
Housewives	25	24	**	19	21	**	25	**	17	13	10	4	9	11	11	20	16	11
Protestants	27	26	25	26	26	21	31	15	20	19	11	9	10	9	15	20	20	16
Catholics	29	21	19	27	25	33	31	15	17	13	12	15	11	7	9	16	15	17
Jews	17	18*	25	41	7	40*	16*	14*	17*	12*	16	23	15	12	26*	13*	27	23*
Other and No Religion	3	3*	0*	26*	18*	11*	4	7*	-8	-6	-6	-20	-16	-11	-9	3	-1	-3
Total Population	27	24	23	27	24	24	29	14	18	16	11	8	8	6	11	17	17	15

Partisan - Independent Balance is proportion "Strong Democrat" and "Strong Republican" minus proportion "Independent Independent" and "Apolitical" (see categories in table 2.1).

Table 2.37
Partisan - Independent Balance by Political Groups, Summarized by a Percentage Difference Index#

	1964	1966	1968	1970	1972	1974	1976	1978	1980	1982	1984	1986
Liberal Self Placement 1	**	**	**	**	29	14	23	11	29	38	38	36
Liberal Self Placement 2	**	**	**	**	7	19	8	8	14	22	19	20
Neutral Self Placement 3	**	**	**	**	10	3	-1	4	7	12	8	9
Conservative Self Placement 4	**	**	**	**	7	15	16	5	6	16	15	7
Conservative Self Placement 5	**	**	**	**	28	17	25	25	29	34	43	35
Liberal Index 1	46	17*	42	46	31	34	31	**	53*	55	44	35
Liberal Index 2	35	17	25	24	15	16	7	**	16	26	22	21
Neutral Index 3	24	6	13	6	6	-6	-1	**	1	5	4	-1
Conservative Index 4	28	18	17	16	14	8	15	**	9	20	21	16
Conservative Index 5	38	37	23	29	20	22	25	**	31	35	53	37
Total Population	29	14	18	16	11	8	8	6	11	17	17	15

Partisan - Independent Balance is proportion "Strong Democrat" and "Strong Republican"
minus proportion "Independent Independent" and "Apolitical" (see categories in table 2.1).

Table 2.38
Strength of Party Identification by Social Groups, Summarized by a Percentage Difference Index#

	1952	1954	1956	1958	1960	1962	1964	1966	1968	1970	1972	1974	1976	1978	1980	1982	1984	1986
1959 or later Cohort	**	**	**	**	**	**	**	**	**	**	**	**	**	14	39	54	53	60
1943 - 1958 Cohort	**	**	**	**	**	**	80*	64	34	54	43	44	47	45	54	68	69	65
1927 - 1942 Cohort	92	66	71	89	88	78	92	73	81	73	65	67	66	69	80	89	91	92
1911 - 1926 Cohort	92	95	93	99	93	93	103	87	88	94	94	78	91	86	95	109	102	110
1895 - 1910 Cohort	104	106	102	110	102	119	121	97	111	97	102	101	102	107	112	116	114	114
Before 1895 Cohort	113	108	120	124	122	122	132	106	123	121	112	130	110	144*	-	-	-	-
Grade School	97	96	95	101	103	107	118	91	109	90	93	89	90	95	93	108	83	112
High School	103	102	92	99	94	91	101	78	84	80	69	64	67	60	66	84	75	71
College	104	93	106	115	103	104	102	91	75	84	72	66	68	66	79	80	86	84
Central cities	101	90	99	115	97	105	107	85	85	89	84	77	86	75	89	91	86	92
Suburbs	103	105	102	100	103	93	101	75	87	78	66	59	58	65	65	79	79	76
Non-urban Areas	100	100	91	99	97	101	108	92	89	84	75	72	73	61	73	86	79	76
Income Percentile 0-16	100	96	93	101	108	101	110	84	107	87	86	71	85	75	88	84	69	81
Income Percentile 17-33	100	92	102	98	98	108	111	84	84	84	76	78	86	70	77	95	87	88
Income Percentile 34-67	104	99	89	106	100	93	106	89	85	83	67	63	64	62	64	89	80	78
Income Percentile 68-95	103	100	98	104	91	103	100	84	78	82	78	66	60	59	79	79	84	76
Income Percentile 95-100	87	101	112	133	105	114	105	80	86	102	78	99	89	80	66	99	86	92
Males	101	102	94	107	94	100	104	87	86	82	69	64	62	58	69	79	76	76
Females	101	95	97	100	103	97	107	83	89	85	78	72	78	73	79	89	84	83
Whites	103	101	97	106	103	99	104	85	82	81	71	67	68	63	70	80	81	75
Blacks	81	83	78	88	61	94	124	84	138	114	102	95	103	101	114	127	89	112
Union Household	106	105	94	109	93	**	113	89	87	82	68	64	65	68	69	84	81	87
Non-union Household	100	96	96	102	101	**	103	83	87	84	77	71	73	66	76	85	81	78
South	105	105	100	103	99	91	116	86	86	80	79	70	80	74	85	94	78	83
Non-south	99	95	94	104	98	103	101	84	88	85	72	68	67	62	69	80	82	78
Professional	102	**	96	108	95	**	103	**	77	83	77	73	68	64	76	87	90	85
White collar	98	**	94	107	108	**	110	**	82	78	72	65	70	65	77	73	80	78
Blue collar	107	**	93	104	95	**	104	**	89	85	72	69	71	64	74	86	78	80
Unskilled	84	**	98	123	86*	**	147*	**	115*	121*	58*	73*	59	38	44*	79*	79	77
Farmers	114	**	112	112	103	**	118	**	107	110	107	115	93	89*	72*	111*	59	81
Housewives	100	**	95	95	99	**	102	**	90	82	78	68	76	77	77	95	86	77
Protestants	103	102	99	104	101	96	110	85	91	89	77	71	75	71	80	89	87	83
Catholics	103	92	90	100	101	110	106	86	85	82	76	78	76	69	70	86	78	83
Jews	85	85*	98	118	60	121*	78*	88*	74*	71*	77	95	78	69	102*	88*	96	84*
Other and No Religion	58	60*	52*	103*	95*	73*	55	70*	51	41	39	20	22	33	42	55	45	50
Total Population	101	98	96	103	98	99	105	85	87	84	74	69	71	66	74	85	81	80

\# Strength of Party Identification is calculated by scoring "Strong Democrat" and "Strong Republican" as +2,
"Weak Democrat" and "Weak Republican" as +1, "Independent Democrat" and "Independent Republican" as 0,
and "Independent Independent" and "Apolitical" as -1 for each respondent (see categories in table 2.1).

Table 2.39
Strength of Party Identification by Political Groups, Summarized by a Percentage Difference Index#

	1964	1966	1968	1970	1972	1974	1976	1978	1980	1982	1984	1986
Liberal Self Placement 1	**	**	**	**	95	72	89	64	92	111	106	106
Liberal Self Placement 2	**	**	**	**	62	86	67	63	78	85	83	87
Neutral Self Placement 3	**	**	**	**	75	60	56	61	69	77	69	71
Conservative Self Placement 4	**	**	**	**	69	84	83	67	68	84	82	71
Conservative Self Placement 5	**	**	**	**	102	80	93	95	97	108	115	106
Liberal Index 1	122	75*	115	127	103	105	106	**	136*	133	111	110
Liberal Index 2	111	86	98	95	75	79	64	**	81	96	90	86
Neutral Index 3	100	77	83	68	66	50	59	**	59	66	59	57
Conservative Index 4	104	88	85	86	81	67	80	**	71	91	87	83
Conservative Index 5	118	109	83	97	89	84	89	**	94	107	133	108
Total Population	105	85	87	84	74	69	71	66	74	85	81	80

Strength of Party Identification is calculated by scoring "Strong Democrat" and "Strong Republican" as +2,
  "Weak Democrat" and "Weak Republican" as +1, "Independent Democrat" and "Independent Republican" as 0,
  and "Independent Independent" and "Apolitical" as -1 (see categories in table 2.1).

Table 2.40
Average Number of Favorable Responses About Political Actors per Respondent

	1952	1954	1956	1958	1960	1962	1964	1966	1968	1970	1972	1974	1976	1978	1980	1982	1984	1986
Democratic Candidate	1.1	**	0.9	**	1.4	**	1.8	**	1.3	**	0.7	**	1.3	**	1.1	**	1.1	**
Republican Candidate	1.7	**	2.0	**	1.5	**	0.8	**	1.5	**	1.4	**	1.2	**	1.0	**	1.5	**
Democratic Party	1.4	**	1.2	1.1	1.1	**	1.2	**	1.1	**	0.8	**	0.9	0.6	0.8	1.1	1.0	0.9
Republican Party	1.1	**	0.9	0.7	0.9	**	0.6	**	0.8	**	0.7	**	0.6	0.4	0.6	0.8	0.8	0.7

Table entries are the average for the total population

Table 2.41
Average Number of Unfavorable Responses About Political Actors per Respondent

	1952	1954	1956	1958	1960	1962	1964	1966	1968	1970	1972	1974	1976	1978	1980	1982	1984	1986
Democratic Candidate	0.7	**	0.9	**	1.0	**	0.8	**	1.3	**	1.4	**	1.1	**	1.6	**	1.1	**
Republican Candidate	0.8	**	0.8	**	0.6	**	1.6	**	1.1	**	0.9	**	1.1	**	1.3	**	1.5	**
Democratic Party	1.2	**	0.7	0.6	0.7	**	0.7	**	1.2	**	0.7	**	0.7	0.5	0.7	0.8	0.7	0.7
Republican Party	1.0	**	0.9	1.0	0.8	**	0.8	**	0.9	**	0.8	**	0.9	0.5	0.6	1.0	0.8	0.9

Table entries are the average for the total population

Table 2.42
Average Affect Toward Political Actors

DESCRIPTION: The affect of a political actor is the number of favorable responses about the political actor minus the number of unfavorable responses, for each respondent. The affect of both candidates is a directional score derived by subtracting the affect of the Republican candidate from the affect of the Democratic candidate, for each respondent. The affect of both parties is also a directional measure derived in a similar manner.

	1952	1954	1956	1958	1960	1962	1964	1966	1968	1970	1972	1974	1976	1978	1980	1982	1984	1986
Democratic Candidate	0.5	**	0.0	**	0.4	**	1.0	**	-0.1	**	-0.6	**	0.3	**	-0.4	**	0.0	**
Republican Candidate	1.0	**	1.2	**	0.9	**	-0.7	**	0.4	**	0.5	**	0.1	**	-0.2	**	0.0	**
Democratic Party	0.1	**	0.5	0.5	0.5	**	0.4	**	-0.2	**	0.1	**	0.2	0.1	0.2	0.3	0.3	0.2
Republican Party	0.1	**	0.1	-0.3	0.1	**	-0.2	**	0.0	**	-0.2	**	-0.3	0.0	0.0	-0.3	0.0	-0.1
Both Candidates	-0.5	**	-1.2	**	-0.4	**	1.7	**	-0.5	**	-1.2	**	0.2	**	-0.2	**	0.0	**
Both Parties	0.0	**	0.4	0.8	0.4	**	0.6	**	-0.1	**	0.2	**	0.5	0.2	0.2	0.6	0.3	0.4

Table entries are the average for the total population

Table 2.43
Average Salience of Political Actors

DESCRIPTION: The salience of a political actor is the total number of favorable and unfavorable responses to that actor, for each respondent. The salience of both candidates is the sum of the salience of the Democratic candidate and the Republican candidate, for each respondent. The salience of both parties is the sum of the salience of the Democratic party and the Republican party, for each respondent. The relative salience of candidates is the salience of the Democratic candidate minus the salience of the Republican candidate, for each respondent. The relative salience of parties is the salience of the Democratic party minus the salience of the Republican party, for each respondent.

	1952	1954	1956	1958	1960	1962	1964	1966	1968	1970	1972	1974	1976	1978	1980	1982	1984	1986
Democratic Candidate	1.8	**	1.8	**	2.4	**	2.6	**	2.6	**	2.1	**	2.4	**	2.7	**	2.2	**
Republican Candidate	2.5	**	2.7	**	2.1	**	2.4	**	2.6	**	2.3	**	2.3	**	2.3	**	3.0	**
Democratic Party	2.6	**	1.9	1.7	1.8	**	1.9	**	2.3	**	1.5	**	1.6	1.0	1.5	1.8	1.6	1.5
Republican Party	2.1	**	1.8	1.7	1.7	**	1.4	**	1.7	**	1.5	**	1.5	0.9	1.2	1.8	1.6	1.6
Both Candidates	4.3	**	4.6	**	4.5	**	5.0	**	5.2	**	4.4	**	4.7	**	5.0	**	5.2	**
Both Parties	4.7	**	3.8	3.4	3.4	**	3.3	**	4.0	**	3.0	**	3.2	1.9	2.7	3.6	3.2	3.1
Relative Salience of Candidates	-0.7	**	-0.9	**	0.2	**	0.2	**	0.0	**	-0.2	**	0.1	**	0.4	**	-0.8	**
Relative Salience of Parties	0.5	**	0.1	0.0	0.1	**	0.4	**	0.6	**	0.0	**	0.1	0.1	0.3	0.1	0.1	-0.1

Table entries are the average for the total population

Table 2.44
Average Number of Favorable Responses About Democratic Candidate per Respondent

	1952	1956	1960	1964	1968	1972	1976	1980	1984
Strong Democrats	1.9	1.8	2.3	2.6	2.5	1.4	2.0	2.1	2.4
Weak Democrats	1.2	1.1	1.7	2.0	1.3	0.8	1.6	1.3	1.4
Independent Democrats	1.7	1.4	2.1	2.1	1.4	1.2	1.7	1.5	1.7
Independent Independents	0.8	0.5	1.2	1.4	0.7	0.4	1.1	0.7	0.7
Independent Republicans	0.7	0.4	0.8	1.3	0.9	0.5	0.9	0.7	0.5
Weak Republicans	0.7	0.5	1.0	1.3	0.6	0.4	0.9	0.7	0.4
Strong Republicans	0.5	0.4	0.6	0.6	0.4	0.3	0.6	0.5	0.2
Total Population	1.1	0.9	1.4	1.8	1.3	0.7	1.3	1.1	1.1

Table entries are the average for the population group

Table 2.45
Average Number of Unfavorable Responses About Democratic Candidate per Respondent

	1952	1956	1960	1964	1968	1972	1976	1980	1984
Strong Democrats	0.3	0.5	0.4	0.3	0.6	0.8	0.5	0.9	0.5
Weak Democrats	0.4	0.7	0.8	0.6	1.2	1.2	0.8	1.2	0.7
Independent Democrats	0.5	0.9	0.6	0.7	1.3	0.9	1.0	1.5	0.8
Independent Independents	0.7	0.9	0.6	0.7	1.2	1.2	1.0	1.6	1.0
Independent Republicans	1.1	1.3	1.5	1.6	2.1	1.9	1.7	2.2	1.8
Weak Republicans	0.9	1.1	1.4	1.1	1.8	1.9	1.4	2.0	1.5
Strong Republicans	1.3	1.6	1.9	1.8	2.2	2.0	2.0	2.6	2.1
Total Population	0.7	0.9	1.0	0.8	1.3	1.4	1.1	1.6	1.1

Table entries are the average for the population group

Table 2.46
Average Affect Toward Democratic Candidate

DESCRIPTION: The affect toward the Democratic candidate is the
number of favorable responses about the candidate minus the number
of unfavorable responses about the candidate for each respondent.

	1952	1956	1960	1964	1968	1972	1976	1980	1984
Strong Democrats	1.6	1.3	1.9	2.3	1.9	0.5	1.6	1.2	2.0
Weak Democrats	0.7	0.5	0.8	1.4	0.2	-0.4	0.8	0.0	0.7
Independent Democrats	1.2	0.4	1.5	1.4	0.1	0.2	0.7	0.0	0.9
Independent Independents	0.1	-0.4	0.5	0.7	-0.5	-0.8	0.1	-0.8	-0.3
Independent Republicans	-0.4	-0.9	-0.7	-0.4	-1.2	-1.4	-0.7	-1.5	-1.3
Weak Republicans	-0.3	-0.6	-0.4	0.2	-1.2	-1.5	-0.4	-1.4	-1.1
Strong Republicans	-0.8	-1.2	-1.3	-1.3	-1.8	-1.8	-1.4	-2.1	-1.9
Total Population	0.5	0.0	0.4	1.0	-0.1	-0.6	0.3	-0.4	0.0

Table entries are the average for the population group

Table 2.47
Average Salience of Democratic Candidate

DESCRIPTION: The salience of the Democratic candidate is the total
number of favorable and unfavorable responses about the candidate
for each respondent.

	1952	1956	1960	1964	1968	1972	1976	1980	1984
Strong Democrats	2.2	2.3	2.7	2.9	3.1	2.2	2.5	2.9	2.9
Weak Democrats	1.6	1.8	2.5	2.6	2.5	2.0	2.4	2.5	2.1
Independent Democrats	2.2	2.3	2.7	2.8	2.7	2.1	2.7	3.0	2.5
Independent Independents	1.5	1.3	1.8	2.2	1.9	1.6	2.1	2.3	1.7
Independent Republicans	1.8	1.6	2.3	2.9	2.9	2.4	2.6	2.8	2.3
Weak Republicans	1.6	1.7	2.4	2.4	2.4	2.3	2.3	2.7	2.0
Strong Republicans	1.8	2.0	2.4	2.4	2.6	2.3	2.6	3.0	2.3
Total Population	1.8	1.8	2.4	2.6	2.6	2.1	2.4	2.7	2.2

Table entries are the average for the population group

Table 2.48
Average Number of Favorable Responses About Republican Candidate per Respondent

	1952	1956	1960	1964	1968	1972	1976	1980	1984
Strong Democrats	0.9	1.0	0.5	0.3	0.4	0.8	0.5	0.4	0.5
Weak Democrats	1.5	1.5	1.2	0.6	1.0	1.2	0.9	0.7	1.0
Independent Democrats	1.5	1.9	0.7	0.6	1.0	0.9	0.9	0.8	0.7
Independent Independents	2.1	2.0	1.3	0.6	1.5	1.3	1.1	0.9	1.3
Independent Republicans	2.7	3.0	2.6	1.6	2.6	2.0	1.9	1.7	2.3
Weak Republicans	2.4	2.7	2.3	1.2	2.4	1.9	1.6	1.6	2.3
Strong Republicans	2.8	3.2	2.9	2.3	3.3	2.5	2.3	2.2	2.8
Total Population	1.7	2.0	1.5	0.8	1.5	1.4	1.2	1.0	1.5

Table entries are the average for the population group

Table 2.49
Average Number of Unfavorable Responses About Republican Candidate per Respondent

	1952	1956	1960	1964	1968	1972	1976	1980	1984
Strong Democrats	1.3	1.5	1.2	2.0	1.7	1.5	1.7	1.8	2.6
Weak Democrats	0.8	0.9	0.9	1.6	1.2	1.0	1.2	1.3	1.8
Independent Democrats	1.2	1.3	1.0	2.0	1.6	1.5	1.5	1.7	2.4
Independent Independents	0.5	0.6	0.4	1.3	0.9	0.6	0.9	1.1	1.1
Independent Republicans	0.5	0.4	0.4	1.1	0.8	0.7	0.9	1.0	0.9
Weak Republicans	0.5	0.4	0.2	1.4	0.7	0.6	0.7	0.9	0.9
Strong Republicans	0.3	0.1	0.1	0.8	0.4	0.3	0.6	0.9	0.6
Total Population	0.8	0.8	0.6	1.6	1.1	0.9	1.1	1.3	1.5

Table entries are the average for the population group

Table 2.50
Average Affect Toward Republican Candidate

DESCRIPTION: The affect toward the Republican candidate is the
number of favorable responses about the candidate minus the number
of unfavorable responses about the candidate, for each respondent.

	1952	1956	1960	1964	1968	1972	1976	1980	1984
Strong Democrats	-0.4	-0.5	-0.7	-1.7	-1.3	-0.7	-1.2	-1.3	-2.1
Weak Democrats	0.6	0.6	0.3	-1.1	-0.1	0.2	-0.3	-0.6	-0.8
Independent Democrats	0.3	0.7	-0.3	-1.4	-0.5	-0.5	-0.7	-0.9	-1.7
Independent Independents	1.6	1.4	0.9	-0.7	0.6	0.7	0.2	-0.2	0.3
Independent Republicans	2.2	2.6	2.3	0.4	1.8	1.3	1.0	0.7	1.4
Weak Republicans	1.9	2.3	2.0	-0.2	1.7	1.3	0.9	0.6	1.4
Strong Republicans	2.5	3.0	2.7	1.6	3.0	2.2	1.7	1.4	2.2
Total Population	1.0	1.2	0.9	-0.7	0.4	0.5	0.1	-0.2	0.0

Table entries are the average for the population group

Table 2.51
Average Salience of Republican Candidate

DESCRIPTION: The salience of the Republican candidate is the total
number of favorable and unfavorable responses about the candidate,
for each respondent.

	1952	1956	1960	1964	1968	1972	1976	1980	1984
Strong Democrats	2.2	2.5	1.7	2.3	2.1	2.3	2.2	2.2	3.2
Weak Democrats	2.3	2.4	2.1	2.2	2.2	2.1	2.2	2.1	2.7
Independent Democrats	2.8	3.2	1.7	2.6	2.6	2.4	2.4	2.5	3.1
Independent Independents	2.7	2.5	1.7	1.9	2.4	1.9	2.0	2.0	2.4
Independent Republicans	3.2	3.4	3.0	2.7	3.4	2.6	2.8	2.7	3.2
Weak Republicans	2.8	3.1	2.5	2.6	3.2	2.6	2.3	2.5	3.2
Strong Republicans	3.1	3.3	3.0	3.1	3.7	2.8	3.0	3.1	3.3
Total Population	2.5	2.7	2.1	2.4	2.6	2.3	2.3	2.3	3.0

Table entries are the average for the population group

Table 2.52
Average Net Affect Toward Candidates

DESCRIPTION: The affect toward candidates is the sum of the
favorable responses to the Democratic candidate and the unfavorable
responses to the Republican candidate minus the sum of the
unfavorable responses to the Democratic candidate and the favorable
responses to the Republican candidate, for each respondent.

	1952	1956	1960	1964	1968	1972	1976	1980	1984
Strong Democrats	1.9	1.8	2.6	4.0	3.2	1.2	2.8	2.5	4.1
Weak Democrats	0.1	-0.1	0.5	2.4	0.3	-0.5	1.1	0.6	1.5
Independent Democrats	0.9	-0.2	1.8	2.8	0.7	0.8	1.4	1.0	2.6
Independent Independents	-1.5	-1.8	-0.3	1.4	-1.1	-1.5	0.0	-0.7	-0.6
Independent Republicans	-2.6	-3.5	-3.0	-0.8	-3.0	-2.8	-1.8	-2.2	-2.7
Weak Republicans	-2.2	-2.9	-2.4	0.4	-2.9	-2.8	-1.3	-2.0	-2.5
Strong Republicans	-3.3	-4.3	-4.0	-2.8	-4.7	-3.9	-3.1	-3.5	-4.1
Total Population	-0.5	-1.2	-0.4	1.7	-0.5	-1.2	0.2	-0.2	0.0

Table entries are the average for the population group

Table 2.53
Average Candidate Salience

DESCRIPTION: Candidate salience is the total number of favorable
and unfavorable responses to both the Democratic and Republican
candidates, for each respondent.

	1952	1956	1960	1964	1968	1972	1976	1980	1984
Strong Democrats	4.4	4.8	4.3	5.2	5.2	4.5	4.8	5.1	6.1
Weak Democrats	3.9	4.2	4.6	4.8	4.7	4.2	4.6	4.6	4.9
Independent Democrats	5.0	5.5	4.4	5.4	5.3	4.5	5.1	5.5	5.6
Independent Independents	4.1	3.9	3.5	4.1	4.3	3.5	4.1	4.3	4.1
Independent Republicans	4.9	5.0	5.3	5.6	6.3	5.1	5.4	5.5	5.5
Weak Republicans	4.4	4.7	4.9	5.1	5.6	4.8	4.6	5.2	5.2
Strong Republicans	4.9	5.3	5.4	5.5	6.2	5.1	5.6	6.1	5.6
Total Population	4.3	4.6	4.5	5.0	5.2	4.4	4.7	5.0	5.2

Table entries are the average for the population group

Evaluations of Party Candidates

Table 2.54
Average Relative Salience of Candidates

DESCRIPTION: Relative salience of candidates is the total number
of favorable and unfavorable responses to the Democratic candidate
minus the total number of favorable and unfavorable responses to
the Republican candidate, for each respondent.

	1952	1956	1960	1964	1968	1972	1976	1980	1984
Strong Democrats	0.1	-0.3	1.0	0.7	1.0	-0.1	0.3	0.8	-0.3
Weak Democrats	-0.7	-0.6	0.4	0.5	0.3	-0.1	0.2	0.4	-0.6
Independent Democrats	-0.6	-0.9	1.1	0.1	0.1	-0.3	0.3	0.5	-0.7
Independent Independents	-1.2	-1.2	0.1	0.2	-0.6	-0.3	0.1	0.3	-0.7
Independent Republicans	-1.4	-1.7	-0.8	0.2	-0.4	-0.2	-0.2	0.2	-1.0
Weak Republicans	-1.2	-1.4	-0.1	-0.2	-0.7	-0.3	0.0	0.2	-1.3
Strong Republicans	-1.2	-1.4	-0.5	-0.7	-1.1	-0.5	-0.4	-0.1	-1.0
Total Population	-0.7	-0.9	0.2	0.2	0.0	-0.2	0.1	0.4	-0.8

Table entries are the average for the population group

Table 2.55
Average Number of Favorable Responses About Democratic Party per Respondent

	1952	1954	1956	1958	1960	1962	1964	1966	1968	1970	1972	1974	1976	1978	1980	1982	1984	1986
Strong Democrats	2.3	**	2.3	2.0	2.1	**	2.1	**	2.1	**	1.7	**	1.7	1.3	1.7	2.0	2.0	1.9
Weak Democrats	1.6	**	1.6	1.3	1.5	**	1.2	**	1.2	**	1.0	**	1.2	0.7	1.1	1.4	1.2	1.1
Independent Democrats	1.8	**	1.7	1.4	1.5	**	1.3	**	1.3	**	1.1	**	1.0	0.6	0.9	1.2	1.2	1.2
Independent Independents	0.9	**	0.7	0.7	0.7	**	0.5	**	0.5	**	0.4	**	0.5	0.1	0.3	0.3	0.4	0.3
Independent Republicans	0.8	**	0.6	0.6	0.7	**	0.7	**	0.6	**	0.4	**	0.5	0.4	0.4	0.9	0.5	0.5
Weak Republicans	0.8	**	0.7	0.4	0.5	**	0.5	**	0.4	**	0.4	**	0.5	0.3	0.5	0.5	0.6	0.5
Strong Republicans	0.5	**	0.3	0.4	0.3	**	0.4	**	0.4	**	0.4	**	0.5	0.3	0.5	0.5	0.4	0.4
Total Population	1.4	**	1.2	1.1	1.1	**	1.2	**	1.1	**	0.8	**	0.9	0.6	0.8	1.1	1.0	0.9

Table entries are the average for the population group

Table 2.56
Average Number of Unfavorable Responses About Democratic Party per Respondent

	1952	1954	1956	1958	1960	1962	1964	1966	1968	1970	1972	1974	1976	1978	1980	1982	1984	1986
Strong Democrats	0.7	**	0.3	0.3	0.2	**	0.3	**	0.7	**	0.5	**	0.3	0.3	0.4	0.4	0.3	0.5
Weak Democrats	0.9	**	0.4	0.4	0.5	**	0.5	**	1.0	**	0.6	**	0.4	0.3	0.5	0.6	0.4	0.4
Independent Democrats	1.1	**	0.7	0.5	0.3	**	0.6	**	1.1	**	0.5	**	0.6	0.4	0.5	0.8	0.5	0.5
Independent Independents	1.3	**	0.5	0.5	0.3	**	0.6	**	1.2	**	0.6	**	0.6	0.2	0.4	0.5	0.3	0.4
Independent Republicans	2.1	**	1.1	0.9	1.1	**	1.4	**	2.1	**	1.0	**	1.2	0.7	1.0	1.4	1.0	1.1
Weak Republicans	1.6	**	1.1	0.7	1.1	**	1.0	**	1.6	**	0.9	**	0.9	0.7	1.0	0.9	0.9	0.7
Strong Republicans	2.3	**	1.5	1.5	1.3	**	1.8	**	2.2	**	1.3	**	1.8	1.2	1.5	1.8	1.5	1.5
Total Population	1.2	**	0.7	0.6	0.7	**	0.7	**	1.2	**	0.7	**	0.7	0.5	0.7	0.8	0.7	0.7

Table entries are the average for the population group

Table 2.57
Average Affect Toward Democratic Party

DESCRIPTION: The affect toward the Democratic party is the number of favorable responses about the party
minus the number of unfavorable responses about the party, for each respondent.

	1952	1954	1956	1958	1960	1962	1964	1966	1968	1970	1972	1974	1976	1978	1980	1982	1984	1986
Strong Democrats	1.6	**	1.9	1.7	1.9	**	1.7	**	1.4	**	1.2	**	1.4	1.0	1.2	1.5	1.7	1.5
Weak Democrats	0.7	**	1.1	0.9	1.0	**	0.8	**	0.2	**	0.4	**	0.7	0.5	0.6	0.8	0.8	0.6
Independent Democrats	0.7	**	1.0	0.9	1.3	**	0.7	**	0.2	**	0.6	**	0.4	0.2	0.4	0.4	0.7	0.7
Independent Independents	-0.4	**	0.2	0.2	0.4	**	-0.1	**	-0.6	**	-0.2	**	-0.1	-0.1	-0.1	-0.2	0.1	-0.1
Independent Republicans	-1.3	**	-0.5	-0.3	-0.5	**	-0.7	**	-1.5	**	-0.6	**	-0.7	-0.3	-0.6	-0.5	-0.5	-0.7
Weak Republicans	-0.9	**	-0.4	-0.3	-0.7	**	-0.5	**	-1.1	**	-0.5	**	-0.5	-0.4	-0.6	-0.4	-0.3	-0.2
Strong Republicans	-1.8	**	-1.2	-1.1	-1.1	**	-1.4	**	-1.7	**	-1.0	**	-1.4	-0.9	-1.0	-1.4	-1.1	-1.1
Total Population	0.1	**	0.5	0.5	0.5	**	0.4	**	-0.2	**	0.1	**	0.2	0.1	0.2	0.3	0.3	0.2

Table entries are the average for the population group

Table 2.58
Average Salience of Democratic Party

DESCRIPTION: The salience of the Democratic party is the total number of favorable and unfavorable responses about the party, for each respondent.

	1952	1954	1956	1958	1960	1962	1964	1966	1968	1970	1972	1974	1976	1978	1980	1982	1984	1986
Strong Democrats	3.0	**	2.6	2.3	2.3	**	2.4	**	2.8	**	2.2	**	2.1	1.6	2.1	2.4	2.3	2.4
Weak Democrats	2.5	**	2.0	1.7	1.9	**	1.7	**	2.2	**	1.5	**	1.6	1.0	1.5	1.9	1.6	1.5
Independent Democrats	2.9	**	2.4	1.9	1.8	**	1.8	**	2.4	**	1.6	**	1.6	1.0	1.4	2.0	1.6	1.7
Independent Independents	2.2	**	1.2	1.3	1.0	**	1.0	**	1.7	**	1.0	**	1.0	0.4	0.6	0.7	0.8	0.7
Independent Republicans	2.9	**	1.7	1.5	1.8	**	2.1	**	2.6	**	1.5	**	1.7	1.1	1.5	2.3	1.5	1.6
Weak Republicans	2.4	**	1.7	1.2	1.6	**	1.4	**	2.0	**	1.3	**	1.4	0.9	1.5	1.4	1.6	1.1
Strong Republicans	2.8	**	1.8	1.9	1.6	**	2.2	**	2.6	**	1.7	**	2.3	1.5	2.0	2.3	2.0	1.8
Total Population	2.6	**	1.9	1.7	1.8	**	1.9	**	2.3	**	1.5	**	1.6	1.0	1.5	1.8	1.6	1.5

Table entries are the average for the population group

Table 2.59
Average Number of Favorable Responses About Republican Party per Respondent

	1952	1954	1956	1958	1960	1962	1964	1966	1968	1970	1972	1974	1976	1978	1980	1982	1984	1986
Strong Democrats	0.3	**	0.3	0.4	0.3	**	0.2	**	0.3	**	0.3	**	0.2	0.2	0.2	0.4	0.3	0.4
Weak Democrats	0.6	**	0.5	0.4	0.5	**	0.3	**	0.5	**	0.4	**	0.4	0.2	0.3	0.4	0.4	0.4
Independent Democrats	0.8	**	0.7	0.5	0.3	**	0.4	**	0.5	**	0.4	**	0.3	0.3	0.3	0.6	0.3	0.4
Independent Independents	1.0	**	0.7	0.6	0.5	**	0.3	**	0.5	**	0.3	**	0.3	0.1	0.3	0.4	0.4	0.4
Independent Republicans	1.8	**	1.5	1.1	1.5	**	1.2	**	1.6	**	0.9	**	1.0	0.7	1.1	1.3	1.3	1.1
Weak Republicans	1.7	**	1.5	1.1	1.5	**	1.0	**	1.3	**	1.1	**	1.0	0.8	1.1	1.1	1.2	1.0
Strong Republicans	2.8	**	2.1	1.9	2.0	**	2.0	**	2.1	**	1.8	**	1.8	1.4	1.8	2.2	2.0	2.0
Total Population	1.1	**	0.9	0.7	0.9	**	0.6	**	0.8	**	0.7	**	0.6	0.4	0.6	0.8	0.8	0.7

Table entries are the average for the population group

Table 2.60
Average Number of Unfavorable Responses About Republican Party per Respondent

	1952	1954	1956	1958	1960	1962	1964	1966	1968	1970	1972	1974	1976	1978	1980	1982	1984	1986
Strong Democrats	1.8	**	1.7	1.6	1.5	**	1.3	**	1.5	**	1.4	**	1.5	0.9	1.2	1.8	1.5	1.7
Weak Democrats	1.0	**	1.0	1.0	0.9	**	0.8	**	0.8	**	0.9	**	1.0	0.5	0.7	1.2	0.9	1.0
Independent Democrats	1.5	**	1.3	1.3	0.9	**	0.8	**	1.1	**	1.1	**	1.1	0.5	0.7	1.5	1.2	1.1
Independent Independents	0.5	**	0.5	0.6	0.5	**	0.4	**	0.7	**	0.6	**	0.7	0.2	0.3	0.3	0.4	0.4
Independent Republicans	0.7	**	0.5	0.9	0.5	**	0.8	**	0.8	**	0.7	**	0.7	0.4	0.4	0.6	0.5	0.6
Weak Republicans	0.5	**	0.5	0.6	0.4	**	0.6	**	0.6	**	0.5	**	0.6	0.3	0.4	0.5	0.6	0.5
Strong Republicans	0.3	**	0.4	0.6	0.3	**	0.5	**	0.4	**	0.5	**	0.7	0.5	0.4	0.8	0.4	0.4
Total Population	1.0	**	0.9	1.0	0.8	**	0.8	**	0.9	**	0.8	**	0.9	0.5	0.6	1.0	0.8	0.9

Table entries are the average for the population group

Table 2.61
Average Affect Toward Republican Party

DESCRIPTION: The affect toward the Republican party is the number of favorable responses about the party minus the number of unfavorable responses about the party, for each respondent.

	1952	1954	1956	1958	1960	1962	1964	1966	1968	1970	1972	1974	1976	1978	1980	1982	1984	1986
Strong Democrats	-1.5	**	-1.3	-1.2	-1.2	**	-1.1	**	-1.1	**	-1.2	**	-1.3	-0.7	-0.9	-1.4	-1.2	-1.3
Weak Democrats	-0.3	**	-0.5	-0.6	-0.4	**	-0.4	**	-0.3	**	-0.5	**	-0.7	-0.2	-0.4	-0.7	-0.4	-0.6
Independent Democrats	-0.7	**	-0.6	-0.8	-0.6	**	-0.4	**	-0.6	**	-0.7	**	-0.7	-0.3	-0.4	-0.9	-0.9	-0.7
Independent Independents	0.5	**	0.2	-0.1	0.0	**	0.0	**	-0.2	**	-0.3	**	-0.4	0.0	0.0	0.1	0.0	0.0
Independent Republicans	1.1	**	1.0	0.2	1.0	**	0.5	**	0.9	**	0.2	**	0.3	0.2	0.7	0.7	0.8	0.4
Weak Republicans	1.2	**	1.0	0.5	1.1	**	0.5	**	0.7	**	0.5	**	0.4	0.4	0.7	0.6	0.6	0.5
Strong Republicans	2.4	**	1.7	1.3	1.7	**	1.4	**	1.8	**	1.3	**	1.1	1.0	1.4	1.4	1.6	1.6
Total Population	0.1	**	0.1	-0.3	0.1	**	-0.2	**	0.0	**	-0.2	**	-0.3	0.0	0.0	-0.3	0.0	-0.1

Table entries are the average for the population group

Table 2.62
Average Salience of Republican Party

DESCRIPTION: The salience of the Republican party is the total number of favorable and unfavorable responses
about the party, for each respondent.

	1952	1954	1956	1958	1960	1962	1964	1966	1968	1970	1972	1974	1976	1978	1980	1982	1984	1986
Strong Democrats	2.1	**	2.0	1.9	1.8	**	1.5	**	1.8	**	1.7	**	1.7	1.2	1.4	2.1	1.9	2.1
Weak Democrats	1.6	**	1.6	1.4	1.4	**	1.1	**	1.3	**	1.3	**	1.4	0.7	1.0	1.6	1.3	1.5
Independent Democrats	2.2	**	2.1	1.8	1.2	**	1.2	**	1.7	**	1.5	**	1.4	0.8	1.0	2.1	1.5	1.5
Independent Independents	1.5	**	1.1	1.2	1.1	**	0.7	**	1.2	**	0.9	**	1.0	0.3	0.6	0.6	0.7	0.7
Independent Republicans	2.6	**	2.0	2.0	2.1	**	2.0	**	2.4	**	1.6	**	1.7	1.1	1.6	1.9	1.7	1.7
Weak Republicans	2.2	**	2.0	1.7	1.9	**	1.6	**	2.0	**	1.6	**	1.6	1.1	1.6	1.6	1.7	1.5
Strong Republicans	3.1	**	2.5	2.6	2.3	**	2.5	**	2.5	**	2.3	**	2.5	1.9	2.2	3.0	2.3	2.4
Total Population	2.1	**	1.8	1.7	1.7	**	1.4	**	1.7	**	1.5	**	1.5	0.9	1.2	1.8	1.6	1.6

Table entries are the average for the population group

Table 2.63
Average Net Affect Toward Parties

DESCRIPTION: The affect toward parties is the sum of the favorable responses to the Democratic party and the unfavorable responses to the Republican party minus the sum of the unfavorable responses to the Democratic party and the favorable responses to the Republican party, for each respondent.

	1952	1954	1956	1958	1960	1962	1964	1966	1968	1970	1972	1974	1976	1978	1980	1982	1984	1986
Strong Democrats	3.1	**	3.2	2.9	3.1	**	2.8	**	2.6	**	2.4	**	2.8	1.6	2.2	3.0	2.9	2.8
Weak Democrats	1.1	**	1.7	1.5	1.4	**	1.2	**	0.5	**	0.9	**	1.4	0.7	1.0	1.5	1.2	1.2
Independent Democrats	1.4	**	1.6	1.6	1.9	**	1.2	**	0.8	**	1.3	**	1.2	0.4	0.8	1.3	1.6	1.4
Independent Independents	-0.9	**	0.0	0.3	0.4	**	-0.1	**	-0.4	**	0.1	**	0.3	-0.1	-0.1	-0.3	0.2	-0.1
Independent Republicans	-2.4	**	1.5	-0.5	-1.4	**	-1.2	**	-2.4	**	-0.9	**	-1.0	-0.6	-1.3	-1.3	-1.3	-1.1
Weak Republicans	-2.1	**	-1.3	-0.8	-1.7	**	-1.0	**	-1.9	**	-1.1	**	-0.8	-0.9	-1.3	-1.0	-0.9	-0.7
Strong Republicans	-4.2	**	-2.9	-2.3	-2.8	**	-2.8	**	-3.5	**	-2.3	**	-2.5	-1.9	-2.3	-2.7	-2.7	-2.7
Total Population	0.0	**	0.4	0.8	0.4	**	0.6	**	-0.1	**	0.2	**	0.5	0.2	0.2	0.6	0.3	0.4

Table entries are the average for the population group

Table 2.64
Average Party Salience

DESCRIPTION: Party salience is the total number of favorable and unfavorable responses to both the Democratic and Republican parties, for each respondent.

	1952	1954	1956	1958	1960	1962	1964	1966	1968	1970	1972	1974	1976	1978	1980	1982	1984	1986
Strong Democrats	5.1	**	4.6	4.2	4.1	**	3.9	**	4.6	**	3.9	**	3.8	2.7	3.5	4.6	4.2	4.5
Weak Democrats	4.1	**	3.6	3.1	3.4	**	2.8	**	3.5	**	2.9	**	3.0	1.7	2.5	3.5	2.9	3.0
Independent Democrats	5.2	**	4.4	3.7	3.0	**	3.1	**	4.1	**	3.0	**	3.0	1.9	2.3	4.1	3.1	3.2
Independent Independents	3.7	**	2.3	2.5	2.1	**	1.8	**	2.9	**	1.9	**	2.0	0.7	1.2	1.4	1.5	1.4
Independent Republicans	5.5	**	3.7	3.4	3.8	**	4.1	**	5.1	**	3.1	**	3.4	2.3	3.0	4.2	3.3	3.3
Weak Republicans	4.6	**	3.7	2.8	3.5	**	3.0	**	4.0	**	2.9	**	3.0	2.0	3.1	3.0	3.3	2.7
Strong Republicans	5.9	**	4.3	4.4	3.9	**	4.7	**	5.1	**	4.0	**	4.8	3.5	4.2	5.3	4.3	4.2
Total Population	4.7	**	3.8	3.4	3.4	**	3.3	**	4.0	**	3.0	**	3.2	1.9	2.7	3.6	3.2	3.1

Table entries are the average for the population group

Evaluations of Parties

Table 2.65
Average Relative Salience of Parties

DESCRIPTION: Relative salience of parties is the total number of favorable and unfavorable responses to the Democratic party minus the total number of favorable and unfavorable responses to the Republican party, for each respondent.

	1952	1954	1956	1958	1960	1962	1964	1966	1968	1970	1972	1974	1976	1978	1980	1982	1984	1986
Strong Democrats	0.9	**	0.6	0.4	0.5	**	0.9	**	1.0	**	0.5	**	0.4	0.4	0.7	0.3	0.5	0.5
Weak Democrats	0.9	**	0.4	0.3	0.5	**	0.6	**	0.9	**	0.2	**	0.3	0.2	0.5	0.3	0.3	0.0
Independent Democrats	0.7	**	0.3	0.1	0.6	**	0.6	**	0.8	**	0.1	**	0.2	0.2	0.4	-0.2	0.1	0.1
Independent Independents	0.7	**	0.1	0.1	-0.1	**	0.3	**	0.5	**	0.1	**	0.0	0.1	0.1	0.1	0.0	0.0
Independent Republicans	0.4	**	-0.3	-0.5	-0.3	**	0.1	**	0.2	**	-0.2	**	0.0	0.0	-0.1	0.3	-0.2	-0.1
Weak Republicans	0.2	**	-0.3	-0.5	-0.3	**	-0.1	**	0.0	**	-0.4	**	-0.3	-0.2	0.0	-0.2	-0.2	-0.4
Strong Republicans	-0.3	**	-0.6	-0.7	-0.7	**	-0.3	**	0.1	**	-0.6	**	-0.3	-0.4	-0.2	-0.7	-0.4	-0.5
Total Population	0.5	**	0.1	0.0	0.1	**	0.4	**	0.6	**	0.0	**	0.1	0.1	0.3	0.1	0.1	-0.1

Table entries are the average for the population group

Table 2.66
Average Feeling Thermometer for Democrats by Social Groups

	1964	1966	1968	1970	1972	1974	1976	1978	1980	1982
1959 or later Cohort	**	**	**	**	**	**	**	**	63.3	59.2
1943 - 1958 Cohort	69.0*	69.7	61.1	63.3	63.6	63.7	59.8	**	60.4	61.5
1927 - 1942 Cohort	71.4	68.0	63.8	67.2	64.5	64.2	60.7	**	62.1	64.9
1911 - 1926 Cohort	72.0	67.6	66.3	69.0	68.4	67.6	65.8	**	69.0	68.2
1895 - 1910 Cohort	71.5	69.0	68.3	69.9	69.3	69.6	68.3	**	67.7	68.9
Before 1895 Cohort	70.8	68.5	66.7	70.4	66.1	72.9	62.1	**	-	-
Grade School	76.1	71.8	72.4	72.9	71.4	71.6	71.2	**	73.0	76.6
High School	72.3	69.5	64.9	68.0	66.8	67.3	63.6	**	64.5	66.3
College	65.0	62.3	60.7	62.2	61.8	60.7	57.9	**	59.7	59.2
Central cities	73.1	73.2	68.1	70.0	68.2	67.4	65.0	**	68.7	66.2
Suburbs	69.3	65.0	62.2	66.3	62.8	64.1	61.0	**	60.1	62.1
Non-urban Areas	72.1	67.3	65.9	67.2	67.3	66.8	62.7	**	63.4	64.8
Income Percentile 0-16	75.4	70.2	72.3	73.5	71.2	68.1	70.7	**	70.7	71.7
Income Percentile 17-33	72.8	73.5	67.4	69.8	66.7	68.8	67.3	**	68.2	66.7
Income Percentile 34-67	75.2	68.1	64.4	68.0	66.4	67.3	62.1	**	62.7	63.9
Income Percentile 68-95	68.0	66.7	62.2	65.1	63.1	63.4	58.9	**	59.4	60.5
Income Percentile 95-100	59.9	64.2	56.3	63.0	59.3	53.9	53.3	**	54.2	55.1
Males	69.6	66.4	63.0	65.5	64.6	64.8	60.4	**	61.0	60.5
Females	73.1	69.9	67.2	69.4	67.3	66.8	64.3	**	65.5	67.1
Whites	69.6	67.0	63.2	66.0	64.8	64.9	60.9	**	61.4	62.4
Blacks	88.8	79.1	84.2	82.6	77.8	75.8	79.5	**	80.2	78.8
Union Household	77.7	72.5	65.9	70.7	67.7	68.1	63.9	**	64.0	65.9
Non-union Household	69.5	66.7	65.2	66.8	65.5	65.1	62.3	**	63.3	63.7
South	75.3	70.9	68.2	69.8	68.7	67.2	66.6	**	66.3	68.6
Non-south	69.8	67.2	64.0	66.6	64.8	65.3	60.8	**	62.0	61.7
Professional	63.2	**	59.1	62.2	62.0	63.6	56.7	**	58.7	59.9
White collar	70.0	**	64.4	65.6	64.9	63.6	61.7	**	62.2	62.4
Blue collar	76.3	**	66.8	70.4	68.8	68.9	65.9	**	66.8	67.3
Unskilled	87.8*	**	77.0*	76.0*	66.0*	67.2*	64.8	**	63.6*	62.7*
Farmers	71.5	**	70.0	71.4	67.2	67.4	68.8	**	60.9*	69.8*
Housewives	72.0	**	66.5	69.2	66.8	65.5	63.8	**	65.3	67.3
Protestants	71.4	66.3	64.9	67.9	65.4	65.7	63.0	**	64.0	64.8
Catholics	73.4	74.3	66.5	69.0	68.7	69.1	63.5	**	63.7	65.4
Jews	72.6*	70.4*	75.7*	69.3*	68.1	65.8	62.6	**	62.7	63.4*
Other and No Religion	62.8	67.2*	59.8	62.1	62.2	59.4	57.7	**	60.7	57.8
Total Population	71.5	68.3	65.3	67.7	66.1	66.0	62.7	**	63.6	64.2

Table entries are the average for the population group

Evaluations of Political Groups

Table 2.67
Average Feeling Thermometer for Democrats by Political Groups

	1964	1966	1968	1970	1972	1974	1976	1978	1980	1982
Strong Democrats	88.9	89.6	86.3	86.0	82.6	83.4	79.6	**	83.1	84.1
Weak Democrats	79.0	76.6	72.0	75.8	71.7	71.4	68.2	**	69.8	72.3
Independent Democrats	74.8	74.4	66.9	65.4	67.0	67.1	64.3	**	64.1	61.8
Independent Independents	58.8	60.1	54.3	57.6	61.1	58.7	57.5	**	55.4	52.5
Independent Republicans	54.0	52.5	52.3	59.4	60.6	55.7	55.2	**	53.3	52.8
Weak Republicans	58.1	54.0	53.0	56.0	57.6	58.7	55.2	**	53.1	52.4
Strong Republicans	46.1	44.2	46.4	50.3	53.8	52.2	49.1	**	50.8	45.4
Liberal Self Placement 1	**	**	**	**	72.0	70.3	69.0	**	73.2	70.2
Liberal Self Placement 2	**	**	**	**	66.5	66.0	62.3	**	64.1	66.3
Neutral Self Placement 3	**	**	**	**	66.9	66.3	62.6	**	63.7	64.6
Conservative Self Placement 4	**	**	**	**	61.0	61.1	56.6	**	57.3	57.0
Conservative Self Placement 5	**	**	**	**	58.3	58.2	55.5	**	54.3	56.8
Liberal Index 1	84.1	77.1*	77.9	82.7	74.7	76.5	69.8	**	81.1*	77.4
Liberal Index 2	78.1	73.7	70.1	73.2	69.4	66.8	66.3	**	68.2	68.1
Neutral Index 3	73.8	69.6	64.8	68.3	64.9	64.3	62.7	**	62.1	62.7
Conservative Index 4	66.6	66.7	65.4	64.6	64.0	64.6	60.1	**	61.7	60.5
Conservative Index 5	46.1	45.1	43.3	57.4	59.0	55.5	47.5	**	48.6	49.0
Total Population	71.5	68.3	65.3	67.7	66.1	66.0	62.7	**	63.6	64.2

Table entries are the average for the population group

Table 2.68
Average Feeling Thermometer for Republicans by Social Groups

	1964	1966	1968	1970	1972	1974	1976	1978	1980	1982
1959 or later Cohort	**	**	**	**	**	**	**	**	54.6	57.0
1943 - 1958 Cohort	55.1*	61.4	59.9	54.7	58.1	54.3	54.1	**	57.3	53.8
1927 - 1942 Cohort	57.4	64.8	61.3	57.8	61.6	56.0	56.5	**	60.0	54.9
1911 - 1926 Cohort	59.2	64.7	61.4	57.6	66.5	59.7	59.9	**	61.2	57.0
1895 - 1910 Cohort	60.7	66.6	64.3	63.0	67.7	62.1	61.1	**	62.4	59.3
Before 1895 Cohort	65.3	66.8	67.0	64.2	68.2	62.7	67.4	**	-	-
Grade School	55.3	62.4	58.1	57.0	63.9	58.7	56.7	**	56.3	50.1
High School	59.7	65.0	62.3	58.0	63.6	57.1	57.6	**	59.1	55.5
College	63.1	67.9	64.9	61.4	61.2	57.1	57.1	**	59.8	56.9
Central cities	56.1	61.5	59.0	54.7	57.4	53.0	56.1	**	55.2	53.1
Suburbs	61.1	67.4	62.4	60.2	62.6	57.6	56.0	**	60.6	56.3
Non-urban Areas	60.5	65.7	63.7	59.8	66.2	60.8	59.7	**	60.4	56.7
Income Percentile 0-16	55.3	61.9	60.2	55.6	61.8	57.7	57.6	**	59.3	51.8
Income Percentile 17-33	57.9	61.4	61.5	58.4	63.7	57.5	56.9	**	57.3	55.2
Income Percentile 34-67	57.9	65.4	62.5	57.8	62.9	56.7	57.1	**	58.8	55.3
Income Percentile 68-95	63.3	66.0	63.4	59.7	62.9	57.6	56.6	**	60.1	56.1
Income Percentile 95-100	61.3	70.3	61.1	65.6	66.1	60.7	61.7	**	64.8	61.5
Males	59.3	62.9	61.0	57.5	61.7	56.7	55.5	**	58.0	55.5
Females	59.5	66.7	63.1	59.3	63.9	57.9	58.7	**	59.9	55.6
Whites	61.8	66.2	63.6	60.4	64.3	58.3	58.4	**	60.3	57.1
Blacks	39.5	56.8	47.8	41.6	50.7	48.5	48.0	**	50.2	42.6
Union Household	55.0	62.6	59.2	52.7	60.8	53.5	53.6	**	56.2	51.2
Non-union Household	60.9	65.9	63.1	60.5	63.6	58.7	58.6	**	60.1	56.7
South	56.5	64.7	58.7	56.5	63.6	58.5	57.7	**	58.8	56.2
Non-south	60.8	65.2	63.7	59.6	62.6	56.9	57.2	**	59.2	55.2
Professional	64.2	**	63.8	60.6	62.2	57.3	56.8	**	59.6	57.6
White collar	61.7	**	62.4	60.5	62.3	57.2	58.7	**	60.7	56.5
Blue collar	54.5	**	59.3	54.9	61.2	56.2	55.2	**	57.4	53.5
Unskilled	46.0*	**	61.6*	42.9*	58.7*	54.0*	53.6	**	58.5*	53.8*
Farmers	53.7	**	61.2	59.2	68.8	67.9	61.1	**	58.9*	59.8*
Housewives	62.1	**	64.2	61.6	66.6	59.7	60.5	**	61.6	55.5
Protestants	60.8	66.4	63.0	60.1	64.0	58.8	59.0	**	60.7	57.7
Catholics	56.7	63.6	62.1	56.9	62.7	56.9	56.5	**	58.5	53.6
Jews	53.5*	54.9*	54.2*	51.5*	52.9	47.8	50.6	**	48.0	46.9*
Other and No Religion	54.6	56.9*	54.3	51.4	54.6	50.3	48.3	**	53.4	47.5
Total Population	59.4	65.0	62.1	58.5	62.9	57.4	57.4	**	59.1	55.6

Table entries are the average for the population group

Table 2.69
Average Feeling Thermometer for Republicans by Political Groups

	1964	1966	1968	1970	1972	1974	1976	1978	1980	1982
Strong Democrats	42.0	53.2	47.5	43.1	52.9	47.9	49.9	**	49.0	41.8
Weak Democrats	56.6	61.1	58.0	53.8	61.0	54.1	53.2	**	55.6	52.8
Independent Democrats	55.1	62.6	57.7	54.8	54.5	52.8	52.8	**	53.8	49.4
Independent Independents	58.6	61.0	60.1	54.6	60.9	55.6	54.2	**	55.0	53.2
Independent Republicans	68.5	71.3	72.8	67.3	66.7	63.5	61.4	**	67.6	64.1
Weak Republicans	76.2	75.8	72.1	73.4	71.5	66.9	64.1	**	66.9	66.7
Strong Republicans	86.9	84.7	85.9	82.8	76.4	76.0	74.8	**	78.0	79.3
Liberal Self Placement 1	**	**	**	**	49.0	48.0	46.0	**	45.0	45.3
Liberal Self Placement 2	**	**	**	**	56.9	52.2	52.4	**	56.0	48.4
Neutral Self Placement 3	**	**	**	**	64.7	59.1	57.9	**	58.0	54.6
Conservative Self Placement 4	**	**	**	**	66.4	60.5	60.2	**	62.4	60.4
Conservative Self Placement 5	**	**	**	**	68.8	63.2	65.6	**	68.6	66.8
Liberal Index 1	37.6	44.8*	42.4	41.2	33.8	35.0	38.6	**	30.5*	36.9
Liberal Index 2	56.0	63.2	56.6	51.0	55.1	53.4	50.4	**	52.2	50.6
Neutral Index 3	56.3	63.1	61.3	59.1	61.8	56.0	55.4	**	57.4	53.7
Conservative Index 4	67.4	69.2	67.6	62.7	68.6	61.8	62.4	**	62.9	62.2
Conservative Index 5	77.3	76.4	69.4	66.2	72.5	65.3	68.7	**	72.9	69.9
Total Population	59.4	65.0	62.1	58.5	62.9	57.4	57.4	**	59.1	55.6

Table entries are the average for the population group

Table 2.70
Average Feeling Thermometer for Democratic Party, by Social Groups

	1978	1980	1982	1984	1986
1959 or later Cohort	57.3	59.9	59.0	58.8	59.6
1943 - 1958 Cohort	60.2	57.8	61.5	59.6	61.3
1927 - 1942 Cohort	62.3	59.0	62.8	64.3	61.7
1911 - 1926 Cohort	64.7	65.6	67.1	65.1	68.7
1895 - 1910 Cohort	66.4	64.8	63.4	63.5	66.0
Before 1895 Cohort	68.2	70.3	53.9	78.5	**
Grade School	71.5	72.0	74.3	70.6	73.2
High School	64.1	62.1	64.9	62.6	63.9
College	57.0	55.8	58.4	59.0	59.1
Central Cities	65.7	66.0	66.0	66.7	66.6
Suburbs	59.8	58.0	61.0	60.8	60.2
Non-urban Areas	62.4	59.6	62.7	59.6	62.7
Income Percentile 0-16	68.7	70.3	71.2	70.9	69.9
Income Percentile 17-33	66.5	63.3	65.6	66.4	65.6
Income Percentile 34-67	61.3	60.1	63.8	60.6	62.4
Income Percentile 68-95	60.3	56.5	58.7	58.5	58.2
Income Percentile 96-100	56.1	47.3	51.1	55.1	53.7
Male	60.5	59.4	60.1	60.0	60.2
Female	63.7	61.7	65.3	63.2	64.5
Whites	60.9	58.5	60.9	59.8	60.1
Blacks	74.5	77.8	79.9	78.4	76.5
Union Household	65.7	62.7	66.3	64.3	65.1
Non-union Household	61.0	59.9	62.1	61.1	61.9
South	64.7	64.1	67.1	64.1	65.7
Non-south	61.0	58.9	60.7	60.7	60.9
Professional	58.0	56.2	58.1	59.4	58.8
White Collar	62.2	58.8	60.0	60.5	61.2
Blue Collar	65.7	64.5	67.0	65.5	65.7
Unskilled	67.8	65.5	68.6	64.4	67.4
Farmers	64.6	56.0	61.1	57.0	63.9
Housewives	60.9	61.0	65.8	59.3	62.4
Protestants	61.3	60.6	62.8	61.0	62.4
Catholics	65.5	62.4	65.1	63.8	64.0
Jews	65.3	63.9	60.5	68.7	59.4
Other and No Religion	59.1	56.3	59.6	59.9	60.3
Total Population	62.3	60.7	62.9	61.8	62.6

Table entries are the average for the population group

Table 2.71
Average Feeling Thermometer for Democratic Party, by Political Groups

	1978	1980	1982	1984	1986
Strong Democrats	82.5	84.3	84.9	84.9	83.2
Weak Democrats	71.6	69.7	72.1	71.0	72.6
Independent Democrats	64.1	61.4	64.6	66.9	67.2
Independent Independents	55.1	53.6	51.7	56.2	55.4
Independent Republicans	51.2	45.5	48.8	51.5	50.8
Weak Republicans	48.7	46.5	47.3	50.2	49.7
Strong Republicans	40.9	39.5	39.8	40.0	39.0
Liberal Self Placement 1	65.4	70.5	72.6	72.1	73.4
Liberal Self Placement 2	65.5	64.3	69.6	67.3	68.1
Neutral Self Placement 3	64.3	62.2	64.2	64.0	63.8
Conservative Self Placement 4	56.4	53.6	54.7	56.3	56.9
Conservative Self Placement 5	51.2	49.3	50.4	48.4	51.0
Liberal Index 1	**	74.6	77.5	74.9	76.4
Liberal Index 2	**	67.8	69.8	69.0	68.3
Neutral Index 3	**	61.2	63.0	60.4	63.6
Conservative Index 4	**	56.8	57.0	56.3	59.5
Conservative Index 5	**	39.6	43.7	35.9	38.3
Total Population	62.3	60.7	62.9	61.8	62.6

Table entries are the average for the population group

Table 2.72
Average Feeling Thermometer for Republican Party, by Social Groups

	1978	1980	1982	1984	1986
1959 or later Cohort	57.7	53.9	55.3	55.3	56.1
1943 - 1958 Cohort	53.6	55.3	52.7	57.2	57.1
1927 - 1942 Cohort	54.4	58.3	52.5	59.1	55.8
1911 - 1926 Cohort	56.4	57.6	53.9	58.1	56.4
1895 - 1910 Cohort	58.7	59.1	57.6	60.5	58.5
Before 1895 Cohort	61.6	61.0	60.3	79.8	**
Grade School	54.1	54.3	47.4	54.9	50.2
High School	54.7	57.3	53.8	57.8	56.1
College	56.0	56.8	54.9	58.2	58.1
Central Cities	50.3	51.9	51.5	51.4	51.8
Suburbs	56.4	57.9	54.8	59.1	59.8
Non-urban Areas	57.4	59.5	54.0	60.2	55.8
Income Percentile 0-16	55.0	55.9	48.2	54.0	51.4
Income Percentile 17-33	52.5	54.6	52.3	55.0	55.1
Income Percentile 34-67	54.5	56.1	53.6	58.1	56.3
Income Percentile 68-95	56.2	58.5	54.6	59.5	60.1
Income Percentile 96-100	56.2	61.3	60.7	66.4	63.7
Male	54.0	57.2	54.3	57.9	57.1
Female	56.0	56.4	53.0	57.5	56.0
Whites	56.4	57.7	55.5	59.5	58.6
Blacks	45.3	49.9	37.9	43.2	43.9
Union Household	51.8	54.7	49.8	52.2	54.1
Non-union Household	56.3	57.6	54.6	59.3	57.2
South	55.4	56.2	53.5	57.5	56.9
Non-south	55.0	57.1	53.7	57.8	56.3
Professional	56.8	57.1	56.4	57.8	58.2
White Collar	54.9	55.8	54.9	59.0	58.1
Blue Collar	52.9	57.1	50.7	55.5	54.1
Unskilled	52.0	55.2	53.0	53.4	57.3
Farmers	55.1	58.2	55.1	66.4	55.6
Housewives	57.5	58.1	53.5	60.4	58.1
Protestants	56.7	59.0	55.7	59.8	57.4
Catholics	53.9	56.0	51.9	57.5	56.8
Jews	45.2	43.6	42.4	45.8	50.7
Other and No Religion	50.8	51.2	46.5	48.0	51.5
Total Population	55.1	56.8	53.6	57.7	56.5

Table entries are the average for the population group

Table 2.73
Average Feeling Thermometer for Republican Party, by Political Groups

	1978	1980	1982	1984	1986
Strong Democrats	41.4	43.1	35.1	37.6	37.4
Weak Democrats	51.5	49.5	49.5	50.4	51.1
Independent Democrats	50.0	52.7	46.2	45.2	48.3
Independent Independents	53.5	56.7	53.3	57.1	55.3
Independent Republicans	60.9	64.7	65.8	68.0	66.1
Weak Republicans	66.4	68.3	67.8	70.6	70.2
Strong Republicans	77.5	81.3	81.2	82.4	81.5
Liberal Self Placement 1	43.8	40.9	39.8	41.0	40.8
Liberal Self Placement 2	50.7	52.0	44.1	50.6	50.3
Neutral Self Placement 3	55.7	57.4	53.2	56.6	56.4
Conservative Self Placement 4	58.9	61.4	60.0	65.8	62.6
Conservative Self Placement 5	64.8	64.3	66.8	69.8	67.2
Liberal Index 1	**	27.6	25.7	24.1	31.0
Liberal Index 2	**	49.5	46.4	51.8	50.5
Neutral Index 3	**	56.7	52.4	57.6	54.5
Conservative Index 4	**	61.1	62.3	65.2	63.6
Conservative Index 5	**	69.2	69.4	76.5	72.5
Total Population	55.1	56.8	53.6	57.7	56.5

Table entries are the average for the population group

Table 2.74
Average Feeling Thermometer for Political Parties in General, by Social Groups

	1980	1982	1984	1986
1959 or later Cohort	57.5	53.8	52.9	54.7
1943 - 1958 Cohort	53.0	54.4	52.4	55.6
1927 - 1942 Cohort	56.8	54.4	56.8	58.8
1911 - 1926 Cohort	56.3	60.1	58.0	59.8
1895 - 1910 Cohort	57.7	57.3	57.0	60.1
Before 1895 Cohort	57.0	60.0	65.0	**
Grade School	57.4	59.2	56.6	58.7
High School	55.1	56.3	55.3	57.0
College	55.4	55.0	53.8	56.5
Central Cities	54.4	56.8	56.2	57.2
Suburbs	55.7	54.9	55.1	57.3
Non-urban Areas	55.7	56.3	53.3	56.2
Income Percentile 0-16	56.2	57.5	57.3	57.1
Income Percentile 17-33	55.8	56.9	55.6	56.6
Income Percentile 34-67	54.8	56.1	53.9	56.8
Income Percentile 68-95	55.1	53.9	54.6	57.8
Income Percentile 96-100	54.3	55.7	55.6	57.6
Male	55.4	55.1	53.8	56.5
Female	55.3	56.6	55.5	57.3
Whites	54.8	55.3	54.5	56.4
Blacks	59.7	60.9	57.8	59.7
Union Household	55.5	55.1	54.5	57.4
Non-union Household	55.2	56.1	54.8	56.9
South	56.6	58.7	56.3	58.8
Non-south	54.7	54.4	54.0	55.9
Professional	55.1	56.1	53.5	56.5
White Collar	55.6	55.4	54.7	56.9
Blue Collar	55.0	55.4	56.2	56.6
Unskilled	54.7	56.0	55.7	56.1
Farmers	53.3	60.7	53.0	59.9
Housewives	55.8	56.3	54.4	59.2
Protestants	56.5	57.0	55.4	57.3
Catholics	56.3	55.8	56.2	58.6
Jews	50.9	52.7	53.3	49.4
Other and No Religion	49.4	49.0	47.3	51.9
Total Population	55.3	55.9	54.7	57.0

Table entries are the average for the population group

Table 2.75
Average Feeling Thermometer for Political Parties in General, by Political Groups

	1980	1982	1984	1986
Strong Democrats	63.2	62.6	60.7	59.7
Weak Democrats	55.6	56.4	54.5	57.7
Independent Democrats	52.2	50.9	49.9	53.3
Independent Independents	50.8	47.6	49.8	50.9
Independent Republicans	48.1	52.4	52.5	54.0
Weak Republicans	55.0	54.6	53.5	56.3
Strong Republicans	61.1	62.2	60.6	65.8
Liberal Self Placement 1	54.9	55.9	56.3	56.8
Liberal Self Placement 2	57.9	57.6	53.7	56.4
Neutral Self Placement 3	55.6	55.1	54.0	55.9
Conservative Self Placement 4	52.4	53.8	55.9	56.5
Conservative Self Placement 5	56.2	57.8	55.9	61.1
Liberal Index 1	59.2	59.4	51.4	55.3
Liberal Index 2	56.4	58.7	55.4	56.3
Neutral Index 3	53.1	53.7	53.3	55.5
Conservative Index 4	53.9	56.3	54.8	58.8
Conservative Index 5	57.5	53.9	57.2	58.2
Total Population	55.3	55.9	54.7	57.0

Table entries are the average for the population group

Table 2.76
Average Feeling Thermometer for Liberals by Social Groups

	1964	1966	1968	1970	1972	1974	1976	1978	1980	1982	1984	1986
1959 or later Cohort	**	**	**	**	**	**	**	**	54.9	48.6	57.6	57.1
1943 - 1958 Cohort	51.9*	56.2	53.6	46.3	56.8	57.6	54.9	**	53.4	48.0	56.9	54.6
1927 - 1942 Cohort	54.4	51.5	51.0	42.9	53.0	50.9	50.3	**	48.9	43.9	54.0	49.8
1911 - 1926 Cohort	53.3	48.6	50.6	41.9	51.8	51.8	50.8	**	50.4	43.4	55.0	50.6
1895 - 1910 Cohort	52.4	50.7	50.8	43.7	51.6	55.1	51.8	**	50.7	40.3	53.2	47.7
Before 1895 Cohort	52.5	47.0	51.0	40.5	55.6	51.0	51.2	**	-	-	-	-
Grade School	52.4	48.2	50.7	41.3	54.1	54.6	56.1	**	51.7	42.5	53.7	53.5
High School	53.9	50.3	49.6	42.1	53.7	54.0	51.5	**	52.1	43.6	56.1	53.3
College	53.2	52.8	54.0	47.2	53.7	54.1	52.2	**	51.2	47.9	56.0	53.0
Central cities	56.0	54.0	52.8	47.7	58.4	58.5	53.8	**	56.4	48.5	59.3	55.9
Suburbs	52.9	49.0	52.3	43.5	52.3	53.2	52.0	**	50.2	45.6	55.3	53.1
Non-urban Areas	51.8	48.7	49.2	40.2	52.1	51.3	51.4	**	49.6	43.4	54.3	51.2
Income Percentile 0-16	53.5	49.3	50.6	47.3	56.7	59.1	58.4	**	55.8	45.8	59.5	55.5
Income Percentile 17-33	53.1	51.3	51.5	45.2	55.8	59.3	53.5	**	53.9	45.9	57.5	55.8
Income Percentile 34-67	54.8	51.8	50.5	42.5	53.5	54.1	53.0	**	53.5	46.9	56.9	52.7
Income Percentile 68-95	52.6	49.5	51.2	41.7	51.9	51.3	50.3	**	48.2	46.8	54.9	52.2
Income Percentile 95-100	50.4	51.9	53.0	48.8	52.1	46.1	48.3	**	46.1	39.6	49.4	52.3
Males	52.5	50.9	50.4	41.5	52.5	52.6	51.2	**	50.3	43.1	53.7	51.0
Females	54.1	49.9	51.6	44.7	54.8	55.2	53.2	**	52.7	47.9	57.6	55.1
Whites	52.4	49.7	50.3	41.3	51.9	53.1	51.1	**	50.0	45.0	55.3	51.5
Blacks	61.5	57.0	57.7	60.3	70.7	64.6	64.8	**	66.1	51.8	61.0	64.7
Union Household	55.7	51.2	51.4	44.1	54.0	54.5	54.8	**	53.3	47.4	56.9	55.3
Non-union Household	52.6	50.0	51.0	43.2	53.7	54.0	51.6	**	51.0	45.2	55.6	52.6
South	51.9	48.3	50.4	40.7	53.4	52.7	52.7	**	50.5	44.2	55.5	52.9
Non-south	54.0	51.2	51.3	44.6	54.0	54.8	52.1	**	52.2	46.4	56.0	53.4
Professional	50.7	**	52.5	44.8	52.1	53.4	50.6	**	49.1	46.5	56.7	53.2
White collar	53.4	**	51.3	43.8	54.3	54.3	52.1	**	50.1	46.6	57.0	52.8
Blue collar	54.9	**	50.5	43.3	56.1	55.2	53.6	**	52.8	44.6	55.6	53.2
Unskilled	51.9*	**	54.4*	56.4*	57.2*	55.0*	56.1	**	58.6*	44.8*	56.1	57.5
Farmers	48.3	**	44.6	43.1	52.2	49.5	50.1	**	50.6*	38.0*	46.9	51.8
Housewives	54.5	**	50.7	40.7	51.3	52.2	50.8	**	52.7	45.2	54.6	53.2
Protestants	52.6	49.0	50.4	42.1	53.2	52.5	51.2	**	50.2	43.6	54.1	52.0
Catholics	53.8	52.3	51.5	41.3	53.4	55.0	53.1	**	53.0	47.0	58.8	54.5
Jews	67.2*	58.4*	62.2*	58.2*	64.0	65.7	58.4	**	63.7	58.3*	60.8	55.7*
Other and No Religion	55.6	56.8*	52.7	53.3	58.0	61.3	56.1	**	53.6	52.0	57.6	56.2
Total Population	53.4	50.4	51.1	43.3	53.8	54.1	52.3	**	51.6	45.7	55.8	53.2

Table entries are the average for the population group

Table 2.77
Average Feeling Thermometer for Liberals by Political Groups

	1964	1966	1968	1970	1972	1974	1976	1978	1980	1982	1984	1986
Strong Democrats	59.2	53.7	57.0	49.0	63.8	64.7	59.7	**	62.0	54.1	64.3	60.4
Weak Democrats	51.6	51.9	50.7	47.2	55.3	56.1	55.3	**	56.2	49.7	59.2	58.5
Independent Democrats	59.5	59.4	56.7	49.5	59.3	59.9	58.7	**	58.0	49.1	62.2	59.7
Independent Independents	51.4	49.8	50.8	38.1	54.5	53.7	52.9	**	50.7	45.0	56.5	54.0
Independent Republicans	49.1	45.3	44.2	38.3	49.6	43.6	45.5	**	44.4	42.1	52.8	46.6
Weak Republicans	49.1	49.0	47.8	38.4	46.4	48.1	46.9	**	43.1	39.3	50.8	47.8
Strong Republicans	46.7	39.2	45.3	33.3	46.1	42.9	42.2	**	38.5	30.5	43.8	38.4
Liberal Self Placement 1	**	**	**	**	76.1	72.8	70.1	**	74.7	68.7	69.9	73.5
Liberal Self Placement 2	**	**	**	**	65.3	63.9	61.0	**	62.3	62.7	63.8	64.4
Neutral Self Placement 3	**	**	**	**	53.0	54.3	52.5	**	53.9	47.3	57.9	55.0
Conservative Self Placement 4	**	**	**	**	45.4	45.7	47.8	**	45.6	38.5	52.3	48.0
Conservative Self Placement 5	**	**	**	**	37.3	38.0	37.3	**	34.7	32.0	42.8	35.3
Liberal Index 1	81.9	81.4*	82.5	83.8	86.6	87.3	82.3	**	86.1*	83.6	84.5	84.4
Liberal Index 2	70.2	67.0	67.1	63.1	70.2	71.2	69.8	**	70.0	65.1	68.5	69.5
Neutral Index 3	53.1	50.8	52.6	46.8	56.8	55.5	54.7	**	56.5	46.8	57.1	55.5
Conservative Index 4	44.9	43.4	42.8	33.7	47.1	47.1	44.7	**	46.3	39.3	47.8	44.9
Conservative Index 5	13.7	14.2	12.7	11.7	15.1	15.1	15.1	**	13.8	8.8	15.9	13.5
Total Population	53.4	50.4	51.1	43.3	53.8	54.1	52.3	**	51.6	45.7	55.8	53.2

Table entries are the average for the population group

Table 2.78
Average Feeling Thermometer for Conservatives by Social Groups

	1964	1966	1968	1970	1972	1974	1976	1978	1980	1982	1984	1986
1959 or later Cohort	**	**	**	**	**	**	**	**	62.7	53.9	59.4	57.1
1943 - 1958 Cohort	56.0*	52.9	55.8	52.4	57.8	56.9	54.9	**	61.2	52.8	59.9	58.8
1927 - 1942 Cohort	54.8	56.6	55.6	52.0	59.8	61.3	59.6	**	63.4	53.7	60.4	59.3
1911 - 1926 Cohort	57.3	55.3	57.2	53.2	64.7	63.5	61.8	**	63.4	53.3	58.9	57.8
1895 - 1910 Cohort	58.1	56.6	58.8	53.3	65.9	67.0	62.9	**	65.4	53.3	61.5	61.4
Before 1895 Cohort	58.5	56.0	58.8	56.2	64.7	68.6	67.0	**	-	-	-	-
Grade School	51.3	52.7	54.2	47.3	61.1	63.3	60.0	**	62.2	46.0	55.1	54.1
High School	57.6	56.2	55.9	52.9	62.3	62.0	59.3	**	61.7	54.5	58.9	58.0
College	60.4	58.9	60.6	57.6	60.1	59.2	57.9	**	63.4	53.0	61.3	59.4
Central cities	55.3	53.3	55.5	50.8	56.2	59.1	57.5	**	60.1	51.1	56.8	55.8
Suburbs	57.4	55.8	57.1	54.3	61.6	61.1	57.7	**	62.6	53.8	60.3	59.4
Non-urban Areas	57.3	57.9	57.6	53.3	64.2	63.1	61.2	**	64.2	54.3	61.1	59.4
Income Percentile 0-16	53.1	54.0	55.7	50.6	59.8	59.9	58.7	**	62.2	52.4	56.8	55.7
Income Percentile 17-33	54.4	55.3	55.5	50.6	61.5	59.9	56.5	**	63.3	49.5	57.3	58.9
Income Percentile 34-67	55.1	55.8	56.7	52.2	61.5	60.7	59.1	**	62.2	53.2	60.1	58.3
Income Percentile 68-95	60.2	56.3	58.1	54.2	61.4	61.3	58.9	**	62.4	55.2	61.4	59.8
Income Percentile 95-100	60.9	58.3	59.7	58.7	62.5	69.5	62.4	**	67.2	58.3	65.1	59.9
Males	57.4	55.9	57.5	53.0	60.8	61.0	58.2	**	62.3	53.7	59.4	58.2
Females	56.2	55.9	56.4	52.9	61.8	61.5	59.4	**	62.7	52.8	60.1	58.7
Whites	57.8	56.2	57.3	53.9	62.5	61.7	59.7	**	63.1	53.8	60.2	58.7
Blacks	47.6	53.2	53.2	43.8	51.2	56.1	49.5	**	58.0	46.5	56.4	56.6
Union Household	53.0	53.8	55.6	49.0	60.9	60.1	56.7	**	60.8	52.0	57.3	57.5
Non-union Household	57.9	56.7	57.4	54.2	61.5	61.6	59.5	**	63.1	53.4	60.5	58.8
South	57.3	57.7	57.9	53.4	63.0	62.2	60.7	**	64.7	56.0	60.9	60.7
Non-south	56.5	55.2	56.4	52.7	60.6	60.7	58.1	**	61.4	51.7	59.3	57.3
Professional	61.4	**	59.4	56.3	61.3	59.6	58.2	**	62.7	54.5	60.1	59.3
White collar	58.5	**	57.1	53.4	61.3	62.5	58.9	**	62.8	53.3	60.9	58.8
Blue collar	53.6	**	55.2	49.6	59.5	60.2	57.5	**	62.5	51.7	58.4	57.1
Unskilled	51.1*	**	57.9*	52.1*	56.3*	59.4*	61.1	**	62.6*	54.1*	53.5	61.5
Farmers	53.6	**	57.8	48.4	67.3	65.8	59.6	**	61.0*	53.2*	63.2	56.2
Housewives	57.0	**	56.7	54.5	64.4	64.5	61.9	**	62.9	54.3	62.2	61.0
Protestants	57.2	57.2	57.4	54.0	62.3	62.7	60.2	**	64.0	54.6	60.5	60.0
Catholics	56.1	54.3	57.2	52.1	62.0	62.1	58.8	**	61.5	52.8	61.4	58.8
Jews	53.3*	50.0*	49.4*	45.1*	47.5	54.3	52.0	**	53.8	44.2*	51.1	55.1*
Other and No Religion	54.4	48.3*	50.2	48.1	51.2	49.5	50.0	**	58.3	47.7	53.3	48.6
Total Population	56.8	55.9	56.9	52.9	61.4	61.3	58.9	**	62.5	53.2	59.8	58.5

Table entries are the average for the population group

Table 2.79
Average Feeling Thermometer for Conservatives by Political Groups

	1964	1966	1968	1970	1972	1974	1976	1978	1980	1982	1984	1986
Strong Democrats	51.2	50.6	52.4	44.9	55.6	58.5	55.2	**	57.8	46.4	53.7	51.9
Weak Democrats	54.6	54.1	54.3	50.1	60.4	57.5	55.4	**	57.9	50.9	55.6	55.9
Independent Democrats	53.4	53.7	53.7	49.5	55.6	57.7	54.7	**	58.6	47.9	53.0	52.1
Independent Independents	54.3	53.3	57.0	51.3	59.8	60.3	56.6	**	59.7	53.8	58.8	56.3
Independent Republicans	64.5	62.3	67.1	63.0	65.0	66.7	64.1	**	70.1	56.4	66.0	64.2
Weak Republicans	61.0	58.4	57.4	57.6	64.8	64.5	62.6	**	65.5	56.3	62.4	63.8
Strong Republicans	70.9	68.9	66.4	67.1	69.7	73.5	69.2	**	76.3	69.7	71.1	69.9
Liberal Self Placement 1	**	**	**	**	45.4	49.9	47.5	**	43.7	39.4	47.1	41.7
Liberal Self Placement 2	**	**	**	**	53.1	50.2	49.9	**	55.1	45.9	52.4	48.9
Neutral Self Placement 3	**	**	**	**	61.9	59.8	58.2	**	62.9	51.0	57.9	56.5
Conservative Self Placement 4	**	**	**	**	68.2	70.2	63.9	**	68.1	57.5	65.8	63.3
Conservative Self Placement 5	**	**	**	**	76.6	77.5	70.8	**	75.2	71.3	73.7	73.2
Liberal Index 1	20.1	18.4*	22.1	18.0	20.0	21.2	21.3	**	20.2*	18.7	21.5	19.1
Liberal Index 2	47.5	46.3	46.6	41.8	48.5	49.2	47.3	**	49.9	44.2	49.0	47.7
Neutral Index 3	53.1	50.8	52.6	46.8	56.8	55.5	54.7	**	56.5	46.8	57.1	55.5
Conservative Index 4	69.7	66.9	67.3	59.9	70.9	71.8	67.3	**	69.3	62.3	71.1	67.7
Conservative Index 5	87.4	87.7	85.1	83.5	85.2	86.7	84.8	**	86.4	83.5	86.5	83.9
Total Population	56.8	55.9	56.9	52.9	61.4	61.3	58.9	**	62.5	53.2	59.8	58.5

Table entries are the average for the population group

Table 2.80
Average Feeling Thermometer for George Wallace within Party Identification

	1968	1970	1972	1974	1976	1978	1980
Strong Democrats	24.0	27.5	42.7	52.4	43.9	41.0	34.6
Weak Democrats	35.0	31.9	48.5	52.4	43.6	45.4	39.0
Independent Democrats	32.1	31.9	43.6	49.2	41.3	40.3	35.8
Independent Independents	34.3	35.0	50.4	53.1	47.4	48.1	39.8
Independent Republicans	39.6	38.2	57.4	57.4	45.4	42.5	43.2
Weak Republicans	31.6	29.9	51.3	54.1	46.3	43.0	39.8
Strong Republicans	23.6	28.6	54.5	57.4	45.0	41.5	43.4
Total Population	31.1	31.2	49.3	53.2	44.6	43.4	38.9

Table entries are the average for the population group

Table 2.81
Average Feeling Thermometer for Hubert Humphrey within Party Identification

	1968	1970	1972	1974	1976
Strong Democrats	81.4	67.8	68.3	65.2	64.9
Weak Democrats	66.5	56.6	58.6	56.3	57.8
Independent Democrats	61.0	52.6	52.9	54.8	54.4
Independent Independents	54.9	44.5	50.0	50.4	50.6
Independent Republicans	46.7	33.9	43.5	42.1	44.2
Weak Republicans	50.3	40.8	46.0	46.2	44.3
Strong Republicans	43.6	30.0	41.9	44.1	41.5
Total Population	61.2	50.3	53.2	53.0	52.6

Table entries are the average for the population group

Table 2.82
Average Feeling Thermometer for Edward Kennedy within Party Identification

	1970	1972	1974	1976	1978	1980	1982	1984
Strong Democrats	69.8	74.3	71.5	76.1	79.0	61.8	70.6	74.1
Weak Democrats	58.7	62.5	60.2	65.6	69.3	54.4	59.2	67.0
Independent Democrats	55.9	64.3	57.3	59.9	67.8	50.7	54.7	62.7
Independent Independents	41.6	54.6	48.9	55.6	61.9	45.0	44.6	56.0
Independent Republicans	30.7	42.0	37.2	44.8	48.1	38.0	32.2	48.1
Weak Republicans	38.2	40.8	40.0	43.0	49.3	36.5	37.9	46.4
Strong Republicans	22.6	32.7	35.1	33.1	35.5	32.5	24.8	34.4
Total Population	49.7	55.2	53.1	56.8	62.1	47.7	50.6	57.0

Table entries are the average for the population group

Evaluations of Political Figures

Table 2.83
Average Feeling Thermometer for Edmund Muskie within Party Identification

	1968	1970	1972
Strong Democrats	73.8	66.6	58.2
Weak Democrats	61.6	61.8	53.4
Independent Democrats	64.5	61.4	53.9
Independent Independents	56.9	53.1	46.9
Independent Republicans	53.0	45.6	44.0
Weak Republicans	55.0	52.0	46.2
Strong Republicans	51.8	40.5	40.5
Total Population	61.1	56.9	49.9

Table entries are the average for the population group

Table 2.84
Average Feeling Thermometer for Richard Nixon within Party Identification

	1968	1970	1972	1974	1976	1978	1980	1982	1984
Strong Democrats	55.0	38.4	47.0	24.1	18.8	19.6	23.1	25.0	28.6
Weak Democrats	60.6	53.5	60.7	33.8	26.4	29.6	27.1	32.2	34.0
Independent Democrats	60.4	47.3	54.1	26.4	22.1	27.6	30.1	29.8	34.0
Independent Independents	64.3	57.7	65.3	38.3	34.0	35.8	36.7	41.9	44.6
Independent Republicans	77.3	74.4	76.2	46.5	39.2	43.4	47.7	42.8	46.9
Weak Republicans	77.2	76.3	80.5	45.3	40.0	47.1	46.2	44.3	45.0
Strong Republicans	84.2	85.9	86.8	60.0	48.5	53.4	56.8	59.6	52.1
Total Population	66.2	58.6	65.6	36.7	31.1	34.3	35.6	36.9	39.8

Table entries are the average for the population group

Table 2.85
Average Feeling Thermometer for Ronald Reagan within Party Identification

	1968	1970	1972	1974	1976	1978	1980	1982	1984	1986
Strong Democrats	41.1	40.7	**	**	46.5	45.6	40.6	31.3	36.2	42.0
Weak Democrats	46.6	46.4	**	**	51.0	54.2	49.5	48.2	51.2	57.9
Independent Democrats	42.5	46.8	**	**	49.0	49.8	48.0	44.1	43.2	49.9
Independent Independents	47.8	51.1	**	**	57.6	56.9	55.7	60.6	64.5	64.5
Independent Republicans	61.9	62.5	**	**	63.4	66.5	68.7	72.9	76.4	76.1
Weak Republicans	53.3	61.5	**	**	65.1	66.9	68.3	74.3	77.6	76.1
Strong Republicans	60.2	71.3	**	**	72.2	75.1	78.8	84.5	86.9	86.0
Total Population	49.1	51.9	**	**	56.4	57.4	56.0	55.1	60.9	62.7

Table entries are the average for the population group

Table 2.86
Average Feeling Thermometer for Nelson Rockefeller within Party Identification

	1968	1970	1972	1974	1976
Strong Democrats	54.6	**	**	48.8	41.2
Weak Democrats	51.7	**	**	51.4	44.4
Independent Democrats	55.4	**	**	49.2	41.8
Independent Independents	50.0	**	**	50.2	44.5
Independent Republicans	53.1	**	**	56.5	47.8
Weak Republicans	57.7	**	**	60.1	51.0
Strong Republicans	54.0	**	**	65.5	56.8
Total Population	53.7	**	**	53.3	46.1

Table entries are the average for the population group

Table 2.87
Average Feeling Thermometer for Spiro Agnew within Party Identification

	1968	1970	1972
Strong Democrats	43.5	31.6	40.2
Weak Democrats	48.5	41.8	49.5
Independent Democrats	45.0	38.5	44.5
Independent Independents	48.9	45.9	50.3
Independent Republicans	57.6	60.6	63.9
Weak Republicans	55.2	55.4	64.7
Strong Republicans	61.6	67.5	76.7
Total Population	50.4	46.0	54.3

Table entries are the average for the population group

Table 2.88
Average Feeling Thermometer for Gerald Ford within Party Identification

	1974	1976	1978	1980	1982	1984
Strong Democrats	54.2	43.2	50.8	47.7	**	49.0
Weak Democrats	58.2	56.0	59.8	55.8	**	56.6
Independent Democrats	57.4	51.7	58.8	56.0	**	51.9
Independent Independents	61.0	63.2	59.8	58.2	**	58.3
Independent Republicans	67.9	70.2	67.8	65.5	**	60.6
Weak Republicans	70.1	71.5	69.1	68.5	**	63.2
Strong Republicans	77.1	80.8	72.1	71.9	**	67.4
Total Population	62.0	60.5	61.3	59.0	**	57.9

Table entries are the average for the population group

Table 2.89
Average Feeling Thermometer for George Bush within Party Identification

	1980	1982	1984	1986
Strong Democrats	47.9	51.5	40.4	44.1
Weak Democrats	52.5	55.1	49.1	54.5
Independent Democrats	53.0	51.3	46.1	47.7
Independent Independents	55.7	56.7	56.9	56.3
Independent Republicans	58.1	60.9	64.3	62.8
Weak Republicans	57.7	61.3	64.0	63.3
Strong Republicans	68.4	68.9	73.1	70.6
Total Population	54.9	56.9	55.3	56.0

Table entries are the average for the population group

Table 2.90
Average Feeling Thermometer for Democratic Presidential Candidate within Party Identification

	1968	1972	1976	1980	1984
Strong Democrats	81.4	68.3	81.7	77.2	80.0
Weak Democrats	66.5	54.7	70.9	64.2	65.8
Independent Democrats	61.0	59.4	68.6	61.8	66.8
Independent Independents	54.9	47.2	59.7	50.7	54.3
Independent Republicans	46.7	36.4	47.9	41.0	44.8
Weak Republicans	50.3	36.7	53.2	43.5	44.6
Strong Republicans	43.6	25.4	38.2	34.7	34.0
Total Population	61.2	48.9	62.8	56.3	57.3

Table entries are the average for the population group

Table 2.91
Average Feeling Thermometer for Democratic Vice Presidential Candidate within Party Identification

	1968	1972	1976	1980	1984
Strong Democrats	73.8	66.1	66.9	67.8	75.7
Weak Democrats	61.6	55.6	57.2	57.8	63.9
Independent Democrats	64.5	56.6	55.4	54.8	65.4
Independent Independents	56.9	44.8	51.9	50.7	55.3
Independent Republicans	53.0	40.4	45.9	44.4	47.7
Weak Republicans	55.0	42.0	47.5	48.5	48.2
Strong Republicans	51.8	34.2	38.4	43.2	36.5
Total Population	61.1	50.1	53.4	54.2	57.2

Table entries are the average for the population group

Table 2.92
Average Feeling Thermometer for Republican Presidential Candidate within Party Identification

	1968	1972	1976	1980	1984
Strong Democrats	55.0	47.0	43.2	40.6	36.2
Weak Democrats	60.6	60.7	56.0	49.5	51.2
Independent Democrats	60.4	54.1	51.7	48.0	43.2
Independent Independents	64.3	65.3	63.2	55.7	64.5
Independent Republicans	77.3	76.2	70.2	68.7	76.4
Weak Republicans	77.2	80.5	71.5	68.3	77.6
Strong Republicans	84.2	86.8	80.8	78.8	86.9
Total Population	66.2	65.6	60.5	56.0	60.9

Table entries are the average for the population group

Table 2.93
Average Feeling Thermometer for Republican Vice Presidential Candidate within Party Identification

	1968	1972	1976	1980	1984
Strong Democrats	43.5	40.2	40.7	47.9	40.4
Weak Democrats	48.5	49.5	45.8	52.5	49.1
Independent Democrats	45.0	44.5	44.6	53.0	46.1
Independent Independents	48.9	50.3	54.4	55.7	56.9
Independent Republicans	57.6	63.9	57.2	58.1	64.3
Weak Republicans	55.2	64.7	57.9	57.7	64.0
Strong Republicans	61.6	76.7	65.7	68.4	73.1
Total Population	50.4	54.3	51.2	55.0	55.4

Table entries are the average for the population group

Table 2.94
Average of Democratic Leader Thermometers within Party Identification

	1968	1972	1976	1980	1984
Strong Democrats	77.7	67.7	74.6	72.5	78.0
Weak Democrats	64.3	55.1	64.3	61.4	64.8
Independent Democrats	63.1	58.6	62.9	58.4	66.1
Independent Independents	56.4	45.8	56.5	50.3	54.7
Independent Republicans	50.0	37.9	47.2	42.6	46.2
Weak Republicans	52.7	39.1	50.3	46.1	46.4
Strong Republicans	47.9	29.8	37.4	38.9	34.9
Total Population	61.4	49.4	58.2	55.2	57.1

Table entries are the average for the population group

Table 2.95
Average of Republican Leader Thermometers within Party Identification

	1968	1972	1976	1980	1984
Strong Democrats	49.3	44.0	42.3	44.3	38.3
Weak Democrats	55.2	55.4	50.8	51.4	50.4
Independent Democrats	52.9	49.6	48.4	50.7	45.0
Independent Independents	57.1	58.2	59.9	56.2	61.2
Independent Republicans	67.6	70.2	64.0	63.7	70.8
Weak Republicans	66.4	72.8	65.8	63.1	71.2
Strong Republicans	73.3	81.9	73.4	73.2	80.5
Total Population	58.7	60.3	56.5	55.8	58.5

Table entries are the average for the population group

Table 2.96
Approve or Disapprove of Way President is Doing His Job

QUESTION: Do you approve or disapprove of the way that (President) is
doing his job?

	1972	1974	1976	1978	1980	1982	1984	1986
Approve	71%	59%	63%	66%	41%	51%	63%	64%
Disapprove	29	41	37	34	59	49	37	36

Table 2.97
Percent of Respondents Who Approve of Way President is Doing His Job, by Social Groups

	1972	1974	1976	1978	1980	1982	1984	1986
1959 or later Cohort	**	**	**	63%	43%	56%	66%	68%
1943 - 1958 Cohort	69%	60%	62%	71	44	50	65	68
1927 - 1942 Cohort	71	59	63	62	33	53	65	61
1911 - 1926 Cohort	74	52	62	63	42	47	59	55
1895 - 1910 Cohort	70	63	64	63	44	55	59	62
Before 1895 Cohort	70	69	78*	-	-	-	-	-
Grade School	64%	58%	55%	71%	51%	37%	50%	49%
High School	72	55	61	67	44	49	62	65
College	72	65	70	62	33	58	68	67
Central Cities	58%	54%	55%	73%	47%	46%	50%	53%
Suburbs	75	60	67	61	40	54	68	70
Non-urban Areas	75	61	65	66	37	53	67	65
Income Percentile 0-16	60%	58%	51%	71%	51%	33%	46%	50%
Income Percentile 17-33	70	52	55	71	48	49	56	58
Income Percentile 34-67	72	58	62	68	40	51	66	69
Income Percentile 68-95	76	59	70	64	33	60	68	70
Income Percentile 96-100	88	79	85	50	21	67	87	76
Males	73%	58%	64%	61%	35%	56%	66%	68%
Females	69	59	62	70	45	47	61	61
Whites	76%	61%	68%	64%	36%	56%	68%	70%
Blacks	25	32	22	82	77	14	23	30
Union Household	61%	49%	54%	68%	43%	43%	53%	60%
Non-union Household	74	62	66	65	40	53	66	65
South	74%	58%	61%	65%	47%	50%	62%	65%
Non-south	70	59	64	66	37	52	64	64
Professional	76%	61%	71%	59%	33%	57%	67%	66%
White Collar	72	56	68	68	38	61	68	68
Blue Collar	66	55	52	68	45	45	58	59
Unskilled	-	53*	65	76*	45*	49*	44*	75
Farmers	70*	72	68	68*	37*	42*	74	61
Housewives	73	64	66	66	48	48	68	68
Protestants	73%	63%	65%	64%	43%	54%	66%	64%
Catholics	70	56	61	72	42	48	64	69
Jews	48*	28*	41	59	20*	-	44*	67*
Other and No Religion	53	34	53	66	34	49	50	56
Total Population	71	59	63	66	41	51	63	64

Table 2.98
Percent of Respondents Who Approve of Way President is Doing His Job, by Political Groups

	1972	1974	1976	1978	1980	1982	1984	1986
Strong Democrats	38%	36%	24%	82%	75%	14%	21%	29%
Weak Democrats	65	54	55	76	53	35	48	57
Independent Democrats	52	49	46	75	45	32	34	44
Independent Independents	73	57	69	72	34	72	75	72
Independent Republicans	87	81	87	45	18	86	89	86
Weak Republicans	92	73	85	43	19	84	92	86
Strong Republicans	94	84	96	32	9	93	97	94
Liberal Self Placement 1	31%	37%	29%	70%	55%	18%	32%	30%
Liberal Self Placement 2	54	58	51	79	45	30	48	51
Neutral Self Placement 3	78	62	66	70	37	46	63	65
Conservative Self Placement 4	92	66	81	56	28	75	82	78
Conservative Self Placement 5	86	69	82	41	22	79	85	80
Liberal Index 1	14%*	22%	21%*	**	52%	8%	13%	17%
Liberal Index 2	54	46	45	**	53	35	47	51
Neutral Index 3	75	58	62	**	47	47	67	63
Conservative Index 4	85	68	76	**	33	69	79	76
Conservative Index 5	85	75	82	**	9	84	93	85
Total Population	71	59	63	66	41	51	63	64

Table 2.99
How Well Does <u>Inspiring</u> Describe Ronald Reagan

QUESTION: I am going to read a list of words and phrases people may use to
describe political figures. Think about Ronald Reagan. The first phrase is
"inspiring." In your opinion, does the phrase "inspiring" describe Reagan
Extremely well, Quite well, Not too well or Not well at all.

	1980	1982	1984	1986
Extremely well	12%	14%	22%	23%
Quite well	37	39	37	38
Not too well	33	31	30	27
Not well at all	18	16	11	11

Table 2.100
How Well Does <u>Knowledgeable</u> Describe Ronald Reagan

	1980	1982	1984	1986
Extremely well	22%	**	29%	28%
Quite well	49	**	48	44
Not too well	22	**	16	20
Not well at all	8	**	7	9

Table 2.101
How Well Does <u>Moral</u> Describe Ronald Reagan

	1980	1982	1984	1986
Extremely well	18%	25%	34%	30%
Quite well	54	49	48	50
Not too well	23	20	14	15
Not well at all	5	7	4	5

Table 2.102
How Well Does <u>Strong Leadership</u> Describe Ronald Reagan

	1980	1982	1984	1986
Extremely well	15%	25%	30%	33%
Quite well	45	43	41	41
Not too well	27	24	21	17
Not well at all	13	8	8	8

Table 2.103
How Well Does <u>Inspiring</u> Describe Ronald Reagan, by Party ID

	1980	1982	1984	1986	
Strong Democrat	8%	8%	7%	13%	Extremely well
	23	25	28	24	Quite well
	41	41	40	39	Not too well
	29	26	25	24	Not well at all
Weak Democrat	8%	7%	13%	16%	Extremely well
	31	32	33	35	Quite well
	38	43	40	34	Not too well
	23	18	14	15	Not well at all
Independent Democrat	7%	12%	9%	9%	Extremely well
	28	28	26	33	Quite well
	39	30	45	38	Not too well
	26	31	21	20	Not well at all
Independent Independent	8%	10%	21%	19%	Extremely well
	38	46	37	46	Quite well
	33	30	35	24	Not too well
	22	14	7	12	Not well at all
Independent Republican	16%	21%	34%	29%	Extremely well
	50	52	47	43	Quite well
	27	26	17	27	Not too well
	6	2	2	2	Not well at all
Weak Republican	16%	19%	27%	32%	Extremely well
	53	53	53	50	Quite well
	24	23	18	16	Not too well
	7	5	2	2	Not well at all
Strong Republican	34%	36%	55%	55%	Extremely well
	47	57	41	37	Quite well
	15	7	4	7	Not too well
	4	0	1	1	Not well at all

Table 2.104
How Well Does <u>Knowledgeable</u> Describe Ronald Reagan, by Party ID

	1980	1982	1984	1986	
Strong Democrat	13%	**	20%	19%	Extremely well
	43	**	38	32	Quite well
	30	**	28	30	Not too well
	14	**	15	18	Not well at all
Weak Democrat	15%	**	22%	23%	Extremely well
	48	**	49	43	Quite well
	26	**	19	22	Not too well
	11	**	9	12	Not well at all
Independent Democrat	12%	**	14%	19%	Extremely well
	47	**	42	39	Quite well
	28	**	28	26	Not too well
	13	**	16	17	Not well at all
Independent Independent	21%	**	30%	24%	Extremely well
	52	**	51	46	Quite well
	21	**	16	20	Not too well
	6	**	2	10	Not well at all
Independent Republican	26%	**	33%	33%	Extremely well
	52	**	58	47	Quite well
	20	**	9	19	Not too well
	2	**	1	2	Not well at all
Weak Republican	31%	**	31%	35%	Extremely well
	55	**	61	54	Quite well
	11	**	7	11	Not too well
	3	**	1	1	Not well at all
Strong Republican	45%	**	56%	45%	Extremely well
	47	**	38	46	Quite well
	6	**	5	10	Not too well
	2	**	1	0	Not well at all

Table 2.105
How Well Does <u>Moral</u> Describe Ronald Reagan, by Party ID

	1980	1982	1984	1986	
Strong Democrat	9%	15%	19%	19%	Extremely well
	47	43	47	43	Quite well
	33	28	23	27	Not too well
	11	14	11	10	Not well at all
Weak Democrat	11%	14%	26%	26%	Extremely well
	52	51	49	48	Quite well
	32	29	20	21	Not too well
	5	6	5	6	Not well at all
Independent Democrat	9%	17%	16%	16%	Extremely well
	55	50	52	60	Quite well
	27	23	26	18	Not too well
	9	10	7	7	Not well at all
Independent Independent	12%	25%	27%	24%	Extremely well
	57	54	58	53	Quite well
	24	15	14	15	Not too well
	6	6	1	8	Not well at all
Independent Republican	26%	41%	46%	37%	Extremely well
	61	52	47	57	Quite well
	12	6	6	6	Not too well
	1	1	1	0	Not well at all
Weak Republican	21%	35%	45%	38%	Extremely well
	66	56	51	56	Quite well
	11	8	3	6	Not too well
	2	1	1	1	Not well at all
Strong Republican	52%	55%	68%	60%	Extremely well
	41	42	32	39	Quite well
	7	3	1	2	Not too well
	0	1	0	0	Not well at all

Table 2.106
How Well Does <u>Strong Leadership</u> Describe Ronald Reagan, By Party ID

	1980	1982	1984	1986	
Strong Democrat	5%	11%	13%	20%	Extremely well
	26	37	31	31	Quite well
	41	33	34	28	Not too well
	27	19	23	21	Not well at all
Weak Democrat	7%	15%	16%	23%	Extremely well
	40	41	45	45	Quite well
	37	35	31	23	Not too well
	17	9	8	10	Not well at all
Independent Democrat	8%	20%	11%	17%	Extremely well
	41	41	38	43	Quite well
	33	29	39	27	Not too well
	19	10	13	13	Not well at all
Independent Independent	11%	24%	24%	30%	Extremely well
	46	51	53	47	Quite well
	32	18	18	16	Not too well
	11	8	6	7	Not well at all
Independent Republican	24%	39%	39%	37%	Extremely well
	60	51	50	50	Quite well
	11	10	9	12	Not too well
	4	0	1	1	Not well at all
Weak Republican	25%	33%	44%	49%	Extremely well
	60	54	49	43	Quite well
	11	12	6	6	Not too well
	4	2	1	2	Not well at all
Strong Republican	45%	63%	71%	69%	Extremely well
	49	36	27	28	Quite well
	5	0	1	3	Not too well
	2	1	1	0	Not well at all

Table 2.107
Has Ronald Reagan Ever Made Respondent Feel Angry

QUESTION: Now we would like to know something about the feelings you have
toward Ronald Reagan. Has Reagan -- because of the kind of person he is,
or because of something he has done -- made you feel angry?

	1980	1982	1984	1986
Yes	24%	43%	48%	48%
No	76	57	52	52

Table 2.108
Has Ronald Reagan Ever Made Respondent Feel Afraid

	1980	1982	1984	1986
Yes	28%	19%	24%	19%
No	72	81	76	81

Table 2.109
Has Ronald Reagan Ever Made Respondent Feel Hopeful

	1980	1982	1984	1986
Yes	48%	63%	60%	65%
No	52	38	40	35

Table 2.110
Has Ronald Reagan Ever Made Respondent Feel Proud

	1980	1982	1984	1986
Yes	31%	50%	55%	64%
No	69	50	45	36

Table 2.111
Ronald Reagan Made Respondent Feel Angry, by Party ID

	1980	1982	1984	1986
Strong Democrat	34%	63%	72%	66%
Weak Democrat	27	49	59	58
Independent Democrat	36	58	70	72
Independent Independent	18	37	38	41
Independent Republican	15	33	35	42
Weak Republican	15	23	30	29
Strong Republican	14	15	20	17

Table 2.112
Ronald Reagan Made Respondent Feel Afraid, by Party ID

	1980	1982	1984	1986
Strong Democrat	38%	34%	42%	30%
Weak Democrat	32	21	35	25
Independent Democrat	44	32	36	30
Independent Independent	22	14	15	15
Independent Republican	22	10	13	11
Weak Republican	19	9	14	11
Strong Republican	13	2	6	3

Table 2.113
Ronald Reagan Made Respondent Feel Hopeful, by Party ID

	1980	1982	1984	1986
Strong Democrat	21%	40%	32%	46%
Weak Democrat	36	53	49	54
Independent Democrat	36	50	41	47
Independent Independent	45	63	59	62
Independent Republican	72	89	82	84
Weak Republican	76	87	82	86
Strong Republican	87	96	92	90

Table 2.114
Ronald Reagan Made Respondent Feel Proud, by Party ID

	1980	1982	1984	1986
Strong Democrat	15%	24%	25%	40%
Weak Democrat	22	35	45	55
Independent Democrat	22	34	35	50
Independent Independent	26	55	53	63
Independent Republican	42	75	77	81
Weak Republican	51	82	77	84
Strong Republican	71	94	92	96

Chapter 3. Positions on Public Policy Issues

The purpose of this chapter is to describe the positions which American citizens take on a variety of public policy issues. Public opinion is often associated with ephemeral issues of the day, but our goal is to concentrate on relatively enduring topics from a limited set of public policy concerns. Monitoring issue attitudes over time provides information that is crucial for understanding the dynamics of attitude change.

At the beginning of the chapter (Tables 3.1-3.32), we present the basic distributions of American opinion on questions in six substantive areas:

1.   Government role in domestic social welfare issues which focus on health care, a government-guaranteed job and a good standard of living for all, and the proper trade-off between government spending and government services (Tables 3.1-3.6).

2.   Issues of law and order which arose from the urban problems of crime and riots in the late sixties (Tables 3.7-3.8).

3.   Race relations issues, including changes in the social situation of black Americans, government assistance to blacks, school integration, and open housing (Tables 3.9-3.15).

4.   Women's and moral issues, including women's equality, participation in politics, abortion, and attitudes about the Bible (Tables 3.16-3.21).

5.   Foreign affairs issues, particularly U.S. involvement in other countries, isolationism, U.S. spending to maintain the armed forces, U.S. relations with Russia (Tables 3.22-3.28).

6.   Assessments of economic conditions, for the respondent and for the nation as a whole, for the last year and the next year (3.29-3.32)

The basic distributions of public opinion in these areas reveal the extent to which policy attitudes are stable or changing. The distributions of political ideology presented in Tables 2.22 and 2.23, for example, reveal relatively stable proportions of liberals and conservatives during the period from 1972 to 1978, whereas Table 3.16 shows a steady change in attitudes toward the role of women in society.

The proportion of Don't Know responses in the basic tables also provides evidence of how concerned the public has been with particular policy questions. Table 3.8, for example,

reveals a good deal of concern about urban riots in 1968 (only 4 percent Don't Know), but a substantial decay in the salience of this issue by 1976 (24 percent Don't Know). This information needs to be taken into account when overall public support or opposition to particular policies is assessed.

In several places in this chapter (for example, Tables 3.4 and 3.5), two tables seem to be reporting on the same survey question. In 1970, the Election Studies began to use seven point scales to elicit respondent opinions on many issues. Although the questions are roughly comparable, it seemed more appropriate to present these questions in adjacent tables, rather than combining them into one table.

The second part of this chapter (Tables 3.33-3.96) presents a series of tables which use the PDI to summarize the relationship between attitudes on issues and the social, political, and ideological characteristics of the survey respondents. Each issue is dealt with in two summary tables. The first table summarizes attitude differences across demographic groupings defined by age cohort, education level, urbanism, income, sex, race, union membership, region, occupation, and religion. The second table in each set presents the relationships among party identification, ideological orientation, and issue attitudes, thus showing the extent to which the attitudes have been politicized. The general assumption underlying the second set of tables is that partisan and ideological orientations influence the positions which citizens take on specific questions of public policy. The summary tables allow the reader to assess the strength of this impact by observing the differences between the PDI values for Democrats and Republicans and for liberals and conservatives.

Next (Tables 3.97-3.99), we address the question of how tightly attitudes on various issues are inter-correlated. We have selected a very small number of issue items for which we present inter-item correlation (gamma) matrices. Each item used in this section is based on the same 7-point scale used to measure issue attitudes; any changes across time are a reflection of real changes or sampling error and not of changes in question wording or format.

Finally, the last series of tables (3.100-3.112) presents how the political parties' positions on major issues are viewed by respondents in relation to their own positions. On the same 7-point issue scale questions for which respondents located themselves, they were also asked to place the political parties, and these tables derive from a comparison of the relative placement of self and of Democratic and Republican parties.

Table 3.1
Power of the Federal Government

QUESTION: Some people are afraid the government in Washington is
getting too powerful for the good of the country and the
individual person. Others feel that the government in Washington
has not gotten too strong for the good of the country. Have you
been interested enough in this to favor one side over the other?

	1964	1966	1968	1970	1972	1974	1976	1978	1980	1982	1984
Government not too strong	36%	27%	30%	33%	27%	**	20%	14%	15%	**	22%
Government too powerful	30	39	41	31	41	**	49	43	49	**	32
Don't know	34	34	29	36	32	**	31	43	36	**	46
Total	100%	100%	100%	100%	100%	**	100%	100%	100%	**	100%
N	1569	1286	1552	1499	1318	**	2856	2276	1405	**	973
PDI#	6	-12	-10	2	-15	**	-30	-29	-33	**	-10

PDI is proportion "not too strong" minus proportion "too powerful"

Table 3.2
Federal Government Support for Comprehensive Health Care

QUESTION: Some say the government in Washington ought to help people get doctors
and hospital care at low cost; others say the government should not get into
this. Have you been interested enough in this to favor one side over the other?
(IF YES) What is your position? Should the government in Washington---

	1956	1958	1960	1962	1964	1968
Help people get care	54%	**	60%	61%	50%	52%
Govt should stay out	26	**	20	24	28	27
Don't know	2	**	2	1	2	46
Total	100%	**	100%	100%	100%	100%
N	1758	**	1918	1283	1563	973
PDI#	28	**	41	38	22	-10

PDI is proportion "help people" minus proportion "stay out"

Table 3.3
Government Health Insurance Scale

QUESTION: There is much concern about the rapid
rise in medical and hospital costs. Some feel
there should be a government insurance plan which
would cover all medical and hospital expenses.
Others feel that medical expenses should be paid
by individuals and through private insurance like
Blue Cross. Where would you place yourself on this
scale?

	1970	1972	1974	1976	1978	1980	1982	1984
Government insurance plan 1	25%	25%	**	22%	24%	**	**	13%
2	8	6	**	7	7	**	**	9
3	7	6	**	6	6	**	**	9
4	13	12	**	10	11	**	**	17
5	5	5	**	7	8	**	**	13
6	8	5	**	8	9	**	**	12
Private insurance plan 7	21	23	**	20	19	**	**	10
Don't know	14	18	**	21	17	**	**	18
Total	100%	100%	**	100%	100%	**	**	100%
N	1489	1355	**	2843	2282	**	**	967
PDI#	4	4	**	1	3	**	**	-3

PDI is proportion "pro government insurance plan" (categories 1,2 and 3) minus proportion
  "pro private insurance plan" (categories 5,6 and 7)

Table 3.4
Federal Government Guarantee Job and a Good Standard of Living (1)

QUESTION: In general some people feel that the government in Washington should see to it
that every person has a job and a good standard of living. Others think the government
should just let each person get ahead on his own. Have you been interested enough in this
to favor one side over the other. (IF YES) Do you think that the government---

	1956	1958	1960	1962	1964	1966	1968
Government Should see to jobs	57%	57%	59%	**	31%	**	31%
Depends	7	7	8	**	11	**	11
Each person on his own	27	26	24	**	43	**	47
Don't know	10	10	10	**	15	**	11
Total	100%	100%	100%	**	100%	**	100%
N	1758	1808	1919	**	1569	**	1551
PDI#	30	30	35	**	-12	**	-16

PDI is proportion "government should see to jobs" minus proportion "each person on his own"

Table 3.5
Federal Government Guarantee Job and a Good Standard of Living (2)

QUESTION: Some people feel that the government in Washington should see to it that every
person has a job and a good standard of living. Others think the government should just
let each person get ahead on his own. And, of course, other people have opinions somewhere
in between. Where would you place yourself on this scale, or haven't you thought much
about this?

	1972	1974	1976	1978	1980	1982	1984	1986
Govt See to Job and Standard of Living 1	13%	12%	11%	7%	10%	10%	10%	10%
2	6	5	5	3	7	6	7	6
3	9	8	8	7	9	9	11	8
4	20	20	17	19	18	20	20	21
5	13	12	10	15	13	16	16	16
6	8	8	11	12	16	13	13	14
Govt Let Each Person Get Ahead on Own 7	19	17	18	17	12	12	9	17
Don't Know	13	18	20	21	16	14	14	7
Total	100%	100%	100%	100%	100%	100%	100%	100%
N	2462	2504	2850	2291	1400	1402	2224	1090
PDI#	-14	-12	-15	-27	-15	-16	-10	-23

PDI is proportion "government should see to jobs" (categories 1, 2 and 3) minus proportion "each person on his own"
  (categories 5, 6, and 7)

Table 3.6
Should Government Provide More/Fewer Services, Increase/Decrease Spending

QUESTION: Some people think the government should provide fewer services, even in areas
such as health and education, in order to reduce spending. Suppose these people are at
one end of the scale at point 1. Other people feel that it is important for the government
to provide more services even if it means an increase in spending. Suppose these people
are at the other end, at point 7. And, of course, some other people have opinions somewhere
in between at points 2, 3, 4, 5, and 6. Where would you place yourself on this scale, or
haven't you thought much about this?

	1980	1982	1984	1986
Govt Should Provide Fewer Services 1	7%	9%	6%	5%
2	9	10	9	6
3	12	13	13	13
4	16	23	26	25
5	11	11	14	17
6	12	6	8	12
Govt Should Provide More Services 7	15	7	7	12
Don't Know	19	20	16	9
Total	100	100	100	100
N	1603	1404	2229	2168
PDI#	-10	8	-1	-17

PDI is proportion "fewer services/reduce spending" (categories 1, 2 and 3) minus proportion "more services/increase spending"
 (categories 5, 6 and 7) .

Table 3.7
Rights of the Accused

QUESTION: Some people are primarily concerned with
doing everything possible to protect the legal
rights of those accused of committing crimes.
Others feel that it is more important to stop
criminal activity even at the risk of reducing the
rights of the accused. Where would you place
yourself on this scale, or haven't you thought
much about this?

	1970	1972	1974	1976	1978
Protect rights of accused 1	17%	16%	18%	15%	11%
2	7	7	8	7	6
3	6	7	7	7	7
4	15	16	16	14	16
5	11	12	12	12	15
6	13	11	8	11	12
Stop crime 7	19	17	15	18	19
Don't know	13	14	18	18	15
Total	100%	100%	100%	100%	100%
N	1493	2255	2482	2848	2285
PDI#	-13	-9	-2	-12	-22

PDI is proportion "protect rights" (categories 1,2 and 3) minus proportion
  "stop crime" (categories 5,6 and 7)

Table 3.8
Response to Urban Unrest

QUESTION: There is much discussion about the best way
to deal with the problem of urban unrest and rioting.
Some say it is more important to use all available
force to maintain law and order--no matter what
results. Others say it is more important to correct
the problems of poverty and unemployment that give
rise to the disturbances. Where would you place
yourself on this scale, or haven't you thought much
about this?

	1968	1970	1972	1974	1976
Solve problems 1	19%	20%	30%	27%	22%
2	11	9	13	10	10
3	10	12	10	10	11
4	28	26	14	16	16
5	10	9	6	6	7
6	7	6	3	4	5
Use all available force 7	12	17	11	9	6
Don't know	4	2	13	18	24
Total	100%	100%	100%	100%	100%
N	1317	1495	1096	2480	2379
PDI#	11	9	32	28	24

PDI is proportion "solve problems" (categories 1,2 and 3) minus proportion
  "use force" (categories 5,6 and 7)

Law and Order

Table 3.9
Change in Situation of Blacks

QUESTION: In the past few years we have heard a lot
about civil rights groups working to improve the
position of the black in this country. How much real
change do you think there has been in the position of
the black in the past few years: a lot, some, not much
at all?

	1964	1966	1968	1970	1972	1974	1976	1978	1980	1982	1984	1986
Not much at all	19%	18%	14%	11%	8%	**	7%	**	**	**	12%	15%
Some	38	39	35	35	35	**	32	**	**	**	41	43
A lot	41	39	50	53	55	**	59	**	**	**	45	39
Don't know	2	4	1	2	2	**	2	**	**	**	3	3
Total	100%	100%	100%	100%	100%	**	100%	**	**	**	100%	100%
N	1561	1283	1552	884	2701	**	2852	**	**	**	968	1081
PDI#	-21	-22	-36	-42	-47	**	-52	**	**	**	-33	-24

PDI is proportion "not much at all" minus proportion "a lot"

Table 3.10
Pace of Civil Rights Leaders' Actions

QUESTION: Some say that the civil rights people
have been trying to push too fast. Others feel they
haven't pushed fast enough. How about you: Do you
think that civil rights leaders are trying to push
too fast, are going too slowly, or are they moving
about the right speed?

	1964	1966	1968	1970	1972	1974	1976	1978	1980	1982	1984	1986
Too slowly	5%	5%	7%	9%	8%	9%	8%	**	13%	**	12%	24%
About right	25	19	28	33	41	44	47	**	48	**	55	59
Too fast	63	65	63	53	46	41	39	**	34	**	30	14
Don't know	6	12	3	5	5	6	5	**	6	**	3	2
Total	100%	100%	100%	100%	100%	100%	100%	**	100%	**	100%	100%
N	1542	1279	1528	874	2677	2447	2826	**	1374	**	945	1072
PDI#	-33	-41	-28	-10	4	11	16	**	27	**	36	69

PDI is proportion "about right" plus "too slowly" minus proportion "too fast"

Table 3.11
Does the Respondent Favor Desegregation or Segregation

QUESTION: What about you? Are you in favor of
desegregation, strict segregation, or something in
between?

	1964	1966	1968	1970	1972	1974	1976	1978
Desegregation	32%	**	36%	40%	41%	**	39%	34%
In between	44	**	47	43	45	**	49	54
Segregation	23	**	16	16	13	**	9	5
Don't know	2	**	1	1	2	**	3	6
Total	100%	**	100%	100%	100%	**	100%	100%
N	1552	**	1496	869	2674	**	2804	2273
PDI#	9	**	21	25	28	**	29	29

PDI is proportion "desegregation" minus proportion "segregation"

Table 3.12
Position on Aid to Minorities

QUESTION: Some people feel that the government in
Washington should make every possible effort to improve the
social and economic position of blacks and other minority
groups. Others feel that the government should not make any
special effort to help minorities because they should help
themselves. Where would you place yourself on this scale,
or haven't you thought much about it?

	1970	1972	1974	1976	1978	1980	1982	1984	1986
Government should help minorities 1	13%	12%	12%	11%	10%	5%	7%	8%	8%
2	7	7	6	7	5	4	5	7	6
3	7	12	10	11	9	10	10	13	12
4	23	21	21	18	22	25	25	27	28
5	11	10	10	10	14	18	14	16	17
6	10	11	8	9	11	11	14	9	11
Minorities should help themselves 7	19	17	19	18	17	12	11	8	8
Don't know	10	11	15	17	11	14	15	13	10
Total	100%	100%	100%	100%	100%	100%	100%	100%	100%
N	1494	2255	2489	2834	2284	1401	1403	2231	1080
PDI#	-13	-8	-9	-7	-18	-23	-18	-5	-10

PDI is proportion "government help" (categories 1,2 and 3) minus proportion "self help" (categories 5,6 and 7)

Table 3.13
Should Federal Government Ensure School Integration&

QUESTION: Some people say that the government in Washington should see to it that
white and black (before 1976: Negro) children are allowed to go to the same schools.
Others claim this is not the government's business. Have you been concerned (1986:
interested) enough about (in) this question to favor one side over the other?
(IF YES) Do you think the government in Washington should--(repeat choice)

	1962	1964	1966	1968	1970	1972	1974	1976	1978	1980	1982	1984	1986
Go to same schools	47%	41%	46%	38%	45%	37%	**	24%	27%	**	**	**	30%
Govt stay out of this area	32	39	34	44	33	45	**	39	41	**	**	**	33
Don't know	21	20	20	18	22	19	**	36	32	**	**	**	37
Total	100%	100%	100%	100%	100%	100%	**	100%	100%	**	**	**	100%
N	1259	1564	1282	1547	885	2694	**	2851	2279	**	**	**	1085
PDI#	15	3	12	-6	12	-8	**	-15	-14	**	**	**	-3

PDI is proportion "go to same schools" minus proportion "government stay out"

& This question appears without lead-in ('Have you been concerned...') and varies slightly in text in 1962.

Table 3.14
Busing to Achieve School Integration

QUESTION: There is much discussion about the best
way to deal with racial problems. Some people
think achieving racial integration of schools is
so important that it justifies busing children to
schools out of their own neighborhoods. Others
think letting children go to their neighborhood
schools is so important that they oppose busing.
Where would you place yourself on this scale, or
haven't you thought much about this?

	1972	1974	1976	1978	1980	1982	1984
Bus to achieve integration 1	5%	4%	5%	**	4%	**	3%
2	2	2	2	**	3	**	2
3	2	2	2	**	3	**	3
4	5	5	6	**	6	**	7
5	3	4	4	**	5	**	9
6	7	9	8	**	16	**	19
Keep children in neighborhood 7	70	62	61	**	57	**	18
Don't know	7	12	11	**	7	**	9
Total	100%	100%	100%	**	100%	**	100%
N	2686	2491	2842	**	1403	**	1963
PDI#	-71	-67	-65	**	-69	**	-69

PDI is proportion "pro busing" (categories 1,2 and 3) minus proportion
  "neighborhood schools" (categories 5,6 and 7)

Minority Relations

Table 3.15
Open Housing

QUESTION: Which of these statements would you agree with: 1) White
people have a right to keep blacks out of their neighborhoods if
they want to or 2) blacks have a right to live wherever they can
afford to just like anybody else.

	1964	1966	1968	1970	1972	1974	1976
Whites can keep blacks out	26%	32%	22%	20%	16%	**	8%
Blacks' rights to choose	57	50	68	70	76	**	85
Don't know	17	18	10	10	8	**	7
Total	100%	100%	100%	100%	100%	**	100%
N	1561	1282	1551	886	2696	**	2851
PDI#	31	17	46	51	61	**	77

PDI is proportion "blacks' rights to choose" minus proportion "whites can keep blacks out"

Table 3.16
Equal Role for Women

QUESTION: Recently there has been a lot of talk
about women's rights. Some people feel that women
should have an equal role with men in running
business, industry, and government. Others feel
that women's place is in the home. Where would
you place yourself on this scale or haven't you
thought much about this?

	1972	1974	1976	1978	1980	1982	1984
Equal role 1	31%	33%	30%	38%	33%	37%	33%
2	9	9	12	10	16	12	12
3	7	8	3	8	10	9	9
4	19	18	18	16	16	17	21
5	6	7	8	7	7	6	7
6	4	5	5	5	6	4	3
Women's place is in the home 7	19	14	11	10	6	7	5
Don't know	5	6	9	6	6	7	10
Total	100%	100%	100%	100%	100%	100%	100%
N	2685	2480	2385	2286	1398	1402	2239
PDI#	17	25	28	35	39	40	39

PDI is proportion "equal role" (categories 1,2 and 3) minus proportion
  "role in home" (categories 5,6 and 7)

Table 3.17
Women Stay Out of Politics

QUESTION: Women should stay out of politics.

	1952	1954	1956	1958	1960	1962	1964	1966	1968	1970	1972
Agree	30%	**	**	**	**	**	**	**	**	**	20%
Disagree	69	**	**	**	**	**	**	**	**	**	80
Don't know	1	**	**	**	**	**	**	**	**	**	1
Total	100%	**	**	**	**	**	**	**	**	**	100%
N	577	**	**	**	**	**	**	**	**	**	2686
PDI#	39	**	**	**	**	**	**	**	**	**	60

PDI is proportion "disagree" minus proportion "agree"

Table 3.18
Abortions (1)

QUESTION: Still on the subject of women's rights, there has
been some discussion about abortion during recent years. Which
one of the opinions on this card best agrees with your view?
You can just tell me the number of the opinion you choose.
(1) Abortion should never be permitted, (2) Abortion should be
permitted only if the life and health of the woman is in
danger, (3) Abortion should be permitted if, due to personal
reasons, the woman would have difficulty in caring for the
child, (4) Abortion should never be forbidden, since one
should not require a woman to have a child she doesn't want.

	1972	1974	1976	1978	1980
Never	11%	**	11%	11%	11%
If health is in danger	46	**	44	43	44
If personal difficulty	17	**	16	16	18
Anytime	24	**	26	27	27
Don't know	3	**	4	4	3
Total	100%	**	100%	100%	100%
N	2692	**	2378	2281	1400
PDI#	13	**	15	16	17

PDI is proportion permit "anytime" minus proportion
  "never" permit

Table 3.19
Abortions (2)

QUESTION: There has been some discussion about abortion during
recent years. Which one of the opinions on this page best
agrees with your view? You can just tell me the number of the
opinion you choose. (1) By law, abortion should never be
permitted, (2) The law should permit abortion only in case of
rape, incest, or when the woman's life is in danger, (3) The
law should permit abortion for reasons other than rape, incest
or danger to the woman's life, but only after the need for the
abortion has been clearly established, (4) By law, a woman
should be able to obtain an abortion as a matter of personal
choice.

	1980	1984	1986
Abortion Never Permitted	11%	13%	13%
Only in Case of Rape, Incest or Danger	32	29	28
Only When Need Clearly Established	18	19	18
As a Matter of Personal Choice	36	35	39
Don't Know	4	3	2
Total	100%	100%	100%
N	1604	2237	2166
PDI#	24	23	25

PDI is proportion permit "as a matter of personal choice"
  minus proportion "never" permit

Table 3.20
Attitudes About the Accuracy of the Bible

QUESTION: Here are four statements about the Bible and I'd like you to tell me
which is closest to your own view. (1) The Bible is God's word and all it says
is true, (2) The Bible was written by men inspired by God but it contains some
human errors, (3) The Bible is a good book because it was written by wise men, but
God had nothing to do with it, (4) The Bible was written by men who lived so long
ago that it is worth very little today.

	1964	1968	1980	1984	1986
Bible is God's Word	53%	54%	47%	50%	51%
Bible Contains Some Human Errors	43	39	44	42	40
Bible Not Written by God	4	6	7	6	6
Bible Worth Very Little Today	1	2	3	2	2
Total	100%	100%	100%	100%	100%
N	1397	1488	1349	1835	2081

Table 3.21
Percent of Respondents Who Consider Religion an Important Part of His/Her Life

QUESTION: Do you consider religion to be an important part of your life, or not?

	1980	1984	1986
Yes	75%	79%	79%
No	25	21	22
Total	100%	100%	100%
N	1398	1911	1071

Women's Issues/Morality

Table 3.22
U.S. Concern with World Problems

QUESTION: This country would be better off if we just stayed home and did not
concern ourselves with problems in other parts of the world.

	1956	1958	1960	1962	1964	1966	1968	1970	1972	1974	1976	1978	1980	1982	1984	1986
Agree	25%	24%	18%	**	**	**	23%	**	20%	**	26%	**	18%	**	24%	29%
Disagree	57	56	66	**	**	**	74	**	77	**	67	**	78	**	73	66
Don't know	18	20	16	**	**	**	3	**	3	**	7	**	5	**	4	5
Total	100%	100%	100%	**	**	**	100%	**	100%	**	100%	**	100%	**	100%	100%
N	1758	1812	1919	**	**	**	1337	**	2688	**	2385	**	1398	**	971	1080
PDI#	32	33	48	**	**	**	51	**	58	**	41	**	60	**	49	37

PDI is proportion "disagree" minus proportion "agree"

Table 3.23
Were We Right in Getting into Korea or Vietnam

QUESTION: Do you think we did the right thing in getting into the fighting in Korea/Vietnam
or should we have stayed out?

	1952	1954	1956	1958	1960	1962	1964	1966	1968	1970	1972
No should have stayed out	43%	**	**	**	**	**	25%	2%	5%	5%	5%
Yes did right thing	41	**	**	**	**	**	38	44	31	30	29
Don't know	17	**	**	**	**	**	37	27	18	20	14
Total	100%	**	**	**	**	**	100%	100%	100%	100%	100%
N	1738	**	**	**	**	**	1443	1278	1549	1496	2701
PDI#	2	**	**	**	**	**	-14	-15	21	19	28

PDI is proportion "should stay out" minus proportion "did right thing"

Table 3.24
Likelihood of Conventional War

QUESTION: (1956, 1960, 1964) Now I'd like to ask you some questions about the chances of our country
getting into war. Would you say that at the present time you are pretty worried about this country
getting into another war, somewhat worried, or not worried at all?
QUESTION: (1982-1986) How about the chances of getting into a conventional war, in which neither side
uses nuclear weapons? Are you pretty worried about this country getting into such a war at the present
time, somewhat worried, or not worried at all?

	1956	1960	1964	1982	1984	1986
Not worried about chance of war	45%	33%	44%	34%	39%	34%
Somewhat worried about chance of war	44	46	45	45	42	51
Pretty worried about chance of war	11	21	11	21	19	16
Total	100%	100%	100%	100%	100%	100%
N	1737	1895	1548	1409	2229	1067
PDI#	33	11	34	12	20	18

PDI is proportion "not worried" minus proportion "pretty worried"

Table 3.25
U.S. Foreign Aid

QUESTION: The United States should give help to foreign countries
even if they don't stand for the same things we do.

	1956	1958	1960	1962	1964	1966	1968	1970	1972	1974	1976
Disagree	26%	20%	21%	**	19%	**	28%	**	52%	**	54%
Agree	43	51	52	**	52	**	40	**	42	**	35
Don't know	31	29	27	**	29	**	32	**	7	**	11
Total	100%	100%	100%	**	100%	**	100%	**	100%	**	100%
N	1755	1809	1913	**	1564	**	1555	**	2678	**	2382
PDI#	18	32	31	**	34	**	12	**	-10	**	-19

PDI is proportion "agree" that US should help ideologically differing countries minus proportion "disagree"

Table 3.26
Military Spending (1)

QUESTION: Some people believe that our armed
forces are already powerful enough and that
we should spend less money for defense.
Others feel that military spending should at
least continue at the present level. How do
you feel -- should military spending be cut,
or should it continue at least at the present
level?

	1972	1974	1976
Cut military spending	35%	**	18%
Continue at present level	57	**	76
Don't know	8	**	6
Total	100%	**	100%
N	1167	**	2849
PDI#	-22	**	-59

PDI is proportion "cut military spending" minus proportion "continue at present level"

Table 3.27
Military Spending (2)

QUESTION: Some people believe that we should spend much less money for defense.   Others
feel that defense spending should be greatly increased. Where would you place
yourself on this scale?

	1980	1982	1984	1986
Greatly Decrease Defense Spending 1	3%	8%	8%	9%
2	2	8	9	10
3	5	12	11	14
4	15	26	28	27
5	21	15	16	17
6	20	7	9	7
Greatly Increase Defense Spending 7	20	4	7	5
Don't Know	15	20	13	11
Total	100%	100%	100%	100%
N	1604	1402	2228	2166
PDI#	-51	2	-4	4

PDI is proportion "decrease defense spending" (categories 1, 2 and 3) minus proportion "increase defense spending"
  (categories 5, 6 and 7).

Table 3.28
Should US Cooperate More or Get Tougher With Russia

QUESTION: Some people feel it is important for us to try to cooperate more with Russia,
while others believe we should be much tougher in our dealings with Russia. Where would
you place yourself on this scale, or haven't you thought much about this?

		1980	1982	1984	1986
Cooperate More With Russia	1	11%	**	10%	8%
	2	10	**	8	7
	3	12	**	11	12
	4	21	**	19	22
	5	12	**	15	15
	6	10	**	10	13
Get Tougher with Russia	7	9	**	11	14
Don't Know		16	**	16	9
Total		100%	**	100%	100%
N		1403	**	2222	2159
PDI#		2	**	-7	-15

PDI is proportion "cooperate more" (categories 1, 2 and 3) minus proportion "get tougher"
  (categories 5, 6 and 7).

Foreign Relations/Defense

Table 3.29
Condition of the Nation's Economy Over the Last Year

	1980	1982	1984	1986
Gotten better	4%	12%	43%	24%
Stayed same	13	18	34	42
Gotten Worse	83	70	24	35
PDI#	-80	-58	19	-11

PDI is percent "gotten better" minus percent "gotten worse"

Table 3.30
Condition of the Nation's Economy Next Year

	1980	1982	1984	1986
Get better	30%	39%	29%	21%
Stay about the same	40	40	51	56
Get worse	31	21	20	23
PDI#	-1	18	9	-2

PDI is proportion "get better" minus proportion "get worse"

Table 3.31
Respondent's Financial Situation over the Last Year

	1962	1964	1966	1968	1970	1972	1974	1976	1978	1980	1982	1984	1986
Gotten Better	34%	**	35%	34%	32%	36%	28%	34%	35%	32%	30%	43%	40%
Stayed the same	47	**	39	47	35	42	31	35	29	25	32	29	33
Gotten Worse	19	**	26	20	34	23	41	31	36	42	38	28	27
PDI#	15	**	10	14	-3	13	-13	3	-2	-10	-8	15	13

PDI is proportion "gotten better" minus proportion "gotten worse"

Table 3.32
Respondent's Financial Situation Over the Next Year

	1956	1958	1960	1962	1964	1966	1968	1970	1972	1974	1976	1978	1980	1982	1984	1986
Get Better	44%	43%	41%	38%	46%	35%	34%	31%	37%	22%	34%	24%	30%	27%	38%	17%
Stay the Same	46	44	50	56	45	53	56	51	54	45	53	47	49	55	53	65
Get Worse	10	13	10	6	9	12	10	18	10	33	13	28	22	18	9	18
PDI#	35	30	31	32	37	23	24	14	27	-11	21	-4	8	8	29	-1

PDI is proportion "get better" minus proportion "get worse"

Table 3.33
Power of the Federal Government by Social Groups, Summarized by a Percentage Difference Index#

	1964	1966	1968	1970	1972	1974	1976	1978	1980	1982	1984
1959 or later Cohort	**	**	**	**	**	**	**	-8	-4	**	9
1943 - 1958 Cohort	-12*	14	-4	12	-16	**	-28	-28	-31	**	-8
1927 - 1942 Cohort	12	-10	-15	1	-18	**	-39	-34	-46	**	-26
1911 - 1926 Cohort	6	-8	-4	3	-12	**	-29	-32	-36	**	-25
1895 - 1910 Cohort	-2	-21	-15	-1	-10	**	-22	-25	-29	**	-55*
Before 1895 Cohort	0	-31	-5	-1	-13*	**	-10	-4*	-	**	-
Grade School	19	-7	1	5	-12	**	-12	-13	-8	**	-36*
High School	6	-10	-9	5	-13	**	-32	-29	-31	**	-24
College	-9	-20	-22	-7	-18	**	-36	-36	-44	**	-7
Central cities	9	0	-1	16	-14	**	-22	-21	-23	**	-12
Suburbs	4	-11	-8	6	-8	**	-29	-29	-38	**	-12
Non-urban Areas	4	-21	-18	-8	-20	**	-36	-37	-37	**	-26
Income Percentile 0-16	15	-10	3	10	-9	**	-10	-22	-21	**	-50
Income Percentile 17-33	14	0	-7	3	-18	**	-25	-19	-24	**	-14
Income Percentile 34-67	13	-9	-12	1	-13	**	-29	-33	-39	**	-19
Income Percentile 68-95	-3	-16	-14	1	-17	**	-38	-33	-36	**	-15
Income Percentile 95-100	-22	-13	-29	-9	-25	**	-54	-42	-52	**	32*
Males	3	-14	-18	-1	-19	**	-35	-32	-40	**	-22
Females	8	-10	-4	5	-11	**	-26	-27	-28	**	-11
Whites	0	-16	-16	-1	-16	**	-34	-32	-38	**	-19
Blacks	52	25	39	35	2	**	4	-7	1	**	7*
Union Household	22	0	-3	7	-13	**	-27	-26	-31	**	4
Non-union Household	0	-16	-13	1	-15	**	-31	-30	-35	**	-23
South	-2	-27	-20	-4	-18	**	-32	-26	-30	**	-17
Non-south	9	-5	-6	5	-13	**	-28	-31	-35	**	-17
Professional	-17	**	-31	-4	-20	**	-33	-38	-46	**	-6
White collar	-2	**	-8	-2	-20	**	-31	-30	-36	**	-31
Blue collar	19	**	-4	10	-13	**	-31	-23	-30	**	-12
Unskilled	42*	**	19*	33*	-15*	**	-33	-24	-10*	**	-
Farmers	15	**	-2	-14	0*	**	-22	-58*	-36*	**	-
Housewives	6	**	-8	0	-13	**	-26	-32	-28	**	-20
Protestants	1	-18	-18	-1	-18	**	-33	-33	-36	**	-25
Catholics	17	4	7	11	-3	**	-21	-23	-30	**	0
Jews	40*	26*	17*	14*	-12*	**	-1	-7	-15*	**	-
Other and No Religion	9	-9*	-5	11	-22	**	-36	-30	-35	**	-19
Total Population	6	-12	-10	2	-14	**	-30	-29	-33	**	-17

PDI is proportion "not too strong" minus proportion "too powerful" (see table 3.1)

Table 3.34
Power of the Federal Government by Political Groups, Summarized by a Percentage Difference Index#

	1964	1966	1968	1970	1972	1974	1976	1978	1980	1982	1984
Strong Democrats	33	18	27	10	-6	**	-14	-13	-2	**	-19
Weak Democrats	31	2	-2	18	-24	**	-40	-41	-40	**	-20
Independent Democrats	50	-10	-5	-8	-32	**	-36	-55	-50	**	-32*
Independent Independents	0	-15	-11	-1	-22	**	-33	-33	-42	**	-4
Independent Republicans	-35	-46	-52	22	-20	**	-56	-61	-73	**	-21
Weak Republicans	-25	-45	-37	-14	-13	**	-50	-61	-66	**	-21
Strong Republicans	-52	-65	-47	-16	-11	**	-48	-50	-69	**	-13
Liberal Self Placement 1	**	**	**	**	-11	**	-22	-21	-12	**	9
Liberal Self Placement 2	**	**	**	**	-18	**	-32	-24	-29	**	-6
Neutral Self Placement 3	**	**	**	**	-6	**	-28	-28	-39	**	-12
Conservative Self Placement 4	**	**	**	**	-17	**	-41	-46	-47	**	-18
Conservative Self Placement 5	**	**	**	**	-29	**	-55	-49	-54	**	-32
Liberal Index 1	32	41*	29	10	-34*	**	2	**	17*	**	-
Liberal Index 2	31	6	2	16	-6	**	-18	**	-16	**	-4
Neutral Index 3	11	-6	-5	4	-12	**	-33	**	-30	**	2
Conservative Index 4	-12	-24	-20	-3	-16	**	-41	**	-46	**	-35
Conservative Index 5	-59	-75	-65	-30	-20	**	-68	**	-68	**	-50*
Total Population	6	-12	-10	2	-14	**	-30	-29	-33	**	-17

PDI is proportion "not too strong" minus proportion "too powerful" (see table 3.1)

Table 3.35
Federal Government Support for Comprehensive Health Care by Social Groups, Summarized by a Percentage Difference Index#

	1956	1958	1960	1962	1964	1966	1968
1959 or later Cohort	**	**	**	**	**	**	**
1943 - 1958 Cohort	**	**	**	**	46*	**	22
1927 - 1942 Cohort	27	**	36	29	19	**	18
1911 - 1926 Cohort	22	**	26	35	19	**	24
1895 - 1910 Cohort	29	**	53	49	25	**	38
Before 1895 Cohort	45	**	64	45	32	**	29
Grade School	56	**	69	72	53	**	52
High School	25	**	39	37	20	**	24
College	-11	**	4	-1	-8	**	6
Central cities	38	**	54	46	31	**	41
Suburbs	17	**	38	33	10	**	19
Non-urban Areas	28	**	36	36	24	**	20
Income Percentile 0-16	55	**	84	63	51	**	48
Income Percentile 17-33	43	**	55	45	31	**	38
Income Percentile 34-67	23	**	40	40	25	**	17
Income Percentile 68-95	10	**	16	17	2	**	16
Income Percentile 95-100	-5	**	14	-15	-11	**	5
Males	29	**	35	39	21	**	27
Females	27	**	45	36	23	**	24
Whites	24	**	35	33	15	**	19
Blacks	77	**	90	87	76	**	82
Union Household	34	**	53	**	32	**	35
Non-union Household	26	**	36	**	18	**	22
South	39	**	42	37	24	**	29
Non-south	23	**	40	38	21	**	24
Professional	1	**	8	**	-4	**	13
White collar	12	**	23	**	6	**	8
Blue collar	39	**	55	**	38	**	39
Unskilled	58	**	65*	**	64*	**	56*
Farmers	39	**	47	**	33	**	25
Housewives	30	**	47	**	25	**	24
Protestants	23	**	35	33	16	**	22
Catholics	40	**	56	49	32	**	28
Jews	52	**	60	57*	62*	**	61*
Other and No Religion	36*	**	29*	50*	41	**	41
Total Population	28	**	40	37	22	**	25

PDI is proportion "help people get care" minus proportion "stay out" (see table 3.2)

Social Welfare

Table 3.36
Federal Government Support for Comprehensive Health Care by Political Groups, Summarized by a Percentage Difference Index#

	1956	1958	1960	1962	1964	1966	1968
Strong Democrats	50	**	65	63	54	**	60
Weak Democrats	46	**	52	59	46	**	55
Independent Democrats	56	**	44	54	51	**	38
Independent Independents	21	**	44	30	23	**	30
Independent Republicans	-2	**	27	0	-24	**	-12
Weak Republicans	17	**	24	40	-1	**	-12
Strong Republicans	2	**	27	-16	-40	**	-4
Liberal Self Placement 1	**	**	**	**	**	**	**
Liberal Self Placement 2	**	**	**	**	**	**	**
Neutral Self Placement 3	**	**	**	**	**	**	**
Conservative Self Placement 4	**	**	**	**	**	**	**
Conservative Self Placement 5	**	**	**	**	**	**	**
Liberal Index 1	**	**	**	**	67	**	71
Liberal Index 2	**	**	**	**	35	**	36
Neutral Index 3	**	**	**	**	32	**	31
Conservative Index 4	**	**	**	**	0	**	13
Conservative Index 5	**	**	**	**	-42	**	-25
Total Population	28	**	40	37	22	**	25

PDI is proportion "help people get care" minus proportion "stay out" (see table 3.2)

Table 3.37
Government Health Insurance by Social Groups, Summarized by a Percent Difference Index#

	1970	1972	1974	1976	1978	1980	1982	1984
1959 or later Cohort	**	**	**	**	-14	**	**	-11
1943 - 1958 Cohort	5	7	**	4	1	**	**	-2
1927 - 1942 Cohort	-5	0	**	-5	-2	**	**	-6
1911 - 1926 Cohort	8	12	**	9	15	**	**	-13
1895 - 1910 Cohort	19	15	**	11	16	**	**	11
Before 1895 Cohort	23	24	**	-2	17	**	**	100
Grade School	24	18	**	16	27	**	**	4
High School	0	0	**	1	3	**	**	-1
College	-7	4	**	-4	-6	**	**	-7
Central Cities	11	20	**	14	15	**	**	6
Suburbs	12	7	**	2	0	**	**	-5
Non-urban Areas	-5	-6	**	-9	-4	**	**	-6
Income Percentile 0-16	35	25	**	33	27	**	**	3
Income Percentile 17-33	30	2	**	12	20	**	**	7
Income Percentile 34-67	-1	5	**	-1	0	**	**	-1
Income Percentile 68-95	-10	-3	**	-11	-6	**	**	-11
Income Percentile 95-100	-26	-25	**	-32	-30	**	**	-42
Males	1	6	**	0	1	**	**	-9
Females	7	4	**	3	4	**	**	2
Whites	-2	0	**	-3	-1	**	**	-6
Blacks	55	43	**	31	26	**	**	15
Union Household	9	13	**	2	9	**	**	4
Non-Union Household	3	1	**	1	0	**	**	-5
South	-4	-3	**	-2	-2	**	**	-3
Non-South	9	8	**	3	5	**	**	-3
Professional	-11	-1	**	-8	-8	**	**	-16
White collar	0	8	**	-7	3	**	**	-4
Blue collar	11	12	**	13	11	**	**	9
Unskilled	42	43	**	5	31	**	**	-24
Farmers	21	5	**	-8	-12	**	**	-10
Housewives	6	-2	**	-6	-4	**	**	-2
Protestants	-4	-4	**	-7	-6	**	**	-7
Catholics	23	17	**	17	18	**	**	3
Jews	35	57	**	44	34	**	**	-9
Other and No Religion	30	36	**	10	14	**	**	9
Total Population	4	4	**	1	3	**	**	-3

PDI is proportion "pro government insurance plan" minus proportion "pro private insurance plan"
  (see table 3.3).

Social Welfare

Table 3.38
Government Health Insurance by Political Groups, Summarized by a Percent Difference Index#

	1970	1972	1974	1976	1978	1980	1982	1984
Strong Democrats	29	26	**	19	26	**	**	18
Weak Democrats	15	4	**	12	13	**	**	-2
Independent Democrats	10	30	**	18	17	**	**	10
Independent Independents	3	5	**	6	2	**	**	4
Independent Republicans	-18	-7	**	-18	-20	**	**	-16
Weak Republicans	-14	-19	**	-19	-23	**	**	-21
Strong Republicans	-31	-14	**	-33	-30	**	**	-21
Liberal Self Placement 1	**	54	**	54	42	**	**	24
Liberal Self Placement 2	**	7	**	16	15	**	**	-8
Neutral Self Placement 3	**	2	**	-5	7	**	**	-4
Conservative Self Placement 4	**	-10	**	-15	-24	**	**	-19
Conservative Self Placement 5	**	2	**	-11	-2	**	**	-24
Liberal Index 1	65	64	**	47	**	**	**	33
Liberal Index 2	21	25	**	30	**	**	**	9
Neutral Index 3	0	-2	**	-1	**	**	**	2
Conservative Index 4	-8	-9	**	-15	**	**	**	-17
Conservative Index 5	-18	-22	**	-48	**	**	**	-42
Total Population	4	4	**	1	3	**	**	-3

PDI is proportion "pro government insurance plan" minus proportion "pro private insurance plan"
 (see table 3.3)

Table 3.39
Federal Government Guarantee Job and a Good Standard of Living (1) by Social Groups, Summarized by a Percentage Difference Index#

	1956	1958	1960	1962	1964	1966	1968
1959 or later Cohort	**	**	**	**	**	**	**
1943 - 1958 Cohort	**	**	**	**	27*	**	-10
1927 - 1942 Cohort	29	38	41	**	-10	**	-9
1911 - 1926 Cohort	23	24	23	**	-15	**	-21
1895 - 1910 Cohort	32	32	43	**	-13	**	-19
Before 1895 Cohort	46	33	47	**	-15	**	-21
Grade School	58	58	60	**	10	**	6
High School	26	31	31	**	-14	**	-21
College	-8	-15	10	**	-33	**	-24
Central cities	42	38	61	**	5	**	-1
Suburbs	20	25	32	**	-32	**	-20
Non-urban Areas	29	29	26	**	-10	**	-22
Income Percentile 0-16	59	60	61	**	15	**	8
Income Percentile 17-33	43	44	45	**	-3	**	-12
Income Percentile 34-67	28	33	39	**	-11	**	-24
Income Percentile 68-95	9	13	18	**	-30	**	-24
Income Percentile 95-100	-10	-35	14	**	-42	**	-22
Males	27	23	31	**	-15	**	-21
Females	32	36	39	**	-10	**	-11
Whites	25	25	30	**	-21	**	-25
Blacks	80	77	84	**	64	**	64
Union Household	43	45	54	**	-6	**	-11
Non-union Household	25	25	28	**	-14	**	-17
South	41	38	34	**	-1	**	-15
Non-south	25	27	36	**	-17	**	-16
Professional	3	-6	13	**	-35	**	-28
White collar	28	7	21	**	-32	**	-25
Blue collar	40	47	45	**	4	**	-6
Unskilled	57	64	57*	**	39*	**	-4*
Farmers	30	47	50	**	0	**	-20
Housewives	31	38	41	**	-10	**	-15
Protestants	28	26	30	**	-13	**	-19
Catholics	34	46	49	**	-15	**	-10
Jews	48	24	69	**	2*	**	24*
Other and No Religion	25*	35*	18*	**	4	**	-17
Total Population	30	30	35	**	-12	**	-16

PDI is proportion "government should see to jobs" minus proportion "each person on his own" (see table 3.4)

Social Welfare

Table 3.40
Federal Government Guarantee Job and Good Standard of Living(1) by Political Groups. Summarized by a Percentage Difference Index#

	1956	1958	1960	1962	1964	1966	1968
Strong Democrats	53	46	55	**	16	**	16
Weak Democrats	37	44	46	**	-3	**	-2
Independent Democrats	30	31	40	**	-5	**	-13
Independent Independents	22	37	48	**	-17	**	-38
Independent Republicans	6	1	-4	**	-37	**	-50
Weak Republicans	26	15	8	**	-32	**	-34
Strong Republicans	10	4	26	**	-50	**	-28
Liberal Self Placement 1	**	**	**	**	**	**	**
Liberal Self Placement 2	**	**	**	**	**	**	**
Neutral Self Placement 3	**	**	**	**	**	**	**
Conservative Self Placement 4	**	**	**	**	**	**	**
Conservative Self Placement 5	**	**	**	**	**	**	**
Liberal Index 1	**	**	**	**	38	**	42
Liberal Index 2	**	**	**	**	-1	**	-1
Neutral Index 3	**	**	**	**	-4	**	-18
Conservative Index 4	**	**	**	**	-32	**	-22
Conservative Index 5	**	**	**	**	-64	**	-60
Total Population	30	30	35	**	-12	**	-16

PDI is proportion "government should see to jobs" minus proportion "each person on his own" (see table 3.4)

Table 3.41
Federal Government Guarantee Jobs and Standard of Living (2) by Social Groups, Summarized by a Percent Difference Index#

	1972	1974	1976	1978	1980	1982	1984	1986
1959 or later Cohort	**	**	**	**	3	0	8	-13
1943 - 1958 Cohort	-4	6	-10	-27	-10	-12	-9	-25
1927 - 1942 Cohort	-19	-30	-19	-33	-27	-23	-20	-23
1911 - 1926 Cohort	-18	-18	-20	-27	-14	-23	-13	-27
1895 - 1910 Cohort	-6	-15	-7	-18	-21	-17	-7	-17
Before 1895 Cohort	1	-6	-19	-8	-22	-29	**	**
Grade School	6	-1	6	-4	8	6	9	-1
High School	-14	-11	-11	-24	-12	-15	-6	-17
College	-20	-21	-29	-38	-26	-24	-17	-33
Central cities	1	2	-5	-16	-1	-2	4	-7
Suburbs	-23	-16	-20	-32	-18	-22	-17	-29
Non-urban Areas	-11	-20	-15	-28	-24	-22	-8	-25
Income Percentile 0-16	14	4	19	6	6	14	26	1
Income Percentile 17-33	1	5	0	-18	-9	0	2	-16
Income Percentile 34-67	-15	-15	-15	-29	-13	-21	-8	-24
Income Percentile 68-95	-25	-22	-32	-42	-27	-30	-28	-37
Income Percentile 95-100	-45	-52	-49	-54	-48	-47	-49	-51
Males	-17	-26	-24	-34	-22	-28	-18	-29
Females	-8	-3	-7	-20	-10	-8	-2	-17
Whites	-20	-19	-21	-32	-23	-24	-16	-32
Blacks	59	54	38	16	39	42	42	28
Union Household	-12	-4	-9	-18	-6	-14	-8	-19
Non-union Household	-13	-15	-15	-29	-19	-17	-9	-24
South	-8	-6	-4	-23	-12	-16	-1	-20
Non-south	-14	-16	-18	-28	-17	-17	-13	-23
Professional	-22	-22	-34	-45	-33	-27	-21	-43
White collar	-18	-15	-20	-27	-21	-22	-12	-28
Blue collar	-2	-5	-4	-17	-4	-10	-1	-14
Unskilled	7	-3	-3	-3	5	-23	-13	17
Farmers	-25	-53	-11	-27	-52	-5	-16	-24
Housewives	-15	-8	-8	-22	-5	-10	-8	-9
Protestants	-14	-14	-16	-29	-15	-20	-10	-24
Catholics	-11	-11	-12	-21	-17	-11	-7	-25
Jews	0	-20	-3	-28	-10	-4	-13	-41
Other and No Religion	3	3	-9	-22	-10	-7	0	-10
Total Population	-14	-12	-15	-27	-15	-16	-10	-23

PDI is proportion "government should see to jobs" minus proportion "each person on his own"
  (see table 3.5)

Social Welfare

Table 3.42
Federal Government Guarantee Job and Standard of Living (2) by Political Groups, Summarized by a Percent Difference Index#

	1972	1974	1976	1978	1980	1982	1984	1986
Strong Democrats	16	12	14	-6	21	16	15	8
Weak Democrats	-6	-7	-2	-14	0	-9	1	-11
Independent Democrats	-3	-4	-10	-20	-14	-10	14	-21
Independent Independents	-12	-16	-23	-25	-24	-18	-3	-17
Independent Republicans	-30	-40	-34	-53	-38	-43	-24	-51
Weak Republicans	-32	-31	-29	-49	-42	-38	-31	-43
Strong Republicans	-32	-48	-49	-58	-48	-57	-47	-50
Liberal Self Placement 1	40	30	17	6	39	44	20	21
Liberal Self Placement 2	-5	2	-6	-30	-8	-24	5	-23
Neutral Self Placement 3	-18	-17	-15	-33	-11	-21	-7	-28
Conservative Self Placement 4	-35	-48	-40	-53	-46	-38	-37	-45
Conservative Self Placement 5	-47	-43	-56	-56	-51	-48	-42	-47
Liberal Index 1	59	48	16	**	72	51	32	30
Liberal Index 2	7	12	7	**	11	8	7	-15
Neutral Index 3	-11	-18	-15	**	-14	-19	-13	-20
Conservative Index 4	-30	-32	-35	**	-36	-37	-28	-42
Conservative Index 5	-53	-51	-64	**	-56	-67	-76	-46
Total Population	-14	-12	-15	-27	-15	-16	-10	-23

PDI is proportion "government should see to jobs" minus proportion "each person on his own"
  (see table 3.5)

Table 3.43
Government Services and Spending by Social Groups, Summarized by a Percent Difference Index#

	1980	1982	1984	1986
1959 or later Cohort	-38	-6	-15	-27
1943 - 1958 Cohort	-15	4	1	-21
1927 - 1942 Cohort	3	14	3	-11
1911 - 1926 Cohort	-6	12	0	-14
1895 - 1910 Cohort	-11	14	0	-5
Before 1895 Cohort	-46	-14	-33	0
Grade School	-26	-4	-10	-22
High School	-14	4	-3	-25
College	-1	14	3	-10
Central Cities	-22	-4	-10	-28
Suburbs	-7	12	-2	-16
Non-urban Areas	-5	12	5	-14
Income Percentile 0-16	-29	-12	-20	-31
Income Percentile 17-33	-20	2	-6	-24
Income Percentile 34-67	-11	7	0	-19
Income Percentile 68-95	4	16	7	-5
Income Percentile 95-100	21	38	20	-7
Males	-5	18	7	-9
Females	-14	-1	-8	-25
Whites	-5	13	3	-12
Blacks	-52	-35	-37	-54
Union Household	-16	-3	-12	-30
Non-union Household	-9	10	1	-15
South	-10	12	-4	-17
Non-South	-11	5	0	-19
Professional	6	17	7	-4
White collar	-3	17	3	-15
Blue collar	-24	-2	-9	-28
Unskilled	-26	-28	-15	-39
Farmers	-12	16	20	2
Housewives	-9	8	-4	-25
Protestants	-7	14	4	-14
Catholics	-14	-2	-8	-25
Jews	-41	0	-41	-34
Other and No Religion	-15	-8	-8	-23
Total Population	-10	8	-1	-17

PDI is proportion "fewer services/reduce spending" minus proportion "more services/increase spending"
  (see table 3.6)

Social Welfare

Table 3.44
Government Services and Spending by Political Groups, Summarized by a Percent Difference Index#

	1980	1982	1982	1986
Strong Democrats	-49	-19	-32	-43
Weak Democrats	-25	-5	-21	-31
Independent Democrats	-19	-14	-22	-39
Independent Independents	-7	13	4	-22
Independent Republicans	22	41	21	8
Weak Republicans	20	34	22	0
Strong Republicans	27	52	36	24
Liberal Self Placement 1	-62	-50	-31	-49
Liberal Self Placement 2	-19	-5	-12	-22
Neutral Self Placement 3	-17	6	-6	-27
Conservative Self Placement 4	22	30	23	12
Conservative Self Placement 5	23	45	31	13
Liberal Index 1	-81	-57	-45	-60
Liberal Index 2	-44	-19	-18	-37
Neutral Index 3	-21	3	-2	-23
Conservative Index 4	4	30	17	-3
Conservative Index 5	52	62	60	32
Total Population	-10	8	-1	-17

PDI is proportion "fewer services/reduce spending" minus proportion "more services/increase spending"
  (see table 3.6)

Social Welfare

Table 3.45
Rights of the Accused by Social Groups, Summarized by a Percentage Difference Index#

	1970	1972	1974	1976	1978
1959 or later Cohort	**	**	**	**	-8
1943 - 1958 Cohort	0	7	21	0	-12
1927 - 1942 Cohort	-11	2	-2	-9	-26
1911 - 1926 Cohort	-11	-20	-18	-23	-33
1895 - 1910 Cohort	-25	-38	-22	-26	-35
Before 1895 Cohort	-30	-13	-16	-24	-28*
Grade School	-24	-28	-17	-18	-27
High School	-13	-11	-3	-16	-24
College	-5	5	9	-3	-19
Central cities	-1	3	9	-8	-19
Suburbs	-14	-5	-3	-9	-25
Non-urban Areas	-20	-19	-9	-16	-22
Income Percentile 0-16	-10	-11	-7	-2	-20
Income Percentile 17-33	-4	-16	14	-10	-16
Income Percentile 34-67	-14	-9	1	-16	-26
Income Percentile 68-95	-20	-5	-6	-13	-26
Income Percentile 95-100	0	-12	-21	-18	-35
Males	-15	-8	-9	-13	-17
Females	-12	-11	3	-11	-27
Whites	-19	-13	-5	-15	-24
Blacks	46	25	26	14	-12
Union Household	-11	-3	3	-12	-23
Non-union Household	-14	-12	-3	-12	-22
South	-15	-16	-9	-18	-22
Non-south	-12	-6	2	-9	-23
Professional	-10	-5	-6	-10	-19
White collar	-3	5	2	-11	-24
Blue collar	-16	-8	3	-12	-21
Unskilled	-12*	15*	-19*	-12	0
Farmers	-30	-23	-24	-22	-37*
Housewives	-16	-26	-11	-18	-33
Protestants	-16	-13	-5	-11	-26
Catholics	-15	-7	-1	-18	-24
Jews	10*	26*	3	3	-15
Other and No Religion	10	10	26	-7	1
Total Population	-13	-9	-2	-12	-22

PDI is proportion "protect rights" minus proportion "stop crime" (see table 3.7)

Table 3.46
Rights of the Accused by Political Groups, Summarized by a Percentage Difference Index#

	1970	1972	1974	1976	1978
Strong Democrats	-1	-3	14	1	-14
Weak Democrats	-4	-8	-7	-10	-21
Independent Democrats	-1	26	23	-2	-10
Independent Independents	-17	-9	2	-10	-23
Independent Republicans	-33	-15	-16	-19	-30
Weak Republicans	-21	-26	-13	-27	-42
Strong Republicans	-33	-31	-36	-32	-52
Liberal Self Placement 1	**	57	41	35	19
Liberal Self Placement 2	**	23	22	1	-14
Neutral Self Placement 3	**	-16	-2	-12	-23
Conservative Self Placement 4	**	-19	-25	-17	-29
Conservative Self Placement 5	**	-42	-28	-38	-53
Liberal Index 1	36	78	61	10	**
Liberal Index 2	1	25	32	12	**
Neutral Index 3	-19	-12	-2	-15	**
Conservative Index 4	-18	-20	-19	-19	**
Conservative Index 5	-44	-46	-44	-45	**
Total Population	-13	-9	-2	-12	-22

PDI is proportion "protect rights" minus proportion "stop crime" (see table 3.7)

Table 3.47
Response to Urban Unrest by Social Groups, Summarized by a Percentage Difference Index#

	1968	1970	1972	1974	1976
1959 or later Cohort	**	**	**	**	**
1943 - 1958 Cohort	15	23	52	43	37
1927 - 1942 Cohort	21	8	36	34	20
1911 - 1926 Cohort	6	8	24	15	17
1895 - 1910 Cohort	2	3	6	14	17
Before 1895 Cohort	6	4	-3*	13	1*
Grade School	0	4	17	13	15
High School	13	9	31	29	24
College	17	16	42	38	30
Central cities	24	23	40	44	34
Suburbs	8	7	36	27	25
Non-urban Areas	5	2	23	18	17
Income Percentile 0-16	12	10	24	25	38
Income Percentile 17-33	15	20	33	42	22
Income Percentile 34-67	9	8	32	28	23
Income Percentile 68-95	9	4	39	29	25
Income Percentile 95-100	3	9	16	11	18
Males	-3	-4	24	21	12
Females	22	20	37	33	34
Whites	4	3	28	26	21
Blacks	69	70	58	59	57
Union Household	8	8	29	35	26
Non-union Household	12	10	32	26	24
South	4	-5	20	14	14
Non-south	14	17	38	36	30
Professional	11	10	32	25	21
White collar	15	14	36	37	27
Blue collar	4	2	27	28	23
Unskilled	-	8*	-	51*	28
Farmers	0	5	-12*	-4	6
Housewives	15	13	34	26	27
Protestants	7	7	27	22	22
Catholics	18	4	39	40	26
Jews	43*	45*	29*	47	40
Other and No Religion	31*	37	53*	41	36
Total Population	11	9	32	28	24

PDI is proportion "solve problems" minus proportion "use force" (see table 3.8)

Law and Order

Table 3.48
Response to Urban Unrest by Political Groups, Summarized by a Percentage Difference Index#

	1968	1970	1972	1974	1976
Strong Democrats	36	20	33	49	39
Weak Democrats	18	21	44	38	40
Independent Democrats	17	24	48	46	35
Independent Independents	-7	4	28	19	22
Independent Republicans	-4	-14	26	5	17
Weak Republicans	-2	2	33	28	17
Strong Republicans	1	-9	15	14	17
Liberal Self Placement 1	**	**	69	73	66
Liberal Self Placement 2	**	**	59	48	44
Neutral Self Placement 3	**	**	37	26	27
Conservative Self Placement 4	**	**	21	18	21
Conservative Self Placement 5	**	**	-1	2	-4
Liberal Index 1	54	64	74*	66	52
Liberal Index 2	26	28	63	57	53
Neutral Index 3	7	6	36	23	28
Conservative Index 4	10	2	17	17	15
Conservative Index 5	-35	-33	-11	-5	-21
Total Population	11	9	32	28	24

PDI is proportion "solve problems" minus proportion "use force" (see table 3.8)

Table 3.49
Change in Situation of Blacks by Social Groups, Summarized by a Percentage Difference Index#

	1964	1966	1968	1970	1972	1974	1976	1978	1980	1982	1984	1986
1959 or later Cohort	**	**	**	**	**	**	**	**	**	**	**	-20
1943 - 1958 Cohort	-15*	-26	-35	-41	-44	**	-45	**	**	**	**	-24
1927 - 1942 Cohort	-20	-21	-35	-38	-52	**	-50	**	**	**	**	-38
1911 - 1926 Cohort	-29	-25	-42	-47	-48	**	-59	**	**	**	**	-50
1895 - 1910 Cohort	-15	-22	-29	-45	-44	**	-59	**	**	**	**	-44
Before 1895 Cohort	-12	-16	-30	-37*	-48	**	-54	**	**	**	**	-
Grade School	-16	-21	-28	-44	-33	**	-50	**	**	**	**	-33
High School	-20	-22	-37	-42	-48	**	-54	**	**	**	**	-37
College	-27	-23	-39	-40	-54	**	-49	**	**	**	**	-27
Central cities	-31	-26	-42	-43	-44	**	-47	**	**	**	**	-26
Suburbs	-23	-26	-33	-37	-54	**	-54	**	**	**	**	-36
Non-urban Areas	-12	-15	-33	-45	-44	**	-54	**	**	**	**	-33
Income Percentile 0-16	-14	-20	-28	-50	-45	**	-52	**	**	**	**	-31
Income Percentile 17-33	-18	-10	-30	-35	-37	**	-47	**	**	**	**	-31
Income Percentile 34-67	-22	-27	-36	-43	-48	**	-52	**	**	**	**	-39
Income Percentile 68-95	-24	-21	-44	-42	-51	**	-56	**	**	**	**	-27
Income Percentile 95-100	-29	-26	-38	-48*	-56	**	-57	**	**	**	**	-40*
Males	-21	-20	-36	-47	-48	**	-50	**	**	**	**	-36
Females	-21	-23	-35	-39	-46	**	-53	**	**	**	**	-30
Whites	-18	-21	-34	-44	-49	**	-57	**	**	**	**	-36
Blacks	-46	-29	-55	-27	-34	**	-14	**	**	**	**	-9
Union Household	-28	-21	-39	-42	-46	**	-51	**	**	**	**	-27
Non-union Household	-19	-22	-35	-43	-48	**	-52	**	**	**	**	-35
South	-29	-32	-47	-47	-52	**	-61	**	**	**	**	-34
Non-south	-18	-18	-31	-40	-44	**	-48	**	**	**	**	-32
Professional	-21	**	-31	-43	-53	**	-52	**	**	**	**	-31
White collar	-30	**	-44	-35	-55	**	-55	**	**	**	**	-35
Blue collar	-22	**	-38	-43	-42	**	-50	**	**	**	**	-31
Unskilled	-39*	**	-48*	-44*	-34*	**	-59	**	**	**	**	-33*
Farmers	14	**	-40	-44*	-40	**	-27	**	**	**	**	-27*
Housewives	-21	**	-31	-43	-47	**	-57	**	**	**	**	-42
Protestants	-18	-21	-38	-42	-47	**	-53	**	**	**	**	-37
Catholics	-26	-23	-32	-47	-52	**	-54	**	**	**	**	-26
Jews	-44*	-26*	-41*	-37*	-54	**	-50	**	**	**	**	-52*
Other and No Religion	-28	-36*	-21	-29	-28	**	-39	**	**	**	**	-21
Total Population	-21	-22	-36	-42	-47	**	-52	**	**	**	**	-33

PDI is proportion "not much at all" minus proportion "a lot" (see table 3.9)

Minority Relations

Table 3.50
Change in Situation of Blacks by Political Groups, Summarized by a Percentage Difference Index#

	1964	1966	1968	1970	1972	1974	1976	1978	1980	1982	1984	1986
Strong Democrats	-31	-26	-38	-36	-41	**	-47	**	**	**	**	-35
Weak Democrats	-24	-22	-36	-43	-50	**	-48	**	**	**	**	-24
Independent Democrats	-27	-16	-44	-38	-44	**	-51	**	**	**	**	-25
Independent Independents	-11	-16	-33	-32	-43	**	-52	**	**	**	**	-27
Independent Republicans	-22	-12	-38	-42	-51	**	-57	**	**	**	**	-31
Weak Republicans	-8	-31	-32	-49	-55	**	-60	**	**	**	**	-32
Strong Republicans	-22	-19	-27	-45	-50	**	-65	**	**	**	**	-47
Liberal Self Placement 1	**	**	**	**	-46	**	-40	**	**	**	**	-13
Liberal Self Placement 2	**	**	**	**	-53	**	-49	**	**	**	**	-46
Neutral Self Placement 3	**	**	**	**	-50	**	-50	**	**	**	**	-35
Conservative Self Placement 4	**	**	**	**	-54	**	-65	**	**	**	**	-42
Conservative Self Placement 5	**	**	**	**	-52	**	-65	**	**	**	**	-38
Liberal Index 1	-41	-23*	-24	-36*	-35	**	-41	**	**	**	**	5*
Liberal Index 2	-37	-32	-40	-40	-52	**	-47	**	**	**	**	-27
Neutral Index 3	-15	-20	-33	-40	-49	**	-51	**	**	**	**	-31
Conservative Index 4	-17	-18	-41	-44	-50	**	-63	**	**	**	**	-44
Conservative Index 5	-9	-22	-30	-44	-59	**	-67	**	**	**	**	-41
Total Population	-21	-22	-36	-42	-47	**	-52	**	**	**	**	-33

PDI is proportion "not much at all" minus proportion "a lot" (see table 3.9)

Table 3.51
Pace of Civil Rights Leaders' Actions by Social Groups, Summarized by a Percentage Difference Index#

	1964	1966	1968	1970	1972	1974	1976	1978	1980	1982	1984	1986
1959 or later Cohort	**	**	**	**	**	**	**	**	46	**	54	65
1943 - 1958 Cohort	-48*	-29	-24	5	20	29	26	**	46	**	43	58
1927 - 1942 Cohort	-28	-42	-21	-13	5	19	21	**	23	**	46	56
1911 - 1926 Cohort	-35	-34	-34	-11	-10	-3	1	**	4	**	7	18
1895 - 1910 Cohort	-37	-53	-37	-14	-5	-9	5	**	6	**	21	2
Before 1895 Cohort	-29	-50	-9	-27*	15	-5	15	**	-	**	-	-
Grade School	-26	-42	-24	-18	-7	-5	10	**	20	**	24	11
High School	-36	-42	-40	-14	-2	4	7	**	17	**	31	41
College	-33	-38	-10	7	22	36	32	**	43	**	46	66
Central cities	-13	-21	-3	23	24	22	29	**	43	**	52	60
Suburbs	-40	-43	-31	-18	0	7	16	**	20	**	35	51
Non-urban Areas	-42	-54	-42	-26	-5	8	6	**	23	**	28	38
Income Percentile 0-16	-11	-34	-13	2	11	15	26	**	33	**	34	39
Income Percentile 17-33	-31	-38	-35	-14	4	17	17	**	22	**	35	34
Income Percentile 34-67	-42	-45	-37	-10	1	3	8	**	30	**	31	52
Income Percentile 68-95	-39	-42	-28	-13	4	21	21	**	27	**	44	57
Income Percentile 95-100	-30	-42	-7	8*	10	24	31	**	33	**	51*	59*
Males	-40	-48	-32	-16	3	3	14	**	22	**	32	48
Females	-27	-35	-26	-6	5	18	18	**	32	**	40	50
Whites	-46	-52	-41	-21	-5	4	8	**	20	**	29	42
Blacks	76	47	86	85	77	82	83	**	85	**	87	86
Union Household	-25	-43	-34	-11	-2	17	7	**	28	**	44	43
Non-union Household	-35	-40	-26	-11	6	10	19	**	27	**	34	51
South	-36	-55	-37	-35	-10	-4	1	**	24	**	32	45
Non-south	-31	-35	-25	2	11	20	23	**	29	**	39	51
Professional	-33	**	-22	0	11	18	21	**	35	**	43	67
White collar	-46	**	-34	-18	7	15	20	**	22	**	34	46
Blue collar	-26	**	-30	-14	2	2	11	**	23	**	37	42
Unskilled	-33*	**	-15*	-	31*	41*	2	**	45*	**	43*	17*
Farmers	-25	**	-18	-10*	1	13	26	**	4*	**	16*	44*
Housewives	-34	**	-32	-14	-7	12	13	**	23	**	32	41
Protestants	-32	-45	-30	-15	2	7	13	**	23	**	29	45
Catholics	-39	-33	-25	1	13	18	17	**	30	**	48	54
Jews	-26*	-30*	-12*	45*	45	20	36	**	48*	**	33*	-
Other and No Religion	-24	-18*	-33	23	20	38	31	**	37	**	51	68
Total Population	-33	-41	-28	-10	4	11	16	**	27	**	36	69

PDI is proportion "about right" plus "too slowly" minus proportion "too fast" (see table 3.10)

Minority Relations

Table 3.52
Pace of Civil Rights Leaders' Actions by Political Groups, Summarized by a Percentage Difference Index#

	1964	1966	1968	1970	1972	1974	1976	1978	1980	1982	1984	1986
Strong Democrats	-26	-35	-1	4	15	31	18	**	39	**	48	49
Weak Democrats	-14	-42	-19	9	1	7	22	**	37	**	56	57
Independent Democrats	-6	-34	-22	3	20	27	21	**	34	**	48	61
Independent Independents	-38	-34	-53	-2	3	1	14	**	15	**	30	52
Independent Republicans	-55	-65	-51	-3	0	-8	10	**	28	**	30	42
Weak Republicans	-39	-47	-35	-13	-7	13	14	**	25	**	26	48
Strong Republicans	-62	-65	-39	-26	-7	4	12	**	2	**	14	35
Liberal Self Placement 1	**	**	**	**	61	56	47	**	68	**	55	79
Liberal Self Placement 2	**	**	**	**	39	38	46	**	46	**	56	67
Neutral Self Placement 3	**	**	**	**	-1	9	14	**	23	**	41	46
Conservative Self Placement 4	**	**	**	**	-7	4	25	**	30	**	43	62
Conservative Self Placement 5	**	**	**	**	-17	-19	-5	**	-1	**	9	23
Liberal Index 1	15	12*	59	63*	76	78	61	**	83*	**	67*	79*
Liberal Index 2	-23	-24	-6	16	43	52	42	**	54	**	48	67
Neutral Index 3	-34	-45	-40	-5	1	10	18	**	35	**	41	49
Conservative Index 4	-42	-48	-35	-24	-4	-6	10	**	18	**	32	45
Conservative Index 5	-62	-67	-59	-36	-33	-30	-16	**	-16	**	-6	28
Total Population	-33	-41	-28	-10	4	11	16	**	27	**	36	69

PDI is proportion "about right" plus "too slowly" minus proportion "too fast" (see table 3.10)

Table 3.53
Does the Respondent Favor Desegregation or Segregation by Social Groups, Summarized by a Percentage Difference Index#

	1964	1966	1968	1970	1972	1974	1976	1978
1959 or later Cohort	**	**	**	**	**	**	**	19
1943 - 1958 Cohort	0*	**	35	38	40	**	38	32
1927 - 1942 Cohort	22	**	31	31	37	**	34	30
1911 - 1926 Cohort	8	**	19	22	19	**	21	28
1895 - 1910 Cohort	1	**	5	18	9	**	14	24
Before 1895 Cohort	-11	**	8	-4*	20	**	5	4*
Grade School	-8	**	-3	7	4	**	13	19
High School	9	**	18	22	24	**	22	26
College	29	**	45	51	52	**	47	38
Central cities	28	**	36	37	38	**	35	35
Suburbs	12	**	22	27	32	**	36	27
Non-urban Areas	-7	**	11	15	20	**	19	27
Income Percentile 0-16	-8	**	8	21	17	**	24	25
Income Percentile 17-33	13	**	15	21	26	**	27	29
Income Percentile 34-67	8	**	18	23	25	**	28	29
Income Percentile 68-95	15	**	31	29	39	**	35	31
Income Percentile 95-100	29	**	45	51*	48	**	45	40
Males	6	**	23	25	31	**	30	32
Females	11	**	19	25	27	**	29	27
Whites	2	**	15	19	24	**	24	27
Blacks	66	**	69	76	66	**	69	45
Union Household	16	**	18	20	25	**	25	27
Non-union Household	7	**	22	26	30	**	31	30
South	-17	**	1	1	16	**	19	28
Non-south	20	**	29	37	35	**	34	30
Professional	22	**	39	46	44	**	45	39
White collar	10	**	20	26	36	**	35	31
Blue collar	9	**	13	20	24	**	22	24
Unskilled	8*	**	12*	-	24*	**	25	37
Farmers	-32	**	14	3*	6	**	11	21*
Housewives	7	**	16	17	19	**	21	24
Protestants	3	**	15	22	25	**	27	27
Catholics	17	**	31	32	31	**	30	29
Jews	56*	**	61*	47*	60	**	46	57
Other and No Religion	38	**	33	28	39	**	39	37
Total Population	9	**	21	25	28	**	29	29

PDI is proportion "desegregation" minus proportion "segregation" (see table 3.11)

Minority Relations

Table 3.54
Does the Respondent Favor Desegregation or Segregation by Political Groups, Summarized by a Percentage Difference Index#

	1964	1966	1968	1970	1972	1974	1976	1978
Strong Democrats	11	**	30	22	32	**	25	37
Weak Democrats	7	**	20	35	26	**	33	31
Independent Democrats	34	**	32	29	44	**	41	39
Independent Independents	10	**	13	22	27	**	23	27
Independent Republicans	7	**	20	35	28	**	34	28
Weak Republicans	15	**	23	23	29	**	25	25
Strong Republicans	13	**	16	35	21	**	28	25
Liberal Self Placement 1	**	**	**	**	76	**	64	56
Liberal Self Placement 2	**	**	**	**	58	**	49	42
Neutral Self Placement 3	**	**	**	**	25	**	33	29
Conservative Self Placement 4	**	**	**	**	35	**	41	32
Conservative Self Placement 5	**	**	**	**	17	**	18	24
Liberal Index 1	38	**	48	81*	79	**	66	**
Liberal Index 2	26	**	37	35	54	**	51	**
Neutral Index 3	3	**	9	16	28	**	29	**
Conservative Index 4	1	**	24	26	24	**	29	**
Conservative Index 5	-6	**	23	14	17	**	23	**
Total Population	9	**	21	25	28	**	29	29

PDI is proportion "desegregation" minus proportion "segregation" (see table 3.11)

Table 3.55
Position on Aid to Minorities by Social Groups, Summarized by a Percentage Difference Index#

	1970	1972	1974	1976	1978	1980	1982	1984	1986
1959 or later Cohort	**	**	**	**	0	-7	-16	1	1
1943 -1958 Cohort	-2	11	9	6	-13	-22	-13	-4	-9
1927 - 1942 Cohort	-13	-10	-16	-9	-30	-26	-22	-9	-13
1911 - 1926 Cohort	-14	-18	-20	-18	-18	-32	-19	-5	-16
1895 - 1910 Cohort	-19	-18	-22	-20	-14	-16	-22	-7	-37
Before 1895 Cohort	-27	-14	-16	-8	4*	-	-	-	-
Grade School	-13	-20	-22	-7	-4	-18	-12	3	-17
High School	-17	-13	-12	-14	-20	-28	-22	-11	-16
College	-6	9	3	3	-19	-19	-14	0	-3
Central cities	2	14	7	4	-2	-4	-2	12	7
Suburbs	-14	-6	-14	-9	-23	-25	-17	-9	-14
Non-urban Areas	-23	-20	-17	-14	-24	-36	-30	-11	-20
Income Percentile 0-16	3	-3	9	15	8	-5	-10	13	0
Income Percentile 17-33	-11	-6	-4	-3	-11	-26	-16	0	-16
Income Percentile 34-67	-16	-12	-9	-9	-21	-22	-15	-10	-15
Income Percentile 68-95	-19	-7	-16	-16	-32	-30	-23	-10	-11
Income Percentile 95-100	-8	-5	-49	-18	-36	-47	-27	-11	-9*
Males	-18	-9	-16	-12	-23	-26	-21	-8	-17
Females	-10	-7	-5	-4	-13	-21	-15	-3	-5
Whites	-23	-15	-17	-15	-25	-29	-24	-10	-16
Blacks	73	63	61	50	38	21	33	36	20
Union Household	-11	-7	-9	-11	-19	-24	-19	-7	-9
Non-union Household	-14	-8	-10	-6	-17	-23	-17	-5	-11
South	-24	-14	-13	-12	-22	-28	-22	-8	-18
Non-south	-7	-5	-8	-5	-15	-20	-15	-4	-6
Professional	-14	0	2	-6	-22	-24	-12	2	-5
White collar	-10	-2	-15	-3	-19	-26	-21	-9	-12
Blue collar	-12	-7	-13	-10	-16	-21	-21	-7	-13
Unskilled	-4*	29*	3*	-1	-2	0*	-5*	-19*	-14*
Farmers	-5	-26	-39	-9	-14*	-39*	-12*	-7	-17*
Housewives	-19	-21	-14	-15	-21	-27	-24	-9	-14
Protestants	-17	-11	-13	-9	-18	-28	-19	-9	-15
Catholics	-12	-4	-11	-10	-23	-20	-16	2	-5
Jews	22*	31*	-2	6	-6	18*	17*	19	-
Other and No Religion	5	12	19	12	-8	-16	-19	-1	0
Total Population	-13	-8	-9	-7	-18	-23	-18	-5	-10

PDI is proportion "government help" minus proportion "self help" (see table 3.12)

Table 3.56
Position on Aid to Minorities by Political Groups, Summarized by a Percentage Difference Index#

	1970	1972	1974	1976	1978	1980	1982	1984	1986
Strong Democrats	8	9	6	2	4	-2	2	15	10
Weak Democrats	-1	-5	-6	5	-17	-18	-16	9	-5
Independent Democrats	-6	14	11	4	-6	-9	0	18	7
Independent Independents	-16	-13	-10	-12	-20	-24	-21	-3	-17
Independent Republicans	-28	-19	-26	-14	-38	-49	-30	-31	-29
Weak Republicans	-26	-21	-30	-27	-38	-46	-37	-25	-22
Strong Republicans	-38	-27	-40	-22	-43	-51	-55	-26	-36
Liberal Self Placement 1	**	58	41	43	21	27	42	34	38
Liberal Self Placement 2	**	32	7	11	-12	-8	-10	13	5
Neutral Self Placement 3	**	-11	-5	-6	-24	-33	-16	-12	-12
Conservative Self Placement 4	**	-21	-31	-21	-35	-30	-33	-13	-15
Conservative Self Placement 5	**	-47	-48	-44	-50	-48	-40	-28	-36
Liberal Index 1	62	69	66	41	**	73*	59	35	46*
Liberal Index 2	9	29	30	25	**	2	5	10	-2
Neutral Index 3	-19	-7	-19	-14	**	-26	-22	-14	-9
Conservative Index 4	-23	-22	-28	-20	**	-36	-26	-14	-19
Conservative Index 5	-42	-45	-42	-51	**	-60	-53	-41	-46
Total Population	-13	-8	-9	-7	-18	-23	-18	-5	-10

PDI is proportion "government help" minus proportion "self help" (see table 3.12)

Table 3.57
Should Federal Government Ensure School Integration by Social Groups, Summarized by a Percentage Difference Index#&

	1962	1964	1966	1968	1970	1972	1974	1976	1978	1980	1982	1984	1986
1959 or later Cohort	**	**	**	**	**	**	**	**	-3	**	**	**	21
1943 - 1958 Cohort	**	-15*	40	3	30	5	**	-7	-8	**	**	**	-9
1927 - 1942 Cohort	20	11	14	1	10	-12	**	-23	-19	**	**	**	-5
1911 - 1926 Cohort	10	5	16	-7	6	-17	**	-19	-23	**	**	**	-11
1895 - 1910 Cohort	13	-2	3	-17	6	-14	**	-21	-7	**	**	**	-4
Before 1895 Cohort	22	-21	-6	-13	-1*	8	**	2	8*	**	**	**	-
Grade School	6	-7	1	-10	4	-2	**	-8	5	**	**	**	3
High School	16	4	14	-6	9	-14	**	-20	-16	**	**	**	-4
College	24	11	22	-2	26	-1	**	-12	-16	**	**	**	-3
Central cities	23	18	31	18	28	5	**	-4	-2	**	**	**	14
Suburbs	31	9	12	-9	7	-13	**	-23	-21	**	**	**	-5
Non-urban Areas	-6	-14	0	-18	5	-11	**	-16	-15	**	**	**	-13
Income Percentile 0-16	8	-4	8	-6	18	3	**	3	1	**	**	**	10
Income Percentile 17-33	10	5	20	1	19	2	**	-8	2	**	**	**	5
Income Percentile 34-67	17	0	10	-11	6	-11	**	-17	-19	**	**	**	-6
Income Percentile 68-95	24	7	17	-5	8	-14	**	-23	-23	**	**	**	-6
Income Percentile 95-100	23	12	18	-6	40*	-11	**	-13	-23	**	**	**	-7*
Males	17	-1	13	-12	9	-9	**	-19	-16	**	**	**	-5
Females	14	6	12	-1	14	-7	**	-13	-12	**	**	**	-1
Whites	12	-4	5	-15	5	-16	**	-23	-22	**	**	**	-13
Blacks	50	56	66	78	77	63	**	52	47	**	**	**	52
Union Household	**	13	16	-5	5	-9	**	-19	-11	**	**	**	-2
Non-union Household	**	0	11	-6	13	-7	**	-14	-14	**	**	**	-3
South	-35	-22	-16	-21	-7	-17	**	-18	-10	**	**	**	-2
Non-south	42	14	25	1	21	-3	**	-14	-15	**	**	**	-3
Professional	**	1	**	1	24	-12	**	-12	-18	**	**	**	-3
White collar	**	-1	**	-13	9	-8	**	-19	-22	**	**	**	-11
Blue collar	**	11	**	-11	11	-5	**	-16	-6	**	**	**	-4
Unskilled	**	6*	**	7*	-	10*	**	-17	7	**	**	**	20*
Farmers	**	-26	**	-5	-3*	18*	**	-11	0	**	**	**	0*
Housewives	**	2	**	-3	4	-15	**	-18	-23	**	**	**	2
Protestants	4	-7	5	-11	10	-10	**	-16	-15	**	**	**	-3
Catholics	43	25	30	8	8	-8	**	-20	-16	**	**	**	-1
Jews	73*	43*	40*	24*	5*	23	**	6	5	**	**	**	-
Other and No Religion	40*	26	30*	-3	42	6	**	-4	-8	**	**	**	-2
Total Population	19	3	12	-6	12	-8	**	-15	-14	**	**	**	-3

PDI is proportion "same schools" minus proportion "government stay out" (see table 3.13)

& Question appears without lead-in ('Have you been concerned...') and varies slightly in text in 1962

Minority Relations

Table 3.58
Should Federal Government Ensure School Integration by Political Groups, Summarized by a Percentage Difference Index#&

	1962	1964	1966	1968	1970	1972	1974	1976	1978	1980	1982	1984	1986
Strong Democrats	18	12	24	21	18	9	**	0	9	**	**	**	15
Weak Democrats	3	11	14	3	31	-14	**	-9	-12	**	**	**	11
Independent Democrats	49	34	25	1	18	-1	**	-17	-10	**	**	**	20
Independent Independents	34	-8	25	-18	0	-3	**	-21	-22	**	**	**	-3
Independent Republicans	5	-15	13	-37	17*	-24	**	-40	-38	**	**	**	-33
Weak Republicans	26	12	3	-15	26	-9	**	-34	-40	**	**	**	-31
Strong Republicans	24	-18	-10	-23	15	-26	**	-39	-40	**	**	**	-18
Liberal Self Placement 1	**	**	**	**	**	43	**	23	22	**	**	**	20
Liberal Self Placement 2	**	**	**	**	**	18	**	2	-20	**	**	**	20
Neutral Self Placement 3	**	**	**	**	**	-18	**	-18	-18	**	**	**	-10
Conservative Self Placement 4	**	**	**	**	**	-23	**	-30	-20	**	**	**	-10
Conservative Self Placement 5	**	**	**	**	**	-35	**	-34	-38	**	**	**	-25
Liberal Index 1	**	28	59*	42	73*	62	**	31	**	**	**	**	34*
Liberal Index 2	**	21	16	10	36	18	**	9	**	**	**	**	10
Neutral Index 3	**	-2	9	-10	-2	-8	**	-16	**	**	**	**	-7
Conservative Index 4	**	-4	18	-8	9	-21	**	-28	**	**	**	**	-13
Conservative Index 5	**	-29	-22	-45	1	-48	**	-44	**	**	**	**	-42
Total Population	15	3	12	-6	12	-8	**	-15	-14	**	**	**	-3

PDI is proportion "same schools" minus proportion "government stay out" (see table 3.13)

& Question appears without lead-in ('Have you been concerned...') and varies slightly in text in 1962

Table 3.59
Busing to Achieve School Integration by Social Groups, Summarized by a Percentage Difference Index#

	1972	1974	1976	1978	1980	1982	1984
1959 or later Cohort	**	**	**	**	-57	**	-24
1943 - 1958 Cohort	-64	-60	-57	**	-62	**	-35
1927 - 1942 Cohort	-73	-64	-69	**	-77	**	-36
1911 - 1926 Cohort	-74	-75	-70	**	-74	**	-38
1895 - 1910 Cohort	-72	-75	-67	**	-78	**	-36
Before 1895 Cohort	-68	-68	-68	**	-	**	-
Grade School	-66	-65	-56	**	-60	**	-28
High School	-78	-71	-69	**	-73	**	-36
College	-61	-61	-62	**	-67	**	-34
Central cities	-55	-53	-53	**	-52	**	-28
Suburbs	-79	-74	-74	**	-76	**	-35
Non-urban Areas	-74	-70	-64	**	-75	**	-37
Income Percentile 0-16	-63	-57	-40	**	-59	**	-25
Income Percentile 17-33	-69	-55	-63	**	-70	**	-32
Income Percentile 34-67	-75	-71	-66	**	-73	**	-38
Income Percentile 68-95	-72	-72	-76	**	-71	**	-35
Income Percentile 95-100	-73	-73	-68	**	-81	**	-35
Males	-71	-71	-68	**	-70	**	-35
Females	-71	-63	-62	**	-69	**	-34
Whites	-78	-72	-73	**	-79	**	-37
Blacks	-13	-15	10	**	-1	**	-11
Union Household	-74	-71	-70	**	-65	**	-36
Non-union Household	-70	-65	-63	**	-71	**	-34
South	-74	-67	-65	**	-71	**	-34
Non-south	-69	-66	-64	**	-68	**	-34
Professional	-67	-63	-68	**	-68	**	-35
White collar	-73	-77	-68	**	-80	**	-35
Blue collar	-70	-65	-60	**	-66	**	-34
Unskilled	-55*	-51*	-64	**	-55*	**	-28*
Farmers	-64	-88	-57	**	-89*	**	-31
Housewives	-77	-70	-69	**	-73	**	-37
Protestants	-72	-70	-63	**	-69	**	-36
Catholics	-78	-70	-73	**	-76	**	-34
Jews	-41	-50	-60	**	-73*	**	-32*
Other and No Religion	-43	-34	-51	**	-60	**	-26
Total Population	-71	-67	-65	**	-69	**	-34

PDI is proportion "pro busing" minus proportion "neighborhood schools" (see table 3.14)

Table 3.60
Busing to Achieve School Integration by Political Groups, Summarized by a Percentage Difference Index#

	1972	1974	1976	1978	1980	1982	1984
Strong Democrats	-46	-43	-55	**	-46	**	-30
Weak Democrats	-76	-77	-62	**	-69	**	-75
Independent Democrats	-68	-71	-71	**	-71	**	-58
Independent Independents	-70	-76	-69	**	-71	**	-35
Independent Republicans	-88	-92	-75	**	-86	**	-82
Weak Republicans	-86	-83	-84	**	-91	**	-87
Strong Republicans	-85	-84	-78	**	-88	**	-43
Liberal Self Placement 1	-16	-32	-33	**	-43	**	-17
Liberal Self Placement 2	-58	-49	-50	**	-64	**	-34
Neutral Self Placement 3	-84	-79	-71	**	-77	**	-34
Conservative Self Placement 4	-88	-86	-75	**	-84	**	-41
Conservative Self Placement 5	-93	-87	-85	**	-82	**	-43
Liberal Index 1	18	7	-17	**	11*	**	-13
Liberal Index 2	-54	-45	-47	**	-57	**	-31
Neutral Index 3	-77	-75	-70	**	-71	**	-34
Conservative Index 4	-87	-82	-75	**	-82	**	-41
Conservative Index 5	-96	-82	-85	**	-93	**	-46
Total Population	-71	-67	-65	**	-69	**	-34

PDI is proportion "pro busing" minus proportion "neighborhood schools" (see table 3.14)

Table 3.61
Open Housing by Social Groups, Summarized by a Percentage Difference Index#

	1964	1966	1968	1970	1972	1974	1976
1959 or later Cohort	**	**	*i	**	**	**	**
1943 - 1958 Cohort	31*	49	59	68	76	**	89
1927 - 1942 Cohort	49	26	54	59	68	**	81
1911 - 1926 Cohort	31	21	49	43	51	**	69
1895 - 1910 Cohort	16	0	30	45	46	**	59
Before 1895 Cohort	8	-12	28	11*	37	**	52
Grade School	10	-9	24	33	34	**	57
High School	33	15	50	47	61	**	76
College	49	51	58	77	80	**	89
Central cities	46	34	62	58	73	**	80
Suburbs	33	23	49	54	65	**	85
Non-urban Areas	19	0	34	43	50	**	68
Income Percentile 0-16	17	6	37	37	50	**	74
Income Percentile 17-33	33	2	37	46	55	**	68
Income Percentile 34-67	32	13	45	48	59	**	79
Income Percentile 68-95	35	30	57	60	71	**	86
Income Percentile 95-100	41	40	68	78*	80	**	88
Males	30	29	49	51	65	**	80
Females	32	8	43	50	58	**	75
Whites	24	10	41	45	56	**	74
Blacks	87	75	96	95	98	**	97
Union Household	33	16	48	51	61	**	79
Non-union Household	30	18	46	50	61	**	77
South	2	-12	19	24	43	**	65
Non-south	44	30	58	64	70	**	83
Professional	38	**	63	70	77	**	88
White collar	35	**	37	45	70	**	86
Blue collar	35	**	44	42	59	**	72
Unskilled	53*	**	56*	-	46*	**	86
Farmers	14	**	42	48*	38	**	71
Housewives	23	**	39	47	47	**	68
Protestants	24	13	40	46	58	**	76
Catholics	45	26	59	55	63	**	78
Jews	85*	56*	86*	79*	85	**	84
Other and No Religion	44	22*	59	77	75	**	84
Total Population	31	17	46	51	61	**	77

PDI is proportion "blacks' rights to choose" minus proportion "whites can keep blacks out" (see table 3.15)

Minority Relations

Table 3.62
Open Housing by Political Groups, Summarized by a Percentage Difference Index#

	1964	1966	1968	1970	1972	1974	1976
Strong Democrats	26	15	57	48	54	**	67
Weak Democrats	37	15	49	67	56	**	83
Independent Democrats	72	38	56	72	78	**	92
Independent Independents	29	21	36	41	71	**	77
Independent Republicans	31	34	53	73	72	**	86
Weak Republicans	54	14	56	54	72	**	83
Strong Republicans	30	21	37	53	59	**	76
Liberal Self Placement 1	**	**	**	**	89	**	88
Liberal Self Placement 2	**	**	**	**	84	**	89
Neutral Self Placement 3	**	**	**	**	60	**	86
Conservative Self Placement 4	**	**	**	**	71	**	86
Conservative Self Placement 5	**	**	**	**	54	**	70
Liberal Index 1	46	67*	78	84*	94	**	80
Liberal Index 2	37	30	60	60	87	**	87
Neutral Index 3	31	8	35	38	57	**	83
Conservative Index 4	25	18	50	59	61	**	79
Conservative Index 5	15	17	44	44	46	**	66
Total Population	31	17	46	51	61	**	77

PDI is proportion "blacks' rights to choose" minus proportion "whites can keep blacks out" (see table 3.15)

Table 3.63
Equal Role for Women by Social Groups, Summarized by a Percentage Difference Index#

	1972	1974	1976	1978	1980	1982	1984
1959 or later Cohort	**	**	**	47	40	45	51
1943 - 1958 Cohort	32	49	45	52	52	54	52
1927 - 1942 Cohort	16	18	31	31	41	39	38
1911 - 1926 Cohort	13	9	16	24	19	27	15
1895 - 1910 Cohort	7	9	4	4	23	12	8
Before 1895 Cohort	-4	-5	-11*	-17*	-	-	-
Grade School	-7	-4	-8	-5	4	-3	8
High School	12	17	18	28	28	28	26
College	43	54	58	59	63	63	61
Central cities	28	32	36	41	43	47	44
Suburbs	24	31	38	40	44	44	43
Non-urban Areas	6	12	12	25	29	30	30
Income Percentile 0-16	7	24	12	18	24	34	21
Income Percentile 17-33	15	20	17	32	36	29	23
Income Percentile 34-67	12	20	29	32	36	41	42
Income Percentile 68-95	30	36	37	51	53	54	52
Income Percentile 95-100	39	29	53	51	56	47	74
Males	20	28	33	40	36	39	43
Females	15	22	24	31	40	40	35
Whites	17	23	27	34	39	38	39
Blacks	22	37	33	41	31	52	34
Union Household	13	19	31	37	35	42	50
Non-union Household	19	27	27	34	39	39	36
South	10	23	20	30	32	35	29
Non-south	21	25	32	38	42	42	43
Professional	40	48	58	59	56	57	63
White collar	39	36	34	53	49	51	45
Blue collar	8	17	25	24	26	34	31
Unskilled	10*	27*	30	46	31*	33*	36*
Farmers	-9	-3	-4	32*	39*	14*	28
Housewives	-1	4	-1	6	21	13	4
Protestants	14	19	20	28	34	32	33
Catholics	19	28	35	40	40	49	45
Jews	65	65	63	64	60*	71*	56
Other and No Religion	34	50	56	55	57	62	57
Total Population	17	24	28	35	39	40	39

PDI is proportion "equal role" minus proportion "role in home" (see table 3.16)

Women's Issues/Morality

Table 3.64
Equal Role for Women by Political Groups, Summarized by a Percentage Difference Index#

	1972	1974	1976	1978	1980	1982	1984
Strong Democrats	12	32	29	31	37	40	42
Weak Democrats	19	30	32	34	41	48	46
Independent Democrats	40	47	42	57	57	52	52
Independent Independents	9	27	28	46	41	47	33
Independent Republicans	28	14	43	42	49	48	41
Weak Republicans	16	17	20	26	36	37	41
Strong Republicans	6	7	21	14	27	17	31
Liberal Self Placement 1	63	71	62	78	74	83	70
Liberal Self Placement 2	51	67	61	78	66	66	68
Neutral Self Placement 3	21	29	40	38	46	52	40
Conservative Self Placement 4	17	16	35	43	48	49	44
Conservative Self Placement 5	5	2	2	4	20	27	27
Liberal Index 1	48	74	50	**	73*	74	71
Liberal Index 2	39	62	56	**	63	67	49
Neutral Index 3	20	22	31	**	43	37	46
Conservative Index 4	14	15	27	**	40	46	38
Conservative Index 5	5	-14	6	**	23	18	35
Total Population	17	24	28	35	39	40	39

PDI is proportion "equal role" minus proportion "role in home" (see table 3.16)

Table 3.65
Women stay out of Politics by Social Groups, Summarized by a Percentage Difference Index#

	1952	1956	1960	1964	1968	1972
1959 or later Cohort	**	**	**	**	**	**
1943 - 1958 Cohort	**	**	**	**	**	72
1927 - 1942 Cohort	41*	**	**	**	**	64
1911 - 1926 Cohort	42	**	**	**	**	59
1895 - 1910 Cohort	49	**	**	**	**	49
Before 1895 Cohort	30	**	**	**	**	4
Grade School	21	**	**	**	**	21
High School	44	**	**	**	**	58
College	85	**	**	**	**	89
Central cities	47	**	**	**	**	67
Suburbs	42	**	**	**	**	71
Non-urban Areas	29	**	**	**	**	48
Income Percentile 0-16	15	**	**	**	**	31
Income Percentile 17-33	12	**	**	**	**	52
Income Percentile 34-67	50	**	**	**	**	62
Income Percentile 68-95	53	**	**	**	**	78
Income Percentile 95-100	-	**	**	**	**	86
Males	45	**	**	**	**	62
Females	36	**	**	**	**	58
Whites	44	**	**	**	**	60
Blacks	6	**	**	**	**	60
Union Household	37	**	**	**	**	60
Non-union Household	43	**	**	**	**	60
South	20	**	**	**	**	53
Non-south	46	**	**	**	**	63
Professional	53	**	**	**	**	86
White collar	58	**	**	**	**	74
Blue collar	39	**	**	**	**	45
Unskilled	0*	**	**	**	**	40*
Farmers	33*	**	**	**	**	37
Housewives	45	**	**	**	**	51
Protestants	34	**	**	**	**	56
Catholics	56	**	**	**	**	67
Jews	-	**	**	**	**	84
Other and No Religion	-	**	**	**	**	72
Total Population	39	**	**	**	**	60

PDI is proportion "disagree" minus proportion "agree" (see table 3.17)

Women's Issues/Morality

Table 3.66
Women stay out of Politics by Political Groups, Summarized by a Percentage Difference Index#

	1952	1956	1960	1964	1968	1972
Strong Democrats	36	**	**	**	**	60
Weak Democrats	43	**	**	**	**	56
Independent Democrats	58	**	**	**	**	73
Independent Independents	32*	**	**	**	**	57
Independent Republicans	73	**	**	**	**	66
Weak Republicans	47	**	**	**	**	62
Strong Republicans	22	**	**	**	**	56
Liberal Self Placement 1	**	**	**	**	**	86
Liberal Self Placement 2	**	**	**	**	**	87
Neutral Self Placement 3	**	**	**	**	**	68
Conservative Self Placement 4	**	**	**	**	**	82
Conservative Self Placement 5	**	**	**	**	**	63
Liberal Index 1	**	**	**	**	**	75
Liberal Index 2	**	**	**	**	**	82
Neutral Index 3	**	**	**	**	**	61
Conservative Index 4	**	**	**	**	**	68
Conservative Index 5	**	**	**	**	**	64
Total Population	39	**	**	**	**	60

PDI is proportion "disagree" minus proportion "agree" (see table 3.17)

Table 3.67
Abortions (1) by Social Groups, Summarized by
a Percentage Difference Index#

	1972	1974	1976	1978	1980
1959 or later Cohort	**	**	**	1	27
1943 - 1958 Cohort	25	**	23	25	22
1927 - 1942 Cohort	18	**	25	13	19
1911 - 1926 Cohort	10	**	11	14	8
1895 - 1910 Cohort	-4	**	-7	0	9
Before 1895 Cohort	-12	**	-16	15*	-
Grade School	-12	**	-16	-15	-12
High School	13	**	12	14	13
College	29	**	34	30	31
Central cities	18	**	17	15	18
Suburbs	23	**	22	24	21
Non-urban Areas	3	**	8	8	13
Income Percentile 0-16	-4	**	-10	1	-6
Income Percentile 17-33	7	**	7	10	14
Income Percentile 34-67	14	**	15	17	21
Income Percentile 68-95	24	**	26	23	28
Income Percentile 95-100	31	**	49	39	37
Males	15	**	18	15	15
Females	11	**	13	17	19
Whites	15	**	17	19	20
Blacks	-3	**	-1	-4	-2
Union Household	17	**	18	16	20
Non-union Household	12	**	15	16	17
South	3	**	6	10	9
Non-south	18	**	20	19	22
Professional	26	**	33	34	29
White collar	20	**	29	25	24
Blue collar	9	**	5	3	6
Unskilled	-10*	**	17	10	8*
Farmers	-17	**	-14	0*	7*
Housewives	6	**	6	11	11
Protestants	13	**	15	15	13
Catholics	1	**	0	2	8
Jews	60	**	76	73	63*
Other and No Religion	48	**	46	37	46
Total Population	13	**	15	16	17

PDI is proportion permit "anytime" minus proportion
"never" permit (see table 3.18)

Table 3.68
Abortions (2) by Social Groups, Summarized with a Percent
Difference Index#

	1980	1984	1986
1959 or later Cohort	41	27	25
1943 - 1958 Cohort	32	32	33
1927 - 1942 Cohort	29	22	26
1911 - 1926 Cohort	11	13	18
1895 - 1910 Cohort	6	-2	-4
Before 1895 Cohort	-	-	-
Grade School	-7	-10	-14
High School	20	17	20
College	40	38	39
Central Cities	25	29	32
Suburbs	29	27	30
Non-urban AReas	19	13	14
Income Percentile 0-16	2	2	6
Income Percentile 17-33	19	19	15
IncomePercentile 34-67	27	25	28
Income Percentile 68-95	35	32	35
Income Percentile 96-100	44	48	58
Males	24	25	25
Females	25	21	26
Whites	26	24	28
Blacks	8	15	12
Union Household	26	29	32
Non-union Household	24	21	24
South	19	12	16
Non-south	28	28	31
Professional	36	39	37
White Collar	32	30	37
Blue Collar	18	16	16
Unskilled	2*	10*	20
Farmers	3*	-9*	-5
Housewives	15	9	14
Protestants	22	17	21
Catholics	13	20	21
Jews	65*	62	81
Other and No Religion	52	56	55
Total Population	24	23	25

PDI is proportion permit "as a matter of personal choice"
minus proportion "never" permit (see table 3.19)

Women's Issues/Morality

Table 3.69
Abortions (1) by Political Groups, Summarized by
a Percentage Difference Index#

	1972	1974	1976	1978	1980
Strong Democrats	1	**	4	3	6
Weak Democrats	10	**	13	13	22
Independent Democrats	29	**	32	29	33
Independent Independents	12	**	20	17	22
Independent Republicans	29	**	20	21	18
Weak Republicans	15	**	16	23	14
Strong Republicans	9	**	18	20	16
Liberal Self Placement 1	32	**	38	34	49
Liberal Self Placement 2	29	**	33	34	41
Neutral Self Placement 3	18	**	24	15	20
Conservative Self Placement 4	22	**	22	21	19
Conservative Self Placement 5	15	**	10	9	5
Liberal Index 1	21	**	32	**	45*
Liberal Index 2	27	**	34	**	35
Neutral Index 3	13	**	17	**	16
Conservative Index 4	14	**	16	**	18
Conservative Index 5	14	**	9	**	12
Total Population	13	**	15	16	17

PDI is proportion permit "anytime" minus proportion
"never" permit (see table 3.18)

Table 3.70
Abortion (2) by Political Groups, Summarized with a Percent
Difference Index#

	1980	1984	1986
Strong Democrats	9	25	18
Weak Democrats	30	29	28
Independent Democrats	34	26	37
Independent Independents	29	18	19
Independent Republicans	30	24	26
Weak Republicans	23	20	32
Strong Republicans	18	12	25
Liberal Self Placement 1	47	53	49
Liberal Self Placement 2	52	44	45
Neutral Self Placement 3	32	29	32
Conservative Self Placement 4	27	27	29
Conservative Self Placement 5	13	8	9
Liberal Index 1	49*	53	53
Liberal Index 2	41	37	39
Neutral Index 3	27	25	30
Conservative Index 4	26	18	23
Conservative Index 5	19	18	8
Total Population	24	23	25

PDI is proportion permit "as a matter of personal choice"
minus proportion "never" permit (see table 3.19)

Table 3.71
Percent of Respondents Who Believe Bible is God's Word, by Social Groups&

	1964	1968	1980	1984	1986
1959 or later Cohort	**	**	48%	58%	54%
1943 - 1958 Cohort	38%*	47%	45	45	47
1927 - 1942 Cohort	47	53	41	48	50
1911 - 1926 Cohort	57	51	54	53	55
1895 - 1910 Cohort	51	57	55	61	61
Before 1895 Cohort	65	71	-	-	-
Grade School	75%	76%	73%	73%	77%
High School	53	57	53	58	59
College	30	29	32	36	36
Central Cities	47%	52%	48%	50%	50%
Suburbs	43	44	36	42	46
Non-urban Areas	64	62	60	60	58
Income Percentile 0-16	71%	76%	68%	70%	67%
Income Percentile 17-33	60	61	54	61	66
Income Percentile 34-67	56	55	45	48	52
Income Percentile 68-95	39	39	34	38	35
Income Percentile 96-100	28	24	26	29	24
Males	46%	47%	43%	43%	44%
Females	58	59	51	56	56
Whites	51%	51%	45%	47%	48%
Blacks	69	79	65	71	68
Union Household	50%	53%	41%	43%	46%
Non-union Household	53	54	49	52	52
South	61%	68%	61%	65%	65%
Non-south	49	47	39	43	43
Professional	33%	32%	34%	34%	33%
White Collar	46	52	44	48	51
Blue Collar	58	59	53	55	60
Unskilled	69*	81*	59*	63*	59
Farmers	80	71	67*	67	66
Housewives	58	61	57	65	61
Protestants	57%	59%	56%	61%	60%
Catholics	48	47	36	38	37
Jews	24*	3*	18*	5*	26*
Other and No Religion	28	33	27	26	27
Total Population	53	54	47	50	51

& See table 3.20 for question description

Table 3.72
Percent of Respondents Who Believe Bible is God's Word, by Political Groups&

	1964	1968	1980	1984	1986
Strong Democrats	58%	66%	57%	55%	55%
Weak Democrats	60	59	50	49	52
Independent Democrats	41	39	38	39	46
Independent Independents	57	50	41	52	52
Independent Republicans	39	46	42	54	47
Weak Republicans	46	46	44	48	49
Strong Republicans	40	50	50	50	49
Liberal Self Placement 1	**	**	26%	31%	33%
Liberal Self Placement 2	**	**	28	32	34
Neutral Self Placement 3	**	**	38	46	47
Conservative Self Placement 4	**	**	35	41	44
Conservative Self Placement 5	**	**	58	58	58
Liberal Index 1	50%	34%	41%*	32%	33%
Liberal Index 2	46	49	32	43	41
Neutral Index 3	62	59	47	52	54
Conservative Index 4	46	53	45	48	47
Conservative Index 5	42	43	51	50	55
Total Population	53	54	47	50	51

& See table 3.20 for question description

Table 3.73
Percent of Respondents Who Consider Religion an Important Part of His/Her Life, by Social Groups&

	1980	1984	1986
1959 or later Cohort	57%	74%	71%
1943 - 1958 Cohort	70	73	75
1927 - 1942 Cohort	77	83	81
1911 - 1926 Cohort	83	89	91
1895 - 1910 Cohort	86	90	81
Before 1895 Cohort	-	-	-
Grade School	88%	89%	84%
High School	76	81	80
College	71	76	75
Central Cities	78%	80%	78%
Suburbs	70	77	77
Non-urban Areas	79	82	82
Income Percentile 0-16	83%-	84%	83%
Income Percentile 17-33	76	86	87
Income Percentile 34-67	75	78	76
Income Percentile 68-95	69	73	79
Income Percentile 96-100	66	76	51
Males	67%	71%	71%
Females	82	86	84
Whites	73%	78%	77%
Blacks	92	92	91
Union Household	72%	78%	71%
Non-union Household	76	80	80
South	84%	86%	86%
Non-south	71	76	74
Professional	69%	76%	73%
White Collar	78	80	82
Blue Collar	76	77	78
Unskilled	71*	80*	72*
Farmers	83*	83	84
Housewives	85	90	88
Protestants	81%	84%	84%
Catholics	82	86	83
Jews	48*	55*	-
Other and No Religion	34	36	35
Total Population	75	79	79

& See table 3.21 for question description

Women's Issues/Morality

Table 3.74
Percent of Respondents Who Consider Religion an Important Part of His/Her Life, by Political Groups&

	1980	1984	1986
Strong Democrats	83%	87%	82%
Weak Democrats	74	79	81
Independent Democrats	65	71	76
Independent Independents	70	81	70
Independent Republicans	71	79	74
Weak Republicans	77	78	82
Strong Republicans	85	79	85
Liberal Self Placement 1	60%	73%	64%
Liberal Self Placement 2	68	68	68
Neutral Self Placement 3	72	77	80
Conservative Self Placement 4	72	81	81
Conservative Self Placement 5	82	83	86
Liberal Index 1	65%*	69%	57%*
Liberal Index 2	67	75	72
Neutral Index 3	74	77	80
Conservative Index 4	76	84	81
Conservative Index 5	80	72	88
Total Population	75	79	79

& See table 3.21 for question description

Table 3.75
U.S. Concern with World Problems by Social Groups, Summarized by a Percentage Difference Index#

	1956	1958	1960	1962	1964	1966	1968	1970	1972	1974	1976	1978	1980	1982	1984	1986
1959 or later Cohort	**	**	**	**	**	**	**	**	**	**	**	**	66	**	47	35
1943 - 1958 Cohort	**	**	**	**	**	**	65	**	63	**	50	**	63	**	59	46
1927 - 1942 Cohort	46	47	54	**	**	**	63	**	64	**	48	**	70	**	60	43
1911 - 1926 Cohort	43	36	57	**	**	**	53	**	58	**	39	**	59	**	36	27
1895 - 1910 Cohort	25	29	44	**	**	**	34	**	44	**	16	**	29	**	6	-7
Before 1895 Cohort	1	12	19	**	**	**	11	**	23	**	-17	**	-	**	-	-
Grade School	-2	6	20	**	**	**	19	**	23	**	-15	**	13	**	-3	-11
High School	40	35	52	**	**	**	53	**	59	**	37	**	55	**	40	25
College	69	69	78	**	**	**	74	**	79	**	70	**	82	**	72	61
Central cities	37	33	55	**	**	**	57	**	55	**	38	**	61	**	49	30
Suburbs	43	43	60	**	**	**	53	**	64	**	47	**	66	**	57	45
Non-urban Areas	24	27	38	**	**	**	47	**	55	**	36	**	53	**	40	31
Income Percentile 0-16	-8	-5	3	**	**	**	12	**	29	**	0	**	32	**	15	5
Income Percentile 17-33	20	26	25	**	**	**	41	**	48	**	23	**	46	**	36	38
Income Percentile 34-67	40	40	51	**	**	**	55	**	62	**	46	**	66	**	56	36
Income Percentile 68-95	52	50	72	**	**	**	74	**	71	**	61	**	81	**	69	61
Income Percentile 95-100	67	65	88	**	**	**	80	**	87	**	69	**	76	**	71	72*
Males	36	42	58	**	**	**	58	**	61	**	47	**	62	**	60	42
Females	29	25	39	**	**	**	46	**	55	**	36	**	59	**	40	33
Whites	36	36	49	**	**	**	52	**	60	**	46	**	62	**	51	41
Blacks	-6	6	34	**	**	**	42	**	35	**	-3	**	47	**	36	21
Union Household	34	30	52	**	**	**	46	**	56	**	43	**	64	**	53	35
Non-union Household	32	34	46	**	**	**	53	**	58	**	40	**	59	**	48	37
South	23	23	38	**	**	**	45	**	60	**	32	**	60	**	43	35
Non-south	36	37	53	**	**	**	54	**	57	**	45	**	61	**	52	38
Professional	59	59	80	**	**	**	68	**	78	**	66	**	80	**	79	59
White collar	46	36	57	**	**	**	68	**	69	**	56	**	64	**	47	36
Blue collar	28	29	54	**	**	**	42	**	48	**	34	**	47	**	39	20
Unskilled	7	36	11*	**	**	**	-	**	32*	**	-22	**	48*	**	29*	35*
Farmers	-7	-2	7	**	**	**	56	**	59	**	13	**	52*	**	23*	38*
Housewives	29	25	31	**	**	**	43	**	49	**	27	**	58	**	31	36
Protestants	32	32	48	**	**	**	48	**	57	**	40	**	58	**	45	39
Catholics	32	32	51	**	**	**	57	**	62	**	35	**	65	**	56	31
Jews	48	61	73	**	**	**	82	**	60	**	83	**	95*	**	78*	-
Other and No Religion	16*	21*	50*	**	**	**	63*	**	51	**	49	**	52	**	47	31
Total Population	32	33	48	**	**	**	51	**	58	**	41	**	60	**	49	37

PDI is proportion "disagree" (that US should not concern itself) minus proportion "agree" (see table 3.22)

Foreign Relations

Table 3.76
U.S. Concern with World Problems by Political Groups, Summarized by a Percentage Difference Index#

	1956	1958	1960	1962	1964	1966	1968	1970	1972	1974	1976	1978	1980	1982	1984	1986
Strong Democrats	28	30	43	**	**	**	51	**	58	**	18	**	61	**	30	22
Weak Democrats	42	48	51	**	**	**	46	**	59	**	40	**	65	**	50	38
Independent Democrats	37	49	77	**	**	**	67	**	51	**	43	**	60	**	36	26
Independent Independents	32	37	47	**	**	**	46	**	44	**	46	**	49	**	49	34
Independent Republicans	51	70	76	**	**	**	71	**	76	**	63	**	65	**	63	50
Weak Republicans	47	36	55	**	**	**	46	**	64	**	44	**	70	**	56	44
Strong Republicans	35	38	57	**	**	**	54	**	71	**	63	**	67	**	69	63
Liberal Self Placement 1	**	**	**	**	**	**	**	**	64	**	49	**	55	**	46	30
Liberal Self Placement 2	**	**	**	**	**	**	**	**	70	**	58	**	77	**	55	34
Neutral Self Placement 3	**	**	**	**	**	**	**	**	69	**	54	**	62	**	52	40
Conservative Self Placement 4	**	**	**	**	**	**	**	**	71	**	61	**	77	**	72	48
Conservative Self Placement 5	**	**	**	**	**	**	**	**	72	**	61	**	65	**	72	52
Liberal Index 1	**	**	**	**	**	**	73	**	55	**	33	**	56*	**	52*	36*
Liberal Index 2	**	**	**	**	**	**	54	**	67	**	46	**	72	**	49	37
Neutral Index 3	**	**	**	**	**	**	37	**	61	**	34	**	60	**	50	41
Conservative Index 4	**	**	**	**	**	**	65	**	70	**	60	**	67	**	63	45
Conservative Index 5	**	**	**	**	**	**	61	**	72	**	71	**	71	**	75	60
Total Population	32	33	48	**	**	**	51	**	58	**	41	**	60	**	49	37

PDI is proportion "disagree" (that US should not concern itself) minus proportion "agree" (see table 3.22)

Table 3.77
Were We Right in Getting into Korea or Vietnam by Social Groups, Summarized by a Percentage Difference Index#

	1952	1954	1956	1958	1960	1962	1964	1966	1968	1970	1972
1959 or later Cohort	**	**	**	**	**	**	**	**	**	**	**
1943 - 1958 Cohort	**	**	**	**	**	**	-43*	-26	3	6	19
1927 - 1942 Cohort	-20	**	**	**	**	**	-22	-30	10	0	16
1911 - 1926 Cohort	-12	**	**	**	**	**	-19	-12	20	28	36
1895 - 1910 Cohort	12	**	**	**	**	**	1	-7	44	41	45
Before 1895 Cohort	20	**	**	**	**	**	5	7	41	41	64
Grade School	20	**	**	**	**	**	6	5	38	39	44
High School	-6	**	**	**	**	**	-16	-19	17	12	26
College	-27	**	**	**	**	**	-29	-31	15	15	21
Central cities	-3	**	**	**	**	**	-17	-16	28	25	39
Suburbs	-1	**	**	**	**	**	-19	-24	11	10	19
Non-urban Areas	9	**	**	**	**	**	-7	-8	25	23	29
Income Percentile 0-16	28	**	**	**	**	**	7	-6	44	44	46
Income Percentile 17-33	15	**	**	**	**	**	-2	3	26	38	35
Income Percentile 34-67	-1	**	**	**	**	**	-18	-17	14	12	21
Income Percentile 68-95	-15	**	**	**	**	**	-27	-21	10	3	21
Income Percentile 95-100	-15	**	**	**	**	**	-33	-47	18	40	30
Males	-12	**	**	**	**	**	-23	-24	11	15	24
Females	13	**	**	**	**	**	-7	-8	30	22	32
Whites	1	**	**	**	**	**	-16	-17	20	17	25
Blacks	10	**	**	**	**	**	2	-2	33	45	55
Union Household	-8	**	**	**	**	**	-19	-17	21	16	23
Non-union Household	5	**	**	**	**	**	-12	-15	22	21	30
South	3	**	**	**	**	**	-10	-16	23	19	23
Non-south	2	**	**	**	**	**	-15	-15	21	19	31
Professional	-22	**	**	**	**	**	-30	**	13	16	23
White collar	-12	**	**	**	**	**	-23	**	22	9	23
Blue collar	-6	**	**	**	**	**	-12	**	16	17	27
Unskilled	9	**	**	**	**	**	-6*	**	19*	33*	54*
Farmers	19	**	**	**	**	**	7	**	37	40	47
Housewives	15	**	**	**	**	**	-6	**	33	26	32
Protestants	7	**	**	**	**	**	-10	-14	22	18	28
Catholics	-9	**	**	**	**	**	-27	-22	12	13	22
Jews	-30	**	**	**	**	**	-8*	-12*	43*	35*	71
Other and No Religion	13	**	**	**	**	**	-3	-18*	44	43	40
Total Population	2	**	**	**	**	**	-14	-15	21	19	28

PDI is proportion "should stay out" minus proportion "did right thing" (see table 3.23)

Table 3.78
Were We Right in Getting into Korea or Vietnam by Political Groups, Summarized by a Percentage Difference Index#

	1952	1954	1956	1958	1960	1962	1964	1966	1968	1970	1972
Strong Democrats	-21	**	**	**	**	**	-19	-12	16	27	36
Weak Democrats	-1	**	**	**	**	**	-24	-29	29	25	35
Independent Democrats	-20	**	**	**	**	**	-32	-23	19	7	41
Independent Independents	13	**	**	**	**	**	-10	-10	20	37	29
Independent Republicans	-10	**	**	**	**	**	-21	-29	21	-10	13
Weak Republicans	28	**	**	**	**	**	-6	-15	29	26	33
Strong Republicans	31	**	**	**	**	**	-9	-15	36	15	17
Liberal Self Placement 1	**	**	**	**	**	**	**	**	**	**	57
Liberal Self Placement 2	**	**	**	**	**	**	**	**	**	**	22
Neutral Self Placement 3	**	**	**	**	**	**	**	**	**	**	20
Conservative Self Placement 4	**	**	**	**	**	**	**	**	**	**	13
Conservative Self Placement 5	**	**	**	**	**	**	**	**	**	**	6
Liberal Index 1	**	**	**	**	**	**	12	6*	32	54	62
Liberal Index 2	**	**	**	**	**	**	-29	-20	13	35	36
Neutral Index 3	**	**	**	**	**	**	-15	-9	27	10	25
Conservative Index 4	**	**	**	**	**	**	-7	-23	19	13	16
Conservative Index 5	**	**	**	**	**	**	-15	-31	13	4	5
Total Population	2	**	**	**	**	**	-14	-15	21	19	28

PDI is proportion "should stay out" minus proportion "did right thing" (see table 3.23)

Table 3.79
Likelihood of Conventional War by Social Groups, Summarized with a Percent Difference Index#

	1956	1960	1964	1982	1984	1986
1959 or later Cohort	**	**	**	9%	13%	8%
1943 - 1958 Cohort	**	**	4%*	15	22	21
1927 - 1942 Cohort	22%	-5%	31	11	20	20
1911 - 1926 Cohort	30	13	31	11	19	19
1895 - 1910 Cohort	42	18	42	11	24	32
Before 1895 Cohort	42	17	39	-	-	-
Grade School	39%	18%	38%	-12%	12%	8%
High School	30	4	31	9	16	16
College	34	19	37	22	27	23
Central Cities	32%	17%	33%	10%	9%	12%
Suburbs	40	14	38	15	21	20
Non-urban Areas	30	7	31	11	26	21
Income Percentile 0-16	38%	10%	37%	1%	1%	8%
Income Percentile 17-33	34	14	25	7	6	6
Income Percentile 34-67	29	11	37	14	23	28
Income Percentile 68-95	35	9	36	18	29	22
Income Percentile 96-100	33	19	34	28	50	18
Males	39%	28%	42%	20%	35%	32%
Females	28	-2	27	6	9	8
Whites	33%	11%	34%	14%	23%	21%
Blacks	41	17	32	-5	-3	3
Union Household	28%	13%	40%	7%	17%	23%
Non-union Household	35	10	32	14	21	17
South	29%	8%	29%	14%	19%	19%
Non-south	35	13	36	11	21	18
Professional	36%	13%	37%	30%	26%	25%
White Collar	26	13	30	6	19	11
Blue Collar	39	23	39	5	22	21
Unskilled	36	43*	31*	0*	10*	40*
Farmers	44	28	46	23*	22	32
Housewives	28	-7	27	8	10	4
Protestants	34%	12%	34%	15%	23%	20%
Catholics	31	7	28	5	14	13
Jews	29	10	49*	17*	-4	-
Other and No Religion	30*	39*	42	10	25	16
Total Population	33	11	34	12	20	18

PDI is proportion "not worried" minus proportion "pretty worried" (see table 3.24)

Table 3.80
Likelihood of Conventional War by Political Groups, Summarized with a Percent Difference Index#

	1956	1960	1964	1982	1984	1986
Strong Democrats	19%	8%	35%	3%	-9%	12%
Weak Democrats	33	2	35	10	9	13
Independent Democrats	16	6	25	2	-2	10
Independent Independents	41	22	30	20	29	18
Independent Republicans	36	25	44	5	36	38
Weak Republicans	34	19	34	22	37	14
Strong Republicans	50	14	34	28	51	32
Liberal Self Placement 1	**	**	**	13%	4%	-11%
Liberal Self Placement 2	**	**	**	16	8	11
Neutral Self Placement 3	**	**	**	12	18	14
Conservative Self Placement 4	**	**	**	15	31	29
Conservative Self Placement 5	**	**	**	22	46	34
Liberal Index 1	**	**	35%	-8%	-15%	13%*
Liberal Index 2	**	**	40	15	5	12
Neutral Index 3	**	**	32	12	21	17
Conservative Index 4	**	**	29	17	33	23
Conservative Index 5	**	**	41	26	64	38
Total Population	33	11	34	12	20	18

PDI is proportion "not worried" minus proportion "pretty worried" (see table 3.24)

Table 3.81
U.S. Foreign Aid by Social Groups, Summarized by a Percentage Difference Index#

	1956	1958	1960	1962	1964	1966	1968	1970	1972	1974	1976
1959 or later Cohort	**	**	**	**	**	**	**	**	**	**	**
1943 - 1958 Cohort	**	**	**	**	46*	**	13	**	-2	**	-20
1927 - 1942 Cohort	10	28	28	**	39	**	23	**	-6	**	-20
1911 - 1926 Cohort	17	31	34	**	41	**	17	**	-20	**	-15
1895 - 1910 Cohort	20	31	30	**	26	**	-4	**	-14	**	-24
Before 1895 Cohort	23	42	32	**	5	**	-13	**	-10	**	-19
Grade School	15	30	27	**	14	**	-8	**	-32	**	-27
High School	15	27	28	**	38	**	7	**	-14	**	-24
College	29	47	46	**	45	**	38	**	12	**	-9
Central cities	22	37	33	**	34	**	20	**	-5	**	-23
Suburbs	23	34	42	**	42	**	19	**	3	**	-13
Non-urban Areas	13	28	25	**	27	**	2	**	-22	**	-22
Income Percentile 0-16	13	32	24	**	15	**	-16	**	-15	**	-18
Income Percentile 17-33	16	25	23	**	29	**	4	**	-23	**	-22
Income Percentile 34-67	11	30	24	**	36	**	13	**	-13	**	-20
Income Percentile 68-95	25	35	43	**	42	**	30	**	-2	**	-17
Income Percentile 95-100	36	60	57	**	56	**	39	**	22	**	-11
Males	19	31	38	**	39	**	16	**	-8	**	-17
Females	16	32	26	**	30	**	9	**	-12	**	-20
Whites	17	31	32	**	34	**	9	**	-9	**	-18
Blacks	24	44	24	**	31	**	36	**	-18	**	-32
Union Household	16	22	30	**	40	**	5	**	-15	**	-18
Non-union Household	18	35	32	**	32	**	14	**	-8	**	-19
South	15	31	24	**	30	**	12	**	-14	**	-31
Non-south	18	32	35	**	35	**	12	**	-8	**	-13
Professional	27	38	39	**	44	**	36	**	8	**	-12
White collar	15	35	27	**	46	**	21	**	-10	**	-16
Blue collar	15	30	35	**	35	**	1	**	-19	**	-23
Unskilled	13	4	16*	**	17*	**	-11*	**	-24*	**	-49
Farmers	5	46	26	**	8	**	2	**	-32	**	-26
Housewives	18	30	29	**	28	**	5	**	-12	**	-18
Protestants	17	31	30	**	30	**	10	**	-12	**	-20
Catholics	17	28	43	**	42	**	13	**	-7	**	-20
Jews	39	69	40	**	59*	**	50*	**	-15	**	-4
Other and No Religion	18*	38*	29*	**	42	**	15	**	11	**	-14
Total Population	18	32	31	**	34	**	12	**	-10	**	-19

PDI is proportion "agree" that U.S. should help ideologically differing countries minus proportion "disagree"
  (see table 3.25)

Foreign Relations

Table 3.82
U.S. Foreign Aid by Political Groups, Summarized by a Percentage Difference Index#

	1956	1958	1960	1962	1964	1966	1968	1970	1972	1974	1976
Strong Democrats	13	26	27	**	38	**	18	**	-21	**	-19
Weak Democrats	32	43	42	**	50	**	17	**	-11	**	-17
Independent Democrats	31	46	63	**	61	**	17	**	12	**	-22
Independent Independents	15	32	26	**	23	**	1	**	-12	**	-22
Independent Republicans	21	42	37	**	48	**	20	**	-13	**	-19
Weak Republicans	20	50	48	**	48	**	23	**	-12	**	-19
Strong Republicans	20	50	42	**	24	**	8	**	-4	**	-25
Liberal Self Placement 1	**	**	**	**	**	**	**	**	18	**	5
Liberal Self Placement 2	**	**	**	**	**	**	**	**	10	**	-4
Neutral Self Placement 3	**	**	**	**	**	**	**	**	-5	**	-15
Conservative Self Placement 4	**	**	**	**	**	**	**	**	-2	**	-16
Conservative Self Placement 5	**	**	**	**	**	**	**	**	-21	**	-32
Liberal Index 1	**	**	**	**	42	**	32	**	8	**	-6
Liberal Index 2	**	**	**	**	53	**	20	**	9	**	-7
Neutral Index 3	**	**	**	**	28	**	5	**	-10	**	-23
Conservative Index 4	**	**	**	**	34	**	15	**	-6	**	-19
Conservative Index 5	**	**	**	**	14	**	10	**	-16	**	-36
Total Population	18	32	31	**	34	**	12	**	-10	**	-19

PDI is proportion "agree" that U.S. should help ideologically differing countries minus proportion "disagree"
  (see table 3.25)

Table 3.83
Military Spending (1) by Social Groups, Summarized by a Percentage Difference Index#

	1972	1974	1976
1959 or later Cohort	**	**	**
1943 - 1958 Cohort	-7	**	-45
1927 - 1942 Cohort	-22	**	-62
1911 - 1926 Cohort	-34	**	-72
1895 - 1910 Cohort	-19	**	-66
Before 1895 Cohort	-36*	**	-53
Grade School	-23	**	-62
High School	-30	**	-65
College	-7	**	-48
Central cities	0	**	-49
Suburbs	-22	**	-58
Non-urban Areas	-33	**	-66
Income Percentile 0-16	-25	**	-55
Income Percentile 17-33	-24	**	-55
Income Percentile 34-67	-20	**	-59
Income Percentile 68-95	-20	**	-61
Income Percentile 95-100	-28	**	-50
Males	-23	**	-62
Females	-20	**	-56
Whites	-24	**	-61
Blacks	5	**	-40
Union Household	-19	**	-61
Non-union Household	-22	**	-58
South	-39	**	-64
Non-south	-13	**	-56
Professional	-17	**	-48
White collar	-2	**	-61
Blue collar	-33	**	-64
Unskilled	-	**	-62
Farmers	-38*	**	-68
Housewives	-24	**	-61
Protestants	-28	**	-64
Catholics	-14	**	-59
Jews	38*	**	-15
Other and No Religion	3	**	-31
Total Population	-22	**	-59

PDI is proportion "cut military spending" minus proportion "continue at present level" (see table 3.26)

Foreign Relations

Table 3.84
Military Spending (1) by Political Groups, Summarized by a Percentage Difference Index#

	1972	1974	1976
Strong Democrats	-3	**	-55
Weak Democrats	-18	**	-58
Independent Democrats	-4	**	-41
Independent Independents	-30	**	-61
Independent Republicans	-39	**	-62
Weak Republicans	-33	**	-73
Strong Republicans	-44	**	-81
Liberal Self Placement 1	44	**	-21
Liberal Self Placement 2	10	**	-25
Neutral Self Placement 3	-30	**	-63
Conservative Self Placement 4	-29	**	-70
Conservative Self Placement 5	-61	**	-79
Liberal Index 1	81*	**	9
Liberal Index 2	8	**	-32
Neutral Index 3	-27	**	-64
Conservative Index 4	-36	**	-68
Conservative Index 5	-67	**	-92
Total Population	-22	**	-59

PDI is proportion "cut military spending" minus proportion "continue at present level" (see table 3.26)

Table 3.85
Military Spending (2) by Social Groups, Summarized by a Percent Difference Index#

	1980	1982	1984	1986
1959 or later Cohort	-32	11	2	11
1943 - 1958 Cohort	-39	12	3	8
1927 - 1942 Cohort	-44	2	-1	3
1911 - 1926 Cohort	-43	2	1	12
1895 - 1910 Cohort	-43	-6	13	12
Before 1895 Cohort	-	-	-	-
Grade School	-42	0	11	13
High School	-44	-2	-3	6
College	-37	14	6	11
Central Cities	-40	10	12	15
Suburbs	-38	10	1	8
Non-urban Areas	-45	-1	-3	4
Income Percentile 0-16	-31	1	10	9
Income Percentile 17-33	-41	16	6	15
Income Percentile 34-67	-46	4	1	8
Income Percentile 68-95	-42	6	2	3
Income Percentile 95-100	-40	2	-4	6
Males	-47	1	-2	2
Females	-36	11	6	14
Whites	-43	5	1	7
Blacks	-25	22	16	19
Union Household	-43	8	6	8
Non-union Household	-41	6	1	9
South	-48	0	-4	1
Non-south	-37	9	5	13
Professional	-36	13	8	12
White Collar	-42	11	4	13
Blue Collar	-49	-5	-2	4
Unskilled	-18*	7*	3*	-13*
Farmers	-39*	4*	-7	14
Housewives	-40	6	-1	7
Protestants	-46	2	-2	6
Catholics	-37	9	3	9
Jews	-31*	30*	15*	20*
Other and No Religion	-27	22	23	21
Total Population	-35	5	2	7

PDI is the proportion in categories 1 and 2 less the proportion in categories 6 and 7 (see table 3.27)

Foreign Relations

Table 3.86
Military Spending (2) by Political Groups, Summarized by a Percent Difference Index#

	1980	1982	1984	1986
Strong Democrats	-52	22	23	25
Weak Democrats	-49	10	10	20
Independent Democrats	-47	24	27	31
Independent Independents	-59	14	-3	-8
Independent Republicans	-69	-11	-22	-14
Weak Republicans	-74	-14	-20	-6
Strong Republicans	-82	-53	-46	-32
Liberal Self Placement 1	-5	61	38	49
Liberal Self Placement 2	-46	48	18	36
Neutral Self Placement 3	-64	10	-1	6
Conservative Self Placement 4	-73	-6	-13	-4
Conservative Self Placement 5	-71	-34	-32	-26
Liberal Index 1	3*	81*	61	63
Liberal Index 2	-40	37	20	23
Neutral Index 3	-60	4	-3	4
Conservative Index 4	-72	-9	-18	-3
Conservative Index 5	-82	-58	-48	-37
Total Population	-51	2	-4	4

PDI is proportion "decrease spending" minus proportion "increase spending" (see table 3.27)

Table 3.87
Cooperation with Russia by Social Groups, Summarized by a Percent Difference Index#

	1980	1982	1984	1986
1959 or later Cohort	-1	**	8	-5
1943 - 1958 Cohort	12	**	-8	-9
1927 - 1942 Cohort	-3	**	-15	-24
1911 - 1926 Cohort	-2	**	-7	-21
1895 - 1910 Cohort	-7	**	-1	-30
Before 1895 Cohort	33	**	C	O
Grade School	5	**	-5	-27
High School	-4	**	-14	-17
College	11	**	2	-8
Central Cities	8	**	3	-10
Suburbs	-2	**	-8	-15
Non-urban Areas	4	**	-11	-17
Income Percentile 0-16	-4	**	3	-18
Income Percentile 17-33	5	**	-5	-11
Income Percentile 34-67	5	**	-2	-13
Income Percentile 68-95	5	**	-11	-14
Income Percentile 95-100	7	**	-16	-9
Males	2	**	-11	-19
Females	3	**	-2	-11
Whites	3	**	-8	-15
Blacks	5	**	4	-11
Union Household	3	**	-2	-16
Non-union Household	2	**	-7	-14
South	2	**	-10	-24
Non-south	3	**	-4	-9
Professional	-3	**	9	-2
White collar	6	**	-8	-16
Blue collar	-4	**	-10	-22
Unskilled	-3	**	2	-30
Farmers	19	**	-24	-30
Housewives	18	**	-20	-14
Protestants	O	**	-11	-19
Catholics	4	**	-4	-10
Jews	23	**	12	-31
Other and No Religion	10	**	18	8
Total Population	2	**	-7	-15

PDI is proportion "cooperate more" minus proportion "get tougher" (see table 3.28)

Foreign Relations

Table 3.88
Cooperation with Russia by Political Groups, Summarized by a Percent Difference Index#

	1980	1982	1984	1986
Strong Democrats	12	**	9	-4
Weak Democrats	3	**	1	-7
Independent Democrats	11	**	24	8
Independent Independents	4	**	-4	-17
Independent Republicans	-5	**	-27	-27
Weak Republicans	-3	**	-15	-24
Strong Republicans	-11	**	-35	-40
Liberal Self Placement 1	38	**	29	26
Liberal Self Placement 2	22	**	20	18
Neutral Self Placement 3	3	**	-5	-16
Conservative Self Placement 4	-10	**	-11	-20
Conservative Self Placement 5	-21	**	-35	-43
Liberal Index 1	39	**	48	28
Liberal Index 2	28	**	11	0
Neutral Index 3	6	**	-4	-11
Conservative Index 4	-5	**	-20	-25
Conservative Index 5	-31	**	-49	-50
Total Population	2	**	-7	-15

PDI is proportion "cooperate more" minus proportion "get tougher" (see table 3.28)

Table 3.89
Condition of the Nation's Economy over the Last Year by Social Groups, Summarized by a Percent Difference Index#

	1980	1982	1984	1986
1959 or later Cohort	-83	-46	24	-4
1943 - 1958 Cohort	-80	-53	28	-6
1927 - 1942 Cohort	-83	-63	18	-11
1911 - 1926 Cohort	-77	-67	6	-26
1895 - 1910 Cohort	-73	-60	1	-36
Before 1895 Cohort	-	-	-	-
Grade School	-72	-74	-12	-28
High School	-79	-64	9	-19
College	-83	-48	38	0
Central Cities	-78	-61	1	-12
Suburbs	-83	-57	29	-3
Non-urban Areas	-76	-57	19	-22
Income Percentile 0-16	-73	-68	-15	-24
Income Percentile 17-33	-80	-62	1	-25
Income Percentile 34-67	-78	-55	23	-11
Income Percentile 68-95	-87	-54	38	1
Income Percentile 96-100	-84	-52	66	27
Males	-78	-50	32	-2
Females	-81	-65	9	-18
Whites	-81	-55	25	-8
Blacks	-72	-82	-34	-35
Union Household	-78	-67	10	-9
Non-union Household	-80	-56	22	-12
South	-73	-55	12	-12
Non-south	-83	-60	23	-11
Professional	-81	-45	40	3
White Collar	-84	-58	19	-11
Blue Collar	-79	-59	8	-18
Unskilled	-77*	-75*	-14	0
Farmers	-67*	-73*	31	-36
Housewives	-81	-70	13	-21
Protestants	-80	-59	20	-15
Catholics	-76	-56	16	-5
Jews	-84	-79*	2*	0*
Other and No Religion	-83	-50	22	-1
Total Population	-80	-58	19	-11

PDI is proportion "gotten better" minus proportion "gotten worse" (see table 3.29)

Table 3.90
Condition of Nation's Economy Over the Last Year by Political Groups, Summarized by a Percent Difference Index#

	1980	1982	1984	1986
Strong Democrats	-68	-77	-27	-32
Weak Democrats	-79	-70	0	-20
Independent Democrats	-77	-64	-10	-17
Independent Independents	-79	-64	21	-15
Independent Republicans	-85	-20	47	10
Weak Republicans	-86	-42	55	-5
Strong Republicans	-90	-25	67	22
Liberal Self Placement 1	-77	-66	8	-20
Liberal Self Placement 2	-75	-61	16	-13
Neutral Self Placement 3	-84	-58	15	-13
Conservative Self Placement 4	-80	-46	44	-3
Conservative Self Placement 5	-88	-35	50	3
Liberal Index 1	-68*	-77	-5	-26
Liberal Index 2	-76	-62	5	-13
Neutral Index 3	-80	-63	16	-15
Conservative Index 4	-82	-50	42	-4
Conservative Index 5	-93	-20	74	8
Total Population	-80	-58	19	-11

PDI is proportion "gotten better" minus proportion "gotten worse" (see table 3.29)

Table 3.91
Condition of Nation's Economy Next Year by Social Groups, Summarized by a Percent Difference Index#

	1980	1982	1984	1986
1959 or later Cohort	-3	12	11	0
1943 - 1958 Cohort	-10	16	12	-1
1927 - 1942 Cohort	2	16	6	-5
1911 - 1926 Cohort	5	20	6	-4
1895 - 1910 Cohort	12	29	-3	4
Before 1895 Cohort	-	-	-	-
Grade School	6	0	1	-3
High School	-3	10	6	-1
College	-2	29	13	-2
Central Cities	5	16	4	0
Suburbs	-4	18	11	-3
Non-urban Areas	-3	18	8	-3
Income Percentile 0-16	2	-5	1	-1
Income Percentile 17-33	-9	15	4	-3
Income Percentile 34-67	-3	17	9	2
Income Percentile 68-95	1	29	14	-4
Income Percentile 96-100	10	36	21	-5
Males	13	29	8	2
Females	-12	8	9	-5
Whites	-2	21	11	-2
Blacks	9	-12	-9	-7
Union Household	4	9	-1	-2
Non-union Household	-3	20	11	-2
South	-3	22	9	4
Non-south	0	15	8	-5
Professional	1	30	12	-6
White Collar	-6	23	10	1
Blue Collar	2	9	4	-4
Unskilled	18*	5*	-21*	2
Farmers	-21*	14*	20	-4
Housewives	-3	13	12	6
Protestants	-4	19	7	-4
Catholics	6	22	14	5
Jews	24*	-8*	12*	0*
Other and No Religion	-6	7	1	-8
Total Population	-1	18	9	-2

PDI is proportion "get better" minus proportion "get worse" (see table 3.30)

Economic Conditions

Table 3.92
Condition of Nation's Economy Next Year by Political Groups, Summarized by a Percent Difference Index#

	1980	1982	1984	1986
Strong Democrats	26	-5	-12	-10
Weak Democrats	-1	5	-3	-2
Independent Democrats	-7	-9	-9	-6
Independent Independents	-5	11	-3	-10
Independent Republicans	-7	53	21	1
Weak Republicans	-16	45	27	3
Strong Republicans	-1	65	42	14
Liberal Self Placement 1	10	-6	-11	-11
Liberal Self Placement 2	9	10	3	-6
Neutral Self Placement 3	2	21	1	-4
Conservative Self Placement 4	2	37	19	0
Conservative Self Placement 5	-18	42	33	2
Liberal Index 1	-4*	-19*	-17	-26
Liberal Index 2	3	8	-5	-3
Neutral Index 3	0	11	5	-3
Conservative Index 4	1	35	24	1
Conservative Index 5	-14	52	47	3
Total Population	-1	18	9	-2

PDI is proportion "get better" minus proportion "get worse" (see table 3.30)

Table 3.93
Respondent's Financial Situation over the Last Year by Social Groups. Summarized by a Percent Difference Index#

	1962	1964	1966	1968	1970	1972	1974	1976	1978	1980	1982	1984	1986
1959 or later Cohort	**	**	**	**	**	**	**	**	6	12	11	34	25
1943 - 1958 Cohort	**	**	50	44	13	33	-5	19	17	-2	0	31	25
1927 - 1942 Cohort	39	**	21	28	3	14	-15	0	-12	-18	-20	7	4
1911 - 1926 Cohort	18	**	7	11	-6	2	-16	-9	-14	-19	-19	-9	-7
1895 - 1910 Cohort	1	**	-2	-9	-19	1	-24	-8	-23	-18	-2	-12	-16
Before 1895 Cohort	-17	**	-20	-16	0*	0*	14	10	-19*	-	-	-	-
Grade School	-4	**	-7	-2	-14	4	-12	-2	-18	-15	-22	-19	-8
High School	18	**	14	13	-2	10	-13	1	-6	-17	-14	9	5
College	31	**	18	28	5	25	-13	11	10	1	2	32	26
Central Cities	14	**	13	14	-2	-2	-14	-4	-9	-11	-7	4	11
Suburbs	23	**	9	19	-4	17	-17	5	0	-10	-4	25	21
Non-urban Areas	8	**	7	11	-3	19	-9	8	2	-9	-13	11	4
Income Percentile 0-16	-17	**	-13	-16	-31	-1	-26	-12	-23	-19	-29	-17	-13
Income Percentile 17-33	-4	**	-3	6	-20	11	-22	-10	-7	-18	-15	-3	0
Income Percentile 34-67	23	**	12	15	0	11	-14	6	-1	-10	-8	20	12
Income Percentile 68-95	37	**	23	35	11	27	-3	15	12	3	4	42	35
Income Percentile 96-100	37	**	25	34	42*	23*	6	19	28	0	11	46	61
Males	20	**	12	19	5	18	-9	7	6	-3	-6	22	21
Females	11	**	8	9	-8	9	-16	1	-8	-15	-10	10	7
Whites	18	**	9	14	-3	15	-12	7	-2	-9	-4	20	15
Blacks	-11	**	11	12	2	-5	-17	-21	-1	-16	-38	-15	-1
Union Household	**	**	11	17	-9	11	-7	4	-1	-9	-4	18	22
Non-union Household	**	**	9	12	-1	14	-16	3	-2	-10	-9	15	11
South	18	**	5	16	4	19	-11	2	-3	-5	-9	9	13
Non-south	14	**	12	13	-6	10	-14	4	-1	-13	-7	18	13
Professional	**	**	**	26	14	22	-6	10	7	3	7	31	25
White Collar	**	**	**	18	-7	14	-14	8	-1	-12	-2	16	17
Blue Collar	**	**	**	15	3	8	-14	0	-2	-18	-14	8	6
Unskilled	**	**	**	-	-	7*	-25	7	-7	13*	-32*	-4*	-2
Farmers	**	**	**	2	-13*	19*	-6	7	2*	7*	-32*	16	-5
Housewives	**	**	**	8	-15	14	-16	4	-11	-19	-17	6	7
Protestants	15	**	11	12	1	12	-10	4	-1	-12	-9	15	10
Catholics	23	**	9	17	-11	17	-22	1	-4	-11	-6	14	17
Jews	-14*	**	2*	19*	-22*	-	-20	5	9	-18*	-21*	2	25*
Other and No Religion	14*	**	-7*	26*	-10	23	-18	10	-3	9	-5	27	22
Total Population	15	**	10	14	-3	13	-13	3	-2	-10	-8	15	13

PDI is proportion "gotten better" minus proportion "gotten worse" (see table 3.31)

Table 3.94
Respondent's Financial Situation Over the Last Year by Political Groups, Summarized by a Percent Difference Index#

	1962	1964	1966	1968	1970	1972	1974	1976	1978	1980	1982	1984	1986
Strong Democrats	14	**	8	13	-6	-10	-20	-19	-10	-13	-23	-18	-1
Weak Democrats	15	**	9	11	-7	15	-9	2	-5	-4	-12	3	14
Independent Democrats	23	**	21	29	-12	15	-3	0	13	-12	-18	0	8
Independent Independents	17	**	17	12	-10	5	-16	11	8	-5	-12	18	1
Independent Republicans	29	**	8	17	20	39	-20	17	-6	-4	14	40	28
Weak Republicans	18	**	8	16	-5	14	-15	6	-4	-14	5	37	17
Strong Republicans	10	**	1	2	22	18	-14	18	-4	-20	19	46	33
Liberal Self Placement 1	**	**	**	**	**	-5	-22	-5	-3	-15	-5	6	8
Liberal Self Placement 2	**	**	**	**	**	11	-9	0	9	10	-11	23	22
Neutral Self Placement 3	**	**	**	**	**	19	-16	4	-5	-13	-5	7	12
Conservative Self Placement 4	**	**	**	**	**	30	-11	20	7	-1	5	33	17
Conservative Self Placement 5	**	**	**	**	**	12	-2	9	-4	-20	4	40	20
Liberal Index 1	**	45	51*	34	-2*	10*	16	38	**	24*	0	11	-17
Liberal Index 2	**	43	23	31	8	26	-1	17	**	15	5	27	8
Neutral Index 3	**	32	27	20	15	32	-13	24	**	10	10	32	-1
Conservative Index 4	**	40	18	26	20	33	-10	19	**	13	17	35	-2
Conservative Index 5	**	34	27	19	18	32	-9	41	**	-4	27	49	6
Total Population	15	**	10	14	-3	13	-13	3	-2	-10	-8	15	13

PDI is proportion "gotten better" minus proportion "gotten worse" (see table 3.31)

Table 3.95
Respondent's Financial Situation over the Next Year by Social Groups, Summarized by a Percent Difference Index#

	1956	1958	1960	1962	1964	1966	1968	1970	1972	1974	1976	1978	1980	1982	1984	1986
1959 or later Cohort	**	**	**	**	**	**	**	**	**	**	**	33	26	17	49	13
1943 - 1958 Cohort	**	**	**	**	72*	56	56	37	52	8	38	16	22	29	44	4
1927 - 1942 Cohort	57	56	64	57	63	41	43	27	36	-11	26	-14	5	-2	25	-8
1911 - 1926 Cohort	43	39	39	35	41	20	17	2	14	-22	3	-22	-9	-10	-1	-7
1895 - 1910 Cohort	28	15	11	15	7	-1	-6	-5	-2	-32	-2	-27	-10	-23	-5	-8
Before 1895 Cohort	-5	-7	-4	-4	-10	-1	-6	-7*	-3*	-25	-2	-	-	-	-	-
Grade School	18	17	16	10	14	5	0	-12	3	-25	4	-25	-12	-22	0	-11
High School	39	31	34	37	41	31	27	20	29	-13	20	-5	8	2	25	-6
College	50	46	42	46	52	26	36	23	39	2	30	4	14	21	41	9
Central Cities	40	38	31	33	41	25	28	9	20	-9	19	2	13	8	27	2
Suburbs	38	32	33	39	43	30	26	12	35	-10	25	-6	4	11	35	7
Non-urban Areas	30	25	30	24	29	17	20	17	26	-12	19	-6	9	5	23	-10
Income Percentile 0-16	13	9	6	8	3	5	7	-1	12	-11	18	-8	3	-14	21	-15
Income Percentil 17-33	31	25	23	22	33	17	15	2	29	-29	10	-1	7	5	23	-13
Income Percentile 34-67	40	35	30	38	50	26	25	14	28	-10	21	-6	12	11	34	-1
Income Percentile 68-95	41	40	42	47	50	33	37	24	36	-1	29	0	10	18	35	13
Income Percentile 96-100	50	40	53	44	45	33	39	37*	32*	13	27	6	16	29	44	45*
Males	38	31	33	36	44	26	27	10	34	-9	26	-2	13	12	33	3
Females	31	28	28	28	31	21	21	17	22	-12	17	-6	4	6	26	-3
Whites	34	28	28	33	34	22	24	14	28	-11	20	-5	7	10	30	1
Blacks	44	52	49	19	64	33	15	12	20	-9	27	3	16	-8	24	-7
Union Household	37	27	27	**	42	25	23	4	26	-12	21	-7	14	7	26	1
Non-union Household	34	31	32	**	35	23	24	17	28	-10	21	-3	6	9	30	-1
South	36	30	32	31	37	17	23	19	29	-14	25	-5	12	8	31	-2
Non-south	34	30	30	33	37	26	24	11	26	-9	19	-3	6	8	29	0
Professional	44	39	47	**	44	**	37	27	35	-2	29	-2	12	19	38	7
White Collar	49	40	33	**	44	**	29	27	33	-9	21	-3	6	19	35	7
Blue Collar	35	31	29	**	41	**	21	12	23	-14	21	-4	5	-2	27	-9
Unskilled	30	31	20*	**	58*	**	-	-	-	10	29	4	31*	0*	20*	7*
Farmers	14	7	15	**	9	**	-5*	-28*	4*	-12	6	-17*	-10*	0*	22*	-10*
Housewives	30	23	25	**	29	**	20	10	22	-15	14	-9	5	1	16	-3
Protestants	33	32	31	30	36	21	21	15	25	-12	20	-3	7	8	27	-3
Catholics	41	21	26	39	41	29	28	14	30	-8	22	-8	9	6	33	0
Jews	44	54	24	41*	38*	47*	41*	15*	-	-16	24	-3	8*	17*	28*	-
Other and No Religion	27*	22*	45*	31*	38	21*	36*	3	30*	-5	23	7	15	18	36	14
Total Population	35	30	31	32	37	23	24	14	27	-11	21	-4	8	8	29	-1

PDI is proportion "get getter" minus proportion "get worse" (see table 3.32)

Table 3.96
Respondent's Financial Situation Over the Next Year by Political Groups, Summarized by a Percent Difference Index#

	1956	1958	1960	1962	1964	1966	1968	1970	1972	1974	1976	1978	1980	1982	1984	1986
Strong Democrats	31	34	26	34	44	28	14	2	11	-19	22	-9	18	-13	10	-10
Weak Democrats	35	33	29	34	34	25	21	11	21	-5	20	-1	2	4	26	0
Independent Democrats	45	26	35	37	42	34	41	8	23	-6	12	-1	5	5	23	-7
Independent Independents	32	16	22	22	27	29	24	9	33	-23	24	1	13	9	37	-6
Independent Republicans	40	18	34	56	43	10	40	36	44	-5	24	-3	3	29	40	9
Weak Republicans	31	35	30	29	36	18	21	24	35	-6	19	-3	8	25	36	1
Strong Republicans	38	23	42	25	28	10	24	20	34	-6	32	-14	14	24	42	18
Liberal Self Placement 1	**	**	**	**	**	**	**	**	16	-12	22	5	16	11	27	-7
Liberal Self Placement 2	**	**	**	**	**	**	**	**	33	4	28	7	23	22	39	14
Neutral Self Placement 3	**	**	**	**	**	**	**	**	28	-8	22	-10	7	8	26	-1
Conservative Self Placement 4	**	**	**	**	**	**	**	**	51	-13	33	-1	20	16	32	5
Conservative Self Placement 5	**	**	**	**	**	**	**	**	16	-13	25	-13	-1	22	45	1
Liberal Index 1	**	**	**	**	45	51*	34*	-2*	10*	15	38*	**	24*	0*	11	17*
Liberal Index 2	**	**	**	**	43	23	31	8	26	-1	17	**	15	5	27	8
Neutral Index 3	**	**	**	**	32	27	20	15	32	-13	24	**	10	10	32	-1
Conservative Index 4	**	**	**	**	40	18	26	20	33	-10	19	**	13	17	35	-2
Conservative Index 5	**	**	**	**	34	27	19	18	32	-9	41	**	-4	27	49	6
Total Population	35	30	31	32	37	23	24	14	27	-11	21	-4	8	8	29	-1

PDI is proportion "get better" minus proportion "get worse" (see table 3.32)

Matrix 3.1
Gammas in 1970 of Issues for Total Population

	Health Insurance Scale	Urban Unrest	Rights of Accused	Aid to Minorities	Busing
Alleviate Causes of Urban Unrest	0.16	.	.	.	.
Protect Rights of Accused	0.12	0.32	.	.	.
Government Aid to Minorities	0.27	0.44	0.30	.	.
Use Busing to Integrate	**	**	**	**	.
Women's Role Equal to Mens'	**	**	**	**	**

Matrix 3.2
Gammas in 1972 of Issues for Total Population

	Health Insurance Scale	Urban Unrest	Rights of Accused	Aid to Minorities	Busing
Alleviate Causes of Urban Unrest	**	.	.	.	.
Protect Rights of Accused	0.12	0.30	.	.	.
Government Aid to Minorities	0.23	0.38	0.34	.	.
Use Busing to integrate	0.30	0.33	0.34	0.47	.
Women's Role Equal to Mens'	0.09	0.09	0.16	0.18	0.19

Matrix 3.3
Gammas in 1974 of Issues for Total Population

	Health Insurance Scale	Urban Unrest	Rights of Accused	Aid to Minorities	Busing
Alleviate Causes of Urban Unrest	**	.	.	.	.
Protect Rights of Accused	**	0.38	.	.	.
Government Aid to Minorities	**	0.30	0.32	.	.
Use Busing to Integrate	**	0.25	0.33	0.50	.
Women's Role Equal to Mens'	**	0.22	0.22	0.28	0.20

Positions on Public Policy Issues

Matrix 3.4
Gammas in 1976 of Issues for Total Population

```
                                  Health Insurance Scale
                                    . Urban Unrest
                                    .        . Rights of Accused
                                    .        .        . Aid to Minorities
                                    .        .        .        . Busing
    Alleviate Causes of Urban Unrest  0.21     .        .        .        .
         Protect Rights of Accused    0.16   0.25       .        .        .
      Government Aid to Minorities     0.26   0.27   0.26       .        .
         Use Busing to Integrate      0.17   0.26   0.30   0.45       .
      Women's Role Equal to Mens'     0.06   0.22   0.17   0.16   0.21
```

Matrix 3.5
Gammas in 1978 of Issues for Total Population

```
                                  Health Insurance Scale
                                    . Urban Unrest
                                    .        . Rights of Accused
                                    .        .        . Aid to Minorities
                                    .        .        .        . Busing
    Alleviate Causes of Urban Unrest    **      .        .        .        .
         Protect Rights of Accused    0.11      **      .        .        .
      Government Aid to Minorities     0.24      **    0.25       .        .
         Use Busing to Integrate        **      **      **       **      .
      Women's Role Equal to Mens'     0.14      **    0.18   0.15       **
```

Matrix 3.6
Gammas in 1980 of Issues for Total Population

```
                                  Health Insurance Scale
                                    . Urban Unrest
                                    .        . Rights of Accused
                                    .        .        . Aid to Minorities
                                    .        .        .        . Busing
    Alleviate Causes of Urban Unrest    **      .        .        .        .
         Protect Rights of Accused      **      **      .        .        .
      Government Aid to Minorities       **      **      **       .        .
         Use Busing to Integrate        **      **      **    0.43       .
      Women's Role Equal to Mens'       **      **      **    0.21   0.04
```

Matrix 3.7
Gammas in 1982 of Issues for Total Population

```
                                 Health Insurance Scale
                                    . Urban Unrest
                                    .      . Rights of Accused
                                    .      .      . Aid to Minorities
                                    .      .      .      . Busing
    Alleviate Causes of Urban Unrest  **     .      .      .      .
          Protect Rights of Accused   **    **      .      .      .
       Government Aid to Minorities   **    **    **       .      .
           Use Busing to Integrate    **    **    **     **       .
      Women's Role Equal to Mens'     **    **    **    0.14     **
```

Matrix 3.8
Gammas in 1984 of Issues for Total Population

```
                                 Health Insurance Scale
                                    . Urban Unrest
                                    .      . Rights of Accused
                                    .      .      . Aid to Minorities
                                    .      .      .      . Busing
    Alleviate Causes of Urban Unrest  **     .      .      .      .
          Protect Rights of Accused   **    **      .      .      .
       Government Aid to Minorities   **    **    **       .      .
           Use Busing to integrate    **    **    **    0.28      .
      Women's Role Equal to Mens'     **    **    **    0.20   0.09
```

Matrix 3.9
Gammas in 1986 of Issues for Total Population

```
                                 Health Insurance Scale
                                    . Urban Unrest
                                    .      . Rights of Accused
                                    .      .      . Aid to Minorities
                                    .      .      .      . Busing
    Alleviate Causes of Urban Unrest  **     .      .      .      .
          Protect Rights of Accused   **    **      .      .      .
       Government Aid to Minorities   **    **    **       .      .
           Use Busing  to integrate   **    **    **     **       .
      Women's Role Equal to Mens'     **    **    **     **     **
```

Positions on Public Policy Issues

Table 3.97
Gammas of Issues with Party Identification&

	1952	1954	1956	1958	1960	1962	1964	1966	1968	1970	1972	1974	1976	1978	1980	1982	1984	1986
Fed Govt Not Too Strong	**	**	**	**	**	**	0.50	0.47	0.41	0.17	0.02	**	0.19	0.24	0.43	**	0.02	**
Govt Help Get Hlth Care	**	**	0.32	**	0.30	0.42	0.52	**	0.43	0.33	0.23	**	0.31	0.32	**	**	**	**
Govt Provide Hlth Insur.	**	**	**	**	**	**	**	**	**	0.21	0.17	**	0.21	0.24	**	**	**	**
Govt Provide Jobs/S L (1)	**	**	0.22	0.23	0.23	**	0.31	**	0.25	**	**	**	**	**	**	**	**	**
Govt Provide Jobs/S L (2)	**	**	**	**	**	**	**	**	**	**	0.18	0.23	0.23	0.23	0.30	0.29	0.26	0.25
Less Govt Svcs/Spending	**	**	**	**	**	**	**	**	**	**	**	**	**	**	-0.19	-0.21	-0.21	-0.21
Protect Rghts of Accused	**	**	**	**	**	**	**	**	**	0.09	0.09	0.11	0.08	0.08	**	**	**	**
Remove Cause Urban Unrst	**	**	**	**	**	**	**	**	0.16	0.13	0.11	0.17	0.16	**	**	**	**	**
Blacks Positn Not Imprvd	**	**	**	**	**	**	-0.09	-0.03	-0.04	0.04	0.06	**	0.11	**	**	**	0.06	0.10
Civ Rghts Move Too Slow	**	**	**	**	**	**	0.17	0.12	0.20	0.13	0.11	0.13	0.09	**	0.17	**	0.23	0.17
Shd Achieve Desegregation	**	**	**	**	**	**	-0.03	**	0.06	0.01	0.04	**	0.02	0.10	**	**	**	**
Govt Shd Prov. Aid to Min	**	**	**	**	**	**	**	**	**	0.16	0.12	0.16	0.13	0.13	0.22	0.13	0.21	0.18
Govt Shd Integrate Schls	**	**	**	**	**	-0.04	0.11	0.12	0.24	0.04	0.11	**	0.25	0.27	**	**	**	0.31
Shd Use Busing- Integrate	**	**	**	**	**	**	**	**	**	**	0.19	0.20	0.11	**	0.21	**	0.09	**
Whites Keep Blacks Out	**	**	**	**	**	**	0.09	0.04	-0.06	-0.01	0.12	**	0.08	**	**	**	**	**
Women's Role Shd be Equal	**	**	**	**	**	**	**	**	**	**	0.01	0.07	0.04	0.05	0.04	0.10	0.08	**
Women Out of Politics	-0.01	**	**	**	**	**	**	**	**	**	0.01	**	**	**	**	**	**	**
Never Permit Abortions(1)	**	**	**	**	**	**	**	**	**	**	0.08	**	0.08	0.11	0.03	**	**	**
Never Permit Abortions(2)	**	**	**	**	**	**	**	**	**	**	**	**	**	**	0.05	**	-0.06	0.03
Bible is God's Word	**	**	**	**	**	**	0.10	**	0.12	**	**	**	**	**	0.05	**	0.03	0.09
Religion is Imprt to Life	**	**	**	**	**	**	**	**	**	**	**	**	**	**	0.06	**	0.08	0.03
Shd Ignore Wrld Problems	-0.23	**	0.06	0.05	0.09	**	**	**	0.03	**	0.08	**	0.19	**	0.03	**	0.20	0.16
Shd Stay Out Korea/Viet.	-0.27	**	**	**	**	**	-0.11	-0.01	-0.06	0.06	0.09	**	**	**	**	-0.11	-0.30	-0.09
Not Worried- Conv. War	**	**	-0.15	**	-0.08	**	0.00	**	**	**	**	**	**	**	**	**	**	**
Shd Deny US Foreign Aid	**	**	0.02	0.17	0.09	**	-0.05	**	-0.04	**	0.04	**	-0.02	**	**	**	**	**
Shd Cut Mil. Spend. (1)	**	**	**	**	**	**	**	**	**	**	0.18	**	0.17	**	**	**	**	**
Shd Cut Mil. Spend. (2)	**	**	**	**	**	**	**	**	**	**	**	**	**	**	0.14	0.22	0.26	0.22
Shd Cooperate w/ Russia	**	**	**	**	**	**	**	**	**	**	**	**	**	**	0.04	**	0.09	0.08
Nat Econ Better Last Yr.	**	**	**	**	**	**	**	**	**	**	**	**	**	**	0.19	-0.25	-0.40	0.19
Nat Econ Better Next Yr.	**	**	**	**	**	**	**	**	**	**	**	**	**	**	0.12	-0.27	-0.28	0.10
R Finances Bettr Last Yr.	**	**	**	**	**	0.02	**	0.01	0.01	-0.10	0.04	-0.01	-0.11	-0.02	0.02	-0.15	-0.25	0.11
R Finances Bettr Next Yr.	**	**	0.00	0.04	-0.02	0.04	0.06	0.05	-0.02	-0.07	0.04	-0.05	-0.01	0.03	0.01	-0.12	-0.09	0.09

& For party identification, see 7 categories per table 2.1. Refer to tables 3.1-3.32 for the codes of issue questions (questions
appear in the same order as above). Labels above reflect first coded position [code 1] for that issue var., with subsequent
codes decreasingly supportive of, or increasingly opposed to, that position.

Table 3.98
Gammas of Issues with Liberal-Conservative Scale&

	1972	1974	1976	1978	1980	1982	1984	1986
Fed Govt Not Too Strong	0.09	**	0.21	0.22	0.32	**	0.18	**
Govt Help Get Hlth Care	0.38	**	0.50	0.40	**	**	**	**
Govt Provide Hlth Insur.	0.28	**	0.34	0.29	**	**	**	**
Govt Provide Jobs/SL (2)	0.31	0.34	0.29	0.27	0.37	0.30	0.29	0.24
Less Govt Svcs/Spending	**	**	**	**	0.12	0.16	0.18	0.08
Protect Rghts of Accused	0.31	0.27	0.24	0.22	**	**	**	**
Remove Cause Urban Unrst	0.28	0.32	0.30	**	**	**	**	**
Blacks Positn Not Imprvd	0.05	**	0.19	**	**	**	0.07	0.20
Civ Rights Move Too Slow	0.35	0.38	0.27	**	0.28	**	0.27	0.27
Shd Achieve Desegregtn	0.31	**	0.25	0.22	**	**	**	**
Govt Shd Prov Aid to Min	0.38	0.37	0.31	0.24	0.29	0.29	0.25	0.26
Govt Shd Integrate Schls	0.37	**	0.36	0.29	**	**	**	0.30
Shd Use Busing-Integrate	0.48	0.39	0.31	**	0.24	**	0.23	**
Whites Keep Blacks Out	-0.25	**	-0.26	**	**	**	**	**
Women's Role Shd be Eql	0.19	0.32	0.25	0.33	0.24	0.29	0.19	**
Women out of Politics	-0.17	**	**	**	**	**	**	**
Never Permit Abortions(1)	-0.14	**	-0.21	-0.19	-0.28	**	**	**
Never Permit Abortions(2)	**	**	**	**	-0.24	**	-0.26	-0.23
Bible is God's Word	**	**	**	**	-0.23	**	-0.21	-0.29
Religion is Important	**	**	**	**	-0.17	**	-0.14	-0.02
Shd Ignore World Probs	0.06	**	0.08	**	0.06	**	0.23	0.13
Shd Stay out Korea/Viet.	0.21	**	**	**	**	**	**	**
Not Worried- Conv. War	**	**	**	**	**	-0.05	-0.23	-0.23
Shd Deny US Foreign Aid	-0.15	**	-0.17	**	**	**	**	**
Shd Cut Mil. Spend. (1)	0.43	**	0.42	**	**	**	**	**
Shd Cut Mil. Spend. (2)	**	**	**	**	0.26	0.38	0.28	0.29
Shd Cooperate w/ Russia	**	**	**	**	0.10	**	0.31	0.25
Nat Econ Better Last Yr.	**	**	**	**	0.05	0.07	0.07	0.03
Nat Econ Better Next Yr.	**	**	**	**	-0.03	0.08	-0.03	0.00
R Finances Bettr Lst Yr.	0.32	-0.05	0.00	0.02	0.04	0.05	0.00	0.04
R Finances Bettr Nxt Yr.	0.31	0.00	-0.01	-0.02	0.12	0.02	0.01	0.03

& For liberal-conservative scale, see 5 categories per table 2.22.   Refer to tables 3.1-3.32 for the codes of issue questions
  (questions appear in the same order as above).   Labels above reflect first coded position [code 1] for that issue var.,
  with subsequent codes decreasingly supportive of, or increasingly opposed to, that position.

Issues

Table 3.99
Gammas of Issues with Liberal-Conservative Index&

	1964	1966	1968	1970	1972	1974	1976	1978	1980	1982	1984	1986
Fed Govt Not Too Strong	0.46	0.42	0.32	0.24	0.05	**	0.27	**	0.44	**	0.24	**
Govt Help Get Hlth Care	0.42	**	0.34	0.31	0.32	**	0.44	**	**	**	**	**
Govt Provide Helth Insur.	**	**	**	0.21	0.23	**	0.29	**	**	**	**	**
Govt Provide Jobs/SL (1)	0.33	**	0.22	**	**	**	**	**	**	**	**	**
Govt Provide Jobs/SL (2)	**	**	**	**	0.29	0.31	0.26	**	0.37	0.34	0.29	0.22
Less Govt Svcs/Spending	**	**	**	**	**	**	**	**	-0.11	-0.01	-0.11	-0.07
Protect Rghts of Accused	**	**	**	0.16	0.31	0.28	0.15	**	**	**	**	**
Remove Cause Urban Unrst	**	**	0.16	0.24	0.33	0.28	0.30	**	**	**	**	**
Blacks Positn Not Imprvd	-0.14	-0.07	0.02	0.06	0.05	**	0.18	**	**	**	0.16	0.17
Civ Rights Move Too Slow	0.22	0.26	0.26	0.36	0.36	0.43	0.27	**	0.37	**	0.23	0.28
Shd Achieve Desegregtn	0.19	**	0.08	0.15	0.28	**	0.21	**	**	**	**	**
Govt Shd Prov Aid to Min	**	**	**	0.24	0.32	0.34	0.25	**	0.33	0.25	0.20	0.21
Govt Shd Integrate Schls	0.23	0.11	0.22	0.23	0.38	**	0.38	**	**	**	**	0.33
Shd Use Busing-Integrate	**	**	**	**	0.47	0.42	0.24	**	0.30	**	0.19	**
Whites Keep Blacks Out	-0.13	-0.11	-0.08	-0.06	-0.32	**	-0.18	**	**	**	**	**
Women's Role Shd be Equal	**	**	**	**	0.15	0.29	0.19	**	0.19	0.19	0.10	**
Women out of Politics	**	**	**	**	-0.12	**	**	**	**	**	**	**
Never Permit Abortions(1)	**	**	**	**	-0.12	**	-0.17	**	-0.17	**	**	**
Never Permit Abortions(2)	**	**	**	**	**	**	**	**	-0.14	**	-0.18	-0.18
Bible is God's Word	0.09	**	0.06	**	**	**	**	**	0.24	**	0.30	-0.20
Religion is Important	**	**	**	**	**	**	**	**	0.41	**	0.46	0.01
Shd Ignore World Probs	**	**	0.10	**	0.09	**	0.22	**	0.01	**	0.17	0.11
Shd Stay Out Korea/Viet.	-0.08	0.11	0.02	0.20	0.21	**	**	**	**	**	**	**
Not Worried- Conv. War	0.05	**	**	**	**	**	**	**	**	-0.07	-0.27	-0.13
Shd Deny US Foreign Aid	-0.18	**	-0.04	**	-0.10	**	-0.10	**	**	**	**	**
Shd Cut Mil. Spend. (1)	**	**	**	**	0.41	**	0.40	**	**	**	**	**
Shd Cut Mil. Spend. (2)	**	**	**	**	**	**	**	**	0.25	0.36	0.28	0.26
Shd Cooperate w/ Russia	**	**	**	**	**	**	**	**	0.43	**	0.10	0.21
Nat Econ Better Last Yr.	**	**	**	**	**	**	**	**	0.06	-0.02	-0.14	0.03
Nat Econ Better Next Yr.	**	**	**	**	**	**	**	**	0.03	-0.04	-0.14	0.01
R Finances Bettr Last Yr	**	-0.01	0.05	-0.07	0.29	-0.03	-0.06	**	0.03	0.01	-0.07	0.03
R Finances Bettr Nxt Yr	0.03	0.04	0.08	-0.08	0.28	0.05	0.01	**	-0.04	-0.04	-0.05	0.09

& For liberal-conservative index, see 5 categories per table 2.23. Refer to tables 3.1-3.32 for the codes of issue questions (questions appear in the same order as above). Labels above reflect first coded position [code 1] for that issue var., with subsequent codes decreasingly supportive of, or increasingly opposed to, that position.

Table 3.100
Respondent's Proximity to Parties on 7-Point Scale Issues&

	1972	1974	1976	1978	1980	1982	1984	1986	
Aid to Minorities	29%	29%	33%	25%	26%	30%	36%	**	Closer to Democrats
	40	43	37	45	26	28	28	**	Equidistant
	31	28	30	30	48	42	36	**	Closer to Republicans
	-2	1	3	-5	-21	-12	0	**	PDI#
Liberal-Conservative Rating	33%	34%	35%	35%	38%	40%	36%	37%	Closer to Democrats
	27	30	27	30	20	20	21	26	Equidistant
	39	36	39	36	42	41	43	37	Closer to Republicans
	-6	-3	-4	-1	-5	-1	-7	0	PDI#
Govt Guarantee Jobs and Std of Living (2)	31%	33%	30%	24%	29%	33%	31%	**	Closer to Democrats
	30	35	31	38	25	24	30	**	Equidistant
	40	32	38	39	46	43	39	**	Closer to Republicans
	-9	1	-8	-15	-17	-10	-8	**	PDI#
Women's Role in Government	23%	**	27%	29%	45%	35%	**	**	Closer to Democrats
	61	**	60	56	36	46	**	**	Equidistant
	16	**	14	15	19	19	**	**	Closer to Republicans
	7	**	13	14	26	16	**	**	PDI#
Military Spending (2)	**	**	**	**	30%	47%	43%	50%	Closer to Democrats
	**	**	**	**	23	21	23	21	Equidistant
	**	**	**	**	47	32	34	29	Closer to Republicans
	**	**	**	**	-17	15	9	21	PDI#
Government Services and Spending	**	**	**	**	36%	37%	39%	41%	Closer to Democrats
	**	**	**	**	23	22	22	26	Equidistant
	**	**	**	**	41	41	40	33	Closer to Republicans
	**	**	**	**	-5	-4	-1	8	PDI#
Rights of the Accused	23%	29%	29%	21%	**	**	**	**	Closer to Democrats
	51	48	45	55	**	**	**	**	Equidistant
	26	23	26	24	**	**	**	**	Closer to Republicans
	-4	6	3	-3	**	**	**	**	PDI#
Busing	26%	24%	31%	**	**	**	**	**	Closer to Democrats
	33	39	33	**	**	**	**	**	Equidistant
	41	37	36	**	**	**	**	**	Closer to Republicans
	-15	-13	-5	**	**	**	**	**	PDI#
Urban Unrest	32%	39%	35%	**	**	**	**	**	Closer to Democrats
	44	39	41	**	**	**	**	**	Equidistant
	24	22	25	**	**	**	**	**	Closer to Republicans
	8	17	10	**	**	**	**	**	PDI#
Health Insurance	36%	**	37%	34%	**	**	**	**	Closer to Democrats
	35	**	29	34	**	**	**	**	Equidistant
	30	**	34	32	**	**	**	**	Closer to Republicans
	6	**	4	2	**	**	**	**	PDI#

PDI is proportion "closer to Republicans" minus proportion "closer to Democrats"

& "Proximity to parties" is R's position on an issue relative to the perceived (by R) position of each major party. It is the absolute difference between the number of R's position on a 7-point scale as subtracted from both the perceived Dem. party position and the perceived Rep. party position, with the 2 results compared in magnitude.

Table 3.101
Respondent's Proximity to Parties on Aid to Minorities by Social Groups, Summarized with a Percent Difference Index#&

	1972	1974	1976	1978	1980	1982	1984
1959 or later Cohort	**	**	**	-2*	-16	-13	11
1943 - 1958 Cohort	8	17	13	-1	-17	-5	-3
1927 - 1942 Cohort	-1	-5	0	-13	-27	-17	4
1911 - 1926 Cohort	-11	-5	-5	-2	-20	-14	-1
1895 - 1910 Cohort	-10	-20	-8	-1	-29	-21	-12
Before 1895 Cohort	-25*	-19*	-	-	-	-	-
Grade School	3	2	21	20	-7	13	14
High School	-6	2	4	0	-21	-9	2
College	0	-1	-4	-14	-23	-17	-3
Central Cities	14	10	13	11	-2	6	19
Suburbs	-7	-6	4	-11	-29	-15	-4
Non-urban Areas	-9	0	-8	-10	-27	-22	-8
Income Percentile 0-16	9	5	33	18	-5	12	31
Income Percentile 17-33	10	17	13	0	-18	8	10
Income Percentile 34-67	-5	3	3	-1	-17	-10	1
Income Percentile 68-95	-7	-2	-1	-15	-29	-21	-12
Income Percentile 96-100	-19	-43	-41	-24	-54	-47	-22
Males	-3	-4	0	-10	-27	-22	-7
Females	-2	6	6	1	-16	-2	7
Whites	-10	-4	-7	-12	-30	-20	-7
Blacks	60	52	68	49	40	67	58
Union Household	-3	17	15	1	-18	-5	9
Non-union Household	-3	-5	-1	-6	-23	-13	-2
South	-2	-3	3	-5	-24	-10	0
Non-south	-3	3	3	-5	-20	-13	1
Professional	-5	2	-9	-14	-26	-18	-4
White Collar	-5	-1	0	0	-27	-20	4
Blue Collar	4	0	15	4	-13	-3	4
Unskilled	-	-	7*	9*	-29*	4*	18*
Farmers	6*	-16*	-18*	-	-	-27*	-17
Housewives	-15	-5	-9	-13	-23	-9	-9
Protestants	-5	-3	-2	-7	-23	-15	-8
Catholics	-5	-3	5	-4	-28	-11	6
Jews	42*	16*	15	22	12*	-	44*
Other and No Religion	21	25	28	-1	-9	-3	22
Total Population	-2	1	3	-5	-21	-12	0

PDI is proportion "closer to Republicans" minus proportion "closer to Democrats"

& "Proximity to parties" is R's position on an issue relative to the perceived (by R) position of each major party. It is the absolute difference between the number of R's position on a 7-point scale as subtracted from both the perceived Dem. party position and the perceived Rep. party position, with the 2 results compared in magnitude.

Table 3.102
Respondent's Proximity to Parties on Aid to Minorities by Political Groups, Summarized with a Percent Difference Index#&

	1972	1974	1976	1978	1980	1982	1984
Strong Democrats	37	37	49	33	17	40	41
Weak Democrats	6	23	24	9	5	8	34
Independent Democrats	20	16	19	11	4	16	37
Independent Independents	-3	-6	-1	-4	-33	-31	-2
Independent Republicans	-32	-37	-27	-34	-61	-48	-40
Weak Republicans	-22	-28	-28	-36	-57	-54	-34
Strong Republicans	-42	-64	-61	-57	-67	-79	-60
Liberal Self Placement 1	55	53	58	32	36	53	43
Liberal Self Placement 2	24	13	22	5	-2	8	23
Neutral Self Placement 3	-9	6	5	-4	-28	1	5
Conservative Self Placement 4	-30	-33	-30	-26	-45	-45	-20
Conservative Self Placement 5	-39	-50	-42	-43	-59	-50	-44
Liberal Index 1	80	86	61	**	87	60	43
Liberal Index 2	26	40	34	**	14	19	30
Neutral Index 3	2	2	9	**	-18	-8	-1
Conservative Index 4	-22	-26	-20	**	-39	-32	-24
Conservative Index 5	-50	-56	-62	**	-73	-67	-65
Total Population	-2	1	3	-5	-21	-12	0

PDI is proportion "closer to Republicans" minus proportion "closer to Democrats"

& "Proximity to parties" is R's position on an issue relative to the perceived (by R) position of each major party. It is the absolute difference between the number of R's position on a 7-point scale as subtracted from both the perceived Dem. party position and the perceived Rep. party position, with the 2 results compared in magnitude.

Table 3.103
Respondent's Proximity to Parties on Liberal-Conservative Rating by Social Groups, Summarized with a Percent Difference Index#&

	1972	1974	1976	1978	1980	1982	1984	1986
1959 or later Cohort	**	**	**	3	5	5	0	5
1943 - 1958 Cohort	14	21	17	10	5	9	-8	6
1927 - 1942 Cohort	-10	-18	-10	-11	-14	-9	-10	-11
1911 - 1926 Cohort	-19	-17	-22	-7	-8	-7	-9	-2
1895 - 1910 Cohort	-18	-10	-29	-5	-21	-29	-4	-15
Before 1895 Cohort	-19*	-17*	-	-	-	-	-	-
Grade School	-1	-1	-8	27	4	23	6	13
High School	-7	0	1	4	-4	-4	-8	3
College	-6	-5	-9	-9	-5	0	-8	-3
Central Cities	15	11	1	15	16	12	14	14
Suburbs	-9	-8	-1	-9	-10	-7	-10	-6
Non-urban Areas	-17	-10	-12	-2	-16	-4	-19	-3
Income Percentile 0-16	14	-1	14	26	9	26	6	18
Income Percentile 17-33	0	18	8	13	-1	8	10	11
Income Percentile 34-67	-8	1	-1	3	-1	13	1	0
Income Percentile 68-95	-9	-8	-3	-8	-14	-13	-20	-5
Income Percentile 96-100	-33	-61	-45	-34	-16	-29	-31	-27
Males	-12	-9	-6	-4	-8	-12	-12	-9
Females	-1	3	-3	3	-2	11	-2	8
Whites	-12	-6	-10	-5	-9	-5	-11	-7
Blacks	55	39	52	51	43	54	32	51
Union Household	-1	9	16	9	6	7	9	7
Non-union Household	-8	-6	-11	-4	-9	-2	-12	-2
South	-10	-10	-11	-4	-2	-5	-11	4
Non-south	-4	1	-2	1	-6	2	-6	-2
Professional	-14	-8	-17	-7	-4	-3	-7	-2
White Collar	-3	-8	-6	4	-12	2	-8	-9
Blue Collar	5	9	9	9	-2	5	-3	8
Unskilled	-	-	22*	33*	-	-	7*	32*
Farmers	-36*	-25*	-27*	-	-	-	-34*	-13*
Housewives	-18	-13	-14	-15	-9	-12	-19	-9
Protestants	-12	-12	-16	-11	-12	-11	-19	-3
Catholics	0	4	6	8	3	8	2	-3
Jews	42*	43	48	24*	32*	-	44*	14*
Other and No Religion	24	27	28	26	5	28	25	18
Total Population	-6	-3	-4	-1	-5	-1	-7	0

PDI is proportion "closer to Republicans" minus proportion "closer to Democrats"

& "Proximity to parties" is R's position on an issue relative to the perceived (by R) position of each major party. It is the absolute difference between the number of R's position on a 7-point scale as subtracted from both the perceived Dem. party position and the perceived Rep. party position, with the 2 results compared in magnitude.

Party Proximity

Table 3.104
Respondent's Proximity to Parties on Liberal-Conservative Rating by Political Groups, Summarized with a Percent Difference Index#&

	1972	1974	1976	1978	1980	1982	1984	1986
Strong Democrats	52	43	49	49	61	65	57	61
Weak Democrats	9	22	30	30	27	26	26	29
Independent Democrats	39	19	33	41	34	47	45	39
Independent Independents	-12	-4	-5	-7	-2	-22	-1	-2
Independent Republicans	-42	-51	-41	-47	-58	-41	-49	-46
Weak Republicans	-43	-39	-48	-57	-56	-50	-53	-40
Strong Republicans	-64	-73	-81	-71	-77	-91	-77	-72
Liberal Self Placement 1	80	72	83	69	79	86	63	73
Liberal Self Placement 2	68	59	70	61	58	71	53	55
Neutral Self Placement 3	-5	-6	4	12	14	20	6	17
Conservative Self Placement 4	-61	-55	-62	-57	-53	-53	-57	-51
Conservative Self Placement 5	-71	-59	-67	-59	-62	-65	-61	-52
Liberal Index 1	81	73	68	**	93	89	85	78
Liberal Index 2	48	53	50	**	56	64	38	39
Neutral Index 3	4	-3	7	**	19	13	-3	10
Conservative Index 4	-38	-38	-36	**	-33	-40	-43	-25
Conservative Index 5	-68	-64	-85	**	-73	-80	-86	-77
Total Population	-6	-3	-4	-1	-5	-1	-7	0

PDI is proportion "closer to Republicans" minus proportion "closer to Democrats"

& "Proximity to parties" is R's position on an issue relative to the perceived (by R) position of each major party. It is the
absolute difference between the number of R's position on a 7-point scale as subtracted from both the perceived Dem. party
position and the perceived Rep. party position, with the 2 results compared in magnitude.

Party Proximity

Table 3.105
Respondent's Proximity to Parties on Government Guaranteed Jobs (2) by Social Groups, Summarized by a Percent Difference Index#&

	1972	1974	1976	1978	1980	1982	1984
1959 or later Cohort	**	**	**	-3*	13	5	3
1943 - 1958 Cohort	-2	14	1	-17	-17	-4	-9
1927 - 1942 Cohort	-8	-6	-14	-21	-28	-17	-15
1911 - 1926 Cohort	-16	-8	-12	-8	-13	-16	-8
1895 - 1910 Cohort	-13	-7	-12	-4	-19	-23	-6
Before 1895 Cohort	-17*	14*	-16*	-	-	-	-
Grade School	7	15	11	13	1	4	21
High School	-10	7	-1	-7	-10	0	-4
College	-14	-10	-22	-28	-26	-21	-15
Central Cities	7	9	5	-5	2	3	12
Suburbs	-18	-6	-13	-23	-23	-15	-17
Non-urban Areas	-12	2	-14	-12	-26	-15	-12
Income Percentile 0-16	17	18	23	9	1	16	21
Income Percentile 17-33	5	10	4	2	4	4	13
Income Percentile 34-67	-10	8	-7	-11	-11	-3	-4
Income Percentile 68-95	-19	-8	-16	-28	-34	-28	-27
Income Percentile 96-100	-37	-55	-47	-47	-61	-42	-45
Males	-10	-6	-15	-20	-24	-21	-18
Females	-7	8	-1	-9	-10	0	1
Whites	-17	-5	-16	-19	-26	-19	-15
Blacks	55	59	52	29	57	63	49
Union Household	-3	15	7	-5	-6	2	7
Non-union Household	-12	-4	-13	-18	-21	-13	-12
South	-6	8	-2	-9	-19	-8	-4
Non-south	-10	-2	-11	-18	-16	-12	-10
Professional	-15	-6	-27	-29	-31	-25	-19
White Collar	-7	-5	-15	-10	-26	-10	-9
Blue Collar	2	7	9	-2	-5	3	1
Unskilled	19*	45*	-1*	8*	16*	-4*	14*
Farmers	-11*	-13*	-23*	-22*	-	-10*	-33*
Housewives	-23	3	-9	-21	-10	-11	-14
Protestants	-14	-2	-13	-18	-17	-16	-12
Catholics	0	5	3	-13	-20	-2	-5
Jews	16*	10	9	-6	-25*	-	24*
Other and No Religion	8	5	-12	-8	-2	2	1
Total Population	-9	1	-8	-15	-17	-10	-8

PDI is proportion "closer to Republicans" minus proportion "closer to Democrats"

& "Proximity to parties" is R's position on an issue relative to the perceived (by R) position of each major party. It is the absolute difference between the number of R's position on a 7-point scale as subtracted from both the perceived Dem. party position and the perceived Rep. party position, with the 2 results compared in magnitude.

Table 3.106
Respondent's Proximity to Parties on Government Guaranteed Jobs(2) by Political Groups, Summarized by a Percent Difference Index#&

	1972	1974	1976	1978	1980	1982	1984
Strong Democrats	40	47	41	23	48	42	43
Weak Democrats	12	28	13	8	2	14	20
Independent Democrats	15	9	10	3	-5	20	27
Independent Independents	-9	-2	-15	-8	-30	-28	-18
Independent Republicans	-47	-40	-45	-55	-55	-66	-40
Weak Republicans	-51	-37	-39	-54	-55	-51	-43
Strong Republicans	-57	-62	-67	-65	-70	-76	-73
Liberal Self Placement 1	50	38	36	21	52	57	37
Liberal Self Placement 2	7	15	12	-7	-10	-10	10
Neutral Self Placement 3	-13	6	-8	-12	-17	-5	1
Conservative Self Placement 4	-40	-32	-42	-38	-39	-40	-41
Conservative Self Placement 5	-53	-41	-51	-44	-63	-50	-52
Liberal Index 1	83	70	37*	**	89*	62*	62
Liberal Index 2	20	36	21	**	29	18	16
Neutral Index 3	-5	-6	-3	**	-20	-5	-8
Conservative Index 4	-33	-21	-33	**	-38	-33	-35
Conservative Index 5	-60	-54	-70	**	-79	-73	-79
Total Population	-9	1	-8	-15	-17	-10	-8

PDI is proportion "closer to Republicans" minus proportion "closer to Democrats"

& "Proximity to parties" is R's position on an issue relative to the perceived (by R) position of each major party. It is the absolute difference between the number of R's position on a 7-point scale as subtracted from both the perceived Dem. party position and the perceived Rep. party position, with the 2 results compared in magnitude.

Table 3.107
Respondent's Proximity to Parties on Role of Women by Social Groups, Summarized with a Percent Difference Index#&

	1972	1974	1976	1978	1980	1982	1984	1986
1959 or later Cohort	**	**	**	8*	39	8	**	**
1943 - 1958 Cohort	15	**	18	22	36	21	**	**
1927 - 1942 Cohort	8	**	11	7	20	14	**	**
1911 - 1926 Cohort	0	**	6	14	11	14	**	**
1895 - 1910 Cohort	-5	**	9	0	16	5	**	**
Before 1895 Cohort	3	**	30*	-	-	-	**	**
Grade School	2	**	22	11	9	8	**	**
High School	3	**	3	8	19	10	**	**
College	13	**	21	21	34	22	**	**
Central Cities	18	**	18	25	38	27	**	**
Suburbs	6	**	16	12	23	16	**	**
Non-urban Areas	-1	**	5	6	18	6	**	**
Income Percentile 0-16	10	**	24	17	15	25	**	**
Income Percentile 17-33	4	**	23	25	35	16	**	**
Income Percentile 34-67	11	**	8	11	25	12	**	**
Income Percentile 68-95	5	**	12	15	28	12	**	**
Income Percentile 96-100	-6	**	13	5	22	21	**	**
Males	4	**	14	16	22	12	**	**
Females	9	**	12	12	29	20	**	**
Whites	4	**	10	10	22	13	**	**
Blacks	23	**	36	46	55	40	**	**
Union Household	9	**	23	16	22	21	**	**
Non-union Household	6	**	9	13	27	15	**	**
South	1	**	13	16	24	15	**	**
Non-south	9	**	13	13	27	16	**	**
Professional	10	**	18	21	31	23	**	**
White Collar	16	**	12	17	20	13	**	**
Blue Collar	5	**	16	14	16	17	**	**
Unskilled	3*	**	11*	25*	48*	-8*	**	**
Farmers	-9*	**	-16*	-	-	0*	**	**
Housewives	0	**	2	-3	28	8	**	**
Protestants	3	**	8	10	19	10	**	**
Catholics	9	**	15	11	25	18	**	**
Jews	46*	**	25*	45	67*	-	**	**
Other and No Religion	19	**	33	28	50	41	**	**
Total Population	7	**	13	14	26	16	**	**

PDI is proportion "closer to Republicans" minus proportion "closer to Democrats"

& "Proximity to parties" is R's position on an issue relative to the perceived (by R) position of each major party. It is the
  absolute difference between the number of R's position on a 7-point scale as subtracted from both the perceived Dem. party
  position and the perceived Rep. party position, with the 2 results compared in magnitude.

Table 3.108
Respondent's Proximity to Parties on Role of Women by Political Groups, Summarized with a Percent Difference Index#&

	1972	1974	1976	1978	1980	1982	1984	1986
Strong Democrats	19	**	30	34	51	43	**	**
Weak Democrats	17	**	22	21	31	28	**	**
Independent Democrats	21	**	22	32	49	32	**	**
Independent Independents	1	**	9	15	23	0	**	**
Independent Republicans	0	**	6	4	23	-11	**	**
Weak Republicans	-16	**	-4	-8	3	-3	**	**
Strong Republicans	-15	**	-7	-27	-12	-26	**	**
Liberal Self Placement 1	38	**	47	44	74	66	**	**
Liberal Self Placement 2	23	**	32	35	47	37	**	**
Neutral Self Placement 3	2	**	10	13	26	12	**	**
Conservative Self Placement 4	-2	**	5	5	23	4	**	**
Conservative Self Placement 5	-15	**	-8	-15	-5	-9	**	**
Liberal Index 1	59	**	51	**	85	68	**	**
Liberal Index 2	19	**	33	**	58	41	**	**
Neutral Index 3	10	**	13	**	29	12	**	**
Conservative Index 4	-4	**	4	**	13	2	**	**
Conservative Index 5	-12	**	-15	**	-15	-22	**	**
Total Population	7	**	13	14	26	16	**	**

PDI is proportion "closer to Republicans" minus proportion "closer to Democrats"

& "Proximity to parties" is R's position on an issue relative to the perceived (by R) position of each major party. It is the absolute difference between the number of R's position on a 7-point scale as subtracted from both the perceived Dem. party position and the perceived Rep. party position, with the 2 results compared in magnitude.

Table 3.109
Respondent's Proximity to Parties on Military Spending (2) by Social Groups, Summarized by a Percent Difference Index#&

	1980	1982	1984	1986
1959 or later Cohort	-7	26	16	19
1943 - 1958 Cohort	-16	19	10	20
1927 - 1942 Cohort	-26	13	7	17
1911 - 1926 Cohort	-9	12	3	31
1895 - 1910 Cohort	-29	-18	0	24
Before 1895 Cohort	-	-	-	-
Grade School	-22	-4	18	32
High School	-14	12	7	21
College	-20	19	9	21
Central Cities	-5	19	28	30
Suburbs	-20	18	4	16
Non-urban Areas	-25	8	1	21
Income Percentile 0-16	-12	27	26	30
Income Percentile 17-33	2	23	23	34
Income Percentile 34-67	-18	14	10	23
Income Percentile 68-95	-24	13	0	7
Income Percentile 96-100	-34	4	-14	16
Males	-23	6	4	9
Females	-12	24	13	32
Whites	-21	11	4	17
Blacks	17	54	54	52
Union Household	-6	31	25	32
Non-union Household	-22	11	4	18
South	-20	7	2	17
Non-south	-16	19	12	23
Professional	-16	16	10	17
White Collar	-19	9	8	29
Blue Collar	-16	13	12	23
Unskilled	-20*	16*	32*	5*
Farmers	-32*	0*	-17*	16*
Housewives	-17	19	1	16
Protestants	-26	7	2	17
Catholics	-7	23	14	26
Jews	31*	-	45*	39*
Other and No Religion	-9	36	30	32
Total Population	-17	15	9	21

PDI is proportion "closer to Republicans" minus proportion "closer to Democrats"

& "Proximity to parties" is R's position on an issue relative to the perceived (by R) position of each major party. It is the absolute difference between the number of R's position on a 7-point scale as subtracted from both the perceived Dem. party position and the perceived Rep. party position, with the 2 results compared in magnitude.

Table 3.110
Respondent's Proximity to Parties on Military Spending (2) by Political Groups, Summarized by a Percent Difference Index#&

	1980	1982	1984	1986
Strong Democrats	35	55	57	65
Weak Democrats	4	39	37	43
Independent Democrats	15	46	56	52
Independent Independents	-28	4	0	12
Independent Republicans	-60	-17	-23	-10
Weak Republicans	-51	-20	-25	-10
Strong Republicans	-80	-59	-55	-41
Liberal Self Placement 1	47	74	54	64
Liberal Self Placement 2	23	53	38	43
Neutral Self Placement 3	-17	26	18	30
Conservative Self Placement 4	-38	-11	-5	3
Conservative Self Placement 5	-58	-29	-37	-20
Liberal Index 1	72*	98*	80*	82
Liberal Index 2	25	57	38	48
Neutral Index 3	-10	18	14	26
Conservative Index 4	-38	-6	-13	3
Conservative Index 5	-66	-51	-69	-42
Total Population	-17	15	9	21

PDI is proportion "closer to Republicans" minus proportion "closer to Democrats"

& "Proximity to parties" is R's position on an issue relative to the perceived (by R) position of each major party. It is the
  absolute difference between the number of R's position on a 7-point scale as subtracted from both the perceived Dem. party
  position and the perceived Rep. party position, with the 2 results compared in magnitude.

Table 3.111
Respondent's Proximity to Parties on Government Services by Social Groups, Summarized with a Percent Difference Index#&

	1980	1982	1984	1986
1959 or later Cohort	20	8	8	13
1943 - 1958 Cohort	0	-1	-3	9
1927 - 1942 Cohort	-19	-10	-3	0
1911 - 1926 Cohort	-8	-7	-1	9
1895 - 1910 Cohort	5	-6	-15	17
Before 1895 Cohort	-	-	-	-
Grade School	24	35	17	33
High School	-1	3	5	14
College	-14	-13	-10	0
Central Cities	16	12	15	23
Suburbs	-11	-10	-4	2
Non-urban Areas	-16	-10	-9	3
Income Percentile 0-16	26	21	34	23
Income Percentile 17-33	10	21	2	23
Income Percentile 34-67	3	-2	5	9
Income Percentile 68-95	-22	-17	-14	-4
Income Percentile 96-100	-56	-35	-39	-23
Males	-13	-15	-8	1
Females	2	7	6	15
Whites	-12	-12	-8	1
Blacks	53	63	59	50
Union Household	2	7	12	31
Non-union Household	-8	-7	-5	2
South	-4	-7	3	8
Non-south	-6	-2	-3	8
Professional	-22	-15	-9	-6
White Collar	-6	-19	-5	7
Blue Collar	8	12	7	20
Unskilled	5*	27*	33*	32*
Farmers	-	5*	-28*	-9*
Housewives	-6	-7	-10	7
Protestants	-9	-11	-9	4
Catholics	-1	4	5	13
Jews	21*	-	51*	7*
Other and No Religion	-2	15	13	20
Total Population	-5	-4	-1	8

PDI is proportion "closer to Republicans" minus proportion "closer to Democrats"

& "Proximity to parties" is R's position on an issue relative to the perceived (by R) position of each major party. It is the absolute difference between the number of R's position on a 7-point scale as subtracted from both the perceived Dem. party position and the perceived Rep. party position, with the 2 results compared in magnitude.

Table 3.112
Respondent's Proximity to Parties on Government Services by Political Groups, Summarized with a Percent Difference Index#&

	1980	1982	1984	1986
Strong Democrats	56	53	59	58
Weak Democrats	34	20	33	33
Independent Democrats	9	34	47	37
Independent Independents	-12	-28	-10	4
Independent Republicans	-54	-53	-46	-34
Weak Republicans	-50	-50	-45	-27
Strong Republicans	-76	-70	-72	-60
Liberal Self Placement 1	57	62	48	60
Liberal Self Placement 2	21	27	23	24
Neutral Self Placement 3	0	4	9	13
Conservative Self Placement 4	-34	-38	-31	-24
Conservative Self Placement 5	-46	-54	-51	-37
Liberal Index 1	88*	85*	61	72
Liberal Index 2	40	39	29	34
Neutral Index 3	10	4	3	17
Conservative Index 4	-31	-41	-30	-14
Conservative Index 5	-70	-71	-78	-55
Total Population	-5	-4	-1	8

PDI is proportion "closer to Republicans" minus proportion "closer to Democrats"

& "Proximity to parties" is R's position on an issue relative to the perceived (by R) position of each major party. It is the absolute difference between the number of R's position on a 7-point scale as subtracted from both the perceived Dem. party position and the perceived Rep. party position, with the 2 results compared in magnitude.

Chapter 4. Support of the Political System

Substantively, this chapter focuses on the citizen's psychological attachment to various aspects of the political system. In general terms, the political system includes the authorities, salient institutions and levels of government, political norms, and, in its broadest sense, the people that compose the political community. The items selected for analysis and presentation tap evaluative orientations toward these political objects. Positive evaluations of these political objects as measured by these items generally include expression of support for government and acceptance of the legitimacy of the political regime. Although negative responses to the survey questions analyzed in this chapter may not reveal support for alternative forms of government, they do suggest a level of discontent with the authorities of the time and the performance of government in general.

Presumably, in a democratic system, periodic elections provide an opportunity to "throw the rascals out" if citizens are disenchanted with the policies and performance of the incumbents. Elections therefore act to maintain citizen satisfaction with the political order, for they offer a peaceful means to change. If, however, dissatisfaction with authorities and government accumulates over a long period of time, the legitimacy of the institutions and political norms may become the targets of discontent. Thus, when monitored across time, these indicators of how positively citizens regard their political leaders and institutions of governance provide an important measure of support for the nation's political system.

The chapter begins with distributions which show how all respondents in the samples answered the individual questions selected to measure attitudes toward components of the political system. We start with questions about the confidence and trust citizens have in government's different levels (national, state, and local; Tables 4.1-4.2) and branches (executive, legislative, and judicial; Tables 4.3-4.5).

Next, we present the over-time distributions for responses to a series of items measuring several concepts in the general domain of system support (Tables 4.6-4.36). The specific questions measuring each of these concepts are then combined into indices, and a further analysis of each index across time is presented (Tables 4.37-4.57). A brief definition of the conceptual meaning of each index is given below.

Trust in government refers to the public's basic evaluative orientation toward the government in Washington. The items in Tables 4.12-4.16 were used to form a cumulative index which selected the following response categories to indicate a cynical answer: 4.12, None or Some of the Time; 4.13, Few Big Interests; 4.14, Waste a Lot; 4.15, Don't Know What They're Doing; 4.16, Quite a Lot. The resulting scale values represent the number of cynical responses to the five questions. The constructed index runs from high trust or confidence in government to distrust or political cynicism. Cynicism thus indicates a negative evaluation of government and reflects the belief that the government is not functioning in accordance with individual expectations of efficiency, honesty and equity.

Internal political efficacy indicates individuals' self-perceptions that they are capable of understanding politics and competent enough to participate in political acts such as voting. The additive index combines the items in Tables 4.17-4.19 and ranges from the least efficacious to the most efficacious, depending on the number of efficacious responses the individual gave to the three survey questions. A sense of efficacy is indicated by a Disagree response to a question.

External political efficacy, unlike internal political efficacy, measures expressed beliefs about political institutions rather than perceptions about one's own abilities. A sense of external efficacy denotes the feeling that an individual and the public can have an impact on the political process because government institutions will respond to their needs. The lack of external efficacy or the feeling of inefficacy indicates the belief that the public cannot influence political outcomes because government leaders and institutions are unresponsive to their needs. The items in Tables 4.20-4.22 were combined in this index by counting the number of items to which the respondent gave an efficacious response (Disagree).

Government responsiveness reflects beliefs about the extent to which specific political institutions (public opinion, parties, and elections) and leaders (congressmen) can bring about responsive government. The index was formed by adding the response to the four items in Tables 4.23-4.26. The answer category A Good Deal was used to indicate the belief that government is responsive. The scale was then constructed to represent the number of such answers to the four items. The resulting index ranges from low to high responsiveness, indicating the extent to which the respondent believes that the institutions mentioned will be effective in making government responsive to the needs of the people. The emphasis is on the responsiveness of political institutions rather than on the effectiveness of individual citizens.

Citizen duty denotes the belief that the individual has a civic responsibility to vote. It therefore implies support for the institution of elections as a democratic norm. How strongly individuals felt about the obligation to vote was measured with a cumulative index which represents the number of Disagree responses to the four survey questions presented in Tables 4.27-4.30. The resulting scale ranges from low to high sense of citizen duty. Those respondents with a high sense of

duty are most strongly committed to the democratic norm of
voting.

Trust in people comes close to capturing a sense of
political community at the interpersonal level. Presumably, an
elementary level of system support requires trust in one's
fellows; otherwise, cooperative activity aimed at meeting
common objectives would be impeded. The three questions from
Tables 4.31-4.33 have to do with whether one can trust most
people, whether most people are fair in their dealings with
others. The number of positive responses to the three items
reflects the extent of trust in people.

Protest approval refers to support of or opposition to
protest activities which are directed at government. This
measure can be interpreted as indicating a predisposition to
support or engage in protest activity and, therefore, comes as
close as we can with our previous surveys to measuring system
support as behavior. The three items from Tables 4.34-4.36,
combined in the additive index, express the degree of approval
for legal protests, disobeying laws, and disrupting government
activities.

Changes in some political support attitudes were quite
dramatic during the decades from 1958 to 1980. Of particular
interest is the downward trend in political trust, government
responsiveness, and external political efficacy. At the same
time, there was an increase in public approval of protest
actions. Citizen duty and internal political efficacy, on the
other hand, showed virtually no change over the same period.

Table 4.1
Level of Government the Respondent Has Most Confidence In

QUESTION: We find that people differ in how much
faith and confidence they have in various levels
of government in this country. In your case, do
you have more faith and confidence in the
national government, the government of this state,
or in the local government around here?

	1968	1970	1972	1974	1976
National Government	39%	**	40%	25%	26%
State government	16	**	21	22	23
Local government	23	**	26	28	31
Don't know	23	**	14	25	20
Total	100%	**	100%	100%	100%
N	1348	**	1070	2515	2401

Table 4.2
Level cf Government the Respondent Has Least Confidence In

QUESTION: Which level do you have the least faith
and confidence in -- the national government, the
government of this state, or the local
government around here?

	1968	1970	1972	1974	1976
National Government	22%	**	22%	32%	35%
State government	16	**	19	11	15
Local government	31	**	38	26	25
Don't know	31	**	22	31	26
Total	100%	**	100%	100%	100%
N	1348	**	1061	2461	2398

Table 4.3
Branch of Government the Respondent Trusts Most

QUESTION: Which part of the government
(on the list) do you most often trust to
do what's right <Congress, Supreme Court,
President, Political Parties>?

	1972	1974	1976
Congress	28%	23%	23%
Supreme Court	23	43	33
President	37	19	25
Political Parties	1	2	2
Don't know	11	13	17
Total	100%	100%	100%
N	1067	2485	2393

Table 4.4
Branch of Government Next Most Trusted by R

QUESTION: Which of the others do you next
often trust to do what's right <Congress,
Supreme Court, President, political parties>?

	1972	1974	1976
Congress	35%	38%	29%
Supreme Court	20	19	20
President	25	23	25
Political Parties	4	4	4
Don't know	17	16	22
Total	100%	100%	100%
N	1058	2464	2383

Table 4.5
Branch of Government the Respondent Trusts Least

QUESTION: Which <part of the government>
do you least often trust to do what's
right <Congress, President, Supreme Court,
or political parties>?

	1972	1974	1976
Congress	4%	5%	9%
Supreme Court	15	6	10
President	9	12	7
Political Parties	57	65	60
Don't know	15	12	15
Total	100%	100%	100%

Table 4.6
Performance Rating of Federal Government

QUESTION: Now, I'd like to ask you how good a job you feel some of the parts of
our government are doing. As I read, please give me the number that best describes
how good a job you feel that part of the government is doing for the country as a whole.

		1974	1976	1980
Very poor job	0	4%	3%	5%
	1	1	1	2
Poor job	2	15	13	19
	3	8	7	12
Fair job	4	39	52	45
	5	12	10	8
Good job	6	16	13	8
	7	2	1	1
Very good job	8	3	1	1
	Total	100%	100%	100%
	N	2343	2221	1341

Table 4.7
Performance Rating of Presidency

		1974	1976	1980
Very poor job	0	6%	3%	5%
	1	2	1	3
Poor job	2	12	11	19
	3	7	6	12
Fair job	4	29	37	33
	5	11	14	11
Good job	6	24	23	13
	7	4	3	2
Very good job	8	4	3	2
	Total	100%	100%	100%
	N	2328	2239	1348

Table 4.8
Performance Rating of the Congress

		1974	1976	1980
Very poor job	0	3%	3%	5%
	1	1	2	2
Poor job	2	10	16	22
	3	7	12	14
Fair job	4	33	41	35
	5	15	13	11
Good job	6	23	13	9
	7	4	1	1
Very good job	8	4	1	1
	Total	100%	100%	100%
	N	2302	2109	1269

Table 4.9
Performance Rating of the Supreme Court

		1974	1976	1980
Very poor job	0	3%	4%	4%
	1	1	2	4
Poor job	2	6	13	12
	3	4	9	11
Fair job	4	23	31	29
	5	11	13	13
Good job	6	30	22	20
	7	10	4	3
Very good job	8	11	2	3
Total		100%	100%	100%
N		2224	1940	1103

Table 4.10
Performance Rating of State Government

		1974	1976	1980
Very poor job	0	2%	2%	2%
	1	1	1	1
Poor job	2	8	12	11
	3	6	8	9
Fair job	4	39	41	42
	5	13	13	14
Good job	6	26	20	20
	7	3	2	1
Very good job	8	3	1	2
Total		100%	100%	100%
N		2316	2182	1303

Table 4.11
Performance Rating of Local Government

		1974	1976	1980
Very poor job	0	5%	3%	3%
	1	3	1	1
Poor job	2	9	12	10
	3	7	8	8
Fair job	4	31	34	36
	5	11	12	14
Good job	6	24	25	22
	7	6	3	3
Very good job	8	4	2	2
Total		100%	100%	100%
N		2285	2166	1308

Table 4.12
Can you Trust the Federal Government

QUESTION: How much of the time do you think you can trust the
government in Washington to do what is right--just about always, most
of the time, or only some of the time?

	1958	1960	1962	1964	1966	1968	1970	1972	1974	1976	1978	1980	1982	1984	1986
None of the time	0%	**	**	0%	3%	0%	0%	1%	1%	1%	4%	4%	3%	1%	2%
Some of the time	23	**	**	22	28	36	44	44	61	62	64	69	62	53	57
Most of the time	57	**	**	62	48	54	47	48	34	30	27	23	31	40	35
Always	16	**	**	14	17	7	7	5	3	3	3	2	2	4	3
Don't know	4	**	**	2	4	2	2	2	2	3	3	2	3	2	2
Total	100%	**	**	100%	100%	100%	100%	100%	100%	100%	100%	100%	100%	100%	100%
N	1774	**	**	1445	1285	1337	1497	2279	2499	2859	2288	1606	1401	1921	1081
PDI#	50	**	**	55	34	25	9	8	-26	-30	-39	-48	-32	-10	-21

PDI is proportion "always or most of the time" minus proportion "some or none of the time"

Table 4.13
Is the Government Run for the Benefit of All

QUESTION: Would you say the government is pretty much run
by a few big interests looking out for themselves or that
it is run for the benefit of all people?

	1964	1966	1968	1970	1972	1974	1976	1978	1980	1982	1984
Few big interests	29%	33%	40%	50%	53%	66%	66%	67%	70%	61%	55%
Benefit of all	64	53	51	41	38	25	24	24	21	29	39
Don't know	8	14	9	9	9	9	10	9	9	10	6
Total	100%	100%	100%	100%	100%	100%	100%	100%	100%	100%	100%
N	1443	1276	1336	1496	2273	2500	2839	2263	1593	1397	1898
PDI#	35	20	12	-9	-16	-42	-42	-42	-49	-32	-16

PDI is proportion "benefit of all" minus proportion "few big interests"

Table 4.14
Do People in Government Waste Tax Money

QUESTION: Do you think that people in the government waste a lot
of money we pay in taxes, waste some of it, or don't waste very
much of it?

	1958	1960	1962	1964	1966	1968	1970	1972	1974	1976	1978	1980	1982	1984
A lot	43%	**	**	47%	**	59%	69%	66%	74%	74%	77%	78%	66%	65%
Some	42	**	**	44	**	34	26	30	22	20	19	18	29	30
Not much	10	**	**	7	**	4	4	2	1	3	2	2	2	4
Don't know	4	**	**	2	**	3	1	2	2	3	2	2	3	2
Total	100%	**	**	100%	**	100%	100%	100%	100%	100%	100%	100%	100%	100%
N	1774	**	**	1447	**	1343	1502	2282	2515	2865	2291	1607	1403	1920
PDI#	9	**	**	4	**	-21	-39	-33	-50	-51	-57	-59	-34	-32

PDI is proportion "not much" and "some" minus proportion "a lot"

Table 4.15
Do Government Officials Know What They Are Doing

QUESTION: Do you feel that almost all of the people running the government are smart
people (who usually know what they are doing), or do you think that quite a few [1970:
quite a lot] of them don't seem to know what they are doing?

	1958	1960	1962	1964	1966	1968	1970	1972	1974	1976	1978	1980
Don't know what they're doing	37%	**	**	27%	**	37%	44%	40%	46%	50%	51%	62%
Know what they're doing	57	**	**	69	**	58	52	55	49	44	41	34
Don't know	6	**	**	4	**	5	4	5	5	7	8	4
Total	100%	**	**	100%	**	100%	100%	100%	100%	100%	100%	100%
N	1781	**	**	1447	**	1342	1502	2275	2506	2851	2266	1595
PDI#	20	**	**	42	**	21	7	15	4	-6	-10	-29

PDI is proportion "know what they're doing" minus proportion "don't know what they're doing"
Parenthetical phrase omitted after 1972

Table 4.16
Are Government Officials Crooked

QUESTION: Do you think that quite a few of the people running the
government are a little crooked not, very many are, or do you
think hardly any of them are crooked at all?

	1958	1960	1962	1964	1966	1968	1970	1972	1974	1976	1978	1980	1982	1984
Quite a lot	24%	**	**	29%	**	25%	32%	36%	45%	42%	40%	47%	**	32%
Not many	44	**	**	49	**	52	49	46	42	40	42	41	**	50
Hardly any	26	**	**	18	**	19	16	14	10	13	13	9	**	14
Don't know	6	**	**	4	**	4	3	4	3	5	6	4	**	4
Total	100%	**	**	100%	**	100%	100%	100%	100%	100%	100%	100%	**	100%
N	1774	**	**	1438	**	1330	1489	2268	2498	2832	2266	1600	**	1905
PDI#	46	**	**	38	**	46	34	24	6	11	15	3	**	32

PDI is proportion "hardly any and not many" minus proportion "quite a lot"

Table 4.17
Is Voting the Only Way People Have a Say in Government

QUESTION: Voting is the only way that people like me can have any say about how
the government runs things.

	1952	1954	1956	1958	1960	1962	1964	1966	1968	1970	1972	1974	1976	1978	1980
Agree	81%	**	73%	**	73%	**	73%	69%	57%	60%	62%	60%	55%	58%	58%
Disagree	17	**	25	**	25	**	26	27	42	39	37	37	42	40	39
Don't know	2	**	2	**	2	**	1	5	1	1	1	3	3	2	3
Total	100%	**	100%	**	100%	**	100%	100%	100%	100%	100%	100%	100%	100%	100%
N	1775	**	1749	**	1917	**	1563	1289	1339	1500	2692	2507	2391	2287	1404
PDI#	-64	**	-48	**	-48	**	-48	-42	-15	-21	-24	-22	-13	-18	-20

PDI is proportion "disagree" minus proportion "agree"

Table 4.18
Do People Have Any Say in What the Government Does

QUESTION: People like me don't have any say about what the government does.

	1952	1954	1956	1958	1960	1962	1964	1966	1968	1970	1972	1974	1976	1978	1980	1982	1984
Agree	31%	**	28%	**	27%	**	29%	34%	41%	36%	40%	40%	41%	45%	39%	45%	33%
Disagree	68	**	71	**	72	**	70	60	59	64	59	57	56	53	59	52	66
Don't know	1	**	1	**	1	**	1	6	0	1	1	3	3	2	2	3	1
Total	100%	**	100%	**	100%	**	100%	100%	100%	100%	100%	100%	100%	100%	100%	100%	100%
N	1769	**	1752	**	1922	**	1564	1290	1337	1504	2693	2519	2394	2291	1403	1402	969
PDI#	37	**	43	**	45	**	40	26	17	28	19	17	15	8	20	7	33

PDI is proportion "disagree" minus proportion "agree"

Table 4.19
Is Politics Too Complicated

QUESTION: Sometimes politics and government seem so complicated that a person
like me can't really understand what's going on.

	1952	1954	1956	1958	1960	1962	1964	1966	1968	1970	1972	1974	1976	1978	1980	1982	1984
Agree	71%	**	64%	**	59%	**	67%	69%	71%	73%	74%	72%	72%	72%	70%	**	71%
Disagree	28	**	36	**	41	**	32	27	29	26	26	26	27	26	28	**	29
Don't know	1	**	1	**	0	**	1	4	0	1	1	2	2	2	2	**	0
Total	100%	**	100%	**	100%	**	100%	100%	100%	100%	100%	100%	100%	100%	100%	**	100%
N	1779	**	1742	**	1900	**	1558	1289	1341	1502	2694	2500	2392	2288	1404	**	2239
PDI#	-42	**	-28	**	-18	**	-35	-43	-42	-47	-48	-46	-45	-46	-42	**	-42

PDI is proportion "disagree" minus proportion "agree"

Table 4.20
Do Public Officials Care What People Think

QUESTION: I don't think public officials care much what people like me think.

	1952	1954	1956	1958	1960	1962	1964	1966	1968	1970	1972	1974	1976	1978	1980	1982	1984	1986
Agree	35%	**	26%	**	25%	**	36%	34%	43%	47%	49%	50%	51%	51%	52%	47%	42%	52%
Disagree	63	**	71	**	73	**	62	57	55	50	49	46	44	45	44	50	57	43
Don't know	2	**	2	**	2	**	2	9	2	3	2	4	5	4	4	4	1	5
Total	100%	**	100%	**	100%	**	100%	100%	100%	100%	100%	100%	100%	100%	100%	100%	100%	100%
N	1765	**	1740	**	1892	**	1557	1289	1337	1502	2689	2505	2387	2281	1397	1402	2229	1082
PDI#	28	**	45	**	49	**	26	22	12	2	0	-4	-7	-6	-9	3	15	-9

PDI is proportion "disagree" minus proportion "agree"

Table 4.21
Do Congressmen Lose Touch with People

QUESTION: Generally speaking, those we elect to
Congress in Washington lose touch with the people
pretty quickly.

	1968	1970	1972	1974	1976	1978	1980
Agree	53%	60%	66%	67%	68%	70%	71%
Disagree	43	37	31	28	26	25	23
Don't know	4	4	3	6	5	5	6
Total	100%	100%	100%	100%	100%	100%	100%
N	1338	1499	2681	2500	2391	2287	1394
PDI#	-10	-23	-35	-39	-42	-45	-48

PDI is proportion "disagree" minus proportion "agree"

Table 4.22
Are Parties Interested in Peoples' Votes or Their Opinions

QUESTION: Parties are only interested in people's
votes but not in their opinions.

	1968	1970	1972	1974	1976	1978	1980
Agree	46%	54%	58%	58%	60%	62%	59%
Disagree	51	43	40	37	34	33	35
Don't know	3	3	3	5	6	5	6
Total	100%	100%	100%	100%	100%	100%	100%
N	1338	1487	2686	2503	2389	2278	1400
PDI#	5	-11	-18	-21	-26	-29	-23

PDI is proportion "disagree" minus proportion "agree"

Table 4.23
How Much Does Government Listen to People

QUESTION: Over the years, how much attention do you
feel the government pays to what the people think
when it decides what to do -- a good deal, some, or
not much?

	1964	1966	1968	1970	1972	1974	1976	1978	1980	1982	1984
Not much	24%	**	29%	24%	24%	28%	33%	28%	41%	41	30%
Some	38	**	42	49	56	59	54	55	49	46	54
A good deal	32	**	23	24	17	11	11	14	8	10	15
Don't know	6	**	6	3	2	2	3	3	2	4	2
Total	100%	**	100%	100%	100%	100%	100%	100%	100%	100%	100%
N	1446	**	1340	910	2183	2518	2399	2287	1408	1399	2239
PDI#	8	**	-6	-1	-7	-17	-22	-15	-32	-31	-15

PDI is proportion "a good deal" minus proportion "not much"

Table 4.24
How Much Do Parties Make Government Listen to People

QUESTION: How much do you feel that political
parties help to make the government pay attention
to what the people think a good deal, some, or not
much?

	1964	1966	1968	1970	1972	1974	1976	1978	1980
Not much	13%	**	16%	19%	18%	19%	26%	22%	28%
Some	39	**	41	43	52	55	53	53	51
A good deal	41	**	37	33	26	22	17	21	18
Don't know	7	**	6	5	4	5	4	5	3
Total	100%	**	100%	100%	100%	100%	100%	100%	100%
N	1443	**	1342	911	2181	2511	2400	2288	1407
PDI#	28	**	20	14	8	3	-9	-1	-10

PDI is proportion "a good deal" minus proportion "not much"

Table 4.25
How Much Do Elections Make Government Pay Attention

QUESTION: And how much do you feel that having
elections makes the government pay attention to
what the people think--a good deal, some, or not
much?

	1964	1966	1968	1970	1972	1974	1976	1978	1980	1982	1984
Not much	7%	9%	8%	8%	8%	11%	10%	10%	13%	**	20%
Some	25	25	29	30	36	36	36	32	35	**	37
A good deal	65	62	60	58	55	50	52	56	51	**	42
Don't know	4	4	4	3	2	3	3	2	2	**	1
Total	100%	100%	100%	100%	100%	100%	100%	100%	100%	**	100%
N	1445	1282	1342	909	2184	2509	2399	2290	1407	**	2243
PDI#	58	53	51	50	47	38	41	46	38	**	22

PDI is proportion "a good deal" minus proportion "not much"

Table 4.26
Are Congressmen Attentive to Their Constituencies

QUESTION: How much attention do you think most
Congressmen pay to the people who elect them when
they decide what to do in Congress, a good deal,
some, or not much?

	1964	1966	1968	1970	1972	1974	1976	1978	1980
Not much	15%	**	19%	22%	19%	26%	22%	21%	25%
Some	38	**	44	45	51	50	56	58	56
A good deal	42	**	32	30	27	20	18	17	17
Don't know	5	**	5	4	3	4	4	3	4
Total	100%	**	100%	100%	100%	100%	100%	100%	100%
N	1443	**	1334	908	2182	2508	2399	2284	1403
PDI#	27	**	14	7	8	-6	-4	-4	-8

PDI is proportion "a good deal" minus proportion "not much"

Table 4.27
With Many Other People Voting, Does It Matter If the Respondent Votes

QUESTION: So many other people vote in the national elections that it doesn't
matter much to me whether I vote or not.

	1952	1954	1956	1958	1960	1962	1964	1966	1968	1970	1972	1974	1976	1978	1980
Agree	12%	**	10%	**	8%	**	**	**	**	**	10%	**	10%	13%	9%
Disagree	87	**	89	**	91	**	**	**	**	**	90	**	89	85	91
Don't know	1	**	1	**	1	**	**	**	**	**	1	**	1	2	0
Total	100%	**	100%	**	100%	**	**	**	**	**	100%	**	100%	100%	100%
N	1777	**	1746	**	1913	**	**	**	**	**	2688	**	2841	2291	1567
PDI#	75	**	80	**	84	**	**	**	**	**	80	**	79	72	82

PDI is proportion "disagree" minus proportion "agree"

Table 4.28
If a Person Doesn't Care about Outcome Should He Vote

QUESTION: If a person doesn't care how an election comes out he shouldn't vote
in it.

	1952	1954	1956	1958	1960	1962	1964	1966	1968	1970	1972	1974	1976	1978	1980	1982	1984
Agree	53%	**	46%	**	44%	**	**	**	**	**	45%	**	46%	48%	41%	**	57%
Disagree	46	**	53	**	55	**	**	**	**	**	54	**	53	49	58	**	43
Don't know	1	**	2	**	2	**	**	**	**	**	1	**	2	3	1	**	1
Total	100%	**	100%	**	100%	**	**	**	**	**	100%	**	100%	100%	100%	**	100%
N	1775	**	1736	**	1908	**	**	**	**	**	2686	**	2838	2290	1559	**	2243
PDI#	-8	**	7	**	11	**	**	**	**	**	8	**	8	1	17	**	-14

PDI is proportion "disagree" minus proportion "agree"

Table 4.29
Is It Important to Vote If Your Party Can't Win

QUESTION: It isn't so important to vote when you know your party doesn't have
any chance to win.

	1952	1954	1956	1958	1960	1962	1964	1966	1968	1970	1972	1974	1976	1978	1980
Agree	11%	**	9%	**	8%	**	**	**	**	**	9%	**	8%	8%	8%
Disagree	88	**	90	**	92	**	**	**	**	**	91	**	91	89	92
Don't know	1	**	1	**	1	**	**	**	**	**	1	**	1	3	0
Total	100%	**	100%	**	100%	**	**	**	**	**	100%	**	100%	100%	100%
N	1779	**	1752	**	1914	**	**	**	**	**	2689	**	2847	2290	1564
PDI#	76	**	80	**	84	**	**	**	**	**	82	**	83	81	84

PDI is proportion "disagree" minus proportion "agree"

Table 4.30
Are Local Elections Not Important

QUESTION: A good many local elections aren't important enough to bother with.

	1952	1954	1956	1958	1960	1962	1964	1966	1968	1970	1972	1974	1976	1978	1980
Agree	18%	**	14%	**	12%	**	**	**	**	**	14%	**	14%	12%	14%
Disagree	81	**	85	**	87	**	**	**	**	**	85	**	85	85	86
Don't know	1	**	1	**	1	**	**	**	**	**	1	**	2	2	0
Total	100%	**	100%	**	100%	**	**	**	**	**	100%	**	100%	100%	100%
N	1779	**	1749	**	1912	**	**	**	**	**	2686	**	2837	2291	1561
PDI#	63	**	71	**	75	**	**	**	**	**	72	**	71	73	72

PDI is proportion "disagree" minus proportion "agree"

Table 4.31
Can People Be Trusted

QUESTION: Generally speaking, would you say that most people can
be trusted, or that you can't be too careful in dealing with
people.

	1964	1966	1968	1970	1972	1974	1976
Can't be too careful	45%	46%	43%	**	52%	52%	46%
Most people can be trusted	53	53	55	**	46	47	51
Don't know	2	2	2	**	2	1	3
Total	100%	100%	100%	**	100%	100%	100%
N	1446	1284	1343	**	2179	2486	2400
PDI#	9	7	12	**	-7	-6	5

PDI is proportion "most people can be trusted" minus proportion "can't be too careful"

Table 4.32
Do People Try to Be Helpful

QUESTION: Would you say that most of the time people try to be
helpful, or that they are mostly just looking out for themselves?

	1964	1966	1968	1970	1972	1974	1976
Just look out for themselves	41%	46%	39%	**	49%	47%	44%
Try to be helpful	54	52	58	**	47	51	52
Don't know	4	2	3	**	4	3	4
Total	100%	100%	100%	**	100%	100%	100%
N	1445	1285	1344	**	2174	2450	2394
PDI#	13	6	20	**	-2	4	8

PDI is proportion "try to be helpful" minus proportion "just look out for themselves"

Table 4.33
Would People Take Advantage of You

QUESTION: Do you think most people would try to take
advantage of you if they got a chance, or would they try to
be fair?

	1964	1966	1968	1970	1972	1974	1976
Would take advantage	29%	**	30%	**	37%	40%	36%
Would try to be fair	67	**	67	**	59	58	60
Don't know	4	**	3	**	4	3	5
Total	100%	**	100%	**	100%	100%	100%
N	1443	**	1342	**	2179	2473	2390
PDI#	39	**	37	**	22	18	24

PDI is proportion "would try to be fair" minus proportion "would take advantage"

Table 4.34
Approval of Legal Protests

QUESTION: How about taking part in protest
meetings or marches that are permitted by the
local authorities? Would you approve of taking
part, disapprove, or would it depend on the
circumstances?

	1968	1970	1972	1974
Disapprove	49%	49%	40%	40%
Depends	25	37	40	42
Approve	18	13	18	16
Don't know	8	1	2	2
Total	100%	100%	100%	100%
N	1344	915	2696	2514
PDI#	-31	-35	-21	-24

PDI is proportion "approve" minus proportion "disapprove"

Table 4.35
Approval of Disobeying Laws

QUESTION: How about refusing to obey a law which
one thinks is unjust, if the person feels so
strongly about it that he is willing to go to
jail rather than obey the law? Would you approve
of a person doing that, disapprove, or would it
depend on the circumstances?

	1968	1970	1972	1974
Disapprove	56%	52%	43%	42%
Depends	22	35	39	41
Approve	13	10	16	15
Don't know	9	2	2	2
Total	100%	100%	100%	100%
N	1344	915	2694	2508
PDI#	-43	-42	-27	-27

PDI is proportion "approve" minus proportion "disapprove"

Table 4.36
Approval of Disruption of Government

QUESTION: Suppose all other methods have failed
and the person decides to try to stop the
government from going about its usual activities
with sit-ins, mass meetings, demonstrations, and
things like that? Would you approve of that
disapprove, or would it depend on the
circumstances?

	1968	1970	1972	1974	1976&
Disapprove	67%	63%	57%	51%	29%
Depends	16	28	33	39	61
Approve	7	6	8	8	6
Don't know	10	2	2	2	4
Total	100%	100%	100%	100%	100%
N	1342	915	2691	2507	2388
PDI#	-60	-57	-50	-43	-22

PDI is proportion "approve" minus proportion "disapprove"

& The deletion of the other two protest questions (Tables 4.34-4.35) from the 1976 study is apparently responsible for most of the
change recorded in 1976

Table 4.37
Trust in Government Index#&

DESCRIPTION: This index collapses a 6 point Guttman scale of trust in government
which is constructed from five items: 1) How much of the time does the
respondent trust the government in Washington to do what is right, 2) Is the
government run by a few big interests or for the benefit of all of the people,
3) Does the government waste a lot of tax money, 4) Are the people running the
government smart people, and 5) Are quite a few of the people running the
government a little crooked (see tables 4.12-4.16). The 6 point scale is
collapsed to 3 codes as follows: 1=1, 2=1, 3=2, 4=2, 5=3, 6=3.

	Five Question Version									Four Question Version@	
	1964	1966	1968	1970	1972	1974	1976	1978	1980	1980	1984
Cynical	19%	**	26%	36%	36%	50%	53%	52%	62%	67%	46%
	18	**	24	25	24	24	23	26	21	10	14
Trusting	61	**	48	38	38	24	22	19	15	19	36
Not scored	2	**	3	1	2	2	2	3	3	1	5
Total	100%	**	100%	100%	100%	100%	100%	100%	100%	100%	100%
N	1450	**	1348	1507	2285	2523	2870	2304	1614	1603	1989
PDI#	42	**	22	2	2	-25	-31	-33	-46	-51	-10

PDI is proportion "most trusting" minus proportion "most cynical"

& The 1958 Index includes item 2 but with its scoring adjusted to match the inter-item correlations in order

@ The Four Question Version collases a 5 point Guttman scale constructed from 4 of the 5 items
   above: 1) How much of the times does the respondent trust the government in Washington to do
   what is right, 2) Is the government run by a few big interests or for the benefit of all of
   the people, 3) Does the government waste a lot of tax money and 5) Are quite a few of the
   people running the government a little crooked (see tables 4.12-4.14, 4.16). The 5 point scale
   is collapsed to 3 codes as follows: 1=1, 2=1, 3=2, 4=3, 5=3.

Table 4.38
Trust in Government Index by Social Groups, Summarized by a Percentage Difference Index#&

	Five Question Version												Four Question Version	
	1958	1960	1962	1964	1966	1968	1970	1972	1974	1976	1978	1980	1980	1984
1959 or later Cohort	**	**	**	**	**	**	**	**	**	**	-8	-25	-28	-1
1943 - 1958 Cohort	**	**	**	43*	**	40	9	7	-11	-27	-26	-51	-57	-5
1927 - 1942 Cohort	57	**	**	51	**	32	8	5	-27	-31	-37	-47	-52	-19
1911 - 1926 Cohort	49	**	**	42	**	14	4	1	-36	-33	-40	-50	-52	-18
1895 - 1910 Cohort	42	**	**	33	**	11	-14	-10	-35	-39	-44	-39	-41	-15
Before 1895 Cohort	37	**	**	30	**	17	-10	-1	-29	-12	-23*	-	-	-
Grade School	36	**	**	32	**	8	-18	-14	-40	-44	-32	-44	-50	-14
High School	50	**	**	48	**	25	5	1	-28	-35	-37	-47	-51	-7
College	57	**	**	40	**	29	15	12	-11	-18	-28	-46	-53	-8
Central cities	51	**	**	47	**	28	7	-6	-23	-30	-33	-45	-34	-24
Suburbs	51	**	**	45	**	28	8	11	-22	-26	-33	-49	-49	-11
Non-urban Areas	43	**	**	36	**	15	-6	-1	-30	-35	-33	-45	-51	-12
Income Percentile 0-16	34	**	**	28	**	19	-12	-9	-33	-28	-38	-38	-51	-9
Income Percentile 17-33	45	**	**	49	**	17	-17	-8	-47	-36	-35	-47	-48	-19
Income Percentile 34-67	52	**	**	45	**	21	1	-1	-16	-30	-36	-46	-52	-4
Income Percentile 68-95	53	**	**	45	**	31	18	13	-22	-24	-28	-49	-51	-12
Income Percentile 95-100	58	**	**	44	**	18	15	36	-11	-31	-23	-61	-46	-14
Males	48	**	**	45	**	18	1	2	-21	-29	-27	-45	-53	-9
Females	46	**	**	40	**	25	2	1	-29	-32	-38	-48	-39	-12
Whites	47	**	**	40	**	20	4	6	-23	-29	-33	-48	-51	-13
Blacks	45	**	**	56	**	39	-25	-38	-55	-53	-34	-36	-52	-12
Union Household	41	**	**	53	**	23	5	-4	-28	-39	-36	-48	-56	-6
Non-union Household	49	**	**	38	**	22	1	4	-24	-28	-32	-46	-53	9
South	36	**	**	43	**	15	-7	1	-31	-32	-30	-44	-48	-8
Non-south	52	**	**	41	**	25	6	2	-22	-30	-35	-48	-59	-14
Professional	57	**	**	43	**	25	10	15	-13	-20	-30	-44	-49	-15
White collar	55	**	**	42	**	30	8	8	-22	-22	-31	-55	-43	-28
Blue collar	41	**	**	44	**	13	-1	-9	-33	-41	-34	-45	-69	-12
Unskilled	39	**	**	59*	**	-	-50*	-26*	-49*	-46	-32	-23*	-55*	5
Farmers	28	**	**	45	**	15	-27	-3	-20	-37	-30*	-69*	-54*	-26
Housewives	48	**	**	38	**	25	2	3	-27	-30	-42	-52	-50	-6
Protestants	47	**	**	39	**	20	1	1	-30	-33	-33	-45	-50	-13
Catholics	49	**	**	54	**	33	10	10	-22	-30	-48		-50	2
Jews	47	**	**	45*	**	3*	5*	-5*	-5	-31	-27	-57	-59	-21
Other and No Religion	46*	**	**	29	**	4*	-12	-28	-43	-42	-42	-48	-55	-25
Total Population	47	**	**	42	**	22	2	2	-25	-31	-33	-46	-51	-10

\# PDI is proportion "most trusting" minus proportion "most cynical"

& Negative values indicate a preponderance of cynical responses whereas positive values indicate a preponderance of trusting
responses. The range is +100 to -100. Subtable at the far right for 1980 and 1984 is based on the Four Question Version
(See Table 4.37).

Table 4.39
Trust in Government Index by Political Groups, Summarized by a Percentage Difference Index#&

	Five Question Version												Four Question Version	
	1958	1960	1962	1964	1966	1968	1970	1972	1974	1976	1978	1980	1980	1984
Strong Democrats	38	**	**	57	**	38	-3	-23	-31	-45	-24	-32	-30	-27
Weak and Leaning Democrats	54	**	**	46	**	24	3	-5	-23	-36	-31	-44	-49	-23
Independent Independents	55	**	**	31	**	-9	-13	-2	-36	-34	-36	-55	-56	-5
Weak and Leaning Republicans	57	**	**	34	**	22	7	20	-17	-22	-40	-57	-63	3
Strong Republicans	57	**	**	17	**	17	18	22	-15	-10	-41	-61	-57	8
Liberal Self Placement 1	**	**	**	**	**	**	**	-33	-32	-36	-36	-42	-45	-34
Liberal Self Placement 2	**	**	**	**	**	**	**	7	-3	-28	-23	-39	-42	-12
Neutral Self Placement 3	**	**	**	**	**	**	**	8	-19	-28	-37	-50	-52	-10
Conservative Self Placement 4	**	**	**	**	**	**	**	20	-19	-11	-27	-49	-58	-4
Conservative Self Placement 5	**	**	**	**	**	**	**	10	-35	-37	-45	-61	-67	-3
Liberal Index 1	**	**	**	45	**	22	-19	-59	-49	-48	**	-39*	-65*	-53
Liberal Index 2	**	**	**	49	**	30	-11	-7	-21	-33	**	-41	-42	-21
Neutral Index 3	**	**	**	55	**	25	8	2	-21	-30	**	-46	-51	-3
Conservative Index 4	**	**	**	31	**	22	9	16	-24	-25	**	-45	-53	1
Conservative Index 5	**	**	**	6	**	-15	4	15	-30	-38	**	-71	-70	-20
Total Population	47	**	**	42	**	22	2	2	-25	-31	-33	-46	-51	-10

PDI is proportion "most trusting" minus proportion "most cynical"

& Negative values indicate a preponderance of cynical responses whereas positive values indicate a preponderance of trusting responses. The range is +100 to -100. Subtable at the far right for 1980 and 1984 is based on the Four Question Version (See Table 4.37).

Table 4.40
Internal Political Efficacy Index

DESCRIPTION: This measure is an additive index of internal political efficacy
constructed from three items: 1) Voting is the only way that people like me can have
any say about how the government runs things, 2) People like me don't have any say
about what the government does, and 3) Sometimes politics and government seem so
complicated that a person like me can't really understand what's going on.

	1952	1954	1956	1958	1960	1962	1964	1966	1968	1970	1972	1974	1976	1978	1980
Least efficacious	23%	**	21%	**	19%	**	22%	25%	28%	25%	29%	26%	26%	28%	23%
	43	**	34	**	34	**	37	30	28	32	31	31	28	31	32
	26	**	31	**	33	**	26	23	26	27	26	26	26	25	28
Most efficacious	6	**	12	**	13	**	12	11	16	14	13	12	14	12	12
Not scored	2	**	2	**	2	**	3	11	2	2	2	5	5	4	5
Total	100%	**	100%	**	100%	**	100%	100%	100%	100%	100%	100%	100%	100%	100%
N	1760	**	1737	**	1897	**	1555	1290	1332	1499	2687	2498	2390	2278	1402
PDI#	-17	**	-9	**	-6	**	-10	-14	-12	-11	-16	-14	-12	-16	-11

PDI is proportion "most efficacious" minus proportion "least efficacious"

Table 4.41
Internal Political Efficacy Index by Social Groups, Summarized by a Percentage Difference Index#

	1952	1954	1956	1958	1960	1962	1964	1966	1968	1970	1972	1974	1976	1978	1980
1959 or later Cohort	**	**	**	**	**	**	**	**	**	**	**	**	*	-9	-13
1943 - 1958 Cohort	**	**	**	**	**	**	-17*	3	6	-9	-10	-2	-10	-10	-5
1927 - 1942 Cohort	-14	**	-5	**	-4	**	2	-6	-2	1	-8	-5	-4	-11	-2
1911 - 1926 Cohort	-12	**	-6	**	-1	**	-11	-9	-13	-11	-17	-20	-13	-24	-22
1895 - 1910 Cohort	-15	**	-9	**	-9	**	-17	-29	-30	-25	-33	-38	-26	-36	-27
Before 1895 Cohort	-28	**	-23	**	-17	**	-31	-37	-27	-31	-30	-26	-20	-8*	-
Grade School	-32	**	-35	**	-25	**	-38	-35	-45	-42	-45	-42	-39	-45	-35
High School	-11	**	-9	**	-6	**	-10	-18	-16	-13	-22	-20	-21	-26	-22
College	10	**	31	**	21	**	20	19	22	23	15	14	13	9	9
Central cities	-16	**	-8	**	-5	**	-7	-13	-7	-6	-12	-7	-9	-20	-8
Suburbs	-16	**	-2	**	-3	**	0	-9	-5	-6	-6	-9	-6	-9	-10
Non-urban Areas	-19	**	-14	**	-8	**	-21	-19	-20	-18	-25	-22	-20	-21	-16
Income Percentile 0-16	-39	**	-37	**	-24	**	-33	-30	-40	-40	-35	-32	-32	-32	-26
Income Percentile 17-33	-25	**	-20	**	-20	**	-21	-26	-24	-26	-26	-23	-25	-27	-20
Income Percentile 34-67	-15	**	-8	**	-8	**	-5	-15	-12	-12	-18	-14	-10	-17	-10
Income Percentile 68-95	-5	**	11	**	5	**	3	-5	9	6	2	3	-2	-2	-1
Income Percentile 95-100	8	**	19	**	33	**	11	23	22	20	19	16	23	8	11
Males	-12	**	-2	**	-1	**	-5	-7	-4	-5	-8	-8	-6	-8	-5
Females	-21	**	-15	**	-10	**	-14	-20	-18	-16	-21	-18	-16	-22	-16
Whites	-14	**	-7	**	-4	**	-9	-13	-9	-9	-14	-12	-10	-14	-9
Blacks	-44	**	-36	**	-20	**	-20	-27	-32	-28	-29	-21	-27	-31	-25
Union Household	-15	**	-10	**	-8	**	-13	-15	-16	-12	-19	-12	-12	-17	-8
Non-union Household	-17	**	-9	**	-5	**	-9	-13	-10	-11	-14	-14	-12	-16	-12
South	-26	**	-20	**	-14	**	-21	-22	-20	-24	-24	-24	-22	-20	-15
Non-south	-13	**	-5	**	-2	**	-5	-11	-8	-5	-11	-8	-7	-14	-9
Professional	3	**	21	**	21	**	9	**	21	21	14	7	16	5	10
White collar	-5	**	3	**	9	**	4	**	-7	-2	-7	-12	-7	-16	-12
Blue collar	-15	**	-14	**	-10	**	-16	**	-27	-23	-28	-21	-26	-25	-22
Unskilled	-34	**	-34	**	-17*	**	-31*	**	-	-33*	-30*	-42*	-26	-27	-20*
Farmers	-30	**	-28	**	-31	**	-30	**	-25	-32	-34	-29	-19	-34*	-33*
Housewives	-21	**	-16	**	-18	**	-16	**	-18	-23	-26	-20	-18	-25	-21
Protestants	-18	**	-10	**	-5	**	-13	-16	-14	-13	-18	-16	-14	-18	-12
Catholics	-16	**	-11	**	-7	**	-4	-12	-8	-9	-15	-13	-11	-13	-9
Jews	-8	**	14	**	10	**	2*	5*	-13*	-10*	10	-12	-4	5	-15*
Other and No Religion	-5	**	-9*	**	-13*	**	-7	-2*	0*	3	-2	8	-3	-13	-10
Total Population	-17	**	-9	**	-6	**	-10	-14	-12	-11	-16	-14	-12	-16	-11

PDI is proportion "most efficacious" minus proportion "least efficacious" (see table 4.40)

Table 4.42
Internal Political Efficacy Index by Political Groups, Summarized by a Percentage Difference Index#

	1952	1954	1956	1958	1960	1962	1964	1966	1968	1970	1972	1974	1976	1978	1980
Strong Democrats	-21	**	-13	**	-12	**	-11	-21	-22	-17	-22	-20	-18	-24	-16
Weak and Leaning Democrats	-18	**	-12	**	-11	**	-12	-13	-14	-11	-19	-13	-13	-16	-16
Independent Independents	-14	**	-1	**	-19	**	-17	-19	-26	-19	-24	-11	-18	-14	-13
Weak and Leaning Republicans	-11	**	-5	**	10	**	-8	-12	4	-8	-8	-11	-9	-12	-2
Strong Republicans	-11	**	1	**	1	**	5	1	-7	4	-1	-11	6	-6	-3
Liberal Self Placement 1	**	**	**	**	**	**	**	**	**	**	0	-1	-5	-2	0
Liberal Self Placement 2	**	**	**	**	**	**	**	**	**	**	7	6	7	3	3
Neutral Self Placement 3	**	**	**	**	**	**	**	**	**	**	-12	-10	-10	-19	-11
Conservative Self Placement 4	**	**	**	**	**	**	**	**	**	**	1	-4	1	-3	0
Conservative Self Placement 5	**	**	**	**	**	**	**	**	**	**	-7	-8	1	-7	-3
Liberal Index 1	**	**	**	**	**	**	-6	12*	-6	-9	6	27	-3	**	0*
Liberal Index 2	**	**	**	**	**	**	0	-9	-8	-4	-1	-1	2	**	-2
Neutral Index 3	**	**	**	**	**	**	-19	-23	-23	-10	-17	-18	-18	**	-18
Conservative Index 4	**	**	**	**	**	**	-7	-9	-6	-6	-7	-12	-3	**	-10
Conservative Index 5	**	**	**	**	**	**	1	1	15	-12	-10	2	7	**	6
Total Population	-17	**	-9	**	-6	**	-10	-14	-12	-11	-16	-14	-12	-16	-11

PDI is proportion "most efficacious" minus proportion "least efficacious" (see table 4.40)

Table 4.43
External Political Efficacy Index

DESCRIPTION: This measure is an additive index of
external political efficacy constructed from three
items: 1) Respondent doesn't think public officials
care much what people like the respondent think, 2)
Generally speaking those elected to Congress in
Washington lose touch with people pretty quickly, and
3) Parties are only interested in people's votes but
not in their opinions.

	1968	1970	1972	1974	1976	1978	1980
Least efficacious	27%	36%	38%	39%	39%	40%	39%
	17	17	18	16	18	20	20
	19	15	17	16	16	15	15
Most efficacious	29	25	21	18	16	15	14
Not scored	7	7	6	12	11	11	12
Total	100%	100%	100%	100%	100%	100%	100%
N	1332	1485	2675	2478	2379	2265	1386
PDI#	2	-11	-17	-21	-23	-25	-24

PDI is proportion "most efficacious" minus proportion "least efficacious"

Table 4.44
External Political Efficacy Index by Social Groups, Summarized by a Percentage Difference Index#

	1968	1970	1972	1974	1976	1978	1980
1959 or later Cohort	**	**	**	**	**	-22	-17
1943 - 1958 Cohort	5	-7	-12	-13	-24	-21	-26
1927 - 1942 Cohort	14	-1	-12	-19	-18	-23	-20
1911 - 1926 Cohort	4	-7	-18	-20	-20	-29	-23
1895 - 1910 Cohort	-16	-25	-30	-34	-36	-40	-36
Before 1895 Cohort	-16	-39	-31	-36	-29	-15*	-
Grade School	-31	-46	-49	-53	-47	-52	-42
High School	1	-8	-20	-27	-28	-29	-32
College	30	20	9	9	-7	-9	-9
Central cities	1	-2	-19	-18	-18	-28	-23
Suburbs	10	-8	-10	-17	-21	-22	-24
Non-urban Areas	-2	-18	-21	-26	-29	-27	-25
Income Percentile 0-16	-31	-44	-41	-33	-39	-38	-35
Income Percentile 17-33	-10	-30	-29	-36	-34	-32	-27
Income Percentile 34-67	8	-14	-17	-19	-22	-26	-22
Income Percentile 68-95	24	12	-2	-10	-14	-16	-15
Income Percentile 95-100	31	31	19	26	-5	6	-18
Males	2	-14	-17	-27	-24	-25	-27
Females	2	-8	-17	-17	-23	-25	-22
Whites	4	-7	-13	-18	-22	-23	-24
Blacks	-11	-45	-49	-50	-37	-37	-28
Union Household	-1	-13	-24	-28	-22	-32	-28
Non-union Household	3	-10	-15	-19	-24	-22	-23
South	-5	-22	-28	-34	-35	-26	-25
Non-south	6	-5	-12	-14	-17	-24	-24
Professional	25	18	7	0	-12	-11	-13
White collar	13	8	-6	-10	-13	-20	-20
Blue collar	-16	-25	-34	-38	-37	-36	-36
Unskilled	-	-44*	-44*	-68*	-32	-32	-31*
Farmers	-15	-61	-28	-23	-29	-39*	-19*
Housewives	3	-16	-21	-20	-22	-26	-24
Protestants	1	-12	-18	-23	-24	-25	-21
Catholics	10	-10	-12	-15	-17	-22	-24
Jews	-12*	-7*	-18	-17	-26	-24	-27*
Other and No Religion	-10*	-6	-30	-13	-35	-34	-40
Total Population	2	-11	-17	-21	-23	-25	-24

PDI is proportion "most efficacious" minus proportion "least efficacious" (see table 4.43)

Table 4.45
External Political Efficacy Index by Political Groups, Summarized by a Percentage Difference Index#

	1968	1970	1972	1974	1976	1978	1980
Strong Democrats	2	-20	-26	-18	-19	-23	-22
Weak and Leaning Democrats	-1	-10	-23	-22	-28	-25	-29
Independent Independents	-13	-18	-27	-37	-34	-34	-36
Weak and Leaning Republicans	11	-6	-4	-12	-19	-25	-19
Strong Republicans	10	13	4	-4	0	-10	-10
Liberal Self Placement 1	**	**	-11	-21	-19	-26	-17*
Liberal Self Placement 2	**	**	5	1	-11	-16	-18
Neutral Self Placement 3	**	**	-6	-12	-19	-23	-26
Conservative Self Placement 4	**	**	-5	0	-14	-11	-19
Conservative Self Placement 5	**	**	-6	-24	-20	-24	-20
Liberal Index 1	2	-19	-26	-9	-37	**	-17*
Liberal Index 2	9	-12	-5	-5	-24	**	-21
Neutral Index 3	-4	-10	-17	-25	-24	**	-31
Conservative Index 4	10	2	-5	-18	-14	**	-16
Conservative Index 5	-4	-14	-8	-4	-24	**	-28
Total Population	2	-11	-17	-21	-23	-25	-24

PDI is proportion "most efficacious" minus proportion "least efficacious" (see table 4.43)

Table 4.46
Government Responsiveness Index

DESCRIPTION: This measure is an additive index of government
responsiveness constructed from four items: 1) Over the years how much
attention does the respondent feel the government pays to what the
people think when it decides what to do, 2) How much does the
respondent feel that political parties help to make the government pay
attention to what the people think, 3) How much does the respondent
feel that having elections makes the government pay attention to what
the people think, and 4) How much attention does the respondent think
most Congressmen pay to the people who elect them when they decide what
to do in Congress.

	1964	1966	1968	1970	1972	1974	1976	1978	1980
Low responsiveness	5%	**	8%	8%	6%	8%	10%	9%	10%
	12	**	15	19	19	24	24	20	24
	16	**	18	16	23	22	19	22	17
	29	**	29	32	33	30	34	35	29
Highest responsiveness	32	**	25	22	17	12	9	12	6
Not scored	5	**	5	4	3	4	3	4	15
Total	100%	**	100%	100%	100%	100%	100%	100%	100%
N	1450	**	1348	915	2191	2523	2402	2304	1614
PDI#	44	**	31	27	24	10	9	17	1

PDI is proportion in two highest responsiveness categories minus proportion in two lowest responsiveness categories

Table 4.47
Government Responsiveness Index by Social Groups, Summarized by a Percentage Difference Index#

	1964	1966	1968	1970	1972	1974	1976	1978	1980
1959 or later Cohort	**	**	**	**	**	**	**	18	8
1943 - 1958 Cohort	48*	**	35	21	31	12	10	18	0
1927 - 1942 Cohort	52	**	33	41	32	14	10	19	4
1911 - 1926 Cohort	48	**	39	41	21	19	9	18	-2
1895 - 1910 Cohort	34	**	21	1	8	-7	8	13	-5
Before 1895 Cohort	23	**	1*	1	-1	-12	-2	12*	-
Grade School	21	**	12	5	-6	-21	-6	-3	-11
High School	49	**	32	29	25	7	5	13	-6
College	55	**	45	43	41	34	21	31	14
Central cities	46	**	33	32	18	13	15	15	3
Suburbs	53	**	34	27	39	15	10	21	-2
Non-urban Areas	35	**	27	24	17	3	4	15	2
Income Percentile 0-16	22	**	15	-8	3	-7	6	4	-3
Income Percentile 17-33	40	**	21	10	11	-12	4	17	-6
Income Percentile 34-67	49	**	31	27	25	15	7	18	1
Income Percentile 68-95	54	**	43	48	38	22	14	26	12
Income Percentile 95-100	64	**	58	58*	57	61	35	40	7
Males	44	**	30	31	28	12	11	22	4
Females	44	**	31	24	20	9	8	13	-2
Whites	43	**	29	30	26	12	11	19	0
Blacks	49	**	45	-1	-3	-10	0	8	7
Union Household	54	**	31	40	22	13	8	17	0
Non-union Household	41	**	31	24	25	9	9	18	1
South	39	**	32	20	23	-2	1	13	7
Non-south	46	**	30	31	24	17	13	20	-3
Professional	47	**	42	48	38	30	20	27	14
White collar	59	**	38	26	33	19	18	20	2
Blue collar	39	**	23	34	15	-2	-3	12	-6
Unskilled	25*	**	-	-	11*	-3*	-2	12	15*
Farmers	26	**	9	-11*	-5	4	13	18*	3*
Housewives	44	**	30	15	20	4	6	12	-10
Protestants	42	**	31	27	23	6	7	16	3
Catholics	53	**	37	32	27	25	15	24	-1
Jews	40*	**	-3*	48*	34*	62	18	36	0
Other and No Religion	37	**	25*	7	14	-5	1	4	-7
Total Population	44	**	31	27	24	10	9	17	1

PDI is proportion in two highest responsiveness categories minus proportion in two lowest
  responsiveness categories (see table 4.46)

Table 4.48
Government Responsiveness Index by Political Groups, Summarized by a Percentage Difference Index#

	1964	1966	1968	1970	1972	1974	1976	1978	1980
Strong Democrats	55	**	36	24	15	24	18	30	14
Weak and Leaning Democrats	44	**	29	33	18	10	5	21	0
Independent Independents	23	**	15	7	15	-9	0	-1	-21
Weak and Leaning Republicans	43	**	34	33	36	16	11	14	4
Strong Republicans	33	**	36	38	39	18	25	33	1
Liberal Self Placement 1	**	**	**	**	17	18	24	23	7
Liberal Self Placement 2	**	**	**	**	39	24	32	28	10
Neutral Self Placement 3	**	**	**	**	29	17	14	23	6
Conservative Self Placement 4	**	**	**	**	44	24	17	33	11
Conservative Self Placement 5	**	**	**	**	32	9	8	14	0
Liberal Index 1	42	**	39	7*	-11	12	0	**	24*
Liberal Index 2	58	**	37	23	31	24	16	**	9
Neutral Index 3	43	**	25	34	22	8	11	**	-12
Conservative Index 4	42	**	36	32	34	15	12	**	10
Conservative Index 5	19	**	24	43	40	21	4	**	-4
Total Population	44	**	31	27	24	10	9	17	1

PDI is proportion in two highest responsiveness categories minus proportion in two lowest
responsiveness categories (see table 4.46)

Table 4.49
Citizen Duty Index

DESCRIPTION: This index is a Guttman scale of sense of citizen duty constructed from four items: 1)
Sometimes so many other people vote in the national elections that it doesn't matter much to the
respondent whether they vote or not, 2) If a person doesn't care how an election comes out he
shouldn't vote in it, 3) It isn't so important to vote when the respondent knows their party
doesn't have any chance to win, and 4) Whether the respondent believes that a good many local
elections aren't important enough to bother with.

	1952	1954	1956	1958	1960	1962	1964	1966	1968	1970	1972	1974	1976	1978	1980
Lowest sense of citizen duty	17%	**	13%	**	10%	**	**	**	**	**	14%	**	14%	15%	12%
	40	**	37	**	37	**	**	**	**	**	36	**	36	36	33
Highest sense of citizen duty	40	**	48	**	49	**	**	**	**	**	49	**	48	45	51
Not scored	3	**	2	**	3	**	**	**	**	**	2	**	3	3	4
Total	100%	**	100%	**	100%	**	**	**	**	**	100%	**	100%	100%	100%
N	1799	**	1762	**	1954	**	**	**	**	**	2705	**	2870	2304	1614
PDI#	22	**	35	**	39	**	**	**	**	**	34	**	34	30	39

PDI is proportion "highest" sense of duty minus proportion "lowest" sense of duty

Table 4.50
Citizen Duty Index by Social Groups, Summarized by a Percentage Difference Index#

	1952	1954	1956	1958	1960	1962	1964	1966	1968	1970	1972	1974	1976	1978	1980
1959 or later Cohort	**	**	**	**	**	**	**	**	**	**	**	**	**	4	21
1943 - 1958 Cohort	**	**	**	**	**	**	**	**	**	**	26	**	23	21	32
1927 - 1942 Cohort	17	**	45	**	51	**	**	**	**	**	43	**	41	37	45
1911 - 1926 Cohort	23	**	34	**	43	**	**	**	**	**	37	**	43	40	49
1895 - 1910 Cohort	27	**	36	**	34	**	**	**	**	**	35	**	34	34	40
Before 1895 Cohort	17	**	21	**	23	**	**	**	**	**	20	**	28	23*	-
Grade School	0	**	3	**	17	**	**	**	**	**	18	**	15	8	20
High School	32	**	45	**	48	**	**	**	**	**	34	**	31	28	37
College	54	**	59	**	50	**	**	**	**	**	47	**	48	41	48
Central cities	24	**	36	**	37	**	**	**	**	**	34	**	28	27	38
Suburbs	24	**	40	**	41	**	**	**	**	**	34	**	37	35	40
Non-urban Areas	19	**	31	**	39	**	**	**	**	**	35	**	35	28	38
Income Percentile 0-16	-8	**	2	**	14	**	**	**	**	**	17	**	15	10	29
Income Percentile 17-33	13	**	25	**	29	**	**	**	**	**	25	**	29	23	38
Income Percentile 34-67	22	**	41	**	50	**	**	**	**	**	35	**	34	35	39
Income Percentile 68-95	39	**	50	**	44	**	**	**	**	**	49	**	42	40	46
Income Percentile 95-100	63	**	61	**	58	**	**	**	**	**	46	**	65	51	49
Males	25	**	36	**	41	**	**	**	**	**	33	**	34	34	36
Females	20	**	34	**	37	**	**	**	**	**	36	**	34	27	41
Whites	27	**	38	**	41	**	**	**	**	**	35	**	36	33	40
Blacks	-23	**	-5	**	23	**	**	**	**	**	27	**	24	13	32
Union Household	24	**	36	**	43	**	**	**	**	**	35	**	37	40	42
Non-union Household	21	**	34	**	38	**	**	**	**	**	34	**	33	27	38
South	-1	**	20	**	26	**	**	**	**	**	26	**	25	23	35
Non-south	31	**	41	**	46	**	**	**	**	**	39	**	38	34	41
Professional	46	**	57	**	50	**	**	**	**	**	49	**	49	45	49
White collar	46	**	52	**	57	**	**	**	**	**	40	**	42	25	47
Blue collar	18	**	29	**	38	**	**	**	**	**	26	**	27	26	29
Unskilled	-7	**	11	**	35*	**	**	**	**	**	2*	**	11	17	31*
Farmers	10	**	4	**	18	**	**	**	**	**	29	**	35	14*	53*
Housewives	20	**	33	**	32	**	**	**	**	**	34	**	31	29	37
Protestants	20	**	33	**	39	**	**	**	**	**	34	**	36	29	42
Catholics	29	**	41	**	44	**	**	**	**	**	38	**	37	40	33
Jews	44	**	57	**	42	**	**	**	**	**	41	**	54	48	55
Other and No Religion	5	**	14*	**	21*	**	**	**	**	**	21	**	1	11	26
Total Population	22	**	35	**	39	**	**	**	**	**	34	**	34	30	39

PDI is proportion "highest" sense fo duty minus proportion "lowest" sense of duty (see table 4.49)

Support of the Political System

Table 4.51
Citizen Duty Index by Political Groups, Summarized by a Percentage Difference Index#

	1952	1954	1956	1958	1960	1962	1964	1966	1968	1970	1972	1974	1976	1978	1980
Strong Democrats	22	**	33	**	44	**	**	**	**	**	42	**	46	35	48
Weak and Leaning Democrats	16	**	34	**	36	**	**	**	**	**	34	**	29	29	37
Independent Independents	25	**	34	**	22	**	**	**	**	**	16	**	15	19	28
Weak and Leaning Republicans	29	**	43	**	52	**	**	**	**	**	40	**	39	40	40
Strong Republicans	42	**	49	**	46	**	**	**	**	**	45	**	58	48	55
Liberal Self Placement 1	**	**	**	**	**	**	**	**	**	**	38	**	40	27	47
Liberal Self Placement 2	**	**	**	**	**	**	**	**	**	**	37	**	36	37	42
Neutral Self Placement 3	**	**	**	**	**	**	**	**	**	**	43	**	43	41	48
Conservative Self Placement 4	**	**	**	**	**	**	**	**	**	**	48	**	47	42	47
Conservative Self Placement 5	**	**	**	**	**	**	**	**	**	**	44	**	53	40	41
Liberal Index 1	**	**	**	**	**	**	**	**	**	**	51	**	29	**	35*
Liberal Index 2	**	**	**	**	**	**	**	**	**	**	37	**	32	**	47
Neutral Index 3	**	**	**	**	**	**	**	**	**	**	32	**	34	**	43
Conservative Index 4	**	**	**	**	**	**	**	**	**	**	44	**	44	**	42
Conservative Index 5	**	**	**	**	**	**	**	**	**	**	53	**	50	**	47
Total Population	22	**	35	**	39	**	**	**	**	**	34	**	34	30	39

PDI is proportion "highest" sense of duty minus proportion "lowest" sense of duty (see table 4.49)

Table 4.52
Trust in People Index

DESCRIPTION: This measure is an additive index of trust in
people constructed from three items: 1)Generally speaking
does the respondent believe that most people can be trusted
or that one can't be too careful in dealing with people, 2)
Would the respondent say that most of the time people try to
be helpful or that they are mostly just looking out for
themselves, and 3) Does the respondent think most people would
try to take advantage of them if they got a chance or would
they try to be fair.

	1964	1966	1968	1970	1972	1974	1976
Trust people the least	21%	**	19%	**	27%	28%	24%
	13	**	14	**	16	16	13
	19	**	18	**	17	18	18
Most trust in people	38	**	41	**	32	33	35
Not scored	9	**	7	**	8	6	10
Total	%100	**	100%	**	100%	100%	100%
N	1440	**	1339	**	2166	2405	2386
PDI#	17	**	22	**	5	5	12

PDI is proportion "most trust in people" minus proportion "trust people the least"

Table 4.53
Trust in People Index by Social Groups, Summarized by a Percentage Difference Index#

	1964	1966	1968	1970	1972	1974	1976
1959 or later Cohort	**	**	**	**	**	**	**
1943 - 1958 Cohort	-5*	**	22	**	-9	-2	5
1927 - 1942 Cohort	19	**	21	**	13	10	20
1911 - 1926 Cohort	23	**	24	**	15	9	17
1895 - 1910 Cohort	10	**	19	**	1	7	5
Before 1895 Cohort	9	**	27	**	-2	6	6
Grade School	-15	**	-4	**	-25	-20	-15
High School	23	**	20	**	4	0	7
College	40	**	46	**	26	28	30
Central cities	13	**	11	**	-8	7	11
Suburbs	27	**	22	**	18	5	19
Non-urban Areas	13	**	29	**	3	3	5
Income Percentile 0-16	-14	**	-3	**	-16	-14	-21
Income Percentile 17-33	12	**	19	**	-12	-8	4
Income Percentile 34-67	25	**	24	**	2	10	15
Income Percentile 68-95	30	**	36	**	25	20	26
Income Percentile 95-100	41	**	44	**	42	17	38
Males	15	**	18	**	5	3	11
Females	19	**	25	**	5	6	12
Whites	22	**	27	**	12	10	18
Blacks	-20	**	-22	**	-57	-41	-40
Union Household	16	**	11	**	-5	-5	10
Non-union Household	18	**	26	**	8	8	12
South	13	**	13	**	-8	-11	-5
Non-south	19	**	26	**	12	14	19
Professional	43	**	46	**	28	20	30
White collar	24	**	41	**	14	21	26
Blue collar	2	**	-2	**	-16	-13	-4
Unskilled	-25*	**	-	**	-37*	-25*	-18
Farmers	-6	**	16	**	-2	16	-5
Housewives	22	**	26	**	11	3	14
Protestants	16	**	21	**	6	5	11
Catholics	23	**	27	**	6	6	14
Jews	51*	**	33*	**	17*	4	21
Other and No Religion	2	**	17*	**	-9	1	10
Total Population	17	**	22	**	5	5	12

PDI is proportion "most trust in people" minus proportion "trust people the least" (see table 4.52)

Table 4.54
Trust in People Index by Political Groups Summarized by a Percentage Difference Index#

	1964	1966	1968	1970	1972	1974	1976
Strong Democrats	13	**	8	**	-8	-2	-1
Weak and Leaning Democrats	16	**	20	**	-1	-1	8
Independent Independents	-6	**	0	**	-2	-8	2
Weak and Leaning Republicans	30	**	43	**	19	25	25
Strong Republicans	30	**	31	**	21	23	32
Liberal Self Placement 1	**	**	**	**	-2	9	7
Liberal Self Placement 2	**	**	**	**	18	18	22
Neutral Self Placement 3	**	**	**	**	12	10	21
Conservative Self Placement 4	**	**	**	**	26	27	28
Conservative Self Placement 5	**	**	**	**	14	9	22
Liberal Index 1	0	**	21	**	-30	0	-8
Liberal Index 2	22	**	24	**	9	8	14
Neutral Index 3	14	**	17	**	7	6	12
Conservative Index 4	23	**	28	**	15	10	22
Conservative Index 5	28	**	31	**	14	12	23
Total Population	17	**	22	**	5	5	12

PDI is proportion "most trust in people" minus proportion "trust people the least" (see table 4.52)

Table 4.55
Approve of Protest Index

DESCRIPTION: This measure is an additive index of
approval of protest constructed from three items:
1) Whether the respondent approves of taking part
in protest meetings or marches that are permitted
by the local authorities, 2) Whether the
respondent approves of refusing to obey a law
which one thinks is unjust, if the person feels
so strongly about it that he is willing to go to
jail rather than obey the law, and 3) Whether the
respondent approves of a person deciding if all
other methods have failed, to try to stop the
government from going about its usual activities
with sit-ins, mass meetings, demonstrations, and
things like that.

	1968	1970	1972	1974
Disapproval	30%	27%	21%	22%
	18	22	18	17
	17	20	21	19
	9	15	18	20
Approval	12	11	17	18
Not scored	15	4	4	4
Total	100%	100%	100%	100%
N	1348	915	2705	2523
PDI#	-28	-23	-4	-1

PDI is proportion in two most approving categories minus proportion in two most disapproving categories

Table 4.56
Approve of Protest Index by Social Groups, Summarized by a Percentage Difference Index#

	1968	1970	1972	1974
1959 or later Cohort	**	**	**	**
1943 - 1958 Cohort	-17	-1	30	25
1927 - 1942 Cohort	-14	-20	-3	-2
1911 - 1926 Cohort	-34	-23	-16	-15
1895 - 1910 Cohort	-40	-42	-34	-27
Before 1895 Cohort	-46	-38*	-51	-26
Grade School	-31	-31	-22	-15
High School	-38	-29	-9	-3
College	-7	-4	16	12
Central cities	-10	-3	11	23
Suburbs	-24	-20	-2	-4
Non-urban Areas	-41	-39	-16	-17
Income Percentile 0-16	-28	-28	-7	-2
Income Percentile 17-33	-31	-15	-1	1
Income Percentile 34-67	-34	-24	-6	-2
Income Percentile 68-95	-24	-27	-2	2
Income Percentile 95-100	-2	-2*	2	-2
Males	-26	-21	-5	-4
Females	-29	-25	-4	1
Whites	-34	-30	-10	-5
Blacks	28	44	42	33
Union Household	-34	-15	0	11
Non-union Household	-25	-25	-6	-5
South	-31	-28	-11	-10
Non-south	-26	-21	-1	4
Professional	-7	-14	-1	3
White collar	-41	-17	2	11
Blue collar	-36	-22	-8	-5
Unskilled	-	-	44*	32*
Farmers	-31	-38*	-39	-37
Housewives	-30	-33	-12	-13
Protestants	-32	-31	-11	-8
Catholics	-20	-21	-1	4
Jews	27*	30*	44	33
Other and No Religion	-19*	17	38	35
Total Population	-28	-23	-4	-1

PDI is proportion in two most approving categories minus proportion in two most disapproving categories (see table 4.55)

Table 4.57
Approve of Protest Index by Political Groups Summarized by a Percentage Difference Index#

	1968	1970	1972	1974
Strong Democrats	-16	-22	5	7
Weak and Leaning Democrats	-25	-12	3	10
Independent Independents	-39	-18	3	6
Weak and Leaning Republicans	-31	-30	-10	-16
Strong Republicans	-41	-59	-39	-28
Liberal Self Placement 1	**	**	55	47
Liberal Self Placement 2	**	**	34	29
Neutral Self Placement 3	**	**	-6	-6
Conservative Self Placement 4	**	**	-13	-10
Conservative Self Placement 5	**	**	-35	-26
Liberal Index 1	44	44*	65	49
Liberal Index 2	-13	12	36	34
Neutral Index 3	-36	-35	1	-8
Conservative Index 4	-30	-33	-17	-11
Conservative Index 5	-55	-55	-41	-39
Total Population	-28	-23	-4	-1

PDI is proportion in two most approving categories minus proportion in two most disapproving categories (see table 4.55)

Chapter 5. Involvement and Turnout

A basic tenet of democratic theory is that citizens generally are interested and involved in politics. Unrestricted suffrage supposedly produces full and equal participation, which acts to ensure acceptance of those leaders selected through elections, thereby securing the legitimacy of authorities and their policy decisions. In reality, citizens do not necessarily participate at the same rate or in the same types of political activities. Data describing who does participate are, therefore, important, for they indirectly reflect the distribution of political influence in the public and allow us to determine whether involved citizens are representative of the population as a whole. Furthermore, voter turnout, when studied over time, provides an indirect measure of active support for the electoral system rather than indicating interest in the outcome of any specific electoral contest.

Legal requirements dealing with registration and voting vary from place to place, thus deterring some citizens from active involvement in politics. Prior to the mid-1960s, for example, legal restrictions kept significant numbers of Southern blacks from voting. During the period covered by the surveys reported in this volume, many legal barriers to registration and participation were removed. Such changes would suggest increased voter turnout; yet participation in the elections after 1960 has declined (Table 5.16).

Clearly, numerous factors other than legal requirements influence political involvement and participation. The purpose of this chapter is twofold: first, to describe the extent of citizen involvement in various political activities; second, to investigate several sociological and political correlates of involvement and electoral turnout.

The array of activities used at the outset of the chapter (Tables 5.1-5.14) to measure political involvement is quite extensive. Some activities, such as attending political meetings, working for a party or candidate, and writing letters to public officials, require considerable time and effort. Other means of involvement, including following campaign events through the media, indicate a relatively lower commitment of time and resources. Finally, we present the data on what may be considered the least demanding form of involvement, self-reported interest in public affairs and campaigns. As expected, the proportion of highly engaged citizens increases as one goes from the most to the least demanding modes of involvement. Few respondents (3-10 percent) report attending political meetings or working in a political campaign. Yet approximately 60 percent of the respondents say they follow what is going on in government and public affairs some or most of the time. Involvement in the most demanding modes of participation was basically stable over the period of the surveys, while general political interest actually increased slightly. These trends are quite interesting, given the decline in electoral turnout which occurred during the same period.

Another regular pattern of involvement differences is apparent when presidential and congressional election years are compared. Presidential elections generally arouse greater citizen participation than congressional contests (Table 5.16). Although previous literature has associated differences in presidential and congressional turnout rates with degree of interest in the campaign, the over-time pattern apparent from Table 5.12 corresponds only weakly to the variation in participation. By contrast, reports of talking to others about the election (Table 5.1) are more numerous for presidential elections than for congressional elections, a pattern which is similar to the one of surge and decline in voter turnout.

After the basic distributions are given for the measures of involvement and turnout, the second half of the chapter presents a series of tables which summarize with a PDI the relationship between involvement and social or political characteristics. Three indicators of involvement are used in this half of the chapter. The first is the number of media (television, newspapers, radio, or magazines) relied on to follow campaign events, the second is simply turnout, that is, the proportion of respondents reporting that they voted in the particular election, and the last is a measure of participation in campaign activities.

A caveat regarding survey estimates of turnout is in order at this point. Self-reports generally produce estimates of participation which are higher than official turnout statistics. While some systematic variation in overreporting turnout occurs across demographic groups, it is not significant enough to distort the differences observed in the tables below. Although the level of turnout suggested by the survey data is higher than that revealed by the official statistics, across-group and over-time comparisons are still valid.

Table 5.1
Tried to Influence Other's Vote

QUESTION: During the campaign, did you talk to any people and try to show
them why they should vote for one of the parties or candidates?

	1952	1954	1956	1958	1960	1962	1964	1966	1968	1970	1972	1974	1976	1978	1980	1982	1984	1986
No	73%	**	72%	83%	67%	82%	69%	78%	67%	73%	68%	85%	63%	79%	64%	78%	68%	79%
Yes	28	**	28	17	34	18	31	22	33	27	32	15	37	22	36	23	32	21
Total	100%	**	100%	100%	100%	100%	100%	100%	100%	100%	100%	100%	100%	100%	100%	100%	100%	100%
N	1708*	**	1762	1784	1828	1287	1447	1286	1346	1505	2189	2523	2400	2291	1406	1402	1939	2172
PDI#	-45	**	-43	-66	-33	-63	-37	-55	-34	-47	-37	-71	-27	-57	-28	-55	-35	-58

PDI is proportion "yes" minus proportion "no"

Table 5.2
Attended Political Meeting

QUESTION: Did you go to any political meetings, rallies, dinners, or things
like that?

	1952	1954	1956	1958	1960	1962	1964	1966	1968	1970	1972	1974	1976	1978	1980	1982	1984	1986
No	93%	**	93%	**	92%	92%	91%	**	91%	91%	91%	94%	94%	91%	93%	91%	92%	93%
Yes	7	**	7	**	8	8	9	**	9	9	9	6	6	10	8	9	8	7
Total	100%	**	100%	**	100%	100%	100%	**	100%	100%	100%	100%	100%	100%	100%	100%	100%	100%
N	1704	**	1761	**	1822	1287	1445	**	1346	1505	2190	2523	2394	2292	1407	1404	1942	2175
PDI#	-86	**	-86	**	-83	-84	-83	**	-82	-81	-82	-88	-87	-81	-85	-81	-84	-87

PDI is proportion "yes" minus proportion "no"

Table 5.3
Worked for a Party or Candidate

QUESTION: Did you do any other work for one of the parties or candidates?

	1952	1954	1956	1958	1960	1962	1964	1966	1968	1970	1972	1974	1976	1978	1980	1982	1984	1986
No	97%	**	97%	**	94%	96%	95%	**	94%	93%	95%	95%	96%	94%	96%	94%	96%	97%
Yes	3	**	3	**	6	4	5	**	6	7	5	5	4	6	4	6	4	3
Total	100%	**	100%	**	100%	100%	100%	**	100%	100%	100%	100%	100%	100%	100%	100%	100%	100%
N	1708	**	1758	**	1825	1286	1444	**	1338	1505	2188	2522	2397	2292	1405	1403	1938	2172
PDI#	-94	**	-94	**	-89	-92	-90	**	-88	-86	-90	-91	-91	-89	-93	-89	-92	-93

PDI is proportion "yes" minus proportion "no"

Table 5.4
Wore a Button or Put a Sticker on the Car

QUESTION: Did you wear a campaign button or put a campaign
sticker on your car?

	1956	1958	1960	1962	1964	1966	1968	1970	1972	1974	1976	1978	1980	1982	1984	1986
No	85%	**	79%	90%	84%	**	85%	91%	86%	95%	92%	91%	93%	92%	91%	93%
Yes	16	**	21	10	17	**	15	9	14	5	8	9	7	8	9	7
Total	100%	**	100%	100%	100%	**	100%	100%	100%	100%	100%	100%	100%	100%	100%	100%
N	1759	**	1826	1284	1444	**	1335	1503	2188	2522	2394	2291	1407	1403	1942	2175
PDI#	-69	**	-58	-81	-67	**	-70	-82	-72	-89	-85	-82	-87	-84	-82	-85

PDI is proportion "yes" minus proportion "no"

Table 5.5
Gave Money to Help a Campaign

QUESTION: Did you give any money or buy any tickets or anything to help the
campaign for one of the parties or candidates?

	1952	1954	1956	1958	1960	1962	1964	1966	1968	1970	1972	1974	1976	1978	1980	1982	1984	1986
No	96%	**	90%	**	88%	91%	89%	92%	91%	**	90%	92%	84%	87%	92%	91%	88%	90%
Yes	4	**	10	**	12	9	11	8	9	**	10	8	16	13	8	9	13	10
Total	100%	**	100%	**	100%	100%	100%	100%	100%	**	100%	100%	100%	100%	100%	100%	100%	100%
N	1708	**	1762	**	1825	1286	1443	1276	1320	**	2191	2516	2394	2292	1404	1406	1938	2158
PDI#	-92	**	-80	**	-77	-81	-79	-83	-82	**	-79	-83	-68	-75	-84	-82	-75	-80

PDI is proportion "yes" minus proportion "no"

Table 5.6
Letter Writing to Public Officials

QUESTION: Have you ever written a letter to any
public officials giving them your opinion about
something that should be done?

	1964	1966	1968	1970	1972	1974	1976
No	83%	**	80%	**	73%	**	72%
Yes	17	**	20	**	27	**	28
Total	100%	**	100%	**	100%	**	100%
N	1447	**	1343	**	2191	**	2393
PDI#	-66	**	-60	**	-46	**	-45

PDI is proportion "yes" minus proportion "no"

Table 5.7
Watched Campaign on TV

QUESTION: How about television-- Did you watch any programs about the
campaign on television? (If yes) How many television programs about the
campaign would you say you watched-- a good many, several, or just one or two?&

	1952	1954	1956	1958	1960	1962	1964	1966	1968	1970	1972	1974	1976	1978	1980	1982	1984	1986
No	49%	**	26%	**	13%	**	11%	**	11%	**	12%	45%	11%	31%	14%	24%	14%	25%
Yes	51	**	74	**	87	**	89	**	89	**	88	55	89	69	86	76	86	75
Total	100%	**	100%	**	100%	**	100%	**	100%	**	100%	100%	100%	100%	100%	100%	100%	100%
N	1656	**	1758	**	1829	**	1448	**	1341	**	1116	2479	2400	2290	1406	1409	1943	2174
PDI#	3	**	48	**	73	**	78	**	78	**	77	10	78	39	72	52	72	51

PDI is proportion "yes" minus proportion "no"

& See question wording for 1974

Table 5.8
Listened to Campaign Radio Programs

QUESTION: How about radio-- Did you listen to any speeches or discussions about the
campaign on the radio? (If yes) How many programs about the campaign did you listen to
on the radio -- a good many, several, or just one or two?

	1952	1954	1956	1958	1960	1962	1964	1966	1968	1970	1972	1974	1976	1978	1980	1982	1984	1986
No	30%	**	55%	**	58%	**	52%	**	59%	**	57%	**	55%	54%	53%	54%	55%	59%
Yes	70	**	45	**	42	**	48	**	41	**	43	**	45	46	47	47	45	41
Total	100%	**	100%	**	100%	**	100%	**	100%	**	100%	**	100%	100%	100%	100%	100%	100%
N	1708	**	1758	**	1823	**	1444	**	1335	**	1116	**	2395	2291	1406	1401	1941	2170
PDI#	40	**	-9	**	-16	**	-4	**	-18	**	-14	**	-10	-8	-6	-7	-10	-19

PDI is proportion "yes" minus proportion "no"

Table 5.9
Read Magazine Articles on the Campaign

QUESTION: How about magazines -- Did you read about the campaign in any
magazines? (If yes) How many magazine articles about the campaign would
you say you read-- a good many, several, or just one or two?

	1952	1954	1956	1958	1960	1962	1964	1966	1968	1970	1972	1974	1976	1978	1980	1982	1984
No	60%	**	69%	**	59%	**	61%	**	64%	**	67%	**	52%	75%	65%	69%	65%
Yes	40	**	31	**	41	**	39	**	36	**	33	**	48	25	35	31	35
Total	100%	**	100%	**	100%	**	100%	**	100%	**	100%	**	100%	100%	100%	100%	100%
N	1706	**	1751	**	1818	**	1446	**	1342	**	1117	**	2397	2293	1403	1406	1942
PDI#	-19	**	-38	**	-18	**	-21	**	-29	**	-34	**	-4	-49	-31	-38	-30

PDI is proportion "yes" minus proportion "no"

Table 5.10
Read about the Campaign in Newspapers

QUESTION: We're interested in this interview in finding out whether people
paid much attention to the election campaign this year. Take newspapers
for instance -- Did you read much about the campaign this year in any
newspapers? (IF YES) How much did you read newspaper articles about the
election--regularly, often, from time to time, or just once in a great while?&

	1952	1954	1956	1958	1960	1962	1964	1966	1968	1970	1972	1974	1976	1978	1980	1982	1984	1986
No	21%	**	32%	**	20%	**	21%	**	25%	**	43%	14%	27%	29%	29%	28%	23%	36%
Yes	79	**	69	**	80	**	79	**	75	**	57	86	73	71	71	72	77	64
Total	100%	**	100%	**	100%	**	100%	**	100%	**	100%	100%	100%	100%	100%	100%	100%	100%
N	1708	**	1760	**	1823	**	1448	**	1348	**	1115	1755	2393	2257	1400	1416	1943	2171
PDI#	58	**	37	**	60	**	57	**	51	**	15	72	47	42	42	44	54	29

PDI is proportion "yes" minus proportion "no"
& Wording was "read about the campaign" before 1972

Table 5.11
General Interest in Public Affairs

QUESTION: Some people seem to follow what's going on in government
and public affairs most of the time whether there's an election
going on or not. Others aren't that interested. Would you say you
follow what's going on in government and public affairs most of
the time some of the time only now and then or hardly at all?&

	1960	1962	1964	1966	1968	1970	1972	1974	1976	1978	1980	1982	1984	1986
Hardly at all	38%	42%	11%	17%	18%	**	11%	11%	12%	17%	15%	15%	14%	15%
Only now and then	**	**	17	18	19	**	16	14	18	25	23	21	23	24
Some of the time	42	43	42	30	31	**	36	36	31	34	35	35	36	35
Most of the time	21	16	30	35	33	**	37	39	38	23	26	29	26	26
Don't know	0	0	0	0	0	**	0	1	1	1	0	0	0	0
Total	100%	100%	100%	100%	100%	**	100%	100%	100%	100%	100%	100%	100%	100%
N	1826	1293	1447	1288	1345	**	2191	2513	2399	2280	1404	1413	1926	2148
PDI#	-17	-26	2	0	-3	**	9	14	8	-19	-12	-7	-11	-13

PDI is proportion interested "most of the time" minus proportion interested "only now and then" and "hardly at all"

& Question wording in 1960 and 1962 is: 'We'd like to know how much attention you pay to what's going on in politics
generally. I mean from day to day, when there isn't any big election campaign going on, would you say you follow
politics very closely, fairly closely or not much at all?'
(For these two years, Very Closely is recoded to 'Most of the time,' Fairly Closely to 'some of the time,' and Not Much At All
to 'hardly at all.' No category appeared in these two years which was recoded to 'only now and then,' and there was no 'Don't
Know' category.)

Table 5.12
Interest in Current Campaign

QUESTION: Some people don't pay much attention to the political campaigns. How about you
would you say that you have been/were very much interested somewhat interested or not
much interested in follow this year?

	1952	1954	1956	1958	1960	1962	1964	1966	1968	1970	1972	1974	1976	1978	1980	1982	1984	1986
Not much interested	29%	**	31%	41%	25%	26%	25%	30%	21%	24%	27%	**	21%	34%	26%	30%	25%	33%
Somewhat interested	34	**	40	33	37	38	37	40	40	43	41	**	42	45	44	44	47	44
Very much interested	37	**	30	27	38	36	38	30	39	34	32	**	37	22	30	26	28	23
Don't know	0	**	0	0	0	0	0	0	0	0	0	**	0	0	0	0	0	0
Total	100%	**	100%	100%	100%	100%	100%	100%	100%	100%	100%	**	100%	100%	100%	100%	100%	100%
N	1776	**	1754	1812	1919	1294	1565	1272	1546	1506	2699	**	2857	2300	1567	1415	2251	2172
PDI#	8	**	-1	-14	13	10	13	1	18	10	4	**	15	-12	4	-4	4	-11

PDI is proportion "very much interested" minus proportion "not much interested"

Table 5.13
Care Who Wins Election

QUESTION: Generally speaking would you say that you personally care/cared a good deal which
party wins/won the presidential election this fall or don't you care very much which party wins/won?

	1952	1954	1956	1958	1960	1962	1964	1966	1968	1970	1972	1974	1976	1978	1980	1982	1984
Don't care or Don't know&	33%	**	37%	**	35%	**	35%	**	35%	**	40%	**	43%	**	44%	**	35%
Care a good deal	67	**	63	**	65	**	66	**	65	**	60	**	57	**	56	**	65
Total	100%	**	100%	**	100%	**	100%	**	100%	**	100%	**	100%	**	100%	**	100%
N	1763	**	1723	**	1873	**	1562	**	1496	**	2682	**	2844	**	1555	**	2241
PDI#	34	**	26	**	30	**	31	**	30	**	21	**	13	**	12	**	30

PDI is proportion "care a good deal" minus proportion "don't care or don't know"

& Don't Know includes Pro-Con, Depends, and Other

Table 5.14
Expected Closeness of Presidential Race

QUESTION: Do you think it will be a close race or will
<the respondent's predicted winning candidate> win by
quite a bit?

	1952	1956	1960	1964	1968	1972	1976	1980	1984
Will win by quite a bit	20%	25%	12%	43%	20%	56%	14%	14%	46%
Close race	61	57	64	42	60	32	70	70	48
Don't know	19	18	25	16	20	13	17	16	6
Total	100%	100%	100%	100%	100%	100%	100%	100%	100%
N	1755	1629	1870	1470	1497	2697	2857	1565	2252
PDI#	41	32	52	-1	40	-24	56	56	1

PDI is proportion "close race" minus proportion "will win by quite a lot"

Table 5.15
Media Exposure Index

DESCRIPTION: This measure of media exposure counts how many of four media the respondent has used. The media activities are: 1) watching any programs about the campaign on television 2) listening to any speeches or discussions about the campaign on the radio 3) reading about the campaign in any magazines and 4) reading about the campaign this year in any newspaper.

	1952	1954	1956	1958	1960	1962	1964	1966	1968	1970	1972	1974	1976	1978	1980	1982	1984
Used no media	6%	**	8%	**	4%	**	3%	**	4%	**	6%	**	5%	12%	6%	10%	6%
	14	**	19	**	13	**	12	**	15	**	21	**	15	19	16	16	14
	30	**	32	**	29	**	30	**	32	**	33	**	23	30	30	30	31
	35	**	28	**	36	**	36	**	34	**	27	**	34	28	32	29	32
Used all four media	15	**	13	**	18	**	19	**	14	**	13	**	23	12	17	16	18
Total	100%	**	100%	**	100%	**	100%	**	100%	**	100%	**	100%	100%	100%	100%	100%
N	1711	**	1762	**	1829	**	1449	**	1350	**	1119	**	2403	2304	1407	1417	1944
PDI#	-5	**	-14	**	0	**	3	**	-5	**	-14	**	3	-19	-5	-10	-2

PDI is proportion "used all four media" minus proportion "used none" and "one"

Table 5.16
Turnout in Current Election

QUESTION: In talking to people about the election we find that a lot of people weren't able to vote because they weren't registered or they were sick or they just didn't have time. How about you did you vote this time?

	1952	1954	1956	1958	1960	1962	1964	1966	1968	1970	1972	1974	1976	1978	1980	1982	1984	1986
No	27%	**	27%	42%	21%	40%	22%	38%	24%	41%	27%	48%	28%	46%	29%	40%	26%	48%
Yes	73	**	73	58	79	60	78	62	76	59	73	53	72	55	71	60	74	53
Total	100%	**	100%	100%	100%	100%	100%	100%	100%	100%	100%	100%	100%	100%	100%	100%	100%	100%
N	1714	**	1762	1806	1829	1293	1450	1288	1391	1493	2283	2512	2403	2292	1407	1406	1989	2174
PDI#	46	**	46	15	58	21	55	25	52	19	46	5	43	9	43	21	47	5

PDI is proportion "Yes" minus proportion "No"

Table 5.17
Electoral Participation Index

DESCRIPTION: This measure compares voting and participation in five other activitites. The
activities are: 1) talking to any people or trying to show people how to vote during the
campaign 2) attending any political meetings rallies dinners or things like that 3)
working for any parties or candidates 4) wearing a campaign button or displaying a bumper
sticker and 5) giving any money or buying any tickets or anything to help the campaign
for one of the parties or candidates.

	1952	1954	1956	1958	1960	1962	1964	1966	1968	1970	1972	1974	1976	1978	1980	1982	1984	1986
Non-participant	23%	**	22%	39%	16%	34%	17%	34%	19%	33%	22%	42%	21%	38%	22%	35%	21%	41%
Voted or Participated	50	**	45	47	45	44	46	44	44	41	42	40	40	37	43	39	43	36
Both	27	**	34	14	40	23	37	22	37	26	36	18	39	25	35	27	37	24
Total	100%	**	100%	100%	100%	100%	100%	100%	100%	100%	100%	100%	100%	100%	100%	100%	100%	100%
N	1708	**	1762	1775	1829	1285	1448	1285	1345	1493	2190	2512	2401	2289	1407	1402	1942	2173
PDI#	4	**	12	-25	24	-11	20	-12	18	-8	13	-24	18	-13	14	-8	16	-17

PDI is proportion "both" minus proportion "non-participant"

Table 5.18
Media Exposure Index by Social Groups, Summarized by a Percentage Difference Index#

	1952	1954	1956	1958	1960	1962	1964	1966	1968	1970	1972	1974	1976	1978	1980	1982	1984
1959 or later Cohort	**	**	**	**	**	**	**	**	**	**	**	**	**	-43	-17	-36	-14
1943 -1958 Cohort	**	**	**	**	**	**	-19*	**	-8	**	-20	**	0	-27	-10	-13	0
1927 - 1942 Cohort	-9	**	-23	**	1	**	3	**	-3	**	-15	**	12	-12	8	-8	4
1911 - 1926 Cohort	-5	**	-12	**	7	**	7	**	0	**	-7	**	3	-10	-4	0	0
1895 - 1910 Cohort	-1	**	-10	**	-3	**	1	**	-12	**	-10	**	-3	-16	-8	-5	2
Before 1895 Cohort	-10	**	-19	**	-12	**	2	**	-10	**	-18*	**	-15	-27*	-	-	-
Grade School	-29	**	-42	**	-21	**	-21	**	-24	**	-31	**	-30	-41	-30	-31	-27
High School	6	**	-11	**	4	**	5	**	-9	**	-20	**	-7	-27	-18	-18	-14
College	26	**	22	**	22	**	25	**	19	**	8	**	31	1	18	4	18
Central cities	4	**	-19	**	-5	**	2	**	1	**	-5	**	10	-24	-4	-8	-2
Suburbs	-5	**	-7	**	4	**	8	**	-5	**	-8	**	7	-13	1	-7	1
Non-urban Areas	-14	**	-16	**	1	**	1	**	-8	**	-22	**	-6	-21	-13	-15	-5
Income Percentile 0-16	-38	**	-41	**	-29	**	-21	**	-22	**	-30	**	-30	-35	-21	-26	-19
Income Percentile 17-33	-15	**	-24	**	-17	**	5	**	-11	**	-19	**	-5	-25	-18	-16	-13
Income Percentile 34-67	-8	**	-14	**	7	**	4	**	-3	**	-13	**	5	-19	-7	-9	-3
Income Percentile 68-95	14	**	3	**	13	**	11	**	7	**	-5	**	15	-9	12	0	14
Income Percentile 95-100	33	**	18	**	23	**	31	**	11	**	14*	**	44	4	39	10	29
Males	0	**	-6	**	4	**	8	**	0	**	-8	**	14	-13	3	-3	6
Females	-10	**	-21	**	-3	**	0	**	-9	**	-18	**	-5	-23	-12	-16	-8
Whites	-1	**	-11	**	3	**	5	**	-5	**	-14	**	5	-17	-2	-9	-1
Blacks	-43	**	-47	**	-23	**	-7	**	-4	**	-13	**	-16	-28	-22	-13	-8
Union Household	-1	**	-21	**	0	**	1	**	-6	**	-19	**	2	-19	-5	-11	3
Non-union Household	-7	**	-12	**	0	**	4	**	-4	**	-11	**	4	-19	-5	-10	-3
South	-24	**	-24	**	-6	**	3	**	-10	**	-17	**	-4	-24	-7	-16	-8
Non-south	2	**	-11	**	3	**	3	**	-3	**	-12	**	6	-16	-4	-7	2
Professional	26	**	17	**	22	**	20	**	13	**	12	**	31	3	22	6	22
White collar	14	**	-9	**	4	**	14	**	-2	**	-7	**	12	-17	-2	-3	-2
Blue collar	-5	**	-23	**	-4	**	-6	**	-14	**	-24	**	-5	-31	-18	-19	-11
Unskilled	-32	**	-43	**	-18	**	-13	**	5	**	-	**	-28	-31	-20*	-15*	-18*
Farmers	-19	**	-17	**	-22	**	-14	**	-11	**	-16*	**	-22	-16*	-3*	-20*	-5
Housewives	-13	**	-19	**	-4	**	0	**	-7	**	-26	**	-11	-23	-20	-22	-17
Protestants	-8	**	-15	**	0	**	5	**	-5	**	-13	**	1	-18	-7	-9	-3
Catholics	3	**	-16	**	-1	**	-1	**	-5	**	-18	**	3	-19	-5	-13	0
Jews	-	**	7	**	21	**	13	**	9	**	26	**	43	22	17*	4*	12*
Other and No Religion	-25	**	-16*	**	0*	**	-2	**	-4*	**	-13	**	6	-33	-1	-13	-1
Total Population	-5	**	-14	**	0	**	3	**	-5	**	-14	**	3	-19	-5	-10	-2

PDI is proportion "used all four media" minus proportion "used none" and "one" (see table 5.15)

Table 5.19
Media Exposure Index by Political Groups, Summarized by a Percentage Difference Index#

	1952	1954	1956	1958	1960	1962	1964	1966	1968	1970	1972	1974	1976	1978	1980	1982	1984
Strong Democrats	-10	**	-14	**	-3	**	2	**	-3	**	-4	**	11	-14	-4	-4	8
Weak and Leaning Democrats	-6	**	-15	**	-3	**	2	**	-9	**	-17	**	1	-22	-11	-11	-7
Independent Independents	-2	**	-16	**	6	**	-20	**	-13	**	-25	**	-4	-30	-17	-31	-13
Weak and Leaning Republicans	-3	**	-11	**	4	**	7	**	1	**	-14	**	3	-10	8	-5	-2
Strong Republicans	12	**	-2	**	12	**	30	**	9	**	4	**	19	5	13	10	i6
Liberal Self Placement 1	**	**	**	**	**	**	**	**	**	**	11	**	22	-7	16	11	16
Liberal Self Placement 2	**	**	**	**	**	**	**	**	**	**	4	**	20	-8	7	-3	9
Neutral Self Placement 3	**	**	**	**	**	**	**	**	**	**	-17	**	7	-13	-2	2	-3
Conservative Self Placement 4	**	**	**	**	**	**	**	**	**	**	-1	**	27	-5	14	5	12
Conservative Self Placement 5	**	**	**	**	**	**	**	**	**	**	-2	**	18	-9	10	-1	12
Liberal Index 1	**	**	**	**	**	**	1	**	4	**	0*	**	9	**	5*	6	32
Liberal Index 2	**	**	**	**	**	**	13	**	10	**	1	**	17	**	7	5	2
Neutral Index 3	**	**	**	**	**	**	-7	**	-15	**	-18	**	-2	**	-17	-14	-10
Conservative Index 4	**	**	**	**	**	**	10	**	-3	**	-7	**	16	**	2	-3	8
Conservative Index 5	**	**	**	**	**	**	26	**	16	**	-3	**	30	**	19	2	26
Total Population	-5	**	-14	**	0	**	3	**	-5	**	-14	**	3	-19	-5	-10	-2

PDI is proportion "used all four media" minus proportion "used none" and "one" (see table 5.15 for media exposure index description)

Table 5.20
Gammas of Social Groups and Political Groups with Media Exposure Index&

	1952	1954	1956	1958	1960	1962	1964	1966	1968	1970	1972	1974	1976	1978	1980	1982	1984
Age Cohorts	-0.04	**	0.04	**	-0.05	**	0.00	**	-0.01	**	0.07	**	-0.01	0.15	0.05	0.14	0.06
Education of Respond	0.51	**	0.45	**	0.38	**	0.40	**	0.38	**	0.34	**	0.46	0.32	0.44	0.30	0.41
Urbanism	-0.12	**	-0.01	**	0.01	**	-0.04	**	-0.08	**	-0.17	**	-0.15	0.00	-0.07	-0.07	-0.04
Family Income	0.40	**	0.30	**	0.32	**	0.25	**	0.21	**	0.20	**	0.30	0.18	0.32	0.20	0.27
Sex of Respondent	-0.12	**	-0.19	**	-0.09	**	-0.09	**	-0.09	**	-0.15	**	-0.21	-0.14	-0.24	-0.17	-0.19
Race of Respondent	-0.53	**	-0.42	**	-0.36	**	-0.21	**	-0.01	**	-0.01	**	-0.23	-0.12	-0.27	-0.03	-0.14
Union Membership	-0.01	**	0.09	**	0.02	**	0.07	**	0.07	**	0.09	**	-0.01	-0.00	-0.02	-0.02	-0.06
Region	0.31	**	0.18	**	0.13	**	0.01	**	0.10	**	0.08	**	0.13	0.10	0.05	0.09	0.14
Occupation of Respond	-0.21	**	-0.16	**	-0.18	**	-0.14	**	-0.13	**	-0.25	**	-0.29	-0.19	-0.30	-0.19	-0.25
Party Identification@	0.11	**	0.07	**	0.11	**	0.10	**	0.07	**	0.03	**	0.03	0.08	0.11	0.04	0.04
Lib-Conserv Self Pl@	**	**	**	**	**	**	**	**	**	**	-0.05	**	0.00	0.01	0.01	-0.02	0.02
Lib to Conserv Index@	**	**	**	**	**	**	0.07	**	-0.01	**	-0.03	**	0.07	**	0.08	0.00	0.06

& See table 5.15 for media exposure index description. Sequence of codes within social and political group vars correspond to their category sequences appearing in 5.18 and 5.19.

@ For party identification var description, see Table 2.1; for Liberal-Conservative Self-placement var description, see Table 2.22; for Liberal-Conservative Index var description, see Table 2.23

Table 5.21
Media Exposure Index by Independent Variables, Summarized by a Percentage Difference Index#

	1952	1954	1956	1958	1960	1962	1964	1966	1968	1970	1972	1974	1976	1978	1980	1982	1984	
Interest Level	**	**	**	**	-25	**	-49	**	-49	**	-68	**	-65	-67	-53	-56	-51	Hardly
	**	**	**	**	**	**	-14	**	-17	**	-33	**	-26	-31	-22	-27	-20	Only now
	**	**	**	**	11	**	6	**	1	**	-12	**	8	-6	5	-8	10	Some
	**	**	**	**	25	**	29	**	21	**	10	**	35	14	24	24	26	Most
Interest in Campaign	-35	**	-47	**	-37	**	-28	**	-40	**	-43	**	-43	-55	-44	-52	-40	Not much
	-5	**	-10	**	1	**	1	**	-9	**	-14	**	3	-9	-3	-3	2	Somewhat
	17	**	14	**	23	**	26	**	16	**	12	**	27	17	23	26	23	Very
Care Who Wins Pres	-24	**	-30	**	-17	**	-12	**	-14	**	-32	**	-9	**	-14	**	-20	Don't care or know
	4	**	-5	**	9	**	11	**	0	**	-3	**	12	**	2	**	8	Care
President Race Close	-8	**	-15	**	-7	**	5	**	-2	**	-9	**	-8	**	-14	**	3	Not close
	4	**	-10	**	7	**	5	**	2	**	-16	**	8	**	-3	**	-2	Close
Trust in Govt	**	**	**	**	**	**	3	**	-4	**	-17	**	1	-18	-5	**	**	Cynical
	**	**	**	**	**	**	9	**	2	**	-11	**	7	-16	-6	**	**	
	**	**	**	**	**	**	3	**	-6	**	-9	**	8	-19	2	**	**	Trusting
Internal Efficacy	-30	**	-40	**	-23	**	-13	**	-22	**	-26	**	-22	-31	-23	**	**	Least efficacious
	-9	**	-21	**	-1	**	-4	**	-5	**	-23	**	3	-21	-8	**	**	
	17	**	3	**	12	**	16	**	4	**	-2	**	19	-8	5	**	**	
	29	**	15	**	20	**	30	**	18	**	9	**	34	7	23	**	**	Most efficacious
External Efficacy	**	**	**	**	**	**	**	**	-16	**	-24	**	-8	-24	-14	**	**	Least efficacious
	**	**	**	**	**	**	**	**	-2	**	-9	**	7	-16	-2	**	**	
	**	**	**	**	**	**	**	**	-3	**	-4	**	20	-10	9	**	**	
	**	**	**	**	**	**	**	**	8	**	-5	**	20	-5	13	**	**	Most efficacious
Govt Responsiveness	**	**	**	**	**	**	-22	**	-26	**	-25	**	-21	-36	-20	**	**	Lowest
	**	**	**	**	**	**	3	**	-10	**	-21	**	1	-25	-10	**	**	
	**	**	**	**	**	**	-3	**	-8	**	-19	**	3	-17	0	**	**	
	**	**	**	**	**	**	8	**	4	**	-6	**	11	-11	1	**	**	
	**	**	**	**	**	**	15	**	8	**	-2	**	24	-8	14	**	**	Highest
Approve of Protest	**	**	**	**	**	**	**	**	-2	**	-15	**	**	**	**	**	**	Disapproval
	**	**	**	**	**	**	**	**	-3	**	-14	**	**	**	**	**	**	
	**	**	**	**	**	**	**	**	4	**	-7	**	**	**	**	**	**	
	**	**	**	**	**	**	**	**	11	**	-4	**	**	**	**	**	**	Approval
Citizen Duty	-41	**	-51	**	-33	**	**	**	**	**	-32	**	-30	-44	-28	**	**	Lowest
	-2	**	-13	**	2	**	**	**	**	**	-15	**	5	-15	-9	**	**	
	9	**	-3	**	8	**	**	**	**	**	-8	**	13	-11	3	**	**	Highest
Trust in People	**	**	**	**	**	**	-13	**	-23	**	-26	**	-14	**	**	**	**	Least
	**	**	**	**	**	**	-3	**	-6	**	-15	**	0	**	**	**	**	
	**	**	**	**	**	**	5	**	-2	**	-5	**	8	**	**	**	**	Most
	**	**	**	**	**	**	15	**	5	**	-6	**	17	**	**	**	**	
Total Population	-5	**	-14	**	0	**	3	**	-5	**	-14	**	3	-19	-5	-10	-2	

PDI is proportion "used all four media" minus proportion "used none" and "one" (see table 5.15). For descriptions
  of independent vars (respective to their order above), see tables 5.11-5.14, 4.37, 4.40, 4.43, 4.46, 4.55, 4.50, 4.52

Media Exposure Index

Table 5.22
Gammas of Independent Variables with Media Exposure Index&

	1952	1954	1956	1958	1960	1962	1964	1966	1968	1970	1972	1974	1976	1978	1980	1982	1984
Interest Level	**	**	**	**	0.47	**	0.50	**	0.50	**	0.49	**	0.63	0.52	0.49	0.53	0.50
Interest in Campaign	0.48	**	0.51	**	0.53	**	0.44	**	0.50	**	0.46	**	0.51	0.59	0.51	0.60	0.49
Care Who Wins Pres	0.40	**	0.32	**	0.38	**	0.28	**	0.23	**	0.37	**	0.28	**	0.20	**	-0.05
President Race Close	0.17	**	0.07	**	0.15	**	0.01	**	0.10	**	-0.09	**	0.20	**	0.16	**	-0.05
Trust in Govt (1)	**	**	**	**	**	**	-0.03	**	-0.05	**	0.05	**	0.05	0.00	0.01	**	**
Internal Efficacy	0.40	**	0.37	**	0.30	**	0.30	**	0.30	**	0.27	**	0.35	0.22	0.28	**	**
External Efficacy	**	**	**	**	**	**	**	**	0.21	**	0.18	**	0.24	0.15	0.21	**	**
Govt Responsiveness	**	**	**	**	**	**	0.18	**	0.18	**	0.14	**	0.18	0.16	0.16	**	**
Approve of Protest	**	**	**	**	**	**	**	**	0.10	**	0.09	**	**	**	**	**	**
Citizen Duty	0.35	**	0.27	**	0.26	**	**	**	**	**	0.17	**	0.25	0.22	0.19	**	**
Trust in People	**	**	**	**	**	**	0.23	**	0.19	**	0.16	**	0.23	**	**	**	**

& See table 5.15 for media exposure index description. Sequence of codes within independent vars correspond to their category sequences appearing in 5.21

Table 5.23
Percent Turnout in Current Election, by Social Groups

	1952	1954	1956	1958	1960	1962	1964	1966	1968	1970	1972	1974	1976	1978	1980	1982	1984	1986
1959 or later Cohort	**	**	**	**	**	**	**	**	**	**	**	**	**	25.7	56.6	28.8	53.0	28.8
1943 - 1958 Cohort	**	**	**	**	**	**	47.6*	38.5	61.1	40.6	66.1	37.5	62.0	43.4	63.1	55.8	74.5	47.0
1927 - 1942 Cohort	58.0	**	58.4	35.5	69.5	48.9	71.4	57.6	75.3	58.3	76.7	53.4	78.9	61.1	78.2	68.5	80.1	66.4
1911 - 1926 Cohort	73.3	**	73.7	60.4	82.6	61.8	82.5	69.4	83.8	66.4	78.5	65.7	79.2	68.0	81.6	73.5	83.4	71.6
1895 - 1910 Cohort	77.8	**	78.2	66.1	81.9	68.4	82.0	67.0	76.1	65.1	72.8	62.8	74.4	60.6	75.7	59.8	69.2	64.2
Before 1895 Cohort	76.6	**	76.3	66.5	78.4	65.6	76.7	57.4	62.2	60.8	55.3	56.1	46.6	73.1*	-	-	-	-
Grade School	62.1	**	60.3	48.9	67.3	51.1	67.8	52.4	60.4	49.3	58.0	43.6	59.8	47.8	58.6	44.8	58.0	45.4
High School	80.1	**	74.4	56.4	81.1	59.8	77.8	61.7	78.3	55.9	70.1	47.8	66.0	48.0	65.4	54.3	66.3	43.6
College	89.5	**	89.7	73.2	90.3	71.9	88.2	74.2	84.1	76.7	86.6	65.5	85.0	66.9	82.6	70.9	85.3	63.6
Central cities	75.5	**	74.7	61.1	83.3	59.1	76.6	55.6	75.3	59.4	73.9	52.1	72.7	54.2	72.7	66.1	75.7	54.8
Suburbs	75.5	**	76.8	61.1	80.4	63.9	80.9	69.5	80.3	63.0	77.2	53.5	71.9	56.7	71.1	58.4	75.7	53.7
Non-urban Areas	68.9	**	69.9	53.7	76.5	57.6	75.9	61.5	73.2	57.1	69.0	52.0	70.5	52.3	70.6	58.0	69.8	49.1
Income Perc 0-16	53.3	**	52.7	41.4	65.4	49.4	63.8	41.4	60.5	42.5	60.1	38.7	54.3	45.7	56.4	45.6	52.7	37.6
Income Perc 17-33	68.6	**	65.3	46.4	70.8	47.4	72.9	53.8	66.1	54.2	62.9	49.1	65.3	46.4	68.0	54.2	69.3	46.3
Income Perc 34-67	75.8	**	76.2	58.9	81.2	62.0	79.0	63.0	79.3	56.0	70.5	49.9	70.9	56.2	72.1	65.7	74.5	52.7
Income Perc 68-95	84.7	**	82.8	71.2	85.4	68.2	85.7	72.4	86.8	71.5	86.2	64.6	80.4	60.7	81.4	67.8	84.4	62.8
Income Perc 95-100	95.0	**	89.6	91.2	94.0	84.1	87.8	81.7	92.5	77.8	90.4	75.0	91.4	72.6	86.7	67.7	91.3	65.1
Males	79.7	**	79.5	66.7	84.1	63.7	80.2	65.2	78.1	61.9	76.4	56.2	76.9	55.3	73.3	63.1	73.6	52.8
Females	69.3	**	67.6	49.6	74.7	57.7	75.6	59.9	74.1	57.5	70.1	49.9	67.8	53.9	69.8	58.1	73.6	52.3
Whites	78.5	**	76.5	59.9	81.9	62.7	79.6	63.4	77.1	60.7	73.8	54.6	72.5	56.2	72.3	60.4	75.2	53.4
Blacks	33.1	**	34.9	35.7	52.9	38.7	64.9	54.4	67.7	47.1	64.7	34.8	65.1	43.7	66.7	62.0	65.6	50.2
Union Household	76.3	**	75.8	61.0	76.9	**	82.8	62.8	76.1	59.7	75.3	49.6	77.4	56.9	74.6	65.0	78.7	55.0
Non-union Household	73.0	**	71.9	56.5	80.2	**	76.1	62.2	75.8	59.3	72.1	53.6	70.0	53.9	70.6	59.2	72.3	51.9
South	49.4	**	54.8	37.4	68.2	45.2	67.3	53.1	67.9	45.3	62.8	43.0	63.8	47.5	69.6	56.2	66.6	44.0
Non-south	82.3	**	80.4	66.1	84.4	68.5	82.3	66.1	79.4	66.7	77.9	57.9	75.3	58.3	72.3	62.7	77.1	57.3
Professional	91.8	**	88.9	72.0	87.9	**	84.6	**	87.5	73.0	85.0	70.0	85.5	68.3	85.9	72.4	87.4	70.6
White collar	84.4	**	83.7	63.5	89.9	**	86.1	**	84.8	67.2	78.0	54.0	78.0	55.6	74.9	61.4	78.8	56.6
Blue collar	76.1	**	70.6	57.1	79.7	**	75.4	**	69.2	55.5	68.8	45.4	65.7	46.8	63.6	54.0	64.7	41.9
Unskilled	53.8	**	56.5	63.0	70.6*	**	62.5*	**	-	45.5*	57.1*	29.7*	57.6	37.3	67.5*	52.6*	59.6*	25.0
Farmers	72.1	**	69.9	66.7	77.9	**	70.8	**	68.4	46.0	75.9	58.9	67.8	61.4*	62.1*	56.8*	62.7	43.9
Housewives	69.6	**	67.6	47.1	69.4	**	74.8	**	73.4	53.1	66.9	47.2	65.3	53.8	66.7	57.0	70.1	50.8
Protestants	71.2	**	69.9	53.1	77.3	56.4	75.9	60.2	75.2	57.8	70.4	50.4	72.3	54.0	72.0	63.4	71.7	53.6
Catholics	84.5	**	80.6	70.2	87.0	73.2	84.0	67.6	79.5	65.7	79.2	59.1	73.5	58.9	72.6	57.2	79.2	54.3
Jews	92.3	**	94.6	80.0	85.5	70.5*	94.7*	81.4*	97.1*	73.8*	90.5*	73.3	82.6	67.2	87.8*	70.8*	86.4*	75.0*
Other and None	50.9	**	68.2*	53.8*	52.6*	60.5*	63.1	52.2*	50.0*	53.2	70.1	46.2	57.0	44.5	60.8	47.3	68.2	36.4
Total Population	73.0	**	72.9	57.6	79.0	60.4	77.7	62.3	75.8	59.4	72.8	52.5	71.6	54.5	71.4	60.4	73.6	52.5

Table 5.24
Percent Turnout in Current Election, by Political Groups

	1952	1954	1956	1958	1960	1962	1964	1966	1968	1970	1972	1374	1976	1978	1980	1982	1984	1986
Strong Democrats	75.4	**	79.1	66.5	83.1	69.4	81.5	69.9	83.0	68.4	79.8	61.7	80.9	69.3	83.7	75.9	85.2	67.1
Weak and Leaning Dem	70.1	**	69.2	52.4	75.8	53.2	72.4	57.6	71.2	51.8	70.8	50.8	69.3	49.2	66.7	57.0	67.3	50.5
Independent Ind	73.6	**	76.8	47.7	73.8	54.5	61.9	45.5	65.0	46.1	53.4	35.2	56.6	38.9	54.5	35.5	60.1	31.2
Weak and Leaning Rep	77.4	**	77.0	56.5	86.2	64.0	84.4	64.3	80.7	64.0	77.9	59.1	73.7	62.7	76.4	60.8	76.2	52.3
Strong Republicans	92.6	**	80.5	76.5	87.8	77.8	91.7	85.4	86.3	80.4	87.3	75.2	92.1	78.1	88.2	80.0	87.1	67.8
Liberal Self Place 1	**	**	**	**	**	**	**	**	**	**	82.4	50.5	73.7	52.3	82.1	73.0	81.6	61.7
Liberal Self Place 2	**	**	**	**	**	**	**	**	**	**	82.1	60.6	84.2	57.3	75.2	63.8	78.7	58.2
Neutral Self Place 3	**	**	**	**	**	**	**	**	**	**	75.6	59.3	73.4	57.2	76.7	65.5	74.1	52.1
Conserv Self Place 4	**	**	**	**	**	**	**	**	**	**	84.2	70.4	82.2	64.7	80.3	69.1	84.5	60.5
Conserv Self Place 5	**	**	**	**	**	**	**	**	**	**	80.6	58.2	82.2	65.3	80.4	69.7	81.5	63.1
Liberal Index 1	**	**	**	**	**	**	69.2	57.1*	73.6	56.7	87.3	62.3	76.5	**	83.8*	84.3	80.6	62.5
Liberal Index 2	**	**	**	**	**	**	83.2	69.2	84.9	66.3	79.9	53.3	78.0	**	68.3	68.8	74.7	53.3
Neutral Index 3	**	**	**	**	**	**	73.5	53.5	67.5	55.9	70.2	50.7	69.8	**	63.0	56.8	70.8	45.3
Conservative Index 4	**	**	**	**	**	**	80 8	68.3	79.7	63.7	78.8	59.8	77.2	**	79.1	64.8	78.6	60.0
Conservative Index 5	**	**	**	**	**	**	90.1	77.1	88.6	72.8	81.4	59.1	88.8	**	83.5	68.3	95.0	70.3
Total Population	73.0	**	72.9	57.6	79.0	60.4	77.7	62.3	75.8	59.4	72.8	52.5	71.6	54.5	71.4	60.4	73.6	52.5

Table 5.25
Gammas of Social Groups and Political Groups with Turnout in Current Election&

	1952	1954	1956	1958	1960	1962	1964	1966	1968	1970	1972	1974	1976	1978	1980	1982	1984	1986
Age Cohorts	0.15	**	0.21	0.31	0.13	0.22	0.19	0.16	0.08	0.22	0.07	0.31	0.18	0.31	0.27	0.31	0.26	0.43
Education of Respond	0.46	**	0.43	0.28	0.42	0.26	0.35	0.27	0.36	0.34	0.43	0.28	0.40	0.29	0.38	0.34	0.45	0.32
Urbanism	-0.12	**	-0.11	-0.12	-0.15	-0.03	-0.03	0.06	-0.07	-0.05	-0.11	0.00	-0.04	-0.03	-0.03	-0.10	-0.11	-0.07
Family Income	0.45	**	0.39	0.38	0.34	0.28	0.33	0.37	0.40	0.32	0.38	0.27	0.34	0.21	0.32	0.23	0.40	0.26
Sex of Respondent	-0.27	**	-0.30	-0.34	-0.28	-0.12	-0.13	-0.11	-0.11	-0.09	-0.16	-0.13	-0.23	-0.03	-0.08	-0.10	0.00	-0.01
Race of Respondent	-0.76	**	-0.72	-0.46	-0.60	-0.45	-0.36	-0.18	-0.23	-0.27	-0.21	-0.38	-0.17	-0.25	-0.13	0.03	-0.23	-0.06
Union Membership	-0.09	**	-0.10	-0.09	0.10	**	-0.20	-0.01	-0.01	-0.01	-0.08	0.08	-0.19	-0.06	-0.10	-0.12	-0.17	-0.06
Region	0.65	**	0.54	0.53	0.43	0.45	0.38	0.26	0.29	0.42	0.35	0.29	0.27	0.21	0.06	0.13	0.26	0.26
Occupation of Respon	-0.28	**	-0.26	-0.25	-0.33	**	-0.18	**	-0.23	-0.23	-0.25	-0.23	-0.23	-0.28	-0.18	-0.29	-0.19	-0.31	-0.30
Party Identif.@	0.18	**	0.06	0.02	0.11	0.06	0.09	0.06	0.04	0.06	0.07	0.05	0.06	0.06	0.03	-0.07	0.04	-0.05
Lib-Conserv Self Pl@	**	**	**	**	**	**	**	**	**	**	0.02	0.10	0.09	0.13	0.04	0.02	0.07	0.05
Lib to Conserv Index@	**	**	**	**	**	**	0.09	0.11	0.05	0.08	0.02	0.08	0.09	**	0.22	-0.03	0.13	0.13

& Turnout var is: 1. No   2. Yes (see table 5.16).   Sequence of codes within social and political group vars correspond to their category sequences appearing in 5.23 and 5.24.

@ For party identification var description, see Table 2.1; for Liberal-Conservative Self-placement var description, see Table 2.22; for Liberal-Conservative Index var description, see Table 2.23

Table 5.26
Percent Turnout in Current Election, by Independent Variables&

	1952	1954	1956	1958	1960	1962	1964	1966	1968	1970	1972	1974	1976	1978	1980	1982	1984	1986	
Interest Level	**	**	**	**	63.7	44.3	50.0	34.1	51.9	**	39.9	15.3	38.4	30.5	45.5	25.2	46.7	23.9	Hardly
	**	**	**	**	**	**	69.7	50.7	70.4	**	56.8	34.1	54.3	46.1	63.7	48.6	64.9	42.0	Only now
	**	**	**	**	86.6	68.2	82.6	67.2	81.3	**	74.2	52.4	77.4	60.3	76.0	64.7	80.3	56.6	Some
	**	**	**	**	91.3	81.6	85.4	77.9	86.3	**	87.6	70.3	86.0	74.2	86.8	82.6	88.2	74.0	Most
Interest in Campaign	55.2	**	58.3	37.6	56.1	33.8	62.3	32.9	52.2	33.3	50.8	**	47.2	29.2	43.6	30.3	50.4	23.8	Not much
	75.1	**	73.6	62.9	81.5	61.9	77.3	65.9	75.8	58.3	75.8	**	71.9	61.4	73.9	66.6	75.5	58.4	Somewhat
	88.0	**	87.1	82.0	90.4	77.9	87.6	86.1	87.5	79.3	85.9	**	84.0	79.6	89.5	84.4	89.2	83.6	Very
Care Who Wins Pres	61.5	**	62.3	**	64.6	**	66.1	**	66.3	**	59.7	**	61.0	**	61.1	**	62.4	**	Don't care or know
	80.1	**	79.5	71.8	86.6	**	83.5	**	80.4	**	80.8	**	79.7	**	78.9	**	79.6	**	Care
President Race Close	73.7	**	68.7	**	73.1	**	80.0	**	78.2	**	76.2	**	65.6	**	68.3	**	76.4	**	Not close
	79.1	**	77.0	**	84.4	**	77.1	**	78.2	**	73.5	**	74.1	**	73.8	**	72.9	**	Close
Trust in Govt (1)	**	**	**	54.9	**	**	72.5	**	72.4	57.4	68.6	49.6	70.2	55.7	72.4	**	**	**	Cynical
	**	**	**	61.1	**	**	80.4	**	77.0	60.4	74.9	53.4	75.5	55.1	69.9	**	**	**	
	**	**	**	58.7	**	**	79.2	**	78.9	61.5	76.6	58.8	74.1	53.7	74.5	**	**	**	Trusting
Internal Efficacy	58.2	**	57.4	**	63.8	**	70.5	53.0	65.0	49.3	61.4	47.4	61.9	51.8	67.4	**	**	**	Least efficacious
	76.0	**	69.6	**	79.2	**	77.1	62.2	76.6	61.0	68.7	49.9	69.2	50.9	66.4	**	**	**	
	84.4	**	83.1	**	85.7	**	80.9	73.6	82.9	63.5	81.9	59.8	79.9	58.0	78.6	**	**	**	
	89.6	**	91.0	**	91.4	**	87.5	71.5	85.7	70.6	87.5	65.9	90.0	68.5	86.7	**	**	**	Most efficacious
External Efficacy	**	**	**	**	**	**	**	**	61.8	51.3	62.4	43.3	64.4	50.9	63.2	**	**	**	Least efficacious
	**	**	**	**	**	**	**	**	75.4	60.9	76.0	50.3	73.1	51.4	72.2	**	**	**	
	**	**	**	**	**	**	**	**	80.3	60.1	76.5	64.1	81.3	62.8	84.0	**	**	**	
	**	**	**	**	**	**	**	**	87.4	69.1	84.2	69.4	88.1	63.2	84.7	**	**	**	Most efficacious
Govt Responsiveness	**	**	**	**	**	**	69.6	**	62.6	48.6	54.3	35.4	57.7	46.3	56.4	**	**	**	Low
	**	**	**	**	**	**	76.8	**	75.4	53.5	66.2	41.9	68.9	50.4	72.6	**	**	**	
	**	**	**	**	**	**	75.7	**	77.4	61.5	71.2	53.1	71.6	57.3	68.6	**	**	**	
	**	**	**	**	**	**	79.9	**	80.4	61.2	79.7	62.4	78.3	56.7	79.1	**	**	**	
	**	**	**	**	**	**	83.1	**	81.3	69.8	77.5	66.1	81.0	62.7	74.5	**	**	**	Highest
Approve of Protest	**	**	**	**	**	**	**	**	76.7	60.3	72.7	57.7	**	**	**	**	**	**	Disapproval
	**	**	**	**	**	**	**	**	81.4	60.8	74.9	47.1	**	**	**	**	**	**	
	**	**	**	**	**	**	**	**	75.1	60.8	74.4	57.2	**	**	**	**	**	**	
	**	**	**	**	**	**	**	**	82.6	60.0	69.1	48.9	**	**	**	**	**	**	
	**	**	**	**	**	**	**	**	77 4	59.0	77.0	54.4	**	**	**	**	**	**	Approval
Citizen Duty	44.4	**	36.0	**	48.7	**	**	**	**	**	38.2	**	37.5	27.0	42.3	**	**	**	Lowest
	77.1	**	74.4	**	78.9	**	**	**	**	**	74.8	**	71.4	54.1	66.8	**	**	**	
	86.0	**	83.7	**	87.5	**	**	**	**	**	81.6	**	82.8	65.6	80.9	**	**	**	Highest
Trust in People	**	**	**	**	**	**	70.4	**	61.1	**	61.4	35.6	59.1	**	**	**	**	**	Least
	**	**	**	**	**	**	72.9	**	70.5	**	65.4	45.3	66.6	**	**	**	**	**	
	**	**	**	**	**	**	75.7	**	75.3	**	74.5	61.3	72.9	**	**	**	**	**	
	**	**	**	**	**	**	83.5	**	84.5	**	83.7	68.0	82.6	**	**	**	**	**	Most
Total Population	73.0	**	72.9	57.6	79.0	60.4	77.7	62.3	75.8	59.4	72.8	52.5	71.6	54.5	71.4	60.4	73.6	52.5	

& For descriptions of independent vars (respective to their order above), see tables 5.11-5.14, 4.37, 4.40, 4.43, 4.46, 4.55, 4.50, 4.52

Table 5.27
Gammas of Independent Variables with Turnout in Current Election&

	1952	1954	1956	1958	1960	1962	1964	1966	1968	1970	1972	1974	1976	1978	1980	1982	1984	1986
Interest Level	**	**	**	**	0.56	0.49	0.40	0.48	0.45	**	0.55	0.53	0.55	0.44	0.47	0.56	0.50	0.48
Interest in Campaign	0.52	**	0.45	0.58	0.56	0.54	0.44	0.66	0.52	0.56	0.51	**	0.49	0.61	0.63	0.66	0.56	0.69
Care Who Wins Pres.	0.43	**	0.4C	**	0.56	**	0.44	**	0.35	**	0.48	**	0.43	**	0.41	**	0.40	**
President Race Close	0.15	**	0.21	**	0.33	**	-0.09	**	0.00	**	-0.07	**	0.20	**	0.13	**	-0.09	**
Trust in Govt (1)	**	**	**	0.01	**	**	0.10	**	0.12	0.06	0.15	0.13	0.09	-0.03	0.00	**	**	**
Internal Efficacy	0.41	**	0.44	**	0.40	**	0.23	0.26	0.32	0.21	0.37	0.20	0.37	0.15	0.26	**	**	**
External Efficacy	**	**	**	**	**	**	**	**	0.41	0.22	0.33	0.33	0.37	0.16	0.36	**	**	**
Govt Responsiveness	**	**	**	**	**	**	0.15	**	0.17	0.18	0.23	0.30	0.23	0.12	0.19	**	**	**
Approve of Protest	**	**	**	**	**	**	**	**	0.02	-0.01	0.01	-0.03	**	**	**	**	**	**
Citizen Duty	0.53	**	0.53	**	0.49	**	**	**	**	**	0.47	**	0.51	0.41	0.47	**	**	**
Trust in People	**	**	**	**	**	**	0.23	**	0.36	**	0.35	0.40	0.35	**	**	**	**	**

& Turnout var is: 1. No 2. Yes (see table 5.16). Sequence of codes within independent vars correspond to their category
sequences appearing in 5.26.

Table 5.28
Electoral Participation Index by Social Groups, Summarized by a Percentage Difference Index#

	1952	1954	1956	1958	1960	1962	1964	1966	1968	1970	1972	1974	1976	1978	1980	1982	1984	1986
1959 or later Cohort	**	**	**	**	**	**	**	**	**	**	**	**	**	-51	4	-42	-8	-48
1943 - 1958 Cohort	**	**	**	**	**	**	-14*	-31	6	-21	13	-36	10	-24	7	-11	20	-21
1927 - 1942 Cohort	-7	**	-5	-47	18	-24	19	-15	24	0	22	-23	29	-1	26	1	26	6
1911 - 1926 Cohort	2	**	15	-23	29	-7	28	-1	27	-3	18	-10	27	2	19	4	26	1
1895 - 1910 Cohort	13	**	19	-14	25	-1	19	-9	12	-11	3	-19	10	-14	6	-15	-4	-16
Before 1895 Cohort	2	**	8	-19	16	-15	5	-27	-13	-29	-30	-35	-33	-8*	-	-	-	-
Grade School	-17	**	-11	-39	-2	-32	-7	-34	-10	-34	-20	-46	-13	-33	-12	-36	-21	-41
High School	14	**	13	-28	28	-11	19	-14	19	-16	7	-32	7	-25	2	-21	3	-32
College	39	**	46	2	51	13	52	18	40	36	44	3	48	13	37	13	40	4
Central cities	8	**	16	-19	24	-12	20	-18	24	-2	18	-15	21	-13	19	0	23	-12
Suburbs	11	**	20	-19	29	-4	28	0	24	-3	23	-24	20	-7	13	-8	19	-16
Non-urban Areas	-5	**	5	-32	21	-18	14	-16	11	-15	4	-31	13	-18	9	-14	9	-22
Income Percentile 0-16	-26	**	-25	-46	-6	-37	-9	-45	-16	-39	-15	-51	-16	-34	-10	-29	-16	-41
Income Percentile 17-33	-11	**	-3	-40	3	-33	11	-26	2	-24	0	-37	5	-28	2	-20	7	-29
Income Percentile 34-67	5	**	17	-24	27	-7	22	-12	27	-15	9	-26	16	-10	15	-3	18	-18
Income Percentile 68-95	24	**	31	-7	41	7	37	6	38	17	39	-5	37	2	32	5	33	1
Income Percentile 95-100	57	**	52	16	58	32	48	35	46	39	59	31	62	23	49	13	58	22
Males	16	**	27	-11	32	-1	28	-4	27	0	23	-17	29	-6	20	-2	19	-13
Females	-5	**	0	-38	17	-19	14	-17	12	-14	7	-29	10	-17	9	-13	14	-20
Whites	11	**	17	-23	28	-9	23	-9	19	-6	15	-21	20	-10	16	-8	19	-15
Blacks	-53	**	-40	-41	-15	-35	5	-31	18	-24	4	-49	3	-28	1	-5	3	-23
Union Household	9	**	19	-17	23	**	27	-9	21	-9	17	-26	25	-8	20	0	24	-13
Non-union Household	3	**	9	-28	25	**	18	-12	17	-7	13	-23	16	-14	12	-10	14	-18
South	-24	**	-11	-48	11	-29	13	-27	11	-27	2	-39	7	-19	9	-15	3	-27
Non-south	15	**	21	-16	30	-2	24	-5	22	2	20	-16	23	-9	16	-4	23	-11
Professional	41	**	41	-4	46	**	43	**	42	22	40	8	46	17	39	17	41	14
White collar	21	**	24	-11	42	**	37	**	31	7	21	-23	31	-10	18	-7	23	-13
Blue collar	12	**	13	-22	21	**	12	**	8	-19	6	-37	9	-26	3	-22	4	-33
Unskilled	-29	**	-13	-23	6*	**	3*	**	-	-36*	6*	-65*	-1	-44	5*	-18*	-5*	-45
Farmers	-6	**	4	-28	18	**	0	**	2	-29	0	-23	-4	-2*	-7*	-14*	-15	-30
Housewives	-7	**	0	-43	9	**	12	**	10	-21	-2	-34	0	-21	-3	-17	5	-28
Protestants	1	**	9	-29	25	-15	18	-14	18	-12	9	-28	18	-13	14	-5	13	-16
Catholics	17	**	19	-14	26	2	28	-8	20	2	22	-17	20	-6	12	-11	24	-16
Jews	27	**	41	0	11	-5*	34*	21*	52*	22*	61*	8	52	13	44*	17*	51*	32*
Other and No Religion	-25	**	0*	-31*	-13*	-11*	6	-20*	-6*	-4	15	-16	2	-28	6	-22	11	-40
Total Population	4	**	12	-25	24	-11	20	-12	18	-8	13	-24	18	-13	14	-8	16	-17

PDI is proportion "both" minus proportion "non-participant" (see table 5.17)

Table 5.29
Electoral Participation Index by Political Groups, Summarized by a Percentage Difference Index#

	1952	1954	1956	1958	1960	1962	1964	1966	1968	1970	1972	1974	1976	1978	1980	1982	1984	1986
Strong Democrats	12	**	24	-8	35	8	25	-4	34	8	22	-10	36	10	33	20	39	8
Weak and Leaning Democrats	-7	**	2	-33	12	-26	9	-21	8	-18	11	-28	12	-22	1	-16	6	-25
Independent Independents	-2	**	9	-42	12	-23	-12	-35	-1	-30	-18	-48	-8	-41	-18	-47	-10	-50
Weak and Leaning Republicans	10	**	18	-31	34	-9	31	-9	24	-6	20	-16	18	3	26	-11	15	-15
Strong Republicans	37	**	32	-2	48	22	57	37	45	32	38	14	66	29	54	34	47	12
Liberal Self Placement 1	**	**	**	**	**	**	**	**	**	**	51	-17	39	-5	40	18	43	5
Liberal Self Placement 2	**	**	**	**	**	**	**	**	**	**	39	-14	40	-1	28	6	25	-5
Neutral Self Placement 3	**	**	**	**	**	**	**	**	**	**	16	-18	21	-10	15	2	15	-18
Conservative Self Placement 4	**	**	**	**	**	**	**	**	**	**	34	5	42	9	28	6	30	-5
Conservative Self Placement 5	**	**	**	**	**	**	**	**	**	**	28	-11	41	8	34	14	36	6
Liberal Index 1	**	**	**	**	**	**	21	-6*	21	0	48	4	37	**	49*	43	37	6
Liberal Index 2	**	**	**	**	**	**	34	-2	40	8	34	-19	31	**	17	11	20	-14
Neutral Index 3	**	**	**	**	**	**	4	-29	-1	-18	10	-28	14	**	0	-18	8	-28
Conservative Index 4	**	**	**	**	**	**	27	0	26	-1	22	-15	30	**	22	2	26	-8
Conservative Index 5	**	**	**	**	**	**	68	28	49	22	29	-2	61	**	45	13	62	23
Total Population	4	**	12	-25	24	-11	20	-12	18	-8	13	-24	18	-13	14	-8	16	-17

PDI is proportion "both" minus proportion "non-participant" (see table 5.17)

Table 5.30
Gammas of Social Groups and Political Groups with Electoral Participation Index&

	1952	1954	1956	1958	1960	1962	1964	1966	1968	1970	1972	1974	1976	1978	1980	1982	1984	1986
Age Cohorts	0.05	**	0.07	0.21	-0.01	0.10	-0.03	0.04	-0.06	0.00	-0.09	0.15	0.01	0.16	0.05	0.15	0.08	0.26
Education of Respond	0.41	**	0.37	0.28	0.37	0.30	0.42	0.34	0.34	0.44	0.42	0.35	0.42	0.34	0.36	0.35	0.42	0.34
Urbanism	-0.10	**	-0.11	-0.14	-0.03	-0.06	-0.07	0.00	-0.11	-0.11	-0.13	-0.11	-0.06	-0.04	-0.07	-0.10	-0.10	-0.07
Family Income	0.39	**	0.36	0.31	0.33	0.32	0.30	0.35	0.33	0.35	0.35	0.30	0.32	0.25	0.28	0.21	0.29	0.26
Sex of Respondent	-0.25	**	-0.30	-0.33	-0.17	-0.19	-0.16	-0.15	-0.18	-0.14	-0.18	-0.15	-0.21	-0.11	-0.13	-0.12	-0.07	-0.06
Race of Respondent	-0.70	**	-0.57	-0.24	-0.44	-0.30	-0.19	-0.25	-0.01	-0.19	-0.11	-0.34	-0.19	-0.18	-0.17	0.03	-0.18	-0.08
Union Membership	-0.08	**	-0.12	-0.12	0.03	**	-0.09	-0.03	-0.05	0.02	-0.04	0.04	-0.09	-0.06	-0.09	-0.11	-0.11	-0.05
Region	0.44	**	0.33	0.41	0.20	0.31	0.11	0.25	0.12	0.30	0.19	0.27	0.17	0.12	0.09	0.12	0.22	0.17
Occupation of Respon	-0.28	**	-0.22	-0.26	-0.24	**	-0.22	**	-0.19	-0.25	-0.24	-0.24	-0.28	-0.22	-0.26	-0.20	-0.26	-0.27
Party Identif.@	0.13	**	0.06	-0.03	0.10	0.03	0.11	0.10	0.04	0.04	0.06	0.05	0.06	0.07	0.08	-0.05	0.02	-0.02
Lib-Cons Self Pl@	**	**	**	**	**	**	**	**	**	**	-0.08	0.07	0.04	0.08	0.02	0.01	0.03	0.05
Lib to Cons Index@	**	**	**	**	**	**	0.10	0.12	0.03	0.06	-0.06	0.05	0.09	**	0.12	-0.01	0.10	0.10

& For electoral parcipitation index description, see table 5.17. Sequence of codes within social and political group vars correspond to their category sequences appearing in 5.28 and 5.29.

@ For party identification var description, see Table 2.1; for Liberal-Conservative Self-placement var description, see Table 2.22; for Liberal-Conservative Index var description, see Table 2.23

Table 5.31
Electoral Participation Index by Independent Variables, Summarized by a Percentage Difference Index#

	1952	1954	1956	1958	1960	1962	1964	1966	1968	1970	1972	1974	1976	1978	1980	1982	1984	1986	
Interest Level	**	**	**	**	-11	-42	-42	-61	-38	**	-50	-80	-47	-60	-40	-69	-37	-68	Hardly
	**	**	**	**	**	**	-2	-40	0	**	-19	-56	-19	-30	-2	-31	-6	-38	Only now
	**	**	**	**	37	4	27	-9	27	**	16	-26	25	0	23	-4	28	-10	Some
	**	**	**	**	60	29	46	25	51	**	45	6	51	26	45	37	49	24	Most
Interest in Campaign	-33	**	-19	-60	-26	-58	-16	-60	-32	-57	-31	**	-29	-57	-36	-60	-28	-66	Not much
	2	**	10	-22	17	-17	15	-15	13	-11	15	**	13	-3	14	-3	15	-10	Somewhat
	37	**	47	23	61	29	48	40	49	32	44	**	48	37	51	43	53	42	Very
Care Who Wins Pres	-25	**	-13	**	-7	**	-7	**	-9	**	-11	**	-5	**	-9	**	-8	**	Don't Care
	19	**	27	-3	39	**	34	**	32	16	28	1	35	17	29	18	29	14	Care
President Race Close	6	**	8	**	16	**	23	**	22	**	19	**	12	**	9	**	21	**	Not close
	14	**	20	**	35	**	22	**	25	**	17	**	23	**	18	**	15	**	Close
Trust in Govt	**	**	**	-24	**	**	17	**	14	-14	6	-30	16	-11	16	**	**	**	Cynical
	**	**	**	-19	**	**	28	**	23	-4	20	-21	27	-8	11	**	**	**	
	**	**	**	-26	**	**	20	**	22	-3	20	-14	18	-17	16	**	**	**	Trusting
Internal Efficacy	-23	**	-16	**	-10	**	3	-33	-5	-30	-12	-40	-3	-23	-4	**	**	**	Least efficacious
	4	**	4	**	25	**	15	-15	18	-7	7	-32	12	-17	5	**	**	**	
	28	**	29	**	37	**	33	11	31	-1	29	-9	36	-5	30	**	**	**	
	39	**	47	**	49	**	44	24	49	25	50	11	55	20	52	**	**	**	Most efficacious
External Efficacy	**	**	**	**	**	**	**	**	-6	-25	-6	-42	5	-21	-1	**	**	**	Least efficacious
	**	**	**	**	**	**	**	**	14	-9	18	-29	23	-12	17	**	**	**	
	**	**	**	**	**	**	**	**	28	4	21	-4	35	2	38	**	**	**	
	**	**	**	**	**	**	**	**	39	11	39	6	45	5	39	**	**	**	Most efficacious
Govt Responsiveness	**	**	**	**	**	**	3	**	-13	-30	-22	-52	-10	-32	-10	**	**	**	Lowest
	**	**	**	**	**	**	22	**	12	-23	2	-39	15	-17	12	**	**	**	
	**	**	**	**	**	**	14	**	26	-10	11	-21	16	-9	15	**	**	**	
	**	**	**	**	**	**	21	**	27	1	28	-12	29	-7	24	**	**	**	
	**	**	**	**	**	**	34	**	31	15	24	3	41	1	27	**	**	**	Highest
Approve of Protest	**	**	**	**	**	**	**	**	25	-4	13	-32	**	**	**	**	**	**	Disapproval
	**	**	**	**	**	**	**	**	20	-1	17	-21	**	**	**	**	**	**	
	**	**	**	**	**	**	**	**	34	-7	12	-26	**	**	**	**	**	**	
	**	**	**	**	**	**	**	**	32	5	30	-14	**	**	**	**	**	**	Approval
Citizen Duty	-39	**	-45	**	-30	**	**	**	**	**	-40	**	-35	-58	-36	**	**	**	Lowest
	10	**	14	**	23	**	**	**	**	**	18	**	18	-10	11	**	**	**	
	21	**	28	**	40	**	**	**	**	**	26	**	35	4	25	**	**	**	Highest
Trust in People	**	**	**	**	**	**	9	**	-2	**	-3	-49	-1	**	**	**	**	**	Least
	**	**	**	**	**	**	6	**	13	**	-2	-39	12	**	**	**	**	**	
	**	**	**	**	**	**	15	**	15	**	20	-13	23	**	**	**	**	**	
	**	**	**	**	**	**	33	**	29	**	32	0	35	**	**	**	**	**	Most
Total Population	4	**	12	-25	24	-11	20	-12	18	-8	13	-24	18	-13	14	-8	16	-17	

PDI is proportion "both" minus proportion "non-participant" (see table 5.17). For descriptions of independent vars (respective to their order above), see tables 5.11-5.14, 4.37, 4.40, 4.43, 4.46, 4.55, 4.50, 4.52

Table 5.32
Gammas of Independent Variables with Electoral Participation Index&

	1952	1954	1956	1958	1960	1962	1964	1966	1968	1970	1972	1974	1976	1978	1980	1982	1984	1986
Interest Level	**	**	**	**	0.56	0.51	0.48	0.54	0.53	**	0.52	0.52	0.55	0.46	0.46	C.56	0.49	0.49
Interest in Campaign	0.55	**	0.47	0.64	0.64	0.61	0.49	0.68	0.55	0.58	0.49	**	0.50	0.60	0.57	0.65	0.54	0.67
Care Who Wins Pres	0.51	**	0.43	**	0.51	**	0.46	**	0.46	**	0.41	**	0.42	**	0.41	**	0.40	**
President Race Close	0.10	**	0.14	**	0.23	**	-0.02	**	0.03	**	-0.03	**	0.13	**	0.10	**	-0.06	**
Trust in Govt (1)	**	**	**	-0.04	**	**	-0.01	**	0.05	0.08	0.10	0.13	0.04	-0.03	-0.02	**	**	**
Internal Efficacy	0.38	**	0.36	**	0.33	**	0.26	0.34	0.34	0.26	0.35	0.28	0.34	0.19	0.30	**	**	**
External Efficacy	**	**	**	**	**	**	**	**	0.31	0.24	0.29	0.34	0.27	0.17	0.30	**	**	**
Govt Responsiveness	**	**	**	**	**	**	0.15	**	0.16	0.24	0.20	0.27	0.20	0.12	0.16	**	**	**
Approve of Protest	**	**	**	**	**	**	**	**	0.09	0.07	0.12	0.04	**	**	**	**	**	**
Citizen Duty	0.36	**	0.38	**	0.37	**	**	**	**	**	0.32	**	0.37	0.33	0.31	**	**	**
Trust in People	**	**	**	**	**	**	0.20	**	0.21	**	0.25	0.36	0.24	**	**	**	**	**

& For electoral participation index description, see table 5.17. Sequence of codes within independent vars correspond to their category sequences appearing in 5.31.

Chapter 6. The Vote

In previous chapters, we described the electorate in terms of socioeconomic groups, partisanship and ideology, policy preference, and level of participation. We now examine how these characteristics are related to and, presumably, influence the vote.

An analysis of the vote decision, the partisan direction of the electoral choice for any single election, provides evidence suggesting the relative impact of partisan ties, policy preferences, and candidate popularity on the election outcome. The study of election outcomes over time, however, goes well beyond the question of what determined a single vote decision and begins to describe larger aspects of the political process. When studied over time, the vote becomes an indicator of broader social and political shifts; the election outcomes serve as an instrument for examining social trends rather than the motivation of individual voters. Viewed within a longer time frame, the vote represents the contours of American politics rather than the events, candidates, issues, and group cleavages which dominate any specific election. Eventually, after data have been gathered at enough points in time, more systematic classifications of elections, not just categorizations of factors affecting election outcomes, may be possible. The data presented in this chapter provide the starting point for such an enterprise.

Employing the various measures introduced earlier, this chapter begins (Tables 6.1-6.8) with a presentation of the presidential vote across time for demographic and political groups. The reader should note that, for parsimonious presentation, only the proportion of respondents voting for the democratic candidate is provided in the tables throughout this chapter. The proportion voting republican can be accurately estimated, except for 1968 and 1980, by subtracting the percentage voting democratic from 100 percent.

As Table 6.5 details, there are a few demographic trends visible in the democratic presidential vote. For example, since 1960 well over 70% of blacks vote for the democratic presidential candidate; with the exception of 1984, the South is not solidly democratic; as levels of income and education rise, the proportion of respondents voting for the democratic presidential candidate falls. The principle message of Table 6.5 is that many of the explanations of the presumed realignment of social group support for the party vote are explanations of changes that really have not occurred. To the extent that the "New Deal Alignments" pit the well-educated against the less well-educated, the rich against the poor, the farm against the central city, or the union family against the non-unionized, 1984 marked an extension and a high point, not the low point, in 30-year trends of partisan polarization on these dimensions. It is true that blue-collar/professional differences were less in 1984 (although not in 1976) than in

the 1950s, the partisan vote differences between protestants and catholics or southerners and nonsoutherners have increased, and gender differences have reversed. But the constancy of many correlates of party identification as illuminated in Chapter 2 are repeated here for the vote with a clarity that undermines much of the overblown prose arguing a new era of dealignment and realignment. The past thirty years have been a time of change, but change of some subtlety and greater complexity that is often portrayed. Many of the nuances are exposed in later tables of this chapter.

We then turn (Tables 6.9-6.14) to an examination of two closely related topics. The first concerns the time of the vote decision, while the second involves the extent of ticket-splitting. Many voters report that they know who they will vote for far in advance of the actual campaign, although that figure has declined for the elections since 1956 (Table 6.09). The recall data on time of vote decision are heavily influenced by strength of party identification (Tables 6.10-6.11), and they suggest that enduring support for a particular party helps partisans to make their decision early. Tables 6.12-6.14, relating party identification to frequency of voting for the same party and ticket-splitting, also reveal more consistent behavior across time for strong partisans.

We subsequently (Tables 6.15-6.24) relate the presidential vote to opinions of Presidential performance, to trust in government, and to a range of policy questions on civil rights, foreign policy and social welfare. Some of the issues seem to be centrally and primarily related to enduring party cleavage-- see Table 6.22, where no matter who the incumbent is, those at one end of the 7-point scale on services and spending or government guarantees of jobs tend to vote democratic, while those at the opposite end do not. Other tables clearly show the interesting effects of party identification and incumbent evaluation (e.g., Table 6.15). Table 6.24, displaying the gamma correlation of selected issues with democratic presidential vote, summarize this series of tables.

The next tables (Tables 6.25 - 6.27) explore the relationship between the two-party vote and the affective feelings toward the candidates and parties. These tables are based on the "likes-dislikes" question series, which are also used (and explained further) in Chapter Two.

In the series of tables which follow (Tables 6.28-6.34), we compare the two-party congressional voting over time, for political and social groups. The chief thing we have noted is the stability of the vote over time. (Chapter 7 incorporates added material on congressional evaluations).

The last series of tables (Tables 6.35-6.40) present ticket splitting over time. Ticket splitting -- that is,

casting votes for different parties and the presidential and
congressional levels -- increased over time. In 1952, only 12%
of the voters ticket-split their vote between the congressional
and presidential candidates. In 1984, 26% of the voters split
their vote.   Democratic Congress members   and republican
presidential candidates benefitted the most from such ticket
splitting.

Table 6.1
Presidential Vote, 2 Major Parties&

	1952	1956	1960	1964	1968	1972	1976	1980	1984
Democratic vote	41.9%	40.4%	49.2%	67.5%	46.2%	35.7%	51.1%	43.7%	41.8%
Republican vote	58.1	59.6	50.8	32.5	53.8	64.3	48.9	56.3	58.2
Total	100%	100%	100%	100%	100%	100%	100%	100%	100%
N	1235	1266	1421	1111	911	1587	1631	877	1376

& Note that all percentages for "Democratic Presidential Vote" following table 6.4 are based on 100% minus Republican vote

Table 6.2
Presidential Vote, 3 Parties

	1952	1956	1960	1964	1968	1972	1976	1980	1984
Democratic vote	41.8%	40.2%	48.9%	67.4%	40.9%	35.3%	50.2%	39.4%	41.4%
Republican vote	57.9	59.4	50.6	32.4	47.6	63.6	47.9	50.8	57.7
Other vote&	0.2	0.3	0.5	0.2	11.5	1.1	1.9	9.8	0.9
Total	100%	100%	100%	100%	100%	100%	100%	100%	100%
N	1238	1270	1428	1113	1029	1605	1663	972	1389

& Most percentages for "other" vote based on small Ns: (see Table 6.4)

Table 6.3
Presidential Vote, for 3 Parties and Non-voters

	1952	1956	1960	1964	1968	1972	1976	1980	1984
Democratic vote	30.5%	20.3%	38.6%	52.2%	30.8%	25.4%	35.6%	27.9%	30.0%
Republican vote	42.2	43.2	39.8	25.1	35.9	45.9	34.0	35.9	41.8
Other vote&	0.2	0.2	0.4	0.1	8.6	0.8	1.4	6.9	0.7
Non-voters	27.2	27.3	21.2	22.5	24.6	27.9	29.1	29.3	27.4
Total	100%	100%	100%	100%	100%	100%	100%	100%	100%
N	1701	1747	1812	1437	1365	2226	2346	1375	1914

& Most percentages for "other" vote based on small Ns: (see Table 6.4)

Table 6.4
Presidential Vote, Sample Size, for 3 Parties and Non-voters&

	1952	1956	1960	1964	1968	1972	1976	1980	1984
Democratic vote	518	511	699	750	421	566	834	383	575
Republican vote	717	755	722	361	490	1021	797	494	801
Other vote	3	4	7	2	118	18	32	95	13
Non-voters	463	477	384	324	336	621	683	403	525
Total	100%	100%	100%	100%	100%	100%	100%	100%	100%
N	1701	1747	1812	1437	1365	2226	2346	1375	1914

& Sample size tables can be derived for tables 6.1 - 6.2 from the data appearing here.

Table 6.5
Democratic Percentage of Two-Party Presidential Vote, for Social Groups&

	1952	1956	1960	1964	1968	1972	1976	1980	1984
1959 or later cohort	**	**	**	**	**	**	**	52%*	42%
1943-1958 cohort	**	**	**	-	49%	47%	53%	41	41
1927-1942 cohort	43%	42%	51%	71%	50	35	47	38	40
1911-1926 cohort	47	41	51	69	43	30	53	47	44
1895-1910 cohort	39	39	50	66	46	32	52	50	42
Before 1895 cohort	38	38	40	56	38*	22*	33*	-	-
Grade school	49%	42%	56%	80%	61%	40%	67%	64%	62%
High school	43	44	53	69	48	33	54	46	42
College	27	31	36	54	37	37	43	37	38
Central cities	50%	45%	60%	73%	58%	50%	57%	63%	60%
Suburbs	38	36	44	63	45	31	50	36	35
Non-urban areas	39	40	47	68	40	30	48	37	39
Income percentile 0-16	43%	41%	46%	74%	49%	44%	67%	60%	64%
Income percentile 17-33	46	44	45	71	48	38	60	52	53
Income percentile 34-67	46	43	55	74	46	37	53	41	43
Income percentile 68-95	40	43	51	60	47	34	45	40	34
Income percentile 95-100	23	23	24	54	33	18	23	18	19
Males	43%	44%	52%	66%	45%	32%	51%	40%	38%
Females	41	37	47	69	47	39	51	47	45
Whites	40%	39%	48%	65%	41%	30%	47%	37%	37%
Blacks	80	64*	71	100	97	87	95	93	91
Union household	56%	53%	64%	83%	56%	43%	64%	55%	57%
Non-union household	36	36	44	62	43	33	47	40	37
South	51%	49%	51%	65%	50%	34%	54%	47%	46%
Non-south	40	38	49	68	45	37	50	42	40
Professional	31%	33%	42%	54%	40%	34%	41%	39%	39%
White collar	35	37	43	66	45	37	47	39	39
Blue collar	56	49	63	80	54	39	66	51	49
Unskilled	66	63	33*	-	-	-	66*	42*	72*
Farmers	36	48	47	65*	42*	20*	44*	-	23*
Housewives	37	35	43	66	44	30	46	44	35
Protestants	36%	36%	37%	63%	39%	31%	47%	43%	37%
Catholics	52	46	83	79	60	40	58	46	46
Jewish	72*	77	89	89*	93*	69*	71*	58*	69*
Other and no religion	54*	57*	-	68*	-	61	64	41	52
Total population	42%	40%	49%	68%	46%	36%	51%	44%	42%

& Note that, in this table and all percentage tables remaining in Chapter 6, percent Democratic Presidential (or Congressional) vote is computed by subtracting the % Republican vote from 100%, i.e. third party and non-voters are not included as valid data

Table 6.6
Democratic Percentage of Two-Party Presidential Vote, for Political Groups

	1952	1956	1960	1964	1968	1972	1976	1980	1984
Strong Democrats	84%	85%	91%	95%	92%	73%	92%	89%	89%
Weak Democrats	62	63	72	82	68	49	75	65	68
Independent Democrats	61	68	90	90	64	61	76	61	79
Independent Independents	20	17	46	77	30	30	43	26	28
Independent Republicans	7	7	12	25	5	13	14	13	7
Weak Republicans	7	7	13	43	11	9	22	5	6
Strong Republicans	2	1	2	10	3	3	3	5	3
Liberal self-placement 1	**	**	**	**	**	83%	84%	92%	77%
Liberal self-placement 2	**	**	**	**	**	56	73	60	67
Neutral self-placement 3	**	**	**	**	**	31	53	39	45
Cons. self-placement 4	**	**	**	**	**	15	26	30	22
Cons. self-placement 5	**	**	**	**	**	10	18	18	15
Liberal index 1	**	**	**	89%	90%*	90%	86%*	100%*	96%*
Liberal index 2	**	**	**	85	64	61	76	72	65
Neutral index 3	**	**	**	77	49	37	60	49	39
Conservative index 4	**	**	**	50	35	18	32	31	23
Conservative index 5	**	**	**	20	9	7	12	5	4
Total population	42%	40%	49%	68%	46%	36%	51%	44%	42%

Table 6.7
Sample Size of All Presidential Voters by Social Groups

	1952	1956	1960	1964	1968	1972	1976	1980	1984
1959 or later cohort	**	**	**	**	**	**	**	44	151
1943-1958 cohort	**	**	**	10	75	403	498	276	529
1927-1942 cohort	76	178	276	342	284	446	425	224	319
1911-1926 cohort	453	516	561	401	313	432	433	224	275
1895-1910 cohort	373	354	390	261	191	253	243	102	88
Before 1895 cohort	264	198	194	96	45	46	23	5	1
Grade school	401	320	366	235	154	241	214	89	98
High school	568	645	693	577	454	761	745	409	585
College	210	295	357	295	303	584	668	376	685
Central cities	410	322	324	320	243	399	441	240	312
Suburbs	383	353	394	360	296	529	582	335	606
Non-urban areas	442	591	703	431	372	659	608	302	458
Income percentile 0-16	167	142	174	168	108	234	157	108	127
Income percentile 17-33	171	245	220	182	160	153	264	124	187
Income percentile 34-67	274	393	409	285	294	568	477	290	452
Income percentile 68-95	493	316	528	353	276	491	525	221	392
Income percentile 95-100	57	120	79	85	55	100	108	51	94
Males	578	613	681	507	390	709	718	395	600
Females	603	653	740	604	521	878	913	482	776
Whites	1127	1213	1340	1014	816	1430	1458	765	1220
Blacks	51	50	75	94	87	138	132	105	129
Union household	330	356	362	290	222	406	395	228	315
Non-union household	843	907	1040	821	687	1166	1219	645	1060
South	237	276	405	297	217	465	475	322	411
Non-south	998	990	1016	814	694	1122	1156	555	965
Professional	208	238	253	228	208	376	408	250	396
White collar	146	147	223	158	142	248	287	163	327
Blue collar	245	307	439	307	234	457	470	269	383
Unskilled	92	60	24	20	10	19	34	24	25
Farmers	86	79	81	49	33	41	47	14	39
Housewives	394	421	374	332	254	391	329	127	176
Protestants	817	884	1028	763	635	1066	1084	581	834
Catholics	287	297	318	272	219	403	414	198	378
Jewish	47	53	53	36	29	36	40	26	36
Other and no religion	26	30	20	40	20	79	90	66	123
Total population	1235	1266	1421	1111	911	1587	1631	877	1376

Table 6.8
Sample Size of All Presidential Voters by Political Groups

	1952	1956	1960	1964	1968	1972	1976	1980	1984
Strong Democrats	262	285	301	319	205	252	270	189	265
Weak Democrats	274	269	339	262	204	396	374	186	256
Independent Democrats	118	80	79	90	77	160	186	81	128
Independent Independents	61	115	113	61	69	130	172	73	109
Independent Republicans	90	108	106	68	87	184	174	98	184
Weak Republicans	170	193	206	162	151	247	250	138	211
Strong Republicans	200	210	253	144	117	211	201	108	216
Liberal self-placement 1	**	**	**	**	**	151	137	63	137
Liberal self-placement 2	**	**	**	**	**	167	158	74	142
Neutral self-placement 3	**	**	**	**	**	421	434	175	320
Cons. self-placement 4	**	**	**	**	**	260	242	130	224
Cons. self-placement 5	**	**	**	**	**	193	261	160	238
Liberal index 1	**	**	**	54	30	61	41	26	49
Liberal index 2	**	**	**	223	204	293	286	122	335
Neutral index 3	**	**	**	431	293	324	456	158	359
Conservative index 4	**	**	**	302	312	536	520	359	417
Conservative index 5	**	**	**	81	53	115	110	95	95
Total population	1235	1266	1421	1111	911	1587	1631	877	1376

Table 6.9
Time of Presidential Election Vote Decision

	1952	1956	1960	1964	1968	1972	1976	1980	1984
Knew All Along	32%	45%	25%	18%	21%	34%	20%	20%	30%
When Candidate Announced	4	15	6	23	14	11	14	20	22
During Convention	32	19	31	25	24	18	21	18	18
Post-Convention	21	12	26	21	19	24	22	15	17
Last 2 wks of Campaign	9	8	9	9	15	8	17	17	10
Election Day	2	2	3	4	7	5	7	9	4
Total	100%	100%	100%	100%	100%	100%	100%	100%	100%
N	1202	1230	1385	1089	960	1487	1638	984	1391
PDI#	0	24	-13	-16	-20	-4	-27	-21	0

PDI is proportion "knew all along" minus proportion "post-convention" through "election day"

Presidential Vote

Table 6.10
Time of Presidential Election Vote Decision, in Percents, for Party Identification Groups

	1952	1956	1960	1964	1968	1972	1976	1980	1984	
Strong Democrats	41%	59%	33%	26%	29%	37%	26%	37%	35%	Knew All Along
	2	6	8	33	18	10	17	20	22	When Candidate Announced
	29	15	31	24	24	17	24	16	19	During Convention
	20	11	22	13	16	21	19	13	14	Post Convention
	7	5	6	4	8	10	9	11	8	Last 2 Wks of Campaign
	2	3	0	1	6	5	4	4	3	Election Day
Weak Democrats	26%	43%	19%	15%	19%	25%	19%	16%	18%	Knew All Along
	2	7	5	23	16	10	12	19	21	When Candidate Announced
	28	21	24	26	16	19	18	16	18	During Convention
	26	14	32	24	23	26	26	19	24	Post Convention
	14	12	15	10	17	12	18	20	15	Last 2 Wks of Campaign
	4	3	5	2	10	8	6	12	5	Election Day
Independent Democrats	21%	32%	21%	9%	10%	26%	8%	8%	25%	Knew All Along
	0	11	4	19	10	9	16	13	14	When Candidate Announced
	26	16	21	29	25	16	16	15	19	During Convention
	30	27	24	22	26	26	20	23	20	Post Convention
	17	10	21	13	18	13	28	20	18	Last 2 Wks of Campaign
	5	4	8	7	9	11	12	20	5	Election Day
Independent Independents	24%	31%	16%	17%	20%	30%	10%	13%	22%	Knew All Along
	5	11	4	23	5	9	6	17	17	When Candidate Announced
	22	17	30	17	16	18	13	13	20	During Convention
	24	17	34	25	19	33	27	24	17	Post Convention
	19	18	14	12	31	7	27	25	17	Last 2 Wks of Campaign
	7	5	2	6	10	4	16	8	7	Election Day
Independent Republicans	23%	43%	20%	3%	17%	28%	19%	19%	30%	Knew All Along
	7	20	6	21	8	11	16	19	22	When Candidate Announced
	42	25	32	21	26	23	24	22	18	During Convention
	25	10	37	37	23	26	15	12	18	Post Convention
	3	3	4	9	17	7	17	17	10	Last 2 Wks of Campaign
	0	0	2	9	9	5	10	12	2	Election Day
Weak Republicans	28%	40%	23%	14%	18%	36%	20%	16%	31%	Knew All Along
	8	25	5	15	15	12	12	24	27	When Candidate Announced
	37	18	28	25	24	21	20	21	17	During Convention
	18	11	29	25	20	21	25	11	18	Post Convention
	7	5	9	15	15	6	19	20	5	Last 2 Wks of Campaign
	2	1	6	6	8	4	5	9	3	Election Day
Strong Republicans	43%	49%	30%	19%	28%	56%	32%	23%	49%	Knew All Along
	4	28	8	18	17	15	17	32	23	When Candidate Announced
	40	18	48	30	44	12	32	28	14	During Convention
	10	3	15	19	7	16	13	8	10	Post Convention
	3	2	0	9	5	1	5	6	3	Last 2 Wks of Campaign
	0	0	0	5	0	1	1	3	1	Election Day

Table 6.11
Time of Presidential Election Vote Decision, for Party Identification Groups, Summarized by a Percentage Difference Index#

	1952	1956	1960	1964	1968	1972	1976	1980	1984
Strong Democrats	12	40	5	9	1	1	-7	10	11
Weak Democrats	-18	14	-33	-21	-30	-21	-32	-35	-26
Independent Democrats	-32	-8	-32	-33	-44	-24	-51	-56	-18
Independent Independents	-25	-9	-33	-26	-40	-13	-61	-44	-20
Independent Republicans	-6	30	-23	-52	-32	-11	-24	-22	0
Weak Republicans	1	23	-20	-32	-25	5	-29	-23	5
Strong Republicans	31	44	15	-15	16	38	14	6	34
Total population	0	24	-13	-16	-20	-4	-27	-21	0

PDI is proportion "knew all along" minus proportion "post-convention" through "election day"

Time of Presidential Vote Decision

Table 6.12
Frequency of Presidential Vote for the Same Party

QUESTION: Have you always voted for the same party or
have you voted for different parties for President?

	1952	1956	1960	1964	1968	1972	1976	1980
Different	29%	38%	42%	39%	43%	54%	53%	57%
Same or mostly same	71	62	58	61	57	46	47	43
Total	100%	100%	100%	100%	100%	100%	100%	100%
N	1369	1388	1571	1267	1240	2073	2280	1260

Table 6.13
Frequency of Presidential Vote for the Same Party, by Party Identification Groups

	1952	1956	1960	1964	1968	1972	1976	1980	
Strong Democrats	8%	16%	15%	15%	14%	24%	30%	26%	Different party
	92	84	85	85	86	76	70	74	Same party or mostly same party
Weak Democrats	20%	38%	49%	42%	41%	57%	52%	53%	Different party
	80	62	51	58	60	43	48	47	Same party or mostly same party
Independent Democrats	54%	59%	71%	62%	58%	64%	70%	82%	Different party
	46	41	29	39	42	36	30	19	Same party or mostly same party
Independent Independents	78%	84%	82%	84%	83%	81%	77%	81%	Different party
	22	17	18	16	17	19	23	19	Same party or mostly same party
Independent Republicans	53%	68%	71%	70%	63%	76%	73%	74%	Different party
	47	32	30	30	37	24	27	26	Same party or mostly same party
Weak Republicans	39%	43%	42%	46%	56%	62%	52%	72%	Different party
	61	57	58	54	44	38	48	29	Same party or mostly same party
Strong Republicans	18%	20%	23%	23%	27%	31%	33%	40%	Different party
	82	80	77	77	73	69	68	61	Same party or mostly same party

Table 6.14
Frequency of Presidential Vote for the Same Party, by Party Identification Groups, Summarized by a Percentage Difference Index#

	1952	1956	1960	1964	1968	1972	1976	1980
Strong Democrats	83	67	69	70	71	51	40	49
Weak Democrats	60	24	2	16	19	-14	-3	-6
Independent Democrats	-8	-18	-42	-23	-16	-28	-41	-63
Independent Independents	-56	-67	-64	-69	-66	-62	-53	-62
Independent Republicans	-5	-35	-41	-40	-27	-53	-47	-48
Weak Republicans	22	15	16	7	-13	-24	-4	-43
Strong Republicans	63	60	54	55	45	38	35	21
Total population	42	23	16	22	14	-9	-7	-14

PDI is proportion "same or mostly same party" minus proportion "different"

Table 6.15
Democratic Percentage of Two-Party Presidential Vote, for Opinion of Presidential Performance

		1956	1960	1964	1968	1972	1976	1980	1984
Do you approve or disapprove of the way the President is handling his job as President?	Approve	**	**	**	**	17%	26%	81%	13%
	Disapprove	**	**	**	**	86	91	18	93

Table 6.16
Democratic Percentage of Two-Party Presidential Vote, for Trust in Government Index (1)
(see Table 4.37 for description of Index)

	1956	1960	1964	1968	1972	1976	1980	1984
Cynical	**	**	42%	40%	49%	55%	39%	**
Mixture	**	**	58	45	37	53	47	**
Trusting	**	**	78	50	24	40	59	**

Table 6.17
Democratic Percentage of Two-Party Presidential Vote, for Power of Federal Government

		1956	1960	1964	1968	1972	1976	1980	1984
Some people are afraid the government in Washington is getting too powerful. Others feel that the government has not gotten too strong for the good of the country. Have you been interested enough in this to favor one side over the other? (IF YES) What is your feeling?	Not too strong	**	**	87%	63%	34%	55%	65%	40%
	Too powerful	**	**	34	28	39	47	28	40

Table 6.18
Democratic Percentage of Two-Party Presidential Vote, for Economic Issues

		1956	1960	1964	1968	1972	1976	1980	1984
How about the economy? Would you say that over the past year the nation's economy has gotten better, stayed the same or gotten worse?	Gotten better	**	**	**	**	**	**	58%*	20%
	Stayed same	**	**	**	**	**	**	71	47
	Gotten worse	**	**	**	**	**	**	39	79
What about the next 12 months? Do you expect the economy to get better, get worse, or stay about the same?	Get better	**	**	**	**	**	**	59%	22%
	Stay same	**	**	**	**	**	**	40	40
	Get worse	**	**	**	**	**	**	34	71
We are interested in how people are getting along financially these days. Would you say you and your family are better off or worse off financially than you were a year ago?	Better off	**	**	**	54%	31%	45%	46%	26%
	Same now	**	**	**	47	30	48	46	45
	Worse off	**	**	**	35	48	62	40	67
Now looking ahead--do you think that a year from now you will be better off financially or worse off or just about the same as now?	Better off	39%	44%	70%	44%	29%	48%	49%	30%
	Same as now	39	53	68	46	30	49	45	44
	Worse off	44	53	59	51	71	66	34	65

Table 6.19
Democratic Percentage of Two-Party Presidential Vote, for Racial Issues

		1964	1968	1972	1976	1980	1984
How much real change do you think there has been	A lot	62%	34%	38%	66%	**	56%
in the position of blacks in the past few years:	Some	67	48	40	55	**	43
a lot, some, or not much at all?	Not much at all	70	48	33	47	**	34
Some say that civil rights people have been trying	Too slowly	90%	70%	73%	78%	71%	70%
to push too fast. Others feel they haven't pushed	About right	82	54	40	50	45	44
fast enough. Do you think civil rights leaders are	Too fast	60	39	25	48	33	24
trying to push too fast... too slowly... or at about							
the right speed?							
What about you? Are you in favor of desegregation,	Desegregation	75%	56%	47%	53%	**	**
strict segregation, or something in between?	In between	65	38	28	49	**	**
	Segregation	62	42	18	56	**	**
Some say that the gov't should see to it that white	Gov't role	77%	58%	50%	63%	**	**
and black children are allowed to go to the same	No gov't role	55	34	23	45	**	**
schools. Others claim this is not the government's							
business. Have you been concerned enough to favor							
one side over the other? (IF YES) Which side?							
Some people think achieving racial integration of	Busing 1	**	**	85%	78%	86%*	-
schools is so important that it justifies busing	2	**	**	87*	77*	82*	-
children out of their own neighborhoods (point 1).	3	**	**	73*	53*	89*	-
others think letting children go to their	4	**	**	51	55	69*	51*
neighborhood schools is so important that they	5	**	**	47	44	45*	52
oppose busing (point 7). Where would you	6	**	**	38	49	36	35
place yourself on this scale?	Nghbrhood schls 7	**	**	26	48	36	33
Which of these statements would you agree with:							
1. White people have a right to keep blacks out of	Stmt.1	61%	34%	22%	52%	**	**
their neighborhoods if they want; 2. Blacks have a	Stmt.2	71	49	39	52	**	**
right to live wherever they can afford to, just							
like anybody else.							
Some feel that the gov't in Washington should make	Gov't help 1	**	**	70%	76%	93%*	82
every possible effort to improve the social and	2	**	**	60	61	85*	67
economic position of blacks and other minority	3	**	**	36	54	55	49
groups (point 1). Others feel that the gov't	4	**	**	33	47	47	42
should not make any special effort to help	5	**	**	20	43	31	31
because they should help themselves (point 7).	6	**	**	19	38	30	21
Where would you place yourself on this scale?	Help selves 7	**	**	27	42	29	23

Table 6.20
Democratic Percentage of Two-Party Presidential Vote, for Religion and Abortion Issues

		1964	1968	1972	1976	1980	1984
Which of these opinions best agrees with your view:	Opinion 1	**	**	37%	57%	45%	**
abortion should be permitted: 1. Never permitted;	Opinion 2	**	**	31	50	44	**
2. Only if the life and health of the woman is in	Opinion 3	**	**	38	47	33	**
danger; 3. If due to personal reasons the woman would	Opinion 4	**	**	41	54	49	**
have difficulty caring for the child; 4. Never forbidden							
Which of these opinions best agrees with your view:	Opinion 1	**	**	**	**	49%	36%
the law should permit abortions: 1. Never permitted;	Opinion 2	**	**	**	**	44	37
2. In case of incest, rape, or when the woman's life is	Opinion 3	**	**	**	**	34	38
in danger; 3. For reasons other than incest, rape	Opinion 4	**	**	**	**	47	50
or danger, but only after need is clearly established;							
4. A woman should always be able to obtain an abortion.							
Do you consider religion to be an important part of your	Yes	**	**	**	**	44%	42%
life or not?	No	**	**	**	**	42	39
Would you say that religion provides some guidance	Some	**	**	**	**	41%	43%
in your day-to-day living, quite a bit of guidance	Quite a bit	**	**	**	**	43	41
or a great deal of guidance?	A great deal	**	**	**	**	47	43
Here are 4 statements about the Bible...Which is closest	Stmt.1	74%	49%	**	**	45%	40%
to your own view? - 1. The Bible is God's word and all	Stmt.2	61	41	**	**	42	41
it says is true; 2. The Bible was written by men inspired	Stmt.3	70*	51	**	**	50*	49
by God but it contains some human errors; 3. The Bible	Stmt.4	-	-	**	**	-	55*
is a good book because it was written by wise men, but							
God had nothing to do with it; 4. The Bible was written							
by men who lived so long ago that it is worth very little							
today.							

Table 6.21
Democratic Percentage of Two-Party Presidential Vote, for Foreign Affairs and National Defense Issues

		1952	1956	1960	1964	1968	1972	1976	1980	1984
This country would be better off if we just stayed home and did not concern ourselves with problems in other parts of the would.6	Agree	33%	41%	55%	**	41%	44%	70%	44%	53%
	Disagree	53	41	47	**	48	34	45	43	37
The U.S. should give help to foreign countries even if they don't stand for the same things we do.	Agree	**	44%	49%	60%	42%	35%	52%	**	**
	Disagree	**	41	48	72	50	38	50	**	**
Some people feel it is important for us to try to cooperate more with Russia (point 1) while others believe we should be much tougher in our dealings with Russia (point 7). Where would you place yourself on this scale?	Cooperate more 1	**	**	**	**	**	**	**	61%	73%
	2	**	**	**	**	**	**	**	46	62
	3	**	**	**	**	**	**	**	45	54
	4	**	**	**	**	**	**	**	40	33
	5	**	**	**	**	**	**	**	32	26
	6	**	**	**	**	**	**	**	26	21
	Get tougher 7	**	**	**	**	**	**	**	32	32
How about our chances of getting into war (a conventional war). Are you pretty worried about this country getting into such a war at the present time, somewhat worried, or not worried?	Not worried	**	36%	47%	66%	**	**	**	**	25%
	Somewhat worried	**	42	48	69	**	**	**	**	48
	Pretty worried	**	53	55	67	**	**	**	**	67
Do you think we did the right thing in getting into the fighting in Korea/ Vietnam, or should we have stayed out?	Shd have stayed out	34%	**	**	57%	43%	43%	**	**	**
	Did right thing	52	**	**	70	49	23	**	**	**
Some people believe that our armed forces are already powerful enough and that we should spend less money for defense. Others feel that military spending should continue at least at the present level. How do you feel?	Cut	**	**	**	**	**	57%	68%	**	**
	Continue	**	**	**	**	**	21	47	**	**
Some people believe that we should spend much less money for defense. Others feel that defense spending should be greatly increased. Where would you place yourself on this scale?	Spend much less 1	**	**	**	**	**	**	**	83%	79%
	2	**	**	**	**	**	**	**	94	67
	3	**	**	**	**	**	**	**	59	57
	4	**	**	**	**	**	**	**	51	33
	5	**	**	**	**	**	**	**	41	25
	6	**	**	**	**	**	**	**	30	18
	Spend much more 7	**	**	**	**	**	**	**	35	22

Table 6.22
Democratic Percentage of Two-Party Presidential Vote, for Government Role in Social Welfare Issues

		1956	1960	1964	1968	1972	1976	1980	1984
Some people think the gov't should provide fewer services even in areas such as health and education in order to reduce spending...(Point 1) other people feel that it is important for the gov't to provide many more services, even if it means an increase in spending (point 7). Other people have opinions in between (points 2,3,4,5,6). Where would you place yourself on this scale?	Decrease 1	**	**	**	**	**	**	20%	17%
	2	**	**	**	**	**	**	8	12
	3	**	**	**	**	**	**	24	20
	4	**	**	**	**	**	**	43	44
	5	**	**	**	**	**	**	52	60
	6	**	**	**	**	**	**	67	67
	Increase 7	**	**	**	**	**	**	74	72
Some say the gov't in Washington ought to help people get doctors and hospital care at low cost; others say the gov't should not get into this. (IF INTERESTED ENOUGH TO SAY) What is your position?	Gov't help	51%	58%	85%	62%	**	**	**	**
	Gov't stay out	25	28	37	24	**	**	**	**
There is much concern about the rapid rise in medical and hospital costs. Some feel there should be a gov't insurance plan that would cover all medical and hospital expenses (point 1). Others feel that medical expenses should be paid by individuals and through private insurance like Blue Cross. Where would you place yourself on this scale?	Gov't plan 1	**	**	**	**	57%	70%	**	61%
	2	**	**	**	**	54	58	**	41
	3	**	**	**	**	27	63	**	53
	4	**	**	**	**	36	53	**	39
	5	**	**	**	**	29	34	**	36
	6	**	**	**	**	16*	38	**	21
	Private plan 7	**	**	**	**	20	35	**	19
Some people feel that the gov't in Washington should see to it that each person has a job and a good standard of living. Others think the government should just let each person get ahead on his own. (IF INTERESTED ENOUGH TO SAY) What is your position?	Gov't role	47%	60%	85%	64%	**	**	**	**
	Neutral	37	35	70	42	**	**	**	**
	No gov't role	32	33	52	36	**	**	**	**
Suppose people who believe that the gov't should see to it that every person has a job and a good standard of living are at one end of the scale-- point 1. And suppose people who believe the gov't should let each person get ahead on his own are the other end--at point 7. Where would you place yourself on this scale?	Gov't role 1	**	**	**	**	72%	80%	80%	71%
	2	**	**	**	**	61	79	56	67
	3	**	**	**	**	50	65	63	59
	4	**	**	**	**	36	50	50	48
	5	**	**	**	**	25	41	40	34
	6	**	**	**	**	16	39	19	16
	No gov't role 7	**	**	**	**	19	39	21	15
There is much discussion about the best way to deal with the problem of urban unrest and rioting. Some say it is more important to use all available force to maintain law and order-- no matter what results. Others say it is more important to correct the problems of poverty and unemployment that gave rise to the disturbances. Where would you place yourself on this scale?	Correct problems 1	**	**	**	69%	51%	69%	**	**
	2	**	**	**	53	46	58	**	**
	3	**	**	**	61	33	44	**	**
	4	**	**	**	38	24	43	**	**
	5	**	**	**	24	22	37	**	**
	6	**	**	**	28	17*	48	**	**
	Use force 7	**	**	**	39	24	39	**	**

Table 6.23
Democratic Percentage of Two-Party Presidential Vote, for Non-racial Civil Rights Issues

		1952	1972	1976	1980	1984
Some people are primarily concerned with doing	Protect rights 1	**	52%	58%	**	**
everything possible to protect the legal rights of	2	**	50%	60%	**	**
those accused of committing crimes. Others feel	3	**	47%	60%	**	**
that it is more important to stop criminal activity	4	**	39%	48%	**	**
even at the risk of reducing the rights of the	5	**	23%	38%	**	**
accused. Where would you place yourself on this	6	**	20%	45%	**	**
scale or haven't you thought much about it?	Stop crime 7	**	27%	51%	**	**
Recently there has been a lot of talk about	Equal role 1	**	40%	55%	49%	51%
women's rights. Some people feel that women	2	**	43%	47%	39%	44%
should have an equal role with men in running	3	**	40%	48%	47%	31%
business, industry and government. Others feel	4	**	27%	50%	43%	34%
that women's place is in the home. Where would	5	**	27%	46%	29%	35%
you place yourself on this scale or haven't you	6	**	40%	61%	25%	24%
thought much about this?	Stay at home 7	**	33%	59%	54%*	36%
Women should stay out of politics	Agree	45%	29%	**	**	**
	Disagree	42%	37%	**	**	**

Table 6.24
Gammas of Selected Issues with Democratic Presidential Vote&
(See Tables 6.15-6.23 for issue descriptions)

	1952	1956	1960	1964	1968	1972	1976	1980	1984
Approve of Pres. Performance	**	**	**	**	**	-.94	-.93	.90	-.98
Trust in Government	**	**	**	-.52	-.14	.37	.19	-.27	**
Fed Gov't Not Too Strong	**	**	**	.86	.64	-.10	.16	.65	.15
Gov't Help Get Health Care	**	.52	.55	.80	.68	**	**	**	**
Gov't Provide Health Insurance	**	**	**	**	**	.44	.37	**	.37
Gov't Provide Jobs/Std Living (1)	**	.27	.46	.57	.42	**	**	**	**
Gov't Provide Jobs/Std Living (2)	**	**	**	**	**	.50	.36	.51	.52
Less Gov't Services/Spending	**	**	**	**	**	**	**	-.59	-.56
Protect Rights of Accused	**	**	**	**	**	.32	.11	**	**
Remove Cause of Urban Unrest	**	**	**	**	.38	.37	.29	**	**
Blacks' Position Not Improved	**	**	**	-.11	-.11	.14	.19	**	.26
Civil Rights Move Too Slowly	**	**	**	.54	.35	.45	.17	.38	.50
Should Achieve Desegregation	**	**	**	.19	.26	.41	.03	**	**
Govt Shd Provide Aid to Min.	**	**	**	**	**	.41	.26	.43	.44
Gov't Should Integrate Schools	**	**	**	.45	.46	.55	.36	**	**
Should Use Busing to Integrate	**	**	**	**	**	.58	.17	.41	.29
Whites Keep Blacks Out-Housing	**	**	**	-.22	-.31	-.39	.01	**	**
Womens' Role Should be Equal	**	**	**	**	**	.12	.04	.12	**
Women Out of Politics	.06	**	**	**	**	-.18	**	**	**
Never Permit Abortions (1)	**	**	**	**	**	-.11	0	-.02	**
Never Permit Abortions (2)	**	**	**	**	**	**	**	0	-.18
Bible is God's Word	**	**	**	.24	.08	**	**	0	-.07
Religion is Important to R's Life	**	**	**	**	**	**	**	.05	.07
Should Ignore World Problems	-.38	.01	.15	**	-.15	.20	.48	.01	.32
Shd Have Stayed Out-Korea/Vietn.	-.37	**	**	-.27	-.14	.43	**	**	**
Not Worried-Conventional War	**	-.17	-.10	-.05	**	**	**	**	-.51
Should Deny U.S. Foreign Aid	**	.04	.02	-.27	-.15	-.08	.04	**	**
Should Cut Military Spending (1)	**	**	**	**	**	.66	.41	**	**
Should Cut Military Spending (2)	**	**	**	**	**	**	**	.29	.51
Should Cooperate With Russia	**	**	**	**	**	**	**	.27	.43
Nat Economy Better in Last Yr.	**	**	**	**	**	**	**	.51	-.69
Nat Economy Better in Next Yr.	**	**	**	**	**	**	**	.32	-.55
R's Finances Better in Last Yr.	**	**	**	**	.22	-.20	-.21	.09	-.52
R's Finances Better in Next Year	**	-.04	-.13	.10	-.06	-.27	-.14	.17	-.35

& (Presidential vote variable is: 1. Democratic vote, 2. Republican vote). Refer to tables 6.15, 4.37 and 3.1-3.32 for
   the codes of issue questions (questions in the same order as above). Labels above reflect the first coded position
   [code 1] for that issue var., with subsequent codes decreasingly supportive of, or increasingly opposed to, that position.

Table 6.25
Democratic Percentage of Two-Party Presidential Vote, for Net Affect toward Parties&

	1952	1956	1960	1964	1968	1972	1976	1980	1984
Maximum Republican	2%	2%	1%	10%	6%	5%	7%	2%	2%
	13	9	15	29	21	18	18	15	11
Neutral	41	22	47	74	38	28	49	37	33
	69	66	74	90	77	55	73	72	65
Maximum Democratic	91	84	92	96	91	78	90	90	89

& Net affect is Democratic party affect minus Republican party affect.

Table 6.26
Democratic Percentage of Two-Party Presidential Vote, for Net Affect Toward Candidates&

	1952	1956	1960	1964	1968	1972	1976	1980	1984
Maximum Republican	6%	6%	4%	6%	6%	5%	8%	4%	2%
	18	26	23	13	22	21	18	19	11
Neutral	48	59	64	61	52	52	46	42	35
	76	78	84	81	78	73	82	74	69
Maximum Democratic	91	93	95	94	93	92	92	93	93

& Net affect is Democratic candidate affect minus Republican candidate affect.

Table 6.27
Gammas of Affect Measures with Presidential Vote&
    (Affect Measures each have eleven categories: -5. Maximum Negative ... 0. Neutral ... 5. Maximum Positive)

	1952	1956	1960	1964	1968	1972	1976	1980	1984
Affect Dem. Candidate	-.77	-.72	-.80	-.80	-.78	-.79	-.77	-.83	-.87
Affect Rep. Candidate	.77	.79	.85	.84	.82	.76	.75	.76	.88
Affect Dem. Party	-.82	-.77	-.82	-.81	-.76	-.59	-.68	-.69	-.73
Affect Rep. Party	.86	.79	.80	.74	.70	.61	.62	.72	.77
Net Affect Candidates@	-.83	-.84	-.89	-.87	-.88	-.85	-.84	-.87	-.92
Net Affect Parties@	-.88	-.84	-.86	-.84	-.81	-.67	-.75	-.79	-.82

& Presidential Vote variable is: 1. Democratic vote, 2. Republican vote

@ This is Democratic party/candidate affect minus Republican party/candidate affect.

Table 6.28
Congressional Vote, 2 Major Parties&

	1952	1954	1956	1958	1960	1962	1964	1966	1968	1970	1972	1974	1976	1978	1980	1982	1984	1986
Democratic vote	49%	**	53%	61%	56%	58%	65%	57%	52%	55%	56%	62%	57%	59%	55%	57%	55%	60%
Republican vote	51	**	47	**	44	**	35	43	48	45	44	38	43	41	45	43	45	40
Total	100%	**	100%	100%	100%	100%	100%	100%	100%	100%	100%	100%	100%	100%	100%	100%	100%	100%
N	1013	**	1157	962	1198	698	957	677	871	683	1337	1120	1317	1009	859	712	1187	981

& Note that all percentages for "Democratic Congressional vote" in tables 6.25 - 6.40 are based on 100% minus Republican vote

Table 6.29
Congressional Vote, 2 Major Parties and Non-voters

	1952	1954	1956	1958	1960	1962	1964	1966	1968	1970	1972	1974	1976	1978	1980	1982	1984	1986
Democratic vote	29%	**	36%	33%	35%	33%	47%	31%	33%	26%	34%	29%	34%	26%	30%	30%	45%	28%
Republican vote	30	**	32	21	28	24	25	23	31	22	27	18	25	19	25	22	37	19
Non-voters	42	**	33	46	37	43	28	46	36	52	39	54	41	55	45	48	19	54
Total	100%	**	100%	100%	100%	100%	100%	100%	100%	100%	100%	100%	100%	100%	100%	100%	100%	100%
N	1741	**	1726	1784	1896	1214	1330	1247	1352	1422	2190	2428	2243	2247	1568	1379	1462	2113

Table 6.30
Congressional Vote, Sample Size

	1952	1954	1956	1958	1960	1962	1964	1966	1968	1970	1972	1974	1976	1978	1980	1982	1984	1986
Democratic vote	497	**	612	582	666	405	620	388	452	372	748	694	753	590	466	409	653	591
Republican vote	516	**	545	380	532	293	337	289	419	311	589	426	565	419	393	303	534	390
Non-voters	728	**	569	822	698	516	373	570	481	739	853	1308	926	238	709	667	275	1132
Total population	1741	**	1726	1784	1896	1214	1330	1247	1352	1422	2190	2428	2243	2247	1568	1379	1462	2113

& Sample size table can be derived for table 6.28 from the data appearing here

Table 6.31
Democratic Percentage of Two-Party Congressional Vote for Social Groups&

	1952	1954	1956	1958	1960	1962	1964	1966	1968	1970	1972	1974	1976	1978	1980	1982	1984	1986
1959 or later cohort	**	**	**	**	**	**	**	**	**	**	**	**	**	-	49%*	27%*	57%	64%
1943-1958 cohort	**	**	**	**	**	**	-	57%*	47%	62%	63%	69%	59%	59%	58	61	55	58
1927-1942 cohort	50%	**	53%	69%	55%	57%	65%	60	53	56	55	63	55	58	52	57	54	54
1911-1926 cohort	55	**	56	61	62	56	67	59	50	55	53	57	59	60	53	61	56	67
1895-1910 cohort	47	**	51	60	52	61	66	51	57	48	57	61	57	58	55	48	51	67
Before 1895 cohort	41	**	48	56	46	56	54	56*	39*	53*	36*	66*	-	-	-	-	-	-
Grade school	55%	**	52%	67%	60%	69%	81%	62%	70%	66%	63%	66%	68%	72%	69%	76%*	64%	80%
High school	47	**	56	67	60	57	66	61	52	55	56	63	59	59	53	63	56	63
College	43	**	47	45	44	52	50	49	43	47	54	60	52	56	53	51	53	55
Central cities	56%	**	61%	68%	62%	66%	67%	68%	60%	60%	66%	65%	62%	72%	72%	66%	65%	77%
Suburbs	44	**	45	55	46	55	59	49	44	47	51	61	61	55	50	57	50	52
Non-urban areas	46	**	53	60	58	56	68	58	53	57	55	62	50	50	46	50	54	58
Inc. percentile 0-16	48%	**	50%	59%	55%	51%	74%	61%	66%	65%	68%	67%	73%	70%	63%	74%	75%	79%
Inc. percentile 17-33	56	**	57	71	58	65%*	66	59%*	55	61	59	75	63	57	65	58	62	72
Inc. percentile 34-67	52	**	59	64	59	62	69	56	51	55	56	65	60	61	52	63	54	59
Inc. percentile 68-95	47	**	51	59	55	57	59	60	48	52	54	56	52	54	51	53	50	53
Inc. percentile 95-100	24*	**	38	22	41	40*	51	46	43	36*	37	46	38	49	41	40	41	52
Males	48%	**	58%	61%	55%	61%	65%	62%	52%	54%	57%	63%	58%	60%	56%	54%	53%	59%
Females	49	**	48	60	56	55	65	53	52	55	56	61	57	58	53	60	57	62
Whites	47%	**	52%	59%	54%	56%	63%	54%	49%	52%	53%	60%	53%	56%	50%	54%	52%	55%
Blacks	92*	**	83*	79	83*	92*	95	90	87	82*	94	94	97	92	95	90	91	91
Union Household	61%	**	62%	78%	69%	**	80%	68%	58%	63%	62%	71%	72%	70%	65%	70%	62%	64%
Non-union household	44	**	49	55	51	**	59	53	50	52	53	59	52	54	51	54	53	59
South	89%	**	76%	78%	73%	68%	76%	70%	66%	67%	69%	70%	67%	80%	65%	64%	60%	76%
Non-south	41	**	47	56	50	55	61	53	47	50	51	59	53	51	49	55	53	54
Professional	39%	**	49%	52%	46%	**	52%	**	46%	46%	52%	63%	50%	54%	49%	48%	54%	58%
White collar	50	**	51	54	49	**	59	**	46	59	57	60	56	54	55	53	57	58
Blue collar	59	**	59	72	65	**	76	**	60	62	64	66	65	66	59	66	59	68
Unskilled	68	**	67	77*	-	**	-	**	-	-	-	-	69*	-	59*	-	-	-
Farmers	44	**	62	63	58	**	70*	**	57*	72*	46*	61*	54*	-	-	-	53*	57*
Housewives	45	**	47	56	57	**	64	**	49	49	49	56	55	57	55	69	41	52
Protestants	45%	**	48%	54%	46%	50%	62%	51%	47%	51%	51%	57%	53%	55%	52%	53%	50%	57%
Catholics	55	**	61	73	81	75	72	68	61	58	66	68	64	64	59	66	61	66
Jewish	75*	**	83	93*	82*	78*	79*	82*	79*	86*	82*	91*	85*	73*	69*	-	80*	61*
Other and none	65*	**	70*	-	-	-	67*	73*	-	69*	59	73	66	61	56	64	64	68
Total population	49%	**	53%	61%	56%	58%	65%	57%	52%	55%	56%	62%	57%	59%	55%	57%	55%	60%

& Note that, in this table and all following, the percent Democratic Congressional vote is computed by subtracting the percent Republican vote from 100%, i.e., third party and non-voters are not included as valid data.

Table 6.32
Sample Size of All Congressional Voters by Social Groups

	1952	1954	1956	1958	1960	1962	1964	1966	1968	1970	1972	1974	1976	1978	1980	1982	1984	1986
1959 or later cohort	**	**	**	**	**	**	**	**	**	**	**	**	**	15	41	30	110	96
1943-1958 cohort	**	**	**	**	**	**	9	28	64	73	311	255	358	300	283	241	462	328
1927-1942 cohort	60	**	152	119	237	162	292	189	274	198	382	253	337	295	223	171	274	256
1911-1926 cohort	369	**	474	390	463	243	348	250	308	205	373	350	392	268	212	213	248	242
1895-1910 cohort	316	**	327	284	331	201	221	158	183	157	222	222	208	116	94	52	79	58
Before 1895 cohort	221	**	186	169	167	87	86	48	39	32	42	32	18	12	5	3	1	0
Grade school	322	**	281	244	291	160	187	148	138	133	195	177	173	90	72	49	80	73
High school	473	**	595	457	587	337	504	332	445	321	634	501	606	477	384	294	505	377
College	179	**	275	251	319	196	263	195	288	228	508	437	538	441	401	369	595	518
Central cities	343	**	303	253	271	175	267	167	217	169	307	301	367	282	230	214	275	250
Suburbs	311	**	323	286	338	286	310	235	272	214	466	422	448	428	336	265	502	435
Non-urban areas	359	**	531	423	589	237	380	275	382	300	564	397	503	299	293	233	410	296
Inc. percentile 0-16	123	**	123	109	132	118	142	86	93	66	199	128	121	110	95	73	98	104
Inc. percentile 17-33	135	**	222	151	178	37	158	49	156	90	119	167	218	138	110	88	161	126
Inc. percentile 34-67	225	**	353	267	342	285	233	210	281	181	460	382	372	300	296	215	399	324
Inc. percentile 68-95	431	**	299	358	465	177	313	257	274	295	435	326	446	270	220	210	346	294
Inc. percentile 95-100	46	**	116	51	71	50	77	54	54	31	89	59	88	86	58	57	76	52
Males	489	**	578	528	584	335	454	324	391	323	604	514	592	452	388	327	522	426
Females	486	**	579	434	614	363	503	353	480	360	733	606	725	557	471	385	665	555
Whites	936	**	1120	902	1146	655	890	614	802	632	1229	1034	1184	919	771	640	1067	828
Blacks	37	**	35	53	46	39	64	57	63	44	93	66	106	72	82	68	95	136
Union Household	287	**	327	251	321	**	250	194	221	157	358	268	322	291	227	170	280	209
Non-union household	682	**	827	707	858	**	707	481	649	517	967	832	985	718	629	539	906	767
South	166	**	238	182	307	177	241	162	220	171	343	316	384	261	288	230	349	287
Non-south	847	**	919	780	891	521	716	515	651	512	994	804	934	748	571	482	838	694
Professional	182	**	227	210	221	**	204	**	202	175	330	326	341	305	265	212	346	335
White collar	129	**	133	121	188	**	140	**	137	98	219	169	243	166	158	140	287	221
Blue collar	202	**	286	282	361	**	265	**	230	186	375	323	387	287	243	201	328	250
Unskilled	69	**	52	31	19	**	15	**	9	7	16	7	24	19	22	12	18	14
Farmers	69	**	73	56	69	**	47	**	35	25	37	41	35	19	16	19	36	21
Housewives	314	**	374	254	313	**	272	**	234	174	318	227	253	189	123	109	149	120
Protestants	681	**	801	659	864	482	661	468	617	481	902	730	866	651	560	486	724	650
Catholics	231	**	276	241	279	169	235	155	204	140	336	277	338	247	187	152	322	238
Jewish	36	**	52	41	34	27	28	28	24	21	33	33	34	37	32	16	30	23
Other and none	23	**	27	19	19	20	33	22	20	39	63	75	76	70	73	55	108	60
Total population	1013	**	1157	962	1198	698	957	677	871	683	1337	1120	1317	1009	859	712	1187	981

Table 6.33
Democratic Percentage of Two-Party Congressional Vote, for Political Groups

	1952	1954	1956	1958	1960	1962	1964	1966	1968	1970	1972	1974	1976	1978	1980	1982	1984	1984
Strong Democrats	90%	**	94%	96%	93%	97%	94%	92%	88%	89%	92%	90%	89%	87%	85%	91%	89%	92%
Weak Democrats	78	**	86	89	86	84	84	82	73	77	81	82	78	80	69	75	70	75
Ind. Democrats	64	**	83	74	87	75*	79	62	63	76	80	87	78	62	70	83	78	73
Ind. Independents	28	**	37	46*	50	63*	73*	53*	50	52	56	56	58	57	56	33*	59	62
Ind. Republicans	19	**	17	24*	26	27*	28	33*	18	35	27	39	32	37	32	37	39	37
Weak Republicans	11	**	12	22	15	16	36	22	22	18	24	31	28	34	26	20	34	35
Strong Republicans	5	**	5	7	8	7	8	13	8	5	15	15	15	20	23	12	15	21
Lib. Self Placement 1	**	**	**	**	**	**	**	**	**	**	86%	79%	86%	74%	81%	85%	79%	87%
Lib. Self Placement 2	**	**	**	**	**	**	**	**	**	**	65	73	70	66	70	70	68	70
Neutral Placement 3	**	**	**	**	**	**	**	**	**	**	56	61	57	60	53	62	64	63
Cons. Self Placement 4	**	**	**	**	**	**	**	**	**	**	43	48	43	50	40	42	45	48
Cons. Self Placement 5	**	**	**	**	**	**	**	**	**	**	41	53	32	35	37	33	29	40
Liberal Index 1	**	**	**	**	**	**	93%*	82%*	78%*	97%*	86%*	87%*	91%*	**	93%*	90%*	93%*	87%*
Liberal Index 2	**	**	**	**	**	**	77	67	64	72	76	74	77	**	77	74	72	72
Neutral Index 3	**	**	**	**	**	**	71	63	54	59	57	67	60	**	59	62	55	67
Conservative Index 4	**	**	**	**	**	**	51	51	42	43	44	50	46	**	42	39˙	45	50
Conservative Index 5	**	**	**	**	**	**	34	30	38	42	43	43	30	**	30	26	20	36
Total Population	49%	**	53%	61%	56%	58%	65%	57%	52%	55%	56%	62%	57%	59%	55%	57%	55%	60%

Table 6.34
Sample Size of All Congressional Voters by Political Groups

	1952	1954	1956	1958	1960	1962	1964	1966	1968	1970	1972	1974	1976	1978	1980	1982	1984	1986
Strong Democrats	208	**	266	302	256	191	277	144	192	156	210	251	230	200	183	179	231	229
Weak Democrats	219	**	247	187	281	145	220	169	198	148	324	217	308	210	163	166	224	205
Ind. Democrats	98	**	72	62	70	44	77	52	83	58	132	148	145	129	93	65	108	97
Ind. Independents	51	**	100	50	100	40	48	49	64	58	112	88	118	98	71	45	88	60
Ind. Republicans	78	**	96	42	86	41	60	46	84	52	150	93	131	109	100	57	163	115
Weak Republicans	143	**	173	166	171	127	143	110	139	120	217	182	202	146	144	104	177	136
Strong Republicans	173	**	198	152	215	107	129	95	110	89	186	141	183	115	102	94	191	137
Lib. Self Placement 1	**	**	**	**	**	**	**	**	**	**	123	133	116	92	78	61	115	83
Lib. Self Placement 2	**	**	**	**	**	**	**	**	**	**	147	102	134	97	79	59	119	120
Neutral Placement 3	**	**	**	**	**	**	**	**	**	**	359	331	333	283	174	177	282	270
Cons. Self Placement 4	**	**	**	**	**	**	**	**	**	**	225	187	202	172	130	105	206	172
Cons. Self Placement 5	**	**	**	**	**	**	**	**	**	**	170	173	229	165	149	117	214	176
Liberal Index 1	**	**	**	**	**	**	40	22	32	30	44	46	39	**	28	39	41	47
Liberal Index 2	**	**	**	**	**	**	197	132	189	121	246	217	231	**	145	117	293	223
Neutral Index 3	**	**	**	**	**	**	367	226	280	154	277	273	357	**	160	224	310	203
Conservative Index 4	**	**	**	**	**	**	265	232	289	236	456	378	430	**	342	202	371	333
Conservative Index 5	**	**	**	**	**	**	76	56	63	84	105	96	104	**	93	58	86	101
Total Population	1013	**	1157	962	1198	698	957	677	871	683	1337	1120	1317	1009	859	712	1187	981

Congressional Vote

Table 6.35
Percent of Voters Ticket-Splitting between Presidential and Congressional Vote

	1952	1956	1960	1964	1968	1972	1976	1980	1984
Dem. Pres./Dem. Congr.	39%	39%	45%	59%	40%	31%	42%	35%	36%
Dem. Pres./Rep. Congr.	2	2	4	9	7	5	9	8	6
Rep. Pres./Dem. Congr.	10	14	10	6	11	25	16	20	20
Rep. Pres./Rep. Congr.	49	45	41	26	42	40	34	38	39
Total	100%	100%	100%	100%	100%	100%	100%	100%	100%
N	1009	1151	1187	947	776	1293	1280	762	1144

Table 6.36
Voters' Ticket-Splitting between Presidential and Congressional Vote, by Party Identification Groups

	1952	1956	1960	1964	1968	1972	1976	1980	1984	
Strong Democrats	82%	85%	88%	91%	84%	71%	84%	79%	81%	Dem. Pres./Dem. Congr.
	2	2	4	5	8	3	7	11	8	Dem. Pres./Rep. Congr.
	9	9	6	3	5	21	5	7	8	Rep. Pres./Dem. Congr.
	7	4	4	1	4	4	4	4	4	Rep. Pres./Rep. Congr.
Weak Democrats	57%	62%	71%	75%	59%	44%	63%	48%	56%	Dem. Pres./Dem. Congr.
	4	3	4	9	13	6	12	15	11	Dem. Pres./Rep. Congr.
	20	24	15	9	12	37	15	21	15	Rep. Pres./Dem. Congr.
	18	11	10	7	15	14	10	17	18	Rep. Pres./Rep. Congr.
Independent Democrats	57%	64%	79%	76%	47%	53%	63%	50%	65%	Dem. Pres./Dem. Congr.
	6	6	11	13	16	8	16	10	13	Dem. Pres./Rep. Congr.
	7	19	8	3	13	26	15	22	12	Rep. Pres./Dem. Congr.
	29	11	3	8	24	14	7	18	9	Rep. Pres./Rep. Congr.
Independent Independents	20%	12%	34%	65%*	26%	24%	35%	19%	22%	Dem. Pres./Dem. Congr.
	2	4	13	13*	2	8	13	5	5	Dem. Pres./Rep. Congr.
	8	25	14	8*	25	34	23	38	37	Rep. Pres./Dem. Congr.
	71	59	40	15*	47	35	30	38	37	Rep. Pres./Rep. Congr.
Independent Republicans	5%	5%	8%	18%	4%	6%	6%	7%	4%	Dem. Pres./Dem. Congr.
	1	2	2	5	1	5	5	6	1	Dem. Pres./Rep. Congr.
	14	12	17	10	14	22	27	24	36	Rep. Pres./Dem. Congr.
	80	81	72	67	81	67	62	64	59	Rep. Pres./Rep. Congr.
Weak Republicans	4%	5%	8%	27%	8%	6%	9%	2%	5%	Dem. Pres./Dem. Congr.
	1	2	4	15	4	3	12	3	2	Dem. Pres./Rep. Congr.
	6	6	7	11	13	18	19	24	30	Rep. Pres./Dem. Congr.
	89	87	81	47	75	73	60	70	64	Rep. Pres./Rep. Congr.
Strong Republicans	2%	1%	2%	2%	3%	1%	1%	3%	1%	Dem. Pres./Dem. Congr.
	0	0	0	7	0	2	1	2	0	Dem. Pres./Rep. Congr.
	4	5	7	5	6	15	13	19	14	Rep. Pres./Dem. Congr.
	95	95	92	85	92	83	85	76	85	Rep. Pres./Rep. Congr.

Table 6.37
Percent of Voters Ticket-Splitting between Presidential and Congressional Vote, by Party Identification Groups

	1952	1956	1960	1964	1968	1972	1976	1980	1984
Strong Democrats	11%	11%	9%	8%	13%	25%	12%	18%	15%
Weak Democrats	24	27	19	18	25	42	27	35	26
Independent Democrats	14	25	18	16	29	34	31	32	25
Independent Independents	10	29	26	21*	26	42	35	43	42
Independent Republicans	15	14	20	15	15	27	32	30	37
Weak Republicans	7	8	11	26	17	21	31	27	32
Strong Republicans	4	5	7	12	6	16	14	21	14
Total Population	13%	16%	14%	15%	18%	30%	25%	28%	25%

Table 6.38
Percent of Voters Ticket-Splitting between Presidential and Senatorial Vote

	1952	1956	1960	1964	1968	1972	1976	1980	1984
Dem. Pres./Dem. Sen.	37%	39%	47%	56%	38%	29%	44%	35%	36%
Dem. Pres./Rep. Sen.	3	2	4	12	5	7	8	7	6
Rep. Pres./Dem. Sen.	9	14	7	5	14	21	15	17	17
Rep. Pres./Rep. Sen.	51	45	42	27	43	43	33	42	41
Total	100%	100%	100%	100%	100%	100%	100%	100%	100%
N	797	878	723	787	603	765	946	539	717

Table 6.39
Voters' Ticket-Splitting between Presidential and Senatorial Vote, by Party Identification Groups

	1952	1956	1960	1964	1968	1972	1976	1980	1984	
Strong Democrats	82%	85%	87%	89%	85%	68%	88%	78%	85%	Dem. Pres./Dem. Sen.
	5	4	2	8	5	9	3	8	4	Dem. Pres./Rep. Sen.
	7	6	5	1	4	13	5	9	4	Rep. Pres./Dem. Sen.
	7	5	5	2	5	10	5	6	7	Rep. Pres./Rep. Sen.
Weak Democrats	59%	64%	67%	78%	62%	37%	68%	59%	60%	Dem. Pres./Dem. Sen.
	4	4	5	9	4	10	11	8	12	Dem. Pres./Rep. Sen.
	16	22	13	6	15	31	10	17	15	Rep. Pres./Dem. Sen.
	21	11	16	8	19	22	11	16	13	Rep. Pres./Rep. Sen.
Independent Democrats	53%	59%	80%*	76%	36%*	38%	59%	55%*	60%	Dem. Pres./Dem. Sen.
	9	7	13*	14	18*	14	15	17*	18	Dem. Pres./Rep. Sen.
	3	19	3*	3	18*	23	17	10*	13	Rep. Pres./Dem. Sen.
	35	15	3*	7	27*	25	9	19*	9	Rep. Pres./Rep. Sen.
Independent Independents	14%*	15%	28%	54%*	13%*	20%	34%	10%*	21%	Dem. Pres./Dem. Sen.
	6*	3	14	20*	11*	10	11	12*	7	Dem. Pres./Rep. Sen.
	14*	32	4	4*	34*	26	30	34*	31	Rep. Pres./Dem. Sen.
	67*	51	54	22*	42*	44	25	44*	41	Rep. Pres./Rep. Sen.
Independent Republicans	4%	6%	14%	15%	0%	1%	9%	7%	4%	Dem. Pres./Dem. Sen.
	2	0	0	11	2	6	3	4	1	Dem. Pres./Rep. Sen.
	9	16	4	17	33	21	30	25	26	Rep. Pres./Dem. Sen.
	85	78	82	57	66	73	58	64	69	Rep. Pres./Rep. Sen.
Weak Republicans	3%	7%	8%	20%	7%	8%	14%	5%	4%	Dem. Pres./Dem. Sen.
	2	1	2	24	5	3	12	2	3	Dem. Pres./Rep. Sen.
	4	10	10	8	14	16	16	27	21	Rep. Pres./Dem. Sen.
	91	82	80	48	74	73	59	66	72	Rep. Pres./Rep. Sen.
Strong Republicans	2%	1%	0%	3%	2%	1%	1%	3%	0%	Dem. Pres./Dem. Sen.
	0	0	0	8	0	1	1	1	2	Dem. Pres./Rep. Sen.
	8	4	3	5	6	12	9	5	15	Rep. Pres./Dem. Sen.
	91	96	97	85	92	86	89	91	83	Rep. Pres./Rep. Sen.

Table 6.40
Percent of Voters Ticket-Splitting between Presidential and Senatorial Vote, by Party Identification Groups

	1952	1956	1960	1964	1968	1972	1976	1980	1984
Strong Democrats	11%	10%	8%	9%	9%	22%	8%	17%	8%
Weak Democrats	20	25	18	15	19	41	21	25	27
Independent Democrats	12	26	17*	17	36*	37	32	26*	31
Independent Independents	19*	34	18	24*	45*	36	41	46*	38
Independent Republicans	10	16	4	28	35	26	33	29	27
Weak Republicans	6	11	12	32	19	19	28	30	24
Strong Republicans	8	4	3	13	6	13	10	7	17
Total Population	12%	16%	11%	17%	19%	29%	24%	24%	23%

Chapter 7. The Congress

This chapter focuses on the citizen's feelings toward, and relationship with, his/her congressperson and the House of Representatives.   To the respondents in these surveys, the Congress is in many ways a body of anonymous representatives. Few respondents can name the candidates for Congress in their district, or can identify more than one thing they like about these candidates.   At the same time, the respondents express positive feelings toward their incumbent congresspersons and overwhelmingly report some form of contact with them.

The reader should keep in mind the fact that a substantial majority of the incumbent congresspeople are democrats. Differences between the democratic and republican congressional candidates are confounded with differences between incumbents and challengers.

This chapter begins with feeling thermometer evaluations of the candidates for Congress.   Tables 7.1 - 7.8 detail the average feeling thermometer scores for the democratic and republican candidates, and for the incumbent and the challenger.   Respondents, on average, felt ten or more degrees warmer toward the incumbent than toward the challenger.   Since a substantial majority of the incumbent representatives are democrats, one might expect that the average feeling thermometer score for democratic candidates would be higher than the same score for republican candidates.   However, although respondents did, in fact, provide a slightly warmer average score for democratic candidates than for republican candidates, the difference in all but one year (1986) is less than five degrees; it is often within only a degree or two.

There are few striking demographic factors in these feeling thermometer scores. Blacks felt slightly warmer toward the democratic candidates than did whites; and blacks also felt slightly less warm toward the republican candidates than did whites. Respondents in older cohorts felt warmer toward all candidates.   Partisanship certainly affects the respondents' feelings toward the democratic and republican candidates: as party identification moves toward "Strong Democrat," respondents provided warmer feeling thermometer scores for democratic candidates, by several degrees. Similarly, more republican respondents felt warmer toward republican candidates than did democratic respondents.

If respondents feel warmly toward their congressperson, this feeling does not seem to be based upon specific likes or dislikes about the candidates (Tables 7.9 - 7.28).   When asked to name anything that they liked about the candidates, respondents on average could name one thing they liked about the incumbent, less for other candidates.   In general, respondents could not name anything that they disliked about any of the candidates.   For all but the most partisan, respondents had positive affect (the number of likes about a candidate less the number of dislikes) toward all candidates.

Warmth toward their congresspersons is not accompanied by high levels of recall of the candidates' names.   Fewer than half of the respondents correctly recalled the name of at least one candidate for Congress (Tables 7.29 - 7.30).   Less than 15% of the respondents could recall at least two candidates' names. There were few striking demographic differences in respondents' ability to recall the candidates' names: higher levels of education brought modest increases in the respondents' recall of at least one candidate's name; wealthier respondents (income percentile 96-100) and professionals correctly recalled at least one candidate's name more often than less wealthy respondents.

If the names of their Representatives are not on the tips of the respondents' tongues, a very large proportion of respondents report some form of contact with the incumbent (Tables 7.33-7.42). More than three-fourths of the respondents report ever having some form of contact with the incumbent. (The modes of contact included: attending a gathering or meeting where the candidate spoke, talking to a member of the candidate's staff, receiving something in the mail from the candidate, reading about the candidate in a newspaper or magazine, hearing the candidate on the radio, or seeing the candidate on TV.)   The proportion of respondents reporting some form of contact with the challenger falls well under 50%, and, at times, is less than half the rate of contact with the incumbent.   A portion of the overwhelming difference between rates of contact with the incumbent and with the challenger must derive from the absence of a time focus for these questions: any contact at any time counts.

The final battery of tables report on approval of the performance of the Congress and the congressional incumbent (Tables 7.43-7.48).   Citizens generally like how their incumbent is doing, but disapprove of the performance of Congress as a whole. More than 85% of the respondents overall approve of the performance of their incumbent.   Far fewer respondents approve of the performance of the Congress as a whole, only 41% in 1980 and 1982, up to 60% in 1984, and 54% in 1986. Approval for the incumbent congressperson fluctuates only slightly across the different social groups and across different years.   Approval of the Congress as a whole fluctuates by as much as 30% across different social groups (from a low of 31% in the 95-100 income percentile to a high of 70% in the youngest age cohort) and by as much as 20% within a social group through different years (e.g., for the 1895-1910 cohort and the 96-100 income percentile).

Table 7.1
Average Feeling Thermometer for Congressional Candidates

	1978	1980	1982	1984	1986
Democratic Candidate	64.2	60.8	62.3	58.9	64.2
Republican Candidate	62.5	59.7	58.7	57.3	58.5
Incumbent Candidate	68.2	64.6	64.6	62.2	65.8
Challenger Candidate	53.0	52.4	53.9	50.4	52.1

Table entries are the average for the total population

Table 7.2
Average Feeling Thermometer for Democratic and Republican Congressional Candidates, by Social Groups

	Democratic Candidate					Republican Candidate				
	1978	1980	1982	1984	1986	1978	1980	1982	1984	1986
1959 or later Cohort	61.1*	54.9	57.0	55.9	61.4	60.0*	54.7*	57.7	55.1	55.7
1943 - 1958 Cohort	61.5	58.3	60.9	56.3	61.0	59.9	56.6	56.4	55.7	56.5
1927 - 1942 Cohort	64.6	60.5	62.9	60.3	64.2	61.7	59.4	58.3	58.1	60.1
1911 - 1926 Cohort	67.0	64.6	65.0	61.6	71.0	65.6	61.5	60.5	60.2	60.8
1895 - 1910 Cohort	68.1	64.9	66.4	67.5	71.8	68.6	71.1	64.5	61.4	69.7*
Before 1895 Cohort	-	-	-	-	-	-	-	-	-	-
Grade School	68.3	70.2	68.2	64.7	70.7	68.5	62.7	62.4	56.8	58.3
High School	64.9	60.7	65.3	59.1	65.5	62.3	59.5	59.6	58.1	59.5
College	61.9	58.6	58.2	57.7	61.4	61.3	59.5	57.3	56.6	57.6
Central Cities	67.3	63.3	64.0	59.3	66.1	57.0	55.1	54.5	55.3	55.5
Suburbs	61.8	59.7	59.7	58.0	62.4	62.6	59.1	57.8	58.5	59.5
Non-urban Areas	64.0	59.9	64.0	59.7	64.9	66.4	63.2	62.9	57.0	58.7
Income Percentile 0-16	68.2	67.9	68.5	61.9	68.5	64.4	63.1	60.2	53.9	59.2
Income Percentile 17-33	64.2	59.7	64.8	60.9	68.3	62.5	60.2	57.7	57.2	57.5
Income Percentile 34-67	64.4	59.6	63.7	59.6	63.8	62.9	60.3	60.4	59.0	58.5
Income Percentile 68-95	63.0	57.2	59.8	57.4	60.4	62.3	58.7	57.4	56.8	57.8
Income Percentile 96-100	59.4	58.6*	54.7	49.0	61.9*	64.5	61.7	56.6	57.6	59.5*
Males	62.7	60.3	60.9	57.3	62.6	61.5	57.7	57.8	56.4	57.9
Females	65.5	61.3	63.6	60.2	65.5	63.3	61.4	59.4	58.1	58.9
Whites	63.1	59.5	61.2	58.3	63.2	63.3	60.1	58.9	58.1	58.6
Blacks	72.9	71.6	72.4	63.3	68.4	52.8	53.0*	55.7	47.5	55.7
Union Household	67.1	61.3	65.4	60.2	64.1	62.3	57.2	54.1	54.3	57.7
Non-union Household	63.1	60.7	61.7	58.5	64.2	62.5	60.6	59.9	58.2	58.6
South	69.5	64.2	64.9	61.3	67.6	59.8	59.1	60.2	57.2	59.5
Non-south	61.1	58.7	60.7	57.6	62.2	63.2	59.9	57.9	57.3	58.1
Professional	62.3	59.0	58.9	57.9	61.6	62.6	58.6	58.8	56.1	56.6
White Collar	62.1	59.9	61.5	59.1	63.3	62.6	59.9	59.5	58.1	59.2
Blue Collar	65.8	62.7	65.4	60.9	66.5	61.6	59.0	58.0	56.7	58.4
Unskilled	64.6*	60.2*	68.3*	53.8*	63.1*	59.8*	-	-	58.8*	57.0*
Farmers	66.5*	-	-	55.8*	62.1*	64.8*	-	70.2*	57.8*	57.5*
Housewives	65.0	62.0	63.7	57.3	65.6	64.8	61.3	59.9	60.7	62.5
Protestants	64.6	61.2	61.8	57.8	64.4	63.9	60.7	61.2	58.9	60.4
Catholics	64.8	62.9	63.9	62.3	64.4	62.1	60.6	54.8	57.0	55.1
Jews	68.8*	56.5*	-	63.3*	62.9*	61.5*	-	-	47.7*	-
Other and No Religion	58.2	55.7	62.5	55.6	61.6	54.6	51.7	52.9	49.5	54.7
Total Population	64.2	60.8	62.3	58.9	64.2	62.5	59.7	58.7	57.3	58.5

Table entries are the average for the population group

Table 7.3
Average Feeling Thermometer for Democratic and Republican Congressional Candidates, by Political Groups

	Democratic Candidate					Republican Candidate				
	1978	1980	1982	1984	1986	1978	1980	1982	1984	1986
Strong Democrats	74.8	73.7	75.4	72.0	75.3	56.7	55.3	50.5	50.3	48.0
Weak Democrats	69.3	63.2	65.5	60.9	67.3	60.4	57.7	58.3	53.7	57.1
Independent Democrats	62.1	61.0	63.0	58.6	66.0	57.7	54.3	46.3	51.4	57.1
Independent Independents	61.3	56.4	58.3	56.2	62.0	61.9	57.1	61.2	55.1	55.1
Independent Republicans	56.8	51.0	54.8	55.7	55.2	64.0	62.0	61.7	58.5	60.9
Weak Republicans	59.0	53.6	53.7	54.3	58.2	66.8	64.1	64.4	62.3	63.2
Strong Republicans	52.9	55.0	43.0	46.8	51.1	75.6	68.6	70.8	65.7	66.7
Liberal Self Placement 1	68.2	65.8	66.4	64.5	68.6	53.3	49.0	45.6	49.4	48.0
Liberal Self Placement 2	66.2	61.2	68.0	59.4	66.5	59.0	56.8	52.8	52.2	53.1
Neutral Self Placement 3	64.2	62.1	63.1	60.7	65.9	61.9	58.4	57.2	56.3	58.7
Conservative Self Placement 4	61.7	56.2	58.7	55.7	60.0	64.6	62.1	61.1	61.7	59.4
Conservative Self Placement 5	59.0	55.7	54.3	52.1	58.5	69.3	64.5	64.4	64.0	62.7
Liberal Index 1	**	67.7*	70.5*	72.0*	65.6	**	-	41.2*	34.5*	41.3*
Liberal Index 2	**	63.8	67.7	62.1	66.3	**	55.0	48.6	53.6	56.5
Neutral Index 3	**	61.8	61.9	56.7	65.5	**	56.6	58.4	54.3	56.1
Conservative Index 4	**	57.8	59.7	57.8	62.5	**	60.7	62.7	61.4	60.2
Conservative Index 5	**	54.4	47.4	43.3	53.9	**	68.5	67.3	69.0	66.0
Total Population	64.2	60.8	62.3	58.9	64.2	62.5	59.7	58.7	57.3	58.5

Table entries are the average for the population group

Table 7.4
Average Feeling Thermometer for Incumbent and Challenger Congressional Candidates, by Social Groups

	Incumbent Candidate					Challenger Candidate				
	1978	1980	1982	1984	1986	1978	1980	1982	1984	1986
1959 or later Cohort	64.2*	57.5	59.0	57.6	62.5	-	49.3*	55.3*	51.5	49.4
1943 - 1958 Cohort	65.0	60.9	63.0	59.4	63.1	53.5	51.9	52.3	49.9	51.2
1927 - 1942 Cohort	67.9	63.9	64.7	64.1	66.2	52.2	53.2	54.6	49.3	52.5
1911 - 1926 Cohort	71.7	69.3	68.0	65.8	71.9	53.2	50.7	54.7	51.2	53.7
1895 - 1910 Cohort	73.5	71.1	68.1	70.8	73.6	52.8*	58.0*	57.7*	52.4*	-
Before 1895 Cohort	-	-	-	-	-	-	-	-	-	-
Grade School	74.4	72.8	69.0	65.8	69.2	52.0	55.3*	57.3*	52.0*	56.0*
High School	68.6	63.4	67.2	62.3	66.9	53.5	52.9	54.5	51.6	53.8
College	66.0	63.8	61.1	61.5	64.2	52.4	51.5	53.1	49.0	50.0
Central Cities	68.6	65.4	62.6	61.5	67.4	50.9	50.5	56.3	51.3	49.0
Suburbs	67.1	62.4	62.2	62.4	65.2	52.6	54.3	53.8	50.4	52.5
Non-urban Areas	69.4	66.2	68.6	62.4	65.4	55.4	51.4	51.0	49.8	54.0
Income Percentile 0-16	70.3	71.0	68.1	63.2	69.4	56.5	54.6	56.4	48.1	54.0
Income Percentile 17-33	70.3	65.0	64.4	62.2	69.1	49.8	49.0	56.2	53.9	53.0
Income Percentile 34-67	68.8	64.2	66.3	62.4	65.0	53.3	53.3	56.4	52.8	51.8
Income Percentile 68-95	67.4	59.7	62.8	62.5	63.5	53.2	54.4	51.9	47.9	51.3
Income Percentile 96-100	66.8	66.2	62.5	59.7	65.5	48.6*	49.3*	46.4*	42.9*	50.0*
Males	66.9	63.9	64.1	61.3	64.7	52.1	50.7	51.4	48.3	51.7
Females	69.4	65.1	65.1	62.9	66.8	53.7	54.0	56.1	52.3	52.5
Whites	67.8	63.7	64.1	62.2	65.1	53.5	52.4	53.4	51.0	52.4
Blacks	72.3	72.2	70.0	61.9	69.1	46.2*	52.6*	59.4*	46.6	49.8
Union Household	69.4	63.1	64.1	61.6	66.7	53.6	54.2	55.0	50.3	51.8
Non-union Household	67.8	65.1	64.8	62.4	65.6	52.7	51.7	53.8	50.4	52.2
South	69.9	66.8	67.3	63.3	68.6	53.2	53.3	54.0	51.0	51.0
Non-south	67.4	63.3	63.0	61.6	64.2	52.9	52.0	53.9	50.1	52.5
Professional	67.5	63.6	62.9	61.9	64.3	52.0	50.2	52.4	47.8	50.2
White Collar	67.6	62.9	65.7	63.3	65.5	50.9	53.6	50.9	49.7	50.1
Blue Collar	68.5	65.1	66.0	63.0	67.4	53.7	53.6	56.5	52.0	54.0
Unskilled	63.6*	62.1*	68.6*	59.7*	61.3*	-	-	-	-	-
Farmers	70.7*	-	72.7*	60.4*	63.9*	-	-	-	48.1*	52.7*
Housewives	70.2	65.6	64.2	60.6	67.3	53.7	56.0	57.7	55.1	54.5
Protestants	69.3	65.3	66.1	61.7	66.6	52.8	52.9	53.6	51.3	53.0
Catholics	68.0	66.0	62.6	65.2	65.4	53.1	54.2	55.5	50.6	50.1
Jews	73.9	59.4*	-	65.7*	62.0*	50.5*	-	-	-	-
Other and No Religion	59.3	58.3	60.9	57.0	61.0	54.0	46.6	51.6*	45.4	53.1*
Total Population	68.2	64.6	64.6	62.2	65.8	53.0	52.4	53.9	50.4	52.1

Table entries are the average for the population group

Feeling Thermometer Scores for Congressional Candidates

Table 7.5
Average Feeling Thermometer for Incumbent Congressional Candidate, by Political Groups

	Incumbent Candidate					Challenger Candidate				
	1978	1980	1982	1984	1986	1978	1980	1982	1984	1986
Strong Democrats	75.6	74.0	70.5	70.4	71.0	50.9	51.5	59.4	49.6	54.0
Weak Democrats	69.5	64.2	65.6	62.3	67.4	54.7	53.9	55.9	48.0	53.5
Independent Democrats	66.0	63.3	57.9	58.8	66.5	49.9	48.4	54.1	47.9	53.7
Independent Independents	65.1	58.5	63.3	59.2	62.2	55.3	54.9	53.2*	49.5	47.7*
Independent Republicans	65.2	61.5	63.6	60.0	61.1	51.0	47.7	50.5*	51.1	53.0
Weak Republicans	67.3	61.9	63.0	61.3	64.1	53.6	53.7	49.8	52.7	51.9
Strong Republicans	67.5	65.3	63.2	59.6	64.5	56.2	55.4	48.1*	52.9	48.6
Liberal Self Placement 1	65.8	65.4	62.5	65.1	70.0	49.7	47.0*	51.5*	45.4	46.1*
Liberal Self Placement 2	69.4	62.6	63.0	59.5	63.7	50.1	55.4*	60.2*	48.9	52.0
Neutral Self Placement 3	68.0	64.4	64.8	63.1	66.7	54.1	53.0	52.4	50.3	53.2
Conservative Self Placement 4	66.9	62.2	64.0	61.5	63.6	53.2	52.3	52.9	54.2	52.0
Conservative Self Placement 5	69.1	65.1	63.4	61.4	65.9	54.2	50.9	51.2	51.4	50.2
Liberal Index 1	**	67.4*	59.9*	65.6	62.3	**	-	-	-	43.0*
Liberal Index 2	**	64.8	63.0	62.5	66.3	**	52.3	54.1	51.1	52.4
Neutral Index 3	**	62.9	64.4	60.0	65.1	**	52.7	53.3	46.9	53.0
Conservative Index 4	**	63.0	65.0	62.7	66.0	**	52.1	54.2	53.0	52.6
Conservative Index 5	**	66.8	64.1	58.6	65.0	**	51.4*	44.3*	50.7*	46.4*
Total Population	68.2	64.6	64.6	62.2	65.8	53.0	52.4	53.9	50.4	52.1

Table entries are the average for the population group

Table 7.6
Average Feeling Thermometer for Congressional Candidates, by Party ID

	1978	1980	1982	1984	1986	
Democratic Candidate	74.8	73.7	75.4	72.0	75.3	Strong Democrats
	69.3	63.2	65.5	60.9	67.3	Weak Democrats
	62.1	61.0	63.0	58.6	66.0	Independent Democrats
	61.3	56.4	58.3	56.2	62.0	Independent Independents
	56.8	51.0	54.8	55.7	55.2	Independent Republicans
	59.0	53.6	53.7	54.3	58.2	Weak Republicans
	52.9	55.0	43.0	46.8	51.1	Strong Republicans
Republican Candidate	56.7	55.3	50.5	50.3	48.0	Strong Democrats
	60.4	57.7	58.3	53.7	57.1	Weak Democrats
	57.7	54.3	46.3	51.4	57.1	Independent Democrats
	61.9	57.1	61.2	55.1	55.1	Independent Independents
	64.0	62.0	61.7	58.5	60.9	Independent Republicans
	66.8	64.1	64.4	62.3	63.2	Weak Republicans
	75.6	68.6	70.8	65.7	66.7	Strong Republicans
Incumbent Candidate	75.6	74.0	70.5	70.4	71.0	Strong Democrats
	69.5	64.2	65.6	62.3	67.4	Weak Democrats
	66.0	63.3	57.9	58.8	66.5	Independent Democrats
	65.1	58.5	63.3	59.2	62.2	Independent Independents
	65.2	61.5	63.6	60.0	61.1	Independent Republicans
	67.3	61.9	63.0	61.3	64.1	Weak Republicans
	67.5	65.3	63.2	59.6	64.5	Strong Republicans
Challenger Candidate	50.9	51.5	59.4	49.6	54.0	Strong Democrats
	54.7	53.9	55.9	48.0	53.5	Weak Democrats
	49.9	48.4	54.1	47.9	53.7	Independent Democrats
	55.3	54.9	53.2*	49.5	47.7*	Independent Independents
	51.0	47.7	50.5*	51.1	53.0	Independent Republicans
	53.6	53.7	49.8	52.7	51.9	Weak Republicans
	56.2	55.4	48.1*	52.9	48.6	Strong Republicans

Table entries are the average for the population group

Table 7.7
Difference between Average Feeling Thermometers for Congressional Candidates, Democrat minus Republican, by Party ID

	1978	1980	1982	1984	1986
Strong Democrats	18.1	18.4	24.9	21.7	27.3
Weak Democrats	8.9	5.5	7.2	7.2	10.2
Independent Democrats	4.4	6.7	16.7	7.2	8.9
Independent Independents	-0.6	-0.7	-2.9	1.1	6.9
Independent Republicans	-7.2	-11.0	-6.9	-2.8	-5.7
Weak Republicans	-7.8	-10.5	-10.7	-8.0	-5.0
Strong Republicans	-22.7	-13.6	-27.8	-18.9	-15.6

Table entries are the difference between average scores within the population group

Table 7.8
Difference between Average Feeling Thermometer for Congressional Candidates, Incumbent minus Challenger, by Party ID

	1978	1980	1982	1984	1986
Strong Democrats	24.7	22.5	11.1	20.8	17.0
Weak Democrats	14.8	10.3	9.7	14.3	13.9
Independent Democrats	16.1	14.9	3.8	10.9	12.8
Independent Independents	9.8	3.6	10.1*	9.7	14.5*
Independent Republicans	14.2	13.8	13.1*	8.9	8.1
Weak Republicans	13.7	8.2	13.2	8.6	12.2
Strong Republicans	11.3	9.9	15.1*	6.7	15.9

Table entries are the difference between average scores within the population group

Table 7.9
Average Number of Likes About Congressional Candidates

	1978	1980	1982	1984	1986
Democratic Candidate	0.8	0.9	1.1	0.8	1.0
Republican Candidate	0.8	0.9	0.9	0.7	0.7
Incumbent Candidate	1.0	1.1	1.2	1.0	1.1
Challenger Candidate	0.3	0.4	0.7	0.4	0.4

Table entries are the average for the total population

Table 7.10
Average Number of Dislikes About Congressional Candidates

	1978	1980	1982	1984	1986
Democratic Candidate	0.2	0.3	0.3	0.2	0.2
Republican Candidate	0.2	0.2	0.3	0.2	0.3
Incumbent Candidate	0.2	0.3	0.3	0.2	0.2
Challenger Candidate	0.2	0.2	0.4	0.2	0.2

Table entries are the average for the total population

Table 7.11
Average Affect Toward Congressional Candidates

(Affect is the number of favorable mentions minus the number of unfavorable mentions about the Candidate)

	1978	1980	1982	1984	1986
Democratic Candidate	0.6	0.6	0.8	0.6	0.8
Republican Candidate	0.5	0.6	0.6	0.5	0.5
Incumbent Candidate	0.8	0.8	0.9	0.8	0.9
Challenger Candidate	0.1	0.2	0.2	0.1	0.2

Table entries are the average for the total population

Table 7.12
Average Salience of Congressional Candidates

(Salience is the total number of mentions, favorable or unfavorable, about the candidate)

	1978	1980	1982	1984	1986
Democratic Candidate	1.1	1.2	1.4	1.1	1.2
Republican Candidate	1.0	1.1	1.2	0.9	1.0
Incumbent Candidate	1.2	1.3	1.5	1.2	1.3
Challenger Candidate	0.8	1.0	1.0	0.8	0.8

Table entries are the average for the total population

Table 7.13
Average Number of Likes about Democratic and Republican Candidates, by Party ID

	Democratic Candidate					Republican Candidate				
	1978	1980	1982	1984	1986	1978	1980	1982	1984	1986
Strong Democrat	1.2	1.3	1.8	1.3	1.5	0.4	0.7	0.7	0.4	0.4
Weak Democrat	1.0	0.8	1.1	0.9	1.0	0.6	0.7	0.8	0.5	0.5
Independent Democrat	0.7	1.0	1.3	0.8	1.2	0.6	0.6	0.6	0.4	0.7
Independent Independent	0.5	0.5	0.6	0.7	0.6	0.6	0.6	0.6	0.4	0.6
Independent Republican	0.8	0.7	0.9	0.8	0.8	1.1	0.9	0.9	0.8	1.0
Weak Republican	0.6	0.6	0.5	0.6	0.7	0.9	1.1	1.1	0.9	0.8
Strong Republican	0.8	0.9	0.6	0.5	0.7	1.4	1.5	1.6	1.3	1.2
Total Population	0.8	0.9	1.1	0.8	1.0	0.8	0.9	0.9	0.7	0.7

Table entries are the average for the population group

Table 7.14
Average Number of Dislikes about Democratic and Republican Candidates, by Party ID

	Democratic Candidate					Republican Candidate				
	1978	1980	1982	1984	1986	1978	1980	1982	1984	1986
Strong Democrat	0.1	0.2	0.2	0.1	0.1	0.3	0.4	0.7	0.4	0.5
Weak Democrat	0.2	0.2	0.2	0.2	0.1	0.3	0.3	0.3	0.2	0.3
Independent Democrat	0.2	0.3	0.3	0.1	0.2	0.2	0.4	0.6	0.2	0.5
Independent Independent	0.2	0.2	0.4	0.2	0.2	0.1	0.2	0.2	0.2	0.2
Independent Republican	0.4	0.4	0.4	0.3	0.4	0.3	0.1	0.2	0.1	0.3
Weak Republican	0.2	0.3	0.4	0.4	0.3	0.1	0.2	0.1	0.2	0.1
Strong Republican	0.6	0.5	0.7	0.5	0.5	0.2	0.2	0.1	0.2	0.1
Total Population	0.2	0.3	0.3	0.2	0.2	0.2	0.2	0.3	0.2	0.3

Table entries are the average for the population group

Table 7.15
Average Affect Towards Democratic and Republican Candidates, by Party ID

(Affect is the number of favorable mentions minus the number of unfavorable mentions about the Candidate)

	Democratic Candidate						Republican Candidate				
	1978	1980	1982	1984	1986		1978	1980	1982	1984	1986
Strong Democrat	1.1	1.1	1.6	1.2	1.4		0.2	0.3	0.0	0.0	-0.1
Weak Democrat	0.8	0.6	0.9	0.7	0.9		0.3	0.5	0.5	0.2	0.3
Independent Democrat	0.6	0.7	0.9	0.6	1.0		0.4	0.2	-0.1	0.2	0.2
Independent Independent	0.3	0.3	0.3	0.5	0.4		0.5	0.4	0.4	0.2	0.4
Independent Republican	0.4	0.3	0.5	0.5	0.4		0.9	0.8	0.7	0.7	0.6
Weak Republican	0.4	0.2	0.1	0.2	0.4		0.8	1.0	1.0	0.7	0.7
Strong Republican	0.2	0.4	-0.1	0.0	0.2		1.2	1.2	1.5	1.1	1.1
Total Population	0.6	0.6	0.8	0.6	0.8		0.5	0.6	0.6	0.5	0.5

Table entries are the average for the population group

Table 7.16
Average Salience of Democratic and Republican Candidates, by Party ID

(Salience is the total number of mentions, favorable or unfavorable, about the candidate)

	Democratic Candidate						Republican Candidate				
	1978	1980	1982	1984	1986		1978	1980	1982	1984	1986
Strong Democrat	1.4	1.6	2.0	1.4	1.6		0.8	1.1	1.4	0.8	0.9
Weak Democrat	1.1	1.0	1.3	1.0	1.2		0.8	1.0	1.2	0.7	0.8
Independent Democrat	1.0	1.4	1.6	0.9	1.5		0.8	1.0	1.2	0.7	1.2
Independent Independent	0.8	0.8	1.0	0.9	0.8		0.7	0.8	0.8	0.7	0.9
Independent Republican	1.2	1.1	1.3	1.1	1.2		1.4	1.0	1.1	0.9	1.3
Weak Republican	0.8	0.9	1.0	1.0	1.0		1.0	1.3	1.3	1.0	1.0
Strong Republican	1.4	1.4	1.3	1.0	1.2		1.6	1.6	1.8	1.4	1.4
Total Population	1.1	1.2	1.4	1.1	1.2		1.0	1.1	1.2	0.9	1.0

Table entries are the average for the population group

Table 7.17
Difference between Average Number cf Likes about Congressional Candidates, Democrat minus Republican, by Party ID

	1978	1980	1982	1984	1986
Strong Democrat	0.8	0.6	1.1	0.9	1.1
Weak Democrat	0.4	0.1	0.3	0.4	0.5
Independent Democrat	0.1	0.4	0.7	0.4	0.5
Independent Independent	-0.1	-0.1	0.0	0.3	0.0
Independent Republican	-0.3	-0.2	0.0	0.0	-0.2
Weak Republican	-0.3	-0.5	-0.6	-0.3	-0.1
Strong Republican	-0.6	-0.6	-1.0	-0.8	-0.5
Total Population	0.0	0.0	0.2	0.1	0.3

Table entries are the difference between averages within the population group

Table 7.18
Difference between Average Number of Dislikes about Congressional Candidates, Democrat minus Republican, by Party ID

	1978	1980	1982	1984	1986
Strong Democrat	-0.2	-0.2	-0.5	-0.3	-0.4
Weak Democrat	-0.1	-0.1	-0.1	0.0	-0.2
Independent Democrat	0.0	-0.1	-0.3	-0.1	-0.3
Independent Independent	0.1	0.0	0.2	0.0	0.0
Independent Republican	0.1	0.3	0.2	0.2	0.1
Weak Republican	0.1	0.1	0.3	0.2	0.2
Strong Republican	0.4	0.3	0.6	0.3	0.4
Total Population	0.0	C.1	0.0	0.0	-0.1

Table entries are the difference between averages within the population group

Table 7.19
Difference between Average Affects Towards Congressional Candidates, Democrat minus Republican, by Party ID

(Affect is the number of favorable mentions minus the number of unfavorable mentions about the candidate)

	1978	1980	1982	1984	1986
Strong Democrat	0.9	0.8	1.6	1.2	1.5
Weak Democrat	0.5	0.1	0.4	0.5	0.6
Independent Democrat	0.2	0.5	1.0	0.4	0.8
Independent Independent	-0.2	-0.1	-0.1	0.3	0.0
Independent Republican	-0.5	-0.5	-0.2	-0.2	-0.2
Weak Republican	-0.4	-0.8	-0.9	-0.5	-0.3
Strong Republican	-1.0	-0.8	-1.6	-1.1	-0.9
Total Population	0.1	0.0	0.2	0.1	0.3

Table entries are the difference between averages within the population group

Table 7.20
Difference between Average Saliences of Congressional Candidates, Democrat minus Republican, by Party ID

(Salience is the total number of mentions, favorable or unfavorable, about the candidate)

	1978	1980	1982	1984	1986
Strong Democrat	0.6	0.5	0.6	0.6	0.7
Weak Democrat	0.3	0.0	0.1	0.3	0.4
Independent Democrat	0.2	0.4	0.4	0.2	0.3
Independent Independent	0.1	0.0	0.2	0.2	-0.1
Independent Republican	-0.2	0.1	0.2	0.2	-0.1
Weak Republican	-0.2	-0.4	-0.3	0.0	0.0
Strong Republican	-0.2	-0.2	-0.5	-0.4	-0.2
Total Population	0.1	0.1	0.2	0.2	0.2

Table entries are the difference between averages within the population group

Table 7.21
Average Number of Likes about Incumbent and Challenger Candidates, by Party ID

	Incumbent Candidate					Challenger Candidate				
	1978	1980	1982	1984	1986	1978	1980	1982	1984	1986
Strong Democrat	1.2	1.4	1.6	1.3	1.3	0.3	0.4	1.1	0.3	0.5
Weak Democrat	1.0	0.9	1.2	0.9	1.0	0.3	0.5	0.6	0.3	0.4
Independent Democrat	0.9	1.1	1.1	0.9	1.3	0.2	0.4	0.7	0.3	0.4
Independent Independent	0.7	0.7	0.8	0.8	0.8	0.3	0.3	0.4	0.2	0.3
Independent Republican	1.2	1.1	1.1	0.9	1.1	0.4	0.3	0.6*	0.5	0.5
Weak Republican	1.0	1.1	1.0	0.9	0.9	0.3	0.3	0.4	0.5	0.3
Strong Republican	1.4	1.5	1.4	1.1	1.2	0.5	0.6*	0.6*	0.5	0.4
Total Population	1.0	1.1	1.2	1.0	1.1	0.3	0.4	0.7	0.4	0.4

Table entries are the average for the population group

Table 7.22
Average Number of Dislikes about Incumbent and Challenger Candidates, by Party ID

	Incumbent Candidate					Challenger Candidate				
	1978	1980	1982	1984	1986	1978	1980	1982	1984	1986
Strong Democrat	0.2	0.3	0.3	0.2	0.2	0.2	0.3	0.5	0.4	0.2
Weak Democrat	0.2	0.2	0.2	0.2	0.2	0.2	0.2	0.3	0.2	0.2
Independent Democrat	0.2	0.3	0.5	0.2	0.3	0.2	0.4	0.4	0.2	0.3
Independent Independent	0.1	0.2	0.3	0.1	0.2	0.1	0.1	0.3	0.3	0.2
Independent Republican	0.3	0.3	0.2	0.3	0.3	0.5	0.2	0.5*	0.1	0.2
Weak Republican	0.1	0.3	0.3	0.3	0.2	0.2	0.2	0.3	0.2	0.2
Strong Republican	0.4	0.4	0.4	0.4	0.3	0.4	0.3	0.7*	0.3	0.3
Total Population	0.2	0.3	0.3	0.2	0.2	0.2	0.2	0.4	0.2	0.2

Table entries are the average for the population group

Table 7.23
Average Affect Towards Incumbent and Challenger Candidates, by Party ID

(Affect is the number of favorable mentions minus the number of unfavorable mentions about the candidate).

	Incumbent Candidate						Challenger Candidate				
	1978	1980	1982	1984	1986		1978	1980	1982	1984	1986
Strong Democrat	1.1	1.1	1.2	1.1	1.2		0.1	0.1	0.5	0.0	0.2
Weak Democrat	0.8	0.6	0.9	0.8	0.9		0.1	0.3	0.3	0.1	0.2
Independent Democrat	0.8	0.8	0.6	0.7	1.0		0.0	-0.1	0.4	0.1	0.1
Independent Independent	0.5	0.5	0.5	0.7	0.5		0.1	0.2	0.1	-0.1	0.1
Independent Republican	0.9	0.8	0.9	0.7	0.8		-0.1	0.1	0.0*	0.4	0.2
Weak Republican	0.9	0.9	0.8	0.6	0.7		0.1	0.1	0.1	0.2	0.1
Strong Republican	1.0	1.1	1.1	0.7	0.9		0.1	0.3*	-0.1*	0.2	0.2
Total Population	0.8	0.8	0.9	0.8	0.9		0.1	0.2	0.2	0.1	0.2

Table entries are the average for the population group

Table 7.24
Average Salience of Incumbent and Challenger Candidates, by Party ID

(Salience is the total number of mentions, favorable or unfavorable, about the candidate).

	Incumbent Candidate						Challenger Candidate				
	1978	1980	1982	1984	1986		1978	1980	1982	1984	1986
Strong Democrat	1.4	1.6	1.9	1.5	1.6		0.6	0.9	1.0	0.7	0.5
Weak Democrat	1.2	1.1	1.4	1.1	1.2		0.7	0.8	0.9	0.6	0.6
Independent Democrat	1.1	1.4	1.5	1.1	1.6		0.7	0.8	0.8	0.6	0.8
Independent Independent	0.8	1.0	1.1	0.9	1.0		0.6	0.6	0.9	0.6	0.7
Independent Republican	1.4	1.3	1.4	1.2	1.4		1.2	0.9	0.9	0.8	1.0
Weak Republican	1.1	1.4	1.3	1.1	1.1		0.9	1.2	1.0	0.9	0.8
Strong Republican	1.7	1.8	1.8	1.4	1.6		1.5	1.5	1.7	1.3	1.3
Total Population	1.2	1.3	1.5	1.2	1.3		0.8	1.0	1.0	0.8	0.8

Table entries are the average for the population group

Likes and Dislikes About Congressional Candidates

Table 7.25
Difference between Average Number of Likes about Congressional Candidates, Incumbent minus Challenger, by Party ID

	1978	1980	1982	1984	1986
Strong Democrat	0.9	1.0	0.5	1.0	0.8
Weak Democrat	0.7	0.4	0.6	0.6	0.6
Independent Democrat	0.7	0.7	0.4	0.6	0.9
Independent Independent	0.4	0.4	0.4	0.6	0.5
Independent Republican	0.8	0.8	0.5*	0.4	0.6
Weak Republican	0.7	0.8	0.6	0.4	0.6
Strong Republican	0.9	0.9*	0.8*	0.6	0.8
Total Population	0.7	0.7	0.5	0.6	0.7

Table entries are the difference between averages within the population group

Table 7.26
Difference between Average Number of Dislikes about Congressional Candidates, Incumbent minus Challenger, by Party ID

	1978	1980	1982	1984	1986
Strong Democrat	0.0	0.0	-0.2	-0.2	0.0
Weak Democrat	0.0	0.0	-0.1	0.0	0.0
Independent Democrat	0.0	-0.1	0.1	0.0	0.0
Independent Independent	0.0	0.1	0.0	-0.2	0.0
Independent Republican	-0.2	0.1	-0.3*	0.2	0.1
Weak Republican	-0.1	0.1	0.0	0.1	0.0
Strong Republican	0.0	0.1	-0.3*	0.1	0.0
Total Population	0.0	0.1	-0.1	0.0	0.0

Table entries are the difference between averages within the population group

Table 7.27
Difference between Average Affects Towards Congressional Candidates, Incumbent - Challenger, by Party ID

(Affect is the number of favorable mentions minus the number of unfavorable mentions for the candidate).

	1978	1980	1982	1984	1986
Strong Democrat	1.0	1.0	0.7	1.1	1.0
Weak Democrat	0.7	0.3	0.6	0.7	0.7
Independent Democrat	0.8	0.9	0.2	0.6	0.9
Independent Independent	0.4	0.3	0.4	0.8	0.4
Independent Republican	1.0	0.7	0.9*	0.3	0.6
Weak Republican	0.8	0.8	0.7	0.4	0.6
Strong Republican	0.9	0.8*	1.2*	0.5	0.7
Total Population	0.7	0.6	0.7	0.7	0.7

Table entries are the difference between averages within the population group

Table 7.28
Difference between Average Saliences of Congressional Candidates, Incumbent - Challenger, by Party ID

(Salience is the total number of mentions, favorable or unfavorable, about the candidate).

	1978	1980	1982	1984	1986
Strong Democrat	0.8	0.7	0.9	0.8	1.1
Weak Democrat	0.5	0.3	0.5	0.5	0.6
Independent Democrat	0.4	0.6	0.7	0.5	0.8
Independent Independent	0.2	0.4	0.2	0.3	0.3
Independent Republican	0.2	0.4	0.5	0.4	0.4
Weak Republican	0.2	0.2	0.3	0.2	0.3
Strong Republican	0.2	0.3	0.1	0.1	0.3
Total Population	0.4	0.3	0.5	0.4	0.5

Table entries are the difference between averages within the population group

Table 7.29
Percent of Respondents Who Correctly Recall At Least 1 Congressional Candidate's Name, by Social Groups

	1978	1980	1982	1984	1986
1959 or later Cohort	20%	10%	23%	14%	12%
1943 - 1958 Cohort	27	24	31	29	23
1927 - 1942 Cohort	39	36	42	34	40
1911 - 1926 Cohort	38	33	43	34	33
1895 - 1910 Cohort	37	36	27	19	30
Before 1895 Cohort	23*	-	-	-	-
Grade School	28%	23%	20%	7%	11%
High School	28	21	32	24	21
College	42	42	43	38	36
Central Cities	34%	27%	34%	23%	23%
Suburbs	34	27	35	30	27
Non-urban Areas	31	33	36	28	28
Income Percentile 0-16	27%	24%	27%	11%	14%
Income Percentile 17-33	28	25	30	24	22
Income Percentile 34-67	33	30	38	30	27
Income Percentile 68-95	39	33	42	37	35
Income Percentile 96-100	48	47	52	40	37
Males	37%	35%	40%	33%	29%
Females	30	24	31	23	24
Whites	34%	30%	36%	30%	29%
Blacks	24	20	27	14	16
Union Household	32%	28%	33%	29%	28%
Non-union Household	33	29	36	27	26
South	31%	32%	41%	26%	21%
Non-south	34	27	32	28	29
Professional	43%	42%	46%	43%	42%
White Collar	31	29	35	28	28
Blue Collar	27	23	32	21	18
Unskilled	27	25*	21*	14	16
Farmers	39*	50*	32*	20	19
Housewives	35	22	29	25	24
Protestants	33%	30%	38%	27%	27%
Catholics	35	27	30	30	26
Jews	49	28	33*	32	44*
Other and No Religion	27	26	29	22	20
Total Population	33%	29%	35%	28%	27%

Table 7.30
Percent of Respondents Who Correctly Recall At Least 1 Congressional Candidate's Name, by Political Groups

	1978	1980	1982	1984	1986
Strong Democrats	38%	31%	41%	33%	28%
Weak Democrats	31	26	33	21	25
Independent Democrats	29	28	30	21	28
Independent Independents	23	18	32	22	16
Independent Republicans	43	37	38	36	35
Weak Republicans	36	32	30	32	24
Strong Republicans	47	41	48	34	36
Liberal Self Placement 1	31%	48%	44%	36%	30%
Liberal Self Placement 2	35	25	45	29	31
Neutral Self Placement 3	34	28	35	30	27
Conservative Self Placement 4	42	40	43	39	32
Conservative Self Placement 5	46	38	47	42	38
Liberal Index 1	**	43*%	57%	44%	28%
Liberal Index 2	**	36	44	31	28
Neutral Index 3	**	24	29	27	22
Conservative Index 4	**	35	43	40	32
Conservative Index 5	**	52	49	56	27
Total Population	33%	29%	35%	28%	27%

Rates of Recall of Congressional Candidates' Names

Table 7.31
Percent of Respondents Who Correctly Recall 2 or More Congressional Candidates' Names, by Social Groups

	1978	1980	1982	1984	1986
1959 or later Cohort	4%	4%	10%	5%	3%
1943 - 1958 Cohort	10	9	14	10	7
1927 - 1942 Cohort	12	14	16	11	10
1911 - 1926 Cohort	10	15	15	12	8
1895 - 1910 Cohort	7	9	9	5	8
Before 1895 Cohort	0*	-	-	-	-
Grade School	4%	8%	5%	0%	4%
High School	8	7	11	8	5
College	14	17	18	14	10
Central Cities	13%	10%	16%	7%	3%
Suburbs	9	10	15	9	8
Non-urban Areas	8	12	11	11	9
Income Percentile 0-16	5%	7%	8%	4%	4%
Income Percentile 17-33	7	8	12	9	6
Income Percentile 34-67	11	13	14	11	7
Income Percentile 68-95	12	13	18	12	11
Income Percentile 96-100	14	17	20	13	9
Males	12%	13%	17%	12%	9%
Females	8	9	12	7	6
Whites	11%	12%	15%	10%	8%
Blacks	4	4	6	3	2
Union Household	10%	11%	15%	11%	8%
Non-union Household	10	11	13	9	7
South	6%	10%	15%	10%	3%
Non-south	12	11	13	9	9
Professional	15%	18%	18%	13%	12%
White Collar	9	11	16	10	6
Blue Collar	7	8	11	8	5
Unskilled	7	8*	10*	4	5
Farmers	9*	16*	9*	8	11
Housewives	11	9	10	8	6
Protestants	10%	11%	15%	9%	7%
Catholics	8	12	12	11	8
Jews	16	6	21*	11*	13*
Other and No Religion	8	9	10	6	7
Total Population	10%	11%	14%	9%	7%

Table 7.32
Percent of Respondents Who Correctly Recall 2 or More Congressional Candidates' Names, by Political Groups

	1978	1980	1982	1984	1986
Strong Democrats	9%	9%	16%	10%	8%
Weak Democrats	8	10	12	8	7
Independent Democrats	8	11	13	8	4
Independent Independents	5	6	13	6	4
Independent Republicans	16	18	19	11	9
Weak Republicans	11	13	13	10	8
Strong Republicans	21	15	18	16	11
Liberal Self Placement 1	10%	20%	21%	11%	14%
Liberal Self Placement 2	11	13	19	8	8
Neutral Self Placement 3	10	9	14	11	7
Conservative Self Placement 4	14	20	19	12	8
Conservative Self Placement 5	17	14	20	16	11
Liberal Index 1	**	11%*	29%	13%	14%
Liberal Index 2	**	18	18	10	7
Neutral Index 3	**	9	11	9	5
Conservative Index 4	**	14	16	15	9
Conservative Index 5	**	17	26	19	11
Total Population	10%	11%	14%	9%	7%

Rates of Recall of Congressional Candidates' Names

Table 7.33
Percent of Respondents Having Any Contact with Congressional Candidates

	1978	1980	1982	1984	1986
Democratic Candidate	65%	63%	66%	64%	63%
Republican Candidate	54%	58%	61%	56%	57%
Incumbent Candidate	76%	79%	79%	77%	78%
Challenger Candidate	37%	39%	47%	38%	34%

Table 7.34
Average Number of Contacts with Congressional Candidates, per Respondent

	1978	1980	1982	1984	1986
Democratic Candidate	1.6	1.5	1.8	1.6	1.7
Republican Candidate	1.4	1.3	1.6	1.4	1.4
Incumbent Candidate	2.1	1.9	2.3	2.0	2.2
Challenger Candidate	0.7	0.7	1.1	0.8	0.7

Table 7.35
Percent of Respondents Having Any Contact with Democratic and Republican Candidates, by Social Groups

	Democratic Candidate					Republican Candidate				
	1978	1980	1982	1984	1986	1978	1980	1982	1984	1986
1959 or later Cohort	53%	51%	62%	59%	58%	49%	51%	56%	49%	50%
1943 - 1958 Cohort	64	59	69	67	64	54	57	61	62	59
1927 - 1942 Cohort	68	68	66	65	66	57	64	68	59	63
1911 - 1926 Cohort	66	67	67	65	64	54	61	61	53	53
1895 - 1910 Cohort	65	66	57	51	54	51	54	53	37	48
Before 1895 Cohort	48*	-	-	-	-	27*	-	-	-	-
Grade School	52%	60%	50%	48%	51%	44%	41%	50%	24%	38%
High School	64	60	64	62	61	53	59	58	55	53
College	71	67	72	71	67	60	63	67	64	64
Central Cities	72%	69%	72%	69%	70%	45%	47%	64%	49%	42%
Suburbs	64	60	68	64	61	56	59	59	62	60
Non-urban Areas	60	60	59	61	61	60	66	61	54	63
Income Percentile 0-16	61%	60%	55%	63%	58%	45%	48%	54%	39%	43%
Income Percentile 17-33	61	67	64	59	65	53	58	57	49	55
Income Percentile 34-67	68	63	70	68	65	55	62	58	59	59
Income Percentile 68-95	71	66	74	67	67	60	63	72	65	65
Income Percentile 96-100	66	59	73	63	58	62	69	71	61*	74
Males	67%	66%	70%	67%	65%	57%	59%	62%	61%	58%
Females	64	60	63	62	61	52	58	60	52	56
Whites	65%	63%	67%	66%	62%	56%	61%	62%	59%	60%
Blacks	69	66	64	51	69	35	32	51	28	42
Union Household	64%	66%	72%	69%	68%	53%	56%	58%	56%	57%
Non-union Household	65	62	64	63	62	55	59	62	56	57
South	72%	70%	73%	62%	66%	45%	60%	65%	52%	59%
Non-south	62	59	62	65	61	57	58	59	58	56
Professional	72%	67%	72%	69%	72%	61%	63%	67%	63%	65%
White Collar	64	62	68	70	60	55	60	63	55	59
Blue Collar	61	62	64	60	61	50	56	57	54	51
Unskilled	63	67	66	57	55	44	58	52	68	54
Farmers	61	64	59	58	60	76	71	74	50	57
Housewives	64	59	63	61	57	51	54	58	51	59
Protestants	66%	64%	68%	62%	64%	58%	61%	66%	55%	58%
Catholics	63	60	64	67	66	50	58	53	59	57
Jews	63	59*	67*	74*	77*	37	21*	67*	48*	64*
Other and No Religion	64	60	57	66	48	51	55	52	56	46
Total Population	65%	63%	66%	64%	63%	54%	58%	61%	56%	57%

Rates of Contact with Congressional Candidates

Table 7.36
Percent of Respondents Having Any Contact with Democratic and Republican Candidates, by Political Groups

	Democratic Candidate					Republican Candidate				
	1978	1980	1982	1984	1986	1978	1980	1982	1984	1986
Strong Democrats	71%	76%	74%	72%	75%	45%	45%	56%	46%	49%
Weak Democrats	66	66	64	63	65	49	52	56	51	53
Independent Democrats	66	65	68	74	66	55	65	55	63	54
Independent Independents	61	51	51	59	61	53	58	55	48	50
Independent Republicans	70	56	73	69	62	62	62	75	61	64
Weak Republicans	62	62	69	54	57	64	68	75	59	65
Strong Republicans	67	60	65	65	54	75	67	75	69	74
Liberal Self Placement 1	62%	67%	76%	71%	73%	47%	48%	67%	59%	48%
Liberal Self Placement 2	71	69	76	69	66	57	58	72	64	54
Neutral Self Placement 3	69	69	72	68	66	56	61	60	57	61
Conservative Self Placement 4	71	70	69	71	65	61	64	73	61	66
Conservative Self Placement 5	68	62	73	63	60	68	63	69	71	68
Liberal Index 1	**	69%*	89%*	67%*	64%	**	30%*	72%*	-	38%
Liberal Index 2	**	69	75	69	70	**	60	64	58	55
Neutral Index 3	**	56	63	64	64	**	55	55	55	52
Conservative Index 4	**	64	71	69	66	**	61	71	61	70
Conservative Index 5	**	64	74	65*	62	**	69	70	80*	71
Total Population	65%	63%	66%	64%	63%	54%	58%	61%	56%	57%

Table 7.37
Average Number of Contacts with Democratic and Republican Candidates, by Social Groups

	Democratic Candidate						Republican Candidate				
	1978	1980	1982	1984	1986		1978	1980	1982	1984	1986
1959 or later Cohort	1.1	0.9	1.1	1.1	1.3		0.9	0.8	1.1	0.9	1.1
1943 - 1958 Cohort	1.5	1.3	1.9	1.7	1.7		1.3	1.2	1.6	1.4	1.4
1927 - 1942 Cohort	1.8	1.7	1.8	1.7	1.8		1.5	1.6	1.8	1.6	1.6
1911 - 1926 Cohort	1.8	1.8	1.9	1.6	1.9		1.4	1.6	1.6	1.3	1.4
1895 - 1910 Cohort	1.8	1.5	1.6	1.1	1.5		1.3	1.1	1.6	1.1	1.2
Before 1895 Cohort	1.1*	-	-	-	-		0.9*	-	-	-	-
Grade School	1.3	1.4	1.1	1.0	1.2		1.0	0.8	1.1	0.7	0.8
High School	1.6	1.3	1.7	1.4	1.4		1.2	1.2	1.4	1.3	1.1
College	1.9	1.7	2.1	1.8	2.0		1.6	1.6	1.9	1.6	1.8
Central Cities	1.9	1.8	2.1	1.8	1.8		1.1	1.1	1.6	1.2	0.9
Suburbs	1.6	1.4	1.7	1.6	1.6		1.3	1.3	1.4	1.5	1.5
Non-urban Areas	1.5	1.3	1.6	1.4	1.6		1.6	1.6	1.8*	1.3	1.5
Income Percentile 0-16	1.3	1.4	1.4	1.5	1.4		0.9	1.0	1.2	0.9	0.9
Income Percentile 17-33	1.4	1.5	1.6	1.4	1.7		1.2	1.2	1.3	1.1	1.2
Income Percentile 34-67	1.7	1.5	1.9	1.7	1.7		1.3	1.5	1.5	1.4	1.4
Income Percentile 68-95	1.9	1.6	2.1	1.8	1.9		1.6	1.4	2.0	1.6	1.7
Income Percentile 96-100	2.1	1.5	2.2	1.4	2.2		1.9	1.9	2.1	1.8	2.2
Males	1.7	1.7	2.0	1.8	1.7		1.4	1.4	1.7	1.5	1.5
Females	1.6	1.3	1.6	1.4	1.6		1.3	1.3	1.5	1.3	1.3
Whites	1.7	1.5	1.8	1.6	1.6		1.4	1.4	1.7	1.4	1.5
Blacks	1.7	1.6	1.7	1.3	1.7		0.6	0.5	1.1	0.6	0.8
Union Household	1.7	1.5	2.0	1.8	1.8		1.3	1.2	1.4	1.4	1.4
Non-union Household	1.6	1.5	1.7	1.5	1.6		1.4	1.4	1.7	1.3	1.4
South	1.9	1.7	2.0	1.5	1.8		1.1	1.3	1.7	1.3	1.4
Non-south	1.5	1.4	1.6	1.6	1.6		1.5	1.3	1.5	1.4	1.4
Professional	2.0	1.7	2.1	2.0	2.3		1.7	1.6	1.9	1.7	1.9
White Collar	1.7	1.5	1.8	1.6	1.7		1.4	1.5	1.7	1.3	1.5
Blue Collar	1.4	1.4	1.7	1.4	1.4		1.1	1.1	1.4	1.2	1.0
Unskilled	1.4	1.5*	1.6*	1.3*	1.1		0.8*	1.3*	1.2*	-	1.1*
Farmers	1.9*	1.8*	1.8*	1.2*	1.2		2.2*	2.4*	2.2*	1.2*	1.7*
Housewives	1.6	1.3	1.5	1.2	1.3		1.3	1.1	1.4	1.2	1.3
Protestants	1.7	1.5	1.8	1.5	1.7		1.5	1.4	1.8	1.3	1.5
Catholics	1.6	1.5	1.7	1.7	1.7		1.2	1.3	1.2	1.5	1.4
Jews	2.0	1.3*	1.9*	1.7*	1.8		1.1	0.6*	1.3*	1.3*	1.6*
Other and No Religion	1.4	1.3	1.5	1.9	1.2		1.1	1.2	1.2	1.2	0.9
Total Population	1.6	1.5	1.8	1.6	1.7		1.4	1.3	1.6	1.4	1.4

Table entries are the average for the population group

Table 7.38
Average Number of Contacts with Democratic and Republican Candidates, by Political Groups

	Democratic Candidate					Republican Candidate				
	1978	1980	1982	1984	1986	1978	1980	1982	1984	1986
Strong Democrats	2.1	2.0	2.3	1.9	2.2	1.0	1.0	1.4	1.1	1.1
Weak Democrats	1.7	1.5	1.7	1.6	1.7	1.1	1.0	1.4	1.2	1.3
Independent Democrats	1.5	1.6	1.9	1.8	1.8	1.3	1.4	1.4	1.3	1.2
Independent Independents	1.5	1.1	1.3	1.4	1.4	1.3	1.3	1.4	1.0	1.1
Independent Republicans	1.9	1.3	1.9	1.6	1.6	1.7	1.5	1.9	1.4	1.7
Weak Republicans	1.4	1.4	1.7	1.2	1.4	1.6	1.7	1.9	1.6	1.7
Strong Republicans	1.8	1.3	1.8	1.5	1.4	2.4	1.8	2.5	1.9	2.0
Liberal Self Placement 1	1.6	2.0	2.1	2.0	2.1	1.1	1.4	1.6	1.4	1.2
Liberal Self Placement 2	1.8	1.7	2.3	1.8	1.8	1.4	1.3	1.7	1.5	1.4
Neutral Self Placement 3	1.8	1.6	2.1	1.8	1.8	1.4	1.3	1.6	1.4	1.5
Conservative Self Placement 4	2.0	1.8	1.9	2.0	1.7	1.7	1.5	2.1	1.6	1.8
Conservative Self Placement 5	1.9	1.5	2.1	1.5	1.7	2.0	1.5	2.1	1.9	1.8
Liberal Index 1	**	2.2*	2.8*	2.3*	1.8	**	0.9*	1.9*	-	1.0
Liberal Index 2	**	1.7	2.2	1.8	1.8	**	1.4	1.6	1.3	1.4
Neutral Index 3	**	1.3	1.6	1.5	1.6	**	1.1	1.4	1.3	1.2
Conservative Index 4	**	1.5	1.9	1.6	1.8	**	1.4	2.0	1.6	1.7
Conservative Index 5	**	1.5	2.1	1.6*	1.6	**	1.9	2.2	2.1*	2.0
Total Population	1.6	1.5	1.8	1.6	1.7	1.4	1.3	1.6	1.4	1.4

Table entries are the average for the population group

Table 7.39
Percent of Respondents Having Any Contact with Incumbent and Challenger Candidates, by Social Groups

	Incumbent Candidate					Challenger Candidate				
	1978	1980	1982	1984	1986	1978	1980	1982	1984	1986
1959 or later Cohort	64%	66%	74%	67%	70%	30%	37%	35%	33%	32%
1943 - 1958 Cohort	75	75	78	81	79	39	36	53	44	38
1927 - 1942 Cohort	79	83	82	81	84	41	45	48	40	37
1911 - 1926 Cohort	80	84	82	78	82	35	40	44	35	27
1895 - 1910 Cohort	74	85	75	64	66	34	34	33	21	28
Before 1895 Cohort	54*	-	-	-	-	-	-	-	-	-
Grade School	64%	72%	68%	55%	63%	26%	26%	30%	16%	25%
High School	75	78	78	75	77	36	38	41	36	29
College	83	82	83	85	83	43	44	55	45	41
Central Cities	75%	78%	82%	70%	75%	37%	33%	55%	38%	31%
Suburbs	78	78	81	80	79	38	39	51	41	34
Non-urban Areas	74	81	75	78	79	36	43	32	35	37
Income Percentile 0-16	68%	73%	72%	66%	68%	32%	29%	32%	29%	26%
Income Percentile 17-33	71	79	76	70	80	32	44	43	35	31
Income Percentile 34-67	80	81	81	82	79	40	41	44	42	37
Income Percentile 68-95	83	83	87	83	84	42	43	57	43	40
Income Percentile 96-100	81	80	80	85*	88	40	42	60	36*	40
Males	77%	81%	79%	82%	79%	42%	40%	50%	43%	36%
Females	75	77	79	73	77	34	38	43	34	33
Whites	77%	80%	81%	81%	79%	39%	40%	48%	41%	35%
Blacks	72	70	72	54	73	25	25	40	21	32
Union Household	78%	79%	80%	80%	82%	34%	40%	50%	39%	35%
Non-union Household	76	79	79	77	77	39	39	46	38	34
South	71%	82%	85%	76%	78%	37%	42%	53%	33%	36%
Non-south	79	77	76	78	78	38	38	44	40	33
Professional	83%	84%	84%	86%	85%	46%	42%	55%	43%	44%
White Collar	76	77	81	82	81	32	42	50	38	31
Blue Collar	72	77	76	72	75	34	36	40	38	30
Unskilled	71	80*	70*	-	73	29*	45*	43*	-	25*
Farmers	75*	85*	85*	73*	78	48*	48*	52*	31*	39*
Housewives	76	76	79	70	73	36	31	41	35	34
Protestants	77%	81%	83%	77%	79%	40%	40%	47%	37%	34%
Catholics	76	76	72	79	79	33	38	44	39	38
Jews	74	66	70	75	97	28	12*	-	-	43*
Other and No Religion	71	75	70	77	65	36	39	44	43	22
Total Population	76%	79%	79%	77%	78%	37%	39%	47%	38%	34%

Rates of Contact with Congressional Candidates

Table 7.40
Percent of Respondents Having Any Contact with Incumbent and Challenger Candidates, by Political Groups

	Incumbent Candidate					Challenger Candidate				
	1978	1980	1982	1984	1986	1978	1980	1982	1984	1986
Strong Democrats	80%	84%	84%	81%	82%	29%	31%	44%	35%	36%
Weak Democrats	75	77	78	74	76	35	36	41	35	34
Independent Democrats	77	77	73	80	77	38	53	51	53	38
Independent Independents	72	70	71	68	72	36	34	38	35	29
Independent Republicans	85	77	78	79	81	42	40	64	42	36
Weak Republicans	77	85	86	76	81	44	43	57	34	33
Strong Republicans	83	81	88	85	84	54	41	46	43	36
Liberal Self Placement 1	72%	77%	84%	85%	75%	34%	36%	63%	44%	38%
Liberal Self Placement 2	83	79	92	82	79	39	45	53	48	35
Neutral Self Placement 3	79	83	84	81	80	41	42	47	41	39
Conservative Self Placement 4	84	83	82	81	84	39	44	57	45	38
Conservative Self Placement 5	81	80	86	86	86	52	42	52	41	35
Liberal Index 1	**	80%*	94%*	81%*	70%*	**	17%*	71%*	53%*	25%
Liberal Index 2	**	78	83	79	82	**	47	53	45	35
Neutral Index 3	**	76	77	78	77	**	35	41	34	32
Conservative Index 4	**	82	85	85	84	**	40	54	40	43
Conservative Index 5	**	85	83	78*	84	**	42	61	60	40
Total Population	70%	79%	79%	77%	78%	37%	39%	47%	38%	34%

Table 7.41
Average Number of Contacts with Incumbent and Challenger Candidates, by Social Groups

	Incumbent Candidate						Challenger Candidate				
	1978	1980	1982	1984	1986		1978	1980	1982	1984	1986
1959 or later Cohort	1.3	1.2	1.4	1.3	1.6		0.5*	0.5	0.6	0.5	0.6
1943 - 1958 Cohort	1.9	1.7	2.3	2.1	2.2		0.8	0.6	1.3	0.9	0.7
1927 - 1942 Cohort	2.3	2.1	2.5	2.2	2.4		0.9	0.9	1.1	0.9	0.8
1911 - 1926 Cohort	2.3	2.3	2.4	2.1	2.5		0.7	0.8	1.1	0.7	0.5
1895 - 1910 Cohort	2.2	2.0	2.3	1.8	2.0		0.6	0.5	0.9	0.4	0.5
Before 1895 Cohort	1.5*	-	-	-	-		-	-	-	-	-
Grade School	1.7	1.6	1.6	1.3	1.5		0.5	0.4	0.6	0.3	0.4
High School	1.9	1.8	2.1	1.8	1.9		0.7	0.7	0.9	0.7	0.5
College	2.4	2.1	2.6	2.3	2.6		0.9	0.9	1.4	0.9	0.9
Central Cities	2.1	1.9	2.4	2.0	2.0		0.7	0.7	1.4	0.9	0.5
Suburbs	2.1	1.8	2.1	2.1	2.2		0.8	0.7	1.1	0.8	0.7
Non-urban Areas	2.1	2.0	2.3	1.9	2.2		0.8	0.7	0.7	0.7	0.8
Income Percentile 0-16	1.6	1.8	1.8	1.6	1.6		0.5	0.6	0.7	0.6	0.5
Income Percentile 17-33	1.9	1.8	2.0	1.7	2.2		0.5	0.7	1.0	0.8	0.6
Income Percentile 34-67	2.2	2.0	2.3	2.1	2.2		0.8	0.8	1.0	0.8	0.6
Income Percentile 68-95	2.4	2.0	2.6	2.3	2.5		0.9	0.8	1.4	0.9	0.9
Income Percentile 96-100	2.7	2.3	2.6	2.5*	3.1		0.8	0.8	1.5	0.6*	1.0
Males	2.2	2.1	2.4	2.2	2.3		0.9	0.8	1.2	0.9	0.7
Females	2.0	1.8	2.2	1.8	2.1		0.7	0.7	1.0	0.7	0.6
Whites	2.1	1.9	2.3	2.1	2.2		0.8	0.8	1.1	0.8	0.7
Blacks	1.7	1.7	1.9	1.5	1.8		0.4	0.4	0.9	0.4	0.5
Union Household	2.2	1.9	2.2	2.1	2.3		0.6	0.8	1.2	1.0	0.7
Non-union Household	2.0	1.9	2.3	2.0	2.2		0.8	0.7	1.1	0.7	0.7
South	2.0	2.0	2.5	2.0	2.2		0.7	0.7	1.2	0.7	0.7
Non-south	2.1	1.9	2.1	2.0	2.2		0.8	0.7	1.0	0.8	0.7
Professional	2.5	2.2	2.7	2.6	2.8		1.0	0.8	1.3	0.9	1.0
White Collar	2.1	2.0	2.3	2.1	2.3		0.7	0.9	1.2	0.7	0.6
Blue Collar	1.8	1.7	2.0	1.7	1.8		0.6	0.7	1.0	0.8	0.5
Unskilled	1.6	1.8*	1.8*	1.9	1.6		0.5*	0.9*	1.0*	-	0.3*
Farmers	2.7*	2.8*	2.6*	1.7*	2.1		1.1*	1.0*	1.6*	0.6*	0.7*
Housewives	2.1	1.7	2.0	1.5	1.8		0.8	0.5	0.9	0.6	0.6
Protestants	2.2	2.0	2.5	1.9	2.2		0.8	0.8	1.2	0.7	0.7
Catholics	2.0	1.8	1.9	2.0	2.2		0.6	0.7	1.0	0.9	0.7
Jews	2.6	1.6*	-	-	2.5*		0.5	0.1*	-	-	0.9*
Other and No Religion	1.7	1.7	1.9	2.2	1.6		0.7	0.7	0.9	0.8	0.5
Total Population	2.1	1.9	2.3	2.0	2.2		0.7	0.7	1.1	0.8	0.7

Table entries are the average for the population group

Table 7.42
Average Number of Contacts with Incumbent and Challenger Candidates, by Political Groups

	Incumbent Candidate						Challenger Candidate				
	1978	1980	1982	1984	1986		1978	1980	1982	1984	1986
Strong Democrats	2.4	2.2	2.6	2.2	2.4		0.6	0.7	1.2	0.8	0.8
Weak Democrats	1.9	1.7	2.2	1.9	2.1		0.7	0.6	0.9	0.7	0.7
Independent Democrats	2.0	2.0	2.1	1.9	2.2		0.7	1.0	1.1	1.1	0.7
Independent Independents	1.8	1.6	1.9	1.7	1.8		0.7	0.7	0.9	0.6	0.6
Independent Republicans	2.5	1.9	2.2	1.9	2.3		0.9	0.8	1.4	0.8	0.6
Weak Republicans	2.0	2.1	2.4	2.0	2.2		0.8	0.8	1.2	0.7	0.6
Strong Republicans	2.6	2.0	2.9	2.4	2.4		1.4	0.8	1.4	0.8	0.8
Liberal Self Placement 1	2.0	2.2	2.5	2.4	2.2		0.7	0.9	1.4	0.9	0.9
Liberal Self Placement 2	2.3	1.9	2.8	2.3	2.3		0.7	1.0	1.3	0.8	0.8
Neutral Self Placement 3	2.2	2.0	2.5	2.1	2.3		0.8	0.7	1.2	0.9	0.7
Conservative Self Placement 4	2.5	2.1	2.4	2.3	2.4		0.9	0.9	1.4	1.0	0.8
Conservative Self Placement 5	2.6	2.0	2.7	2.4	2.5		1.2	0.8	1.3	0.9	0.7
Liberal Index 1	**	2.3*	3.0*	2.9*	2.0		**	0.4*	2.0*	-	0.7
Liberal Index 2	**	2.0	2.5	2.1	2.3		**	0.9	1.3	0.9	0.7
Neutral Index 3	**	1.7	2.1	2.0	2.1		**	0.6	0.9	0.7	0.6
Conservative Index 4	**	2.0	2.5	2.2	2.5		**	0.8	1.4	0.9	0.8
Conservative Index 5	**	2.2	2.7	2.3*	2.6		**	0.9	1.5	1.0*	0.7
Total Population	2.1	1.9	2.3	2.0	2.2		0.7	0.7	1.1	0.8	0.7

Table entries are the average for the population group

Table 7.43
Approval of Performance of Congressional Incumbent&

	1980	1982	1984	1986
Approve	88%	86%	88%	88%
Disapprove	12	14	12	12

& Running incumbent only (not 'retiring' Congressperson)

Table 7.44
Approval of Performance of Congress

	1980	1982	1984	1986
Approve	41%	41%	60%	54%
Disapprove	59	59	40	46

Table 7.45
Percent of Respondents Who Approve of Performance of Incumbent Congressperson, by Social Groups&

	1980	1982	1984	1986
1959 or later Cohort	86%*	85%	85%	89%
1943 - 1958 Cohort	86	85	88	87
1927 - 1942 Cohort	89	84	86	86
1911 - 1926 Cohort	90	90	92	91
1895 - 1910 Cohort	87	91	92	90
Before 1895 Cohort	-	-	-	-
Grade School	93%	91%	93%	91%
High School	88	88	90	88
College	86	83	86	88
Central Cities	84%	82%	88%	87%
Suburbs	86	86	87	87
Non-urban Areas	93	91	90	90
Income Percentile 0-16	87%	89%	87%	88%
Income Percentile 17-33	92	90	91	90
Income Percentile 34-67	88	87	90	87
Income Percentile 68-95	84	84	85	88
Income Percentile 96-100	88*	86	90	91
Males	86%	85%	85%	86%
Females	89	88	91	90
Whites	88%	87%	88%	89%
Blacks	90	81	91	86
Union Household	84%	85%	88%	86%
Non-union Household	89	87	88	88
South	91%	87%	87%	91%
Non-south	86	86	89	86
Professional	89%	84%	86%	89%
White Collar	88	90	89	88
Blue Collar	87	88	90	87
Unskilled	80*	88*	84*	83*
Farmers	-	87*	83*	88*
Housewives	89	85	90	90
Protestants	90%	88%	88%	88%
Catholics	85	84	89	89
Jews	85*	-	97*	-
Other and No Religion	82	84	83	85
Total Population	88%	86%	88%	88%

& Running incumbent only (not 'retiring' Congressperson)

Table 7.46
Percent of Respondents Who Approve of Performance of Incumbent Congressman, by Political Groups&

	1980	1982	1984	1986
Strong Democrats	92%	84%	89%	87%
Weak Democrats	89	90	90	90
Independent Democrats	85	81	90	86
Independent Independents	79	94	88	88
Independent Republicans	88	84	88	88
Weak Republicans	89	88	87	89
Strong Republicans	85	84	84	87
Liberal Self Placement 1	85%	78%	87%	83%
Liberal Self Placement 2	83	84	89	87
Neutral Self Placement 3	89	86	88	89
Conservative Self Placement 4	85	83	86	85
Conservative Self Placement 5	87	86	84	90
Liberal Index 1	91%	75%	84%	79%
Liberal Index 2	86	83	87	86
Neutral Index 3	91	89	91	88
Conservative Index 4	87	85	88	90
Conservative Index 5	87	86	70	89
Total Population	88%	86%	88%	88%

& Running incumbent only (not 'retiring' Congressperson)

Table 7.47
Percent of Respondents Who Approve of Performance of Congress, by Social Groups

	1980	1982	1984	1986
1959 or later Cohort	69%	59%	70%	64%
1943 - 1958 Cohort	43	42	62	54
1927 - 1942 Cohort	40	41	61	50
1911 - 1926 Cohort	36	35	51	50
1895 - 1910 Cohort	31	33	52	51
Before 1895 Cohort	-	-	-	-
Grade School	49%	35%	62%	60%
High School	42	37	62	56
College	38	46	59	52
Central Cities	44%	45%	58%	52%
Suburbs	40	37	62	57
Non-urban Areas	40	43	60	52
Income Percentile 0-16	47%	34%	58%	58%
Income Percentile 17-33	39	47	58	54
Income Percentile 34-67	41	43	63	52
Income Percentile 68-95	44	42	59	56
Income Percentile 96-100	31	47	57	55
Males	36%	39%	55%	51%
Females	46	43	65	57
Whites	40%	42%	61%	54%
Blacks	55	34	53	53
Union Household	41%	38%	63%	53%
Non-union Household	41	42	60	54
South	41%	44%	60%	55%
Non-south	41	39	61	54
Professional	34%	43%	56%	50%
White Collar	46	48	63	58
Blue Collar	42	35	60	53
Unskilled	53*	52*	60*	57*
Farmers	35*	35*	52	57
Housewives	42	37	68	56
Protestants	40%	42%	59%	53%
Catholics	48	39	66	59
Jews	44*	-	72*	41*
Other and No Religion	37	42	53	55
Total Population	41%	41%	60%	54%

Table 7.48
Percent of Respondents Who Approve of Performance of Congress, by Political Groups

	1980	1982	1984	1986
Strong Democrats	51%	39%	59%	55%
Weak Democrats	50	44	72	60
Independent Democrats	42	35	52	53
Independent Independents	36	41	57	52
Independent Republicans	34	41	57	42
Weak Republicans	33	51	63	56
Strong Republicans	32	35	54	55
Liberal Self Placement 1	42%	49%	60%	46%
Liberal Self Placement 2	52	42	65	60
Neutral Self Placement 3	43	45	63	55
Conservative Self Placement 4	37	39	56	49
Conservative Self Placement 5	26	35	53	48
Liberal Index 1	42%	33%	42%	40%
Liberal Index 2	46	53	65	56
Neutral Index 3	46	41	66	58
Conservative Index 4	42	43	58	54
Conservative Index 5	19	26	30	39
Total Population	41%	41%	60%	54%